PARAGON
ISSUES IN
PHILOSOPHY

THE PARAGON ISSUES
IN PHILOSOPHY SERIES

At colleges and universities, interest in the traditional areas of philosophy remains strong. Many new currents flow within them, too, but some of these—the rise of cognitive science, for example, or feminist philosophy—went largely unnoticed in undergraduate philosophy courses until the end of the 1980s. The Paragon Issues in Philosophy Series responds to both perennial and newly influential concerns by bringing together a team of able philosophers to address the fundamental issues in philosophy today and to outline the state of contemporary discussion about them.

More than twenty volumes are scheduled; they are organized into three major categories. The first covers the standard topics—metaphysics, theory of knowledge, ethics, and political philosophy—stressing innovative developments in those disciplines. The second focuses on more specialized but still vital concerns in the philosophies of science, religion, history, sport, and other areas. The third category explores new work that relates philosophy and fields such as feminist criticism, medicine, economics, technology, and literature.

The level of writing is aimed at undergraduate students who have little previous experience studying philosophy. The books provide brief but accurate introductions that appraise the state of the art in their fields and show how the history of thought about their topics developed. Each volume is complete in itself but also complements others in the series.

Traumatic change characterizes these last years of the twentieth century: all of it involves philosophical issues. The editorial staff at Paragon House has worked with us to develop this series. We hope it will encourage the understanding needed in our times, which are as complicated and problematic as they are promising.

John K. Roth
Claremont McKenna College

Frederick Sontag
Pomona College

PARAGON ISSUES IN PHILOSOPHY

MEANING
AND
TRUTH

ALSO BY JAY L. GARFIELD:

Foundations of Cognitive Science: The Essential Readings

Cognitive Science: An Introduction (with N. Stillings, M. Feinstein, E. Rissland, D. Rosenbaum, S. Weisler, and L. Baker-Ward)

Modularity in Knowledge Representation and Natural Language Understanding

Belief in Psychology: A Study in the Ontology of Mind

Abortion: Moral and Legal Perspectives (with P. Hennessey)

JAY L. GARFIELD &
HAMPSHIRE COLLEGE,
AMHERST, MASSACHUSETTS
MURRAY KITELEY
SMITH COLLEGE,
NORTHAMPTON, MASSACHUSETTS

MEANING AND TRUTH: ESSENTIAL READINGS IN MODERN SEMANTICS

PARAGON
ISSUES IN
PHILOSOPHY

PARAGON HOUSE · NEW YORK

FIRST EDITION, 1991

PUBLISHED IN THE UNITED STATES BY
PARAGON HOUSE
90 FIFTH AVENUE
NEW YORK, NY 10011

SERIES DESIGN BY KATHY KIKKERT

LIBRARY OF CONGRESS CATALOGING-IN-PUBLICATION DATA

MEANING AND TRUTH : ESSENTIAL READINGS IN MODERN SEMANTICS
   JAY L. GARFIELD AND MURRAY KITELEY, EDITORS. — 1ST ED.
      P.   CM. — (PARAGON ISSUES IN PHILOSOPHY)
   INCLUDES BIBLIOGRAPHICAL REFERENCES.
   ISBN 1-55778-300-4 : $18.95
   1. SEMANTICS (PHILOSOPHY) 2. MEANING (PHILOSOPHY) 3. TRUTH.
I. GARFIELD, JAY L., 1955–   . II. KITELEY, MURRAY, 1929–
III. SERIES.
B840.M455 1990
121'.68—DC20   90-31315
                                                 CIP

MANUFACTURED IN THE UNITED STATES OF AMERICA
10 9 8 7 6 5 4 3 2 1

FOR BLAINE AND JEAN

CONTENTS

ACKNOWLEDGMENTS

"On Denoting" by Bertrand Russell originally appeared in *Mind*, vol. 14, 1905. It is reprinted by permission of the Oxford University Press.

"Two Types of Quantifiers" by Norbert Hornstein originally appeared in his book *Logic as Grammar*, 1985, MIT Press. It is reprinted by permission of the author and the publisher.

"Propositions" by Robert Stalnaker originally appeared in *Issues in the Philosophy of Language*, edited by A. F. Mackey and D. D. Merrill, New Haven, Yale University Press. It is reprinted by the permission of the author and the publisher.

"Metaphorese" by Harold Skulsky originally appeared in *Nous*, vol. 20 (1986): 351–369. It is reprinted by permission of the author and of the editor of *Nous*.

"The Problem of the Essential Indexical" by John Perry originally appeared in *Nous*, vol. 13 (1979): 3–21. It is reprinted with permission of the author and of the editor of *Nous*.

"A Logical Theory of Verb Phrases Deletion" by Ivan Sag originally appeared in *Papers from the Twelfth Regional Meeting of the Chicago Linguistics Society*, edited by S. S. Mufwene, C. A. Walker, and S. B. Steever. It is reprinted with the permission of the author.

"Mr. Strawson on Referring" by Bertrand Russell originally appeared in his book, *In My Philosophical Development*, Unwin Hyman Limited, London: 238–245. It is reprinted by permission of the publisher.

"The Semantic Conception of Truth" by Alfred Tarski originally appeared in *Philosophy and Phenomenological Research 4 (1944)*. It is reprinted by permission of the estate of Alfred Tarski.

"Possible Worlds" by David Lewis originally appeared in his book *Counterfactuals*, Blackwell and Harvard University Press, Cambridge, MA, 1973: 84–91. It is reprinted by permission of the author and the publisher.

"Tarski's Theory of Truth" by Harry Field originally appeared in *The*

Journal of Philosophy, LXIX: 13 (July 13, 1972): 347–375. It is reprinted by permission of the author and the publisher.

"The Trouble With Possible Worlds" by William Lycan originally appeared in *The Possible and the Actual*, edited by Michael Loux, copyright 1979 by Cornell University. It is reprinted by permission of the author and of Cornell University Press.

"Structured Meanings" and "Structural Ambiguity" by Max Cresswell originally appeared in his book *Structured Meanings*. It is reprinted with permission of MIT Press.

"The Method of Intension and Extension" by Rudolph Carnap originally appeared in his book *Meaning and Necessity*, copyright 1947, 1956 by the University of Chicago Press, Chicago. It is reprinted with permission of the University of Chicago Press.

"Truth and Meaning" by Donald Davidson originally appeared in *Synthèse*, XVII.3: 304–323. It is reprinted with permission of the author and the publisher.

"Speaker's Reference and Semantic Reference," first printed in *Contemporary Perspectives in the Philosophy of Language*, Peter A. French, Theodore F. Uehling, Jr., and Howard K. Wettstein, eds. (Minneapolis: University of Minnesota Press, 1977), pp. 6–27 © 1977 by Saul Kripke.

"Presupposition and Two-Dimensional Logic" by Merrie Bergmann originally appeared in the *Journal of Philosophical Logic*, 10 (1981): 27–53. It is reprinted with permission of the publisher.

"Physicalism and Primitive Denotation: Field on Tarski" by John McDowell originally appeared in *Erkenntnis*, 13 (1978): 131–152. It is reprinted by permission of the publisher.

"Actualism and Possible Worlds" by Alvin Plantinga originally appeared in *Theoria*, 42, 1976. It is reprinted by permission of the publisher.

"Metaphorical Assertions" by Merrie Bergmann originally appeared in *Philosophical Review*, XCI, 2 (1982): 229–245. It is reprinted by permission of the author and the publisher.

"Reference and Definite Description" by Keith Donnellan originally appeared in *Philosophical Review*, 75 (1966): 281–304. It is reprinted by permission of the author and of the publisher.

"Dthat" by David Kaplan originally appeared in *Syntax and Semantics*, vol. 9, Peter Cole, ed., Academic Press, New York, 1978: 221–252. It is reprinted by permission of the author.

"On the Logic of Demonstratives" by David Kaplan originally appeared in *Journal of Philosophical Logic*, vol. 8 (1979). It is reprinted by permission of the author.

PREFACE

This volume is intended as a companion to Ken Taylor's *Introduction to Modern Semantics*, also in the Paragon Issues in Philosophy Series. The essays collected herein present alternative and sometimes conflicting positions on issues raised in that text. It is hoped that when these texts are used in tandem students will receive both a general introduction to a set of questions and problems and a taste of the primary literature and recent debate they occasion. While many of these essays are somewhat challenging, all are accessible to intermediate or advanced undergraudate students of philosophy, linguistics, or cognitive science. It would be folly to pretend that every major topic in contemporary semantic theory is represented, or that every significant position taken on the topics addressed is presented. We have tried as much as possible to avoid duplicating any of the many excellent anthologies on the philosophy of language now available, and to present a selection of readings that recognizes the interdisciplinary character of semantics, and in particular to represent what might be called the more "linguistic" side of that enterprise to a greater degree than it is represented in other anthologies. The selection of essays was determined in part by the availability of primary material accessible to students using that text, and, unfortunately, in part by the reasonableness of publishers in setting fees for permission to reprint scholarly articles. This last problem deserves some comment: In producing an anthology for textbook use, it is obviously essential to keep costs down, so that the resulting volume will be affordable to students. While many publishers recognize this, and charge modest fees, or no fees at all, for permission, and while some others willingly modify their price structure in recognition of this problem, others ask such exorbitant fees that it is for all practical purposes impossible to reprint material originally published by them, even despite the requests of authors for abatement of fees. This, in our view, is a serious impediment to the dissemination of scholarly work, and to its use in the classroom. We urge all scholars before publishing articles, chapters, or books to pay close attention to the policies regarding the reprinting of their work, and to take steps to ensure its broad availability to scholars and students.

We thank the authors and publishers who granted permission to reprint the work contained herein, Don Fehr of Paragon House for editorial support and encouragement, and Donna Gunn, Ruth Hammen, and Leni Bowen for administrative and secretarial support. Special thanks go to Kirsten Hekler and Diane Schroeder, whose tireless, intelligent, and precise research, correspondence, filing, and editorial work made this project possible. And for skilled and heroic proofreading of the galleys, special thanks to Mary O'Conner Hume and Barbara Kostolecki. We cannot imagine having completed the project without their skilled assistance. Thanks also to Emmon Bach, Merrie Bergmann, Jill de Villiers, Mark Feinstein, David Kaplan, Barbara Partee, Tom Tymoczko, Steven Weisler, and Edwin Williams for advice on this volume's contents. Special thanks to Merrie Bergmann and Steve Weisler for inflicting an earlier version of this anthology on their semantics courses. We also thank our families for putting up with our frequent physical and psychological absence while this volume was in preparation.

Jay L. Garfield
Murray Kiteley

JAY L. GARFIELD AND MURRAY KITELEY

GENERAL INTRODUCTION

Aristotle defines truth this way: to say of what is that it is, or to say of what is not that it is not, is the true; to say of what is not that it is, or to say of what is that it is not, is the false. This, one of the more stunningly monosyllabic moments in the history of philosophy, connects the two great ideas of semantics, Meaning and Truth. For to say something about something is to convey meaning, and if Aristotle is right, the truth value of utterances depends just upon their meanings and the fit of those meanings to the world (and not, say, upon the nature of the utterer, or the language of the utterance). Plausibly, utterances, or at least assertions, have as a principal function the expression of belief. More controversially, but yet plausibly, belief can be understood either as a form of internal assertion or as a disposition to make internal assertions. If either of these plausible theses is true, belief must be understood as another concept central to semantics.

It is unsurprising, therefore, that semantics intersects the three disciplines of philosophy, linguistics, and cognitive psychology. Its long dalliance with logic is however less obvious. Mill in his *Logic* alludes not only to semantic doctrines of earlier nineteenth-century logicians, but also to the great flowering of semantic studies in the high Middle Ages. The fact that valid inferences carry one from truths to truths might be urged to explain the medieval logicians' fascination with semantics, but this would not be sufficient, for all that is important in understanding validity is the truth-preserving character of valid argument forms. Any account of the nature of truth, or, more importantly, of the nature of meaning, would be far afield from any specifically *logical* concerns. Whatever explains this semantic golden age hence must make reference to the philosophical importance of semantics in its own right.

This marginal relevance of truth to inference, however, became central in the late nineteenth and early twentieth centuries with the conception of a logical theory as a language with both a syntax and a semantics, a semantics fixed for the logical vocabulary, open for the nonlogical, open, i.e., to various interpretations of the schematic letters. A logic could hence be conceived of as a *partially interpreted* language: the specifically logical terms, such as '&', '~' etc., are assigned meanings, but the propositional, predicate or individual variables (p, F, x, etc.) are left uninterpreted. The variable or uninterpreted semantics of such formal languages does not, however, prevent one from defining truth in them. They are unfixed semantically only at the places that make no difference to the logical truths of that language, logical truths that define in full generality the kinds of valid inferences of which the system treats. While the semantics of such a language does not assign a truth-value to every well-formed formula of the language, it does tell us, in a perfectly intuitive way, *what it is for a sentence in such a language to be true*. Moreover, such a semantics tells us which sentences of the language are *logically true* or *logically false*—true or false no matter what semantic values we assign to the variables in the language.

Truth then in the form of logical truth is very much the business of logic, but, again, this does not by itself demonstrate the importance or relevance of meaning for logic. But here is the idea: Do we know the meaning of (the logician's) 'and' when we know that 'p and q' is true *iff* 'p' is true and 'q' is true? Once you know this, its truth-clause, having previously mastered the recursive rule for its syntax, what else is there to know about it? To answer "nothing more" to this question is to plump for the Tarski-Davidsonian thesis on the shape of the semantic enterprise, a thesis that has defined the quarry of formal semantics for some and been a target for others (Hartry Field, "Tarski's Theory of Truth"). This is to see meaning as *defined by truth-conditions*, and hence sees truth and meaning as belonging to the same domain, and not as attributes of entities as different as words and sentences on the one side and nonlinguistic propositions or acts of assertion on the other. It further takes the truth definition of a contrived language (logic) as paradigmatic for the enterprise of giving the semantics of a much less recently contrived language such as English.

As Tarski shows in his paper ("The Semantic Conception of Truth and the Foundations of Semantics"), however, the paradigm itself is bedeviled by that antique antimony known as Epimenides' Paradox of the Liar: The sentence "This sentence is false" (or "I am lying") is incapable of being assigned a stable truth-value, even though it *seems* to have a meaning. Various complex strategies for avoiding Epimenidean sentences, of which "this sentence is false" is only one, have been canvassed, some less painful than others. The pain comes in such forms as denying meaning to sentences we feel we understand, or assigning to them an undefined semantic value between truth and falsity when we have been able to deduce the truth of the sentence from its falsity and its falsity from its truth. Understanding what such a third (or fourth) truth-value would be, or how to assign it in a principled way is no straightforward matter. (Indeed, sometimes sentences seem to be perfectly unparadoxical when examined for meaning, but only become paradoxical—

and hence apparently meaningless—by accident, so to speak, as in "Everything in the book now being read by _____ [fill in your name] is false." This sentence wasn't strange when it was written, and had a perfectly determinate truth-value, assuming that you were reading a book at that time, but it is now deeply paradoxical.)

Is the paradigm from logic then a will-o'-the-wisp? Another arena in which this question has been hotly debated is that concerned with the interpretation of natural language quantifiers. Much of this debate centers on 'the'-phrases, the so-called definite descriptions (prominently including "the present king of France"). One attitude, to put it roughly, holds natural languages to be too messy for the sharp edges of the logic template. Those who reject this counsel of despair, classically articulated by Strawson ("On Referring"), have to weigh imponderable choices between alternative logics and alternatives within logic. Carnap (*Meaning and Necessity*) surveys options of the second sort for the logical semantics of definite descriptions in which the uniqueness condition fails. Bergmann does the second. She postulates two semantic evaluations, one giving truth-value, the other telling whether the uniqueness condition is satisfied ("security value"). She hence avoids postulating Strawson's semantic relation of presupposition and thus having to choose some version of three-valued logic for sentences with failed descriptions. Russell in his reply to Strawson appears to think of the fit of logic to a natural language as like that of Procrustes' bed to one of his guests, a bed he thinks it on the whole salubrious to make speech fit.

Contemporary semantic theory is rife with theoretical disputes of this kind, disputes not only about the proper account of the meaning of a class of words or constructions, but about the general shape that a semantic theory ought to have. There is even dispute about the *possibility* of semantic theory. As in any science, and most particularly as in any unsettled period in the history of a science, just how one decides between competing theories is never clear. The data are often conflicting, and the crucial phenomena are often remote from everyday concerns. So, for instance, the decision between theories of quantifier interpretation may turn on their ability to make correct (or intelligible) predictions about the meanings of sentences such as "The boy who really loved her kissed the girl who always adored him" (so-called Bach-Peters sentences, in which the interpretation of each quantified noun-phrase depends upon that of the other). Just as we rarely observe the exotic astronomical events that are crucial to deciding highly abstract disputes in physics, we often rarely assert or hear the highly exotic sentences that decide abstract semantic disputes. But semantic theory, like any science, aims at generality, and so, as in any science, we put plausible theories of the everyday to stiff test in the remote reaches of language.

In some ways it is more fun to bog down in the endlessly entertaining details and complexities of the institution of speech than to study the somewhat arid formalities and technicalities of semantic theories. So it must also be said, in defense of the theorizing, that many charming eccentricities of language are only visible against a background of abstract theory. This phenomenon is just the familiar reciprocity between the evidence that supports a theory and the theory that defines the evidence. Such semantic attributes as vagueness, indexicality, ambiguity, figurative speech, and amphiboly (structural ambiguity) are both theory breakers and theory makers. The amphiboly of Pierce's "everyone loves someone" could not be explained by traditional logic but could be by Pierce's. As Quine says in a short essay that could well serve as this introduction regarding another quandary "it owes its very existence to insights from the side of modern logic" ("Logic as a Source of Syntactic Insights," *Ways of Paradox*, p. 48). The slogan might be, to figuratively invoke a false etymon, "no anomaly without nomos."

Semantics is arguably the humanistic science *par excellence*. What institution or artifact is of greater moment than that of language? And what feature of language is more important than meaning? The rebirth of semantics in this century thus marks a return to an enterprise not the less exciting for its spotty career, not less humanistic for its abstract character, and not the less scientific for the elusiveness of its quarry.

Semantics studies meaning and that study includes both the interpretation of natural languages such as Manx and artificial languages such as Pascal. If, however, one thinks of a language as its vocabulary—whether that vocabulary is descriptive or logical—one would collapse semantics into lexicography. It is, however, highly misleading to think that semantics is exhausted by—or even that it is devoted primarily to—the study of the meanings of individual words taken in isolation. While the study of individual word meaning—lexical semantics—is an important part of the entire enterprise, it is but one area of study among many, and arguably not even at the center of current semantic research. Even here semanticists characteristically do not worry about the meaning of individual words, but rather about that of certain uses of words, such as token reflexive uses like "I" or "here," or metaphorical uses.

Words are not enough. When someone comes to understand a linguistic complex, whether on-line as a listener (or reader), or at leisure in the course of theorizing, it is overwhelmingly probable that one does not use some magical semantic intuition to go straight from the uttered words and their surface structure (as organized) to the meaning conveyed. The same would seem as true for the construction of utterances as it is for their interpretation or understanding: Intermediate processing stages probably lie between content and surface form. Depending on the details of one's psycholinguistic, syntactic, and semantic theory, there may occur such intermediate levels of linguistic structure as these: syntactic deep structures, levels of logical form at which structural disambiguation, pronominal interpretation, anaphor resolution, and other kindred operations occur, and a level of nonlinguistic discourse representation.

While the problems addressed by semanticists have inspired an enormous variety of different proposals (many represented in this volume), behind many there nonetheless lies a common idea. The idea, to express it in one misleading, difficult word is that of *intensionality*. A large part of twentieth-century semantic theorizing is prompted by and devoted to this variously described idea or phenomenon. Because of intensionality, the meaning of a linguistic whole is not always compositionally determined by the meanings of its linguistic parts—or at least not straightforwardly so. Thus the mechanisms by which meanings are composed are not always apparent on the surface of language. Many lie underneath, and are revealed only by theoretical analysis. Semantic theory has as one part of its task, therefore, the inquiry into the nature of these underlying compositional structures, their relation to surface structure, and the complex relationships between meaning and surface and underlying linguistic and logical structure. Not only does language apparently come in multiple levels—surface structure, syntactic deep structure, logical form—but meaning may also be a multitiered affair: Phrases and sentence may have as semantic values not simply their extensions or denotations, but, as Frege argued, their intensions or senses, and may only denote as a function of intension and context. This crucial role of intension—signaled by the failure of substitutivity *salve veritate* of coreferential terms, and the failure of generalization and instantiation of quantificational phrases—is particularly evident in modal and intentional contexts (though it is arguably a perfectly general phenomenon). These include those determined by expressions such as "I believe that . . . ," or "Necessarily. . . ." The truth-value sentences of these forms cannot be determined solely by knowing the truth-values of the sentences embedded in them (as in "Fred believes that the blue whale is extinct"—knowing whether or not that species is extinct is insufficient to determine the truth or falsity of the belief-ascribing sentence). Nor are their truth-values necessarily preserved when we substitute coreferential terms in the embedded contexts (Oedipus wanted to marry Jocasta, not his mother). As a consequence, the study of these so-called intensional contexts, and of the role of intensionality in semantics, has become a central area of semantic research.

Each aspect of semantics here described—the study of the meaning of words, phrases, and sentences, and of the routes thereto, as well as the study of intensional obstacles along these routes—concerns the determination of the meaning and truth-conditions of a linguistic structure thought of as an abstract linguistic object. This, of course, is an idealization of the actual linguistic objects whose meanings typically concern us, but an idealization that is theoretically justified. The unabstracted or nonidealized linguistic objects are actual utterances or inscriptions by particular utterers in particular social and conversational contexts. Knowing the meaning—in a broad and intuitively compelling sense often seemingly absent from consideration in more formal truth-conditional semantic theory—of these bits of language requires more than knowing the semantic values of each of their atoms, and combining these values according to a recursive set of semantic rules. One must also make use of the conventions regarding the use of speech act being performed whether it be that of asserting, questioning, promising, greeting, or whatever. Then one must connect the utterance being evaluated to the larger conversational context and understand the way that portions of the utterance or the speech act itself might be used figuratively as well as literally. The domain of semantics hence includes the study of figurative speech, speech act theory, implicature, pragmatics, and discourse effects on linguistic meaning.

The reach of semantics is hence wide. Its goal is no less than the understanding of what linguistic meaning is, how it is represented in language, and how we can decode the linguistic message to arrive at it. The inquiry hence trespasses into and makes use of the theoretical and technical resources of logic, linguistics, the philosophy of language, and psycholinguistics. While each of the subdomains of semantic theory can be seen as indeed a subspecialty of semantics, inasmuch as each is at the same time a natural and well-entrenched subspecialty of another discipline, semantics can be seen as the interdiscipline of cognitive science par excellence, uniting in a single study philosophy, psychology, linguistics and even computer science.

Semantics hence lacks insularity; border disputes are its birthright. Is it a branch of logic or of psychology or of rhetoric? There seems to have been since ancient Greece a discipline of questions about the truth and meaning of speech (Aristotle's *Organon*). Aristotle follows Plato (*Sophist*) in several ways: in his definition of truth and falsity, in his noting the compositional complexity of those property's bearers, (*vide Cratylus*) and in drawing a parallel between the sentences of speech and the language-transcending thoughts to which they give utterance. (In the *Theatetus*, Socrates describes thinking as the soul's eristic debate with itself and belief as its resolution.) This latter point and its parallel in the Stoic's notion of *lekton* (what is meant/said) as the true or false thing a sentence means, became a standard late medieval doctrine. The meaning and truth of oral or written sentences belongs to them solely in virtue of the mental sentences they give voice to. (The Stoic *lekta* were probably not mental sentences inasmuch as they were said to be incorporeal, and the Stoics held even the soul to be corporeal [Kneales, *The Development of Logic*].) So it is that semantics trespasses sometimes into linguistics, sometimes into psychology, and sometimes into philosophy and logic.

Whether or not meaning and truth ultimately reside in sentences, thoughts, speech acts, or abstract propositions is an issue perhaps less critical to semantics than is the claim that wherever they reside they cohabit. For if they do not reside in the same place, one cannot make the meaningfulness of a sentence a condition of its having a truth-value. Of course, what, one might ask, is the relevant notion of proximity and what, for that matter, is meaning? Is not the speech act of assertion close enough to the sentence so asserted that the nonsense of the latter might deprive the former of bivalent truth-value? And what kind of nonsense is it to say that the present king of France is bald or to say "This sentence is false"? It could well be that the answers to any or all of these questions are equally important for several or all of the disciplines in cognitive science.

In order to answer these questions concerning the nature of meaning, Frege introduced two semantic functions or relations to every part of speech—reference, or denotation, and sense—in order to solve problems of intensional or attitudinative semantics, in particular the problem of why the substitution of one coreferring expression such as 'the evening star' for another, 'the morning star', can make a true and informative identity trivial. ("The evening star = The evening star" is uninformative; "The evening star = The morning star" tells us something interesting. How can that be, if the meanings of the referring expressions are their referents?) Salmon calls this "Frege's puzzle." It inspires a vast literature on the problem of opacity or the failure of substitutivity and Frege is often seen as its pioneer. But it, like the Paradoxes of the Liar (above) and the Heap, is a puzzle discovered or recorded by the Stoics. They called it the Hooded Man and stated it thus: You know your brother; you don't know that hooded man; but he is your brother. Their solution(s) are lost. (Kneales, *The Development of Logic*).

Frege's proposed solution requires his distinction between sense (or intension) and reference (extension), which parallels in interesting ways Mill's distinction (adopted from the medieval semanticists) between connotation and denotation. But there are two features of Frege's distinction that set it off from the older distinction that Mill draws between denotative and connotative terms: its scope and its application. His distinction, unlike Mill's, cannot be used to classify the parts of speech because both kinds of meaning belong to them all, and even to phrases, clauses, and sentences. For Mill, proper names and demonstratives are solely denotative and unlike such connotative names as 'white,' which denotes (its extension of) all white things and connotes the attribute of whiteness (which defines that extension). Mill straddles Occam's notion of connotation and Frege's notion of sense. Occam and other schoolmen used the word 'connote' literally to mean co-noted: 'white' co-notes white things and the attribute of whiteness. They were not postulating two different semantic relations as they might have done in the case of Quine's "Giorgione is so-called for his size," the phrase 'so-called' giving the nickname both as they would say personal supposition to the painter and material supposition to itself. Mill and Frege, however, say there are two ways words and other expressions relate. They thus possibly do not agree on what is so related, since Mill's connotation or attribute may not be the same as Frege's sense or mode of presentation. Their views, however, do definitely diverge on the extent of the application of these two relations. In addition, Frege uses his distinction to solve the problem of the failure of the substitutivity of identicals. And he presciently sees the threat that that failure represents for the principle of compositionality: If the meanings of semantic wholes are determined by the meanings of their parts, then since parts of semantic units may often share certain aspects of meaning (as "the evening star" and "the morning star" share the property of denoting Venus), there had better be enough components of meaning available to semantic theory to explain the semantic divergence of the wholes that differ only in containing one member of these pairs rather than the other. Otherwise, we will have the disturbing phenomenon of semantic wholes of identical structure that diverge in meaning, but whose corresponding parts are identical in meaning. Compositionality would fail, and we would be at a loss to explain how language can be understood.

One of the preoccupations of medieval semantics (*Cambridge History of Later Medieval Philosophy*) was the partial or incomplete meaning of the so-called syncategoremata, which roughly are those particles of speech that cannot stand alone as either the subject term or predicate term of a sentence, e.g., 'the'. There is an echo of this notion in Russell's view that definite descriptions are "incomplete symbols." He held them to be semantically incomplete despite their competence to be the subject of a sentence because on analysis they disappeared in favor of a sentence containing no phrase synonymous with them. This of course is true of all standard quantifier noun-phrases (QNPs) as classically understood. 'A satellite exploded' is parsed as Vx(x is a satellite & *x* exploded) with no obvious part that can be pointed to as either the grammatical or logical subject (*vide* Strawson). Occam and others attempted to do both the grammar and the semantics of QNP sentences within the semantics of supposition theory, positing various kinds of confused supposition to account for various kinds of QNP sentences. (Supposition is the medieval term for what is variously and of course not completely uniformly called *Bedeutung*, denotation, or reference.) Something similar has been done recently with great elegance and a lot of set theory for all QNPs whether standard like 'the/a/any . . . satellite' or nonstandard like 'most/at least half/ every other . . . satellite' by Barwise and Cooper. But it means reversing the order of the truth definition, to which at any rate the notion of subject and predicate probably must be relativized anyway. A sentence of the surface form 'the F is G' is construed as '{G} belongs to the family of super sets of the unit set of F'. The set term, {G}, is thus the subject of the sentence and the description now understood to be a term for a family of sets is the predicate. If, then, by incomplete symbol Russell meant an expression that on analysis of the sentence into its logical form, its deep grammar, becomes a non subject-term, this is true of all QNPs for Barwise and Cooper, and of all standard ones for Montague. This is but one illustration of the remarkable progress that can be made by bringing to bear the *prima facie* conceptually distant apparatus of modern logic in these very old philosophical problems concerning the natures of and relations between meaning and truth, and hence of the fruitfulness of semantics as an interdiscipline.

This book could have been organized in many equally good ways, reflecting different theoretical or pedagogical proclivities of particular scholars or teachers. But we had to organize it in some way, so we organized it our way, at the same time realizing that some will find it counterintuitive. We begin with a historical section in which we collect classic articles that have shaped semantics and some discussions of them. Here many of the specific topics that are treated more systematically later in the book are introduced, such as compositionality, intensionality, logical form, and presupposition, and some of the historical roots of semantics in logic and the philosophy of language are laid bare. The second section addresses the surprisingly central questions posed by the interpretation of definite descriptions, such as "the present king of France." The semantic puzzles this class of expressions poses were noted early on, and have motivated a great deal of subsequent theory regarding semantic topics as diverse as the nature of logical form, and the role presupposition and other pragmatic phenomena in semantic interpretation.

In the third section, we take up a second theme raised by early work in semantics—the consequences of Tarski's pioneering work in the theory of truth for the structure of semantic theory. Represented here are two such programmatic consequences—Davidson's truth-theoretic semantic programme, and the debate over the possibility and character of semantics in a physical universe.

The fourth section focuses directly on approaches to intensionality, with particular attention to propositional attitude contexts. Again, while we cannot pretend to completeness, our goal has been variety and representativeness. We introduce two principal programs in semantic theory, as well as some discussion of the philosophical problems raised by subjectivity and the propositional attitudes for semantic theory.

The problem of the relation between meaning and underlying levels of linguistic analysis, such as syntactic or logical form representations, is taken up in the fifth section. These selections are heavily formal in character. They mobilize the resources of syntactic theory and of higher-order logic and model theory quite directly in the service of semantics. While we have not by any means provided an exhaustive inventory of theoretical approaches to intermediate levels of representation and their role in interpretation, we have tried to provide an instructive sampling.

The semantics of natural language, in virtue of the profusion of intensional constructs that must be interpreted, requires—at least according to many prominent theoretical programs—a rich model. The models most often proposed make liberal use of "possible worlds." But given the nonactuality of most of these possible worlds, significant metaphysical problems are posed by their apparent indispensability to semantic theory: What are they? Are they real? What are their contents? Does the reliance upon such nonactual entities impugn the scientific status of semantics? These and other unavoidable philosophical questions posed by the current methodology of semantics are addressed in the sixth section.

The noninsular and interdisciplinary character of semantics is nowhere more evident than in its complex relation to pragmatics. Such problems as the interpretation of metaphor, the distinction between figurative and literal meaning, and the interpretation of indexicals require attention not only to the literal meanings of words and the linguistic structure of the sentences in which they appear, but to features of the discourse in which they figure, such as shared presuppositions, and the identity of the participants. These inescapably pragmatic yet ineliminably semantic questions are taken up in the final section of this book.

Depending on the structure of the course in which this text is used, there are a number of alternative groupings of these essays. For instance, the essays of Frege, Davidson, Kripke, Weisler, Cresswell, Plantinga, and Lycan could be usefully grouped as a section on the sense/reference distinctions and its formal and philosophical ramifications. Or those of Russell, Strawson, Donellan, Bergmann, Hornstein, Kaplan, Quine, and Weisler form a natural group of logical form. Strawson, Donnellan, and Bergmann all address presupposition. And so on. We urge teachers and students to consider alternative orderings and to pursue semantics as a wonderfully tangled interdiscipline.

PART ONE

THE BEGINNINGS

INTRODUCTION

Though semantics as a discipline is arguably as old as philosophy itself, with virtually every significant philosophical tradition exploring the nature of linguistic meaning early on, modern semantics as the systematic investigation into the formal mechanisms by which language encodes meaning has a recognizable beginning with the logical and philosophical work of Frege. For it was Frege who first took seriously the problem of compositionality—of how to construct the meaning of a complex linguistic item on the basis of the meanings of its parts, and attempted a solution that makes use of the resources of logic. And this formal or quasi-formal approach to this central problem is the hallmark of the discipline as it has evolved in this century. But though Frege may be the father of modern semantics, the lineage is certainly older. While one could with justice represent progenitors from Plato in the West and the Nyaya in the East of the Fregean semantic program, we begin with Mill. For in Mill we see represented for the first time the particular constellation of classical and medieval semantic insights that form the foundation for Frege's program.

In *Logic*, Mill justifies the study of language and its terms as a proper part of a study of reasoning, language being "one of the principal instruments or helps of thought." He draws a number of distinctions in his characteristically lucid way, but only one, perhaps, falls within the purview of twentieth-century semanics, viz., the words in which he sets out "a third great division of names, into connotative and non-connotative." Unlike either Frege after (as we shall see) or the medieval logicians before, Mill thinks of these, not so much as of two kinds of semantic relation (two kinds of medieval supposition or notation) as of two disjoint classes of words. The non-connotative are what are now called Millian names—proper names and also descriptions whose descriptive content has decayed: "Dartmouth" is his example, since it would remain so-called even were the Dart river to move. All other words or names whether of general or singular import are connotative, e.g., the word "white" that as he says "denotes all white things . . . and implies or, in the language of the schoolmen, connotes the attribute whiteness." The connoted attribute determines the extension of all white things and is thus in recent usage (Putnam, Carnap) the expression's intension. Mill argues that meanings are not ideas, anticipating Putnam's conclusions, and a fascinating footnote quotes Bain on the word "stone": "there is no quality uniformly present in the cases where it is applied and uniformly absent in the cases where it is not applied," a word showing demonstrable but surprising kinship to "game."

Frege's "Sense and Nominatum," begins with a puzzle that invites the mobilization of exactly this distinction drawn by Mill. The puzzle is how statements of identity can vary in information conveyed when they appear to say the same thing: "The morning star is (=) the morning star" tells us little; "the evening star is the morning star" tells us much; yet they differ only in how one of the identicals is designated ($a = a$ vs. $a = b$) both therefore talking about the same heavenly object and saying the same thing of that object.

Frege uses his famous distinction between Sinn and Bedeutung to solve this puzzle, arguing that while "the morning star" and "the evening star" may have the same *reference* (or *nominatum*), they differ in *sense*, and that sense is what we grasp when we understand a term or a sentence, even though reference may ultimately determine truth. Frege's twofold semantics of sense and reference is justly famous; a measure of that fame is the controversy surrounding even the translation of the German words he chose to denominate it. "Bedeutung" first was rendered by Herbert Feigl as "nominatum," later by Geach and Black as "reference," but in the latest edition of their translation of Frege's essays as "meaning." "Sinn," on the other hand, is pretty uniformly given as "sense," but what it means and what Frege's frequent paraphrase of it as "mode of presentation" means is another matter.

Whatever meaning is, and whatever its components or varieties are, it must be possible to determine the meanings of whole linguistic items—such as phrases or sentences—based on the meanings of their parts. Otherwise, we would need, in order to understand our language, to learn individually each of the infinitely many meanings we are capable of expressing with each of the infinitely many strings of words our language is capable of generating. And if, as Frege argues, there are two varieties or components of meaning, there must then be two levels at which meanings compose to form larger meanings. Perhaps the most imposing feature of Frege's essay is then not so much his famous distinction between two kinds or levels of meaning as is his repeated emphasis on semantic compositionality and his mobilization of compositionality as a constraint on semantic theory. Whatever the semantic values are, they must compose. The value of the whole must be computable from or determined by those of its parts, whether that value is Sinn or Bedeutung. It follows from this doctrine that the wholes must be given the same kind of semantic value as are given to their parts whether that be Sinn or Bedeutung. (This accounts for his slightly odd notion that both a name like "Frege" and a sentence like "Frege is a man" have a Bedeutung, a designation or a reference: in the first case, the man Frege; in the second case, the sentence's truth-value, True.)

The great *prima facie* obstacle to compositionality is the failure of substitutivity. The compositional function ought not to care what the parts look like so long as they have the same semantic value: if they have the same value they ought to be substitutable for each other. For the whole point of insisting on compositionality is to capture the intuition that the semantic value of a whole is a *function* of the semantic values of its parts. That explains how we can understand and produce novel sentences and phrases. But in many cases, as Frege amply illustrates, we encounter sentence structures wherein if we substitute constituents that appear to have identical semantic values, the semantic value of the entire sentence (its truth-value, or the proposition it expresses) changes, as in the "Venus sentences" alluded to above. The truth-value of the subordinate sentence in indirect discourse or in sentences that report beliefs and thoughts (called propositional attitudes) makes no difference to the truth-value of the whole sentence that reports that discourse or that attitude, as one might think it would if the truth-value is, as Frege argues, the reference of a sentence, and if the reference of the whole sentence is a function of the reference of its parts. One can say and believe falsities as well as truths. This apparent obstacle to compositionality led Frege to an instance of a strategy followed by Russell in the next essay, viz., to postulate another semantic value as argument for the compositional function. If the truth-value of what I say or believe is not relevant to whether or not I say or believe it, then perhaps something else, sense, is relevant, relevant to the sense of the whole. So, the theory goes, while the *truth-value* of "I believe that Frege was Scott" is not dependent on the truth-value of "Frege was a Scott," the sense of the whole sentence is dependent upon the sense of that embedded sentence. And the sense of the whole determines its truth-value. Since on Frege's theory sense is what the mind grasps—is the cognitive value of a sentence, the difference in sense between "the morning star" and "the evening star" predicts the difference in cognitive value of the two "Venus" sentences.

    The two essays that comprise the rest of this section are respectively the subject or inspiration for the essays in sections II and III. Both draw inspiration from, and attempt to pursue—albeit in somewhat non-Fregean fashion—the program to develop a formal compositional semantics for natural language announced by Frege's essay. Russell begins a line of inquiry about the semantics of what he calls denoting phrases (quantifier noun-phrases), the most troublesome of which are those beginning with "the" or "a." Tarski's more informal 1944 reprise of his famous Wahrheitsbegriff (1933) makes a substantial contribution to our understanding of the semantics of just such phrases by means of model theory. It does so at least to the extent that natural languages can translate into the rigorous formal language of the predicate calculus, something Tarski is less sanguine about than is Davidson in "Meaning and Truth." It does a good deal more, however. Tarski argues that it is impossible to define truth for any reasonably rich but semantically closed language. But he shows that the satisfaction of predicates of arbitrary recursive complexity is sufficient to explain the semantics of the classical part (the classical truth-functions and quantifiers) of any natural language. Since the inverse of the satisfaction relation is the relation of a predicate's "being true of," this amounts to the reduction of a large part of the theory of meaning to the theory of truth, a suggestion that inspires Davidson's Tarskian semantic program (infra).[1]

Russell in "On Denoting" presents an acute diagnosis of scope ambiguity such as occurs in his example of the guest's gauche "I thought your yacht was larger than it is." He sees the ambiguity of such utterances not as deriving from the presence in the sentence of any ambiguous term, for in this sentence there is no such ambiguous term. Rather, he points out, this is an example of scope ambiguity, or in Whately's terminology, amphiboly. In such cases, linguistic operators function to bind variables that occur within their scope. But since these operators and variables are not apparent as such in the surface structure of the sentence, a single surface structure may possibly encode several quite distinct underlying "logical forms," each of which might represent distinct variable binding possibilities. This is a semantic phenomenon that occurs famously in the case of descriptions. If two operators appear in the same sentence and they are unmarked as to which has superior scope over the other, amphiboly occurs, e.g., with the negation and the description in "It is not the case that the present king of France is bald," and with wonder and the author of *Waverley* in "George IV wondered whether Scott was the author of *Waverley*." If a term (what it denotes) has wide or superior scope over another, Russell says it has primary occurrence, the other secondary. How to identify and rank the two operators in the yacht example is, like much else in this essay, not easy—the size is such (primary occurrence) he thought it smaller than it is vs. he thought the size (secondary occurrence) smaller than it is.

Russell's essay contains many more puzzles than the three he lists. And many are of great semantic interest. Following on the heels of Frege's discovery of the centrality of logic and logical functors to semantics, Russell's deployment of logic in the service of the analysis is ground breaking. He presents the first genuine theory of logical form, and a persuasive account of the logical form of denoting phrases and its relation to surface structure. He mobilizes this account to explain the effect of the failure of the uniqueness condition of 'the'-phrases on truth-value; the causes of the failure of substitutivity to preserve truth-value or information content (or relations of scope); and the relation between the underlying logical form of a sentence and a speech act. Thus, this essay is one of the most significant contributions to modern semantics, and demonstrates for the first time the power of formal methods to solve problems in the theory of meaning. Its influence on subsequent semantic theory is hard to exaggerate.

NOTES

1. A measure of the ambitiousness of this program is the means needed to make tractable some of its obstacles. Tarski thought the Liar Paradox made truth definable only for a language that does not contain its own truth-predicate. Otherwise some of the sentences falling within the extension of "true" or "false" might end with those adjectives and, worse, be self-referring. This obstacle has recently been overcome by Kripke et al., but only at some cost, both in technical machinery and in truth-definability. To construct the extension and counterextension of the word "true" some sentences must be allowed to belong to neither.

JOHN STUART MILL

OF NAMES AND PROPOSITIONS

CHAPTER I. OF THE NECESSITY
OF COMMENCING WITH AN ANALYSIS OF LANGUAGE

§ 1. It is so much the established practice of writers on logic to commence their treatises by a few general observations (in most cases, it is true, rather meagre) on Terms and their varieties, that it will, perhaps, scarcely be required from me in merely following the common usage, to be as particular in assigning my reasons, as it is usually expected that those should be who deviate from it.

The practice, indeed, is recommended by considerations far too obvious to require a formal justification. Logic is a portion of the Art of Thinking: Language is evidently, and by the admission of all philosophers, one of the principal instruments or helps of thought; and any imperfection in the instrument, or in the mode of employing it, is confessedly liable, still more than in almost any other art, to confuse and impede the process, and destroy all ground of confidence in the result. For a mind not previously versed in the meaning and right use of the various kinds of words, to attempt the study of methods of philosophising, would be as if some one should attempt to become an astronomical observer, having never learned to adjust the focal distance of his optical instruments so as to see distinctly.

Since Reasoning, or Inference, the principal subject of logic, is an operation which usually takes place by means of words, and in complicated cases can take place in no other way; those who have not a thorough insight into the signification and purposes of words will be under chances, amounting almost to certainty, of reasoning or inferring incorrectly. And logicians have generally felt that unless, in the very first stage, they removed this source of error; unless they taught their pupil to put away the glasses which distort the object, and to use those which are adapted to his purpose in such a manner as to assist, not perplex, his vision; he would not be in a condition to practise the remaining part of their discipline with any prospect of advantage. Therefore it is that an inquiry into language, so far as is needful to guard against the errors to which it gave rise, has at all times been deemed a necessary preliminary to the study of logic.

But there is another reason, of a still more fundamental nature, why the import of words should be the earliest subject of the logician's consideration: because without it he cannot examine into the import of Propositions. Now this is a subject which stands on the very threshold of the science of logic.

The object of logic, as defined in the Introductory Chapter, is to ascertain how we come by that portion of our knowledge (much the greatest portion) which is not intuitive: and by what criterion we can, in matters not self-evident, distinguish between things proved and things not proved, between what is worthy and what is unworthy of belief. Of the various questions which present themselves to our inquiring faculties, some receive an answer from direct consciousness, others, if resolved at all, can only be resolved by means of evidence. Logic is concerned with these last. But before inquiring into the mode of resolving questions, it is necessary to inquire what are those which offer themselves; what questions are conceivable; what inquiries are there, to which mankind have either obtained, or been able to imagine it possible that they should obtain, an answer. This point is best ascertained by a survey and analysis of Propositions.

§ 2. The answer to every question which it is possible to frame, must be contained in a Proposition, or Assertion. Whatever can be an object of belief, or even of disbelief, must, when put into words, assume the form of a proposition. All truth and all error lie in propositions. What, by a convenient misapplication of an abstract term, we call a Truth, means simply a True Proposition; and errors are false propositions. To know the import of all possible propositions, would be to know all questions which can be raised, all matters which are susceptible of being either believed or disbelieved. How many kinds of inquiries can be propounded; how many kinds of judgments can be made; and how many kinds of propositions is it possible to frame with a meaning; are but different forms of one and the same question. Since, then, the objects of all Belief and of all Inquiry express themselves in propositions; a sufficient scrutiny of Propositions and of their varieties will apprize us what questions mankind have actually asked of themselves, and what, in the nature of answers to those questions, they have actually thought they had grounds to believe.

Now the first glance at a proposition shows that it is formed by putting together two names. A proposition, according to the common simple definition, which is sufficient for our purpose, is, *discourse, in which something is affirmed or denied of something*. Thus, in the proposition, Gold is yellow, the quantity *yellow* is affirmed of the substance *gold*. In the proposition, Franklin was not born in England, the fact expressed by the words *born in England* is denied of the man Franklin.

Every proposition consists of three parts: the Subject, the Predicate, and the Copula. The predicate is the name denoting that which is affirmed or denied. The subject is the name denoting the person or thing which something is affirmed or denied of. The copula is the sign denoting that there is an affirmation or denial; and thereby enabling the hearer or reader to distinguish a proposition from any other kind of discourse. Thus, in the proposition, the earth is round, the Predicate is the word *round*, which denotes the quality affirmed, or (as the phrase is) predicated: *the earth*, words denoting the object which that quality is affirmed of, compose the Subject; the word *is*, which serves as the connecting mark between the subject and predicate, to show that one of them is affirmed of the other, is called the Copula.

Dismissing, for the present, the copula, of which more will be said hereafter, every proposition, then, consists of at least two names; brings together two names, in a particular manner. This is already a first step towards what we are in quest of. It appears from this, that for an act of belief, *one* object is not sufficient; the simplest act of belief supposes, and has something to do with, *two* objects: two names, to say the least; and (since the names must be names of something) two *nameable things*. A large class of thinkers would cut the matter short by saying, two *ideas*. They would say, that the subject and predicate are both of them names of ideas, the idea of gold, for instance, and the idea of yellow; and that what takes place (or part of what takes place) in the act of belief, consists in bringing (as it is often expressed) one of these ideas under the other. But this we are not yet in a condition to say: whether such be the correct mode of describing the phenomenon, is an after consideration. The result with which for the present we must be contented, is, that in every act of belief *two* objects are in some manner taken cognizance of; that there can be no belief claimed, or question propounded, which does not embrace two distinct (either material or intellectual) subjects of thought; each of them capable, or not, of being conceived by itself, but incapable of being believed by itself.

I may say, for instance, "the sun." The word has a meaning, and suggests that meaning to the mind of any one who is listening to me. But suppose I ask him, Whether it is true: whether he believes it? He can give no answer. There is as yet nothing to believe, or to disbelieve. Now, however, let me make, of all possible assertions respecting the sun, the one which involves the least of reference to any object besides itself; let me say, "the sun exists." Here, at once, is something which a person can say he believes. But here instead of only one, we find two distinct objects of conception: the sun is one object; existence is another. Let it not be said that this second conception, existence, is involved in the first; for the sun may be conceived as no longer existing. "The sun" does not convey all the meaning that is conveyed by "the sun exists": "my father" does not include all the meaning of "my father exists," for he may be dead; "a round square" does not include the meaning of "a round square exists," for it does not and cannot exist. When I say "the sun," "my father," or "a round square," I do not call upon the hearer for any belief or disbelief, nor can either the one or the other be afforded me; but if I say, "the sun exists," "my father exists," or a "round square exists," I call for belief; and should in the first of the three instances, meet with it; in the second, with belief or disbelief, as the case might be; in the third, with disbelief.

§ 3. This first step in the analysis of the object of belief, which, though so obvious, will be found to be not unimportant, is the only one which we shall find it practicable to make without a preliminary survey of language. If we attempt to proceed further in the same path, that is, to analyse any further the import of Propositions, we find forced upon us, as a subject of previous consideration, the import of Names. For every proposition consists of two names; and every proposition affirms or denies one of these names, of the other. Now what we do, what passes in our mind, when we affirm or deny two names of one another, must depend on what they are names of; since it is with reference to that, and not to the mere names themselves, that we make the affirmation or denial. Here, therefore, we find a new reason why the signification of names, and the relation generally between names and the things signified by them, must occupy the preliminary stage of the inquiry we are engaged in.

It may be objected that the meaning of names can guide us at most only to the opinions, possibly the foolish and groundless opinions, which mankind have formed concerning things, and that as the object of philosophy is truth, not opinion, the philosopher should dismiss words and look into things themselves, to ascertain what questions can be asked and answered in regard to them. This advice (which no one has it in his power to follow) is in reality an exhortation to discard the whole fruits of the labours of his predecessors, and conduct himself as if he were the first person who had ever turned an inquiring eye upon nature. What does any one's personal knowledge of Things amount to, after subtracting all which he has acquired by means of the words of other people? Even after he has learned as much as people usually do learn from others, will the notions of things contained in his individual mind afford as sufficient a basis for a *catalogue raisonné* as the notions which are in the minds of all mankind?

In any enumeration and classification of Things, which does not set out from their names, no varieties of things will of course be comprehended but those recognised by the particular inquirer; and it will still remain to be established, by a subsequent examination of names, that the enumeration has omitted nothing which ought to have been included. But if we begin with names, and use them as our clue to the things, we bring at once before us all the distinctions which have been recognised, not by a single inquirer, but by all inquirers taken together. It doubtless may, and I believe it will, be found, that mankind have multiplied the varieties unnecessarily, and have imagined distinctions among things, where there were only distinctions in the manner of naming them. But we are not entitled to assume this in the commencement. We must begin by recognising the distinctions made by ordinary language. If some of these appear, on a close examination, not to be fundamental, the enumeration of the different kinds of realities may be abridged accordingly. But to impose upon the facts in the first instance the yoke of a theory, while the grounds of the theory are reserved for discussion in a subsequent stage, is not a course which a logician can reasonably adopt.

CHAPTER II. OF NAMES

§ 1. "A name," says Hobbes,[1] "is a word taken at pleasure to serve for a mark which may raise in our mind a thought like to some thought we had before, and which being pronounced to others, may be to them a sign of what thought the speaker had[2] before in his mind." This simple definition of a name, as a word (or a set of words) serving the double purpose of a mark to recall to ourselves the likeness of a former thought, and a sign to make it known to others, appears unexceptionable. Names, indeed, do much more than this; but whatever else they do, grows out of, and is the result of this; as will appear in its proper place.

Are names more properly said to be the names of things, or of our ideas of things? The first is the expression in common use; the last is that of some metaphysicians, who conceived that in adopting it they were introducing a highly important distinction. The eminent thinker, just quoted, seems to countenance the latter opinion. "But seeing," he continues, "names ordered in speech (as is defined) are signs of our conceptions, it is manifest they are not signs of the things themselves; for that the sound of this word *stone* should be the sign of a stone, cannot be understood in any sense but this, that he that hears it collects that he that pronounces it thinks of a stone."

If it be merely meant that the conception alone, and not the thing itself, is recalled by the name, or imparted to the hearer, this of course cannot be denied. Nevertheless, there seems good reason for adhering to the common usage, and calling (as indeed Hobbes himself does in other places) the word *sun* the name of the sun, and not the name of our idea of the sun. For names are not intended only to make the bearer conceive what we conceive, but also to inform him what we believe. Now, when I use a name for the purpose of expressing a belief, it is a belief concerning the thing itself, not concerning my idea of it. When I say, "the sun is the cause of day," I do not mean that my idea of the sun causes or excites in me the idea of day: or in other words, that thinking of the sun makes me think of day. I mean, that a certain physical fact, which is called the sun's presence (and which, in the ultimate analysis, resolves itself into sensations, not ideas) causes another physical fact, which is called day. It seems proper to consider a word as the *name* of that which we intend to be understood by it when we use it; of that which any fact that we assert of it is to be understood of; that, in short, concerning which, when we employ the word, we intend to give information. Names, therefore, shall always be spoken of in this work as the names of things themselves, and not merely of our ideas of things.

But the question now arises, of what things? and to answer this it is necessary to take into consideration the different kinds of names.

§ 2. It is usual, before examining the various classes into which names are commonly divided, to begin by distinguishing from names of every description, those words which are not names, but only parts of names. Among such are reckoned particles, as *of*, *to*, *truly*, *often*; the inflected cases of nouns substantive, as *me*, *him*, *Johns*; and even adjectives, as *large*, *heavy*. These words do not express things of which anything can be affirmed or denied. We cannot say, Heavy fell, or A heavy fell; Truly or A truly, was asserted; Of, or An of, was in the room. Unless, indeed, we are speaking of the mere words themselves, as when we say, Truly is an English word, or, Heavy is an adjective. In that case they are complete names, viz. names of those particular sounds, or of those particular collections of written characters. This employment of a word to denote the mere letters and syllables of which it is composed, was termed by the schoolmen the *suppositio materialis* of the word. In any other sense we cannot introduce one of these words into the subject of a proposition, unless in combination with other words; as, A heavy *body* fell, A truly *important fact* was asserted, A *member* of *parliament* was in the room.

An adjective, however, is capable of standing by itself as the predicate of a proposition; as when we say, Snow is white; and occasionally even as the subject, for we may say, White is an agreeable colour. The adjective is often said to be so used by a grammatical ellipsis: Snow is white, instead of snow is a white object: White is an agreeable colour, instead of, A white colour, or, The colour white, is agreeable. The Greeks and Romans were allowed, by the rules of their language, to employ this ellipsis universally in the subject as well as in the predicate of a proposition. In English this cannot, generally speaking, be done. We may say, The earth is round; but we cannot say, Round is easily moved; we must say, A round object. This distinction, however, is rather grammatical than logical. Since there is no difference of meaning between *round*, and *a round object*, it is only custom which prescribes that on any given occasion one shall be used, and not the other. We shall, therefore, without scruple, speak of adjectives as names, whether in their own right, or as representative of the more circuitous forms of expression above exemplified. The other classes of subsidiary words have no title whatever to be considered as names. An adverb, or an accusative case, cannot under any circumstances (except when their mere letters and syllables are spoken of) figure as one of the terms of a proposition.

Words which are not capable of being used as names, but only as parts of names, were called by some of the schoolmen Syncategorematic terms: from σὺν, with, and κατᾳγορέω, to predicate, because it was only *with* some other word that they could be predicated. A word which could be used either as the subject or predicate of a proposition without being accompanied by any other word, was termed by the same authorities a Categorematic term. A combination of one or more Categorematic, and one or more Syncategorematic words, as A heavy body, or A court of justice, they sometimes called a *mixed* term; but this seems a needless multiplication of technical expressions. A mixed term is, in the only useful sense of the word, Categorematic. It belongs to the class of what have been called many-worded names.

For, as one word is frequently not a name, but only part of a name, so a number of words often compose one single name, and no more. These words, "The place which the wisdom or policy of antiquity had destined for the residence of the Abyssinian princes," form in the estimation of the logician only one name; one Categorematic term. A mode of determining whether any set of words makes only one name, or more than one, is by predicating something of it, and observing whether, by this predication, we make only one assertion or several. Thus, when we say, John Nokes, who was the mayor of the town, died yesterday—by this predication we make but one assertion; whence it appears that "John Nokes, who was the mayor of the town," is no more than one name. It is true that in this proposition, besides the assertion that John Nokes died yesterday, there is included another insertion, namely, that John Nokes was mayor of the town. But this last assertion was already made: we did not make it by adding the predicate, "died yesterday." Suppose, however, that the words had been, John Nokes *and* the mayor of the town, they would have formed two names instead of one. For when we say, John Nokes and the mayor of the town died yesterday, we make two assertions: one, that John Nokes died yesterday; the other, that the mayor of the town died yesterday.

It being needless to illustrate at any greater length the subject of many-worded names, we proceed to the distinctions which have been established among names, not according to the words they are composed of, but according to their signification.

§ 3. All names are names of something, real or imaginary; but all things have not names appropriated to them individually. For some individual objects we require, and consequently have, separate distinguishing names; there is a name for every person, and for every remarkable place. Other objects, of which we have not occasion to speak so frequently, we do not designate by a name of their own; but when the necessity arises for naming them, we do so by putting together several words, each of which, by itself, might be and is used for an indefinite number of other objects; as when I say, *this stone*: "this" and "stone" being, each of them, names that may be used of many other objects besides the particular one meant, though the only object of which they can both be used at the given moment, consistently with their signification, may be the one of which I wish to speak.

Were this the sole purpose for which names, that are common to more things than one, could be employed; if they only served, by mutually limiting each other, to afford a designation for such individual objects as have no names of their own: they could only be ranked among contrivances for economizing the use of language. But it is evident that this is not their sole function. It is by their means that we are enabled to assert *general* propositions; to affirm or deny any predicate of an indefinite number of things at once. The distinction, therefore, between *general* names, and *individual* or *singular* names, is fundamental; and may be considered as the first grand division of names.

A general name is familiarly defined, a name which is capable of being truly affirmed, in the same sense, of each of an indefinite number of things. An individual or singular name is a name which is only capable of being truly affirmed, in the same sense, of one thing.

Thus, *man* is capable of being truly affirmed of John, George, Mary, and other persons without assignable limit; and it is affirmed of all of them in the same sense; for the word man expresses certain qualities, and when we predicate it of those persons, we assert that they all possess those qualities. But *John* is only capable of being truly affirmed of one single person, at least in the same sense. For, though there are many persons who bear that name, it is not conferred upon them to indicate any qualities, or anything which belongs to them in common; and cannot be said to be affirmed of them in any *sense* at all, consequently not in the same sense. "The king who succeeded William the Conqueror," is also an individual name. For, that there cannot be more than one person of whom it can be truly affirmed, is implied in the meaning of the words. Even "*the* king," when the occasion or the context defines the individual of whom it is to be understood, may justly be regarded as an individual name.

It is not unusual, by way of explaining what is meant by a general name, to say that it is the name of a *class*. But this, though a convenient mode of expression for some purposes, is objectionable as a definition, since it explains the clearer of two things by the more obscure. It would be more logical to reverse the proposition, and turn it into a definition of the word *class*: "A class is the indefinite multitude of individuals denoted by a general name."

It is necessary to distinguish *general* from *collective* names. A general name is one which can be predicated of *each* individual of a multitude; a collective name cannot be predicated of each separately, but only of all taken together. "The 76th regiment of foot in the British army," which is a collective name, is not a general but an individual name; for though it can be predicated of a multitude of individual soldiers taken jointly, it cannot be predicated of them severally. We may say, Jones is a soldier, and Thompson is a soldier, and Smith is a soldier, but we cannot say, Jones is the 76th regiment, and Thompson is the 76th regiment, and Smith is the 76th regiment. We can only say, Jones, and Thompson, and Smith, and Brown, and so forth (enumerating all the soldiers), are the 76th regiment.

"The 76th regiment" is a collective name, but not a general one: "a regiment" is both a collective and a general name. General with respect to all individual regiments, of each of which separately it can be affirmed: collective with respect to the individual soldiers of whom any regiment is composed.

§ 4. The second general division of names is into *concrete* and *abstract*. A concrete name is a name which stands for a thing; an abstract name is a name which stands for an attribute of a thing. Thus *John*, *the sea*, *this table*, are names of things. *White*, also, is the name of a thing, or rather of things. Whiteness, again, is the name of a quality or attribute of those things. Man is a name of many things; humanity is a name of an attribute of those things. *Old* is a name of things; *old age* is a name of one of their attributes.

I have used the words concrete and abstract in the sense annexed to them by the schoolmen, who, notwithstanding the imperfections of their philosophy, were unrivalled in the construction of technical language, and whose definitions, in logic at least, though they never went more than a little way into the subject, have seldom, I think, been altered but to be spoiled. A practice, however, has grown up in more modern times, which, if not introduced by Locke, has gained currency chiefly from his example, of applying the expression "abstract name" to all names which are the result of abstraction or generalisation, and consequently to all general names, instead of confining it to the names of attributes. The metaphysicians of the Condillac school,—whose admiration of Locke, passing over the profoundest speculations of that truly original genius, usually fastens with peculiar eagerness upon his weakest points,—have gone on imitating him in this abuse of language, until there is now some difficulty in restoring the word to its original signification. A more wanton alteration in the meaning of a word is rarely to be met with; for the expression *general name*, the exact equivalent of which exists in all languages I am acquainted with, was already available for the purpose to which *abstract* has been misappropriated, while the misappropriation leaves that important class of words, the names of attributes, without any compact distinctive appellation. The old acceptation, however, has not gone so completely out of use, as to deprive those who still adhere to it of all chance of being understood. By *abstract*, then, I shall always, in Logic proper, mean the opposite of *concrete*; by an abstract name, the name of an attribute; by a concrete name, the name of an object.

Do abstract names belong to the class of general, or to that of singular names? Some of them are certainly general. I mean those which are names not of one single and definite attribute, but of a class of attributes. Such is the word *colour*, which is a name common to whiteness, redness &c. Such is even the word whiteness, in respect of the different shades of whiteness to which it is applied in common: the word magnitude, in respect of the various degrees of magnitude and the various dimensions of space; the word weight, in respect of the various degrees of weight. Such also is the word *attribute* itself, the common name of all particular attributes. But when only one attribute, neither variable in degree nor in kind, is designated by the name; as visibleness; tangibleness; equality; squareness; milkwhiteness; then the name can hardly be considered general; for though it denotes an attribute of many different objects, the attribute itself is always conceived as one, not many.[3] To avoid needless logomachies, the best course would probably be to consider these names as neither general nor individual, and to place them in a class apart.

It may be objected to our definition of an abstract name, that not only the names which we have called abstract, but adjectives, which we have placed in the concrete class, are names of attributes; that *white*, for example, is as much the name of the colour as *whiteness* is. But (as before remarked) a word ought to be considered as the name of that which we intend to be understood by it when we put it to its principal use, that is, when we employ it in predication. When we say snow is white, milk is white, linen is white, we do not mean it to be understood that snow, or linen, or milk, is a colour. We mean that they are things having the colour. The reverse is the case with the word whiteness; what we affirm to *be* whiteness is not snow, but the colour of snow. Whiteness, therefore, is the name of the colour exclusively: white is a name of all things whatever having the colour; a name, not of the quality of whiteness, but of every white object. It is true, this name was given to all those various objects on account of the quality; and we may therefore say, without impropriety, that the quality forms part of its signification; but a name can only be said to stand for, or to be a name of, the things of which it can be predicated. We shall presently see that all names which can be said to have any signification, all names by applying which to an individual we give any information respecting that individual, may be said to *imply* an attribute of some sort; but they are not names of the attribute; it has its own proper abstract name.

§ 5. This leads to the consideration of a third great division of names, into *connotative* and *non-connotative*, the latter sometimes, but improperly, called *absolute.* This is one of the most important distinctions which we shall have occasion to point out, and one of those which go deepest into the nature of language.

A non-connotative term is one which signifies a subject only, or an attribute only. A connotative term is one which denotes a subject, and implies an attribute. By a subject is here meant anything which possesses attributes. Thus John, or London, or England, are names which signify a subject only. Whiteness, length, virtue, signify an attribute only. None of these names, therefore, are connotative. But *white, long, virtuous*, are connotative. The word white, denotes all white things, as snow, paper, the foam of the sea, &c., and implies, or in the language of the schoolmen, *connotes*,[4] the attribute *whiteness*. The word white is not predicated of the attribute, but of the subjects, snow, &c.; but when we predicate it of them, we convey the meaning that the attribute whiteness belongs to them. The same may be said of the other words above cited. Virtuous, for example, is the name of a class, which includes Socrates, Howard, the Man of Ross, and an undefinable number of other individuals, past, present, and to come. These individuals, collectively and severally, can alone be said with propriety to be denoted by the word: of them alone can it properly be said to be a name. But it is a name applied to all of them in consequences of an attribute which they are supposed to possess in common, the attribute which has received the name of virtue. It is applied to all beings that are considered to possess this attribute; and to none which are not so considered.

All concrete general names are connotative. The word *man*, for example, denotes Peter, Jane, John, and an indefinite number of other individuals, of whom, taken as a class, it is the name. But it is applied to them, because they possess, and to signify that they possess, certain attributes. These seem to be, corporeity, animal life, rationality, and a certain external form, which for distinction we call the human. Every existing thing, which possessed all these attributes, would be called a man; and anything which possessed none of them, or only one, or two, or even three of them without the fourth, would not be so called. For example, if in the interior of Africa there were to be discovered a race of animals possessing reason equal to that of human beings, but with the form of an elephant, they would not be called men. Swift's Houyhnhnms would not be so called. Or if such newly-discovered beings possessed the form of man without any vestige of reason, it is probable that some other name than that of man would be found for them. How it happens that there can be any doubt about the matter, will appear hereafter. The word *man*, therefore, signifies all these attributes, and all subjects which possess these attributes. But it can be predicated only of the subjects. What we call men, are the subjects, the individual Stiles and Nokes; not the qualities by which their humanity is constituted. The name, therefore, is said to signify the subjects *directly*, the attributes *indirectly*; it *denotes* the subjects, and implies, or involves, or indicates, or as we shall say henceforth *connotes*, the attributes. It is a connotative name.

Connotative[5] names have hence been also called *denominative*, because the subject which they denote is denominated by, or receives a name from, the attribute which they connote. Snow, and other objects, receive the name white, because they possess the attribute which is called whiteness; Peter, James, and others receive the name man because they possess the attributes which are considered to constitute humanity. The attribute, or attributes, may therefore be said to denominate those objects, or to give them a common name.

It has been seen that all concrete general names are connotative. Even abstract names, though the names only of attributes, may in some instances be justly considered as connotative; for attributes themselves may have attributes ascribed to them; and a word which denotes attributes may connote an attribute of those attributes. Of this description, for example, is such a word as *fault*; equivalent to *bad* or *hurtful quality*. This word is a name common to many attributes, and connotes hurtfulness, an attribute of those various attributes. When, for example, we say that slowness, in a horse, is a fault, we do not mean that the slow movement, the actual change of place of the slow horse, is a bad thing, but that the property or peculiarity of the horse, from which it derives that name, the quality of being a slow mover, is an undesirable peculiarity.

In regard to those concrete names which are not general but individual, a distinction must be made.

Proper names are not connotative: they denote the individuals who are called by them; but they do not indicate or imply any attributes as belonging to those individuals. When we name a child by the name of Paul, or a dog by the name Cæsar, these names are simply marks used to enable those individuals to be made subjects of discourse. It may be said, indeed, that we must have had some reason for giving them those names rather than any others; and this is true; but the name, once given, is independent of the reason. A man may have been named John, because that was the name of his father; a town may have been named Dartmouth, because it is situated at the mouth of the Dart. But it is no part of the signification of the word John, that the father of the person so called bore the same name; nor even of the word Dartmouth, to be situated at the mouth of the Dart. If sand should choke up the mouth of the river, or an earthquake change its course, and remove it to a distance from the town, the name of the town would not necessarily be changed. That fact, therefore, can form no part of the signification of the word; for otherwise, when the fact confessedly ceased to be true, no one would any longer think of applying the name. Proper names are attached to the objects themselves, and are not dependent on the continuance of any attribute of the object.

But there is another kind of names, which, although they are individual names, that is, predictable only of one object, are really connotative. For, though we may give to an individual a name utterly unmeaning, which we call a proper name,—a word which answers the purpose of showing what thing it is we are talking about, but not of telling anything about it; yet a name peculiar to an individual is not necessarily of this description. It may be significant of some attribute, or some union of attributes, which, being possessed by no object but one, determines the name exclusively to that individual. "The sun" is a name of this description; "God," when used by a monotheist, is another. These, however, are scarcely examples of what we are not attempting to illustrate, being, in strictness of language, general, not individual names: for, however they may be *in fact* predictable only of one object, there is nothing in the meaning of the words themselves which implies this: and, accordingly, when we are imagining and not affirming, we may speak of many suns; and the majority of mankind have believed, and still believe, that there are many gods. But it is easy to produce words which are real instances of connotative individual names. It may be part of the meaning of the connotative name itself, that there can exist but one individual possessing the attribute which it connotes: as for instance, "the *only* son of John Stiles;" "the *first* emperor of Rome." Or the attribute connoted may be a connexion with some determinate event, and the connexion may be of such a kind as only one individual could have; or may at least be such as only one individual actually had; and this may be implied in the form of the expression. "The father of Socrates" is an example of the one kind (since Socrates could not have had two fathers); "the author of the Iliad," "the murderer of Henri Quatre," of the second. For, though it is conceivable that more persons than one might have participated in the authorship of the Iliad, or in the murder of Henri Quatre, the employment of the article *the* implies that, in fact, this was not the case. What is here done by the word *the*, is done in other cases by the context: thus, "Cæsar's army" is an individual name, if it appears from the context that the army meant is that which Cæsar commanded in a particular battle. The still more general expressions, "the Roman army," or "the Christian army," may be individualised in a similar manner. Another case of frequent occurrence has already been noticed; it is the following. The name, being a many-worded one, may consist, in the first place, of a *general* name, capable therefore in itself of being affirmed of more things than one, but which is, in the second place, so limited by other words joined with it, that the entire expression can only be predicated of one object, consistently with the meaning of the general term. This is exemplified in such an instance as the following: "the present Prime Minister of England." Prime Minister of England is a general name; the attributes which it connotes may be possessed by an indefinite number of persons: in succession however, not simultaneously; since the meaning of the name itself imports (among other things) that there can be only one such person at a time. This being the case, and the application of the name being afterwards limited by the article and the word *present*, to such individuals as possess the attributes at one indivisible point of time, it becomes applicable only to one individual. And as this appears from the meaning of the name, without any extrinsic proof, it is strictly an individual name.

From the preceding observations it will easily be collected, that whenever the names given to objects convey any information, that is, whenever they have properly any meaning, the meaning resides not in what they *denote*, but in what they *connote*. The only names of objects which connote nothing are *proper* names; and these have, strictly speaking, no signification.[6]

If, like the robber in the Arabian Nights, we make a mark with chalk on a house to enable us to know it again, the mark has a purpose, but it has not properly any meaning. The chalk does not declare anything about the house; it does not mean, This is such a person's house, or This is a house which contains booty. The object of making the mark is merely distinction. I say to myself, All these houses are so nearly alike that if I lose sight of them I shall not again be able to distinguish that which I am now looking at, from any of the others; I must therefore contrive to make the appearance of this one house unlike that of the others, that I may hereafter know when I see the mark—not indeed any attribute of the house—but simply that it is the same house which I am now looking at. Morgiana chalked all the other houses in a similar manner, and defeated the scheme: how? simply by obliterating the difference of appearance between that house and the others. The chalk was still there, but it no longer served the purpose of a distinctive mark.

When we impose a proper name, we perform an operation in some degree analogous to what the robber intended in chalking the house. We put a mark, not indeed upon the object itself, but, so to speak, upon the idea of the object. A proper name is but an unmeaning mark which we connect in our minds with the idea of the object, in order that whenever the mark meets our eyes or occurs to our thoughts, we may think of that individual object. Not being attached to the thing itself, it does not, like the chalk, enable us to distinguish the object when we see it; but it enables us to distinguish it when it is spoken of, either in the records of our own experience, or in the discourse of others; to know that what we find asserted in any proposition of which it is the subject, is asserted of the individual thing with which we were previously acquainted.

When we predicate of anything its proper name; when we say, pointing to a man, this is Brown or Smith, or pointing to a city, that it is York, we do not, merely by so doing, convey to the reader any information about them, except that those are their names. By enabling him to identify the individuals, we may connect them with information previously possessed by him; by saying, This is York, we may tell him that it contains the Minster. But this is in virtue of what he has previously heard concerning York; not by anything implied in the name. It is otherwise when objects are spoken of by connotative names. When we say, The town is built of marble, we give the hearer what may be entirely new information, and this merely by the signification of the many-worded connotative name, "built of marble." Such names are not signs of the mere objects, invented because we have occasion to think and speak of those objects individually; but signs which accompany an attribute: a kind of livery in which the attribute clothes all objects which are recognised as possessing it. They are not mere marks, but more, that is to say, significant marks; and the connotation is what constitutes their significance.

As a proper name is said to be the name of the one individual which it is predicated of, so (as well from the importance of adhering to analogy, as for the other reasons formerly assigned) a connotative name ought to be considered a name of all the various individuals which it is predicable of, or in other words *denotes*, and not of what it connotes. But by learning what things it is a name of, we do not learn the meaning of the name: for to the same thing we may, with equal propriety, apply many names, not equivalent in meaning. Thus, I call a certain man by the name Sophroniscus: I call him by another name, The father of Socrates. Both these are names of the same individual, but their meaning is altogether different; they are applied to that individual for two different purposes: the one, merely to distinguish him from other persons who are spoken of; the other to indicate a fact relating to him, the fact that Socrates was his son. I further apply to him these other expressions: a man, a Greek, an Athenian, a sculptor, an old man, an honest man, a brave man. All these are, or may be, names of Sophroniscus, not indeed of him alone, but of him and each of an indefinite number of other human beings. Each of these names is applied to Sophroniscus for a different reason, and by each whoever understands its meaning is apprised of a distinct fact or number of facts concerning him; but those who knew nothing about the names except that they were applicable to Sophroniscus, would be altogether ignorant of their meaning. It is even possible that I might know every single individual of whom a given name could be with truth affirmed, and yet could not be said to know the meaning of the name. A child knows who are its brothers and sisters, long before it has any definite conception of the nature of the facts which are involved in the signification of those words.

In some cases it is not easy to decide precisely how much a particular word does or does not connote; that is, we do not exactly know (the case not having arisen) what degree of difference in the object would occasion a difference in the name. Thus, it is clear that the word man, besides animal life and rationality, connotes also a certain external form; but it would be impossible to say precisely what form; that is, to decide how great a deviation from the form ordinarily found in the beings whom we are accustomed to call men, would suffice in a newly-discovered race to make us refuse them the name of man. Rationality, also, being a quality which admits of degrees, it has never been settled what is the lowest degree of that quality which would entitle any creature to be considered a human being. In all such cases, the meaning of the general name is so far unsettled and vague; mankind have not come to any positive agreement about the matter. When we come to treat of Classification, we shall have occasion to show under what conditions this vagueness may exist without practical inconvenience; and cases will appear in which the ends of language are better promoted by it than by complete precision; in order that, in natural history for instance, individuals or species of no very marked character may be ranged with those more strongly characterised individuals or species, to which, in all their properties taken together, they bear the nearest resemblance.

But this partial uncertainty in the connotation of names can only be free from mischief when guarded by strict precautions. One of the chief sources, indeed, of lax habits of thought, is the custom of using connotative terms without a distinctly ascertained connotation, and with no more precise notion of their meaning than can be loosely collected from observing what objects they are used to denote. It is in this manner that we all acquire, and inevitably so, our first knowledge of our vernacular language. A child learns the meaning of the words *man*, or *white*, by hearing them applied to a variety of individual objects, and finding out, by a process of generalization and analysis which he could not himself describe, what those different objects have in common. In the case of these two words the process is so easy as to require not assistance from culture; the objects called human beings, and the objects called white, differing from all others by qualities of a peculiarly definite and obvious character. But in many other cases, objects bear a general resemblance to one another, which leads to their being familiarly classed together under a common name, while, without more analytic habits than the generality of mankind possess, it is not immediately apparent what are the particular attributes, upon the possession of which in common by them all, their general resemblance depends. When this is the case, people use the name without any recognised connotation, that is, without any precise meaning; they talk, and consequently think, vaguely, and remain contented to attach only the same degree of significance to their own words, which a child three years old attaches to the words brother and sister. The child at least is seldom puzzled by the starting up of new individuals, on whom he is ignorant whether or not to confer the title; because there is usually an authority close at hand competent to solve all doubts. But a similar resource does not exist in the generality of cases; and new objects are continually presenting themselves to men, women, and children, which they are called upon to class *proprio motu*. They, accordingly, do this on no other principle than that of superficial similarity, giving to each new object the name of that familiar object, the idea of which it most readily recalls, or which, on a cursory inspection, it seems to them most to resemble: as an unknown substance found in the ground will be called, according to its texture, earth, sand, or a stone. In this manner, names creep on from subject to subject, until all traces of a common meaning sometimes disappear, and the word comes to denote a number of things not only independently of any common attribute, but which have actually no attribute in common; or none but what is shared by other things to which the name is capriciously refused.[7] Even scientific writers have aided in this perversion of general language from its purpose; sometimes because, like the vulgar, they knew no better; and sometimes in deference to that aversion to admit new words, which induces mankind, on all subjects not considered technical to attempt to make the original stock of names serve with but little augmentation to express a constantly increasing number of objects and distinctions, and, consequently, to express them in a manner progressively more and more imperfect.

To what a degree this loose mode of classing and denominating objects has rendered the vocabulary of mental and moral philosophy unfit for the purposes of accurate thinking, is best known to whoever has most meditated on the present condition of those branches of knowledge. Since, however, the introduction of a new technical language as the vehicle of speculations on subjects belonging to the domain of daily discussion, is extremely difficult to effect, and would not be free from inconvenience even if effected, the problem for the philosopher, and one of the most difficult which he has to resolve, is, in retaining the existing phraseology, how best to alleviate its imperfections. This can only be accomplished by giving to every general concrete name which there is frequent occasion to predicate, a definite and fixed connotation; in order that it may be known what attributes, when we call an object by that name, we really mean to predicate of the object. And the question of most nicety is, how to give this fixed connotation to a name, with the least possible change in the objects which the name is habitually employed to denote; with the least possible disarrangement, either by adding or substracting, of the group of objects which, in however imperfect a manner, it serves to circumscribe and hold together; and with the least vitiation of the truth of any propositions which are commonly received as true.

This desirable purpose, of giving a fixed connotation where it is wanting, is the end aimed at whenever any one attempts to give a definition of a general name already in use; every definition of a connotative name being an attempt either merely to declare, or to declare and analyse, the connotation of the name. And the fact, that no questions which have arisen in the moral sciences have been subjects of keener controversy than the definitions of almost all the leading expressions, is a proof how great an extent the evil to which we have adverted has attained.

Names with indeterminate connotation are not to be confounded with names which have more than one connotation, that is to say, ambiguous words. A word may have several meanings, but all of them fixed and recognised ones; as the word *post*, for example, or the word *box*, the various senses of which it would be endless to enumerate. And the paucity of existing names, in comparison with the demand for them, may often render it advisable and even necessary to retain a name in this multiplicity of acceptations, distinguishing these so clearly as to prevent their being confounded with one another. Such a word may be considered as two or more names, accidentally written and spoken alike.[8]

§ 6. The fourth principal division of names is into *positive* and *negative*. Positive, as *man*, *tree*, *good*; negative, as *not-man*, *not-tree*, *not-good*. To every positive concrete name, a corresponding negative one might be framed. After giving a name to any one thing, or to any plurality of things, we might create a second name which should be a name of all things whatever, except that particular thing or things. These negative names are employed whenever we have occasion to speak collectively of all things other than some thing or class of things. When the positive name is connotative, the corresponding negative name is connotative likewise; but in a peculiar way, connoting not the presence but the absence of an attribute. Thus, *not-white* denotes all things whatever except white things; and connotes the attribute of not possessing whiteness. For the non-possession of any given attribute is also an attribute, and may receive a name as such; and thus negative concrete names may obtain negative abstract names to correspond to them.[9]

Names which are positive in form are often negative in reality, and others are really positive though their form is negative. The word *inconvenient*, for example, does not express the mere absence of convenience; it expresses a positive attribute, that of being the cause of discomfort or annoyance. So the word *unpleasant*, notwithstanding its negative form, does not connote the mere absence of pleasantness, but a less degree of what is signified by the word *painful*, which, it is hardly necessary to say, is positive. *Idle*, on the other hand, is a word which, though positive in form, expresses nothing but what would be signified either by the phrase *not working*, or by the phrase *not disposed to work*; and *sober*, either by *not drunk* or by *not drunken*.

There is a class of names called *privative*. A privative name is equivalent in its signification to a positive and a negative name taken together; being the name of something which has once had a particular attribute, or for some other reason might have been expected to have it, but which has it not. Such is the word *blind*, which is not equivalent to *not seeing*, or to *not capable of seeing*, for it would not, except by a poetical or rhetorical figure, be applied to stocks and stones. A thing is not usually said to be blind, unless the class to which it is most familiarly referred, or to which it is referred on the particular occasion, be chiefly composed of things which can see, as in the case of a blind man, or a blind horse; or unless it is supposed for any reason that it ought to see; as in saying of a man, that he rushed blindly into an abyss, or of philosophers or the clergy that the greater part of them are blind guides. The names called privative, therefore, connote two things; the absence of certain attributes, and the presence of others, from which the presence also of the former might naturally have been expected.

§ 7. The fifth leading division of names is into *relative* and *absolute*, or let us rather say, *relative* and *non-relative*; for the word absolute is put upon much too hard duty in metaphysics, not to be willingly spared when its services can be dispensed with. It resembles the word *civil* in the language of jurisprudence, which stands for the opposite of criminal, the opposite of ecclesiastical, the opposite of military, the opposite of political—in short, the opposite of any positive word which wants a negative.

Relative names are such as father, son; ruler, subject; like, equal; unlike, unequal; longer, shorter; cause, effect. Their characteristic property is, that they are always given in pairs. Every relative name which is predicated of an object, supposes another object (or objects), of which we may predicate either that same name or another relative name which is said to be the *correlative* of the former. Thus, when we call any person a son, we suppose other persons who must be called parents. When we call any event a cause, we suppose another event which is an effect. When we say of any distance that it is longer, we suppose another distance which is shorter. When we say of any object that it is like, we mean that it is like some other object, which is also said to be like the first. In this last case both objects receive the same name; the relative term is its own correlative.

It is evident that these words, when concrete, are, like other concrete general names, connotative; they denote a subject, and connote an attribute; and each of them has or might have a corresponding abstract name, to denote the attribute connoted by the concrete. Thus the concrete *like* has its abstract *likeness*; the concretes, father and son, have, or might have, the abstracts, paternity, and filiety, or sonship. The concrete name connotes an attribute, and the abstract name which answers to it denotes that attribute. But of what nature is the attribute? Wherein consists the peculiarity in the connotation of a relative name?

The attribute signified by a relative name, say some, is a relation; and this they give, if not as a sufficient explanation, at least as the only one attainable. If they are asked, What, then, is a relation? they do not profess to be able to tell. It is generally regarded as something peculiarly recondite and mysterious. I cannot, however, perceive in what respect it is more so than any other attribute; indeed, it appears to me to be so in a somewhat less degree. I conceive rather, that it is by examining into the signification of relative names, or, in other words, into the nature of the attribute which they connote, that a clear insight may best be obtained into the nature of all attributes: of all that is meant by an attribute.

It is obvious, in fact, that if we take any two correlative names, *father* and *son* for instance, though the objects *de*-noted by the names are different, they both, in a certain sense, connote the same thing. They cannot, indeed, be said to connote the same *attribute*: to be a father, is not the same thing as to be a son. But when we call one man a father, another a son, what we mean to affirm is a set of facts, which are exactly the same in both cases. To predicate of A that he is the father of B, and of B that he is the son of A, is to assert one and the same fact in different words. The two propositions are exactly equivalent: neither of them asserts more or asserts less than the other. The paternity of A and the filiety of B are not two facts, but two modes of expressing the same fact. That fact, when analysed, consists of a series of physical events or phenomena, in which both A and B are parties concerned, and from which they both derive names. What those names really connote, is this series of events: that is the meaning, and the whole meaning, which either of them is intended to convey. The series of events may be said to *constitute* the relation; the schoolmen called it the foundation of the relation, *fundamentum relationis*.

In this manner any fact, or series of facts, in which two different objects are implicated, and which is of facts, in which two different may be either considered as constituting an attribute of the one, or an attribute of the other. According as we consider it in the former, or in the latter aspect, it is connoted by the one or the other of the two correlative names. *Father* connotes the fact, regarded as constituting an attribute of A; *son* connotes the same fact, as constituting an attribute of B. It may evidently be regarded with equal propriety in either light. And all that appears necessary to account for the existence of relative names, is, that whenever there is a fact in which two individuals are concerned, an attribute grounded on that fact may be ascribed to either of these individuals.

A name, therefore, is said to be relative, when, over and above the object which it denotes, it implies in its signification the existence of another object, also deriving a denomination from the same fact which is the ground of the first name. Or (to express the same meaning in other words) a name is relative, when, being the name of one thing, its signification cannot be explained but by mentioning another. Or we may state it thus—when the name cannot be employed in discourse so as to have a meaning, unless the name of some other thing than what it is itself the name of, be either expressed or understood. These definitions are all, at bottom, equivalent, being modes of variously expressing this one distinctive circumstance—that every other attribute of an object might, without any contradiction, be conceived still to exist if no object besides that one had ever existed;[10] but those of its attributes which are expressed by relative names, would on that supposition be swept away.

§ 8. Names have been further distinguished into *univocal* and *æquivocal*: these, however, are not two kinds of names, but two different modes of employing names. A name is univocal, or applied univocally, with respect to all things of which it can be predicated *in the same sense*; it is æquivocal, or applied æquivocally, as respects those things of which it is predicated in different senses. It is scarcely necessary to give instances of a fact so familiar as the double meaning of a word. In reality, as has been already observed, an æquivocal or ambiguous word is not one name, but two names, accidentally coinciding in sound. *File* meaning a steel instrument, and *file* meaning a line of soldiers, have no more title to be considered one word, because written alike, than *grease* and *Greece* have, because they are pronounced alike. They are one sound, appropriated to form two different words.

An intermediate case is that of a name used *analogically* or metaphorically; that is, a name which is predicated of two things, not univocally, or exactly in the same signification, but in significations somewhat similar, and which being derived one from the other, one of them may be considered the primary, and the other a secondary signification. As when we speak of a brilliant light and a brilliant achievement. The word is not applied in the same sense to the light and to the achievement; but having been applied to the light in its original sense, that of brightness to the eye, it is transferred to the achievement in a derivative signification, supposed to be somewhat like the primitive one. The word, however, is just as properly two names instead of one, in this case, as in that of the most perfect ambiguity. And one of the commonest forms of fallacious reasoning arising from ambiguity, is that of arguing from a metaphorical expression as if it were literal; that is, as if a word, when applied metaphorically, were the same name as when taken in its original sense: which will be seen more particularly in its place.

CHAPTER III. OF THE THINGS DENOTED BY NAMES

§ 1. Looking back now to the commencement of our inquiry, let us attempt to measure how far it has advanced. Logic, we found, is the Theory of Proof. But proof supposes something provable, which must be a Proposition or Assertion; since nothing but a Proposition can be an object of belief, or therefore of proof. A Proposition is, discourse which affirms or denies something of some other thing. This is one step: there must, it seems, be two things concerned in every act of belief. But what are these Things? They can be no other than those signified by the two names, which being joined together by a copula constitute the Proposition. If, therefore, we knew what all names signify, we should know everything which, in the existing state of human knowledge, is capable either of being made a subject of affirmation or denial, or of being itself affirmed or denied of a subject. We have accordingly, in the preceding chapter, reviewed the various kinds of Names, in order to ascertain what is signified by each of them. And we have now carried this survey far enough to be able to take an account of its results, and to exhibit an enumeration of all kinds of Things which are capable of being made predicates, or of having anything predicated of them: after which to determine the import of Predication, that is, of Propositions, can be no arduous task.

The necessity of an enumeration of Existence, as the basis of Logic, did not escape the attention of the schoolmen, and of their master Aristotle, the most comprehensive, if not also the most sagacious, of the ancient philosophers. The Categories, or Predicaments—the former a Greek word, the latter its literal translation in the Latin language—were believed to be an enumeration of all things capable of being named; an enumeration by the *summa genera*, *i.e.*, the most extensive classes into which things could be distributed; which, therefore, were so many highest Predicates, one or other of which was supposed capable of being affirmed with truth of every nameable thing whatsoever. The following are the classes into which, according to this school of philosophy, Things in general might be reduced:—

Οὐσία,	Substantia.
Ποσὸν,	Quantitas.
Ποιόν,	Qualitas.
Πρός τι,	Relatio.
Ποιεῖν,	Actio.
Πάσχειν,	Passio.
Ποῦ,	Ubi.
Πότε,	Quando.
Κεῖσθαι,	Situs.
Ἔχειν,	Habitus.

The imperfections of this classification are too obvious to require, and its merits are not sufficient to reward, a minute examination. It is a mere catalogue of the distinctions rudely marked out by the language of familiar life, with little or no attempt to penetrate, by philosophic analysis, to the *rationale* even of those common distinctions. Such an analysis, however superficially conducted, would have shown the enumeration to be both redundant and defective. Some objects are omitted, and others repeated several times under different heads. It is like a division of animals into men, quadrupeds, horses, asses, and ponies. That, for instance, could not be a very comprehensive view of the nature of Relation which could exclude action, passivity, and local situation from that category. The same observation applies to the categories Quando (or position in time), and Ubi (or position in space);

while the distinction between the latter and Situs is merely verbal. The incongruity of erecting into a *summum genus* the class which forms the tenth category is manifest. On the other hand, the enumeration takes no notice of anything besides substances and attributes. In what category are we to place sensations, or any other feelings and states of mind; as hope, joy, fear; sound, smell, taste; pain, pleasure; thought, judgment, conception, and the like? Probably all these would have been placed by the Aristotelian school in the categories of *actio* and *passio*; and the relation of such of them as are active, to their objects, and of such of them as are passive, to their causes, would rightly be so placed; but the things themselves, the feelings or states of mind, wrongly. Feelings, or states of consciousness, are assuredly to be accounted among realities, but they cannot be reckoned either among substances or attributes.[11]

§ 2. Before recommencing, under better auspices, the attempt made with such imperfect success by the early logicians, we must take notice of an unfortunate ambiguity in all the concrete names which correspond to the most general of all abstract terms, the word Existence. When we have occasion for a name which shall be capable of denoting whatever exists, as contradistinguished from non-entity or Nothing, there is hardly a word applicable to the purpose which is not also, and even more familiarly, taken in a sense in which it denotes only substances. But substances are not all that exists; attributes, if such things are to be spoken of, must be said to exist; feelings certainly exist. Yet when we speak of an *object*, or of a *thing*, we are almost always supposed to mean a substance. There seems a kind of contradiction in using such an expression as that one *thing* is merely an attribute of another thing. And the announcement of a Classification of Things would, I believe, prepare most readers for an enumeration like those in natural history, beginning with the great divisions of animal, vegetable, and mineral, and subdividing them into classes and orders. If, rejecting the word Thing, we endeavour to find another of a more general import, or at least more exclusively confined to that general import, a word denoting all that exists, and connoting only simple existence; no word might be presumed fitter for such a purpose than *being*: originally the present participle of a verb which in one of its meanings is exactly equivalent to the verb *exists*; and therefore suitable, even by its grammatical formation, to be the concrete of the abstract *existence*. But this word, strange as the fact may appear, is still more completely spoiled for the purpose which it seemed expressly made for, than the word Thing. *Being* is, by custom, exactly anonymous with substance; except that it is free from a slight taint of a second ambiguity; being applied impartially to matter and to mind, while substance, though originally and in strictness applicable to both, is apt to suggest in preference the idea of matter. Attributes are never called Beings; nor are feelings. A being is that which excites feelings, and which possesses attributes. The soul is called a Being; God and angels are called Beings; but if we were to say, extension, colour, wisdom, virtue, are beings, we should perhaps be suspected of thinking with some of the ancients, that the cardinal virtues are animals; or, at the least, of holding with the Platonic school the doctrine of self-existent Ideas, or with the followers of Epicurus that of Sensible Forms, which detach themselves in every direction from bodies, and by coming in contact with our organs, cause our perceptions. We should be supposed, in short, to believe that Attributes are Substances.

In consequence of this perversion of the word Being, philosophers looking about for something to supply its place, laid their hands upon the word Entity, a piece of barbarous Latin, invented by the schoolmen to be used as an abstract name, in which class its grammatical form would seem to place it; but being seized by logicians in distress to stop a leak in their terminology, it has ever since been used as a concrete name. The kindred word *essence*, born at the same time and of the same parents, scarcely underwent a more complete transformation when, from being the abstract of the verb *to be*, it came to denote something sufficiently concrete to be enclosed in a glass bottle. The word Entity, since it settled down into a concrete name, has retained its universality or signification somewhat less impaired than any of the names before mentioned. Yet the same gradual decay to which, after a certain age, all the language of psychology seems liable, has been at work even here. If you call virtue an *entity*, you are indeed somewhat less strongly suspected of believing it to be a substance than if you called it a *being*; but you are by no means free from the suspicion. Every word which was originally intended to connote mere existence, seems, after a time, to enlarge its connotation to *separate* existence, or existence freed from the condition of belonging to a substance; which condition being precisely what constitutes an attribute, attributes are gradually shut out; and along with them feelings, which in ninety-nine cases out of a hundred have no other name than that of the attribute which is grounded on them. Strange that when the greatest embarrassment felt by all who have any considerable number of thoughts to express, is to find a sufficient variety of precise words fitted to express them, there should be no practice to which even scientific thinkers are more addicted than that of taking valuable words to express ideas which are sufficiently expressed by other words already appropriated to them.

When it is impossible to obtain good tools, the next best thing is to understand thoroughly the defects of those we have. I have therefore warned the reader of the ambiguity of the names which, for want of better, I am necessitated to employ. It must now be the writer's endeavour so to employ them as in no case to leave the meaning doubtful or obscure. No one of the above terms being altogether unambiguous, I shall not confine myself to any one, but shall employ on each occasion the word which seems least likely in the particular case to lead to misunderstanding; nor do I pretend to use either these or any other words with a rigorous adherence to one single sense. To do so would often leave us without a word to express what is signified by a known word in some one or other of its senses: unless authors had an unlimited licence to coin new words, together with (what it would be more difficult to assume) unlimited power of making readers understand them. Nor would it be wise in a writer, on a subject involving so much of abstraction, to deny himself the advantage derived from even an improper use of a term, when, by means of it, some familiar association is called up which brings the meaning home to the mind, as it were by a flash.

The difficulty both to the writer and reader, of the attempt which must be made to use vague words so as to convey a precise meaning, is not wholly a matter of regret. It is not unfitting that logical treatises should afford an example of that, to facilitate which is among the most important uses of logic. Philosophical language will for a long time, and popular language still longer, retain so much of vagueness and ambiguity, that logic would be of little value if it did not, among its other advantages exercise the understanding in doing its work neatly and correctly with these imperfect tools.

After this preamble it is time to proceed to our enumeration. We shall commence with Feelings, the simplest class of nameable things; the term Feeling being of course understood in its most enlarged sense.

NOTES

1. *Computation or Logic*, chap. ii.
2. In the original "had, *or had not.*" These last words, as involving a subtlety foreign to our present purpose, I have forborne to quote.
3. Vide infra, note at the end of § 3, book ii, chap. ii.
4. *Notare*, to mark; *Con*notare, to mark *along with*; to mark one thing *with* or *in addition* to another.
5. Archbishop Whately, who, in the later editions of his *Elements of Logic*, aided in reviving the important distinction treated of in the text, proposes the term "Attributive" as a substitute for "Connotative" (p. 22, 9th ed.). The expression is, in itself, appropriate; but as it has not the advantage of being connected with any verb, of so markedly distinctive a character as "to connote," it is not, I think, fitted to supply the place of the word Connotative in scientific use.
6. A writer who entitles his book *Philosophy; or, The Science of Truth*, charges me in his very first page (referring at the foot of it to this passage) with asserting that *general* names have properly no signification. And he repeats this statement many times in the course of his volume, with comments, not at all flattering, thereon. It is well to be now and then reminded to how great a length perverse misquotation (for, strange as it appears, I do not believe that the writer is dishonest) can sometimes go. It is a warning to readers when they see an author accused, with volume and page referred to, and the apparent guarantee of inverted commas, of maintaining something more than commonly absurd, not to give implicit credence to the assertion without verifying the reference.
7. "Take the familiar term Stone. It is applied to mineral and rocky materials, to the kernels of fruit, to the accumulations in the gall-bladder and in the kidney; while it is refused to polished

minerals (called gems), to rocks that have the cleavage suited for roofing (slates), and to baked clay (bricks). It occurs in the designation of the magnetic oxide of iron (loadstone), and not in speaking of other metallic ores. Such a term is wholly unfit for accurate reasoning, unless hedged round on every occasion by other phrases; as building stone, precious stone, gall stone, etc. Moreover, the methods of definition are baffled for want of sufficient community to ground upon. There is no quality uniformly present in the cases where it is applied, and uniformly absent where it is not applied; hence the definer would have to employ largely the licence of striking off existing applications, and taking in new ones."—Bain, *Logic*, ii. 172.

8. Before quitting the subject of connotative names, it is proper to observe, that the first writer who, in our times, has adopted from the schoolmen the word *to connote*, Mr. James Mill, in his *Analysis of the Phenomena of the Human Mind*, employs it in a signification different from that in which it is here used. He uses the word in a sense coextensive with its etymology, applying it to every case in which a name, while pointing directly to one thing (which is consequently termed its signification), includes also a tacit reference to some other thing. In the case considered in the text, that of concrete general names, his language and mine are the converse of one another. Considering (very justly) the signification of the name to lie in the attribute, he speaks of the word as *noting* the attribute, and *connoting* the things possessing the attribute. And he describes abstract names as being properly concrete names with their connotation dropped: whereas, in my view, it is the *de*notation which would be said to be dropped, what was previously connoted becoming the whole signification.

In adopting a phraseology at variance with that which so high an authority, and one which I am less likely than any other person to undervalue, has deliberately sanctioned, I have been influenced by the urgent necessity for a term exclusively appropriated to express the manner in which a concrete general name serves to mark the attributes which are involved in its signification. This necessity can scarcely be felt in its full force by any one who has not found by experience how vain is the attempt to communicate clear ideas on the philosophy of language without such a word. It is hardly an exaggeration to say, that some of the most prevalent of the errors with which Logic has been infected and a large part of the cloudiness and confusion of ideas which have enveloped it, would, in all probability, have been avoided, if a term had been in common use to express exactly what I have signified by the term to connote. And the schoolmen to whom we are indebted for the greater part of our logical language, gave us this also, and in this very sense. For though some of their general expressions countenance the use of the word in the more extensive and vague acceptation in which it is taken by Mr. Mill, yet when they had to define it specifically as a technical term, and to fix its meaning as such, with that admirable precision which always characterises their definitions, they clearly explained that nothing was said to be connoted except *forms*, which word may generally, in their writings, be understood as synonymous with *attributes*.

Now, if the word *to connote*, so well suited to the purpose to which they applied it, be diverted from that purpose by being taken to fulfil another, for which it does not seem to me to be at all required; I am unable to find any expression to replace it, but such as are commonly employed in a sense so much more general, that it would be useless attempting to associate them peculiarly with this precise idea. Such are the words, to involve, to imply, &c. By employing these, I should fail of attaining the object for which alone the name is needed, namely, to distinguish this particular kind of involving and implying from all other kinds, and to assure to it the degree of habitual attention which its importance demands.

9. Professor Bain (*Logic*, i. 56) thinks that negative names are not names of all things whatever except those denoted by the correlative positive name, but only for all things of some particular class: *not-white*, for instance, he deems not to be a name for everything in nature except white things, but only for every *coloured* thing other than white. In this case, however, as in all others, the test of what a name denotes is what it can be predicated of: and we can certainly predicate of a sound, or a smell, that it is not white. The affirmation and the nega-

tion of the same attribute cannot but divide the whole field of predication between them.

10. Or rather, all objects except itself and the percipient mind; for, as we shall see hereafter, to ascribe any attribute to an object, necessarily implies a mind to perceive it.

The simple and clear explanation given in the text, of relation and relative names, a subject so long the opprobrium of metaphysics, was given (as far as I know) for the first time, by Mr. James Mill, in his Analysis of the Phenomena of the Human Mind.

11. On the preceding passage Professor Bain remarks (*Logic*, i. 265): "The Categories do not seem to have been intended as a classification of Nameable Things, in the sense of 'an enumeration of all kinds of Things which are capable of being made predicates, or of having anything predicated of them.' They seem to have been rather intended as a generalization of *predicates*; an analysis of the final import of predication. Viewed in this light, they are not open to the objections offered by Mr. Mill. The proper question to ask is not—In what Category are we to place sensations or other feelings or states of mind? but, Under what Categories can we predicate regarding states of mind? Take, for example, Hope. When we say that it is a state of mind, we predicate Substance: we may also describe how great it is (Quantity), what is the quality of it, pleasurable or painful (Quality), what it has reference to (Relation). Aristotle seems to have framed the Categories on the plan—Here is an individual; what is the final analysis of all that we can predicate about him?"

This is doubtless a true statement of the leading idea in the classification. The Category Οὐεια was certainly understood by Aristotle to be a general name for all possible answers to the questions Quid sit? when asked respecting a concrete individual; as the other Categories are names comprehending all possible answers to the questions Quantum sit? Quale sit? &c. In Aristotle's conception, therefore, the Categories may not have been a classification of Things; but they were soon converted into one by his scholastic followers, who certainly regarded and treated them as a classification of Things, and carried them out as such, dividing down the Category Substance as a naturalist might do, into the different classes of physical or metaphysical objects as distinguished from attributes, and the other Categories into the principal varieties of quantity, quality, relation, &c. It is, therefore, a just subject of complaint against them, that they had no Category of Feeling. Feeling is assuredly predicable as a summum genus, of every particular kind of feeling, for instance, as in Mr. Bain's example, of Hope: but it cannot be brought within any of the Categories as interpreted either by Aristotle or by his followers.

GOTTLOB FREGE

ON SENSE AND NOMINATUM[1]

The idea of Sameness[2] challenges reflection. It raises questions which are not quite easily answered. Is Sameness a relation? A relation between objects? Or between names or signs of objects? I assumed the latter alternative in my *Begriffsschrift*. The reasons that speak in its favor are the following: "a = a" and "a = b" are sentences of obviously different cognitive significance: "a = a" is valid *a priori* and according to Kant is to be called analytic, whereas sentences of the form "a = b" often contain very valuable extensions of our knowledge and cannot always be justified in an *a priori* manner. The discovery that it is not a different and novel sun which rises every morning, but that it is the very same, certainly was one of the most consequential ones in astronomy. Even nowadays the re-cognition (identification) of a planetoid or a comet is not always a matter of self-evidence. If we wished to view identity as a relation between the objects designated by the names 'a' and 'b' then "a = b" and "a = a" would not seem different if "a = b" is true. This would express a relation of a thing to itself, namely, a relation such that it holds between every thing and itself but never between one thing and another. What one wishes to express with "a = b" seems to be that the signs or names 'a' and 'b' name the same thing; and in that case we would be dealing with those signs: a relation between them would be asserted. But this relation could hold only inasmuch as they name or designate something. The relation, as it were, is mediated through the connection of each sign with the same nominatum. This connection, however, is arbitrary. You cannot forbid the use of an arbitrarily produced process or object as a sign for something else. Hence, a sentence like "a = b" would no longer refer to a matter of fact but rather to our manner of designation; no genuine knowledge would be expressed by it. But this is just what we do want to express in many cases. If the sign "a" differs from the sign "b" only as an object (here by its shape) but not by its rôle as a sign, that is to say, not in the manner in which it designates anything, then the cognitive significance of "a = a" would be essentially the same as that of "a = b", if "a = b" is true.

A difference could arise only if the difference of the signs corresponds to a difference in the way in which the designated objects are given. Let a, b, c be straight lines which connect the corners of a triangle with the midpoints of the opposite sides. The point of intersection of a and b is then the same as that of b and c. Thus we have different designations of the same point and these names ('intersection of a and b', 'intersection of b and c') indicate also the manner in which these points are presented. Therefore the sentence expresses a genuine cognition.

Now it is plausible to connect with a sign (name, word combination, expression) not only the designated object, which may be called the nominatum of the sign, but also the sense (connotation, meaning) of the sign in which is contained the manner and context of presentation. Accordingly, in our examples the *nominata* of the expressions 'the point of intersection of a and b' and 'the point of intersection of b and c' would be the same;—not their senses. The nominata of 'evening star' and 'morning star' are the same but not their senses.

From what has been said it is clear that I here understand by 'sign' or 'name' any expression which functions as a proper name, whose nominatum accordingly is a definite object (in the widest sense of this word). But no concept or relation is under consideration here. These matters are to be dealt with in another essay. The designation of a single object may consist of several words or various signs. For brevity's sake, any such designation will be considered as a proper name.

The sense of a proper name is grasped by everyone who knows the language or the totality of designations of which the proper name is a part;[3] this, however, illuminates the nominatum, if there is any, in a very one-sided fashion. A complete knowledge of the nominatum would require that we could tell immediately in the case of any given sense whether it belongs to the nominatum. This we shall never be able to do.

The regular connection between a sign, its sense and its nominatum is such that there corresponds a definite sense to the sign and to this sense there corresponds again a definite nominatum; whereas not one sign only belongs to one nominatum (object). In different languages, and even in one language, the same sense is represented by different expressions. It is true, there are exceptions to this rule. Certainly there should be a definite sense to each expression in a complete configuration of signs, but the natural languages in many ways fall short of this requirement. We must be satisfied if the same word, at least in the same context, has the same sense. It can perhaps be granted that an expression has a sense if it is formed in a grammatically correct manner and stands for a proper name. But as to whether there is a denotation corresponding to the connotation is hereby not decided. The words 'the heavenly body which has the greatest distance from the earth' have a sense; but it is very doubtful as to whether they have a nominatum. The expression 'the series with the least convergence' has a sense; but it can be proved that it has no nominatum, since for any given convergent series, one can find another one that is less convergent. Therefore the grasping of a sense does not with certainty warrant a corresponding nominatum.

When words are used in the customary manner then what is talked about are their nominata. But it may happen that one wishes to speak about the words themselves or about their senses. The first case occurs when one quotes someone else's words in direct (ordinary) discourse. In this case one's own words immediately name (denote) the words of the other person and only the latter words have the usual nominata. We thus have signs of signs. In writing we make use of quotes enclosing the word-icons. A word-icon in quotes must therefore not be taken in the customary manner.

If we wish to speak of the sense of an expression 'A' we can do this simply through the locution 'the sense of the expression 'A' '. In indirect (oblique) discourse we speak of the sense, e.g., of the words of someone else. From this it becomes clear that also in indirect discourse words do not have their customary nominata; they here name what customarily would be their sense. In order to formulate this succinctly we shall say: words in indirect discourse are used *indirectly*, or have *indirect* nominata. Thus we distinguish the *customary* from the *indirect* nominatum of a word; and similarly, its *customary* sense from its *indirect* sense. The indirect nominatum of a word is therefore its customary sense. Such exceptions must be kept in mind if one wishes correctly to comprehend the manner of connection between signs, senses and nominata in any given case.

Both the nominatum and the sense of a sign must be distinguished from the associated image. If the nominatum of a sign is an object of sense perception, my image of the latter is an inner picture[4] arisen from memories of sense impressions and activities of mine, internal or external. Frequently this image is suffused with feelings; the definiteness of its various parts may vary and fluctuate. Even with the same person the same sense is not always accompanied by the same image. The image is subjective; the image of one person is not that of another. Hence, the various differences between the images connected with one and the same sense. A painter, a rider, a zoölogist probably connect very different images with the name 'Bucephalus'. The image thereby differs essentially from the connotation of a sign, which latter may well be common property of many and is therefore not a part or mode of the single person's mind; for it cannot well be denied that mankind possesses a common treasure of thoughts which is transmitted from generation to generation.[5]

While, accordingly, there is no objection to speak without qualification of the sense in regard to images, we must, to be precise, add *whose* images they are and at what time they occur. One might say: just as words are connected with different images in two different persons, the same holds of the senses also. Yet this difference would consist merely in the manner of association. It does not prevent both from apprehending the same sense, but they cannot have the same image. *Si duo idem faciunt, non est idem.* When two persons imagine the same thing, each still has his own image. It is true, occasionally we can detect differences in the images or even in the sensations of different persons. But an accurate comparison is impossible because these images cannot be had together in one consciousness.

The nominatum of a proper name is the object itself which is designated thereby; the image which we may have along with it is quite subjective; the sense lies in between, not subjective as is the image, but not the object either. The following simile may help in elucidating these relationships. Someone observes the moon through a telescope. The moon is comparable with the nominatum; it is the object of the observation which is mediated through the real image projected by the object lens into the interior of the telescope, and through the retinal image of the observer. The first may be compared with the sense, the second with the presentation (or image in the psychological sense). The real image inside the telescope, however, is relative; it depends upon the standpoint; yet, it is objective in that it can serve several observers. Arrangements could be made such that several observers could utilize it. But every one of them would have only his own retinal image. Because of the different structures of the eyes not even geometrical congruence could be attained; a real coincidence would in any case be impossible. One could elaborate the simile by assuming that the retinal image of *A* could be made visible to *B*; or *A* could see his own retinal image in a mirror. In this manner one could possibly show how a presentation itself can be made into an object; but even so, it would never be to the (outside) observer what it is to the one who possesses the image. However, these lines of thought lead too far afield.

We can now recognize three levels of differences of words, expressions and complete sentences. The difference may concern at most the imagery, or else the sense but not the nominatum, or finally also the nominatum. In regard to the first level, we must note that, owing to the uncertain correlation of images with words, a difference may exist for one person that another does not discover. The difference of a translation from the original should properly not go beyond the first level. Among the differences possible in this connection we mention the shadings and colorings which poetry seeks to impart to the senses. These shadings and colorings are not objective. Every listener or reader has to add them in accordance with the hints of the poet or speaker. Surely, art would be impossible without some kinship among human imageries; but just how far the intentions of the poet are realized can never be exactly ascertained.

We shall henceforth no longer refer to the images and picturizations; they were discussed only lest the image evoked by a word be confused with its sense or its nominatum.

In order to facilitate brief and precise expression we may lay down the following formulations:

A proper name (word, sign, sign-compound, expression) expresses its sense, and designates or signifies its nominatum. We let a *sign express* its sense and *designate* its nominatum.

Perhaps the following objection, coming from idealistic or skeptical quarters, has been kept in abeyance for some time: "You have been speaking without hesitation of the moon as an object; but how do you know that the name 'the moon' has in fact a nominatum? How do you know that anything at all has a nominatum?" I reply that it is not our intention to speak of the image of the moon, nor would we be satisfied with the sense when we say 'the moon'; instead, we presuppose a nominatum here. We should miss the meaning altogether if we assumed we had reference to images in the sentence "the moon is smaller than the earth". Were this intended we would use some such locution as 'my image of the moon'. Of course, we may be in error as regards that assumption, and such errors have occurred on occasion. However, the question whether we could possibly always be mistaken in this respect may here remain unanswered; it will suffice for the moment to refer to our intention in speaking and thinking in order to justify our reference to the nominatum of a sign; even if we have to make the proviso: if there is such a nominatum.

Thus far we have considered sense and nominatum only of such expressions, words and signs which we called proper names. We are now going to inquire into the sense and the nominatum of a whole declarative sentence. Such a sentence contains a proposition.[6] Is this thought to be regarded as the sense or the nominatum of the sentence? Let us for the moment assume that the sentence has a nominatum! If we then substitute a word in it by another word with the same nominatum but with a different sense, then this substitution cannot affect the nominatum of the sentence. But we realize that in such cases the proposition is changed; e.g., the proposition of the sentence "the morning star is a body illuminated by the sun" is different from that of "the evening star is a body illuminated by the sun". Someone who did not know that the evening star is the same as the morning star could consider the one proposition true and the other false. The proposition can therefore not be the nominatum of the sentence; it will instead have to be regarded as its sense. But what about the nominatum? Can we even ask this question? A sentence as a whole has perhaps only sense and no nominatum? It may in any case be expected that there are such sentences, just as there are constituents of sentences which do have sense but no nominatum. Certainly, sentences containing proper names without nominata must be of this type. The sentence "Odysseus deeply asleep was disembarked at Ithaca" obviously has a sense. But since it is doubtful as to whether the name 'Odysseus' occurring in this sentence has a nominatum, so it is also doubtful that the whole sentence has one. However, it is certain that whoever seriously regards the sentence either as true or as false also attributes to the name 'Odysseus' a nominatum, not only a sense; for it is obviously the nominatum of this name to which the predicate is either ascribed or denied. He who does not acknowledge the nominatum cannot ascribe or deny a predicate to it. It might be urged that the consideration of the nominatum of the name is going farther than is necessary; one could be satisfied with the sense, if one stayed with the proposition. If all that mattered were only the sense of the sentence (i.e., the proposition) then it would be unnecessary to be concerned with the nominata of the sentence-components, for only the sense of components can be relevant for the sense of the sentence. The proposition remains the same, no matter whether or not the name 'Odysseus' has a nominatum. The fact that we are at all concerned about the nominatum of a sentence-component indicates that we generally acknowledge or postulate a nominatum for the sentence itself. The proposition loses in interest as soon as we recognize that one of its parts is lacking a nominatum. We may therefore be justified to ask for a nominatum of a sentence, in addition to its sense. But why do we wish that every proper name have not only a sense but also a nominatum? Why is the proposition alone not sufficient? We answer: because what matters to us is the truth-value. This, however, is not always the case. In listening to an epic, for example, we are fascinated by the euphony of the language and also by the sense of the sentences and by the images and emotions evoked. In turning to the question of truth we disregard the artistic appreciation and pursue scientific considerations. Whether the name 'Odysseus' has a nominatum is therefore immaterial to us as long as we accept the poem as a work of art.[7] Thus, it is the striving for truth which urges us to penetrate beyond the sense to the nominatum.

We have realized that we are to look for the nominatum of a sentence whenever the nominata of the sentence-components are the thing that matters; and that is the case whenever and only when we ask for the truth value.

Thus we find ourselves persuaded to accept the *truth-value* of a sentence as its nominatum. By the truth-value of a sentence I mean the circumstance of its being true or false. There are no other truth-values. For brevity's sake I shall call the one the True and the other the False. Every declarative sentence, in which what matters are the nominata of the words, is therefore to be considered as a proper name; and its nominatum, if there is any, is either the True or the False. These two objects are recognized, even if only tacitly, by everyone who at all makes judgments, holds anything as true, thus even by the skeptic. To designate truth-values as objects may thus far appear as a capricious idea or as a mere play on words, from which no important conclusion should be drawn. What I call an object can be discussed only in connection with the nature of concepts and relations. That I will reserve for another essay. But this might be clear even here: in every judgment[8]—no matter how obvious—a step is made from the level of propositions to the level of the nominata (the objective facts).

It may be tempting to regard the relation of a proposition to the True not as that of sense to nominatum but as that of the subject to the predicate. One could virtually say: "the proposition that 5 is a prime number is true". But on closer examination one notices that this does not say any more than is said in the simple sentence "5 is a prime number". This makes clear that the relation of a proposition to the True must not be compared with the relation of subject and predicate. Subject and predicate (interpreted logically) are, after all, components of a proposition; they are on the same level as regards cognition. By joining subject and predicate we always arrive only at a proposition; in this way we never move from a sense to a nominatum or from a proposition to its truth-value. We remain on the same level and never proceed from it to the next one. Just as the sun cannot be part of a proposition, so the truth-value, because it is not the sense, but an object, cannot be either.

If our conjecture (that the nominatum of a sentence is its truth value) is correct, then the truth-value must remain unchanged if a sentence-component is replaced by an expression with the same nominatum but with a different sense. Indeed, Leibnitz declares: *"Eadem sunt, quae sibi mutuo substitui possunt, salva veritate"*. What else, except the truth-value, could be found, which quite generally belongs to every sentence and regarding which the nominata of the components are relevant and which would remain invariant for substitutions of the type indicated?

Now if the truth-value of a sentence is its nominatum, then all true sentences have the same nominatum, and likewise all false ones. This implies that all detail has been blurred in the nominatum of a sentence. What interests us can therefore never be merely the nominatum; but the proposition alone, does not give knowledge; only the proposition together with its nominatum, i.e., its truth-value, does. Judging may be viewed as a movement from a proposition to its nominatum, i.e., its truth-value. Of course this is not intended as a definition. Judging is indeed something peculiar and unique. One might say that judging consists in the discerning of parts within the truth-value. This discernment occurs through recourse to the proposition. Every sense that belongs to a truth-value would correspond in its own manner to the analysis. I have, however, used the word 'part' in a particular manner here: I have transferred the relation of whole and part from the sentence to its nominatum. This I did by viewing the nominatum of a word as part of the nominatum of a sentence, when the word itself is part of the sentence. True enough, this way of putting things is objectionable since as regards the nominatum the whole and one part of it does not determine the other part; and also because the word 'part' in reference to bodies has a different customary usage. A special expression should be coined for what has been suggested above.

We shall now further examine the conjecture that the truth-value of a sentence is its nominatum. We have found that the truth-value of a sentence remains unaltered if an expression within the sentence is replaced by a synonymous one. But we have as yet not considered the case in which the expression-to-be-replaced is itself a sentence. If our view is correct, then the truth-value of a sentence, which contains another sentence as a part, must remain unaltered when we substitute for the part another of the same truth-value. Exceptions are to be expected if the whole or the part are either in direct or indirect discourse; for as we have seen, in that case the nominata of the words are not the usual ones. A sentence in direct discourse nominates again a sentence but in indirect discourse it nominates a proposition.

Our attention is thus directed to subordinate sentences (i.e., dependent clauses). These present themselves of course as parts of a sentence-structure which from a logical point of view appears also as a sentence, and indeed as if it were a main clause. But here we face the question whether in the case of dependent clauses it also holds that their nominata are truth-values. We know already that this is not the case with sentences in indirect discourse. The grammarians view clauses as representatives of sentence-parts and divide them accordingly into subjective, relative, and adverbial clauses. This might suggest that the nominatum of a clause is not a truth-value but rather that it is of similar nature as that of a noun or of an adjective or of an adverb; in short, of a sentence-part whose sense is not a proposition but only part thereof. Only a thorough investigation can provide clarity in this matter. We shall herein not follow strictly along grammatical lines, but rather group together what is logically of comparable type. Let us first seek out such instances in which, as we just surmised, the sense of a clause is not a self-sufficient proposition.

Among the abstract clauses beginning with 'that' there is also the indirect discourse, of which we have seen that in it the words have their indirect (oblique) nominata which coincide with what are ordinarily their senses. In this case then the clause has as its nominatum a proposition, not a truth-value; its sense is not a proposition but it is the sense of the words 'the proposition that . . .', which is only a part of the proposition corresponding to the total sentence-structure. This occurs in connection with 'to say', 'to hear', 'to opine', 'to be convinced', 'to infer' and similar words.[9] The situation is different, and rather complicated in connection with such words as 'to recognize', 'to know', 'to believe', a matter to be considered later.

One can see that in these cases the nominatum of the clause indeed consists in the proposition, because whether that proposition is true or false is immaterial for the truth of the whole sentence. Compare, e.g., the following two sentences: "Copernicus believed that the planetary orbits are circles" and "Copernicus believed that the appearance of the sun's motion is produced by the real motion of the earth". Here the one clause can be substituted for the other without affecting the truth. The sense of the principal sentence together with the clause is the single proposition; and the truth of the whole implies neither the truth nor the falsity of the clause. In cases of this type it is not permissible to replace in the clause one expression by another of the same nominatum. Such replacement may be made only by expressions of the same indirect nominatum, i.e., of the same customary sense. If one were to infer: the nominatum of a sentence is not its truth-value ("because then a sentence could always be replaced by another with the same truth-value"), he would prove too much; one could just as well maintain that the nominatum of the word 'morning star' is not Venus, for one cannot always substitute 'Venus' for 'morning star'. The only correct conclusion is that the nominatum of a sentence is *not always* its truth-value, and that 'morning star' does not always nominate the planet Venus; for this is indeed not the case when the word is used with its indirect nominatum. Such an exceptional case is before us in the clauses just considered, whose nominatum is a proposition.

When we say "it seems that . . ." then we mean to say "it seems to me that . . ." or "I opine that . . .". This is the same case over again. Similarly with expressions such as: 'to be glad', 'to regret', 'to approve', 'to disapprove', 'to hope', 'to fear'. When Wellington, toward the end of the battle of Belle-Alliance was glad that the Prussians were coming, the ground of his rejoicing was a conviction. Had he actually been deceived, he would not have been less glad, as long as his belief persisted; and before he arrived at the conviction that the Prussians were coming he could not have been glad about it, even if in fact they were already approaching.

Just as a conviction or a belief may be the ground of a sentiment, so it can also be the ground of another conviction such as in inference. In the sentence "Columbus inferred from the roundness of the earth that he could, traveling westward, reach India" we have, as nominata of its parts two propositions: that the earth is round, and that Columbus traveling westward could reach India. What matters here is only that Columbus was convinced of the one as well as of the other and that the one conviction furnishes the ground for the other. It is irrelevant for the truth of our sentence whether the earth is really round and whether Columbus could have reached India in the manner he fancied. But it is not irrelevant whether for 'the earth' we substitute 'the planet accompanied by one satellite whose diameter is larger than one-fourth of its own diameter'. Here also we deal with the indirect nominata of the words.

Adverbial clauses of purpose with 'so that', likewise belong here; obviously the purpose is a proposition; therefore: indirect nominata of the words, expressed in subjunctive form.

The clause with 'that' after 'to command', 'to request', 'to forbid' would appear in imperative form in direct discourse. Imperatives have no nominata; they have only sense. It is true, commands or requests are not propositions, but they are of the same type as propositions. Therefore the words in the dependent clauses after 'to command', 'to request', etc. have indirect nominata. The nominatum of such a sentence is thus not a truth-value but a command, a request, and the like.

We meet a similar situation in the case of dependent questions in phrases like 'to doubt if', 'not to know what'. It is easy to see that the words, here too, have to be interpreted in terms of their indirect nominata. The dependent interrogatory clauses containing 'who', 'what', 'where', 'when', 'how', 'whereby', etc. often apparently approximate closely adverbial clauses in which the words have their ordinary nominata. These cases are linguistically distinguished through the mode of the verb. In the subjunctive we have a dependent question and the indirect nominata of the words, so that a proper name cannot generally be replaced by another of the same object.

In the instances thus far considered the words in the clause had indirect nominata; this made it intelligible that the nominatum of the clause itself is indirect, i.e., not a truth-value, but a proposition, a command, a request, a question. The clause could be taken as a noun; one might even say, as a proper name of that proposition, command, etc., in whose rôle it functions in the context of the sentence-structure.

We are now going to consider clauses of another type, in which the words do have their customary nominata although there does not appear a proposition as the sense or a truth-value as the nominatum. How this is possible will best be elucidated by examples.

"He who discovered the elliptical shape of the planetary orbits, died in misery".

If, in this example, the sense of the clause were a proposition, it would have to be expressible also in a principal sentence. But this cannot be done because the grammatical subject 'he who' has no independent sense. It merely mediates the relations to the second part of the sentence: 'died in misery'. Therefore the sense of the clause is not a complete proposition and its nominatum is not a truth-value, but Kepler. It might be objected that the sense of the whole does include a proposition as its part; namely, that there was someone who first recognized the elliptical shape of the planetary orbits; for if we accept the whole as true we cannot deny this part. Indubitably so; but only because otherwise the clause "he who discovered the elliptical shape, etc." would have no nominatum. Whenever something is asserted then the presupposition taken for granted is that the employed proper names, simple or compound, have nominata. Thus, if we assert "Kepler died in misery" it is presupposed that the name 'Kepler' designates something. However, the proposition that the name 'Kepler' designates something is, the foregoing notwithstanding, not contained in the sense of the sentence "Kepler died in misery". If that were the case the denial would not read "Kepler did not die in misery" but "Kepler did not die in misery, or the name 'Kepler' is without nominatum". That the name 'Kepler' designates something is rather the presupposition of the assertion "Kepler died in misery" as well as of its denial. Now, it is a defect of languages that expressions are possible within them, which, in their grammatical form, seemingly determined to designate an object, nevertheless do not fulfill this condition in special cases; because this depends on the truth of the sentence. Thus it depends upon the truth of the sentence "there was someone who discovered the ellipticity of the orbits" whether the clause 'he who discovered the ellipticity of the orbits' really designates an object, or else merely evokes the appearance thereof, while indeed being without nominatum. Thus it may seem as if our clause, as part of its sense, contained the proposition that there existed someone who discovered the ellipticity of the orbits. If this were so, then the denial would have to read "he who first recognized the ellipticity of the orbits did not die in misery, or there was no one who discovered the ellipticity of the orbits." This, it is obvious, hinges upon an imperfection of language of which, by the way, even the symbolic language of analysis is not entirely free; there, also, sign compounds may occur which appear as if they designated something, but which at least hitherto are without nominatum, e.g., divergent infinite series. This can be avoided, e.g., through the special convention that the nominatum of divergent infinite series be the number 0. It is to be demanded that in a logically perfect language (logical symbolism) every expression constructed as a proper name in a grammatically correct manner out of already introduced symbols, in fact designate an object; and that no symbol be introduced as a proper name without assurance that it have a nominatum. It is customary in logic texts to warn against the ambiguity of expressions as a source of fallacies. I deem it at least as appropriate to issue a warning against apparent proper names that have no nominata. The history of mathematics has many a tale to tell of errors which originated from this source. The demagogic misuse is close (perhaps closer) at hand as in the case of ambiguous expressions. 'The will of the people' may serve as an example in this regard; for it is easily established that there is no generally accepted nominatum of that expression. Thus it is obviously not without importance to obstruct once for all the source of these errors, at least as regards their occurrence in science. Then such objections as the one discussed above will become impossible, for then it will be seen that whether a proper name has a nominatum can never depend upon the truth of a proposition.

Our considerations may be extended from these subjective clauses to the logically related relative and adverbial clauses.

Relative clauses, too, are employed in the formation of compound proper names—even if, in contradistinction to subjective clauses, they are not sufficient by themselves for this purpose. These relative clauses may be regarded as equivalent to appositions. Instead of 'the square root of 4 which is smaller than 0' we can also say 'the negative square root of 4'. We have here a case in which out of a conceptual expression a compound proper name is formed, with the help of the definite article in the singular. This is at any rate permissible when one and only one object is comprised by the concept.[10] Conceptual expression can be formed in such a fashion that their characteristics are indicated through relative clauses as in our example through the clause 'which is smaller than 0'. Obviously, such relative clauses, just as the subjective clauses above, do not refer to a proposition as their sense nor to a truth-value as their nominatum. Their sense is only a part of a proposition, which in many cases, can be expressed by a simple apposition. As in the subjective clauses an independent subject is missing and it is therefore impossible to represent the sense of the clause in an independent principal sentence.

Places, dates and time-intervals are objects from a logical point of view; the linguistic symbol of a definite place, moment or span of time must therefore be viewed as a proper name. Adverbial clauses of space or time can then be used in the formation of such proper names in a fashion analogous to the one we have just remarked in the case of subjective and relative clauses. Similarly, expressions for concepts which comprise places, etc., can be formed. Here too, it is to be remarked, the sense of the subordinate clauses cannot be rendered in a principal clause, because an essential constituent, namely the determination of place and time, is missing and only alluded to by a relative pronoun or a conjunction.[11]

In conditional clauses also, there is, just as we have realized in the case of subjective, relative and adverbial clauses, a constituent with indeterminate indication corresponding to which there is a similar one in the concluding clause. In referring to one another the two clauses combine into a whole which expresses, as a rule, only one proposition. In the sentence "if a number is smaller than 1 and greater than 0, then its square also is smaller than 1 and greater than 0" this constitutent in the conditional clause is 'a number' and in the concluding clause it is 'its'. Just through this indeterminacy the sense acquires the universal character which one expects of a law. But it is in this way also that it comes about that the conditional clause alone does not possess a complete proposition as its sense, and that together with the concluding clause it expresses a single proposition whose parts are no longer propositions. It is not generally the case that a hypothetical judgment correlates two judgments. Putting it in that (or a similar) manner would amount to using the word 'judgment' in the same sense that I have attributed to the word 'proposition'. In that case I would have to say: in a hypothetical proposition two propositions are related to each other. But this could be the case only if an indeterminately denoting constituent were absent;[12] but then universality would also be missing.

If a time point is to be indeterminately indicated in a conditional and a concluding clause, then this is not infrequently effected by *tempus praesens* of the verb, which in this case does not connote the present time. It is this grammatical form which takes the place of the indeterminately indicating constituent in the main and the dependent clause. "When the sun is at the Tropic of Cancer, the northern hemisphere has its longest day" is an example. Here, too, it is impossible to express the sense of the dependent clause in a main clause. For this sense is not a complete proposition; if we said: "the sun is at the Tropic of Cancer" we would be referring to the present time and thereby alter the sense. Similarly, the sense of the main clause is not a proposition either, only the whole consisting of main and dependent clause contains a proposition. Further, it may occur that several constituents common to conditional and concluding clause are indeterminately indicated.

 It is obvious that subjective clauses containing 'who', 'what', and adverbial clauses with 'where', 'when', 'wherever', 'whenever' are frequently to be interpreted, inasmuch as their sense is concerned, as conditional sentences; e.g., "He who touches pitch soils himself".

Conditional clauses can also be replaced by relative clauses. The sense of the previously mentioned sentence can also be rendered by "the square of a number which is smaller than 1 and larger than 0, is smaller than 1 and larger than 0."

Quite different is the case in which the common constituent of main and dependent clause is represented by a proper name. In the sentence: "Napoleon who recognized the danger to his right flank, personally led his troops against the enemy's position" there are expressed two propositions:

1. Napoleon recognized the danger to his right flank.
2. Napoleon personally led his troops against the enemy's position.

When and where this happened can indeed be known only from the context, but is to be viewed as thereby determined. If we pronounce our whole sentence as an assertion we thereby assert simultaneously its two component sentences. If one of the components is false the whole is false. Here we have a case in which the dependent clause by itself has a sense in a complete proposition (if supplemented by temporal and spatial indications). The nominatum of such a clause is therefore a truth-value. We may therefore expect that we can replace it by a sentence of the same truth value without altering the truth of the whole. This is indeed the case; but it must be kept in mind that for a purely grammatical reason, its subject must be 'Napoleon'; because only then can the sentence be rendered in the form of a relative clause attaching to 'Napoleon'. If the demand to render it in this form and if the conjunction with 'and' is admitted, then this limitation falls away.

Likewise, in dependent clauses with 'although' complete propositions are expressed. This conjunction really has no sense and does not affect the sense of the sentence; rather, it illuminates it in a peculiar fashion.[13] Without affecting the truth of the whole the implicate may be replaced by one of the same truth value; but the illumination might then easily appear inappropriate, just as if one were to sing a song of sad content in a cheerful manner.

In these last instances the truth of the whole implied the truth of the component sentences. The situation is different if a conditional sentence expresses a complete proposition; namely, when in doing so it contains instead of a merely indicating constituent a proper name or something deemed equivalent to a proper name. In the sentence: "if the sun has already risen by now, the sky is heavily overcast", the tense is the present—therefore determinate. The place also is to be considered determinate. Here we can say that a relation is posited such that the case does not arise in which the antecedent sentence nominates the True and the consequent sentence nominates the False. Accordingly, the given (whole) sentence is true if the sun has not as yet risen (no matter whether or no the sky be heavily overcast), and also if the sun has risen and the sky is heavily overcast. Since all that matters are only the truth-values, each of the component sentences can be replaced by another one of the same truth-value, without altering the truth-value of the whole sentence. In this case also, the illumination would usually seem inappropriate; the proposition could easily appear absurd; but this has nothing to do with the truth-value of the sentence. It must always be remembered that associated thoughts are evoked on the side; but these are not really expressed and must therefore not be taken account of; their truth-values cannot be relevant.[14]

We may hope we have considered the simple types of sentences. Let us now review what we have found out!

The sense of a subordinate clause is usually not a proposition but only part of one. Its nominatum is therefore not a truth-value. The reason for this is *either*: that the words in the subordinate clause have only indirect nominata, so that the nominatum, not the sense, of the clause is a proposition, *or*, that the clause, because of a contained indeterminately indicating constituent, is incomplete, such that only together with the principal clause does it express a proposition. However, there are also instances in which the sense of the dependent clause is a complete proposition, and in this case it can be replaced by another clause of the same truth-value without altering the truth-value of the whole; that is, inasmuch as there are no grammatical obstacles in the way.

In a survey of the various occurrent clauses one will readily encounter some which will not properly fit within any of the considered divisions. As far as I can see, the reason for that is that these clauses do not have quite so simple a sense. It seems that almost always we connect associated propositions with the main proposition which we express; these associated propositions, even if unexpressed, are associated with our words according to psychological laws also by the listener. And because they appear as associated automatically with our words (as in the case of the main proposition) we seem to wish, after all, to express such associated propositions along with the main propositions. The sense of the sentence thereby becomes richer and it may well happen that we may have more simple propositions than sentences. In some cases the sentence may be interpreted in this way, in others, it may be doubtful whether the associated proposition belongs to the sense of the sentence or whether it merely accompanies it.[15] One might find that in the sentence: "Napoleon, who recognized the danger to his right flank, personally led his troops against the enemy's position" there are not only the previously specified two propositions, but also the proposition that the recognition of the danger was the reason why he led his troops against the enemy. One may indeed wonder whether this proposition is merely lightly suggested or actually expressed. Consider the question whether our sentence would be false if Napoleon's resolution had been formed before the recognition of the danger. If our sentence were true even despite this, then the associated proposition should not be regarded as part of the sense of the sentence. In the alternative case the situation is rather complicated: we should then have more simple propositions than sentences. Now if we replaced the sentence: "Napoleon recognized the danger for his right flank" by another sentence of the same truth-value, e.g., by: "Napoleon was over 45 years old" this would change not only our first but also our third proposition; and this might thereby change also the truth-value of the third proposition—namely, if his age was not the reason for his resolution to lead the troops against the enemy. Hence, it is clear that in such instances sentences of the same truth-value cannot always be substituted for one another. The sentence merely by virtue of its connection with another expresses something more than it would by itself alone.

Let us now consider cases in which this occurs regularly. In the sentence: "Bebel imagines that France's desire for vengeance could be assuaged by the restitution of Alsace-Lorraine" there are expressed two propositions, which, however, do not correspond to the main and the dependent clause—namely:

1. Bebel believes that France's desire for vengeance could be assuaged by the restitution of Alsace-Lorraine;
2. France's desire for vengeance cannot be assuaged by the restitution of Alsace-Lorraine.

In the expression of the first proposition the words of the dependent clause have indirect nominata; while the same words, in the expression of the second proposition, have their usual nominata. Hence, we see that the dependent clause of our original sentence really is to be interpreted in a twofold way; i.e., with different nominata, one of which is a proposition and the other a truth-value. An analogous situation prevails with expressions like 'to know', 'to recognize', 'it is known'.

A condition clause and its related main clause express several propositions which, however, do not correspond one-to-one to the clauses. The sentence: "Since ice is specifically lighter than water, it floats on water" asserts:

1. Ice is specifically lighter than water.
2. If something is specifically lighter than water, it floats on water.
3. Ice floats on water.

The third proposition, being implied by the first two, would perhaps not have to be mentioned expressly. However, neither the first and the third, nor the second and the third together would completely render the sense of our sentence. Thus we see that the dependent clause 'since ice is specifically lighter than water' expresses both our first proposition and part of the second. Hence, our clause cannot be replaced by another of the same truth-value; for thereby we are apt to alter our second proposition and could easily affect its truth-value.

A similar situation holds in the case of the sentence: "If iron were lighter than water it would float on water". Here we have the two propositions that iron is not lighter than water and that whatever is lighter than water floats on water. The clause again expresses the one proposition and part of the other. If we interpret the previously discussed sentence: "After Schleswig-Holstein was separated from Denmark, Prussia and Austria fell out with one another" as containing the proposition that Schleswig-Holstein once was separated from Denmark, then we have: firstly, this proposition, secondly, the proposition that, at a time more precisely determined by the dependent clause, Prussia and Austria fell out with one another. Here, too, the dependent clause expresses not only one proposition but also part of another. Therefore, it may not generally be replaced by another clause of the same truth-value.

It is difficult to exhaust all possibilities that present themselves in language; but I hope, in essence at least, to have disclosed the reasons why, in view of the invariance of the truth of a whole sentence, a clause cannot always be replaced by another of the same truth-value. These reasons are:

1. that the clause does not denote a truth-value in that it expresses only a part of a proposition;
2. that the clause, while it does denote a truth-value, is not restricted to this function in that its sense comprises, beside one proposition, also a part of another.

The first case holds

a. with the indirect nominata of the words;
b. if a part of the sentence indicates only indirectly without being a proper name.

In the second case the clause is to be interpreted in a twofold manner; namely, once with its usual nominatum; the other time with its indirect nominatum; or else, the sense of a part of the clause may simultaneously be a constituent of another proposition which, together with the sense expressed in the dependent clause, amounts to the total sense of the main and the dependent clause.

This makes it sufficiently plausible that instances in which a clause is not replaceable by another of the same truth-value do not disprove our view that the nominatum of a sentence is its truth-value and its sense a proposition.

Let us return to our point of departure now.

When we discerned generally a difference in cognitive significance between "a = a" and "a = b" then this is now explained by the fact that for the cognitive significance of a sentence the sense (the proposition expressed) is no less relevant than its nominatum (the truth-value). If a = b, then the nominatum of 'a' and of 'b' is indeed the same and therefore also the truth-value of "a = b" is the same as that of "a = a". Nevertheless, the sense of 'b' may differ from the sense of 'a'; and therefore the proposition expressed by "a = b" may differ from the proposition expressed by "a = a"; in that case the two sentences do not have the same cognitive significance. Thus, if, as above, we mean by 'judgment' the transition from a proposition to its truth-value, then we can also say that the judgments differ from one another.

NOTES

1. Translated by H. F. from the article "Ueber Sinn and Bedeutung", *Zeitschr. f. Philos. und Philos. Kritik*; 100, 1892. The terminology adopted is largely that used by R. Carnap in *Meaning and Necessity*, Univ. of Chicago Press, 1947.

2. I use this word in the sense of identity and understand "a = b" in the sense of "a is the same as b" or "a and b coincide".

3. In the case of genuinely proper names like 'Aristotle' opinions as regards their sense may diverge. As such may, e.g., be suggested: Plato's disciple and the teacher of Alexander the Great. Whoever accepts this sense will interpret the meaning of the statement "Aristotle was born in Stagira" differently from one who interpreted the sense of 'Aristotle' as the Stagirite teacher of Alexander the Great. As long as the nominatum remains the same, these fluctuations in sense are tolerable. But they should be avoided in the system of a demonstrative science and should not appear in a perfect language.

4. With the images we can align also the percepts in which the sense impressions and activities themselves take the place of those traces left in the mind. For our purposes the difference is unimportant, especially since besides sensations and activities recollections of such help in completing the intuitive presentation. 'Percept' may also be understood as the object, inasmuch as it is spatial or capable of sensory apprehension.

5. It is therefore inexpedient to designate fundamentally different things by the one word 'image' (or 'idea').

6. By 'proposition' I do not refer to the subjective activity of thinking but rather to its objective content which is capable of being the common property of many.

7. It would be desirable to have an expression for signs which have sense only. If we call them 'icons' then the words of an actor on the stage would be icons; even the actor himself would be an icon.

8. A judgment is not merely the apprehension of a thought or proposition but the acknowledgment of its truth.

9. In "*A* lied, that he had seen *B*" the clause denotes a proposition of which it is said, firstly, that *A* asserted it as true, and, secondly, that *A* was convinced of its falsity.

10. According to our previous remarks such an expression should always be assured of a nominatum, e.g., through the special convention that the nominatum be the number 0 if there is no object or more than one object denoted by the expression.

11. Regarding these sentences, however, several interpretations are easily conceivable. The sense of the sentence "after Schleswig-Holstein was torn away from Denmark, Prussia and Austria fell out with one another" could also be rendered by "after the separation of Schl.-H. from Denmark, Prussia and Austria fell out with one another." In this formulation it is sufficiently clear that we should not regard it as part of this sense that Schleswig-Holstein once was separated from Denmark; but rather that this is the necessary presupposition for the very existence of a nominatum of the expression 'after the separation of Schl.-H. was once separated from D. This case will be considered later. In order to grasp the difference more clearly, let us identify ourselves with the mind of a Chinese who, with his trifling knowledge of European history, regards it as false that Schl.-H. ever was separated from D. This Chinese will regard as neither true nor false the sentence as interpreted in the first manner. He would deny to it any nominatum because the dependent clause would be lacking a nominatum. The dependent clause would only apparently indicate a temporal determination. But if the Chinese interprets our sentence in the second manner, then he will find it expressing a proposition which he would consider false, in addition to a component which, for him, would be without nominatum.

12. Occasionally there is no explicit linguistic indication and the interpretation has to depend upon the total context.

13. Similarly in the cases of 'but', 'yet'.

14. The proposition of the sentence could also be formulated thus: "either the sun has not as yet risen or the sky is heavily overcast". This shows how to interpret this type of compound sentence.

15. This may be of importance in the question as to whether a given assertion be a lie, an oath or a perjury.

ALFRED TARSKI

THE SEMANTIC CONCEPTION OF TRUTH AND THE FOUNDATIONS OF SEMANTICS

This paper consists of two parts; the first has an expository character, and the second is rather polemical.

In the first part I want to summarize in an informal way the main results of my investigations concerning the definition of truth and the more general problem of the foundations of semantics. These results have been embodied in a work which appeared in print several years ago.[1] Although my investigations concern concepts dealt with in classical philosophy, they happen to be comparatively little known in philosophical circles, perhaps because of their strictly technical character. For this reason I hope I shall be excused for taking up the matter once again.[2]

Since my work was published, various objections, of unequal value, have been raised to my investigations; some of these appeared in print, and others were made in public and private discussions in which I took part.[3] In the second part of the paper I should like to express my views regarding these objections. I hope that the remarks which will be made in this context will not be considered as purely polemical in character, but will be found to contain some constructive contributions to the subject.

In the second part of the paper I have made extensive use of material graciously put at my disposal by Dr. Marja Kokoszyńska (University of Lwów). I am especially indebted and grateful to Professors Ernest Nagel (Columbia University) and David Rynin (University of California, Berkeley) for their help in preparing the final text and for various critical remarks.

I. EXPOSITION

1. The Main Problem—A Satisfactory Definition of Truth

Our discussion will be centered around the notion[4] of *truth*. The main problem is that of giving a *satisfactory definition* of this notion, i.e., a definition which is *materially adequate* and *formally correct*. But such a formulation of the problem, because of its generality, cannot be considered unequivocal, and requires some further comments.

In order to avoid any ambiguity, we must first specify the conditions under which the definition of truth will be considered adequate from the material point of view. The desired definition does not aim to specify the meaning of a familiar word used to denote a novel notion; on the contrary, it aims to catch hold of the actual meaning of an old notion. We must then characterize this notion precisely enough to enable anyone to determine whether the definition actually fulfills its task.

Secondly, we must determine on what the formal correctness of the definition depends. Thus, we must specify the words or concepts which we wish to use in defining the notion of truth; and we must also give the formal rules to which the definition should conform. Speaking more generally, we must describe the formal structure of the language in which the definition will be given.

The discussion of these points will occupy a considerable portion of the first part of the paper.

2. The Extension of the Term "True"

We begin with some remarks regarding the extension of the concept of truth which we have in mind here.

The predicate "true" is sometimes used to refer to psychological phenomena such as judgments or beliefs, sometimes to certain physical objects, namely, linguistic expressions and specifically sentences, and sometimes to certain ideal entities called "propositions." By "sentence" we understand here what is usually meant in grammar by "declarative sentence"; as regards the term "proposition," its meaning is notoriously a subject of lengthy disputations by various philosophers and logicians, and it seems never to have been made quite clear and unambiguous. For several reasons it appears most convenient to *apply the term "true" to sentences*, and we shall follow this course.[5]

Consequently, we must always relate the notion of truth, like that of a sentence, to a specific language; for it is obvious that the same expression which is a true sentence in one language can be false or meaningless in another.

Of course, the fact that we are interested here primarily in the notion of truth for sentences does not exclude the possibility of a subsequent extension of this notion to other kinds of objects.

3. The Meaning of the Term "True"

Much more serious difficulties are connected with the problem of the meaning (or the intension) of the concept of truth.

The word "true," like other words from our everyday language, is certainly not unambiguous. And it does not seem to me that the philosophers who have discussed this concept have helped to diminish its ambiguity. In works and discussions of philosophers we meet many different conceptions of truth and falsity, and we must indicate which conception will be the basis of our discussion.

We should like our definition to do justice to the intuitions which adhere to the *classical Aristotelian conception of truth*—intuitions which find their expression in the well-known words of Aristotle's *Metaphysics*:

To say of what is that it is not, or of what is not that it is, is false, while to say of what is that it is, or of what is not that it is not, is true.

If we wished to adapt ourselves to modern philosophical terminology, we could perhaps express this conception by means of the familiar formula:

The truth of a sentence consists in its agreement with (or correspondence to) reality.

(For a theory of truth which is to be based upon the latter formulation the term "correspondence theory" has been suggested.)

If, on the other hand, we should decide to extend the popular usage of the term "designate" by applying it not only to names, but also to sentences, and if we agreed to speak of the designata of sentences as "states of affairs," we could possibly use for the same purpose the following phrase:

A sentence is true if it designates an existing state of affairs.[6]

However, all these formulations can lead to various misunderstandings, for none of them is sufficiently precise and clear (though this applies much less to the original Aristotelian formulation than to either of the others); at any rate, none of them can be considered a satisfactory definition of truth. It is up to us to look for a more precise expression of our intuitions.

4. A Criterion for the Material Adequacy of the Definition[7]

Let us start with a concrete example. Consider the sentence "snow is white." We ask the question under what conditions this sentence is true or false. It seems clear that if we base ourselves on the classical conception of truth, we shall say that the sentence is true if snow is white, and that it is false if snow is not white. Thus, if the definition of truth is to conform to our conception, it must imply the following equivalence:

The sentence "snow is white" is true if, and only if, snow is white.

Let me point out that the phrase "snow is white" occurs on the left side of this equivalence in quotation marks, and on the right without quotation marks. On the right side we have the sentence itself, and on the left the name of the sentence. Employing the medieval logical terminology we could say that on the right side the words "snow is white" occur in *suppositio formalis*, and on the left in *suppositio materialis*. It is hardly necessary to explain why we must have the name of the sentence, and not the sentence itself, on the left side of the equivalence. For, in the first place, from the point of view of the grammar of our language, an expression of the form "*X* is true" will not become a meaningful sentence if we replace in it '*X*' by a sentence or by anything other than a name—since the subject of a sentence may be only a noun or an expression functioning like a noun. And, in the second place, the fundamental conventions regarding the use of any language require that in any utterance we make about an object it is the name of the object which must be employed, and not the object itself. In consequence, if we wish to say something about a sentence, for example that it is true, we must use the name of this sentence, and not the sentence itself.[8]

It may be added that enclosing a sentence in quotation marks is by no means the only way of forming its name. For instance, by assuming the usual order of letters in our alphabet, we can use the following expression as the name (the description) of the sentence "snow is white":

the sentence constituted by three words, the first of which consists of the 19th, 14th, 15th, and 23rd letters, the second of the 9th and 19th letters, and the third of the 23rd, 8th, 9th, 20th, and 5th letters of the English alphabet.

We shall now generalize the procedure which we have applied above. Let us consider an arbitrary sentence; we shall replace it by the letter '*p.*' We form the name of this sentence and we replace it by another letter, say '*X.*' We ask now what is the logical relation between the two sentences "*X* is true" and '*p.*' It is clear that from the point of view of our basic conception of truth these sentences are equivalent. In other words, the following equivalence holds:

(T) X is true if, and only if, p.

We shall call any such equivalence (with '*p*' replaced by any sentence of the language to which the word "true" refers, and '*X*' replaced by a name of this sentence) an "*equivalence of the form* (T)."

Now at last we are able to put into a precise form the conditions under which we will consider the usage and the definition of the term "true" as adequate from the material point of view: we wish to use the term "true" in such a way that all equivalences of the form (T) can be asserted, and *we shall call a definition of truth "adequate" if all these equivalences follow from it.*

It should be emphasized that neither the expression (T) itself (which is not a sentence, but only a schema of a sentence) nor any particular instance of the form (T) can be regarded as a definition of truth. We can only say that every equivalence of the form (T) obtained by replacing '*p*' by a particular sentence, and '*X*' by a name of this sentence, may be considered a partial definition of truth, which explains wherein the truth of this one individual sentence consists. The general definition has to be, in a certain sense, a logical conjunction of all these partial definitions.

(The last remark calls for some comments. A language may admit the construction of infinitely many sentences; and thus the number of partial definitions of truth referring to sentences of such a language will also be infinite. Hence to give our remark a precise sense we should have to explain what is meant by a "logical conjunction of infinitely many sentences"; but this would lead us too far into technical problems of modern logic.)

5. Truth as a Semantic Concept

I should like to propose the name *"the semantic conception of truth"* for the conception of truth which has just been discussed.

Semantics is a discipline which, speaking loosely, *deals with certain relations between expressions of a language and the objects* (or "states of affairs") *"referred to"* by *those expressions*. As typical examples of semantic concepts we may mention the concepts of *designation, satisfaction,* and *definition* as these occur in the following examples:

the expression "the father of his country" designates (denotes) George Washington;

snow satisfies the sentential function (the condition) "x is white";

the equation "2•x = 1" defines (uniquely determines) the number ½.

While the words "designates," "satisfies," and "defines" express relations (between certain expressions and the objects "referred to" by these expressions), the word "true" is of a different logical nature: it expresses a property (or denotes a class) of certain expressions, viz., of sentences. However, it is easily seen that all the formulations which were given earlier and which aimed to explain the meaning of this word (cf. sections 3 and 4) referred not only to sentences themselves, but also to objects "talked about" by these sentences, or possibly to "states of affairs" described by them. And, moreover, it turns out that the simplest and the most natural way of obtaining an exact definition of truth is one which involves the use of other semantic notions, e.g., the notion of satisfaction. It is for these reasons that we count the concept of truth which is discussed here among the concepts of semantics, and the problem of defining truth proves to be closely related to the more general problem of setting up the foundations of theoretical semantics.

It is perhaps worthwhile saying that semantics as it is conceived in this paper (and in former papers of the author) is a sober and modest discipline which has no pretensions of being a universal patent-medicine for all the ills and diseases of mankind, whether imaginary or real. You will not find in semantics any remedy for decayed teeth or illusions of grandeur or class conflicts. Nor is semantics a device for establishing that everyone except the speaker and his friends is speaking nonsense.

From antiquity to the present day the concepts of semantics have played an important role in the discussions of philosophers, logicians, and philologists. Nevertheless, these concepts have been treated for a long time with a certain amount of suspicion. From a historical standpoint, this suspicion is to be regarded as completely justified. For although the meaning of semantic concepts as they are used in everyday language seems to be rather clear and understandable, still all attempts to characterize this meaning in a general and exact way miscarried. And what is worse, various arguments in which these concepts were involved, and which seemed otherwise quite correct and based upon apparently obvious premises, led frequently to paradoxes and antinomies. It is sufficient to mention here the *antinomy of the liar*, Richard's *antinomy of definability* (by means of a finite number of words), and Grelling-Nelson's *antinomy of heterological terms*.[9]

I believe that the method which is outlined in this paper helps to overcome these difficulties and assures the possibility of a consistent use of semantic concepts.

6. Languages with a Specified Structure

Because of the possible occurrence of antinomies, the problem of specifying the formal structure and the vocabulary of a language in which definitions of semantic concepts are to be given becomes especially acute; and we turn now to this problem.

There are certain general conditions under which the structure of a language is regarded as *exactly specified*. Thus, to specify the structure of a language, we must characterize unambiguously the class of those words and expressions which are to be considered *meaningful*. In particular, we must indicate all words which we decide to use without defining them, and which are called "*undefined* (or *primitive*) *terms*"; and we must give the so-called *rules of definition* for introducing new or *defined terms*. Furthermore, we must set up criteria for distinguishing within the class of expressions those which we call "*sentences*." Finally, we must formulate the conditions under which a sentence of the language can be *asserted*. In particular, we must indicate all *axioms* (or *primitive sentences*), i.e., those sentences which we decide to assert without proof; and we must give the so-called *rules of inference* (or *rules of proof*) by means of which we can deduce new asserted sentences from other sentences which have been previously asserted. Axioms, as well as sentences deduced from them by means of rules of inference, are referred to as *"theorems"* or *"provable sentences."*

If in specifying the structure of a language we refer exclusively to the form of the expressions involved, the language is said to be *formalized*. In such a language theorems are the only sentences which can be asserted.

At the present time the only languages with a specified structure are the formalized languages of various systems of deductive logic, possibly enriched by the introduction of certain nonlogical terms. However, the field of application of these languages is rather comprehensive; we are able, theoretically, to develop in them various branches of science, for instance, mathematics and theoretical physics.

(On the other hand, we can imagine the construction of languages which have an exactly specified structure without being formalized. In such a language the assertability of sentences, for instance, may depend not always on their form, but sometimes on other, nonlinguistic factors. It would be interesting and important actually to construct a language of this type, and specifically one which would prove to be sufficient for the development of a comprehensive branch of empirical science; for this would justify the hope that languages with specified structure could finally replace everyday language in scientific discourse.)

The problem of the definition of truth obtains a precise meaning and can be solved in a rigorous way only for those languages whose structure has been exactly specified. For other languages—thus, for all natural, "spoken" languages—the meaning of the problem is more or less vague, and its solution can have only an approximate character. Roughly speaking, the approximation consists in replacing a natural language (or a portion of it in which we are interested) by one whose structure is exactly specified, and which diverges from the given language "as little as possible."

7. The Antinomy of the Liar

In order to discover some of the more specific conditions which must be satisfied by languages in which (or for which) the definition of truth is to be given, it will be advisable to begin with a discussion of that antinomy which directly involves the notion of truth, namely, the antinomy of the liar.

To obtain this antinomy in a perspicuous form,[10] consider the following sentence:

The sentence printed in this book on p. 59, line 36 is not true.

For brevity we shall replace the sentence just stated by the letter 's.'

According to our convention concerning the adequate usage of the term 'true', we assert the following equivalence of the form (T):

(1) 's' is true if, and only if, the sentence printed in this paper on p. 52, column B, ll. 28–29 is not true.

On the other hand, keeping in mind the meaning of the symbol 's,' we establish empirically the following fact:

(2) 's' is identical with the sentence printed in this paper on p. 52, column B, ll. 28–29.

Now, by a familiar law from the theory of identity (Leibniz's law), it follows from (2) that we may replace in (1) the expression "the sentence printed in this paper on p. 59, line 36" by the symbol " 's.' " We thus obtain what follows:

(3) 's' is true if, and only if, 's' is not true.

In this way we have arrived at an obvious contradiction.

In my judgment, it would be quite wrong and dangerous from the standpoint of scientific progress to depreciate the importance of this and other antinomies, and to treat them as jokes or sophistries. It is a fact that we are here in the presence of an absurdity, that we have been compelled to assert a false sentence [since (3), as an equivalence between two contradictory sentences, is necessarily false]. If we take our work seriously, we cannot be reconciled with this fact. We must discover its cause, that is to say, we must analyze premises upon which the antinomy is based; we must then reject at least one of these premises, and we must investigate the consequences which this has for the whole domain of our research.

It should be emphasized that antinomies have played a preeminent role in establishing the foundations of modern deductive sciences. And just as class-theoretical antinomies, and in particular Russell's antinomy (of the class of all classes that are not members of themselves), were the starting point for the successful attempts at a consistent formalization of logic and mathematics, so the antinomy of the liar and other semantic antinomies give rise to the construction of theoretical semantics.

8. The Inconsistency of Semantically Closed Languages[7]

If we now analyze the assumptions which lead to the antinomy of the liar, we notice the following:

(I) We have implicitly assumed that the language in which the antinomy is constructed contains, in addition to its expressions, also the names of these expressions, as well as semantic terms such as the term *"true"* referring to sentences of this language; we have also assumed that all sentences which determine the adequate usage of this term can be asserted in the language. A language with these properties will be called *"semantically closed."*

(II) We have assumed that in this language the ordinary laws of logic hold.

(III) We have assumed that we can formulate and assert in our language an empirical premise such as the statement (2) which has occurred in our argument.

It turns out that the assumption (III) is not essential, for it is possible to reconstruct the antinomy of the liar without its help.[11] But the assumptions (I) and (II) prove essential. Since every language which satisfies both of these assumptions is inconsistent, we must reject at least one of them.

It would be superfluous to stress here the consequences of rejecting the assumption (II), that is, of changing our logic (supposing this were possible) even in its more elementary and fundamental parts. We thus consider only the possibility of rejecting the assumption (I). Accordingly, we decide *not to use any language which is semantically closed* in the sense given.

This restriction would of course be unacceptable for those who, for reasons which are not clear to me, believe that there is only one "genuine" language (or, at least, that all "genuine" languages are mutually translatable). However, this restriction does not affect the needs or interests of science in any essential way. The languages (either the formalized languages or—what is more frequently the case—the portions of everyday language) which are used in scientific discourse do not have to be semantically closed. This is obvious in case linguistic phenomena and, in particular, semantic notions do not enter in any way into the subject matter of a science; for in such a case the language of this science does not have to be provided with any semantic terms at all. However, we shall see in the next section how semantically closed languages can be dispensed with even in those scientific discussions in which semantic notions are essentially involved.

The problem arises as to the position of everyday language with regard to this point. At first blush it would seem that this language satisfies both assumptions (I) and (II), and that therefore it must be inconsistent. But actually the case is not so simple. Our everyday language is certainly not one with an exactly specified structure. We do not know precisely which expressions are sentences, and we know even to a smaller degree which sentences are to be taken as assertible. Thus the problem of consistency has no exact meaning with respect to this language. We may at best only risk the guess that a language whose structure has been exactly specified and which resembles our everyday language as closely as possible would be inconsistent.

9. Object Language and Metalanguage

Since we have agreed not to employ semantically closed languages, we have to use two different languages in discussing the problem of the definition of truth and, more generally, any problems in the field of semantics. The first of these languages is the language which is "talked about" and which is the subject matter of the whole discussion; the definition of truth which we are seeking applies to the sentences of this language. The second is the language in which we "talk about" the first language, and in terms of which we wish, in particular, to construct the definition of truth for the first language. We shall refer to the first language as "the object language," and to the second as "the metalanguage."

It should be noticed that these terms "object language" and "metalanguage" have only a relative sense. If, for instance, we become interested in the notion of truth applying to sentences, not of our original object language, but of its metalanguage, the latter becomes automatically the object language of our discussion; and in order to define truth for this language, we have to go to a new metalanguage—so to speak, to a metalanguage of a higher level. In this way we arrive at a whole hierarchy of languages.

The vocabulary of the metalanguage is to a large extent determined by previously stated conditions under which a defintion of truth will be considered materially adequate. This definition, as we recall, has to imply all equivalences of the form (T):

(T) X is true if, and only if, p.

The definition itself and all the equivalences implied by it are to be formulated in the metalanguage. On the other hand, the symbol 'p' in (T) stands for an arbitrary sentence of our object language. Hence it follows that every sentence which occurs in the object language must also occur in the metalanguage; in other words, the metalanguage must contain the object language as a part. This is at any rate necessary for the proof of the adequacy of the definition—even though the definition itself can sometimes be formulated in a less comprehensive metalanguage which does not satisfy this requirement.

[The requirement in question can be somewhat modified, for it suffices to assume that the object-language can be translated into the metalanguage; this necessitates a certain change in the interpretation of the symbol 'p' in (T). In all that follows we shall ignore the possibility of this modification.]

Furthermore, the symbol 'X' in (T) represents the name of the sentence which 'p' stands for. We see therefore that the metalanguage must be rich enough to provide possibilities of constructing a name for every sentence of the object language.

In addition, the metalanguage must obviously contain terms of a general logical character, such as the expression "if, and only if."[12]

It is desirable for the metalanguage not to contain any undefined terms except such as are involved explicitly or implicitly in the remarks above, i.e.:

terms of the object language; terms referring to the form of the expressions of the object language, and used in building names for these expressions; and terms of logic. In particular, we desire *semantic terms* (referring to the object language) *to be introduced into the metalanguage only by definition*. For, if this postulate is satisfied, the definition of truth, or of any other semantic concept, will fulfill what we intuitively expect from every definition; that is, it will explain the meaning of the term being defined in terms whose meaning appears to be completely clear and unequivocal. And, moreover, we have then a kind of guarantee that the use of semantic concepts will not involve us in any contradictions.

We have no further requirements as to the formal structure of the object language and the metalanguage; we assume that it is similar to that of other formalized languages known at the present time. In particular, we assume that the usual formal rules of definition are observed in the metalanguage.

10. Conditions for a Positive Solution of the Main Problem

Now, we have already a clear idea both of the conditions of material adequacy to which the definition of truth is subjected, and of the formal structure of the language in which this definition is to be constructed. Under these circumstances the problem of the definition of truth acquires the character of a definite problem of a purely deductive nature.

The solution of the problem, however, is by no means obvious, and I would not attempt to give it in detail without using the whole machinery of contemporary logic. Here I shall confine myself to a rough outline of the solution and to the discussion of certain points of a more general interest which are involved in it.

The solution turns out to be sometimes positive, sometimes negative. This depends upon some formal relations between the object language and its metalanguage; or, more specifically, upon the fact whether the metalanguage in its logical part is *"essentially richer"* than the object language or not. It is not easy to give a general and precise definition of this notion of "essential richness." If we restrict ourselves to languages based on the logical theory of types, the condition for the metalanguage to be "essentially richer" than the object language is that it contain variables of a higher logical type than those of the object language.

If the condition of "essential richness" is not satisfied, it can usually be shown that an interpretation of the metalanguage in the object language is possible; that is to say, with any given term of the metalanguage a well-determined term of the object language can be correlated in such a way that the assertible sentences of the one language turn out to be correlated with assertible sentences of the other. As a result of this interpretation, the hypothesis that a satisfactory definition of truth has been formulated in the metalanguage turns out to imply the possibility of reconstructing in that language the antinomy of the liar; and this in turn forces us to reject the hypothesis in question.

(The fact that the metalanguage, in its nonlogical part, is ordinarily more comprehensive than the object language does not affect the possibility of interpreting the former in the latter. For example, the names of expressions of the object language occur in the metalanguage, though for the most part they do not occur in the object language itself; but, nevertheless, it may be possible to interpret these names in terms of the object language.)

Thus we see that the condition of "essential richness" is necessary for the possibility of a satisfactory definition of truth in the metalanguage. If we want to develop the theory of truth in a metalanguage which does not satisfy this condition, we must give up the idea of defining truth with the exclusive help of those terms which were indicated above (in section 8). We have then to include the term "true," or some other semantic term, in the list of undefined terms of the metalanguage, and to express fundamental properties of the notion of truth in a series of axioms. There is nothing essentially wrong in such an axiomatic procedure, and it may prove useful for various purposes.[13]

It turns out, however, that this procedure can be avoided. For *the condition of the "essential richness" of the metalanguage proves to be, not only necessary, but also sufficient for the construction of a satisfactory definition of truth;* i.e., if the metalanguage satisfies this condition, the notion of truth can be defined in it. We shall now indicate in general terms how this construction can be carried through.

11. The Construction (in Outline) of the Definition[14]

A definition of truth can be obtained in a very simple way from that of another semantic notion, namely, of the notion of *satisfaction*.

Satisfaction is a relation between arbitrary objects and certain expressions called *"sentential functions."* These are expressions like "*x* is white," "*x* is greater than *y*," etc. Their formal structure is analogous to that of sentences; however, they *may* contain the so-called free variables (like '*x*' and '*y*' in "*x* is greater than *y*"), which cannot occur in sentences.

In defining the notion of a sentential function in formalized languages, we usually apply what is called a "recursive procedure"; i.e., we first describe sentential functions of the simplest structure (which ordinarily presents no difficulty), and then we indicate the operations by means of which compound functions can be constructed from simpler ones. Such an operation may consist, for instance, in forming the logical disjunction or conjunction of two given functions, i.e., by combining them by the word "or" or "and." A sentence can now be defined simply as a sentential function which contains no free variables.

As regards the notion of satisfaction, we might try to define it by saying that given objects satisfy a given function if the latter becomes a true sentence when we replace in it free variables by names of given objects. In this sense, for example, snow satisfies the sentential function "x is white" since the sentence "snow is white" is true. However, apart from other difficulties, this method is not available to us, for we want to use the notion of satisfaction in defining truth.

To obtain a definition of satisfaction we have rather to apply again a recursive procedure. We indicate which objects satisfy the simplest sentential functions; and then we state the conditions under which given objects satisfy a compound function—assuming that we know which objects satisfy the simpler functions from which the compound one has been constructed. Thus, for instance, we say that given numbers satisfy the logical disjunction "x is greater than y or x is equal to y" if they satisfy at least one of the functions "x is greater than y" or "x is equal to y."

Once the general definition of satisfaction is obtained, we notice that it applies automatically also to those special sentential functions which contain no free variables, i.e., to sentences. It turns out that for a sentence only two cases are possible: a sentence is either satisfied by all objects, or by no objects. Hence we arrive at a definition of truth and falsehood simply by saying that *a sentence is true if it is satisfied by all objects, and false otherwise.*[15]

(It may seem strange that we have chosen a roundabout way of defining the truth of a sentence, instead of trying to apply, for instance, a direct recursive procedure. The reason is that compound sentences are constructed from simpler sentential functions, but not always from simpler sentences; hence no general recursive method is known which applies specifically to sentences.)

From this rough outline it is not clear where and how the assumption of the "essential richness" of the metalanguage is involved in the discussion; this becomes clear only when the construction is carried through in a detailed and formal way.[16]

12. Consequences of the Definition

The definition of truth which was outlined above has many interesting consequences.

In the first place, the definition proves to be not only formally correct, but also materially adequate (in the sense established in section 4); in other words, it implies all equivalences of the form (T). In this connection it is important to notice that the conditions for the material adequacy of the definition determine uniquely the extension of the term "true." Therefore, every definition of truth which is materially adequate would necessarily be equivalent to that actually constructed. The semantic conception of truth gives us, so to speak, no possibility of choice between various nonequivalent definitions of this notion.

Moreover, we can deduce from our definition various laws of a general nature. In particular, we can prove with its help the *laws of contradiction and of excluded middle*, which are so characteristic of the Aristotelian conception of truth; i.e., we can show that one and only one of any two contradictory sentences is true. These semantic laws should not be identified with the related logical laws of contradiction and excluded middle; the latter belong to the sentential calculus, i.e., to the most elementary part of logic, and do not involve the term "true" at all.

Further important results can be obtained by applying the theory of truth to formalized languages of a certain very comprehensive class of mathematical disciplines; only disciplines of an elementary character and a very elementary logical structure are excluded from this class. It turns out that for a discipline of this class *the notion of truth never coincides with that of provability*; for all provable sentences are true, but there are true sentences which are not provable.[17] Hence it follows further that every such discipline is consistent, but incomplete; that is to say, of any two contradictory sentences at most one is provable, and—what is more—there exists a pair of contradictory sentences neither of which is provable.[18]

13. *Extensions of the Results to Other Semantic Notions*

Most of the results at which we arrived in the preceding sections in discussing the notion of truth can be extended with appropriate changes to other semantic notions, for instance, to the notion of satisfaction (involved in our previous discussion), and to those of *designation* and *definition*.

Each of these notions can be analyzed along the lines followed in the analysis of truth. Thus, criteria for an adequate usage of these notions can be established; it can be shown that each of these notions, when used in a semantically closed language according to those criteria, leads necessarily to a contradiction;[19] a distinction between the object language and the metalanguage becomes again indispensable; and the "essential richness" of the metalanguage proves in each case to be a necessary and sufficient condition for a satisfactory definition of the notion involved. Hence the results obtained in discussing one particular semantic notion apply to the general problem of the foundations of theoretical semantics.

Within theoretical semantics we can define and study some further notions, whose intuitive content is more involved and whose semantic origin is less obvious; we have in mind, for instance, the important notions of *consequence, synonymity,* and *meaning*.[20]

We have concerned ourselves here with the theory of semantic notions related to an individual object language (although no specific properties of this language have been involved in our arguments). However, we could also consider the problem of developing *general semantics* which applies to a comprehensive class of object languages. A considerable part of our previous remarks can be extended to this general problem; however, certain new difficulties arise in this connection, which will not be discussed here. I shall merely observe that the axiomatic method (mentioned in section 10) may prove the most appropriate for the treatment of the problem.[21]

II. POLEMICAL REMARKS

14. Is the Semantic Conception of Truth the "Right" One?

I should like to begin the polemical part of the paper with some general remarks.

I hope nothing which is said here will be interpreted as a claim that the semantic conception of truth is the "right" or indeed the "only possible" one. I do not have the slightest intention to contribute in any way to those endless, often violent discussions on the subject: "What is the right conception of truth?"[22] I must confess I do not understand what is at stake in such disputes, for the problem itself is so vague that no definite solution is possible. In fact, it seems to me that the sense in which the phrase "the right conception" is used has never been made clear. In most cases one gets the impression that the phrase is used in an almost mystical sense based upon the belief that every word has only one "real" meaning (a kind of Platonic or Aristotelian idea), and that all the competing conceptions really attempt to catch hold of this one meaning; since, however, they contradict each other, only one attempt can be successful, and hence only one conception is the "right" one.

Disputes of this type are by no means restricted to the notion of truth. They occur in all domains where—instead of an exact, scientific terminology— common language with its vagueness and ambiguity is used; and they are always meaningless, and therefore in vain.

It seems to me obvious that the only rational approach to such problems would be the following: We should reconcile ourselves with the fact that we are confronted, not with one concept, but with several different concepts which are denoted by one word; we should try to make these concepts as clear as possible (by means of definition, or of an axiomatic procedure, or in some other way); to avoid further confusions, we should agree to use different terms for different concepts; and then we may proceed to a quiet and systematic study of all concepts involved, which will exhibit their main properties and mutual relations.

Referring specifically to the notion of truth, it is undoubtedly the case that in philosophical discussions—and perhaps also in everyday usage—some incipient conceptions of this notion can be found that differ essentially from the classical one (of which the semantic conception is but a modernized form). In fact, various conceptions of this sort have been discussed in the literature, for instance, the pragmatic conception, the coherence theory, etc.[6]

It seems to me that none of these conceptions have been put so far in an intelligible and unequivocal form. This may change, however; a time may come when we find ourselves confronted with several incompatible, but equally clear and precise, conceptions of truth. It will then become necessary to abandon the ambiguous usage of the word "true," and to introduce several terms instead, each to denote a different notion. Personally, I should not feel hurt if a future world congress of the "theoreticians of truth" should decide— by a majority of votes—to reserve the word "true" for one of the nonclassical conceptions, and should suggest another word, say, "frue," for the conception considered here. But I cannot imagine that anybody could present cogent arguments to the effect that the semantic conception is "wrong" and should be entirely abandoned.

15. Formal Correctness of the Suggested Definition of Truth

The specific objections which have been raised to my investigations can be divided into several groups; each of these will be discussed separately.

I think that practically all these objections apply, not to the special definition I have given, but to the semantic conception of truth in general. Even those which were leveled against the definition actually constructed could be related to any other definition which conforms to this conception.

This holds, in particular, for those objections which concern the formal correctness of the definition. I have heard a few objections of this kind; however, I doubt very much whether anyone of them can be treated seriously.

As a typical example let me quote in substance such an objection.[23] In formulating the definition we use necessarily sentential connectives, i.e., expressions like "if . . . , then," "or," etc. They occur in the definiens; and one of them, namely, the phrase "if, and only if" is usually employed to combine the definiendum with the definiens. However, it is well known that the meaning of sentential connectives is explained in logic with the help of the words "true" and "false"; for instance, we say that an equivalence, i.e., a sentence of the form "p if, and only if, q," is true if either both of its members, i.e., the sentences represented by 'p' and 'q,' are true or both are false. Hence the definition of truth involves a vicious circle.

If this objection were valid, no formally correct definition of truth would be possible; for we are unable to formulate any compound sentence without using sentential connectives, or other logical terms defined with their help. Fortunately, the situation is not so bad.

It is undoubtedly the case that a strictly deductive development of logic is often preceded by certain statements explaining the conditions under which sentences of the form "if p, then q," etc., are considered true or false. (Such explanations are often given schematically, by means of the so-called truth-tables.) However, these statements are outside of the system of logic, and should not be regarded as definitions of the terms involved. They are not formulated in the language of the system, but constitute rather special consequences of the definition of truth given in the metalanguage. Moreover, these statements do not influence the deductive development of logic in any way. For in such a development we do not discuss the question whether a given sentence is true, we are only interested in the problem whether it is provable.[24]

On the other hand, the moment we find ourselves within the deductive system of logic—or of any discipline based upon logic, e.g., of semantics— we either treat sentential connectives as undefined terms, or else we define them by means of other sentential connectives but never by means of semantic terms like "true" or "false." For instance, if we agree to regard the expressions "not" and "if . . . , then" (and possibly also "if, and only if") as undefined terms, we can define the term *"or"* by stating that a sentence of the form "*p* or *q*" is equivalent to the corresponding sentence of the form "if not *p*, then *q*." The definition can be formulated e.g., in the following way:

(*p* or *q*) if, and only if, (if not *p*, then *q*).

This definition obviously contains no semantic terms.

However, a vicious circle in definition arises only when the definiens contains either the term to be defined itself, or other terms defined with its help. Thus we clearly see that the use of sentential connectives in defining the semantic term *"true"* does not involve any circle.

I should like to mention a further objection which I have found in the literature and which seems also to concern the formal correctness, if not of the definition of truth itself, then at least of the arguments which lead to this definition.[25]

The author of this objection mistakenly regards scheme (T) (from section 4) as a definition of truth. He charges this alleged definition with "inadmissible brevity, i.e., incompleteness," which "does not give us the means of deciding whether by 'equivalence' is meant a logical-formal, or a nonlogical and also structurally nondescribable relation." To remove this "defect" he suggests supplementing (T) in one of the two following ways:

(T') *X* is true if, and only if, *p* is true,

or

(T'') *X* is true if, and only if, *p* is the case (i.e., if what *p* states is the case).

Then he discusses these two new "definitions," which are supposedly free from the old, formal "defect," but which turn out to be unsatisfactory for other, nonformal reasons.

This new objection seems to arise from a misunderstanding concerning the nature of sentential connectives (and thus to be somehow related to that previously discussed). The author of the objection does not seem to realize that the phrase "if, and only if" (in opposition to such phrases as "are equivalent" or "is equivalent to") expresses no relation between sentences at all since it does not combine names of sentences.

In general, the whole argument is based upon an obvious confusion between sentences and their names. It suffices to point out that—in contradistinction to (T)—schemata (T') and (T") do not give any meaningful expressions if we replace in them 'p' by a sentence; for the phrases "p is true" and "p is the case" (i.e., "what p states is the case") become meaningless if 'p' is replaced by a sentence, and not by the name of a sentence (cf. section 4).[26]

While the author of the objection considers schema (T) "inadmissibly brief," I am inclined, on my part, to regard schemata (T') and (T") as "inadmissibly long." And I think even that I can rigorously prove this statement on the basis of the following definition: An expression is said to be "inadmissibly long" if (i) it is meaningless, and (ii) it has been obtained from a meaningful expression by inserting superfluous words.

16. Redundancy of Semantic Terms—Their Possible Elimination

The objection I am going to discuss now no longer concerns the formal correctness of the definition, but is still concerned with certain formal features of the semantic conception of truth.

We have seen that this conception essentially consists in regarding the sentence "X is true" as equivalent to the sentence denoted by 'X' (where 'X' stands for a name of a sentence of the object language). Consequently, the term "true" when occurring in a simple sentence of the form "X is true" can easily be eliminated, and the sentence itself, which belongs to the metalanguage, can be replaced by an equivalent sentence of the object language; and the same applies to compound sentences provided the term "$true$" occurs in them exclusively as a part of the expressions of the form "X is true."

Some people have therefore urged that the term "true" in the semantic sense can always be eliminated, and that for this reason the semantic conception of truth is altogether sterile and useless. And since the same considerations apply to other semantic notions, the conclusion has been drawn that semantics as a whole is a purely verbal game and at best only a harmless hobby.

But the matter is not quite so simple.[27] The sort of elimination here discussed cannot always be made. It cannot be done in the case of universal statements which express the fact that all sentences of a certain type are true, or that all true sentences have a certain property. For instance, we can prove in the theory of truth the following statement:

All consequences of true sentences are true.

However, we cannot get rid here of the word "true" in the simple manner contemplated.

Again, even in the case of particular sentences having the form "X is true" such a simple elimination cannot always be made. In fact, the elimination is possible only in those cases in which the name of the sentence which is said to be true occurs in a form that enables us to reconstruct the sentence itself. For example, our present historical knowledge does not give us any possibility of eliminating the word "true" from the following sentence:

The first sentence written by Plato is true.

Of course, since we have a definition for truth and since every definition enables us to replace the definiendum by its definiens, an elimination of the term "true" in its semantic sense is always theoretically possible. But this would not be the kind of simple elimination discussed above, and it would not result in the replacement of a sentence in the metalanguage by a sentence in the object language.

If, however, anyone continues to urge that—because of the theoretical possibility of eliminating the word "true" on the basis of its definition—the concept of truth is sterile, he must accept the further conclusion that all defined notions are sterile. But this outcome is so absurd and so unsound historically that any comment on it is unnecessary. In fact, I am rather inclined to agree with those who maintain that the moments of greatest creative advancement in science frequently coincide with the introduction of new notions by means of definition.

17. Conformity of the Semantic Conception of Truth with Philosophical and Common-sense Usage

The question has been raised whether the semantic conception of truth can indeed be regarded as a precise form of the old, classical conception of this notion.

Various formulations of the classical conception were quoted in the early part of this paper (section 3). I must repeat that in my judgment none of them is quite precise and clear. Accordingly, the only sure way of settling the question would be to confront the authors of those statements with our new formulation, and to ask them whether it agrees with their intentions. Unfortunately, this method is impractical since they died quite some time ago.

As far as my own opinion is concerned, I do not have any doubts that our formulation does conform to the intuitive content of that of Aristotle. I am less certain regarding the later formulations of the classical conception, for they are very vague indeed.[28]

Furthermore, some doubts have been expressed whether the semantic conception does reflect the notion of truth in its common-sense and everyday usage. I clearly realize (as I already indicated) that the common meaning of the word "true"—as that of any other word of everyday language—is to some extent vague, and that its usage more or less fluctuates. Hence the problem of assigning to this word a fixed and exact meaning is relatively unspecified, and every solution of this problem implies necessarily a certain deviation from the practice of everyday language.

In spite of all this, I happen to believe that the semantic conception does conform to a very considerable extent with the common-sense usage—although I readily admit I may be mistaken. What is more to the point, however, I believe that the issue raised can be settled scientifically, though of course not by a deductive procedure, but with the help of the statistical questionnaire method. As a matter of fact, such research has been carried on, and some of the results have been reported at congresses and in part published.[29]

I should like to emphasize that in my opinion such investigations must be conducted with the utmost care. Thus, if we ask a high-school boy, or even an adult intelligent man having no special philosophical training, whether he regards a sentence to be true if it agrees with reality, or if it designates an existing state of affairs, it may simply turn out that he does not understand the question; in consequence his response, whatever it may be, will be of no value for us. But his answer to the question whether he would admit that the sentence "it is snowing" could be true although it is not snowing, or could be false although it is snowing, would naturally be very significant for our problem.

Therefore, I was by no means surprised to learn (in a discussion devoted to these problems) that in a group of people who were questioned only 15% agreed that "true" means for them "agreeing with reality," while 90% agreed that a sentence such as "it is snowing" is true if, and only if, it is snowing. Thus, a great majority of these people seemed to reject the classical conception of truth in its "philosophical" formulation, while accepting the same conception when formulated in plain words (waiving the question whether the use of the phrase "the same conception" is here justified).

18. The Definition in Its Relation to "The Philosophical Problem of Truth" and to Various Epistemological Trends

I have heard it remarked that the formal definition of truth has nothing to do with "the philosophical problem of truth."[30] However, nobody has ever pointed out to me in an intelligible way just what this problem is. I have been informed in this connection that my definition, though it states necessary and sufficient conditions for a sentence to be true, does not really grasp the "essence" of this concept. Since I have never been able to understand what the "essence" of a concept is, I must be excused from discussing this point any longer.

In general, I do not believe that there is such a thing as "the philosophical problem of truth." I do believe that there are various intelligible and interesting (but not necessarily philosophical) problems concerning the notion of truth, but I also believe that they can be exactly formulated and possibly solved only on the basis of a precise conception of this notion.

While on the one hand the definition of truth has been blamed for not being philosophical enough, on the other a series of objections have been raised charging this definition with serious philosophical implications, always of a very undesirable nature. I shall discuss now one special objection of this type; another group of such objections will be dealt with in the next section.

It has been claimed that—due to the fact that a sentence like "snow is white" is taken to be semantically true if snow is *in fact* white (italics by the critic)—logic finds itself involved in a most uncritical realism.[31]

If there were an opportunity to discuss the objection with its author, I should raise two points. First, I should ask him to drop the words "in fact," which do not occur in the original formulation and which are misleading, even if they do not affect the content. For these words convey the impression that the semantic conception of truth is intended to establish the conditions under which we are warranted in asserting any given sentence, and in particular any empirical sentence. However, a moment's reflection shows that this impression is merely an illusion; and I think that the author of the objection falls victim to the illusion which he himself created.

In fact, the semantic definition of truth implies nothing regarding the conditions under which a sentence like (1):

(1) snow is white

can be asserted. It implies only that, whenever we assert or reject this sentence, we must be ready to assert or reject the correlated sentence (2):

(2) the sentence "snow is white" is true.

Thus, we may accept the semantic conception of truth without giving up any epistemological attitude we may have had; we may remain naive realists, critical realists or idealists, empiricists or metaphysicians—whatever we were before. The semantic conception is completely neutral toward all these issues.

In the second place, I should try to get some information regarding the conception of truth which (in the opinion of the author of the objection) does not involve logic in a most naive realism. I would gather that this conception must be incompatible with the semantic one. Thus, there must be sentences which are true in one of these conceptions without being true in the other. Assume, e.g., the sentence (1) to be of this kind. The truth of this sentence in the semantic conception is determined by an equivalence of the form (T):

The sentence "snow is white" is true if, and only if, snow is white.

Hence in the new conception we must reject this equivalence, and consequently we must assume its denial:

The sentence "snow is white" is true if, and only if, snow is not white (*or perhaps:* snow, in fact, is not white).

This sounds somewhat paradoxical. I do not regard such a consequence of the new conception as absurd; but I am a little fearful that someone in the future may charge this conception with involving logic in a "most sophisticated kind of irrealism." At any rate, it seems to me important to realize that every conception of truth which is incompatible with the semantic one carries with it consequences of this type.

I have dwelt a little on this whole question, not because the objection discussed seems to me very significant, but because certain points which have arisen in the discussion should be taken into account by all those who for various epistemological reasons are inclined to reject the semantic conception of truth.

19. Alleged Metaphysical Elements in Semantics

The semantic conception of truth has been charged several times with involving certain metaphysical elements. Objections of this sort have been made to apply not only to the theory of truth, but to the whole domain of theoretical semantics.[32]

I do not intend to discuss the general problem whether the introduction of a metaphysical element into a science is at all objectionable. The only point which will interest me here is whether and in what sense metaphysics is involved in the subject of our present discussion.

The whole question obviously depends upon what one understands by "metaphysics." Unfortunately, this notion is extremely vague and equivocal. When listening to discussions in this subject, sometimes one gets the impression that the term "metaphysical" has lost any objective meaning, and is merely used as a kind of professional philosophical invective.

For some people metaphysics is a general theory of objects (ontology)—a discipline which is to be developed in a purely empirical way, and which differs from other empirical sciences only by its generality. I do not know whether such a discipline actually exists (some cynics claim that it is customary in philosophy to baptize unborn children); but I think that in any case metaphysics in this conception is not objectionable to anybody, and has hardly any connections with semantics.

For the most part, however, the term "metaphysical" is used as directly opposed—in one sense or another—to the term "empirical"; at any rate, it is used in this way by those people who are distressed by the thought that any metaphysical elements might have managed to creep into science. This general conception of metaphysics assumes several more specific forms.

Thus, some people take it to be symptomatic of a metaphysical element in a science when methods of inquiry are employed which are neither deductive nor empirical. However, no trace of this symptom can be found in the development of semantics (unless some metaphysical elements are involved in the object language to which the semantic notions refer). In particular, the semantics of formalized languages is constructed in a purely deductive way.

Others maintain that the metaphysical character of a science depends mainly on its vocabulary and, more specifically, on its primitive terms. Thus, a term is said to be metaphysical if it is neither logical nor mathematical, and if it is not associated with an empirical procedure which enables us to decide whether a thing is denoted by this term or not. With respect to such a view of metaphysics it is sufficient to recall that a metalanguage includes only three kinds of undefined terms: (i) terms taken from logic, (ii) terms of the corresponding object language, and (iii) names of expressions in the object language. It is thus obvious that no metaphysical undefined terms occur in the metalanguage (again, unless such terms appear in the object language itself).

There are, however, some who believe that, even if no metaphysical terms occur among the primitive terms of a language, they may be introduced by definitions; namely, by those definitions which fail to provide us with general criteria for deciding whether an object falls under the defined concept. It is argued that the term "true" is of this kind, since no universal criterion of truth follows immediately from the definition of this term, and since it is generally believed (and in a certain sense can even be proved) that such a criterion will never be found. This comment on the actual character of the notion of truth seems to be perfectly just. However, it should be noticed that the notion of truth does not differ in this respect from many notions in logic, mathematics, and theoretical parts of various empirical sciences, e.g., in theoretical physics.

In general, it must be said that if the term "metaphysical" is employed in so wide a sense as to embrace certain notions (or methods) of logic, mathematics, or empirical sciences, it will apply a fortiori to those of semantics. In fact, as we know from part I of the paper, in developing the semantics of a language we use all the notions of this language, and we apply even a stronger logical apparatus than that which is used in the language itself. On the other hand, however, I can summarize the arguments given above by stating that in no interpretation of the term "metaphysical" which is familiar and more or less intelligible to me does semantics involve any metaphysical elements peculiar to itself.

I should like to make one final remark in connection with this group of objections. The history of science shows many instances of concepts which were judged metaphysical (in a loose, but in any case derogatory sense of this term) before their meaning was made precise; however, once they received a rigorous, formal definition, the distrust in them evaporated. As typical examples we may mention the concepts of negative and imaginary numbers in mathematics. I hope a similar fate awaits the concept of truth and other semantic concepts; and it seems to me, therefore, that those who have distrusted them because of their alleged metaphysical implications should welcome the fact that precise definitions of these concepts are now available. If in consequence semantic concepts lose philosophical interest, they will only share the fate of many other concepts of science, and this need give rise to no regret.

20. Applicability of Semantics to Special Empirical Sciences

We come to the last and perhaps the most important group of objections. Some strong doubts have been expressed whether semantic notions find or can find applications in various domains of intellectual activity. For the most part such doubts have concerned the applicability of semantics to the field of empirical science—either to special sciences or to the general methodology of this field; although similar skepticism has been expressed regarding possible applications of semantics to mathematical sciences and their methodology.

I believe that it is possible to allay these doubts to a certain extent, and that some optimism with respect to the potential value of semantics for various domains of thought is not without ground.

To justify this optimism, it suffices I think to stress two rather obvious points. First, the development of a theory which formulates a precise definition of a notion and establishes its general properties provides *eo ipso* a firmer basis for all discussions in which this notion is involved; and, therefore, it cannot be irrelevant for anyone who uses this notion, and desires to do so in a conscious and consistent way. Secondly, semantic notions are actually involved in various branches of science, and in particular of empirical science.

The fact that in empirical research we are concerned only with natural languages and that theoretical semantics applies to these languages only with certain approximation, does not affect the problem essentially. However, it has undoubtedly this effect that progress in semantics will have but a delayed and somewhat limited influence in this field. The situation with which we are confronted here does not differ essentially from that which arises when we apply laws of logic to arguments in everyday life—or, generally, when we attempt to apply a theoretical science to empirical problems.

Semantic notions are undoubtedly involved, to a larger or smaller degree, in psychology, sociology, and in practically all the humanities. Thus, a psychologist defines the so-called intelligence quotient in terms of the numbers of *true* (right) and *false* (wrong) answers given by a person to certain questions; for a historian of culture the range of objects for which a human race in successive stages of its development possesses adequate *designations* may be a topic of great significance; a student of literature may be strongly interested in the problem whether a given author always uses two given words with the same *meaning*. Examples of this kind can be multiplied indefinitely.

The most natural and promising domain for the applications of theoretical semantics is clearly linguistics—the empirical study of natural languages. Certain parts of this science are even referred to as "semantics," sometimes with an additional qualification. Thus, this name is occasionally given to that portion of grammar which attempts to classify all words of a language into parts of speech, according to what the words mean or designate. The study of the evolution of meanings in the historical development of a language is sometimes called "historical semantics." In general, the totality of investigations on semantic relations which occur in a natural language is referred to as "descriptive semantics." The relation between theoretical and descriptive semantics is analogous to that between pure and applied mathematics, or perhaps to that between theoretical and empirical physics; the role of formalized languages in semantics can be roughly compared to that of isolated systems in physics.

It is perhaps unnecessary to say that semantics cannot find any direct applications in natural sciences such as physics, biology, etc.; for in none of these sciences are we concerned with linguistic phenomena, and even less with semantic relations between linguistic expressions and objects to which these expressions and objects which these expressions refer. We shall see, however, in the next section that semantics may have a kind of indirect influence even on those sciences in which semantic notions are not directly involved.

21. *Applicability of Semantics to the Methodology of Empirical Science*

Besides linguistics, another important domain for possible applications of semantics is the methodology of science; this term is used here in a broad sense so as to embrace the theory of science in general. Independent of whether a science is conceived merely as a system of statements or as a totality of certain statements and human activities, the study of scientific language constitutes an essential part of the methodological discussion of a science. And it seems to me clear that any tendency to eliminate semantic notions (like those of truth and designation) from this discussion would make it fragmentary and inadequate.[33] Moreover, there is no reason for such a tendency today, once the main difficulties in using semantic terms have been overcome. The semantics of scientific language should be simply included as a part in the methodology of science.

I am by no means inclined to charge methodology and, in particular, semantics—whether theoretical or descriptive—with the task of clarifying the meanings of all scientific terms. This task is left to those sciences in which the terms are used, and is actually fulfilled by them (in the same way in which, e.g., the task of clarifying the meaning of the term *"true"* is left to, and fulfilled by, semantics). There may be, however, certain special problems of this sort in which a methodological approach is desirable or indeed necessary (perhaps, the problem of the notion of causality is a good example here); and in a methodological discussion of such problems semantic notions may play an essential role. Thus, semantics may have some bearing on any science whatsoever.

The question arises whether semantics can be helpful in solving general and, so to speak, classical problems of methodology. I should like to discuss here with some detail a special, though very important, aspect of this question.

One of the main problems of the methodology of empirical science consists in establishing conditions under which an empirical theory or hypothesis should be regarded as acceptable. This notion of acceptability must be relativized to a given stage of the development of a science (or to a given amount of presupposed knowledge). In other words, we may consider it as provided with a time coefficient; for a theory which is acceptable today may become untenable tomorrow as a result of new scientific discoveries.

It seems a priori very plausible that the acceptability of a theory somehow depends on the truth of its sciences, and that consequently a methodologist in his (so far rather unsuccessful) attempts at making the notion of acceptability precise, can expect some help from the semantic theory of truth. Hence we ask the question: Are there any postulates which can be reasonably imposed on acceptable theories and which involve the notion of truth? And, in particular, we ask whether the following postulate is a reasonable one:

An acceptable theory cannot contain (or imply) any false sentences.

The answer to the last question is clearly negative. For, first of all, we are practically sure, on the basis of our historical experience, that every empirical theory which is accepted today will sooner or later be rejected and replaced by another theory. It is also very probable that the new theory will be incompatible with the old one; i.e., will imply a sentence which is contradictory to one of the sentences contained in the old theory. Hence, at least one of the two theories must include false sentences, in spite of the fact that each of them is accepted at a certain time. Secondly, the postulate in question could hardly ever be satisfied in practice; for we do not know, and are very unlikely to find, any criteria of truth which enables us to show that no sentence of an empirical theory is false.

The postulate in question could be at most regarded as the expression of an ideal limit for successively more adequate theories in a given field of research; but this hardly can be given any precise meaning.

Nevertheless, it seems to me that there is an important postulate which can be reasonably imposed on acceptable empirical theories and which involves the notion of truth. It is closely related to the one just discussed, but is essentially weaker. Remembering that the notion of acceptability is provided with a time coefficient, we can give this postulate the following form:

As soon as we succeed in showing that an empirical theory contains (or implies) false sentences, it cannot be any longer considered acceptable.

In support of this postulate, I should like to make the following remarks.

I believe everybody agrees that one of the reasons which may compel us to reject an empirical theory is the proof of its inconsistency: a theory becomes untenable if we succeed in deriving from it two contradictory sentences. Now we can ask what are the usual motives for rejecting a theory on such grounds. Persons who are acquainted with modern logic are inclined to answer this question in the following way: A well-known logical law shows that a theory which enables us to derive two contradictory sentences enables us also to derive every sentence; therefore, such a theory is trivial and deprived of any scientific interest.

I have some doubts whether this answer contains an adequate analysis of the situation. I think that people who do not know modern logic are as little inclined to accept an inconsistent theory as those who are thoroughly familiar with it; and probably this applies even to those who regard (as some still do) the logical law on which the argument is based as a highly controversial issue, and almost as a paradox. I do not think that our attitude toward an inconsistent theory would change even if we decided for some reasons to weaken our system of logic so as to deprive ourselves of the possibility of deriving every sentence from any two contradictory sentences.

It seems to me that the real reason of our attitude is a different one: We know (if only intuitively) that an inconsistent theory must contain false sentences; and we are not inclined to regard as acceptable any theory which has been shown to contain such sentences.

There are various methods of showing that a given theory includes false sentences. Some of them are based upon purely logical properties of the theory involved; the method just discussed (i.e., the proof of inconsistency) is not the sole method of this type, but is the simplest one, and the one which is not frequently applied in practice. With the help of certain assumptions regarding the truth of empirical sentences, we can obtain methods to the same effect which are no longer of a purely logical nature. If we decide to accept the general postulate suggested above, then a successful application of any such method will make the theory untenable.

22. Applications of Semantics to Deductive Science

As regards the applicability of semantics to mathematical sciences and their methodology, i.e., to metamathematics, we are in a much more favorable position than in the case of empirical sciences. For, instead of advancing reasons which justify some hopes for the future (and thus making a kind of pro-semantics propaganda), we are able to point out concrete results already achieved.

Doubts continue to be expressed whether the notion of a true sentence—as distinct from that of a provable sentence—can have any significance for mathematical disciplines and play any part in a methodological discussion of mathematics. It seems to me, however, that just this notion of a true sentence constitutes a most valuable contribution to metamathematics by semantics. We already possess a series of interesting metamathematical results gained with the help of the theory of truth. These results concern the mutual relations between the notion of truth and that of provability; establish new properties of the latter notion (which, as well known, is one of the basic notions of metamathematics); and throw some light on the fundamental problems of consistency and completeness. The most significant among these results have been briefly discussed in section 12.[34]

Furthermore, by applying the method of semantics we can adequately define several important metamathematical notions which have been used so far only in an intuitive way—such as, e.g., the notion of definability or that of a model of an axiom system; and thus we can undertake a systematic study of these notions. In particular, the investigations on definability have already brought some interesting results, and promise even more in the future.[35]

We have discussed the applications of semantics only to metamathematics, and not to mathematics proper. However, this distinction between mathematics and metamathematics is rather unimportant. For metamathematics is itself a deductive discipline and hence, from a certain point of view, a part of mathematics; and it is well known that—due to the formal character of deductive method—the results obtained in one deductive discipline can be automatically extended to any other discipline in which the given one finds an interpretation. Thus, for example, all metamathematical results can be interpreted as results of number theory. Also from a practical point of view there is no clearcut line between metamathematics and mathematics proper; for instance, the investigations on definability could be included in either of these domains.

23. Final Remarks

I should like to conclude this discussion with some general and rather loose remarks concerning the whole question of the evaluation of scientific achievements in terms of their applicability. I must confess I have various doubts in this connection.

Being a mathematician (as well as a logician, and perhaps a philosopher of a sort), I have had the opportunity to attend many discussions between specialists in mathematics, where the problem of applications is especially acute, and I have noticed on several occasions the following phenomenon: If a mathematician wishes to disparage the work of one of his colleagues, say, A, the most effective method he finds for doing this is to ask where the results can be applied. The hard-pressed man, with his back against the wall, finally unearths the researches of another mathematician B as the locus of the application of his own results. If next B is plagued with a similar question, he will refer to another mathematician C. After a few steps of this kind we find ourselves referred back to the researches of A, and in this way the chain closes.

Speaking more seriously, I do not wish to deny that the value of a man's work may be increased by its implications for the research of others and for practice. But I believe, nevertheless, that it is inimical to the progress of science to measure the importance of any research exclusively or chiefly in terms of its usefulness and applicability. We know from the history of science that many important results and discoveries have had to wait centuries before they were applied in any field. And, in my opinion, there are also other important factors which cannot be disregarded in determining the value of a scientific work. It seems to me that there is a special domain of very profound and strong human needs related to scientific research, which are similar in many ways to aesthetic and perhaps religious needs. And it also seems to me that the satisfaction of these needs should be considered an important task of research. Hence, I believe, the question of the value of any research cannot be adequately answered without taking into account the intellectual satisfaction which the results of that research bring to those who understand it and care for it. It may be unpopular and out-of-date to say—but I do not think that a scientific result which gives us a better understanding of the world and makes it more harmonious in our eyes should be held in lower esteem than, say, an invention which reduces the cost of paving roads, or improves household plumbing.

It is clear that the remarks just made become pointless if the word "application" is used in a very wide and liberal sense. It is perhaps not less obvious that nothing follows from these general remarks concerning the specific topics which have been discussed in this paper; and I really do not know whether research in semantics stands to gain or lose by introducing the standard of value I have suggested.

NOTES

1. Compare Tarski [2] (see References following Notes). This work may be consulted for a more detailed and formal presentation of the subject of the paper, especially of the material

included in sections 6 and 9–13. It contains also references to my earlier publications on the problems of semantics (a communication in Polish, 1930; the article Tarski [1] in French, 1931; a communication in German, 1932; and a book in Polish, 1933). The expository part of the present paper is related in its character to Tarski [3]. My investigations on the notion of truth and on theoretical semantics have been reviewed or discussed in Hofstadter [1], Juhos [1], Kokoszyńska [1] and [2], Kotarbiński [2], Scholz [1], Weinberg [1], et al.

2. It may be hoped that the interest in theoretical semantics will now increase, as a result of the recent publication of the important work Carnap [2].

3. This applies, in particular, to public discussions during the I. International Congress for the Unity of Science (Paris, 1935) and the Conference of International Congresses for the Unity of Science (Paris, 1937); cf., e.g., Neurath [1] and Gonseth [1].

4. The words "notion" and "concept" are used in this paper with all of the vagueness and ambiguity with which they occur in philosophical literature. Thus, sometimes they refer simply to a term, sometimes to what is meant by a term, and in other cases to what is denoted by a term. Sometimes it is irrelevant which of these interpretations is meant; and in certain cases perhaps none of them applies adequately. While on principle I share the tendency to avoid these words in any exact discussion, I did not consider it necessary to do so in this informal presentation.

5. For our present purposes it is somewhat more convenient to understand by "expressions," "sentences," etc., not individual inscriptions, but classes of inscriptions of similar form (thus, not individual physical things, but classes of such things).

6. For the Aristotelian formulation see Aristotle [1], γ, 7, 27. The other two formulations are very common in the literature, but I do not know with whom they originate. A critical discussion of various conceptions of truth can be found, e.g., in Kotarbiński [1] (so far available only in Polish), pp. 123ff., and Russell [1], pp. 362ff.

7. For most of the remarks contained in sections 4 and 8, I am indebted to the late S. Leśniewski who developed them in his unpublished lectures in the University of Warsaw (in 1919 and later). However, Leśniewski did not anticipate the possibility of a rigorous development of the theory of truth, and still less of a definition of this notion; hence, while indicating equivalences of the form (T) as premises in the antinomy of the liar, he did not conceive them as any sufficient conditions for an adequate usage (or definition) of the notion of truth. Also the' remarks in section 8 regarding the occurrence of an empirical premiss in the antinomy of the liar, and the possibility of eliminating this premiss, do not originate with him.

8. In connection with various logical and methodological problems involved in this paper the reader may consult Tarski [6].

9. The antinomy of the liar (ascribed to Eubulides or Epimenides) is discussed here in sections 7 and 8. For the antinomy of definability (due to J. Richard) see, e.g., Hilbert-Bernays [1], vol. 2, pp. 263ff.; for the antinomy of heterological terms see Grelling-Nelson [1], p. 307.

10. Due to Professor J. Łukasiewicz (University of Warsaw).

11. This can roughly be done in the following way. Let S be any sentence beginning with the words "Every sentence." We correlate with S a new sentence S^* by subjecting S to the following two modifications: we replace in S the first word, "Every," by "The"; and we insert after the second word, "sentence," the whole sentence S enclosed in quotation marks. Let us agree to call the sentence S "(self-)applicable" or "non-(self-)applicable" dependent on whether the correlated sentence S^* is true or false. Now consider the following sentence:

Every sentence is nonapplicable.

It can easily be shown that the sentence just stated must be both applicable and nonapplicable; hence a contradiction. It may not be quite clear in what sense this formulation of the antinomy does not involve an empirical premiss; however, I shall not elaborate on this point.

12. The terms "logic" and "logical" are used in this paper in a broad sense, which has

become almost traditional in the last decades; logic is assumed here to comprehend the whole theory of classes and relations (i.e., the mathematical theory of sets). For many different reasons I am personally inclined to use the term "logic" in a much narrower sense, so as to apply it only to what is sometimes called "elementary logic," i.e., to the sentential calculus and the (restricted) predicate calculus.

13. Cf. here, however, Tarski [3], pp. 5f.

14. The method of construction we are going to outline can be applied—with appropriate changes—to all formalized languages that are known at the present time; although it does not follow that a language could not be constructed to which this method would not apply.

15. In carrying through this idea a certain technical difficulty arises. A sentential function may contain an arbitrary number of free variables; and the logical nature of the notion of satisfaction varies with this number. Thus, the notion in question when applied to functions with one variable is a binary relation between these functions and single objects; when applied to functions with two variables it becomes a ternary relation between functions and couples of objects; and so on. Hence, strictly speaking, we are confronted, not with one notion of satisfaction, but with infinitely many notions; and it turns out that these notions cannot be defined independently of each other, but must all be introduced simultaneously.

To overcome this difficulty, we employ the mathematical notion of an infinite sequence (or, possibly, of a finite sequence with an arbitrary number of terms). We agree to regard satisfaction, not as a many-termed relation between sentential functions and an indefinite number of objects, but as a binary relation between functions and sequences of objects. Under this assumption the formulation of a general and precise definition of satisfaction no longer presents any difficulty; and a true sentence can now be defined as one which is satisfied by every sequence.

16. To define recursively the notion of satisfaction, we have to apply a certain form of recursive definition which is not admitted in the object-language. Hence the "essential richness" of the metalanguage may simply consist in admitting this type of definition. On the other hand, a general method is known which makes it possible to eliminate all recursive definitions and to replace them by normal, explicit ones. If we try to apply this method to the definition of satisfaction, we see that we have either to introduce into the metalanguage variables of a higher logical type than those which occur in the object language; or else to assume axiomatically in the metalanguage the existence of classes that are more comprehensive than all those whose existence can be established in the object-language. See here Tarski [2], pp. 393ff., and Tarski [5], p. 110.

17. Due to the development of modern logic, the notion of mathematical proof has undergone a far-reaching simplification. A sentence of a given formalized discipline is provable if it can be obtained from the axioms of this discipline by applying certain simple and purely formal rules of inference, such as those of detachment and substitution. Hence to show that all provable sentences are true, it suffices to prove that all the sentences accepted as axioms are true, and that the rules of inference when applied to true sentences yield new true sentences; and this usually presents no difficulty.

On the other hand, in view of the elementary nature of the notion of provability, a precise definition of this notion requires only rather simple logical devices. In most cases, those logical devices which are available in the formalized discipline itself (to which the notion of provability is related) are more than sufficient for this purpose. We know, however, that as regards the definition of truth just the opposite holds. Hence, as a rule, the notions of truth and provability cannot coincide; and since every provable sentence is true, there must be true sentences which are not provable.

18. Thus the theory of truth provides us with a general method for consistency proofs for formalized mathematical disciplines. It can be easily realized, however, that a consistency proof obtained by this method may possess some intuitive value—i.e., may convince us, or strengthen our belief, that the discipline under consideration is actually consistent—only in case we succeed

in defining truth in terms of a metalanguage which does not contain the object language as a part (cf. here a remark in section 9). For only in this case the deductive assumptions of the metalanguage may be intuitively simpler and more obvious than those of the object-language— even though the condition of "essential richness" will by formally satisfied. Cf. here also Tarski [3], p. 7.

The incompleteness of a comprehensive class of formalized disciplines constitutes the essential content of a fundamental theorem of K. Gödel; cf. Gödel [1], pp. 187ff. The explanation of the fact that the theory of truth leads so directly to Gödel's theorem is rather simple. In deriving Gödel's result from the theory of truth we make an essential use of the fact that the definition of truth cannot be given in a metalanguage which is only as "rich" as the object language (cf. note 17); however, in establishing this fact, a method of reasoning has been applied which is very closely related to that used (for the first time) by Gödel. It may be added that Gödel was clearly guided in his proof by certain intuitive considerations regarding the notion of truth, although this notion does not occur in the proof explicitly; cf. Gödel [1], pp. 174f.

19. The notions of designation and definition lead respectively to the antinomies of Grelling-Nelson and Richard (cf. note 9). To obtain an antinomy for the notion of satisfaction, we construct the following expression:

The sentential function X does not satisfy X.

A contradiction arises when we consider the question whether this expression, which is clearly a sentential function, satisfies itself or not.

20. All notions mentioned in this section can be defined in terms of satisfaction. We can say, e.g., that a given term designates a given object if this object satisfies the sentential function "x is identical with T" where 'T' stands for the given term. Similarly, a sentential function is said to define a given object if the latter is the only object which satisfies this function. For a definition of consequence see Tarski [4], and for that of synonymity, Carnap [2].

21. General semantics is the subject of Carnap [2]. Cf. here also remarks in Tarski [2], pp. 388f.

22. Cf. various quotations in Ness [1], pp. 13f.

23. The names of persons who have raised objections will not be quoted here, unless their objections have appeared in print.

24. It should be emphasized, however, that as regards the question of an alleged vicious circle the situation would not change even if we took a different point of view, represented, e.g., in Carnap [2]; i.e., if we regarded the specification of conditions under which sentences of a language are true as an essential part of the description of this language. On the other hand, it may be noticed that the point of view represented in the text does not exclude the possibility of using truth-tables in a deductive development of logic. However, these tables are to be regarded then merely as a formal instrument for checking the provability of certain sentences; and the symbols 'T' and 'F' which occur in them and which are usually considered abbreviations of "true" and "false" should not be interpreted in any intuitive way.

25. Cf. Juhos [1]. I must admit that I do not clearly understand von Juhos' objections and do not know how to classify them; therefore, I confine myself here to certain points of a formal character. Von Juhos does not seem to know my definition of truth; he refers only to an informal presentation in Tarski [3] where the definition has not been given at all. If he knew the actual definition, he would have to change his argument. However, I have no doubt that he would discover in this definition some "defects" as well. For he believes he has proved that "on ground of principle it is impossible to give such a definition at all."

26. The phrases "p is true" and "p is the case" (or better "it is true that p" and "it is the case that p") are sometimes used in informal discussions, mainly for stylistic reasons; but they are considered then as synonymous with the sentence represented by 'p'. On the other hand, as

far as I understand the situation, the phrases in question cannot be used by von Juhos synonymously with '*p*'; for otherwise the replacement of (T) by (T') or (T") would not constitute any "improvement."

27. Cf. the discussion of this problem in Kokoszyńska [1], pp. 161ff.

28. Most authors who have discussed my work on the notion of truth are of the opinion that my definition does conform with the classical conception of this notion; see, e.g., Kotarbiński [2] and Scholz [1].

29. Cf. Ness [1]. Unfortunately, the results of that part of Ness' research which is especially relevant for our problem are not discussed in his book; compare p. 148, footnote 1.

30. Though I have heard this opinion several times, I have seen it in print only once and, curiously enough, in a work which does not have a philosophical character—in fact, in Hilbert-Bernays [1], vol. II, p. 269 (where, by the way, it is not expressed as any kind of objection). On the other hand, I have not found any remark to this effect in discussions of my work by professional philosophers (cf. note 1).

31. Cf. Gonseth [1], pp. 187f.

32. See Nagel [1], and Nagel [2], pp. 471f. A remark which goes, perhaps, in the same direction is also to be found in Weinberg [1], p. 77; cf., however, his earlier remarks, pp. 75f.

33. Such a tendency was evident in earlier works of Carnap (see, e.g., Carnap [1], especially part V) and in writings of other members of Vienna Circle. Cf. Kokoszyńska [1] and Weinberg [1].

34. For other results obtained with the help of the theory of truth see Gödel [2]; Tarski [2], pp. 401ff.; and Tarski [5], pp. 111f.

35. An object—e.g., a number or a set of numbers—is said to be definable (in a given formalism) if there is a sentential function which defines it; cf. note 20. Thus, the term "definable," though of a metamathematical (semantic) origin, is purely mathematical as to its extension, for it expresses a property (denotes a class) of mathematical objects. In consequence, the notion of definability can be redefined in purely mathematical terms, though not within the formalized discipline to which this notion refers; however, the fundamental idea of the definition remains unchanged. Cf. here—also for further bibliographic references—Tarski [1]; various other results concerning definability can also be found in the literature, e.g., in Hilbert-Bernays [1], vol. I, pp. 354ff., 369ff., 456ff., etc., and in Lindenbaum-Tarski [1]. It may be noticed that the term "definable" is sometimes used in another, metamathematical (but not semantic), sense; this occurs, for instance, when we say that a term is definable in other terms (on the basis of a given axiom system). For a definition of a model of an axiom system see Tarski [4].

REFERENCES

Aristotle [1]. *Metaphysica.* (*Works,* vol. VIII.) English translation by W. D. Ross. (Oxford: 1908).

Carnap, R. [1]. *Logical Syntax of Language* (London and New York: 1937).

——— [2]. *Introduction to Semantics.* (Cambridge: 1942).

Gödel, K. [1]. "Über formal unentscheidbare Sätze der *Principia Mathematica* und verwandter Systeme, I." *Monatshefte für Mathematik und Physik*, XXXVIII (1931), pp. 173–198.

——— [2]. "Über die Länge von Beweisen." *Ergebnisse eines mathematischen Kolloquiums*, vol. VII (1936), pp. 23–24.

Gonseth, F. [1]. "Le Congrès Descartes. Questions de Philosophie scientifique." *Revue thomiste*, vol. XLIV (1938), pp. 183–193.

Grelling, K., and Nelson, L. [1]. "Bemerkungen zu den Paradoxien von Russell und Burali-Forti." *Abhandlungen der Fries'schen Schule*, vol. II (new series), (1908), pp. 301–334.

Hofstadter, A. [1]. "On Semantic Problems." *The Journal of Philosophy*, vol. XXXV (1938), pp. 225–232.

86 • THE BEGINNINGS

Hilbert, D., and Bernays, P. [1]. *Grundlagen der Mathematik.* 2 vols. (Berlin: 1934–1939).
Juhos, B. von. [1]. "The Truth of Empirical Statements." *Analysis*, vol. IV (1937), pp. 65–70.
Kokoszyńska, M. [1]. "Über den absoluten Wahrheitsbegriff und einige andere semantische Begriffe." *Erkenntnis*, vol. VI (1936), pp. 143–165.
———— [2]. "Syntax, Semantik und Wissenschafts-logik." *Actes du Congrès International de Philosophie Scientifique*, vol. III (Paris: 1936), pp. 9–14.
Kotarbiński, T. [1]. *Elementary teorji poznania, logiki formalnej i metodologji nauk.* (*Elements of Epistemology, Formal Logic, and the Methodology of Sciences*, in Polish.) (Lwów: 1929).
———— [2], "W sprawie pojęcia prawdy." (*"Concerning the Concept of Truth,"* in Polish.) *Przeglgd filozoficzny*, vol. XXXVII, pp. 85–91.
Lindenbaum, A., and Tarski, A. [1]. "Über die Beschränktheit der Ausdruccksmittel deduktiver Theorien." *Ergebnisse eines mathematischen Kolloquiums*, vol. VII, (1936), pp. 15–23.
Nagel, E. [1]. Review of Hofstadter [1]. *The Journal of Symbolic Logic*, vol. III, (1938), p. 90.
———— [2]. Review of Carnap [2]. *The Journal of Philosophy*, vol. XXXIX, (1942), pp. 468–473.
Ness, A. [1]. " 'Truth' As Conceived by Those Who Are Not Professional Philosophers." *Skrifter utgitt av Det Norske VIdenskaps-Akademi i Oslo, II. Hist.-Filos. Klasse*, vol. IV (Oslo: 1938).
Neurath, O. [1]. "Erster Internationaler Kongress für Einheit der Wissenschaft in Paris 1935." *Erkenntnis*, vol. V (1935), pp. 377–406.
Russell, B. [1]. *An Inquiry Into Meaning and Truth.* (New York: 1940).
Scholz, H. [1]. Review of *Studia philosophica*, vol. I. *Deutsche Literaturzeitung*, vol. LVIII (1937). pp. 1914–1917.
Tarski, A. [1]. "Sur les ensembles définissables de nombres réels. I." *Fundamenta mathematicae*, vol. XVII (1931), pp. 210–239.
———— [2]. "Der Wahrheitsbegriff in den formalisierten Sprachen." (German translation of a book in Polish, 1933.) *Studia philosophica*, vol. I (1935), pp. 261–405.
———— [3]. "Grundlegung der wissenschaftlichen Semantik." *Actes du Congrès International de Philosophie Scientifique*, vol. III (Paris: 1936), pp. 1–8.
———— [4]. "Über den Begriff der logischen Folgerung." *Actes du Congrès International de Philosophie Scientifique*, vol. VII (Paris: 1937), pp. 1–11.
———— [5]. "On Undecidable Statements in Enlarged Systems of Logic and the Concept of Truth." *The Journal of Symbolic Logic*, vol. IV, 1939, pp. 105–112.
———— [6]. *Introduction to Logic.* (New York: 1941).
Weinberg, J. [1]. Review of *Studia philosophica*, vol. I. *The Philosophical Review*, vol. XLVII, pp. 70–77.

BERTRAND RUSSELL

ON DENOTING

By a "denoting phrase" I mean a phrase such as any one of the following: a man, some man, any man, every man, all men, the present King of England, the present King of France, the centre of mass of the Solar System at the first instant of the twentieth century, the revolution of the earth round the sun, the revolution of the sun round the earth. Thus a phrase is denoting solely in virtue of its *form*. We may distinguish three cases: (1) A phrase may be denoting, and yet not denote anything; e.g., "the present King of France". (2) a phrase may denote one definite object; e.g., "the present King of England" denotes a certain man. (3) A phrase may denote ambiguously; e.g., "a man" denotes not many men, but an ambiguous man. The interpretation of such phrases is a matter of considerable difficulty; indeed, it is very hard to frame any theory not susceptible of formal refutation. All the difficulties with which I am acquainted are met, so far as I can discover, by the theory which I am about to explain.

The subject of denoting is of very great importance not only in logic and mathematics, but also in theory of knowledge. For example, we know that the centre of mass of the Solar System at a definite instant is some definite point, and we can affirm a number of propositions about it; but we have no immediate *acquaintance* with this point, which is only known to us by description. The distinction between *acquaintance* and *knowledge about* is the distinction between the things we have presentations of, and the things we only reach by means of denoting phrases. It often happens that we know that a certain phrase denotes unambiguously, although we have no acquaintance with what it denotes; this occurs in the above case of the centre of mass. In perception we have acquaintance with the objects of perception, and in thought we have acquaintance with objects of a more abstract logical character but we do not necessarily have acquaintance with the objects denoted by phrases composed of words with whose meanings we are acquainted. To take a very important instance: There seems no reason to believe that we are ever acquainted with other people's minds, seeing that these are not directly perceived; hence what we know about them is obtained through denoting. All thinking has to start from acquaintance; but it succeeds in thinking *about* many things with which we have no acquaintance.

The course of my argument will be as follows. I shall begin by stating the theory I intend to advocate;[1] I shall then discuss the theories of Frege and Meinong, showing why neither of them satisfies me; then I shall give the grounds in favour of my theory; and finally I shall briefly indicate the philosophical consequences of my theory.

My theory, briefly, is as follows. I take the notion of the *variable* as fundamental; I use "$C(x)$" to mean a proposition[2] in which x is a constituent, where x, the variable, is essentially and wholly undetermined. Then we can consider the two notions "$C(x)$ is always true" and "$C(x)$ is sometimes true".[3] Then *everything* and *nothing* and *something* (which are the most primitive of denoting phrases) are to be interpreted as follows:

C (everything) means "$C(x)$ is always true";
C (nothing) means " '$C(x)$ is false' is always true";
C (something) means "It is false that '$C(x)$ is false' is always true".[4]

Here the notion "$C(x)$ is always true" is taken as ultimate and indefinable, and the others are defined by means of it. *Everything*, *nothing*, and *something*, are not assumed to have any meaning in isolation, but a meaning is assigned to *every* proposition in which they occur. This is the principle of the theory of denoting I wish to advocate: that denoting phrases never have any meaning in themselves, but that every proposition in whose verbal expression they occur has a meaning. The difficulties concerning denoting are, I believe, all the result of a wrong analysis of propositions whose verbal expressions contain denoting phrases. The proper analysis, if I am not mistaken, may be further set forth as follows.

Suppose now we wish to interpret the proposition, "I met a man". If this is true, I met some definite man; but that is not what I affirm. What I affirm is, according to the theory I advocate:

" 'I met x, and x is human' is not always false".

Generally, defining the class of men as the class of objects having the predicate *human*, we say that:

"C (a man)" means " '$C(x)$ and x is human' is not always false".

This leaves "a man," by itself, wholly destitute of meaning, but gives a meaning to every proposition in whose verbal expression "a man" occurs.

Consider next the proposition "all men are mortal". This proposition[5] is really hypothetical and states that *if* anything is a man, it is mortal. That is, it states that if x is a man, x is mortal, whatever x may be. Hence, substituting 'x is human' for 'x is a man,' we find:

"All men are mortal" means " 'If x is human, x is mortal' is always true".

This is what is expressed in symbolic logic by saying that "all men are mortal" means " 'x is human' implies 'x is mortal' for all values of x". More generally, we say:

"C (all men)" means " 'If x is human, then C (x) is true' is always true."

Similarly

"C (no men)" means " 'If x is human, then C (x) is false' is always true".

"C (some men)" will mean the same as "C (a man),"[6] and

"C (a man)" means "It is false that 'C (x) and x is human' is always false".

"C (every man)" will mean the same as "C (all men)".

If remains to interpret phrases containing *the*. These are by far the most interesting and difficult of denoting phrases. Take as an instance "the father of Charles II was executed." This asserts that there was an x who was the father of Charles II and was executed. Now *the*, when it is strictly used, involves uniqueness; we do, it is true, speak of "*the* son of So-and-so" even when So-and-so has several sons, but it would be more correct to say "a son of So-and-so". Thus for our purposes we take *the* as involving uniqueness. Thus when we say "x was *the* father of Charles II" we not only assert that x had a certain relation to Charles II, but also that nothing else had this relation. The relation in question, without the assumption of uniqueness, and without any denoting phrases, is expressed by "*x begat Charles II*". To get an equivalent of "x was the father of Charles II," we must add, "If y is other than x, y did not beget Charles II," or, what is equivalent, "If y begat Charles II, y is identical with x" Hence "x is the father of Charles II" becomes "x begat Charles II; and 'if y begat Charles II, y is identical with x' is always true of y".

Thus "the father of Charles II was executed" becomes:

"It is not always false of x that x begat Charles II and that x was executed and that 'if y begat Charles II, y is identical with x' is always true of y"

This may seem a somewhat incredible interpretation; but I am not at present giving reasons, I am merely *stating* the theory.

To interpret "C (the father of Charles II)," where C stands for any statement about him, we have only to substitute C (x) for "x was executed" in the above. Observe that, according to the above interpretation, whatever statement C may be, "C (the father of Charles II)" implies:

"It is not always false of x that 'if y begat Charles II, y is identical with x' is always true of y,"

which is what is expressed in common language by "Charles II had one father and no more". Consequently if this condition fails, *every* proposition of the form "C (the father of Charles II)" is false. Thus, e.g., every proposition of the form "C (the present King of France)" is false. This is a great advantage in the present theory. I shall show later that it is not contrary to the law of contradiction, as might be at first supposed.

The above gives a reduction of all propositions in which denoting phrases occur to forms in which no such phrases occur. Why it is imperative to effect such a reduction, the subsequent discussion will endeavour to show.

The evidence for the above theory is derived from the difficulties which seem unavoidable if we regard denoting phrases as standing for genuine constituents of the propositions in whose verbal expressions they occur. Of the possible theories which admit such constituents the simplest is that of Meinong.[7] This theory regards any grammatically correct denoting phrase as standing for an *object*. Thus "the present King of France," "the round square," etc., are supposed to be genuine objects. It is admitted that such objects do not *subsist*, but nevertheless they are supposed to be objects. This is in itself a difficult view; but the chief objection is that such objects, admittedly, are apt to infringe the law of contradiction. It is contended, for example, that the existent present King of France exists, and also does not exist; that the round square is round, and also not round; etc. But this is intolerable; and if any theory can be found to avoid this result, it is surely to be preferred.

The above breach of the law of contradiction is avoided by Frege's theory. He distinguishes, in a denoting phrase, two elements, which we may call the *meaning* and the *denotation*.[8] Thus "the centre of mass of the Solar System at the beginning of the twentieth century" is highly complex in *meaning*, but its *denotation* is a certain point, which is simple. The Solar System, the twentieth century, etc., are constituents of the *meaning*; but the *denotation* has no constituents at all.[9] One advantage of this distinction is that it shows why it is often worth while to assert identity. If we say "Scott is the author of *Waverley*," we assert an identity of denotation with a difference of meaning. I shall, however, not repeat the grounds in favour of this theory, as I have urged its claims elsewhere (*loc. cit.*), and am now concerned to dispute those claims.

One of the first difficulties that confront us, when we adopt the view that denoting phrases *express* a meaning and *denote* a denotation,[10] concerns the cases in which the denotation appears to be absent. If we say "the King of England is bald," that is, it would seem, not a statement about the complex *meaning* "the King of England," but about the actual man denoted by the meaning. But now consider "the King of England is bald". By parity of form, this also ought to be about the denotation of the phrase "the King of France". But this phrase, though it has a *meaning* provided "the King of England" has a meaning, has certainly no denotation, at least in any obvious sense. Hence one would suppose that "the King of France is bald" ought to be nonsense; but it is not nonsense, since it is plainly false. Or again consider such a proposition as the following: "If *u* is a class which has only one member, then that one member is a member of *u*," or, as we may state it, "If *u* is a unit class, *the u* is a *u*". This proposition ought to be *always* true, since the conclusion is true whenever the hypothesis is true. But "the *u*" is a denoting phrase, and it is the denotation, not the meaning, that is said to be a *u*. Now if *u* is *not* a unit class, "the *u*" seems to denote nothing; hence our proposition would seem to become nonsense as soon as *u* is not a unit class.

Now it is plain that such propositions do *not* become nonsense merely because their hypotheses are false. The King in "The Tempest" might say, "If Ferdinand is not drowned, Ferdinand is my only son". Now "my only son" is a denoting phrase, which, on the face of it, has a denotation when, and only when, I have exactly one son. But the above statement would nevertheless have remained true if Ferdinand had been in fact drowned. Thus we must either provide a denotation in cases in which it is at first sight absent, or we must abandon the view that the denotation is what is concerned in propositions which contain denoting phrases. The latter is the course that I advocate. The former course may be taken, as by Meinong, by admitting objects which do not subsist, and denying that they obey the law of contradiction; this, however, is to be avoided if possible. Another way of taking the same course (so far as our present alternative is concerned) is adopted by Frege, who provides by definition some purely conventional denotation for the cases in which otherwise there would be none. Thus "the King of France," is to denote the null-class; "the only son of Mr. So-and-so" (who has a fine family of ten), is to denote the class of all his sons; and so on. But this procedure, though it may not lead to actual logical error, is plainly artificial, and does not give an exact analysis of the matter. Thus if we allow that denoting phrases, in general, have the two sides of meaning and denotation, the cases where there seems to be no denotation cause difficulties both on the assumption that there really is a denotation and on the assumption that there really is none.

A logical theory may be tested by its capacity for dealing with puzzles, and it is a wholesome plan, in thinking about logic, to stock the mind with as many puzzles as possible, since these serve much the same purpose as is served by experiments in physical science. I shall therefore state three puzzles which a theory as to denoting ought to be able to solve; and I shall show later that my theory solves them.

1. If *a* is identical with *b*, whatever is true of the one is true of the other, and either may be substituted for the other in any proposition without altering the truth or falsehood of that proposition. Now George IV wished to know whether Scott was the author of *Waverley*; and in fact Scott *was* the author of *Waverley*. Hence we may substitute *Scott* for *the author* of *"Waverley,"* and thereby prove that George IV wished to know whether Scott was Scott. Yet an interest in the law of identity can hardly be attributed to the first gentleman of Europe.

2. By the law of excluded middle, either "A is B" or "A is not B" must be true. Hence either "the present King of France is bald" or "the present King of France is not bald" must be true. Yet if we enumerated the things that are bald, and then the things that are not bald, we should not find the present King of France in either list. Hegelians, who love a synthesis, will probably conclude that he wears a wig.

3. Consider the proposition "A differs from B". If this is true, there is a difference between A and B, which fact may be expressed in the form "the difference between A and B subsists". But if it is false that A differs from B, then there is no difference between A and B, which fact may be expressed in the form "the difference between A and B does not subsist". But how can a non-entity be the subject of a proposition? "I think, therefore I am" is no more evident than "I am the subject of a proposition, therefore I am," provided "I am" is taken to assert subsistence or being,[11] not existence. Hence, it would appear, it must always be self-contradictory to deny the being of anything; but we have seen, in connexion with Meinong, that to admit being also sometimes leads to contradictions. Thus if A and B do not differ, to suppose either that there is, or that there is not, such an object as "the difference between A and B" seems equally impossible.

The relation of the meaning to the denotation involves certain rather curious difficulties, which seem in themselves sufficient to prove that the theory which leads to such difficulties must be wrong.

When we wish to speak about the *meaning* of a denoting phrase, as opposed to its *denotation*, the natural mode of doing so is by inverted commas. Thus we say:

The centre of mass of the Solar System is a point, not a denoting complex;
"The centre of mass of the Solar System" is a denoting complex, not a point.

Or again,

The first line of Gray's *Elegy* states a proposition.
"The first line of Gray's *Elegy*" does not state a proposition.

Thus taking any denoting phrase, say C, we wish to consider the relation between C and "C", where the difference of the two is of the kind exemplified in the above two instances.

We say, to begin with, that when C occurs it is the *denotation* that we are speaking about; but when "C" occurs, it is the *meaning*. Now the relation of meaning and denotation is not merely linguistic through the phrase: there must be a logical relation involved, which we express by saying that the meaning denotes the denotation. But the difficulty which confronts us is that we cannot succeed in *both* preserving the connexion of meaning and denotation *and* preventing them from being one and the same; also that the meaning cannot be got at except by means of denoting phrases. This happens as follows.

The one phrase C was to have both meaning and denotation. But if we speak of "the meaning of C", that gives us the meaning (if any) of the denotation. "The meaning of the first line of Gray's *Elegy*" is the same as "The meaning of 'The curfew tolls the knell of parting day'," and is not the same as "The meaning of 'the first line of Gray's *Elegy*' ". Thus in order to get the meaning we want, we must speak not of "the meaning of C", but of "the meaning of 'C'," which is the same as "C" by itself. Similarly "the denotation of C" does not mean the denotation we want, but means something which, if it denotes at all, denotes what is denoted by the denotation we want. For example, let "C" be "the denoting complex occurring in the second of the above instances". Then C = "the first line of Gray's *Elegy*", and the denotation of C = The curfew tolls the knell of parting day. But what we *meant* to have as the denotation was "the first line of Gray's *Elegy*". Thus we have failed to get what we wanted.

The difficulty in speaking of the meaning of a denoting complex may be stated thus: The moment we put the complex in a proposition, the proposition is about the denotation; and if we make a proposition in which the subject is "the meaning of C", then the subject is the meaning (if any) of the denotation, which was not intended. This leads us to say that, when we distinguish meaning and denotation, we must be dealing with the meaning: the meaning has denotation and is a complex, and there is not something other than the meaning, which can be called the complex, and be said to *have* both meaning and denotation. The right phrase, on the view in question, is that some meanings have denotations.

But this only makes our difficulty in speaking of meanings more evident. For suppose C is our complex; then we are to say that C *is* the meaning of the complex. Nevertheless, whenever C occurs without inverted commas, what is said is not true of the meaning, but only of the denotation, as when we say: The centre of mass of the Solar System is a point. Thus to speak of C itself, i.e., to make a proposition about the meaning, our subject must not be C, but something which denotes C. Thus "C", which is what we use when we want to speak of the meaning, must be not the meaning, but something which denotes the meaning. And C must not be a constituent of this complex (as it is of "the meaning of C"); for if C occurs in the complex, it will be its denotation, not its meaning, that will occur, and there is no backward road from denotations to meanings, because every object can be denoted by an infinite number of different denoting phrases.

Thus it would seem that "C" and C are different entities, such that "C" denotes C; but this cannot be an explanation, because the relation of "C" to C remains wholly mysterious; and where are we to find the denoting complex "C" which is to denote C? Moreover, when C occurs in a proposition, it is not *only* the denotation that occurs (as we shall see in the next paragraph); yet, on the view in question, C is only the denotation, the meaning being wholly relegated to "C". This is an inextricable tangle, and seems to prove that the whole distinction of meaning and denotation has been wrongly conceived.

That the meaning is relevant when a denoting phrase occurs in a proposition is formally proved by the puzzle about the author of *Waverley*. The proposition "Scott was the author of *Waverley*" has a property not possessed by "Scott was Scott," namely the property that George IV wished to know whether it was true. Thus the two are not identical propositions; hence the meaning of "the author of *Waverley*" must be relevant as well as the denotation, if we adhere to the point of view to which this distinction belongs. Yet, as we have just seen, so long as we adhere to this point of view, we are compelled to hold that only the denotation can be relevant. Thus the point of view in question must be abandoned.

It remains to show how all the puzzles we have been considering are solved by the theory explained at the beginning of this article.

According to the view which I advocate, a denoting phrase is essentially *part* of a sentence, and does not, like most single words, have any significance on its own account. If I say "Scott was a man," that is a statement of the form "*x* was a man," and it has "Scott" for its subject. But if I say "the author of *Waverley* was a man," that is not a statement of the form "*x* was a man," and does not have "the author of *Waverley*" for its subject. Abbreviating the statement made at the beginning of this article, we may put, in place of "the author of *Waverley* was a man," the following "One and only one entity wrote *Waverley*, and that one was a man". (This is not so strictly what is meant as what was said earlier; but it is easier to follow.) And speaking generally, suppose we wish to say that the author of *Waverley* had the property ϕ, what we wish to say is equivalent to "One and only one entity wrote *Waverley*, and that one had the property ϕ".

The explanation of *denotation* is now as follows. Every proposition in which "the author of *Waverley*" occurs being explained as above, the proposition "Scott was the author of *Waverley*" (i.e., "Scott was identical with the author of *Waverley*") becomes "One and only one entity wrote *Waverley*, and Scott was identical with that one"; or, reverting to the wholly explicit form: "It is not always false of x that x wrote *Waverley*, that it is always true of y that if y wrote *Waverley* y is identical with x, and that Scott is identical with x". Thus if "C" is a-denoting phrase, it may happen that there is one entity x (there cannot be more than one) for which the proposition "x is identical with C" is true, this proposition being interpreted as above. We may then say that the entity x is the denotation of the phrase "C". Thus Scott is the denotation of "the author of *Waverley*". The "C" in inverted commas will be merely the *phrase*, not anything that can be called the *meaning*. The phrase *per se* has no meaning, because in any proposition in which it occurs the proposition, fully expressed, does not contain the phrase, which has been broken up.

The puzzle about George IV's curiosity is now seen to have a very simple solution. The proposition "Scott was the author of *Waverley*," which was written out in its unabbreviated form in the preceding paragraph, does not contain any constituent "the author of *Waverley*" for which we could substitute "Scott". This does not interfere with the truth of inferences resulting from making what is *verbally* the substitution of "Scott" for "the author of *Waverley*," so long as "the author of *Waverley*" has what I call a *primary* occurrence in the proposition considered. The difference of primary and secondary occurrences of denoting phrases is as follows:

When we say: "George IV wished to know whether so-and-so," or when we say "So-and-so is surprising" or "So-and-so is true," etc., the "so-and-so" must be a proposition. Suppose now that "so-and-so" contains a denoting phrase. We may either eliminate this denoting phrase from the subordinate proposition "so-and-so," or from the whole proposition in which "so-and-so" is a mere constituent. Different propositions result according to which we do. I have heard of a touchy owner of a yacht to whom a guest, on first seeing it, remarked, "I thought your yacht was larger than it is"; and the owner replied, "No, my yacht is not larger than it is". What the guest meant was, "The size that I thought your yacht was is greater than the size your yacht is"; the meaning attributed to him is, "I thought the size of your yacht was greater than the size of your yacht". To return to George IV and *Waverley*, when we say, "George IV wished to know whether Scott was the author of *Waverley*," we normally mean "George IV wished to know whether one and only one man wrote *Waverley* and Scott was that man"; but we *may* also mean: "One and only one man wrote *Waverley*, and George IV wished to know whether Scott was that man". In the latter, "the author of *Waverley*" has a *primary* occurrence; in the former, a *secondary*. The latter might be expressed by "George IV wished to know, concerning the man who in fact wrote *Waverley*, whether he was Scott". This would be true, for example, if George IV had seen Scott at a distance, and had asked "Is that Scott?" A *secondary* occurrence of a denoting phrase may be defined as one in which the phrase occurs in a proposition ρ which is a mere constituent of the proposition we are considering, and the substitution for the denoting phrase is to be effected in ρ, not in the whole proposition concerned. The ambiguity as between primary and secondary occurrences is hard to avoid in language; but it does no harm if we are on our guard against it. In symbolic logic it is of course easily avoided.

The distinction of primary and secondary occurrences also enables us to deal with the question whether the present King of France is bald or not bald, and generally with the logical status of denoting phrases that denote nothing. If "C" is a denoting phrase, say "the term having the property F," then

"C has the property ϕ" means "one and only one term has the property F, and that one has the property ϕ".[12]

If now the property F belongs to no terms, or to several, it follows that "C has the property ϕ" is false for *all* values of ϕ. Thus "the present King of France is bald" is certainly false; and "the present King of France is not bald" is false if it means

"There is an entity which is now King of France and is not bald,"

but is true if it means

"It is false that there is an entity which is now King of France and is bald".

That is, "the King of France is not bald" is false if the occurrences of "the King of France" is *primary*, and true if it is *secondary*. Thus all propositions in which "the King of France" has a primary occurrence are false; the denials of such propositions are true, but in them "the King of France" has a secondary occurrence. Thus we escape the conclusion that the King of France has a wig.

We can now see also how to deny that there is such an object as the difference between A and B in the case when A and B do not differ. If A and B do differ, there is one and only one entity x such that "x is the difference between A and B" is a true proposition; if A and B do not differ, there is no such entity x. Thus according to the meaning of denotation lately explained, "the difference between A and B" has a denotation when A and B differ, but not otherwise. This difference applies to true and false propositions generally. If "$a \, R \, b$" stands for "a has the relation R to b", then when $a \, R \, b$ is true, there is such an entity as the relation R between a and b; when a R b is false, there is no such entity. Thus out of any proposition we can make a denoting phrase, which denotes an entity if the proposition is true, but does not denote an entity if the proposition is false. E.g., it is true (at least we will suppose so) that the earth revolves round the sun, and false that the sun revolves round the earth; hence "the revolution of the earth round the sun" denotes an entity, while "the revolution of the sun round the earth" does not denote an entity.[13]

The whole realm of non-entities, such as "the round square," "the even prime other than 2," "Apollo," "Hamlet," etc., can now be satisfactorily dealt with. All these are denoting phrases which do not denote anything. A proposition about Apollo means what we get by substituting what the classical dictionary tells us is meant by Apollo, say "the sun-god". All propositions in which Apollo occurs are to be interpreted by the above rules for denoting phrases. If "Apollo" has a primary occurrence, the proposition containing the occurrence is false; if the occurrence is secondary, the proposition may be true. So again "the round square is round" means "there is one and only one entity x which is round and square, and that entity is round," which is a false proposition, not, as Meinong maintains, a true one. "The most perfect Being has all perfections; existence is a perfection; therefore the most perfect Being exists" becomes:

"There is one and only one entity x which is most perfect; that one has all perfections; existence is a perfection; therefore that one exists". As a proof, this fails for want of a proof of the premiss "there is one and only one entity x which is most perfect".[14]

Mr. MacColl (*Mind*, N.S., No. 54, and again No. 55, p. 401) regards individuals as of two sorts, real and unreal; hence he defines the null-class as the class consisting of all unreal individuals. This assumes that such phrases as "the present King of France," which do not denote a real individual, do, nevertheless, denote an individual, but an unreal one. This is essentially Meinong's theory, which we have seen reason to reject because it conflicts with the law of contradiction. With our theory of denoting, we are able to hold that there are no unreal individuals; so that the null-class is the class containing no members, not the class containing as members all unreal individuals.

It is important to observe the effect of our theory on the interpretation of definitions which proceed by means of denoting phrases. Most mathematical definitions are of this sort: for example, "$m - n$ means the number which, added to n, gives m". Thus $m - n$ is defined as meaning the same as a certain denoting phrase; but we agreed that denoting phrases have no meaning in isolation. Thus what the definition really ought to be is: "any proposition containing $m - n$ is to mean the proposition which results from substituting for '*m* − *n*' 'the number which, added to *n*, gives *m*' '". The resulting proposition is interpreted according to the rules already given for interpreting propositions whose verbal expression contains a denoting phrase. In the case where *m* and *n* are such that there is one and only one number *x* which, added to *n*, gives *m*, there is a number *x* which can be substituted for *m* −*n* in any proposition containing *m* − *n* without altering the truth or falsehood of the proposition. But in other cases, all propositions in which "*m* − *n*" has a primary occurrence are false.

The usefulness of *identity* is explained by the above theory. No one outside a logic-book ever wishes to say "*x* is *x*," and yet assertions of identity are often made in such forms as "Scott was the author of *Waverley*" or "thou art the man". The meaning of such propositions cannot be stated without the notion of identity, although they are not simply statements that Scott is identical with another term, the author of *Waverley*, or that thou art identical with another term, the man. The shortest statement of "Scott is the author of *Waverley*" seems to be: "Scott wrote *Waverley*; and it is always true of *y* that if *y* wrote *Waverley*, *y* is identical with Scott". It is in this way that identity enters into "Scott is the author of *Waverley*"; and it is owing to such uses that identity is worth affirming.

One interesting result of the above theory of denoting is this: when there is anything with which we do not have immediate acquaintance, but only definition by denoting phrases, then the propositions in which this thing is introduced by means of a denoting phrase do not really contain this thing as a constituent, but contain instead the constituents expressed by the several words of the denoting phrase. Thus in every proposition that we can apprehend (i.e., not only in those whose truth or falsehood we can judge of, but in all that we can think about), all the constituents are really entities with which we have immediate acquaintance. Now such things as matter (in the sense in which matter occurs in physics) and the minds of other people are known to us only by denoting phrases, i.e., we are not *acquainted* with them, but we know them as what has such and such properties. Hence, although we can form propositional functions C (*x*) which must hold of such and such a material particle, or of So-and-so's mind, yet we are not acquainted with the propositions which affirm these things that we know must be true, because we cannot apprehend the actual entities concerned. What we know is "So-and-so has a mind which has such and such properties" but we do not know "A has such and such properties," where A *is* the mind in question. In such a case, we know the properties of a thing without having acquaintance with the thing itself, and without, consequently, knowing any single proposition of which the thing itself is a constituent.

Of the many other consequences of the view I have been advocating, I will say nothing. I will only beg the reader not to make up his mind against the view—as he might be tempted to do, on account of its apparently excessive complication—until he has attempted to construct a theory of his own on the subject of denotation. This attempt, I believe, will convince him that, whatever the true theory may be, it cannot have such a simplicity as one might have expected beforehand.

NOTES

1. I have discussed this subject in *Principles of Mathematics*, ch. v, and § 476. The theory there advocated is very nearly the same as Frege's, and is quite different from the theory to be advocated in what follows.

2. More exactly, a propositional function.

3. The second of these can be defined by means of the first, if we take it to mean, "It is not true that 'C (x) is false' is always true".

4. I shall sometimes use, instead of this complicated phrase, the phrase "C (x) is not always false," or "C (x) is sometimes true," supposed *defined* to mean the same as the complicated phrase.

5. As has been ably argued in Mr. Bradley's *Logic*, Book 1, ch. ii.

6. Psychologically "C (a man)" has a suggestion of *only one*, and "C (some men)" has a suggestion of *more than one*; but we may neglect these suggestions in a preliminary sketch.

7. See *Untersuchungen zur Gegenstandstheorie und Psychologie*, Leipzig, 1904, the first three articles (by Meinong, Ameseder and Mally respectively).

8. See his "On Sense and Nominatum," in this volume.

9. Frege distinguishes the two elements of meaning and denotation everywhere, and not only in complex denoting phrases. Thus it is the *meanings* of the constituents of a denoting complex that enter into its *meaning*, not their *denotation*. In the proposition "Mont Blanc is over 1,000 metres high," it is, according to him, the *meaning* of "Mont Blanc," not the actual mountain, that is a constituent of the *meaning* of the proposition.

10. In this theory, we shall say that the denoting phrase *expresses* a meaning; and we shall say both of the phrase and of the meaning that they *denote* a denotation. In the other theory, which I advocate, there is no *meaning*, and only sometimes a *denotation*.

11. I use these as synonyms.

12. This is the abbreviated, not the stricter, interpretation.

13. The propositions from which such entities are derived are not identical either with these entities or with the propositions that these entities have being.

14. The argument can be made to prove validly that all members of the class of most perfect Beings exist; it can also be proved formally that this class cannot have more than one member; but, taking the definition of perfection as possession of all positive predicates, it can be proved almost equally formally that the class does not have even one member.

PART TWO

ON
DESCRIPTIONS

INTRODUCTION

The amount of intellectual effort, controversy, and technical machinery that has been directed at the definite article "the" is one reason philosophy of language is baffling when one first comes to it. Russell makes wry fun of himself by comparing himself to Browning's grammarian who, were he dead from the waist down, would still deliver the doctrine of the Greek enclitic "de" ("A Grammarian's Funeral"). Our obsession with "the" doubtlessly can be justified several ways: One way is evident in Strawson's reply to Russell. Large issues concerning the nature of language and its fundamental semantic properties are raised by Russell's account of "the." Are there more than two truth-values? Do they, or does meaning, attach to propositions, sentences, or just to particular uses or utterances of sentences? To what extent do they function like proper names or demonstratives, and to what extent like other quantifier noun phrases? When you assert a sentence with a description, how responsible are you for the aptness of the description? What are we to make of the fact that they are incomplete symbols, i.e., that they can only be defined for a given syntactic context? Why do they have variable scope when proper names and demonstratives always seem to have wide scope? And, of course, the Great Methodological Issue he provocatively pretends to settle with his last seven words: "for ordinary language has no exact logic."

Strawson announces what might be called "the subject/predicate doctrine," the doctrine that a theory of meaning for part of a language (in this case definite description phrases) should leave intact our well-motivated intuition that what we do with a declarative sentence is to predicate something of a definite subject. The theory of descriptions ought not, he suggests, undercut our sound sense of what we are talking about when we use a description to say something; and, admittedly, before reading Russell one had little sense that one was talking about both *something* and *everything* when using a "the"-phrase. (But then one had little sense before reading modern logicians that one was using a hidden "if-then" in one's sentence when talking about every eighteenth-century novelist.) It is worth noting at this stage that mobilizing and defending the intuitions Strawson articulates immediately takes one beyond the domain of semantics per se, and into ontology. This propensity to cross its own border is one of the most salient and exciting features of semantics as a discipline. Similarly, epistemological considerations turn on his notion of acquaintance that moved Russell to suggest demonstratives as ultimate names and on Quine's puzzle as to how to avoid being committed to the existence of a nonexistent object as a subject in a sentence denying its existence (as in "Pegasus does not exist").

The selection from Carnap's *Meaning and Necessity*, apart from being a brief and clear introduction to the theory of definite descriptions, pleasantly evinces a cool and unpolemical attitude toward various technical treatments of failed uniqueness conditions. It provides a nice illustration of how Russell's program articulates in the history of modern semantics.

Keith Donnellan's paper, on the other hand, extends Strawson's philosophical program, using Strawson's pragmatic approach to defend a deeper penetration of semantics by pragmatics than Strawson himself envisioned. One of Strawson's criticisms of Russell is that such semantic relations as reference should properly be ascribed not to parts of speech but to their use by a speaker. Donnellan goes one step further. He distinguishes two classes of uses of definite descriptions distinguished not by syntax but by circumstance. They are sometimes used *referentially* "to enable [one's] audience to pick out whom and what [one] is talking about" (nnn); but sometimes they are only used *attributively* where the speaker states something about whomever or whatever is in fact the one satisfying the description, even if the speaker does not know who in fact does. These two uses are not marked by syntax. Thus our capacity to distinguish them results from being cued by the occasion of the utterance, as Donnellan's ingenious parade of examples shows. "Occasion" here reaches well beyond the containing sentence and even beyond those indexical features of a situation that determines the choice of pronoun or tense. What determines whether a definite description is being used referentially or attributively? Is it an intention or belief of the speaker or an expectation of her audience? These questions, as well as many others, are thoroughly canvassed in Kripke's essay.

Donnellan calls attention to a pervasive feature of our interpretation of what people say, viz., our capacity to infer what they are talking about in the absence of wholly reliable, accurate or even *any* verbal indications of what that may be. And sometimes such extraverbal indicators become conventional, e.g., salience where there is more than one possible subject of discourse of a kind. Any fully general account of the meaning of phrases containing descriptions must then explain such pragmatic phenomena. A larger, more programmatic, issue suggested by Donnellan's paper hence concerns the power of formalisms from the predicate calculus to capture the full structural resources or expressive power of natural languages. How sanguine one is about the power will depend, *inter alia*, on whether or not one thinks of English "the"-phrases as cousins of the class and functional abstracts ("the sine of . . . ," "the set of . . .") that are used in mathematics or whether one thinks of them as cousins of "that" ("that man"). The functional abstracts, one suspects, caught Carnap's eye; the demonstratives Donnellan's.

Kripke's essay is largely methodological. It serves therefore as an excellent survey of large programs in the philosophy of language that form the background of the debate over descriptions. It contains, nonetheless, many interesting observations and arguments on the particulars of the logicist-pragmatist debate. For example, in disputing the idea that Donnellan's distinction is one of scope, he argues persuasively that no merely two-way distinction can handle the multiple amphiboly caused by the interaction of descriptions with modal, epistemic, or truth-functional operators. The greater the number of operators with their relative scope unmarked the greater the degree of scope ambiguity.

Merrie Bergmann's paper in a way shows how to model the interaction between pragmatic presupposition and truth-conditions. She proposes to evaluate sentences with descriptions twice, once for the two classical truth-values and once for their presupposition-value. She then shows how the truth-functions operate on these pairs of values. The final pages of her paper sets out a model theoretic semantics of a language with descriptions and the classical quantifers. An interesting point of coincidence with Kripke's paper is revealed in her remarks about her truth-security table for the unary connective "it is true that." Because this connective implies semantic ascent—joining it to a sentence makes that sentence no longer about its subject's referent but about itself or the proposition it expresses—its security-value is always positive. In arguing against Donnellan's suggestion that, although we would not find Linsky's sentence "her husband is attentive" said of an unmarried woman's lover (believed by both speaker and listener to be her husband) false (assuming the lover to be attentive), we (in the know) would be unwilling to say, "He just said that her husband is attentive." Kripke gets at this point by noting that quotation insulates the quoter from the sentence's anomalousness. "True that" and "says that" can both be seen as inducing semantic ascent. Hence, sentences in which they occur would always be secure. Presupposition is a semantic feature of other denoting phrases (QNPs) as well, as Strawson's sentence about childless John ("All John's children are asleep") shows. Bergmann's semantics, by restricting such QNPs to just that part of the domain that is John's children, evaluate this sentence as insecure but true. (The mad hatter felt his invitation to Alice to have more tea was quite secure despite her having had none; less tea than none he agreed would be insecure since impossible.)

Bergmann's paper illustrates an interesting if puzzling feature of modern formal semantics. Russell's account of descriptions is syntactic in the sense that the logical notation that translates the various natural language definite descriptions is introduced as an abbreviation of something syntactically very different, a compound conjunctive sentence with quantifiers. Other denoting phrases receive a similar if not quite so radical treatment. "All camels . . ." becomes "everything is such that if it is a camel, then . . ." In Bergmann's treatment, the surface syntax is left virtually untouched and simple, a virtue shared by the treatment of Montague and his followers (see Weisler's essay in this volume), with the complexity deferred to the semantics.

David Kaplan's "Dthat" begins with Donnellan's distinction between the attributive and referential use of descriptions but quickly moves to the topic of sense and connotation, a topic that Donnellan's distinction raises: If one were to package all the descriptive content of a definite description with a such-that operator, thus ("The man such that he is standing in the corner drinking the martini . . ."), and then include in this content nonverbal elements such as pointing or looking, might not this complex property so expressed, Kaplan asks, be what medieval semanticists thought was co-(de?)noted and what Frege thought of as sense? If we understand sense in this way, we can, he argues, explain some of the referential uses Donnellan illustrates, e.g., how one is able to pick out the referent of a description that is nonetheless false.

Kaplan, however, does not like the ontology this suggests. What a declarative sentence says is called by those in the Russell-Moore tradition a proposition and by Frege a Gedanken, objective Platonic entities in either case. Kaplan suggests a representation of propositions that preserves the naive subject-predicate view of all sentences: every proposition is an ordered pair, $<x, y>$, consisting of what the sentence talks about and what it says of it. (The difficulty in deciding what the sentence "nothing is immaterial" and its cousins talk about, is handled by putting the denoting phrase in quotation marks: $<$"nothing", $\lambda x(x$ is immaterial)$>$. This, then, would represent a great number of ordered pairs, since the sentence says of each and every object in one's universe of discourse that it is not immaterial.)

Frege, however, distinguishes between what sentences denote and the sense they express. The former is their truth value, the latter a proposition. The difference between the Fregean sense of a sentence about John and a Russellian proposition expressed by a similar sentence that is Russell's actually contains John himself, whereas Frege's is a combination of senses one of which is the sense of the proper name "John." Kaplan represents the Russellian singular proposition about John by sticking John in it: $<John, F>$. By contrast, a proposition that is about John via a definite description of him, say "the guy sitting over there holding a copy of *Garfield and Kiteley* and thinking about Russellian propositions," looks like any general proposition, any one with a denoting phrase, to wit: $<<'the', G> F>$. These look like two very different ways of being about John. At this point Kaplan seems to have given us the means of interpreting Donellan's distinction. Referentially used, "the G is F" $<John, F>$ and context may be needed for the listener to get to a non-G John. Attributively used "the G is F" expresses $<<'the', G>$ $F>$. Why does he not do this? Possibly because he is anxious to explore just how context can get one to the referent, to John, when G is not true of him, whether the setting of an utterance is any part of its content.

Since the topic of scope has been an almost constant countermelody to the theory of quantifiers and descriptions, a further word on it is in order. The classic quantifiers of Aristotle's *Prior Analytics*, "some," "all," and "none" are carefully punctuated in formal logic to avoid scope amphiboly. The same is true of the truth-functions, and, or, and not to which the former can be reduced where the domain of individuals is finite. The amphiboly of "everyone loves someone" results from the uncertain superiority of the quantifier everyone over someone. Ambiguity of scope can be seen to be very different from that of a word or phrase, lexical ambiguity. The meaning of "everyone" and "someone" does not change in the two readings of the "love"-sentence; just their position. Scope amphiboly, however, in common with lexical ambiguity, can affect truth-value.

These papers hardly exhaust the range of questions that might be asked or models that might be proposed in an effort to understand the meanings of quantified noun phrases. But they do reflect the roots and branches of the traditions that have dominated modern semantic theory in this domain.

P. F. STRAWSON

ON REFERRING

I

We very commonly use expressions of certain kinds to mention or refer to some individual person or single object or particular event or place or process, in the course of doing what we should normally describe as making a statement about that person, object, place, event, or process. I shall call this way of using expressions the 'uniquely referring use'. The classes of expressions which are most commonly used in this way are: singular demonstrative pronouns ("this" and "that"); proper names e.g. "Venice," "Napoleon," "John"); singular personal and impersonal pronouns ("he," "she," "I," "you," "it"); and phrases beginning with the definite article followed by a noun, qualified or unqualified, in the singular (e.g. "the table," "the old man," "the king of France"). Any expression of any of these classes can occur as the subject of what would traditionally be regarded as a singular subject-predicate sentence; and would, so occurring, exemplify the use I wish to discuss.

I do not want to say that expressions belonging to these classes never have any other use than the one I want to discuss. On the contrary, it is obvious that they do. It is obvious that anyone who uttered the sentence, "The whale is a mammal," would be using the expression "the whale" in a way quite different from the way it would be used by anyone who had occasion seriously to utter the sentence, "The whale struck the ship." In the first sentence one is obviously *not* mentioning, and in the second sentence one obviously *is* mentioning, a particular whale. Again if I said, "Napoleon was the greatest French soldier," I should be using the word "Napoleon" to mention a certain individual, but I should not be using the phrase, "the greatest French soldier," to mention an individual, but to say something about an individual I had already mentioned. It would be natural to say that in using this sentence I was talking *about* Napoleon and that what I was *saying* about him was that he was the greatest French soldier. But of course I *could* use the expression, "the greatest French soldier," to mention an individual; for example, by saying: "The greatest French soldier died in exile." So it is obvious that at least some expressions belonging to the classes I mentioned *can* have uses other than the use I am anxious to discuss. Another thing I do not want to say is that in any given sentence there is never more than one expression used in the way I propose to discuss. On the contrary, it is obvious that there may be more than one. For example, it would be natural to say that, in seriously using the sentence, "The whale struck the ship," I was saying something about both a certain whale and a certain ship, that I was using each of the expressions "the whale" and "the ship" to mention a particular object; or, in other words, that I was using each of these expressions in the uniquely referring way. In general, however, I shall confine my attention to cases where an expression used in this way occurs as the grammatical subject of a sentence.

I think it is true to say that Russell's theory of descriptions, which is concerned with the last of the four classes of expressions I mentioned above (i.e. with expressions of the form "the so-and-so"), is still widely accepted among logicians as giving a correct account of the use of such expressions in ordinary language. I want to show in the first place, that this theory, so regarded, embodies some fundamental mistakes.

What question or questions about phrases of the form "the so-and-so" was the theory of descriptions designed to answer? I think that at least one of the questions may be illustrated as follows. Suppose someone were now to utter the sentence, "The king of France is wise." No one would say that the sentence which had been uttered was meaningless. Everyone would agree that it was significant. But everyone knows that there is not at present a king of France. One of the questions the theory of descriptions was designed to answer was the question: How can such a sentence as "The king of France is wise" be significant even when there is nothing which answers to the description it contains, i.e., in this case, nothing which answers to the description "The king of France"? And one of the reasons why Russell thought it important to give a correct answer to this question was that he thought it important to show that another answer which might be given was wrong. The answer that he thought was wrong, and to which he was anxious to supply an alternative, might be exhibited as the conclusion of either of the following two fallacious arguments. Let us call the sentence "The king of France is wise" the sentence S. Then the first argument is as follows:

(1) The phrase, "the king of France," is the subject of the sentence S.
Therefore (2) if S is a significant sentence, S is a sentence *about* the king of France.
But (3) if there in no sense exists a king of France, the sentence is not about anything, and hence not about the king of France.
Therefore (4) since S is significant, there must in some sense (in some world) exist (or subsist) the king of France.

And the second argument is as follows:

(1) If S is significant, it is either true or false.

(2) S is true if the king of France is wise and false if the king of France is not wise.

(3) But the statement that the king of France is wise and the statement that the king of France is not wise are alike true only if there is (in some sense, in some world) something which is the king of France.

Hence (4) since S is significant, there follows the same conclusion as before.

These are fairly obviously bad arguments, and, as we should expect, Russell rejects them. The postulation of a world of strange entities, to which the king of France belongs, offends, he says, against "that feeling for reality which ought to be preserved even in the most abstract studies." The fact that Russell rejects these arguments is, however, less interesting than the extent to which, in rejecting their conclusion, he concedes the more important of their principles. Let me refer to the phrase, "the king of France," as the phrase D. Then I think Russell's reasons for rejecting these two arguments can be summarized as follows. The mistake arises, he says, from thinking that D, which is certainly the *grammatical* subject of S, is also the *logical* subject of S. But D is not the logical subject of S. In fact S, although grammatically it has a singular subject and a predicate, is not logically a subject-predicate sentence at all. The proposition it expresses is a complex kind of *existential* proposition, part of which might be described as a "uniquely existential" proposition. To exhibit the logical form of the proposition, we should rewrite the sentence in a logically appropriate grammatical form, in such a way that the deceptive similarity of S to a sentence expressing a subject-predicate proposition would disappear, and we should be safeguarded against arguments such as the bad ones I outlined above. Before recalling the details of Russell's analysis of S, let us notice what his answer, as I have so far given it, seems to imply. His answer seems to imply that in the case of a sentence which is similar to S in that (1) it is grammatically of the subject-predicate form and (2) its grammatical subject does not refer to anything, then the only alternative to its being meaningless is that it should not really (i.e. logically) be of the subject-predicate form at all, but of some quite different form. And this in its turn seems to imply that if there are any sentences which are genuinely of the subject-predicate form, then the very fact of their being significant, having a meaning, guarantees that there *is* something referred to by the logical (and grammatical) subject. Moreover, Russell's answer seems to imply that there are such sentences. For if it is true that one may be misled by the grammatical similarity of S to other sentences into thinking that it is logically of the subject-predicate form, then surely there must be other sentences grammatically similar to S, which *are* of the subject-predicate form.

To show not only that Russell's answer seems to imply these conclusions, but that he accepted at least the first two of them, it is enough to consider what he says about a class of expressions which he calls "logically proper names" and contrasts with expressions, like D, which he calls "definite descriptions." Of logically proper names Russell says or implies the following things:

(1) That they and they alone can occur as subjects of sentences which are genuinely of the subject-predicate form.

(2) That an expression intended to be a logically proper name is *meaningless* unless there is some single object for which it stands: for the *meaning* of such an expression just is the individual object which the expression designates. To be a name at all, therefore, it *must* designate something.

It is easy to see that if anyone believes these two propositions, then the only way for him to save the significance of the sentence S is to deny that it is a logically subject-predicate sentence. Generally, we may say that Russell recognizes only two ways in which sentences which seem, from their grammatical structure, to be about some particular person or individual object or event, can be significant:

(1) The first is that their grammatical form should be misleading as to their logical form, and that they should be analyzable, like S, as a special kind of existential sentence.

(2) The second is that their grammatical subject should be a logically proper name, of which the meaning is the individual thing it designates.

I think that Russell is unquestionably wrong in this, and that sentences which are significant, and which begin with an expression used in the uniquely referring way, fall into neither of these two classes. Expressions used in the uniquely referring way are never either logically proper names or descriptions, if what is meant by calling them "descriptions" is that they are to be analyzed in accordance with the model provided by Russell's theory of descriptions.

There are no logically proper names and there are no descriptions (in this sense).

Let us now consider the details of Russell's analysis. According to Russell, anyone who asserted S would be asserting that:

(1) There is a king of France
(2) There is not more than one king of France
(3) There is nothing which is king of France and is not wise

It is easy to see both how Russell arrived at this analysis, and how it enables him to answer the question with which we began, viz. the question: How can the sentence S be significant when there is no king of France? The way in which he arrived at the analysis was clearly by asking himself what would be the circumstances in which we would say that anyone who uttered the sentence

S had made a true assertion. And it does seem pretty clear, and I have no wish to dispute, that the sentences (1)–(3) above do describe circumstances which are at least *necessary* conditions of anyone making a true assertion by uttering the sentence S. But, as I hope to show, to say this is not at all the same thing as to say that Russell has given a correct account of the use of the sentence S or even that he has given an account which, though incomplete, is correct as far as it goes; and is certainly not at all the same thing as to say that the model translation provided is a correct model for all (or for any) singular sentences beginning with a phrase of the form "the so-and-so."

It is also easy to see how this analysis enables Russell to answer the question of how the sentence S can be significant, even when there is no king of France. For, if this analysis is correct, anyone who utters the sentence S today would be jointly asserting three propositions, one of which (viz. that there is a king of France) would be false; and since the conjunction of three propositions, of which one is false, is itself false, the assertion as a whole would be significant, but false. So neither of the bad arguments for subsistent entities would apply to such an assertion.

II

As a step towards showing that Russell's solution of his problem is mistaken, and towards providing the correct solution, I want now to draw certain distinctions. For this purpose I shall, for the remainder of this section, refer to an expression which has a uniquely referring use as "an expression" for short; and to a sentence beginning with such an expression as "a sentence" for short. The distinctions I shall draw are rather rough and ready, and, no doubt, difficult cases could be produced which would call for their refinement. But I think they will serve my purpose. The distinctions are between:

(A1) a sentence
(A2) a use of a sentence
(A3) an utterance of a sentence

and, correspondingly, between:

(B1) an expression
(B2) a use of an expression
(B3) an utterance of an expression

Consider again the sentence, "The king of France is wise." It is easy to imagine that this sentence was uttered at various times from, say, the beginning of the seventeenth century onwards, during the reigns of each successive French monarch; and easy to imagine that it was also uttered during the subsequent periods in which France was not a monarchy. Notice that it was natural for me to speak of "the sentence" or "this sentence" being uttered at various times during this period; or, in other words, that it would be natural and correct to speak of *one and the same* sentence being uttered on all these various occasions. It is in the sense in which it would be correct to speak of one and the same sentence being uttered on all these various occasions that I want to use the expression (A1) "a sentence." There are, however, obvious differences between different *occasions of the use* of this sentence. For instance, if one man uttered it in the reign of Louis XIV and another man uttered it in the reign of Louis XV, it would be natural to say (to assume) that they were respectively talking about different people; and it might be held that the first man, in using the sentence, made a true assertion, while the second man, in using the same sentence, made a false assertion. If on the other hand two different men simultaneously uttered the sentence (e.g. if one wrote it and the other spoke it) during the reign of Louis XIV, it would be natural to say (assume) that they were both talking about the same person, and, in that case, in using the sentence, they *must* either both have made a true assertion or both have made a false assertion. And this illustrates what I mean by *a use* of a sentence. The two men who uttered the sentence, one in the reign of Louis XV and one in the reign of Louis XIV, each made a different use of the same sentence; whereas the two men who uttered the sentence simultaneously in the reign of Louis XIV, made the same use[1] of the same sentence. Obviously in the case of this sentence, and equally obviously in the case of many others, we cannot talk of *the sentence* being true or false, but only of its being used to make a true or false assertion or (if this is preferred) to express a true or a false proposition. And equally obviously we cannot talk of *the sentence* being *about* a particular person, for the same sentence may be used at different times to talk about quite different particular persons, but only of *a use* of the sentence to talk about a particular person. Finally it will make sufficiently clear what I mean by an utterance of a sentence if I say that the two men who simultaneously uttered the sentence in the reign of Louis XIV made two different utterances of the same sentence, though they made the same *use* of the sentence.

If we now consider not the whole sentence, "The king of France is wise," but that part of it which is the expression, "the king of France," it is obvious that we can make analogous, though not identical distinctions between (1) the expression, (2) a use of the expression, and (3) an utterance of the expression. The distinctions will not be identical; we obviously cannot correctly talk of the expression "the king of France" being used to express a true or false proposition, since in general only sentences can be used truly or falsely; and similarly it is only by using a sentence and not by using an expression alone, that you can talk about a particular person. Instead, we shall say in this case that you *use* the expression to *mention* or *refer to* a particular person in the course of using the sentence to talk about him. But obviously in this case, and a great many others, the *expression* (B1) cannot be said to mention, or refer to, anything, any more than the *sentence* can be said to be true or false. The same expression can have different mentioning-uses, as the same sentence can be used to make statements with different truth-values. 'Mentioning', or 'referring', is not something an expression does; it is something that someone can use an expression to do. Mentioning, or referring to, something is a characteristic of *a use* of an expression, just as 'being about' something, and truth-or-falsity, are characteristics of *a use* of a sentence.

A very different example may help to make these distinctions clearer. Consider another case of an expression which has a uniquely referring use, viz. the expression "I"; and consider the sentence, "I am hot." Countless people may use this same sentence; but it is logically impossible for two different people to make *the same use* of this sentence: or, if this is preferred, to use it to express the same proposition. The expression "I" may correctly be used by (and only by) any one of innumerable people to refer to himself. To say this is to say something about the expression "I": it is, in a sense, to give its meaning. This is the sort of thing that can be said about *expressions*. But it makes no sense to say of the *expression* "I" that it refers to a particular person. This is the sort of thing that can be said only of a particular use of the expression.

Let me use "type" as an abbreviation for "sentence or expression." Then I am not saying that there are sentences and expressions (types), *and* uses of them, *and* utterances of them, as there are ships *and* shoes *and* sealing-wax. I am saying that we cannot say *the same things* about types, uses of types, and utterances of types. And the fact is that we do talk about types; and that confusion is apt to result from the failure to notice the differences between what we can say about these and what we can say only about the *uses* of types. We are apt to fancy we are talking about sentences and expressions when we are talking about the uses of sentences and expressions.

This is what Russell does. Generally, as against Russell, I shall say this. Meaning (in at least one important sense) is a function of the sentence or expression; mentioning and referring and truth or falsity, are functions of the use of the sentence or expression. To give the meaning of an expression (in the sense in which I am using the word) is to give *general directions* for its use to refer to or mention particular objects or persons; to give the meaning of a sentence is to give *general directions* for its use in making true or false assertions. It is not to talk about any particular occasion of the use of the sentence or expression. The meaning of an expression cannot be identified with the object it is used, on a particular occasion, to refer to. The meaning of a sentence cannot be identified with the assertion it is used, on a particular occasion, to make. For to talk about the meaning of an expression or sentence is not to talk about its use on a particular occasion, but about the rules, habits, conventions governing its correct use, on all occasions, to refer or to assert.

So the question of whether a sentence or expression *is significant or not* has nothing whatever to do with the question of whether the sentence, *uttered on a particular occasion*, is, on that occasion, being used to make a true-or-false assertion or not, or of whether the expression is, on that occasion, being used to refer to, or mention, anything at all.

The source of Russell's mistake was that he thought that referring or mentioning, if it occurred at all, must be meaning. He did not distinguish (B1) from (B2); he confused expressions with their use in a particular context; and so confused meaning with mentioning, with referring. If I talk about my handkerchief, I can, perhaps, produce the object I am referring to out of my pocket. I cannot produce the meaning of the expression, "my handkerchief," out of my pocket. Because Russell confused meaning with mentioning, he thought that if there were any expressions having a uniquely referring use, which were what they seemed (i.e. logical subjects) and not something else in disguise, their meaning must *be* the particular object which they were used to refer to. Hence the troublesome mythology of the logically proper name. But if someone asks me the meaning of the expression "this"—once Russell's favorite candidate for this status—I do not hand him the object I have just used the expression to refer to, adding at the same time that the meaning of the word changes every time it is used. Nor do I hand him all the objects it ever has been, or might be, used to refer to. I explain and illustrate the conventions governing the use of the expression. This *is* giving the meaning of the expression. It is quite different from giving (in any sense of giving) the object to which it refers; for the expression itself does not refer to anything; though it can be used, on different occasion, to refer to innumerable things. Now as a matter of fact there is, in English, a sense of the word "mean" in which this word does approximate to "indicate, mention or refer to"; e.g. when somebody (unpleasantly) says, "I mean you"; or when I point and say, "That's the one I mean." But *the one I meant* is quite different from *the meaning of the expression* I used to talk of it. In this special sense of "mean," it is people who mean, not expressions. People use expressions to refer to particular things. But the meaning of an expression is not the set of things or the single thing it may correctly be used to refer to: the meaning is the set of rules, habits, conventions for its use in referring.

It is the same with sentences: even more obviously so. Everyone knows that the sentence, "The table is covered with books," is significant, and everyone knows what it means. But if I ask, "What object is that sentence about?" I am asking an absurd question—a question which cannot be asked about the sentence, but only about some use of the sentence: and in this case the sentence has not been used to talk about something, it has only been taken as an example. In knowing what it means, you are knowing how it could correctly be used to talk about things: so knowing the meaning has nothing to do with knowing about any particular use of the sentence to talk about anything. Similarly, if I ask: "Is the sentence true or false?" I am asking an absurd question, which becomes no less absurd if I add, "It must be one or the other since it is significant." The question is absurd, because the *sentence* is neither true nor false any more than it is *about* some object. Of course the fact that it is significant is the same as the fact that it *can* correctly be used to talk about something and that, in so using it, someone will be making a true or false assertion. And I will add that it will be used to make a true or false assertion *only* if the person using it *is* talking about something. If, when he utters it, he is not talking about anything, then his use is not a genuine one, but a spurious or pseudo-use: he is not making either a true or a false assertion, though he may think he is. And this points the way to the correct answer to the puzzle to which the theory of descriptions gives a fatally incorrect answer. The important point is that the question of whether the sentence is significant or not is quite independent of the question that can be raised about a particular use of it, viz. the question whether it is a genuine or a spurious use, whether it is being used to talk about something, or in make-believe, or as an example in philosophy. The question whether the sentence is significant or not is the question whether there exist such language habits, conventions or rules that the sentence logically could be used to talk about something; and is hence quite independent of the question whether it is being so used on a particular occasion.

III

Consider again the sentence, "The king of France is wise," and the true and false things Russell says about it.

There are at least two true things which Russell would say about the sentence:

(1) The first is that it is significant; that if anyone were now to utter it, he would be uttering a significant sentence.

(2) The second is that anyone now uttering the sentence would be making a true assertion only if there in fact at present existed one and only one king of France, and if he were wise.

What are the false things which Russell would say about the sentence? They are:

(1) That anyone now uttering it would be making a true assertion or a false assertion.

(2) That part of what he would be asserting would be that there at present existed one and only one king of France.

I have already given some reasons for thinking that these two statements are incorrect. Now suppose someone were in fact to say to you with a perfectly serious air: "The king of France is wise." Would you say, "That's untrue"? I think it is quite certain that you would not. But suppose he went on to *ask* you whether you thought that what he had just said was true, or was false; whether you agreed or disagreed with what he had just said. I think you would be inclined, with some hesitation, to say that you did not do either; that the question of whether his statement was true or false simply *did not arise*, because there was no such person as the king of France. You might, if he were obviously serious (had a dazed astray-in-the-centuries look), say something like: "I'm afraid you must be under a misapprehension. France is not a monarchy. There is no king of France." And this brings out the point that if a man seriously uttered the sentence, his uttering it would in some sense be *evidence* that he *believed* that there was a king of France. It would not be evidence for his believing this simply in the way in which a man's reaching for his raincoat is evidence for his believing that it is raining. But nor would it be evidence for his believing this in the way in which a man's saying, "It's raining," is evidence for his believing that it is raining. We might put it as follows. To say "The king of France is wise" is, in some sense of 'imply', to *imply* that there is a king of France. But this is a very special and odd sense of 'imply'. 'Implies' in this sense is certainly not equivalent to 'entails' (or 'logically implies'). And this comes out from the fact that when, in response to his statement, we say (as we should) "There is no king of France," we should certainly *not* say we were *contradicting* the statement that the king of France is wise. We are certainly not saying that it is false. We are, rather, giving a reason for saying that the question of whether it is true or false simply does not arise.

And this is where the distinction I drew earlier can help us. The sentence, "The king of France is wise," is certainly significant; but this does not mean that any particular use of it is true or false. We use it truly or falsely when we use it to talk about someone; when, in using the expression, "The king of France," we are in fact mentioning someone. The fact that the sentence and the expression, respectively, are significant just is the fact that the sentence *could* be used, in certain circumstances, to say something true or false, that the expression *could* be used, in certain circumstances, to mention a particular person: and to know their meaning is to know what sort of circumstances these are. So when we utter the sentence without in fact mentioning anybody by the use of the phrase, "The king of France," the sentence does not cease to be significant: We simply *fail* to say anything true or false because we simply fail to mention anybody by this particular use of that perfectly significant phrase. It is, if you like, a spurious use of the sentence, and a spurious use of the expression; though we may (or may not) mistakenly think it a genuine use.

And such spurious uses[2] are very familiar. Sophisticated romancing, sophisticated fiction,[3] depend upon them. If I began, "The king of France is wise," and went on, "and he lives in a golden castle and has a hundred wives", and so on, a hearer would understand me perfectly well, without supposing *either* that I was talking about a particular person, *or* that I was making a false statement to the effect that there existed such a person as my words described. (It is worth adding that where the use of sentences and expressions is overtly fictional, the sense of the word "about" may change. As Moore said, it is perfectly natural and correct to say that some of the statements in *Pickwick Papers* are *about* Mr. Pickwick. But where the use of sentences and expressions is not overtly fictional, this use of "about" seems less correct; i.e. it would not *in general* be correct to say that a statement was about Mr. X or the so-and-so, unless there were such a person or thing. So it is where the romancing is in danger of being taken seriously that we might answer the question, "Who is he talking about?" with "He's not talking about anybody"; but, in saying this, we are not saying that what he is saying is either false or nonsense.)

Overtly fictional uses apart, however, I said just now that to use such an expression as "The king of France" at the beginning of a sentence was, in some sense of 'imply', to imply that there was a king of France. When a man uses such an expression, he does not *assert*, nor does what he says *entail*, a uniquely existential proposition. But one of the conventional functions of the definite article is to act as a *signal* that a unique reference is being made—a signal, not a disguised assertion. When we begin a sentence with "the such-and-such" the use of "the" shows, but does not state, that we are, or intended to be, referring to one particular individual of the species "such-and-such." *Which* particular individual is a matter to be determined from context, time, place, and any other features of the situation of utterance. Now, whenever a man uses any expression, the presumption is that he thinks he is using it correctly: so when he uses the expression, "the such-and-such," in a uniquely referring way, the presumption is that he thinks both that there is *some* individual of that species, and that the context of use will sufficiently determine which one he has in mind. To use the word "the" in this way is then to imply (in the relevant sense of 'imply') that the existential conditions described by Russell are fulfilled. But to use "the" in this way is not to *state* that those conditions are fulfilled. If I begin a sentence with an expression of the form, "the so-and-so," and then am prevented from saying more, I have made no statement of any kind; but I may have succeeded in mentioning someone or something.

The uniquely existential assertion supposed by Russell to be part of any assertion in which a uniquely referring use is made of an expression of the form "the so-and-so" is, he observes, a compound of two assertions. To say that there is a ϕ is to say something compatible with there being several ϕs; to say there is not more than one ϕ is to say something compatible with there being none. To say there is one φ and one only is to compound these two assertions. I have so far been concerned mostly with the alleged assertion of existence and less with the alleged assertion of uniqueness. An example which throws the emphasis on the latter will serve to bring out more clearly the sense of 'implied' in which a uniquely existential assertion is implied, but not entailed, by the use of expressions in the uniquely referring way. Consider the sentence, "The table is covered with books." It is quite certain that in any normal use of this sentence, the expression "the table" would be used to make a unique reference, i.e. to refer to some one table. It is a quite strict use of the definite article, in the sense in which Russell talks on p. 30 of *Principia Mathematica,* of using the article "*strictly,* so as to imply uniqueness." On the same page Russell says that a phrase of the form "the so-and-so," used strictly, "will only have an application in the event of there being one so-and-so and no more." Now it is obviously quite false that the phrase "the table" in the sentence "the table is covered with books," used normally, will "only have an application in the event of there being one table and no more." It is indeed tautologically true that, in such a use, the phrase will have an application only in the event of there being one table and no more *which is being referred to*, and that it will be understood to have an application only in the event of there being one table and no more which it is understood as being used to refer to. To use the sentence is not to assert, but it is (in the special sense discussed) to imply, that there is only one thing which is *both* of the kind specified (i.e. a table) *and is being referred to* by the speaker. It is obviously not to assert this. To refer is not to say you are referring. To say there is *some table or other* to which you are referring is not the same as referring to a particular table. We should have no use for such phrases as "the individual I referred to" unless there were something which counted as referring. (It would make no sense to say you had pointed if there were nothing which counted as pointing.) So once more I draw the conclusion that referring to or mentioning a particular thing cannot be dissolved into any kind of assertion. To refer is not to assert, though you refer in order to go on to assert.

Let me now take an example of the uniquely referring use of an expression not of the form, "the so-and-so." Suppose I advance my hands, cautiously cupped, towards someone, saying, as I do so, "This is a fine red one." He, looking into my hands and seeing nothing there, may say: "What is? What are you talking about?" Or perhaps, "But there's nothing in your hands." Of course it would be absurd to say that, in saying "But you've got nothing in your hands," he was *denying* or *contradicting* what I said. So "this" is not a disguised description in Russell's sense. Nor is it a logically proper name. For one must know what the sentence means in order to react in that way to the utterance of it. It is precisely because the significance of the word "this" is independent of any particular reference it may be used to make, though not independent of the way it may be used to refer, that I can, as in this example, use it to *pretend* to be referring to something.

The general moral of all this is that communication is much less a matter of explicit or disguised assertion than logicians used to suppose. The particular application of this general moral in which I am interested is its application to the case of making a unique reference. It is a part of the significance of expressions of the kind I am discussing that they can be used, in an immense variety of contexts, to make unique references. It is no part of their significance to assert that they are being used or that the conditions of their being so used are fulfilled. So the wholly important distinction we are required to draw is between

(1) using an expression to make a unique reference; and

(2) asserting that there is one and only one individual which has certain characteristics (e.g. is of a certain kind, or stands in a certain relation to the speaker, or both).

This is, in other words, the distinction between

(1) sentences containing an expression used to indicate or mention or refer to a particular person or thing; and

(2) uniquely existential sentences.

What Russell does is progressively to assimilate more and more sentences of class (1) to sentences of class (2), and consequently to involve himself in insuperable difficulties about logical subjects, and about values for individual variables generally: difficulties which have led him finally to the logically disastrous theory of names developed in the *Enquiry into Meaning and Truth* and in *Human Knowledge*. That view of the meaning of logical-subject-expressions which provides the whole incentive to the Theory of Descriptions at the same time precludes the possibility of Russell's ever finding any satisfactory substitutes for those expressions which, beginning with substantival phrases, he progressively degrades from the status of logical subjects.[4] It is not simply, as is sometimes said, the fascination of the relation between a name and its bearer, that is the root of the trouble. Not even names come up to the impossible standard set. It is rather the combination of two more radical misconceptions: first, the failure to grasp the importance of the distinction (section II above) between what may be said of an expression and what may be said of a particular use of it; second, a failure to recognize the uniquely referring use of expressions for the harmless, necessary thing it is, distinct from, but complementary to, the predicative or ascriptive use of expressions. The expressions which can in fact occur as singular logical subjects are expressions of the class I listed at the outset (demonstratives, substantival phrases, proper names, pronouns): to say this is to say that these expressions, together with context (in the widest sense), are what one uses to make unique references. The point of the conventions governing the uses of such expressions is, along with the situation of utterance, to secure uniqueness of reference. But to do this, enough is enough. We do not, and we cannot, while referring, attain the point of complete explicitness at which the referring function is no longer performed. The actual unique reference made, if any, is a matter of the particular use in the particular context; the significance of the expression used is the set of rules or conventions which permit such references to be made. Hence we can, using significant expressions, pretend to refer, in make-believe or in fiction, or mistakenly think we are referring when we are not referring to anything.[5]

This shows the need for distinguishing two kinds (among many others) of linguistic conventions or rules: rules for referring, and rules for attributing and ascribing; and for an investigation of the former. If we recognize this distinction of use for what it is, we are on the way to solving a number of ancient logical and metaphysical puzzles.

My last two sections are concerned, but only in the barest outline, with these questions.

IV

One of the main purposes for which we use language is the purpose of stating facts about things and persons and events. If we want to fulfill this purpose we must have some way of forestalling the question, "What (who, which one) are you talking about?" as well as the question, "What are you saying about it (him, her)?" The task of forestalling the first question is the referring (or identifying) task. The task of forestalling the second is the attributive (or descriptive or classificatory or ascriptive) task. In the conventional English sentence which is used to state, or to claim to state, a fact about an individual thing or person or event, the performance of these two tasks can be roughly and approximately assigned to separable expressions.[6] And in such a sentence, this assigning of expressions to thier separate rôles corresponds to the conventional grammatical classification of subject and predicate. There is nothing sacrosanct about the employment of separable expressions for these two tasks. Other methods could be, and are, employed. There is, for instance, the method of uttering a single word or attributive phrase in the conspicuous presence of the object referred to; or that analogous method exemplified by, e.g., the painting of the words "unsafe for lorries" on a bridge, or the tying of a label reading "first prize" on a vegetable marrow. Or one can imagine an elaborate game in which one never used an expression in the uniquely referring way at all, but uttered only uniquely existential sentences, trying to enable the hearer to identify what was being talked of by means of an accumulation of relative clauses. (This description of the purposes of the game shows in what sense it would be a game: this is not the normal use we make of existential sentences.) Two points require emphasis. The first is that the necessity of performing these two tasks in order to state particular facts requires no transcendental explanation: To call attention to it is partly to elucidate the meaning of the phrase, "stating a fact." The second is that even this elucidation is made in terms derivative from the grammar of the conventional singular sentence; that even the overtly functional, linguistic distinction between the identifying and attributive rôles that words may play in language is prompted by the fact that ordinary speech offers us separable expressions to which the different functions may be plausibly and approximately assigned. And this functional distinction has cast long philosophical shadows. The distinctions between particular and universal, between substance and quality, are such pseudo-material shadows, cast by the grammar of the conventional sentence, in which separable expressions play distinguishable roles.[7]

To use a separate expression to perform the first of these tasks is to use an expression in the uniquely referring way. I want now to say something in general about the conventions of use for expressions used in this way, and to contrast them with conventions of ascriptive use. I then proceed to the brief illustration of these general remarks and to some further applications of them.

What in general is required for making a unique reference is, obviously, some device, or devices, for showing both *that* a unique reference is intended and *what* unique reference it is; some device requiring and enabling the hearer or reader to identify what is being talked about. In securing this result, the context of utterance is of an importance which it is almost impossible to exaggerate; and by "context" I mean, at least, the time, the place, the situation, the identity of the speaker, the subjects which form the immediate focus of interest, and the personal histories of both the speaker and those he is addressing. Besides context, there is, of course, convention—linguistic convention. But, except in the case of genuine proper names, of which I shall have more to say later, the fulfillment of more or less precisely stateable contextual conditions is *conventionally* (or, in a wide sense of the word, *logically*) required for the correct referring use of expressions in a sense in which this is not true of correct ascriptive uses. The requirement for the correct application of an expression in its ascriptive use to a certain thing is simply that the thing should be of a certain kind, have certain characteristics. The requirement for the correct application of an expression in its referring use to a certain thing is something over and above any requirement derived from such ascriptive meaning as the expression may have; it is, namely, the requirement that the thing should be in a certain relation to the speaker and to the context of utterance. Let me call this the contextual requirement. Thus, for example, in the limiting case of the word "I" the contextual requirement is that the thing should be identical with the speaker; but in the case of most expressions which have a referring use this requirement cannot be so precisely specified. A further, and perfectly general, difference between conventions for referring and conventions for describing is one we have already encountered, viz. that the fulfillment of the conditions for a correct ascriptive use of an expression is a part of what is stated by such a use; but the fulfillment of the conditions for a correct referring use of an expression is never part of what is stated, though it is (in the relevant sense of 'implied') implied by such a use.

Conventions for referring have been neglected or misinterpreted by logicians. The reasons for this neglect are not hard to see, though they are hard to state briefly. Two of them are, roughly: (1) the preoccupation of most logicians with definitions; (2) the preoccupation of some logicians with formal systems.

(1) A definition, in the most familiar sense, is a specification of the conditions of the correct ascriptive or classificatory use of an expression. Definitions take no account of contextual requirements. So that in so far as the search for the meaning or the search for the analysis of an expression is conceived as the search for a definition, the neglect or misinterpretation of conventions other than ascriptive is inevitable. Perhaps it would be better to say (for I do not wish to legislate about "meaning" or "analysis") that logicians have failed to notice that problems of use are wider than problems of analysis and meaning.

(2) The influence of the preoccupation with mathematics and formal logic is most clearly seen (to take no more recent examples) in the cases of Leibniz and Russell. The constructor of calculuses, not concerned or required to make factual statements, approaches applied logic with a prejudice. It is natural that he should assume that the types of convention with whose adequacy in one field he is familiar should be really adequate, if only one could see how, in a quite different field—that of statements of fact. Thus we have Leibniz striving desperately to make the uniqueness of unique references a matter of logic in the narrow sense, and Russell striving desperately to do the same thing, in a different way, both for the implication of uniqueness and for that of existence.

It should be clear that the distinction I am trying to draw is primarily one between different roles or parts that expressions may play in language, and not primarily one between different groups of expressions; for some expressions may appear in either role. Some of the kinds of words I shall speak of have predominantly, if not exclusively, a referring role. This is most obviously true of pronouns and ordinary proper names. Some can occur as wholes or parts of expressions which have a predominantly referring use, and as wholes or parts of expressions which have a predominantly ascriptive or classificatory use. The obvious cases are common nouns; or common nouns preceded by adjectives, including participial adjectives; or, less obviously, adjectives or participial adjectives alone. Expressions capable of having a referring use also differ from one another in at least the three following, not mutually independent, ways.

(1) They differ in the extent to which the reference they are used to make is dependent on the context of their utterance. Words like "I" and "it" stand at one end of this scale—the end of maximum dependence—and phrases like "the author of *Waverley*" and "the eighteenth king of France" at the other.

(2) They differ in the degree of 'descriptive meaning' they possess: by 'descriptive meaning' I intend 'conventional limitation, in application, to things of a certain general kind, or possessing certain general characteristics'. At one end of this scale stand the proper names we most commonly use in ordinary discourse; men, dogs, and motor-bicycles may be called "Horace." The pure name has no descriptive meaning (except such as it may acquire *as a result of* some one of its use as a name). A word like "he" has minimal descriptive meaning, but has some. Substantival phrases like "the round table" have the maximum descriptive meaning. An interesting intermediate position is occupied by 'impure' proper names like "The Round Table"—substantival phrases which have grown capital letters.

(3) Finally, they may be divided into the following two classes: (i) those of which the correct referring use is regulated by some *general* referring-cum-ascriptive conventions; (ii) those of which the correct referring use is regulated by no general conventions, either of the contextual or the ascriptive kind, but by conventions which are ad hoc for each particular use (though not for each particular utterance). To the first class belong both pronouns (which have the least descriptive meaning) and substantival phrases (which have the most). To the second class belong, roughly speaking, the most familiar kind of proper names. Ignorance of a man's name is not ignorance of the language. This is why we do not speak of the meaning of proper names. (But it won't do to say they are meaningless.) Again an intermediate position is occupied by such phrases as "The Old Pretender." Only an old pretender may be so referred to; but to know which old pretender is not to know a general, but an ad hoc, convention.

In the case of phrases of the form "the so-and-so" used referringly, the use of "the" together with the position of the phrase in the sentence (i.e. at the beginning, or following a transitive verb or preposition) acts as a signal *that* a unique reference is being made; and the following noun, or noun and adjective, together with the context of utterance, shows *what* unique reference is being made. In general the functional difference between common nouns and adjective is that the former are naturally and commonly used referringly, while the latter are not commonly, or so naturally, used in this way, except as qualifying nouns; though they can be, and are, so used alone. And of course this functional difference is not independent of the descriptive force peculiar to each word. In general we should expect the descriptive force of nouns to be such that they are more efficient tools for the job of showing what unique reference is intended when such a reference is signalized; and we should also expect the descriptive force of the words we naturally and commonly use to make unique references to mirror our interest in the salient, relatively permanent and behavioral characteristics of things. These two expectations are not independent of one another; and, if we look at the differences between the commoner sort of common nouns and the commoner sort of adjectives, we find them both fulfilled. These are differences of the kind that Locke quaintly reports, when he speaks of our ideas of substances being *collections* of simple ideas; when he says that "powers make up a great part of our ideas of substances"; and when he goes on to contrast the identity of real and nominal essence in the case of simple ideas with their lack of identity and the shiftingness of the nominal essence in the case of substances. 'Substance' itself is the troublesome tribute Locke pays to his dim awareness of the difference in predominant linguistic function that lingered even when the noun had been expanded into a more or less indefinite string of adjectives. Russell repeats Locke's mistake with a difference when, admitting the inference from syntax to reality to the extent of feeling that he can get rid of this metaphysical unknown only if he can purify language of the referring function altogether, he draws up his program for "abolishing particulars"; a programme, in fact, for abolishing the distinction of logical use which I am here at pains to emphasize.

The contextual requirement for the referring use of pronouns may be stated with the greatest precision in some cases (e.g. "I" and "you") and only with the greatest vagueness in others ("it" and "this"). I propose to say nothing further about pronouns, except to point to an additional symptom of the failure to recognize the uniquely referring use for what it is; the fact, namely, that certain logicians have actually sought to elucidate the nature of a variable by offering such *sentences* as "he is sick," "it is green," as examples of something in ordinary speech like a *sentential function*. Now of course it is true that the word "he" may be used on different occasions to refer to different people or different animals: so may the word "John" and the phrase "the cat." What deters such logicians from treating these two expressions as quasi-variables is, in the first case, the lingering superstition that a name is logically tied to a single individual, and, in the second case, the descriptive meaning of the word "cat." But "he," which has a wide range of applications and minimal descriptive force, only acquires a use as a referring word. It is this fact, together with the failure to accord to expressions, used referringly, the place in logic which belongs to them (the place held open for the mythical logically proper name), that accounts for the misleading attempt to elucidate the nature of the variable by reference to such words as "he," "she," "it."

Of ordinary proper names it is sometimes said that they are essentially words each of which is used to refer to just one individual. This is obviously false. Many ordinary personal names—names *par excellence*—are correctly used to refer to numbers of people. An ordinary personal name is, roughly, a word, used referringly, of which the use is *not* dictated by any descriptive meaning the word may have, and is *not* prescribed by any such general rule for use as a referring expression (or a part of a referring expression) as we find in the case of such words as "I," "this" and "the," but is governed by ad hoc conventions for each particular set of applications of the word to a given person. The important point is that the correctness of such applications does not follow from any *general* rule or convention for the use of the word as such. (The limit of absurdity and obvious circularity is reached in the attempt to treat names as disguised description in Russell's sense; for what is in the special sense implied, but not entailed, by my now referring to someone by name is simply the existence of someone, *now being referred to*, who is *conventionally referred to* by that name) Even this feature of names, however, is only a sympton of the purpose for which they are employed. At present our choice of names is partly arbitrary, partly dependent on legal and social observances. It would be perfectly possible to have a thorough-going *system* of names, based e.g. on dates of birth, or on a minute classification of physiological and anatomical differences. But the success of any such system would depend entirely on the convenience of the resulting name-allotments for the purpose of making unique references; and this would depend on the multiplicity of the classifications used and the degree to which they cut haphazardly across normal social groupings. Given a sufficient degree of both, the selectivity supplied by context would do the rest; just as in the case with our present naming habits. Had we such a system, we could use name-words descriptively (as we do at present, to a limited extent and in a different way, with some famous names) as well as referringly. But it is by criteria derived from consideration of the requirements of the referring task that we should assess the adequacy of any system of naming. From the naming point of view, no kind of classification would be better or worse than any other simply because of the kind of classification—natal or anatomical—that it was.

I have already mentioned the class of quasi-names, of substantival phrases which grow capital letters, and of which such phrases as "the Glorious Revolution," "the Great War," "the Annunciation," "the Round Table" are examples. While the descriptive meaning of the words which follow the definite article is still relevant to their referring role, the capital letters are a sign of that extralogical selectivity in their referring use, which is characteristic of pure names. Such phrases are found in print or in writing when one member of some class of events or things is of quite outstanding interest in a certain society. These phrases are embryonic names. A phrase may, for obvious reasons, pass into, and out of, this class (e.g. "the Great War").

V

I want to conclude by considering, all too briefly, three further problems about referring uses.

(a) *Indefinite references:* Not all referring uses of singular expressions forestall the question "What (who, which one) are you talking about?" There are some which either invite this question, or disclaim the intention or ability to answer it. Examples are such sentence-beginnings as "A man told me that . . . ," "Someone told me that . . ." The orthodox (Russellian) doctrine is that such sentences are existential, but not uniquely existential. This seems wrong in several ways. It is ludicrous to suggest that part of what is asserted is that the class of men or persons is not empty. Certainly this is *implied* in the by now familiar sense of implication; but the implication is also as much an implication of the *uniqueness* of the particular object of reference as when I begin a sentence with such a phrase as "the table." The difference between the use of the definite and indefinite articles is, very roughly, as follows. We use "the" either when a previous reference has been made, and when "the" signalizes that the same reference is being made; or when, in the absence of a previous indefinite reference, the context (including the hearer's assumed knowledge) is expected to enable the hearer to tell *what* reference is being made. We use "a" either when these conditions are not fulfilled, or when, although a definite reference *could* be made, we wish to keep dark the identity of the individual to whom, or to which, we are referring. This is the *arch* use of such a phrase as "a certain person" or "someone"; where it could be expanded, not into "someone, but you wouldn't (or I don't) know who" but into "someone, but I'm not telling you who."

(b) *Identification statements:* By this label I intend statements like the following:

(i*a*) That is the man who swam the channel twice on one day.

(ii*a*) Napoleon was the man who ordered the execution of the Duc d'Enghien.

The puzzle about these statements is that their grammatical predicates do not seem to be used in a straightforwardly ascriptive way as are the grammatical predicates of the statements:

(i*b*) That man swam the channel twice in one day.

(ii*b*) Napoleon ordered the execution of the Duc d'Enghien.

But if, in order to avoid blurring the difference between (i*a*) and (i*b*) and (ii*a*) and (ii*b*), one says that the phrases which form the grammatical complements of (i*a*) and (ii*a*) are being used referringly, one becomes puzzled about what is being said in these sentences. We seem then to be referring to the same person twice over and either saying nothing about him and thus making no statement, or identifying him with himself and thus producing a trivial identity.

The bogy of triviality can be dismissed. This only arises for those who think of the object referred to by the use of an expression as its meaning, and thus think of the subect and complement of these sentences as meaning the same because they could be used to refer to the same person.

I think the differences between sentences in the (*a*) group and sentences in the (*b*) group can best be understood by considering the differences between the circumstances in which you would say (i*a*) and the circumstances in which you would say (i*b*). You would say (i*a*) instead of (i*b*) if you knew or believed that your hearer knew or believed that *someone* had swum the channel twice in one day. You say (i*a*) when you take your hearer to be in the position of one who can ask: "Who swam the channel twice in one day?" (And in asking this, he is not saying that anyone did, though his asking it implies—in the relevant sense—that someone did.) Such sentences are like answers to such questions. They are better called 'identification-statements' than 'identities'. Sentence (i*a*) does not assert more or less than sentence (i*b*). It is just that you say (i*a*) to a man whom you take to know certain things that you take to be unknown to the man to whom you say (i*b*).

This is, in the barest essentials, the solution to Russell's puzzle about 'denoting phrases' joined by "is"; one of the puzzles which he claims for the theory of descriptions the merit of solving.

(3) *The logic of subjects and predicates:* Much of what I have said of the uniquely referring use of expressions can be extended, with suitable modifications, to the non-uniquely referring use of expressions; i.e. to some uses of expressions consisting of "the," "all the," "all," "some," "some of the," etc. followed by a noun, qualified or unqualified, in the *plural*; to some uses of "they," "them," "those," "these"; and to conjunctions of names. Expressions of the first kind have a special interest. Roughly speaking, orthodox modern criticism, inspired by mathematical logic, of such traditional doctrines as that of the Square of Opposition and of some of the forms of the syllogism traditionally recognized as valid, rests on the familiar failure to recognize the special sense in which existential assertions may be implied by the referring use of expressions. The universal propositions of the fourfold schedule, it is said, must *either* be given a negatively existential interpretation (e.g. for A, "there are no Xs which are not Ys") *or* they must be interpreted as conjunctions of negatively and positively existential statements of, e.g., the form (for A) "there are no Xs which are not Ys, and there are Xs." The I and O forms are normally given a positively existential interpretation. It is then seen that, whichever of the above alternatives is selected, some of the traditional laws have to be abandoned. The dilemma, however, is a bogus one. If we interpret the propositions of the schedule as neither positively, nor negatively, nor positively *and* negatively, existential, but as sentences such that *the ques-*

tion of whether they are being used to make true or false assertions does not arise except when the existential condition is fulfilled for the subject term, then all the traditional laws hold good together. And this interpretation is far closer to the most common uses of expressions beginning with "all" and "some" than is any Russellian alternative. For these expressions are most commonly used in the referring way. A literal-minded and childless man asked whether all his children are asleep will certainly not answer "Yes" on the ground that he has none; but nor will he answer "No" on this ground. Since he has no children, the question does not arise. To say this is not to say that I may not use the sentence, "All my children are asleep," with the intention of letting someone know that I have children, or of deceiving him into thinking that I have. Nor is it any weakening of my thesis to concede that singular phrases of the form "the so-and-so" may sometimes be used with a similar purpose. Neither Aristotelian nor Russellian rules give the exact logic of any expression of ordinary language; for ordinary language has no exact logic.

NOTES

1. This usage of "use" is, of course, different from (a) the current usage in which 'use' (of a particular word, phrase, sentence) = (roughly) 'rules for using' = (roughly) 'meaning'; and from (*b*) my own usage in the phrase "uniquely referring use of expressions" in which "use" = (roughly) 'way of using'.

2. The choice of the word "spurious" now seems to me unfortunate, at least for some nonstandard uses. I should now prefer to call some of these "secondary" uses.

3. The unsophisticated kind begins: "Once upon time there was . . . ."

4. And this in spite of the danger-signal of that phrase, "*misleading* grammatical form."

5. This sentence now seems to me objectionable in a number of ways, notably because of an unexplicitly restrictive use of the word 'refer'. It could be more exactly phrased as follows: 'Hence we can, using significant expressions, refer in secondary ways, as in make-believe or in fiction, or mistakenly think we are referring to something in the primary way when we are not, in that way, referring to anything'.

6. I neglect relational sentences; for these require, not a modification in the principle of what I say, but a complication of the detail.

7. What is said or implied in the last two sentences of this paragraph no longer seems to me true, unless considerably qualified.

BERTRAND RUSSELL

MR. STRAWSON ON REFERRING

Mr. P. F. Strawson published in *Mind* of 1950 an article called 'On Referring'. This article is reprinted in *Essays in Conceptual Analysis,* selected and edited by Professor Antony Flew. The references that follow are to this reprint. The main purpose of the article is to refute my theory of descriptions. As I find that some philosophers whom I respect consider that it has achieved its purpose successfully, I have come to the conclusion that a polemical reply is called for. I may say, to begin with, that I am totally unable to see any validity whatever in any of Mr. Strawson's arguments. Whether this inability is due to senility on my part or to some other cause, I must leave readers to judge.

The gist of Mr. Strawson's argument consists in identifying two problems which I have regarded as quite distinct—namely, the problem of descriptions and the problem of egocentricity. I have dealt with both these problems at considerable length, but as I have considered them to be different problems, I have not dealt with the one when I was considering the other. This enables Mr. Strawson to pretend that I have overlooked the problem of egocentricity.

He is helped in this pretence by a careful selection of material. In the article in which I first set forth the theory of descriptions, I dealt specially with two examples: 'The present King of France is bald' and 'Scott is the author of *Waverly*'. The latter example does not suit Mr. Strawson, and he therefore entirely ignores it except for one quite perfunctory reference. As regards 'the present King of France', he fastens upon the egocentric word 'present' and does not seem able to grasp that, if for the word 'present' I had substituted the words 'in 1905', the whole of his argument would have collapsed.

Or perhaps not quite the whole, for reasons which I had set forth before Mr. Strawson wrote. It is, however, not difficult to give other examples of the use of descriptive phrases from which egocentricity is wholly absent. I should like to see him apply his doctrine to such sentences as the following: 'the square-root of minus one is half the square-root of minus four', or 'the cube of three is the integer immediately preceding the second perfect number'. There are no egocentric words in either of these two sentences, but the problem of interpreting the descriptive phrases is exactly the same as if there were.

There is not a word in Mr. Strawson's article to suggest that I ever considered egocentric words, still less that the theory which he advocates in regard to them is the very one which I had set forth at great length and in considerable detail.[1] The gist of what he has to say about such words is the entirely correct statement that what they refer to depends upon when and where they are used. As to this, I need only quote one paragraph from *Human Knowledge* (page 107):

'This' denotes whatever, at the moment when the word is used, occupies the centre of attention. With words which are not egocentric, what is constant is something about the object indicated, but 'this' denotes a different object on each occasion of its use: what is constant is not the object denoted, but its relation to the particular use of the word. Whenever the word is used, the person using it is attending to something, and the word indicates this something. When a word is not egocentric, there is no need to distinguish between different occasions when it is used, but we must make this distinction with egocentric words, since what they indicate is something having a given relation to the particular use of the word.

I must refer, also, to the case that I discuss (page 101 ff.) in which I am walking with a friend on a dark night. We lose touch with each other and he calls 'Where are you?' and I reply 'Here I am!' It is of the essence of a scientific account of the world to reduce to a minimum the egocentric element in an assertion, but success in this attempt is a matter of degree, and is never complete where empirical material is concerned. This is due to the fact that the meanings of all empirical words depend ultimately upon ostensive definitions, that ostensive definitions depend upon experience, and that experience is egocentric. We can, however, by means of egocentric words, *describe* something which is not egocentric; it is this that enables us to use a common language.

All this may be right or wrong, but, whichever it is, Mr. Strawson should not expound it as if it were a theory that he had invented, whereas, in fact, I had set it forth before he wrote, though perhaps he did not grasp the purport of what I said. I shall say no more about egocentricity since, for the reasons I have already given, I think Mr. Strawson completely mistaken in connecting it with the problem of descriptions.

I am at a loss to understand Mr. Strawson's position on the subject of names. When he is writing about me, he says: 'There are no logically proper names and there are no descriptions (in this sense)' (page 26). But when he is writing about Quine, in *Mind,* October 1956, he takes a quite different line. Quine has a theory that names are unnecessary and can always be replaced by descriptions. This theory shocks Mr. Strawson for reasons which, to me, remain obscure. However, I will leave the defence of Quine to Quine, who is quite capable of looking after himself. What is important for my purpose is to elucidate the meaning of the words 'in this sense' which Mr. Strawson puts in brackets. So far as I can discover from the context, what he objects to is the belief that there are words which are only significant because there is something that they mean, and if there were not this something, they would be emtpy noises, not words. For my part, I think that there must be such words if language is to have any relation to fact. The necessity for such words is made obvious by the process of ostensive definition. How do we know what is meant by such words as 'red' and 'blue'? We cannot know what these words mean unless we have seen red and seen blue. If there were no red and no blue in our experience, we might, perhaps, invent some elaborate description which we could substitute for the word 'red' or for the word 'blue'. For example, if you were dealing with a blind man, you could hold a red-hot poker near enough for him to feel the heat, and you could tell him that red is what he would see if he could see—but of course for the word 'see' you would have to substitute another elaborate description. Any description which the blind man could understand would have to be in terms of words expressing experiences which he had had. Unless fundamental words in the individual's vocabulary had this kind of direct relation to fact, language in general would have no such relation. I defy Mr. Strawson to give the usual meaning to the word 'red' unless there is something which the word designates.

This brings me to a further point. 'Red' is usually regarded as a predicate and as designating a universal. I prefer for purposes of philosophical analysis a language in which 'red' is a subject, and, while I should not say that it is a positive error to call it a universal, I should say that calling it so invites confusion. This is connected with what Mr. Strawson calls my 'logically disastrous theory of names' (page 39). He does not deign to mention why he considers this theory 'logically disastrous'. I hope that on some future occasion he will enlighten me on this point.

This brings me to a fundamental divergence between myself and many philosophers with whom Mr. Strawson appears to be in general agreement. They are persuaded that common speech is good enough, not only for daily life, but also for philosophy. I, on the contrary, am persuaded that common speech is full of vagueness and inaccuracy, and that any attempt to be precise and accurate requires modification of common speech both as regards vocabulary and as regards syntax. Everybody admits that physics and chemistry and medicine each require a language which is not that of everyday life. I fail to see why philosophy, alone, should be forbidden to make a similar approach towards precision and accuracy. Let us take, in illustration, one of the commonest words of everyday speech: namely, the word 'day'. The most august use of this word is in the first chapter of Genesis and in the Ten Commandments. The desire to keep holy the Sabbath 'day' has led orthodox Jews to give a precision to the word 'day' which it does not have in common speech: they have defined it as the period from one sunset to the next. Astronomers, with other reasons for seeking precision, have three sorts of day: the true solar day; the mean solar day; and the sidereal day. These have different uses: the true solar day is relevant if you are considering lighting-up time; the mean solar day is relevant if you are sentenced to fourteen days without the option; and the sidereal day is relevant if you are trying to estimate the influence of the tides in retarding the earth's rotation. All these four kinds of day—decalogical, true, mean, and sidereal—are more precise than the common use of the word 'day'. If astronomers were subject to the prohibition of precision which some recent philosophers apparently favour, the whole science of astronomy would be impossible.

For technical purposes, technical languages differing from those of daily life are indispensable. I feel that those who object to linguistic novelties, if they had lived a hundred and fifty years ago, would have stuck to feet and ounces, and would have maintained that centimetres and grammes savour of the guillotine.

In philosophy, it is syntax, even more than vocabulary, that needs to be corrected. The subject-predicate logic to which we are accustomed depends for its convenience upon the fact that at the usual temperatures of the earth there are approximately permanent 'things'. This would not be true at the temperature of the sun, and is only roughly true at the temperatures to which we are accustomed.

My theory of descriptions was never intended as an analysis of the state of mind of those who utter sentences containing descriptions. Mr. Strawson gives the name 'S' to the sentence 'The King of France is wise', and he says of me 'The way in which he arrived at the analysis was clearly by asking himself what would be the circumstances in which we would say that anyone who uttered the sentence S had made a true assertion'. This does not seem to me a correct account of what I was doing. Suppose (which God forbid) Mr. Strawson were so rash as to accuse his charlady of thieving: she would reply indignantly, 'I ain't never done no harm to no one'. Assuming her a pattern of virtue, I should say that she was making a true assertion, although, according to the rules of syntax which Mr. Strawson would adopt in his own speech, what she said should have meant: 'there was at least one moment when I was injuring the whole human race'. Mr. Strawson would not have supposed that this was what she meant to assert, although he would not have used her words to express the same sentiment. Similarly, I was concerned to find a more accurate and analysed thought to replace the somewhat confused thoughts which most people at most times have in their heads.

Mr. Strawson objects to my saying that 'the King of France is wise' is false if there is no King of France. He admits that the sentence is significant and not true, but not that it is false. This is a mere question of verbal convenience. He considers that the word 'false' has an unalterable meaning which it would be sinful to regard as adjustable, though he prudently avoids telling us what this meaning is. For my part, I find it more convenient to define the word 'false' so that every significant sentence is either true or false. This is a purely verbal question; and although I have no wish to claim the support of common usage, I do not think that he can claim it either. Suppose, for example, that in some country there was a law that no person could hold public office if he considered it false that the Ruler of the Universe is wise. I think an avowed atheist who took advantage of Mr. Strawson's doctrine to say that he did not hold this proposition false, would be regarded as a somewhat shifty character.

It is not only as to names and as to falsehood that Mr. Strawson shows his conviction that there is an unalterably right way of using words and that no change is to be tolerated however convenient it may be. He shows the same feeling as regards universal affirmatives—i.e. sentences of the form 'All A is B'. Traditionally, such sentences are supposed to imply that there are As, but it is much more convenient in mathematical logic to drop this implication and to consider that 'All A is B' is true if there are no As. This is wholly and solely a question of convenience. For some purposes the one convention is more convenient, and for others, the other. We shall prefer the one convention or the other according to the purpose we have in view. I agree, however, with Mr. Strawson's statement (page 52) that ordinary language has no exact logic.

Mr. Strawson, in spite of his very real logical competence, has a curious prejudice against logic. On page 43, he has a sudden dithyrambic outburst, to the effect that life is greater than logic, which he uses to give a quite false interpretation of my doctrines.

Leaving detail aside, I think we may sum up Mr. Strawson's argument and my reply to it as follows:

There are two problems, that of descriptions and that of egocentricity. Mr. Strawson thinks they are one and the same problem, but it is obvious from his discussion that he has not considered as many kinds of descriptive phrases as are relevant to the argument. Having confused the two problems, he asserts dogmatically that it is only the egocentric problem that needs to be solved, and he offers a solution of this problem which he seems to believe to be new, but which in fact was familiar before he wrote. He then thinks that he has offered an adequate theory of descriptions, and announces his supposed achievement with astonishing dogmatic certainty. Perhaps I am doing him an injustice, but I am unable to see in what respect this is the case.

NOTES

1. Cf. *An Inquiry into Meaning and Truth*, Chapter VII, and *Human Knowledge*, Part II, Chapter IV.

RUDOLF CARNAP

MEANING AND NECESSITY

7. INDIVIDUAL DESCRIPTIONS

An (individual) *description* is an expression of the form '(ix) $(. . x . .)$'; it means 'the one individual such that . . x . . '. If there is one and only one individual such that . . x . . , we say that the description satisfies the uniqueness condition. In this case the *descriptum*, i.e., the entity to which the description refers, is that one individual. Logicians differ in their interpretations of descriptions in cases where the uniqueness condition is not satisfied. The methods of Hilbert and Bernays and of Russell are here discussed; that of Frege will be discussed in the next section.

We use the term *'individual'* not for one particular kind of entity but, rather, relative to a language system S, for those entities which are taken as the elements of the universe of discourse in S, in other words, the entities of lowest level (we call it level zero) dealt with in S, no matter what these entities are. For one system the individuals may be physical things, for another space-time points, or numbers, or anything else. Consequently, we call the variables of level zero individual variables, the constants individual constants, and all expressions of this level, whether simple (variables and constants) or compound, *individual expressions*. The most important kinds of compound individual expressions are: (1) full expressions of functors (e.g., '3 + 4', where '+' is a functor and '3' and '4' are individual constants); within our systems, expressions of this kind occur only in S_3, not in S_1 and S_2; (2) individual descriptions. We shall use here the term 'description' mostly in the sense of 'individual description'. Descriptions of other types do not occur in our systems; a few remarks on them will be made at the end of section 8.

A *description* in S_1 has the form '(ix) $(. . x . .)$'; it is interpreted as 'the one individual x such that . . x . .'. '(ix)' is called an iota-operator; the scope '. . x . .' is a sentential matrix with 'x' as a free variable. For example, '(ix) $(Px . \sim Qx)$' means the same as 'the one individual which is P and not Q'.

The entity for which a description stands (if there is such an entity) will be called its *descriptum*; here, in the case of individual descriptions, the descriptum is an individual. With respect to a given description, there are two possible cases: either (1) there is exactly one individual which fulfils the condition expressed by the scope, or (2) this does not hold, that is, there are none or several such individuals. In the first case we shall say of the scope, and also of the whole description, that it satisfies the uniqueness condition:

7-1

Definition. Let '. . x . .' be a (sentential) matrix (in S_1) with 'x' as the only free variable '. . x . .' (and '(ix) $(. . x . .)$') satisfies the **uniqueness condition** (in S_1) = $_{Df}$ '$(\exists z)$ (x) $[. . x . . \equiv (x \equiv z)]$' is true (in S_1). ('$x \equiv z$' means 'x is the same individual as z'; see 3-3.)

In the case of a description satisfying the uniqueness condition, there is general agreement among logicians with respect to its interpretation; the one individual satisfying the scope is taken as descriptum. In the other case, however, there is, so far, no agreement. Various methods have been proposed. We shall outline three of them, those proposed by Hilbert and Bernays (I), Russell (II), and Frege (III). Then we shall adopt Frege's method for our systems. It should be noticed that the various conceptions now to be discussed are not to be understood as different opinions, so that at least one of them must be wrong, but rather as different proposals. The different interpretations of descriptions are not meant as assertions about the meaning of phrases of the form 'the so-and-so' in English, but as proposals for an interpretation and, consequently, for deductive rules, concerning descriptions in symbolic systems. Therefore, there is no theoretical issue of right or wrong between the various conceptions, but only the practical question of the comparative convenience of different methods.

In order to make the following discussions more concrete, let us suppose that two (sentential) matrices are given, each with exactly one free variable; we indicate them here with the help of dots and dashes: '. . x . .' and '- - y - -' (e.g., 'Axw' and 'Hy'). We construct the description with the first as scope and substitute it for 'y' in the second:

7-2

'- - (ix) $(. . x . .)$ - -'. (*Example:* '$H(ix)$ (Axw)'.)

METHOD I

Hilbert and Bernays,[1] in a system with natural numbers as individuals, permit the use of a description only if it satisfies the uniqueness condition. Since the system is constructed as a calculus, not as a semantical system, the formula of uniqueness is required to be C-true (provable) instead of true. It seems that this method is quite convenient for practical work with a logico-arithmetical system; one uses a description only after he has proved the uniqueness. However, this method has a serious disadvantage, although of a chiefly theoretical nature: the rules of formation become indefinite, i.e., there is no general procedure for determining whether any given expression of the form 7-2 is a sentence of the system (no matter whether true or false, provable or not). For systems also containing factual sentences, the disadvantage would be still greater, because here the question of whether a given expression is a sentence or not would, in general, depend upon the contingency of facts.

METHOD II

Russell[2] takes the whole expression 7-2 in any case as a sentence. The uniqueness condition is here taken not as a precondition for the sentential character of the expression but rather as one of the conditions for its truth—in other words, as part of its content. Thus the translation of 7-2 into M is as follows:

7-3
'There is an individual y such that y is the only individual for which . . y . . holds, and - - y - -' (for example, 'there is an individual y such that y is the only individual which is an author of Waverley, and y is human').

Hence, 7-2 is here interpreted as meaning the same as the following (with a certain restriction, see below):

7-4
'$(\exists y) [(x) (. . x . . \equiv (x \equiv y)) \bullet - - y - -]$'. (In the example, '$(\exists y) [(x) (Axw \equiv (x \equiv y)) \bullet Hy]$'.)

In order to incorporate this interpretation into his system, Russell lays down a contextual definition for descriptions; 7-2 is the definiendum, 7-4 the definiens. If we prefer to take the iota-operator as primitive instead of defining it, we can reach the same result by framing the semantical rules in such a way that any two sentences of the forms 7-2 and 7-4 become L-equivalent.

In comparison with Hilbert's method, Russell's has the advantage that an expression of the form 7-2 is always a sentence. In comparison with Frege's method, which will soon be explained, it has the disadvantage that the rules for descriptions are not so simple as those for other individual expressions, especially those for individual constants. In particular, the inferences of specification, leading from '$(y) (- - y - -)$' to '- - a - -', and of existential generalization, leading from '- -a - -' to '$(\exists y) (- - y - -)$', are, in general, not valid if a description takes the place of the individual constant 'a'; here the uniqueness sentence for the description must be taken as an additional premise. A further disadvantage of Russell's method is the following: A sentence like '$\sim Q(\imath x)$'

(x)' can be transformed in two ways. Either this whole sentence is taken as 7-2 and transformed into the corresponding sentence of the form 7-4; or the part '$Q(ix)$ (Px)' is taken as 7-2, transformed into the corresponding sentence of the form 7-4, and then prefixed again with the sign of negation. The two resulting sentences are not L-equivalent (in distinction to Frege's method); hence Russell has to lay down an additional convention, which determines for each case what is to be taken as the context 7-2.

8. FREGE'S METHOD FOR DESCRIPTIONS

We adopt for our systems a method proposed by Frege for interpreting individual descriptions in cases of nonuniqueness. This method consists in choosing once for all an individual to be taken as descriptum for all such cases.

METHOD III

Frege[3] regards it as a defect in the logical structure of natural languages that in some cases an expression of the grammatical form 'the so-and-so' is a name[4] of one object while in other cases it is not; in our terminology: that some descriptions have a descriptum but others not. Therefore, he suggests that the rules of a language system should be constructed in such a way that every description has a descriptum. This requires certain conventions which are more or less arbitrary; but this disadvantage seems small in comparison with the gain in simplicity for the rules of the system. For instance, specification and existential generalization are here valid also for descriptions (at least in extensional contexts).

Frege's requirement can be fulfilled in various ways. The choice of a convenient procedure depends upon the particular features of the language system, especially upon the range of values of the variables in question. There are chiefly two methods which deserve consideration; we call them IIIa and IIIb. We shall explain them and then use IIIb for our systems.

METHOD IIIa

Frege[5] himself constructs a system without type difference between individuals and classes; that is to say, he counts both classes and their elements as objects, i.e., as values of the individual variables. To any of those descriptions which do not satisfy the condition of uniqueness he assigns as descriptum the class of those objects which fulfil the scope. Thus different descriptions of this kind may have different descripta.

METHOD IIIb

A simpler procedure consists in selecting, once for all, a certain entity from the range of values of the variables in question and assigning it as descriptum to all descriptions which do not satisfy the condition of uniqueness. This has been done in various ways.

(i) If the individuals of the system are numbers, the number 0 seems to be the most natural choice. Frege[6] has already mentioned this possibility. It has been applied by Gödel[7] for his epsilon-operator and by myself[8] for the K-operator.

(ii) For variables to whose values the null class Λ belongs, this class seems to be the most convenient choice. Such a choice has been made by Quine,[9] in whose system there is, as in Frege's, no type difference between individuals and classes.

(iii) How can Method IIIb be applied to a language system whose individuals are physical things or events? At first glance, it seems impossible to make here an even moderately natural choice of an individual as common descriptum for all individual descriptions which do not satisfy the condition of uniqueness. To select, say, Napoleon would be just as arbitrary as to select this dust particle on my paper. However, a natural solution offers itself if we construct the system in such a way that the spatiotemporal part-whole relation is one of its concepts.[10] Every individual in such a system, that is, every thing or event, corresponds to a class of space-time points in a system with space-time points as individuals. Therefore, it is possible, although not customary in the ordinary language, to count among the things also the *null thing*, which corresponds to the null class of space-time points. In the language system of things it is characterized as that thing which is part of every thing.[11] Let us take 'a_0' as the name for the null thing; the other things may be called non-null things. If a system S includes a_0 among its individuals, then a_0 seems a natural and convenient choice as descriptum for those descriptions which do not satisfy the uniqueness condition. It is true that this procedure requires certain deviations from the ordinary language for the forms of sentences in S; but these deviations are smaller than we might expect at first glance. For most of the universal and existential sentences, the translation into S is straightforward, i.e., without change in structure; in other cases 'non-null' must be inserted. [*Examples:* The sentence 'There is no thing which is identical with the king of France in 1905' is translated into a sentence of S of the form 'There is no non-null thing . . .'. On the other hand, no such change in form is necessary for the sentence 'All men are mortal' and not even for 'There is no man who is identical with the king of France in 1905', because it follows from any suitably framed definition for 'man' that every man is a non-null thing.]

In our further discussions we assume for our system S_1 that Frege's

Method IIIb is applied and that the individual constant 'a*' is used for the common descriptum of all descriptions which do not satisfy the uniqueness condition. We leave it open which individual is meant by 'a*'; it may be the null thing a_0, if this belongs to the individuals in S_1; it may be 0, if numbers belong to the individuals (as, for instance, in S_3), but it may as well be any other individual. Consequently, a sentence containing a description is now interpreted in a way different from Russell's. The translation of 7-2 into M is now as follows (instead of 7-3):

8-1

Either there is an individual y such that y is the only individual for which . . y . . holds, and - -y - -; or there is no such individual, and - - a* - -'. [In the previous example: 'Either there is an individual y such that y is the only author of Waverley, and y is human; or there is no such individual y (that is to say, there is either no author or several authors of Waverley), and a* is human'.]

Hence, the sentence 7-2 containing the description is L-equivalent in S_1 to the following (instead of to 7-4):

8-2

'$(\exists y) \left[(x) (. \; . \; x \; . \; . \equiv (x \equiv y)) \bullet - - y - -\right] \vee \left[\sim (\exists y)(x) (. \; . \; x \; . \; . \equiv (x \equiv y)) \bullet - - a^* - -\right]$'. (In the example: '$(\exists y) \left[(x) (Axw \equiv (x \equiv y)) \bullet Hy\right] \vee \left[\sim (\exists y)(x) (Axw \equiv (x \equiv y)) \bullet Ha^*\right]$'.)

Here again, as in the case of Russell's method, we may set up either a contextual definition for 7-2 with 8-2 as definiens, or semantical rules for the iota-operator as a primitive sign such that 7-2 becomes L-equivalent to 8-2.

The accompanying table gives a survey of the various methods just explained for dealing with descriptions in the case of nonuniqueness. The case of uniqueness is not represented because its treatment is the same with all authors.

Some brief remarks may be made on *descriptions with variables of other than individual type*, especially predicator variables, functor variables, and sentential variables. (This is a digression from the study of our systems S_1, etc., which contain only individual variables.) Here it is easy to make a natural choice of a value of the variable as a descriptum for those descriptions which do not satisfy the condition of uniqueness. If an individual has been chosen as a* (it may be a_0 or 0 or anything else), then we might call one entity in every type the null entity of that type, in the following way: In the type of individuals it would be a*; in any predicator type, the null class or null relation of that type, e.g., for level one and degree one the null class Λ; in the type of propositions, the L-false proposition; in any type of functions, that function

INTERPRETATION OF DESCRIPTIONS IN THE CASE
OF NONUNIQUENESS

HILBERT-BERNAYS	RUSSELL	FREGE		QUINE	SYSTEM OF THINGS	SYSTEM S_1
		(a)	(b)			
Method I	Method II	Method IIIa	Method IIIb	Method IIIb	Method IIIb	Method IIIb
Description is meaningless	No descriptum; the sentence is meaningful but false	$\hat{x}(.. x..)$	o	Λ	Null thing a_0	a*

which has as value for all arguments the null entity of the type in question. Then we may take as descriptum in the case of nonuniqueness the null entity of the type of the description variable.

For the sake of simplicity, the following explanations are restricted to extensional systems. Let 'f' and 'g' be predicator variables of level one and degree one. Let '- - $(if)(. . f . .) - -$' indicate, in analogy to 7-2, a sentence containing a description of the type of 'f', hence a description for a class or property. This sentence is L-equivalent to the following, in analogy to 8-2:

'$(\exists g) \left[(f) (. . f . . \equiv (f \equiv g) g) \right] \bullet - - g - -\right] \vee \left[\sim (\exists g)(f) (. . f . . \equiv (f \equiv g)) \bullet - - \Lambda - -\right]$'.

The uniqueness condition here occurring says that there is a property g, such that for those f and only those, which are equivalent to g, . . f . . ; in other words, there is exactly one class g such tht . . g . . . Hence here the uniqueness applies to extensions, not to intentions. This is in analogy to 7-1 and 7-3; for, as we shall see later, the extensions of individual expressions are individuals.

However, if the system contains lambda-operators for the formation of predicators, then descriptions with predicator variables are not necessary, they can be replaced by lambda-expressions. In this case we can transform not only a sentence containing the description as in the earlier case but the description itself into an L-equivalent expression. The description '$(if)(. . f . .)$' is L-equivalent to the lambda-predicator '$(\lambda x) \left[(\exists g) ((f) \left[. . f . . \equiv (f \equiv g) \right] \bullet gx) \right]$'.

In a similar way, for every description of a function (containing an iota-operator with a functor variable) there is an L-equivalent functor formed with a lambda-operator. And for every description containing an iota-operator with a sentential variable there is an L-equivalent sentence without an iota-operator; however, in an extensional system these descriptions with sentential variables are rather useless anyway.

In view of these results, it seems convenient in the primitive notation of a system (at least in an extensional one) to use the iota-operator, if at all, for individual descriptions only, and then to use the lambda-operator for the formation of predicators and functors.[12]

NOTES

1. [Grundlagen I], p. 384.
2. The reasons for this method are explained in detail by Russell in [Denoting]; it has been applied by Russell and Whitehead in the construction of the system of [P.M.], see I, 66 ff. and 173 ff.
3. [Sinn], pp. 39–42.
4. For the question of English translations for Frege's terms, see below, p. 118, n. 21.
5. [Grundgesetze], I, 19.
6. [Sinn], p. 42 n.
7. K. Gödel, "Ueber formal unentscheidbare Sätze der Principia Mathematic und verwandter Systeme", *Monashefte f. Math. u. Physik*, XXXVIII (1931), 173–198.
8. [Syntax], § 7.
9. [M.L.], p. 147.
10. This is, for instance, the case with the following systems: a system for certain biological concepts by J. H. Woodger (*The Axiomatic Method in Biology* [1937]; *The Technique of Theory Construction* ["International Encyclopedia of Unified Science", Vol. II, No. 5 (1939)]); a calculus of individuals by H. S. Leonard and N. Goodman ("The Calculus of Individuals and Its Uses", *Journal of Symbolic Logic*, V [1940], 45–55); and a general system of logic recently constructed by R. M. Martin ("A Homogeneous System for Formal Logic", *Journal of Symbolic Logic*, VIII [1943], 1–23), where the customary symbol of inclusion and the term 'inclusion' apparently refer to the part-whole relation among things.
11. In the system by Martin mentioned in the preceding footnote the null thing is indeed introduced (see *op. cit.*, p. 3, and D7, p. 9), while in the paper by Leonard and Goodman there is an explicit "refusal to postulate a null element" (*op. cit.*, p. 46).
12. Several forms of systems with predicators and functors built with lambda-operators have been constructed by Church, see especially *The Calculi of Lambda-Conversion* ("Ann. of Math. Studies", No. 6 [1941]).

KEITH DONNELLAN

REFERENCE
AND DEFINITE DESCRIPTIONS

I

Definite descriptions, I shall argue, have two possible functions. They are used to refer to what a speaker wishes to talk about, but they are also used quite differently. Moreover, a definite description occurring in one and the same sentence may, on different occasions of its use, function in either way. The failure to deal with this duality of function obscures the genuine referring use of definite descriptions. The best-known theories of definite descriptions, those of Russell and Strawson, I shall suggest, are both guilty of this. Before discussing this distinction in use, I will mention some features of these theories to which it is especially relevant.

On Russell's view a definite description may denote an entity: "If '*C*' is a denoting phrase [as definite descriptions are by definition], it may happen that there is one entity *x* (there cannot be more than one) for which the proposition '*x* is identical with *C*' is true. . . . We may then say that the entity *x* is the denotation of the phrase '*C*.' "[1] In using a definite description, then, a speaker may use an expression which denotes some entity, but this is the only relationship between that entity and the use of the definite description recognized by Russell. I shall argue, however, that there are two uses of definite descriptions. The definition of denotation given by Russell is applicable to both, but in one of these the definite description serves to do something more. I shall say that in this use the speaker uses the definite description to *refer* to something, and call this use the "referential use" of a definite description. Thus, if I am right, referring is not the same as denoting and the referential use of definite descriptions is not recognized on Russell's view.

Furthermore, on Russell's view the type of expression that comes closest to performing the function of the referential use of definite descriptions turns out, as one might suspect, to be a proper name (in "the narrow logical sense"). Many of the things said about proper names by Russell can, I think, be said about the referential use of definite descriptions without straining senses unduly. Thus the gulf Russell thought he saw between names and definite descriptions is narrower than he thought.

Strawson, on the other hand, certainly does recognize a referential use of definite definitions. But what I think he did not see is that a definite description may have a quite different role—may be used nonreferentially, even as it occurs in one and the same sentence. Strawson, it is true, points out nonreferential uses of definite descriptions,[2] but which use a definite description has seems to be for him a function of the kind of sentence in which it occurs; whereas, if I am right, there can be two possible uses of a definite description in the same sentence. Thus, in "On Referring," he says, speaking of expressions used to refer, "Any expression of any of these classes [one being that of definite descriptions] can occur as the subject of what would traditionally be regarded as a singular subject-predicate sentence; and would, so occurring, exemplify the use I wish to discuss."[3] So the definite description in, say, the sentence "The Republican candidate for president in 1968 will be a conservative" presumably exemplifies the referential use. But if I am right, we could not say this of the sentence in isolation from some particular occasion on which it is used to state something; and then it might or might not turn out that the definite description has a referential use.

Strawson and Russell seem to me to make a common assumption here about the question of how definite descriptions function: that we can ask how a definite description functions in some sentence independently of a particular occasion upon which it is used. This assumption is not really rejected in Strawson's arguments against Russell. Although he can sum up his position by saying, " 'Mentioning' or 'referring' is not something an expression does; it is something that someone can use an expression to do,"[4] he means by this to deny the radical view that a "genuine" referring expression *has* a referent, functions to refer, independent of the context of some use of the expression. The denial of this view, however, does not entail that definite descriptions cannot be identified as referring expressions in a sentence unless the sentence is being used. Just as we can speak of a function of a tool that is not at the moment performing its function, Strawson's view, I believe, allows us to speak of the referential function of a definite description in a sentence even when it is not being used. This, I hope to show, is a mistake.

A second assumption shared by Russell's and Strawson's account of definite descriptions is this. In many cases a person who uses a definite descriptions can be said (in some sense) to presuppose or imply that something fits the description.[5] If I state that the king is on his throne, I presuppose or imply that there is a king. (At any rate, this would be a natural thing to say for anyone who doubted that there is a king.) Both Russell and Strawson assume that where the presupposition or implication is false, the truth value of what the speaker says is affected. For Russell the statement made is false; for Strawson it has no truth value. Now if there are two uses of definite descriptions, it may be that the truth value is affected differently in each case by the falsity of the presupposition or implication. This is what I shall in fact argue. It will turn out, I believe, that one or the other of the two views, Russell's or Strawson's, may be correct about the nonreferential use of definite descriptions, but neither fits the referential use. This is not so surprising about Russell's view, since he did not recognize this use in any case, but it is surprising about Strawson's since the referential use is what he tries to explain and defend. Furthermore, on Strawson's account, the result of there being nothing which fits the description is a failure of reference.[6] This too, I believe, turns out not to be true about the referential use of definite descriptions.

II

There are some uses of definite descriptions which carry neither any hint of a referential use nor any presupposition or implication that something fits the description. In general, it seems, these are recognizable from the sentence frame in which the description occurs. These uses will not interest us, but it is necessary to point them out if only to set them aside.

An obvious example would be the sentence "The present King of France does not exist," used, say, to correct someone's mistaken impression that de Gaulle is the King of France.

A more interesting example is this. Suppose someone were to ask, "Is de Gaulle the King of France?" This is the natural form of words for a person to use who is in doubt as to whether de Gaulle is King or President of France. Given this background to the question, there seems to be no presupposition or implication that someone is the King of France. Nor is the person attempting to refer to someone by using the definite description. On the other hand, reverse the name and description in the question and the speaker probably would be thought to presuppose or imply this. "Is the King of France de Gaulle?" is the natural question for one to ask who wonders whether it is de Gaulle rather than someone else who occupies the throne of France.[7]

Many times, however, the use of a definite description does carry a presupposition or implication that something fits the description. If definite descriptions do have a referring role, it will be here. But it is a mistake, I think, to try, as I believe both Russell and Strawson do, to settle this matter without further ado. What is needed, I believe, is the distinction I will now discuss.

III

I will call the two uses of definite descriptions I have in mind the attributive use and the referential use. A speaker who uses a definite description attributively in an assertion states something about whoever or whatever is the so-and-so. A speaker who uses a definite description referentially in an assertion, on the other hand, uses the description to enable his audience to pick out whom or what he is talking about and states something about that person or thing. In the first case the definite description might be said to occur essentially, for the speaker wishes to assert something about whatever or whoever fits that description; but in the referential use the definite description is merely one tool for doing a certain job—calling attention to a person or thing—and in general any other device for doing the same job, another description or a name, would do as well. In the attributive use, the attribute of being the so-and-so is all important, while it is not in the referential use.

To illustrate this distinction, in the case of a single sentence, consider the sentence, "Smith's murderer is insane." Suppose first that we come upon poor Smith foully murdered. From the brutal manner of the killing and the fact that Smith was the most lovable person in the world, we might exclaim, "Smith's murderer is insane." I will assume, to make it a simpler case, that in a quite ordinary sense we do not know who murdered Smith (though this is not in the end essential to the case). This, I shall say, is an attributive use of the definite description.

The contrast with such a use of the sentence is one of those situations in which we expect and intend our audience to realize whom we have in mind when we speak of Smith's murderer and, most importantly, to know that it is this person about whom we are going to say something.

For example, suppose that Jones has been charged with Smith's murder and has been placed on trial. Imagine that there is a discussion of Jones's odd behavior at his trial. We might sum up our impression of his behavior by saying, "Smith's murderer is insane." If someone asks to whom we are referring, by using this description, the answer here is "Jones." This, I shall say, is a referential use of the definite description.

That these two uses of the definite description in the same sentence are really quite different can perhaps best be brought out by considering the consequences of the assumption that Smith had no murderer (for example, he in fact committed suicide). In both situations, in using the definite description "Smith's murderer," the speaker in some sense presupposes or implies that there is a murderer. But when we hypothesize that the presupposition or implication is false, there are different results for the two uses. In both cases we have used the predicate "is insane," but in the first case, if there is no murderer, there is no person of whom it could be correctly said that we attributed insanity to him. Such a person could be identified (correctly) only in case someone fitted the description used. But in the second case, where the definite description is simply a means of identifying the person we want to talk about, it is quite possible for the correct identification to be made even though no one fits the description we used.[8] We were speaking about Jones even though he is not in fact Smith's murderer and, in the circumstances imagined, it was his behavior we were commenting upon. Jones might, for example, accuse us of saying false things of him in calling him insane and it would be no defense, I should think, that our description, "the murderer of Smith," failed to fit him.

It is, moreover, perfectly possible for your audience to know to whom we refer, in the second situation, even though they do not share our presupposition. A person hearing our comment in the context imagined might know we are talking about Jones even though he does not think Jones guilty.

Generalizing from this case, we can say, I think, that there are two uses of sentences of the form, "The ϕ is ψ." In the first, if nothing is the ϕ then nothing has been said to be ψ. In the second, the fact that nothing is the ϕ does not have this consequence.

With suitable changes the same difference in use can be formulated for uses of language other than assertions. Suppose one is at a party and, seeing an interesting-looking person holding a martini glass, one asks, "Who is the man drinking a martini?" If it should turn out that there is only water in the glass, one has nevertheless asked a question about a particular person, a question that it is possible for someone to answer. Contrast this with the use of the same question by the chairman of the local Teetotalers Union. He has just been informed that a man is drinking a martini at their annual party. He responds by asking his informant, "Who is the man drinking a martini?" In asking the question the chairman does not have some particular person in mind about whom he asks the question; if no one is drinking a martini, if the information is wrong, no person can be singled out as the person about whom the question was asked. Unlike the first case, the attribute of being the man drinking a martini is all-important, because if it is the attribute of no one, the chairman's question has no straight-forward answer.

This illustrates also another difference between the referential and the attributive use of definite descriptions. In the one case we have asked a question about a particular person or thing even though nothing fits the description we used; in the other this is not so. But also in the one case our question can be answered; in the other it cannot be. In the referential use of a definite description we may succeed in picking out a person or thing to ask a question about even though he or it does not really fit the description; but in the attributive use if nothing fits the description, no straightforward answer to the question can be given.

This further difference is also illustrated by commands or orders containing definite descriptions. Consider the order, "Bring me the book on the table." If "the book on the table" is being used referentially, it is possible to fulfill the order even though there is no book on the table. If, for example, there is a book *beside* the table, though there is none *on* it, one might bring that book back and ask the issuer of the order whether this is "the book you meant." And it may be. But imagine we are told that someone has laid a book on our prize antique table, where nothing should be put. The order,

"Bring me the book on the table" cannot now be obeyed unless there is a book that has been placed on the table. There is no possibility of bringing back a book which was never on the table and having it be the one that was meant, because there is no book that in that sense was "meant." In the one case the definite description was a device for getting the other person to pick the right book; if he is able to pick the right book even though it does not satisfy the description, one still succeeds in his purpose. In the other case, there is, antecedently, no "right book" except one which fits the description; the attribute of being the book on the table is essential. Not only is there no book about which an order was issued, if there is no book on the table, but the order itself cannot be obeyed. When a definite description is used attributively in a command or question and nothing fits the description, the command cannot be obeyed and the question cannot be answered. This suggests some analogous consequence for assertions containing definite descriptions used attributively. Perhaps the analogous result is that the assertion is neither true nor false: this is Strawson's view of what happens when the presupposition of the use of a definite description is false. But if so, Strawson's view works not for definite descriptions used referentially, but for the quite different use, which I have called the attributive use.

I have tried to bring out the two uses of definite descriptions by pointing out the different consequences of supposing that nothing fits the description used. There are still other differences. One is this: when a definite description is used referentially, not only is there in some sense a presupposition or implication that someone or something fits the description, as there is also in the attributive use, but there is a quite different presupposition; the speaker presupposes of some *particular* someone or something that he or it fits the description. In asking, for example, "Who is the man drinking a martini?" where we mean to ask a question about that man over there, we are presupposing that that man over there is drinking a martini—not just that *someone* is a man drinking a martini. When we say, in a context where it is clear we are referring to Jones, "Smith's murderer is insane," we are presupposing that Jones is Smith's murderer. No such presupposition is present in the attributive use of definite descriptions. There is, of course, the presupposition that someone *or other* did the murder, but the speaker does not presuppose of someone in particular—Jones or Robinson, say—that he did it. What I mean by this second kind of presupposition that someone or something in particular fits the description—which is present in a referential use but not in an attributive use—can perhaps be seen more clearly by considering a member of the speaker's audience who believes that Smith was not murdered at all. Now in the case of the referential use of the description, "Smith's murderer," he could accuse the speaker of mistakenly presupposing both that someone or other is the murderer and that also Jones is the murderer, for even though he believes Jones not to have done the deed, he knows that the speaker was referring to Jones. But in the case of the attributive use, he can accuse the speaker of having only the first, less specific presupposition; he cannot pick out some person and claim that the speaker is presupposing that that person is Smith's murderer. Now the more particular presuppositions that we find present in referential uses are clearly not ones we can assign to a definite description in some particular sentence in isolation from a context of use. In order to know that a person presupposes that Jones is Smith's murderer in using the sentence "Smith's murderer is insane," we have to know that he is using the description referentially and also to whom he is referring. The sentence by itself does not tell us any of this.

IV

From the way in which I set up each of the previous examples it might be supposed that the important difference between the referential and the attributive use lies in the beliefs of the speaker. Does he believe of some particular person or thing that he or it fits the description used? In the Smith murder example, for instance, there was in the one case no belief as to who did the deed, whereas in the contrasting case it was believed that Jones did it. But this is, in fact, not an essential difference. It is possible for a definite description to be used attributively even though the speaker (and his audience) believes that a certain person or thing fits the description. And it is possible for a definite description to be used referentially where the speaker believes that nothing fits the description. It is true—and this is why, for simplicity, I set up the examples the way I did—that if a speaker does not believe that anything fits the description or does not believe that he is in a position to pick out what does fit the description, it is likely that he is not using it referentially. It is also true that if he and his audience would pick out some particular thing or person as fitting the description, then a use of the definite description is very likely referential. But these are only presumptions and not entailments.

To use the Smith murder case again, suppose that Jones is on trial for the murder and I and everyone else believe him guilty. Suppose that I comment that the murderer of Smith is insane, but instead of backing this up, as in the example previously used, by citing Jone's behavior in the dock, I go on to outline reasons for thinking that *anyone* who murdered poor Smith in that particularly horrible way must be insane. If now it turns out that Jones was not the murderer after all, but someone else was, I think I can claim to have been right if the true murderer is after all insane. Here, I think, I would be using the definite description attributively, even though I believe that a particular person fits the description.

It is also possible to think of cases in which the speaker does not believe that what he means to refer to by using the definite description fits the de-

scription, or to imagine cases in which the definite description is used referentially even though the speaker believes *nothing* fits the description.
Admittedly, these cases may be parasitic on a more normal use; nevertheless,
they are sufficient to show that such beliefs of the speaker are not decisive
as to which use is made of a definite description.

Suppose the throne is occupied by a man I firmly believe to be not the
king, but a usurper. Imagine also that his followers as firmly believe that he
is the king. Suppose I wish to see this man. I might say to his minions, "Is
the king in his countinghouse?" I succeed in referring to the man I wish to
refer to without myself believing that he fits the description. It is not even
necessary, moreover, to suppose that his followers believe him to be the king.
If they are cynical about the whole thing, know he is not the king, I may still
succeed in referring to the man I wish to refer to. Similarly, neither I nor the
people I speak to may suppose that *anyone* is the king and, finally, each party
may know that the other does not so suppose and yet the reference may go
through.

V

Both the attributive and the referential use of definite descriptions seem
to carry a presupposition or implication that there is something which fits the
description. But the reasons for the existence of the presupposition or implication are different in the two cases.

There is a presumption that a person who uses a definite description
referentially believes that what he wishes to refer to fits the description.
Because the purpose of using the description is to get the audience to pick
out or think of the right thing or person, one would normally choose a
description that he believes the thing or person fits. Normally a misdescription
of that to which one wants to refer would mislead the audience. Hence, there
is a presumption that the speaker believes *something* fits the description—
namely, that to which he refers.

When a definite description is used attributively, however, there is not
the same possibility of misdescription. In the example of "Smith's murderer"
used attributively, there was not the possibility of misdescribing Jones or
anyone else; we were not referring to Jones nor to anyone else by using the
description. The presumption that the speaker believes *someone* is Smith's
murderer does not arise here from a more specific presumption that he believes Jones or Robinson or someone else whom he can name or identify is
Smith's murderer.

The presupposition or implication is borne by a definite description used
attributively because if nothing fits the description the linguistic purpose of
the speech act will be thwarted. That is, the speaker will not succeed in saying
something true, if he makes an assertion; he will not succeed in asking a

question that can be answered, if he has asked a question; he will not succeed in issuing an order that can be obeyed, if he has issued an order. If one states that Smith's murderer is insane, when Smith has no murderer, and uses the definite description nonreferentially, then one fails to say anything *true*. If one issues the order "Bring me Smith's murderer" under similar circumstances, the order cannot be obeyed; nothing would count as obeying it.

When the definite description is used referentially, on the other hand, the presupposition or implication stems simply from the fact that normally a person tries to describe correctly what he wants to refer to because normally this is the best way to get his audience to recognize what he is referring to. As we have seen, it is possible for the linguistic purpose of the speech act to be accomplished in such a case even though nothing fits the description; it is possible to say something true or to ask a question that gets answered or to issue a command that gets obeyed. For when the definite description is used referentially, one's audience may succeed in seeing to what one refers even though neither it nor anything else fits the description.

VI

The result of the last section shows something to be wrong with the theories of both Russell and Strawson; for though they give differing accounts of the implication or presupposition involved, each gives only one. Yet, as I have argued, the presupposition or implication is present for a quite different reason, depending upon whether the definite description is used attributively or referentially, and exactly what presuppositions or implications are involved is also different. Moreover, neither theory seems a correct characterization of the referential use. On Russell's there is a logical entailment: "The ϕ is ψ" entails "There exists one and only one ϕ." Whether or not this is so for the attributive use, it does not seem true of the referential use of the definite description. The "implication" that something is the ϕ, as I have argued, does not amount to an entailment; it is more like a presumption based on what is *usually* true of the use of a definite description to refer. In any case, of course, Russell's theory does not show—what is true of the referential use—that the implication that *something* is the ϕ comes from the more specific implication that *what is being referred to* is the ϕ. Hence, as a theory of definite descriptions, Russell's view seems to apply, if at all, to the attributive use only.

Russell's definition of denoting (a definite description denotes an entity if that entity fits the description uniquely) is clearly applicable to either use of definite descriptions. Thus whether or not a definite description is used referentially or attributively, it may have a denotation. Hence, denoting and referring, as I have explicated the latter notion, are distinct and Russell's view recognizes only the former. It seems to me, moreover, that this is a welcome result, that denoting and referring should not be confused. If one tried to maintain that they are the same notion, one result would be that a speaker might be referring to something without knowing it. If someone said, for example, in 1960 before he had any idea that Mr. Goldwater would be the Republican nominee in 1964, "The Republican candidate for president in 1964 will be a conservative," (perhaps on the basis of an analysis of the views of party leaders) the definite description here would *denote* Mr. Goldwater. But would we wish to say that the speaker had referred to, mentioned, or talked about Mr. Goldwater? I feel these terms would be out of place. Yet if we identify referring and denoting, it ought to be possible for it to turn out (after the Republican Convention) that the speaker had, unknown to himself, referred in 1960 to Mr. Goldwater. On my view, however, while the definite description used did *denote* Mr. Goldwater (using Russell's definition), the speaker used it *attributively* and did not *refer* to Mr. Goldwater.

Turning to Strawson's theory, it was supposed to demonstrate how definite descriptions are referential. But it goes too far in this direction. For there are nonreferential uses of definite descriptions also, even as they occur in one and the same sentence. I believe that Strawson's theory involves the following propositions:

(1) If someone asserts that the ϕ is ψ he has not made a true or false statement if there is no ϕ.[9]

(2) If there is no ϕ then the speaker has failed to refer to anything.[10]

(3) The reason he has said nothing true or false is that he has failed to refer.

Each of these propositions is either false or, at best, applies to only one of the two uses of definite descriptions.

Proposition (1) is possibly true of the attributive use. In the example in which "Smith's murderer is insane" was said when Smith's body was first discovered, an attributive use of the definite description, there was no person to whom the speaker referred. If Smith had no murderer, nothing true was said. It is quite tempting to conclude, following Strawson, that nothing true *or* false was said. But where the definite description is used referentially, something true may well have been said. It is possible that something true was said of the person or thing referred to.[11]

Proposition (2) is, as we have seen, simply false. Where a definite description is used referentially it is perfectly possible to refer to something though nothing fits the description used.

The situation with proposition (3) is a bit more complicated. It ties together, on Strawson's view, the two strands given in (1) and (2). As an account of why, when the presupposition is false, nothing true or false has been stated, it clearly cannot work for the attributive use of definite descriptions, for the reason it supplies is that reference has failed. It does not then give the reason why, if indeed this is so, a speaker using a definite description attributively fails to say anything true or false if nothing fits the description. It does, however, raise a question about the referential use. Can reference fail when a definite description is used referentially?

I do not fail to refer merely because my audience does not correctly pick out what I am referring to. I can be referring to a particular man when I use the description "the man drinking a martini," even though the people to whom I speak fail to pick out the right person or any person at all. Nor, as we have stressed, do I fail to refer when nothing fits the description. But perhaps I fail to refer in some extreme circumstances, when there is nothing that *I* am willing to pick out as that to which I referred.

Suppose that I think I see at some distance a man walking and ask, "Is the man carrying a walking stick the professor of history?" We should perhaps distinguish four cases at this point. (a) There is a man carrying a walking stick: I have then referred to a person and asked a question about him that can be answered if my audience has the information. (b) The man over there is not carrying a walking stick, but an umbrella; I have still referred to someone and asked a question that can be answered, though if my audience sees that it is an umbrella and not a walking stick, they may also correct my apparently mistaken impression. (c) It is not a man at all, but a rock that looks like one; in this case, I think I still have referred to something, to the thing over there that happens to be a rock but that I took to be a man. But in this case it is not clear that my question can be answered correctly. This, I think, is not because I have failed to refer, but rather because, given the true nature of what I referred to, my question is not appropriate. A simple "No, that is not the professor of history" is at least a bit misleading if said by someone who realizes that I mistook a rock for a person. It may, therefore, be plausible to conclude that in such a case I have not asked a question to which there is a straightforwardly correct answer. But if this is true, it is not because nothing fits the description I used, but rather because what I referred to is a rock and my question has no correct answer when asked of a rock. (d) There is finally the case in which there is nothing at all where I thought there was a man with a walking stick; and perhaps here we have a genuine failure to refer at all, even though the description was used for the purpose of referring. There is no rock, nor anything else, to which I meant to refer; it was, perhaps, a trick of light that made me think there was a man there. I cannot say of anything, "That is what I was referring to, though I now see that it's not a man carrying a walking stick." This failure of reference, however, requires circumstances much more radical than the mere nonexistence of anything fitting the description used. It requires that there be nothing of which it can be said, "That is what he was referring to." Now perhaps also in such cases, if the speaker has asserted something, he fails to state anything true or false if there is nothing that can be identified as that to which he referred. But if so, the failure of reference and truth value does not come about merely because nothing fits the description he used. So (3) may be true of some cases of the referential use of definite descriptions; it may be true that a failure of reference results in a lack of truth value. But these cases are of a much more extreme sort than Strawson's theory implies.

I conclude, then, that neither Russell's nor Strawson's theory represents a correct account of the use of definite descriptions—Russell's because it ignores altogether the referential use, Strawson's because it fails to make the distinction between the referential and the attributive and mixes together truths about each (together with some things that are false).

VII

It does not seem possible to say categorically of a definite description in a particular sentence that it is a referring expression (of course, one could say this if he meant that it *might* be used to refer). In general, whether or not a definite description is used referentially or attributively is a function of the speaker's intentions in a particular case. "The murderer of Smith" may be used either way in the sentence "The murderer of Smith is insane." It does not appear plausible to account for this, either, as an ambiguity in the sentence. The grammatical structure of the sentence seems to me to be the same whether the description is used referentially or attributively: that is, it is not syntactically ambiguous. Nor does it seem at all attractive to suppose an ambiguity in the meaning of the words; it does not appear to be semantically ambiguous. (Perhaps we could say that the sentence is pragmatically ambiguous: the distinction between roles that the description plays is a function of the speaker's intentions.) These, of course, are intuitions; I do not have an argument for these conclusions. Nevertheless, the burden of proof is surely on the other side.

This, I think, means that the view, for example, that sentences can be divided up into predicates, logical operators, and referring expressions is not generally true. In the case of definite descriptions one cannot always assign the referential function in isolation from a particular occasion on which it is used.

There may be sentences in which a definite description can be used only attributively or only referentially. A sentence in which it seems that the definite description could be used only attributively would be "Point out the man who is drinking my martini," I am not so certain that any can be found in which the definite description can be used only referentially. Even if there are such sentences, it does not spoil the point that there are many sentences, apparently not ambiguous either syntactically or semantically, containing definite descriptions that can be used either way.

If it could be shown that the dual use of definite descriptions can be accounted for by the presence of an ambiguity, there is still a point to be made against the theories of Strawson and Russell. For neither, so far as I can see, has anything to say about the possibility of such an ambiguity and, in fact, neither seems compatible with such a possibility. Russell's does not recognize the possibility of the referring use, and Strawson's, as I have tried to show in the last section, combines elements from each use into one unitary account. Thus the view that there is an ambiguity in such sentences does not seem any more attractive to these positions.

VIII

Using a definite description referentially, a speaker may say something true even though the description correctly applies to nothing. The sense in which he may say something true is the sense in which he may say something true about someone or something. This sense is, I think, an interesting one that needs investigation. Isolating it is one of the byproducts of the distinction between the attributive and referential uses of definite descriptions.

For one thing, it raises questions about the notion of a statement. This is brought out by considering a passage in a paper by Leonard Linsky in which he rightly makes the point that one can refer to someone although the definite description used does not correctly describe the person:

. . . said of a spinster that "Her husband is kind to her" is neither true nor false. But a speaker might very well be referring to someone using these words, for he may think that someone is the husband of the lady (who in fact is a spinster). Still, the statement is neither true nor false, for it presupposes that the lady has a husband, which she has not. This last refutes Strawson's thesis that if the presupposition of existence is not satisfied, the speaker has failed to refer.[12]

There is much that is right in this passage. But because Linsky does not make the distinction between the referential and the attributive uses of definite descriptions, it does not represent a wholly adequate account of the situation. A perhaps minor point about this passage is that Linsky apparently thinks it sufficient to establish that the speaker in his example is referring to someone by using the definite description "her husband," that he *believe* that someone is her husband. This will only approximate the truth provided that the "someone" in the description of the belief means "someone in particular" and is not merely the existential quantifier, "there is someone or other." For in both the attributive and the referential use the belief that someone *or other* is the husband of the lady is very likely to be present. If, for example, the speaker has just met the lady and, noticing her cheerfulness and radiant good health, makes his remark from his conviction that these attributes are always the result of having good husbands, he would be using the definite description attributively. Since she has no husband, there is no one to pick out as the person to whom he was referring. Nevertheless, the speaker believed that *someone or other* was her husband. On the other hand, if the use of "her husband" was simply a way of referring to a man the speaker has just met whom he assumed to be the lady's husband, he would have referred to that man even though neither he nor anyone else fits the description. I think it is likely that in this passage Linsky did mean by "someone," in his description of the belief, "someone in particular." But even then, as we have seen, we have neither a sufficient nor a necessary condition for a referential use of the definite description. A definite description can be used attributively even when the speaker believes that some particular thing or person fits the description, and it can be used referentially in the absence of this belief.

My main point, here, however, has to do with Linsky's view that because the presupposition is not satisfied, the *statement* is neither true nor false. This seems to me possibly correct *if* the definite description is thought of as being used attributively (depending upon whether we go with Strawson or Russell). But when we consider it as used referentially, this categorical assertion is no longer clearly correct. For the man the speaker referred to may indeed be kind to the spinster; the speaker may have said something true about that man. Now the difficulty is in the notion of "the statement." Suppose that we know that the lady is a spinster, but nevertheless know that the man referred to by the speaker is kind to her. It seems to me that we shall, on the one hand, want to hold that the speaker said something true, but be reluctant to express this by "It is true that her husband is kind to her."

This shows, I think, a difficulty in speaking simply about "the statement" when definite descriptions are used referentially. For the speaker stated something, in this example, about a particular person, and his statement, we may suppose, was true. Nevertheless, we should not like to agree with his statement by using the sentence he used; we should not like to identify the true statement via the speaker's words. The reason for this is not so hard to find. If we say, in this example, "It is true that her husband is kind to her," *we* are now using the definite description either attributively or referentially. But we should not be subscribing to what the original speaker truly said if we use the description attributively, for it was only in its function as referring to a particular person that the definite description yields the possibility of saying something true (since the lady has no husband). Our reluctance, however, to endorse the original speaker's statement by using the definite description referentially to refer to the same person stems from quite a different consideration. For if we too were laboring under the mistaken belief that this man was the lady's husband, we could agree with the original speaker using his exact words. (Moreover, it is possible, as we have seen, deliberately to use a definite description to refer to someone we believe not to fit the description.) Hence, our reluctance to use the original speaker's words does not arise from the fact that if we did we should not succeed in stating anything true or false. It rather stems from the fact that when a definite description is used referentially there is a presumption that the speaker believes that what he refers to fits the description. Since we, who know the lady to be a spinster, would not normally want to give the impression that we believe otherwise, we would not like to use the original speaker's way of referring to the man in question.

How then would we express agreement with the original speaker without involving ourselves in unwanted impressions about our beliefs? The answer shows another difference between the referential and attributive uses of definite descriptions and brings out an important point about genuine referring.

When a speaker says, "The ϕ is ψ," where "the ϕ" is used attributively, if there is no ϕ, we cannot correctly report the speaker as having said *of* this or that person or thing that it is ψ. But if the definite description is used referentially we can report the speaker as having attributed ψ to something. And *we* may refer to what the speaker referred to, using whatever description or name suits our purpose. Thus, if a speaker says, "Her husband is kind to her," referring to the man he was just talking to, and if that man is Jones, we may report him as having said *of Jones* that he is kind to her. If Jones is also the president of the college, we may report the speaker as having said *of the president of the college* that he is kind to her. And finally, if we are talking to Jones, we may say, referring to the original speaker, "He said of you that *you* are kind to her." It does not matter here whether or not the woman has a husband or whether, if she does, Jones is her husband. If the original speaker referred to Jones, he said of him that he is kind to her. Thus where the definite description is used referentially, but does not fit what was referred to, we can report what a speaker said and agree with him by using a description or name which does fit. In doing so we need not, it is important to note, choose a description or name which the original speaker would agree fits what he was referring to. That is, we can report the speaker in the above case to have said truly of Jones that he is kind to her even if the original speaker did not know that the man he was referring to is named Jones or even if he thinks he is not named Jones.

Returning to what Linsky said in the passage quoted, he claimed that, were someone to say "Her husband is kind to her," when she has no husband, *the statement* would be neither true nor false. As I have said, this is a likely view to hold if the definite description is being used attributively. But if it is being used referentially it is not clear what is meant by "the statement." If we think about what the speaker said about the person he referred to, then there is no reason to suppose he has not said something true or false about him, even though he is not the lady's husband. And Linsky's claim would be wrong. On the other hand, if we do not identify the statement in this way, what is the statement that the speaker made? To say that the statement he made was that her husband is kind to her lands us in difficulties. For we have to decide whether in using the definite description here in the identification of the statement, we are using it attributively or referentially. If the former, then we misrepresent the linguistic performance of the speaker; if the latter, then we are ourselves referring to someone and reporting the speaker to have said something of that person, in which case we are back to the possibility that he did say something true or false of that person.

I am thus drawn to the conclusion that when a speaker uses a definite description referentially he may have stated something true or false even if nothing fits the description, and that there is not a clear sense in which he has made a statement which is neither true nor false.

IX

I want to end by a brief examination a picture of what a genuine referring expression is that one might derive from Russell's views. I want to suggest that this picture is not so far wrong as one might suppose and that strange as this may seem, some of the things we have said about the referential use of definite descriptions are not foreign to this picture.

Genuine proper names, in Russell's sense, would refer to something without ascribing any properties to it. They would, one might say, refer to the thing itself, not simply the thing in so far as it falls under a certain description.[13] Now this would seem to Russell something a definite description could not do, for he assumed that if definite descriptions were capable of referring at all, they would refer to something only in so far as that thing satisfied the description. Not only have we seen this assumption to be false, however, but in the last section we saw something more. We saw that when a definite description is used referentially, a speaker can be reported as having said something *of* something. And in reporting what it was of which he said something we are not restricted to the description he used, or synonyms of it; we may ourselves refer to it using any descriptions, names, and so forth, that will do the job. Now this seems to give a sense in which we are concerned with the thing itself and not just the thing under a certain description, when we report the linguistic act of a speaker using a definite description referentially. That is, such a definite description comes closer to performing the function of Russell's proper names than certainly he supposed.

Secondly, Russell thought, I believe, that whenever we use descriptions, as opposed to proper names, we introduce an element of generality which ought to be absent if what we are doing is referring to some particular thing. This is clear from his analysis of sentences containing definite descriptions. One of the conclusions we are supposed to draw from that analysis is that such sentences express what are in reality completely general propositions: there is a ϕ and only one such and any ϕ is ψ. We might put this in a slightly different way. If there is anything which might be identified as reference here, it is reference in a very weak sense—namely, reference to *whatever* is the one and only one φ, if there is any such. Now this is something we might well say about the attributive use of definite descriptions, as should be evident from the previous discussion. But this lack of particularity is absent from the referential use of definite descriptions precisely because the description is here merely a device for getting one's audience to pick out or think of the thing to be spoken about, a device which may serve its function even if the description is incorrect. More importantly perhaps, in the referential use as opposed to the attributive, there is a *right* thing to be picked out by the audience and its being the right thing is not simply a function of its fitting the description.

ACKNOWLEDGMENTS

I should like to thank my colleagues, John Canfield, Sydney Shoemaker, and Timothy Smiley, who read an earlier draft and gave me helpful suggestions. I also had the benefit of the valuable and detailed comments of the referee for the paper, to whom I wish to express my gratitude.

NOTES

1. "On Denoting," reprinted in *Logic and Knowledge*, ed. Robert C. Marsh (London: 1956), p. 51.
2. "On Referring," reprinted in *Philsophy and Ordinary Language*, ed. Charles C. Caton (Urbana: 1963), pp. 162–163.
3. *Ibid.*, p. 162.
4. *Ibid.*, p. 170.
5. Here and elsewhere I use the disjunction "presuppose or imply" to avoid taking a stand that would side me with Russell or Strawson on the issue of what the relationship involved is. To take a stand here would be beside my main point as well as being misleading, since later on I shall argue that the presupposition or implication arises in a different way depending upon the use to which the definite description is put. This last also accounts for my use of the vagueness indicator, "in some sense."
6. In a footnote added to the original version of "On Referring" (*op. cit.*, p. 181) Strawson seems to imply that where the presupposition is false, we still succeed in referring in a "secondary" way, which seems to mean "as we could be said to refer to fictional or make-believe things." But his view is still that we cannot refer in such a case in the "primary" way. This is, I believe, wrong. For a discussion of this modification of Strawson's view see Charles E. Caton, "Strawson on Referring," *Mind*, LXVIII (1959), 539–544.
7. This is an adaptation of an example (used for a somewhat different purpose) given by Leonard Linsky in "Reference and Referents," in *Philosophy and Ordinary Language*, p. 80.
8. In "Reference and Referents" (pp. 74–75, 80). Linsky correctly points out that one does not fail to refer simply because the description used does not in fact fit anything (or fits more than one thing). Thus he pinpoints one of the difficulties in Strawson's view. Here, however, I use this fact about referring to make a distinction I believe he does not draw, between two uses of definite descriptions. I later discuss the second passage from Linsky's paper.
9. In "A Reply to Mr. Sellars," *Philosophical Review*, LXIII (1954), 216–121, Strawson admits that we do not always refuse to ascribe truth to what a person says when the definite description he uses fails to fit anything (or fits more than one thing). To cite one of his examples,

a person who said, "The United States Chamber of Deputies contains representatives of two major parties," would be allowed to have said something true even though he had used the wrong title. Strawson thinks this does not constitute a genuine problem for his view. He thinks that what we do in such cases, "where the speaker's intended reference is pretty clear, is simply to amend his statement in accordance with his guessed intentions and assess the amended statement for truth or falsity; we are not awarding a truth value at all to the original statement" (p. 230).

The notion of an "amended statement," however, will not do. We may note, first of all, that the sort of case Strawson has in mind could arise only when a definite description is used referentially. For the "amendment" is made by seeing the speaker's intended reference. But this could happen only if the speaker had an intended reference, a particular person or thing in mind, independent of the description he used. The cases Strawson has in mind are presumably not cases of slips of the tongue or the like; presumably they are cases in which a definite description is used because the speaker believes, though he is mistaken, that he is describing correctly what he wants to refer to. We supposedly amend the statement by knowing to what he intends to refer. But what description is to be used in the amended statement? In the example, perhaps, we could use "the United States Congress." But this description might be one the speaker would not even accept as correctly describing what he wants to refer to, because he is misinformed about the correct title. Hence, this is not a case of deciding what the speaker meant to say as opposed to what he in fact said, for the speaker did not mean to say "the United States Congress." If this is so, then there is no bar to the "amended" statement containing any description that does correctly pick out what the speaker intended to refer to. It could be, e.g., "The lower house of the United States Congress." But this means that there is no one unique "amended" statement to be assessed for truth value. And, in fact, it should now be clear that the notion of the amended statement really plays no role anyway. For if we can arrive at the amended statement only by first knowing to what the speaker intended to refer, we can assess the truth of what he said simply by deciding whether what he intended to refer to has the properties he ascribed to it.

10. As noted earlier (note 6), Strawson may allow that one has possibly referred in a "secondary" way, but, if I am right, the fact that there is no φ does not preclude one from having referred in the same way one does if there is a φ.

11. For a further discussion of the notion of saying something true of someone or something, see section VIII.

12. "Reference and Referents," p. 80. It should be clear that I agree with Linsky in holding that a speaker may refer even though the "presupposition of existence" is not satisfied. And I agree in thinking this an objection to Strawson's view. I think, however, that this point, among others, can be used to define two distinct uses of definite descriptions which, in turn, yields a more general criticism of Strawson. So, while I develop here a point of difference, which grows out of the distinction I want to make, I find myself in agreement with much of Linsky's article.

13. "The Philosophy of Logical Atomism," reprinted in Logic and Knowledge, p. 200.

SAUL KRIPKE

SPEAKER'S REFERENCE AND SEMANTIC REFERENCE[1]

I am going to discuss some issues inspired by a well-known paper of Keith Donnellan, "Reference and Definite Descriptions,"[2] but the interest—to me—of the contrast mentioned in my title goes beyond Donnellan's paper: I think it is of considerable constructive as well as critical importance to the philosophy of language. These applications, however, and even everything I might want to say relative to Donnellan's paper, cannot be discussed in full here because of problems of length.

Moreover, although I have a considerable interest in the substantive issues raised by Donnellan's paper, and by related literature, my own conclusions will be methodological, not substantive. I can put the matter this way: Donnellan's paper claims to give decisive objections both to Russell's theory of definite descriptions (taken as a theory about English) and to Strawson's. My concern is *not* primarily with the question: is Donnellan right, or is Russell (or Strawson)? Rather, it is with the question: do the considerations *in Donnellan's paper* refute Russell's theory (or Strawson's)? For definiteness, I will concentrate on Donnellan versus Russell, leaving Strawson aside. And about this issue I will draw a definite conclusion, one which I think will illuminate a few methodological maxims about language. Namely, I will conclude that the considerations in Donnellan's paper, *by themselves*, do *not* refute Russell's theory.

Any conclusions about Russell's views *per se*, or Donnellan's, must be tentative. If I were to be asked for a tentative stab about Russell, I would say that although his theory does a far better job of handling ordinary discourse than many have thought, and although many popular arguments against it are inconclusive, probably it ultimately fails. The considerations I have in mind have to do with the existence of "improper" definite descriptions, such as "the table," where uniquely specifying conditions are not contained in the description itself. Contrary to the Russellian picture, I doubt that such descriptions can always be regarded as elliptical with some uniquely specifying conditions added. And it may even be the case that a true picture will resemble various aspects of Donnellan's in important respects. But such questions will largely be left aside here.

I will state my preference for one substantive conclusion (although I do not feel completely confident of it either): that unitary theories, like Russell's, are preferable to theories that postulate an ambiguity. And much, though not all, of Donnellan's paper seems to postulate a (semantic) ambiguity between his "referential" and "attributive" uses. But—as we shall see—Donnellan is not entirely consistent on this point, and I therefore am not sure whether I am expressing disagreement with him even here.[3]

1. PRELIMINARY CONSIDERATIONS

Donnellan claims that a certain linguistic phenomenon argues against Russell's theory. According to Russell, if someone says, "The x such that $\phi(x)$ ψ's," he means that there is an x which uniquely satisfies "$\phi(x)$" and that any such x satisfies "$(\psi(x)$." [I.e., $(\exists x)$ $(\phi!(x) \wedge \psi(x))$, where "$\phi!(x)$" abbreviates "$\phi(x) \wedge (y)(\phi(y) \supset y = x$"]. Donnellan argues that some phenomenon of the following kind tells against Russell: Suppose someone at a gathering, glancing in a certain direction, says to his companion.

(1) "The man over there drinking champagne is happy tonight."

Suppose both the speaker and hearer are under a false impression, and that the man to whom they refer is a teetotaler, drinking sparkling water. He may, nevertheless, be happy. Now, if there is no champagne drinker over there, Russell would regard (1) as false, and Frege and Strawson would give it a truth-value gap. Nevertheless, as Donnellan emphasizes, we have a substantial intuition that the speaker said something true of the man to whom he referred in spite of his misimpression.

Since no one is really drinking champagne, the case involves a definite description that is empty, or vacuous, according to both Russell and Frege. So as to avoid any unnecessary and irrelevant entanglements of the present question with the issues that arise when definite descriptions are vacuous, I shall modify this case (and all other cases where, in Donnellan's paper, the description was vacuous).[4] Suppose that "over there," exactly one man *is* drinking champagne, although his glass is not visible to the speaker (nor to his hearer). Suppose that he, unlike the teetotaler to whom the speaker refers, has been driven to drink precisely by his misery. Then *all* the classical theories (both Russellian and Fregean) would regard (1) as false (since exactly one man over there is drinking champagne, and he is *not* happy tonight). Now the speaker has spoken *truly* of the man to whom he refers (the teetotaler), yet this dimension is left out in all the classical analyses, which would assign falsehood to his assertion solely on the basis of the misery of *someone else* whom *no one* was talking about (the champagne drinker). Previously Linsky had given a similar example. He gave it as an empty case; once again I modify it to make the description nonvacuous. Someone sees a woman with a man. Taking the man to be her husband, and observing his attitude towards her, he says, "Her husband is kind to her," and someone else may nod, "Yes, he seems to be." Suppose the man in question is not her husband. Suppose he is her lover, to whom she has been driven precisely by her husband's cruelty. Once again both the Russellian analysis and the Fregean analysis would assess the statement as false, and both would do so on the basis of the cruelty of a man neither participant in the dialogues was talking about.

Again, an example suggested to me by a remark of L. Crocker: suppose a religious narrative (similar, say, to the Gospels) consistently refers to its main protagonist as "The Messiah." Suppose a historian wishes to assess the work for *historical accuracy*—that is, he wishes to determine whether it gives an accurate account of the life of its hero (whose identity we assume to be established). Does it matter to this question whether the hero really was the Messiah, as long as the author took him to be so, and addressed his work to a religious community that shared this belief? Surely not. And note that it is no mere "principle of charity" that is operating here. On the contrary, if someone other than the person intended were really the Messiah, and if, by a bizarre and unintended coincidence, the narrative gave a fairly true account of *his* life, we would not for that reason call it "historically true." On the contrary, we would regard the work as historically *false* if the events mentioned were false of its intended protagonist. Whether the story happened to fit the true Messiah—who may have been totally unknown to the author and even have lived after the time the work was composed—would be irrelevant. Once again, this fact seems inconsistent with the positions both of Frege and of Russell.

On the basis of such examples, Donnellan distinguishes two uses of definite descriptions. In the "attributive" use, a speaker "states something about whoever or whatever is the so-and-so." In the "referential" use, a speaker "uses the description to enable his audience to pick out whom or what he is talking about and states something about that person or thing. In the first [attributive] case, the definite description might be said to occur essentially, for the speaker wishes to assert something about whatever or whoever fits that description; but in the referential use the definite description is merely one tool for . . . calling attention to a person or thing . . . and . . . any other device for doing the same job, another description or name, would do as well."[5] For example, suppose I come upon Smith foully murdered. The condition of Smith's body moves me to say, "Smith's murderer is (must be) insane." Then we have an *attributive* use: we speak of the murderer, whoever he may be. On the other hand, suppose that Jones is on trial for Smith's murder and that I am among the spectators in the courtroom. Observing the wild behavior of the defendant at the dock, I may say, "Smith's murderer is insane." (I forgot the defendant's name, but am firmly convinced of his guilt.) Then my use is referential: whether or not Jones was the real murderer, and even if someone else was, if Jones accused me of libel, his failure to fit my description would give me no defense. All of the previous cases, (the teetotaling "champagne" drinker, the lover taken for a husband, the false Messiah), are all referential in Donnellan's sense.

An intuitive mark of the attributive use is the legitimacy of the parenthetical comment, "whoever he is." In the first case, we may say "Smith's murderer, whoever he is, is insane," but not in the second. But we should not be misled: a definite description may be used attributively even if the speaker believes that a certain person, say, Jones, fits it, provided that he is talking about *whoever* fits, and his belief that Jones in fact fits is not relevant. In the case where I deduce the murderer's insanity from the condition of Smith's body, I use the description attributively even if I suspect, or even am firmly convinced, that Jones is the culprit.

I have no doubt that the distinction Donnellan brings out exists and is of fundamental importance, though I do not regard it as exclusive or exhaustive. But Donnellan also believes that Russell's theory applies, if at all, only to attributive uses, and that referential uses of definite descriptions are close to proper names, even to Russell's "logically proper" names. And he appears to believe that the examples of the referential uses mentioned above are inexplicable on Russell's theory. It is these views that I wish to examine.

2. SOME ALLEGED APPLICATIONS OF THE DISTINCTION

Some alleged applications of Donnellan's distinction have entered the oral tradition, and even to an extent, the written tradition, that are not in Donnellan's paper. I will mention some that I find questionable. Unfortunately I will have to discuss these applications more briefly than the issues in question really deserve, since they are ancillary to the main theme.

2a. De Dicto–De Re

Many able people, in and out of print, have implied that Donnellan's distinction has something to do with, can be identified with, or can replace, the *de dicto–de re* distinction, or the small scope–large scope distinction in modal or intensional contexts.

"The number of planets is necessarily odd" can mean two things, depending on whether it is interpreted *de dicto* or *de re*. If it is interpreted *de dicto*, it asserts that the proposition that the number of planets is odd is a necessary truth—something I take to be false (there might have been eight planets). If it is interpreted *de re*, it asserts that the actual number of planets (nine) has the property of necessary oddness (essentialists like me take this to be true). Similarly, if we say, "Jones believes that the richest debutante in Dubuque will marry him," we may mean that Jones's belief has a certain content, viz., that the richest debutante in Dubuque will marry him; or we may mean that he believes, *of* a girl who is (in fact) the richest in Dubuque, that she will marry him. The view in question suggests that the *de dicto* case is to be identified with Donnellan's *attributive* use, the *de re* with the *referential*.

Any such assimilation, in my opinion, is confused. (I don't think Donnellan makes it.) There are many objections; I will mention a few. First, the *de dicto* use of the definite description cannot be identified with either the *referential* or the *attributive* use. Here the basic point was already noticed by Frege. If a description is embedded in a (*de dicto*) intensional context, we cannot be said to be talking *about* the thing described, either *qua* its satisfaction of the description or *qua* anything else. Taken *de dicto*, "Jones believes that the richest debutante in Dubuque will marry him," can be asserted by someone who thinks (let us suppose, wrongly) that there are *no* debutantes in Dubuque; certainly then, he is in no way talking about the richest debutante, even "attributively." Similarly, "It is possible that (France should have a monarchy in 1976, and that) the King of France in 1976 should have been bald" is true, if read *de dicto*; yet we are not using "the King of France in 1976" attributively to speak of the King of France in 1976, for there is none. Frege concluded that "the King of France in 1976" refers, in these contexts, to its ordinary sense; at any rate, if we wish to speak of "reference" here, it cannot be to the nonexistent king. Even if there were such a king, the quoted assertion would say nothing about *him*, if read *de dicto*: to say that *he* might have been bald, would be *de re* (indeed, this *is* the distinction in question).

Second, and even more relevantly, Donnellan's referential use cannot be identified with the *de re* use. (I think Donnellan would agree.) Suppose I have no idea how many planets there are, but (for some reason) astronomical theory dictates that that number must be odd. If I say, "The number of planets (whatever it may be) is odd," my description is used attributively. If I am an essentialist, I will also say, "The number of planets (whatever it may be) is necessarily odd," on the grounds that all odd numbers are necessarily odd; and my usage is just as attributive as in the first case. In "Smith's murderer, whoever he may be, is known to the police, but they're not saying," or, more explicitly, "The police know concerning Smith's murderer, whoever he is, that he committed the murder; but they're not saying who he is," "Smith's murderer" is used attributively, but is *de re*.

Finally: Russell wished to handle the *de dicto–de re* distinction by his notion of the *scope* of a description. Some have suggested that Donnellan's referential–attributive distinction can replace Russell's distinction of scope. But *no* twofold distinction can do this job. Consider:

(2) The number of planets might have been necessarily even.

In a natural use, (2) can be interpreted as true; for example, there might have been exactly eight planets, in which case the number of planets would have been even, and hence necessarily even. (2), interpreted as true, is neither *de re* nor *de dicto*; that is, the definite description neither has the largest nor the smallest possible scope. Consider:

(2a) $\Diamond \Box (\exists x)$ (There are exactly x planets and x is even).

(2b) $(\exists x)$ (There are exactly x planets and $\Diamond \Box (x$ is even)).

(2c) $\Diamond (\exists x)$ (There are exactly x planets and $\Box (x$ is even)).

(2a)–(2c) give three alternative Russellian analyses of (2). (2a) gives the description the smallest possible scope (*de dicto*); it says, presumably falsely, that it might have been necessary that there was an even number of planets. (2b) gives the description the largest possible scope (*de re*); it says, still falsely, of the actual number of planets (viz., nine) that it might have been necessarily even. (2c) is the interpretation which makes (2) true. When intensional operators are iterated, intermediate scopes are possible. Three analogous interpretations are possible, say, for "Jones doubts that Holmes believes that Smith's murderer is insane"; or (using an indefinite description) for "Hoover charged that the Berrigans plotted to kidnap a high American official." (I actually read something like this last in a newspaper and wondered what was meant.[6] This may mean: (a) there is a particular high official such that Hoover charged that the Berrigans plotted to kidnap him (largest scope, *de re*, this was the interpretation intended); or (b) Hoover charged that the Berrigans plotted as follows: let's kidnap a high official (smallest scope, *de dicto*); or (c) Hoover charged that there was a high official (whose identity may have been unknown to Hoover) whom the Berrigans planned to kidnap (intermediate scope).

As intensional (or other) constructions are iterated, there are more and more possible scopes for a definite description. No *twofold* distinction can replace Russell's notion of scope.[7] In particular, neither the *de dicto–de re* distinction nor the referential–attributive distinction can do so.

2b. Rigid Definite Descriptions

If definite descriptions, $\iota x \phi(x)$, are taken as primitive and assigned reference, then the conventional nonrigid assignment assigns to such a description, with respect to each possible world, the unique object, if any, which would have ϕ'd in that world. (Forget the vacuous case, which requires a further convention.) For example, "the number of planets" denotes eight, speaking of a counterfactual situation where there would have been eight planets (and "the number of planets is even" is true of such a situation).

Another type of definite description, $\iota x \phi x$, a "rigid" definite description, could be introduced semantically by the following stipulation: let $\iota x \phi x$ denote, with respect to all possible worlds, the unique object that (actually) ϕ's (then "the number of planets is odd," as interpreted, expresses a necessary truth). Both kinds of definite descriptions can obviously be introduced, theoretically, into a single formal language, perhaps by the notations just given. Some have suggested that definite descriptions, in English, are *ambiguous* between the two readings. It has further been suggested that the two types of definite descriptions, the nonrigid and the rigid, are the source of the *de dicto–de re* distinction and should replace Russell's notion of scope for the purpose. Further, it has been suggested that they amount to the same thing as Donnellan's attributive–referential distinction.[8]

My comments will be brief, so as to avoid too much excursus. Although I have an open mind on the subject, I am not yet convinced that there is any clear evidence for such an ambiguity. Being a twofold distinction, the ambiguity alleged cannot replace Russell's notion of scope, for the reasons given above. Once Russell's notion is available, it can be used to handle the *de dicto–de re* distinction; a further ambiguity seems unnecessary. More relevant to the present context, the "rigid" sense of a definite description, if it exists, cannot be identified with Donnellan's "referential" use. I take it that the identification of the referential use with the rigid definite description was inspired by some line of reasoning like this: Donnellan holds that referential descriptions are those close to proper names, even to Russell's "logically proper names." But surely proper names, or at least, Russellian "logically proper names," are rigid. Hence Donnellan's referential descriptions are just the rigid definite descriptions.

If we assume that Donnellan thinks of names as rigid, as I think of them, his referential definite descriptions *would* most plausibly be taken to refer rigidly to their referents. But it is not clear that he does agree with me on the rigidity of such reference.[9] More important, a rigid definite description, as defined above, still determines its referent via its unique satisfaction of the associated property—and this fact separates the notion of such a description from that of a referential description, as Donnellan defines it. David Kaplan has suggested that a demonstrative "that" can be used, in English, to make any definite description rigid. "That bastard—the man who killed Smith, whoever he may be—is surely insane!" The subject term rigidly designates Smith's murderer, but it is still attributive in Donnellan's sense.[10]

2c. Referential Descriptions

In "Naming and Necessity,"[11] one argument I presented against the description (or cluster-of-descriptions) theory of proper names concerned cases where the referent of a name, the person named by the name, did not satisfy the descriptions usually associated with it, and someone else did. For example, the name "Gödel" might be taken to mean "the man who proved the incompleteness of arithmetic"; but even if Gödel had been a fraud, who had proved nothing at all and had misappropriated his work from an unknown named "Schmidt," our term "Gödel" would refer to the fraud, not to the man who really satisfied the definite description. Against this it has been said that although the argument does succeed in its main purpose of refuting the description theory as a theory of reference (that is, it shows that the descriptive properties cited do not determine the referent), it does nothing to show that names are not abbreviated definite descriptions, because we could take the descriptions in question to be referential in Donnellan's sense. Referential descriptions can easily refer to things that fail to satisfy the descriptions; nothing in my argument shows that names are not synonymous with such descriptions.[12]

My reaction to such an argument may become clearer later. For the moment, (too) briefly: In the case of "Her husband is kind to her," and similar cases, "her husband" can refer to her lover, as long as we are under the misapprehension that the man to whom we refer (the lover) *is* her husband. Once we are apprised of the true facts, we will no longer so refer to him. Similarly, someone can use "the man who proved the incompleteness of arithmetic," as a referential definite description, to refer to Gödel; it might be so used, for example, by someone who had forgotten his name. If the hypothetical fraud were discovered, however, the description is no longer usable as a device to refer to Gödel; henceforth it can be used only to refer to Schmidt. We would withdraw any previous assertions using the description to refer to Gödel (unless they also were true of Schmidt). We would *not* similarly withdraw the *name* "Gödel," even after the fraud was discovered; "Gödel" would still be used to name Gödel, not Schmidt. The name and the description, therefore, are not synonymous. (See also note 27 below.)

3. THE MAIN PROBLEM

3a. A Disagreement with Russell?

Do Donnellan's observations provide an argument against Russell's theory? Do his *views* contradict Russell's? One might think that if Donnellan is right, Russell must be wrong, since Donnellan's truth conditions for statements containing referential definite descriptions differ from Russell's. Unfortunately, this is not so clear. Consider the case of "Her husband is kind to her," mistakenly said of the lover. If Donnellan had roundly asserted that the quoted statement is true if and only if the *lover* is kind to her, regardless of the kindness of the husband, the issue between him and Russell would be clearly joined. But Donnellan doesn't say this: rather he says that the speaker has referred to a certain person, the lover, and said of *him* that he is kind to her. But if we ask, "Yes, but was the statement he made true?", Donnellan would hedge. For if *we* are not under the misimpression that the man the speaker referred to was her husband, *we* would not express the same assertion by "Her husband is kind to her." "If it ['her husband'] is being used referentially, it is not clear what is meant by 'the statement.' . . . To say that the statement he made was that her husband is kind to her lands us in difficulties. For we [in so reporting what the speaker said must use the definite description] either attributively or referentially. If the former, then we misrepresent the linguistic performance of the speaker; if the latter, then we ourselves are referring to someone," and ordinarily we can refer to someone as "her husband" only if we take him to be her husband.[13]

Since Donnellan does not clearly assert that the statement "her husband is kind to her" ever has non-Russelian truth conditions, he has *not*, so far, clearly contradicted Russell's theory. His argument, as he presents it, that there is a problem in reporting "the statement" is questionable, in two ways.

First, it uses the premise that if we say, "Jones said that her husband is kind to her," we ourselves must use the description attributively or referentially; but, as we saw, a definite description in indirect discourse is *neither* referential nor attributive.[14]

Second, there is an important problem about the nature of the referential–attributive distinction. Donnellan says that his distinction is neither syntactic nor semantic:

The grammatical structure of the sentence seems to me to be the same whether the description is used referentially or attributively: that is, it is not syntactically ambiguous. Nor does it seem at all attractive to suppose an ambiguity in the meaning of the words; it does not appear to be semantically ambiguous. (Perhaps we could say that the sentence is pragmatically ambiguous: the distinction between roles that the description plays is a function of the speaker's intentions.) These, of course, are intuitions; I do not have an argument for these conclusions. Nevertheless, the burden of proof is surely on the other side.[15]

Suppose for the moment that this is so. Then if the referential–attributive distinction is pragmatic, rather than syntactic or semantic, it is presumably a distinction about speech acts. There is no reason to suppose that in making an indirect discourse report on what someone else has said I myself must have similar intentions, or be engaged in the same kind of speech act; in fact, it is clear that I am not. If I say "Jones said the police were around the corner," Jones may have said it as a warning, but *I* need not say it as a warning. If the referential–attributive distinction is neither syntactic nor semantic, there is no reason, without further argument, to suppose that my usage, in indirect discourse, should match the man on whom I report, as referential or attributive. The case is quite different for a genuine semantic ambiguity. If Jones says, "I have never been at a bank," and I report this, saying, "Jones denied that he was ever at a bank," the sense I give to "bank" must match Jones's if my report is to be accurate.

Indeed, the passage seems inconsistent with the whole trend of Donnellan's paper. Donnellan suggests that there is no syntactic or semantic ambiguity in the statement, "Her husband is kind to her." He also suggests that Russell may well give a correct analysis of the attributive use but not of the referential use. Surely this is not coherent. It is not "uses," in some pragmatic sense, but *senses* of a sentence which can be analyzed. If the sentence is *not* (syntactically or) semantically ambiguous, it has only *one* analysis; to say that it has two distinct analyses is to attribute a syntactic or semantic ambiguity to it.

Donnellan's arguments for his refusal to give a truth value to the speaker's assertion, "Her husband is kind to her," seem to be fallacious. My own suggested account of the matter below—in terms of a theory of speech acts—creates no problem about "the statement"; it is simply the statement that her husband is kind to her. But Donnellan's cautious refusal to say, under the circumstances mentioned, that "Her husband is kind to her" is true, seems nevertheless to be intuitively correct. The man to whom the speaker refers is—let us suppose—kind to her. But it seems hard for us to say that when he uttered, "Her husband is kind to her," it expressed a truth, if *we* believe that her husband is unkind to her.

Now Donnellan thinks that he has refuted Russell. But all he has clearly claimed, let alone established, is that a speaker can refer to the lover and say, of him, that he is kind to her by saying "Her husband is kind to her." So, first, we can ask: *If* this claim is correct, does it conflict with Russell's views?

Second, since Donnellan's denial that he advocates a semantic ambiguity in definite descriptions seems inconsistent with much of his paper, we can try ignoring the denial, and take his paper to be arguing for such an ambiguity. Then we may ask: has Donnellan established a (semantic) ambiguity inconsistent with Russell's theory?

3b. General Remarks: Apparatus

We need a general apparatus to discuss these questions. Some of the apparatus is well known, but I review it for its intrinsic importance and interest. First, let us distinguish, following Grice,[16] between what *the speaker's words meant*, on a given occasion, and what *he meant*, in saying these words, on that occasion. For example, one burglar says to another, "The cops are around the corner." What *the words meant* is clear: the police were around the corner. But *the speaker may well have meant*, "We can't wait around collecting any more loot: Let's split!" That is not *the meaning of the words*, even on that occasion, though that is *what he meant in saying those words, on that occasion.* Suppose he had said, "The cops are inside the bank." Then on that occasion, "bank" meant a commercial bank, not a river bank, and this is relevant to what the *words* meant, on that occasion. (On other occasions, the same words might mean that the police were at a river bank.) But, if the speaker *meant* "Let's split," this is no part of the *meaning of his words*, even on that occasion.

Again (inspired by an example of Grice)[17] A magician makes a handkerchief change color. Someone says, recalling the trick, "Then he put the red handkerchief on the side of the table"; and someone else interjects, cautiously, "It *looked* red." The words meant, on that occasion, that the object referred to (the handkerchief) looked red. What we speak of when we speak of the meaning of his words, on that occasion, includes a disambiguation of the utterance. (Perhaps, on some occasions, where "it" refers to a book, a phonetically identical utterance might mean, "It looked read," well-thumbed and well-perused). But the speaker meant, on this occasion, to suggest that perhaps the handkerchief wasn't really red, that perhaps the trick relied on some kind of illusion. (Note that, on this occasion, not only do the *words* "it looked red" mean what they mean, but also the *speaker* means that it looked red, as well as that it may not have been red. On the other hand, the speaker has no intention of producing a belief in the hearer that the handkerchief looked red, or a belief in the hearer that he (the speaker) believed it looked red. Both facts are common knowledge. The same *could* hold for "The cops are around the corner."[18] Do these examples contradict Grice's analysis of "meaning"? Grice's theory has become very complex and I am not quite sure.)

The notion of what words can mean, in the language, is semantical: it is given by the conventions of our language. What they mean, on a given occasion, is determined, on a given occasion, by these conventions, together with the intentions of the speaker and various contextual features. Finally what the speaker meant, on a given occasion, in saying certain words, derives from various further special intentions of the speaker, together with various general principles, applicable to all human languages regardless of their special conventions. (Cf. Grice's "conversational maxims.") For example, "It looks red" replaced a categorical affirmation of redness. A plausible general principle of human discourse would have it that if a second speaker insists that a stronger assertion should be replaced by a weaker one, he thereby wishes to cast doubt on the stronger assertion; whence, knowing the semantics of English, and the meaning of the speaker's words on this occasion, we can deduce what was meant (the Gricean "conversational implicature").[19]

Let us now speak of speaker's reference and semantic reference: these notions are special cases of the Gricean notions discussed above. If a speaker has a designator in his idiolect, certain conventions of his idiolect[20] (given various facts about the world) determine the referent in the idiolect: that I call the *semantic referent* of the designator. (If the designator is ambiguous, or contains indexicals, demonstratives, or the like, we must speak of the semantic referent on a given occasion. The referent will be determined by the conventions of the language plus the speaker's intentions and various contextual features.)

Speaker's reference is a more difficult notion. Consider, for example, the following case, which I have mentioned elsewhere.[21] Two people see Smith in the distance and mistake him for Jones. They have a brief colloquy: "What is Jones doing?" "Raking the leaves." "Jones," in the common language of both, is a name of Jones; it *never* names Smith. Yet, in some sense, on this occasion, clearly both participants in the dialogue have referred to Smith, and the second participant has said something true about the man he referred to if and only if Smith was raking the leaves (whether or not Jones was). How can we account for this? Suppose a speaker takes it that a certain object a fulfills the conditions for being the semantic referent of a designator, "d." Then, wishing to say something about a, he uses "d" to speak about a; say, he says "$\phi(d)$." Then, he said, of a, on that occasion, that it ϕ'd; in the appropriate Gricean sense (explicated above), he *meant* that $a\phi$'d. This is true even if a is not really the semantic referent of "d." If it is not, then *that* a ϕ's is included in what he meant (on that occasion), but not in the meaning of his words (on that occasion).

So, we may tentatively define the speaker's referent of a designator to be that object which the speaker wishes to talk about, on a given occasion, and believes fulfills the conditions for being the semantic referent of the designator. He uses the designator with the intention of making an assertion about the object in question (which may not really be the semantic referent, if the speaker's belief that it fulfills the appropriate semantic conditions is in error). The speaker's referent is the thing the speaker referred to by the designator, though it may not be the referent of the designator, in his idiolect. In the example above, Jones, the man named by the name, is the semantic referent. Smith is the speaker's referent, the correct answer to the question, "To whom were you referring?"[22]

Below, the notion of speaker's reference will be extended to include more cases where existential quantification rather than designation is involved.

In a given idiolect, the semantic referent of a designator (without indexicals) is given by a *general* intention of the speaker to refer to a certain object whenever the designator is used. The speaker's referent is given by a *specific* intention, on a given occasion, to refer to a certain object. If the speaker believes that the object he wants to talk about, on a given occasion, fulfills the conditions for being the semantic referent, then he believes that there is no clash between his general intentions and his specific intentions. My hypothesis is that Donnellan's referential-attributive distinction should be generalized in this light. For the speaker, on a given occasion, may believe that his specific intention coincides with his general intention for one of two reasons. In one case (the "simple" case), his specific intention is simply to refer to the semantic referent: that is, his specific intention *is* simply his general semantic intention. (For examples, he uses "Jones" as a name of Jones—elaborate this according to your favorite theory of proper names—and, on this occasion, simply wishes to use "Jones" to refer to Jones.) Alternatively—the "complex" case—he has a specific intention, which is distinct from his general intention, but which he believes, as a matter of fact, to determine the same object as the one determined by his general intention. (For example, he wishes to refer to the man "over there" but believes that he *is* Jones.) In the "simple" case, the speaker's referent is, *by definition*, the semantic referent. In the "complex" case, they may coincide, if the speaker's belief is correct, but they need not. (The man "over there" may be Smith and not Jones.) To anticipate, my hypothesis will be that Donnellan's "attributive" use is nothing but the "simple" case, specialized to definite descriptions, and that the "referential" use is, similarly, the "complex" case. If such a conjecture is correct, it would be wrong to take Donnellan's "referential" use, as he does, to be a use of a description as if it were a proper name. For the distinction of simple and complex cases will apply to proper names just as much as to definite descriptions.

3c. Donnellan's Argument against Russell:
Methodological and Substantive Considerations

In the light of the notions just developed, consider the argument Donnellan adduces against Russell. Donnellan points to a phenomenon which he alleges to be inexplicable on a Russellian account of English definite descriptions. He accounts for it by positing an ambiguity. Alternatively, we wish to account for the phenomenon on pragmatic grounds, encapsulated in the distinction between speaker's reference and semantic reference. How can we see whether Donnellan's phenomenon conflicts with a Russellian account?

I propose the following test for any alleged counterexample to a linguistic proposal: If someone alleges that a certain linguistic phenomenon in English is a counterexample to a given analysis, consider a hypothetical language which (as much as possible) is like English except that the analysis is *stipulated* to be correct. Imagine such a hypothetical language introduced into a community and spoken by it. *If the phenomenon in question would still arise in a community that spoke such a hypothetical language (which may not be English), then the fact that it arises in English cannot disprove the hypothesis that the analysis is correct for English.* An example removed from the present discussion: Some have alleged that identity cannot be the relation that holds between, and only between, each thing and itself, for if so, the nontriviality of identity statements would be inexplicable. If it is conceded, however, that such a relation makes sense, and if it can be shown that a hypothetical language involving such a relation would generate the same problems, it will follow that the existence of these problems does not refute the hypothesis that "identical to" stands for this same relation in English.[23]

By "the weak Russell language," I will mean a language similar to English except that the truth conditions of sentences with definite descriptions are *stipulated* to coincide with Russell's: for example, "The present King of France is bald" is to be true iff exactly one person is King of France, and that person is bald. On the weak Russell language, this effect can be achieved by assigning semantic reference to definite descriptions: the semantic referent of a definite description is the unique object that satisfies the description, if any; otherwise there is no semantic referent. A sentence of the simple subject-predicate form will be true if the predicate is true of the (semantic) referent of its subject; false, if either the subject has no semantic referent or the predicate is not true of the semantic referent of the subject.

Since the weak Russell language takes definite descriptions to be primitive designators, it is not fully Russellian. By "the intermediate Russell language," I mean a language in which sentences containing definite descriptions are taken to be abbreviations or paraphrases of their Russellian analyses: for example, "The present King of France is bald" *means* (or has a "deep structure" like) "Exactly one person is at present King of France, and he is bald," or the like. Descriptions are not terms, and are not assigned reference or meaning in isolation. The "strong Russell language" goes further: definite descriptions are actually *banned* from the language and Russellian paraphrases are used in their place. Instead of saying "Her husband is kind to her," a speaker of this language must say "Exactly one man is married to her, and he is kind to her," or even (better), "There is a unique man who is married to her, and every man who is married to her is kind to her," or the like. If Russell is right, long-windedness is the only defect of these versions.

Would the phenomenon Donnellan adduces arise in communities that spoke these languages? Surely speakers of these languages are no more infallible than we. They too will find themselves at a party and mistakenly think someone is drinking champagne even though he is actually drinking sparkling water. If they are speakers of the weak or intermediate Russell languages, they will say, "The man in the corner drinking champagne is happy tonight." They will say this precisely because *they think, though erroneously, that the Russellian truth conditions are satisfied*. Wouldn't we say of these speakers that they are referring to the teetotaler, under the misimpression that he is drinking champagne? And, if he is happy, are they not saying of him, *truly*, that he is happy? Both answers seem obviously affirmative.

In the case of the weak Russell language, the general apparatus previously developed seems fully adequate to account for the phenomenon. The semantic referent of a definite description is given by the conditions laid down above:

it is a matter of the specific conventions of the (weak) Russell language, in this case that the referent is the unique object satisfying the descriptive conditions. The speaker's referent, on the other hand, is determined by a general theory of speech acts, applicable to all languages: it is the object to which the speaker wishes to refer, and which he believes fulfills the Russellian conditions for being the semantic referent. Again, in asserting the sentence he does, the speaker means that the speaker's referent (the teetotaler) satisfied the predicate (is happy). Thus the rough theoretical apparatus above accounts fully for our intuitions about this case.

What about the other Russellian languages? Even in the strong Russell language, where explicit descriptions are outlawed, the same phenomena can occur. In fact, they occur in English in "arch" uses of existential quantification: "Exactly *one person* (or: *some* person or other) is drinking champagne in that corner, and I hear he is romantically linked with Jane Smith." The circumlocution, in English, expresses the delicacy of the topic, but the speaker's reference (in quite an ordinary sense) may well be clear, even if he in fact is drinking sparkling water. In English such circumlocutions are common only when the speaker wishes to achieve a rather arch and prissy effect, but in the strong Russell language (which of course isn't English), they would be made more common because the definite article is prohibited.

This example leads to an extension of the notion of speaker's reference. When a speaker asserts an existential quantification, $(\exists x) (\phi x \wedge \psi x)$, it may be clear which thing he has in mind as satisfying "ϕx," and he may wish to convey to his hearers that that thing satisfies "ψx." In this case, the thing in question (which may or may not actually satisfy "ϕx") is called the "speaker's referent" when he makes the existential assertion. In English, as I have mentioned, such cases ("arch" uses) are rather rare; but they can be carried off even if the existential quantification is expressed in a highly roundabout and apparently nonreferring fashion. "Not *everyone* in this room is abstaining from champagne, and any such nonabstainer. . . ."[24]

If the notion of speaker's reference applies to the strong Russell language, it can apply to the intermediate Russell language as well, since the speaker's referent of "$\psi(\iota x \phi) (x))$" is then the thing he has in mind as uniquely instantiating "$\phi(x)$" and about which he wishes to convey that it ψ's.

Since the phenomenon Donnellan cites *would* arise in all the Russell languages, if they *were* spoken, the fact that they *do* arise in English, as *actually* spoken, can be no argument that English is not a Russell language.

We may contrast the Russell languages with what may be called the D-languages. In the D-languages the apparent ambiguity between referential and attributive definite descriptions is explicitly built into the semantics of the language and affects truth conditions. (The D-languages are meant to suggest "Donnellan," but are not called the "Donnellan languages," since Donnellan, as we have seen, is "ambiguous" as to whether he posits a semantic ambiguity.) The *unambiguous D-languge* contains two distinct words, "the" and "ze" (rhymes with "the"). A statement of the form ". . . the F . . ." is true iff the predicate represented by the dots is true of the unique object fulfilling F (we need not specify what happens if there is no such thing; if we wish to follow Russell, take it to be false). A statement of the form ". . . ze F . . ." is to be true iff the predicate represented by the dots is true of the unique thing the speaker thinks F is true of. (Once again, we leave free what happens if there is no such thing.) *The ambiguous D-language* is like the unambiguous D-language except that "the," ambiguously, can be interpreted according to the semantics either of "the" *or* of "ze." The general impression conveyed by Donnellan's paper, in spite of his statement at one point to the contrary, is that English is the ambiguous D-language; only on such a hypothesis could we say that the "referential use" (really, referential *sense*) diverges from Russell's theory. The truth-conditions of statements containing "ze," and therefore of one sense of "the" in the ambiguous D-language, *are* incompatible with Russell's theory.[25]

We have two hypotheses: one says that English is a Russell language, while the other says that English is the ambiguous D-language. Which hypothesis is preferable? Since, as we have argued, the phenomena Donnellan adduces would arise in a hypothetical society that spoke any of the Russell languages, the existence in English of such phenomena provides no argument against the hypothesis that English is a Russell language. If Donnellan had possessed a clear intuition that "Her husband is kind to her," uttered in reference to the kind lover of a woman married to a cruel husband, expressed the literal truth, then he *would* have adduced a phenomenon that conforms to the ambiguous D-language but is incompatible with any Russell language. But Donnellan makes no such assertion: he cautiously, and correctly, confines himself to the weaker claim that the speaker spoke truly of the man to whom he referred. This weaker claim, we have seen, *would* hold for a speaker of a Russell language.

So Donnellan's examples provide, in themselves, no evidence that English is the ambiguous D-language rather than a Russell language. Granting that this is so, we can ask whether there is any reason to favor the Russell language hypothesis over the D-language hypothesis. I think there are several general methodological considerations that are relevant.

The Russell language theory, or any other unitary account (that is, any account that postulates no semantic ambiguity), accounts for Donnellan's referential–attributive phenomenon by a general pragmatic theory of speech acts, applicable to a very wide range of language; the D-language hypothesis accounts for these same phenomena by positing a semantic ambiguity. The unitary account appeals to a general apparatus that applies to cases, such as the "Smith-Jones" case, where it is completely implausible that a semantic ambiguity exists. According to the unitary account, far from the referential use constituting a special namelike use of definite descriptions, the referential–attributive distinction is simply a special case of a general distinction, applicable to proper names as well as to definite descriptions, and illustrated in practice by the (leaf-raking) Smith-Jones case. And anyone who compares the Smith-Jones case, where presumably no one is tempted to posit a special semantic ambiguity, with Donnellan's cases of definite descriptions, must surely be impressed by the similarity of the phenomena.[26]

Under these circumstances, surely general methodological principles favor the existing account. The apparatus of speaker's reference and semantic reference, and of simple and complex uses of designators, is needed *anyway*, to explain the Smith-Jones case; it is applicable to all languages.[27] Why posit a semantic ambiguity when it is both insufficient in general and superfluous for the special case it seeks to explain?[28] And why are the phenomena regarding proper names so similar to those for definite descriptions, if the one case involves no semantic ambiguity while the other does?

It is very much the lazy man's approach in philosophy to posit ambiguities when in trouble. If we face a putative counterexample to our favorite philosophical thesis, it is always open to us to protest that some key term is being used in a special sense, different from its use in the thesis. We may be right, but the ease of the move should counsel a policy of caution: Do not posit an ambiguity unless you are really forced to, unless there are really compelling theoretical or intuitive grounds to suppose that an ambiguity really is present.

Let me say a bit more in defense of this. Many philosophers, for example, have advocated a "strong" account of knowledge according to which it is very hard to know anything; stiff requirements must be satisfied. When such philosophers have been confronted with intuitive counterexamples to such strong requirements for knowledge they either have condemned them as popular and loose usages or they have asserted that "know" is being used in a different "weak" sense. The latter move—distinguishing two or more "strong" and "weak" senses of "know"—strikes me as implausible. There *are* different senses of "know," distinguished in German as "kennen" and "wissen," and in French as "connaître" and "savoir"; a person is usually known in the one sense, a fact in the other. It is no surprise that other languages use distinct words for these various senses of "know"; there is no reason for the ambiguity to be preserved in languages unrelated to our own. But what about the uses of "know" that characteristically are followed by that-clauses, knowing that *p*? Are these ambiguous? I would be very surprised to be told that the Eskimos have two separate words, one for (say) Hintikka's "strong" sense of "know," another for his "weak" sense. Perhaps this indicates that we think of knowledge as a unitary concept, unlikely to be "disambiguated" by two separate words in any language.

We thus have two methodological considerations that can be used to test any alleged ambiguity. "Bank" is ambiguous; we would expect the ambiguity to be disambiguated by separate and unrelated words in some other languages. Why should the two separate senses be reproduced in languages unrelated to English? First, then, we can consult our linguistic intuitions, independently of any empirical investigation. Would we be surprised to find languages that used two separate words for the two alleged senses of a given word? If so, then, to that extent our linguistic intuitions are really intuitions of a unitary concept, rather than of a word that expresses two distinct and unrelated senses. Second, we can ask empirically whether languages are in fact found that contain distinct words expressing the allegedly distinct senses. If no such language is found, once again this is evidence that a unitary account of the word or phrase in question should be sought.

As far as our main question is concerned, the first of these two tests, that of our intuitive expectation, seems to me overwhelmingly to favor a unitary account of descriptions, as opposed to the ambiguity postulated in the ambiguous D-language. If English really is the ambiguous D-language, we should expect to find other languages where the referential and attributive uses are expressed by two separate words, as in the *unambiguous* D-language. I at least would find it quite surprising to learn that say, the Eskimo, used two separate words "the" and "ze," for the attributive and referential uses. To the extent that I have this intuition, to that extent I think of "the" as a unitary concept. I should have liked to be able to report that I have reinforced this guess by an actual empirical examination of other languages—the second test—but as of now I haven't done so.[29]

Several general methodological considerations favor the Russell language (or some other unitary account) against the ambiguous D-language as a model for English. First, the unitary account conforms to considerations of economy in that it does not "multiply senses beyond necessity." Second, the metalinguistic apparatus invoked by the unitary account to explain the referential–attributive distinction is an apparatus that is needed in *any case* for other cases, such as proper names. The separate referential sense of descriptions postulated by the D-language hypothesis, is an idle wheel that does no work: if it were absent, we would be able to express everything we wished to express, in the same way. Further, the resemblance between the case of descriptions and that of proper names (where presumably no one would be tempted to postulate an ambiguity) is so close that any attempt to explain the cases differently is automatically suspect. Finally, we would not expect the alleged ambiguity to be disambiguated in other languages, and this means we probably regard ourselves as possessing a unitary concept.

Aside from methodological considerations, is there any direct evidence that would favor one of our two rival accounts? As I remarked above, if we had a direct intuition that "Her husband is kind to her" could be true even when her actual husband is cruel, then we would have decisive evidence for the D-language model; but Donnellan rightly disclaims any such intuition.

On the other hand, I myself feel that such a sentence expresses a falsehood, even when "her husband" is used referentially to refer to a kind man; but the popularity of Donnellan's view has made me uncertain that this intuition should be pressed very far. In the absence of such direct intuitions that would settle the matter conclusively, it would seem that the actual practice of English speakers is compatible with either model, and that only general methodological considerations favor one hypothesis rather than another. Such a situation leaves me uneasy. If there really is no direct evidence to distinguish the two hypotheses, how are they different hypotheses? If two communities, one of whom spoke the ambiguous D-language and the other of whom spoke the (weak) Russell language, would be able to intermingle freely without detecting any linguistic difference, do they really speak two different languages? If so, wherein is the difference?

Two hypothetical communities, one of which was explicitly taught the ambiguous D-language and the other of which was taught the (weak) Russell language (say, in school), would have direct and differing intuitions about the truth-value of "Her husband was kind to her"; but it is uncertain whether English speakers have any such intuitions. If they have none, is this a respect in which English differs from both the Russell languages and the D-languages, and thus differentiates it from both? Or, on the contrary, is there a pragmatic consideration, deriving no doubt from the fact that the relevant rules of language are not explicitly taught, that will explain why we lack such intuitions (if we do) without showing that neither the D-language nor the Russell language is English?

Some commentators on the dispute between Russell and Frege and Strawson over sentences containing vacuous definite descriptions have held that no direct linguistic phenomena conclusively decide between the two views: we should therefore choose the most economical and theoretically satisfying model. But if this is so, are there really two views, and if there are, shouldn't we perhaps say that neither is correct? A hypothetical community that was explicitly taught Russellian or Frege-Strawsonian truth-conditions for sentences containing vacuous definite descriptions would have no difficulty producing direct intuitions that decide the Russell-Strawson dispute. If the commentators in question are correct, speakers of English have no such intuitions. Surely this fact, too, would be a significant fact about English, for which linguistic theory should give an account. Perhaps pragmatic considerations suffice for such an account; or, perhaps, the alleged lack of any such intuition must be accounted for by a feature built into the semantics of English itself. In the latter case, neither the Russellian nor the Frege-Strawsonian truth-conditions would be appropriate for English. Similar considerations would apply to the issue between Donnellan and Russell.[30]

I am uncertain about these questions. Certainly it would be best if there were directly observable phenomena that differentiated between the two hypotheses. Actually I can think of one rather special and localized phenomenon that may indeed favor the Russellian hypothesis, or some other unitary hypothesis. Consider the following two dialogues:

Dialogue I: A: "Her husband is kind to her."
            B: "No, he isn't. The man you're referring to isn't her husband."
Dialogue II: A: "Her husband is kind to her."
            B: "He is kind to her, but he isn't her husband."

In the first dialogue the respondent (B) uses "he" to refer to the semantic referent of "her husband" as used by the first speaker (A); in the second dialogue the respondent uses "he" to refer to the speaker's referent. My tendency is to think that both dialogues are proper. The unitary account can explain this fact, by saying that pronominalization can pick up *either* a previous semantic reference or a previous speaker's reference.[31,32] In the case of the two contrasting dialogues, these diverge.

If English were the ambiguous D-language, the second dialogue would be easy to explain. "He" refers to the object that is both the semantic referent and the speaker's referent of "her husband." (Recall that the notions of speaker's reference and semantic reference are general notions applicable to all languages, even to the D-languages.[33]) The first dialogue, however, would be much more difficult, perhaps impossible, to explain. When A said "her husband," according to the D-language hypothesis he was using "her husband" in the referential sense. Both the speaker's referent and the semantic referent would be the kind lover; only if B had misunderstood A's use as attributive could he have used "he" to refer to the husband, but such a misunderstanding is excluded by the second part of B's utterance. If the first dialogue is proper, it seems hard to fit it into the D-language model.[34]

4. CONCLUSION

I said at the beginning that the main concern of this paper was methodological rather than substantive. I do think that the considerations in this paper make it overwhelmingly probable that an ultimate account of the phenomena behind Donnellan's distinction will make use of the pragmatic ambiguity between "simple" and "complex" uses, as I defined them above, rather than postulating an ambiguity of the D-language type. But any ultimate substantive conclusion on the issue requires a more extensive and thorough treatment than has been given here. First, I have not here examined theories that attempt to explain Donnellan's distinction as a *syntactic* ambiguity, either of scope or of restrictive and nonrestrictive clauses in deep structure.[35] Both these views, like the line suggested in the present paper, are compatible with a unitary hypothesis such as the hypothesis that English is a Russell language.

Although I am not inclined to accept either of these views, some others have found them plausible and unless they are rebutted, they too indicate that Donnellan's observations cannot be taken as providing a conclusive argument against Russell without further discussion.

Second, and most important, no treatment of definite descriptions can be complete unless it examines the complete range of uses of the definite article and related linguistic phenomena. Such a treatment should attempt, as I have argued above, to make it clear why the same construction with a definite article is used for a wide range of cases. It would be wrong for me not to mention the phenomena most favorable to Donnellan's intuitions. In a demonstrative use such as "that table," it seems plausible, as I have mentioned above,[36] that the term rigidly designates its referent. It also seems plausible that the reference of such a demonstrative construction can be an object to which the descriptive adjectives in the construction do not apply (for example, "that scoundrel" may be used to refer to someone who is not, in fact, a scoundrel) and it is not clear that the distinction between speaker's reference and semantic reference should be invoked to account for this. As I also said above, it seems to me to be likely that "indefinite" definite descriptions[37] such as "the table" present difficulties for Russellian analysis. It is somewhat tempting to assimilate such descriptions to the corresponding demonstratives (for example, "that table") and to the extent that such a temptation turns out to be plausible, there may be new arguments in such cases for the intuitions of those who have advocated a rigid vs. nonrigid ambiguity in definite descriptions, or for Donnellan's intuitions concerning the referential case, or for both.[38]

Because I have not yet worked out a complete account that satisfies me, and because I think it would be wrong to make any definitive claim on the basis of the restricted class of phenomena considered here, I regard the primary lessons of this paper as methodological. They illustrate some general methodological considerations and apparatus that I think should be applied to the problems discussed here and to other linguistic problems. They show in the present case that the argument Donnellan actually presents in his original paper shows nothing against a Russellian or other unitary account, and they make it highly probable to me that the problems Donnellan handles by semantic ambiguity should instead be treated by a general theory of speech acts. But at this time nothing more definitive can be said. I think that the distinction between semantic reference and speaker's reference will be of importance not only (as in the present paper) as a critical tool to block postulation of unwarranted ambiguities, but also will be of considerable constructive importance for a theory of language. In particular, I find it plausible that a diachronic account of the evolution of language is likely to suggest that what was originally a mere speaker's reference may, if it becomes habitual in a community, evolve into a semantic reference. And this consideration may be *one* of the factors needed to clear up some puzzles in the theory of reference.[39,40]

ACKNOWLEDGMENTS

I should like to thank Margaret Gilbert and Howard Wettstein for their assistance in the preparation of this paper.

NOTES

1. Versions of this paper—not read from the present manuscript—were given from 1971 onward to colloquia at New York University, M.I.T., the University of California (Los Angeles), and elsewhere. The present version was written on the basis of a transcript of the M.I.T. version prepared by the editors of this volume. Donnellan himself heard the talk at U.C.L.A., and his "Speaker Reference, Descriptions, and Anaphora," to a large extent appears to be a comment on considerations of the type mentioned here. (He does not, however, specifically refer to the present paper.) I decided *not* to alter the paper I gave in talks to take Donnellan's later views into account: largely I think the earlier version stands on its own, and the issues Donnellan raises in the later paper can be discussed elsewhere. Something should be said here, however, about the pronominalization phenomena. In his paper, Donnellan seems to think that these phenomena are incompatible with the suggestion that speaker's reference is a pragmatic notion. On the contrary, at the end of the present paper (and of the talk Donnellan heard), I emphasize these very phenomena and argue that they support this suggestion. See also note 31 below.

2. See also Keith S. Donnellan, "Putting Humpty Dumpty Together Again," *The Philosophical Review*, 77 (1968): 203–215.

3. In his later paper mentioned above in note 1, Donnellan seems more clearly to advocate a semantic ambiguity; but he hedges a bit even in the later paper.

4. I will also avoid cases of "improper" descriptions, where the uniqueness condition fails. Such descriptions may or may not be important for an ultimate evaluation of Donnellan's position, but none of the arguments in his paper rest on them.

5. "Reference and Definite Descriptions," p. 144ff. My discussion in this paragraph and the next is based on Donnellan's paper, pp. 285.

6. At the time, it had not yet been revealed that Kissinger was the official in question.

7. In fact, no *n*-fold distinction can do so, for any fixed *n*. Independently of the present writer, L. Kartunnen has argued similarly that no dual or *n*-fold distinction can replace scope distinctions. I discussed the matter briefly in "Identity and Necessity," *Identity and Individuation*, ed. M. Munitz (New York: 1972), p. 149, n. 10.

8. See the papers of Stalnaker and Partee in *The Semantics of Natural Language*, eds. D. Davidson and G. Harman (Dordrecht: 1971) for such suggestions and also for some of the views mentioned in the previous section. I should emphasize that most of the stimulating discussion in these papers can be made independent of any of the identifications of Donnellan's distinction with others which are rejected here.

9. See his paper "The Contingent *A Priori* and Rigid Designators," [in which] Donnellan asks whether I think proper names (in natural language) are *always* rigid: obviously, he thinks, proper names *could* be introduced to abbreviate nonrigid definite descriptions. My view is that proper names (except perhaps, for some quirky and derivative uses, that are not uses as *names*) *are* always rigid. In particular this applies to "Neptune." It would be logically possible to have single words that abbreviated nonrigid definite descriptions, but these would not be *names*. The point is not merely terminological: I mean that such abbreviated nonrigid definite descriptions would differ in an important semantical feature from (what we call) typical proper names in our

actual speech. I merely state my position and do not argue it; nor can I digress to comment on the other points raised in Donnellan's paper.

10. See Kaplan's paper "Dthat." In that paper, however, he also has some tendency to confuse rigidity with Donnellan's referentiality.

11. In the Davidson-Harman volume mentioned in note 8.

12. For this view, see Jerrold J. Katz, "Logic and Language: An Examination of Recent Criticisms of Intensionalism," in *Minnesota Studies in the Philosophy of Science*, vol. VII (Minneapolis: 1975), pp. 36–130. See especially sections 5.1 and 5.2. As far as proper names are concerned, Katz thinks that *other* arguments tell against the description theory even as a theory of meaning.

13. See Donnellan, "Reference and Definite Descriptions," this volume.

14. So I argued in the talks, and rightly, if Donnellan is taken literally. See note 25 below, however, for a more charitable reading, which probably corresponds to Donnellan's intent. We must, however, take descriptions to be *semantically* ambiguous if we are to maintain the reading in question: see the point raised immediately after this one.

15. "Reference and Definite Descriptions," this volume.

16. For Grice, see the following papers, which I follow loosely in a good deal of the discussion at the beginning of this section: "The Causal Theory of Perception," *Proceedings of the Aristotelian Society*, supplementary vol. 35 (1961); "Logic and Conversation" [reprinted in this volume]; "Meaning," *Philosophical Review* 66 (1957): 337–88; "Utterer's Meaning, Sentence-Meaning and Word-Meaning," *Foundations of Language* 4 (1968): 225–242; "Utterer's Meaning and Intentions."

17. In "The Causal Theory of Perception."

18. Suppose the second burglar is well aware of the proximity of the police, but procrastinates in his greed for more loot. Then the first burglar imparts no *information* by saying what he does, but simply urges the second burglar to "split."

19. Although conversational principles are applicable to *all languages*, they may apply differently to *different societies*. In a society where blunt statement was considered rude, where "it looks red" replaced "it is red" just because of such a custom, "it looks red" might carry different conversational implicatures from our own. This might be the case even though the members of the society spoke *English*, just as we do. Conversational principles are matters for the psychology, sociology, and anthropology of linguistic communities; they are applicable to these communities no matter what language they may speak, though the applicable principles may very somewhat with the communities (and may even, to some extent, be conditioned by the fact that they speak languages with certain structures.) Often, of course, we can state widely applicable, "cross-cultural," general conversational principles. Semantic and syntactic principles, on the other hand, are matters of the conventions of a language, in whatever cultural matrix it may be spoken. *Perhaps* sometimes it is difficult to draw the line, but it exists in general nonetheless.

20. If the views about proper names I have advocated in "Naming and Necessity" are correct (Donnellan, in fact, holds similar views), the conventions regarding names in an idiolect usually involve the fact that the idiolect is no mere idiolect, but part of a common language, in which reference may be passed from link to link.

As the present paper attests, my views on proper names in "Naming and Necessity" have no special connection with the referential–attributive distinction.

21. "Naming and Necessity," p. 343, n. 3.

22. Donnellan shows in his paper that there are "referential" uses, of a somewhat exceptional kind, where the speaker, or even both the speaker and the hearer, are aware that the description used does not apply to the thing they are talking about. For example, they use "the King," knowing him to be a usurper, but fearing the secret police. Analogous cases can be given for proper names: If Smith is a lunatic who thinks he is Napoleon, they may humor him. Largely

for the sake of simplicity of exposition, I have excluded such both from the notion of speaker's reference and from Donnellan's "referential" use (and the "D-languages" below). I do not think that the situation would be materially altered if both notions were revised so as to admit these cases, in a more refined analysis. In particular, it would probably weaken the case for a semantic ambiguity if these cases were allowed: for they shade into ironical and "inverted commas" cases. "He is a 'fine friend'," may be ironical (whether or not inverted commas are used in the transcription). " 'The King' is still in power"; " 'Napoleon' has gone to bed" are similar, whether or not explicit inverted commas are used. It is fairly clear that "fine friend," "brilliant scholar," etc., do not have ironical and inverted commas *senses*: irony is a certain form of speech act, to be accounted for by pragmatic considerations. The case for a semantic ambiguity in definite descriptions is similarly *weakened* if we include such cases as referential uses.

In ordinary discourse, we say that the speaker was referring to someone under a wide variety of circumstances, including linguistic errors, verbal slips, and deliberate misuses of language. (If Mrs. Malaprop says, "The geography teacher said that equilateral triangles are equiangular," she *refers* to the geometry teacher.) The more such phenomena one includes in the notion of speaker's reference, the further one gets from any connection of the notion with semantical matters.

23. See the discussion of "schmidentity" in "Naming and Necessity."

24. Or, using variables explicitly, "There is a person x such that . . ." Notice that in an utterance of "$(\exists x) (\phi x \wedge \psi x)$," as long as it is clear *which* thing allegedly satisfying "ϕx" the speaker has in mind, there can be a speaker's referent, even if both the speaker and the hearer are aware that many things satisfy "ϕx."

25. This description of the D-languages specifies nothing about semantical features more "intensional" than truth conditions. It is plausible to assume that "ze F" is a *rigid* designator of the thing believed to be uniquely F, but this is not explicitly included in the extensional truth conditions. Nor has anything been said about the behavior of "ze F" in belief and indirect discourse contexts. *If* we stipulate that "ze F," even in such contexts, designates the thing the speaker believes uniquely F's, then indeed "Jones said that ze man she married is kind to her," will not be a proper way of reporting Jones's utterance "Ze man she married is kind to her" (even if Jones and the speaker happen to have the same belief as to who her husband is; the difficulty is more obvious if they do not.) No doubt it is this fact that lies behind Donnellan's view that, in the referential case, it is hard to speak of "the statement," even though his exposition of the matter seems to be defective. Such implications, which are not present in the Russell language, lend only further implausibility to the supposition that English is the ambiguous D-language.

To repeat note 22, actually there are many other ways, other than taking something uniquely to satisfy "F," that might be included under referential uses of "the F." The best short way to specify the semantics of "ze F" would seem to be this: "ze F" refers, in the unambiguous D-language, to what would have been the speaker's referent of "the F" in the weak Russell language (under the same circumstances)! But this formulation makes it very implausible that the ambiguous D-language is anything but a chimerical model for English.

26. There is one significant difference between the case of proper names and that of definite descriptions. If someone uses "Jones" to refer to Smith, he has *misidentified* Smith as Jones, taken Smith for someone else. To some extent I *did* think that *Jones* was raking the leaves. (I assume that "Jones" is already in his idiolect as a name of Jones. If I am introduced to an impostor and am told, "This man is none other than Albert Einstein," if I am fooled I will have *taken* him, falsely, to be Einstein. Someone else, who has never heard of Einstein before, may merely be mistaken as to the impostor's name.) On the other hand, if I think that someone is "her husband" and so refer to him, I need not at all have confused two people. I merely think that one person possesses a property—that of being married to her—that in fact he lacks. The real husband is irrelevant.

27. In terms of this apparatus, I can sharpen the reply to Katz, note 12 above. If Schmidt had discovered the incompleteness of arithmetic but I had thought it was Gödel who did so, a complex ("referential") use of the description has a semantic reference to Schmidt but a speaker's reference to Gödel. Once I am apprised of the true facts, speaker's reference and semantic reference will coincide thereafter and I will no longer use the description to refer to Gödel. The name "Gödel," on the other hand, has Gödel as its *semantic* referent: the name will always be applied to Gödel in the presence of correct information. Whether a term would be withdrawn in the presence of correct information (without changing the language) is a good intuitive test for divergence of semantic reference and speaker's reference (disregarding the cases in note 22).

28. There is another problem for any theory of semantic ambiguity. Donnellan says that if I say "Smith's murderer is insane," solely on the basis of the grisly conditions of Smith's body, my use of "Smith's murderer" is attributive (even if I in fact have a belief as to who the murderer is), but if I say it on the basis of the supposed murderer's behavior at the dock, my use is referential. Surely, however, my reasons can be mixed: perhaps neither consideration would have sufficed by itself, but they suffice jointly. What is my use then? A user of the unambiguous D-language would have to choose between "the" and "ze." It seems very implausible to suppose that the speaker is confused and uncertain about what sense he gives to his description; but what else can we say if we suppose that English is the ambiguous D-language? (This problem arises even if the man at the dock is guilty, so that in fact there is no conflict. It is more obvious if he is innocent.)

A pragmatic theory of the referential–attributive distinction can handle such cases much more easily. Clearly there can be borderline cases between the simple and the complex use— where, to some extent the speaker wishes to speak of the semantic referent and to some extent he wishes to speak of something he believes to be the semantic referent. He need not sort out his motives carefully, since he thinks these things are one and the same!

Given such mixed motives, the speaker's reference may be partially to one thing and partially to another, even when the semantic reference is unambiguous. This is especially likely in the case of proper names, since divergences between speaker's referent and semantic referent are characteristically *misidentifications* (see note 26). Even if the speaker's referent of "Jones" in "Jones is raking the leaves" is Smith, to some extent I have said *of Jones* that he is raking the leaves. There are gradations, depending on the speaker's interests and intentions, as to what extent the speaker's reference was to Jones and to what extent it was to Smith. The problem is less common in the case of descriptions, where misidentification need not have occurred.

29. Of course these tests must be used with some caution. The mere fact that some language subdivides the extension of an English word into several subclasses, with their own separate words, and has no word for the whole extension, does not show that the English word was ambiguous (think of the story that the Eskimos have different words for different kinds of snow). If many unrelated languages preserve a single word, this in itself is evidence for a unitary concept. On the other hand, a word may have different senses that are obviously related. One sense may be metaphorical for another (though in that case, it may not really be a separate sense, but simply a common metaphor.) "Statistics" can mean both statistical data and the science of evaluating such data. And the like. The more we can explain relations among senses, and the more "natural" and "inevitable" the relationship, the more we will expect the different senses to be preserved in a wide variety of other languages.

The test, therefore, needs further exploration and refinement. It is certainly wrong to postulate an ambiguity without any explanation of some connection between the "senses" that explains why they occur in a wide variety of languages. In the referential–attributive case, I feel that any attempt to explain the connection between the referential and the attributive uses will be so close to the kind of pragmatic account offered here as to render any assumptions of distinct senses inplausible and superfluous.

30. That is, the *concept* of truth conditions is somehow inappropriate for the semantics of

English. The vague uneasiness expressed in these paragraphs expresses my own rather confused occasional doubts and is ancillary to the main theme. Moore's "paradox of analysis" may be a related problem.

Quine's philosophy of language characteristically is based on a naturalistic doubt about building any "rules" or "conventions" into a language that are not recoverable from actual linguistic practices, even if such rules may be necessary to stipulate the language. In this sense, the uneasiness expressed is Quinean in spirit. I find Quine's emphasis on a naturalistic approach to some extent salutary. But I also feel that our intuitions of semantic rules as speakers should not be ignored cavalierly.

31. Geach, in his book "Reference and Generality," emended ed. (Ithaca: 1970), and elsewhere, has argued vigorously against speaking of pronominalization as picking up a previous reference. I do not wish to argue the extent to which he is right here. I use the terminology given in the text for convenience, but to the extent Geach's views are correct I think the example could presumably be reformulated to fit his scheme. I think the views expressed in this paper are very much in the spirit of Geach's remarks on definite descriptions and speaker's reference in the book just cited. See Geach's discussion, e.g., on p. 8.

32. Donnellan, in "Speaker Reference, Descriptions, and Anaphora," thinks that the fact that pronouns can pick up a previous semantic reference somehow casts doubt on a view that makes speaker's reference a nonsemantical notion. I don't see why: "he," "she," "that," etc., can, under various circumstances, refer to anything salient in an appropriate way. Being physically distinguished against its background is a property that may make an object salient; having been referred to by a previous speaker is another. In "Naming and Necessity," note 3, I suggested tentatively that Donnellan's "remarks about reference have little to do with semantics or truth conditions." The point would be put more exactly if I had said that Donnellan's distinction is not itself a semantical one, though it is relevant to semantics through pronominalization, as many other nonsemantical properties are.

Pronominalization phenomena are relevant to another point. Often one hears it argued against Russell's existential analysis of *indefinite* descriptions that an indefinite description may be anaphorically referred to by a pronoun that seems to preserve the reference of the indefinite description. I am not sure that these phenomena do conflict with the existential analysis. (I am not completely sure there are some that don't, either.) In any event, many cases can be accounted for (given a Russellian theory) by the facts that: (i) existential statements can carry a speaker's reference; (ii) pronouns can refer to the speaker's referent.

33. The use of "ze" in the unambiguous D-language is such that the semantic reference automatically coincided with the speaker's reference, but nevertheless, the notions are applicable. So are the notions of simple and complex uses of designators. However, speakers of the un-ambiguous D-language might be less likely ever to use "the" in a complex case: for, one might be inclined to argue, if such are their intentions, why not use "ze"?

34. Various moves might be tried, but none that I can think of seem to me to be plausible. It has been suggested to me that sometimes the respondent in a dialogue deliberately feigns to misunderstand an ambiguous phrase used by the first speaker, and that, given the supposed ambiguity of "her husband" in the ambiguous D-language, the first dialogue can be interpreted as such a case. For example, the following dialogue: "Jones put the money in a bank." "He put the money in one all right, but it wasn't a commercial bank; he was so much afraid it would be discovered that he hid it near the river." It seems implausible to me that the first dialogue in the text fits into such a very jocular model. But notice further that the joke consists in a mock *confirmation* of the first speaker's assertion. It would be rather bizarre to respond, "He didn't put the money in the bank, and it wasn't a commercial bank." The first dialogue would have to conform to such a bizarre pattern on the hypothesis in question.

Alternatively, it might be suggested that B uses "he" as a pronoun of laziness for A's "her husband," taken in the supposed referential sense. This move seems to be excluded, since B may well be in no position to use "her husband" referentially. He may merely have heard that she is married to a cruel man.

35. I believe that Kartunnen has advocated the view that the referential–attributive distinction arises from a scope ambiguity; I do not know whether this has been published. Since the referential–attributive "ambiguity" arises even in simple sentences such as "Smith's murderer is insane," where there appears to be no room for any scope ambiguity, such a view seems forced to rely on acceptance of Ross's suggestion that all English assertive utterances begin with an initial "I say that," which is suppressed in "surface structure" but present in "deep structure."

For the view that derives the referential–attributive "ambiguity" from a distinction of restrictive and nonrestrictive clauses in "deep structure," see J. M. Bell, "What Is Referential Opacity?", *The Journal of Philosophical Logic*, 2 (1973): 155–180. See also the work of Emmon Bach on which Bell's paper is based, "Nouns and Noun Phrases," in *Universals in Linguistic theory*, ed. E. Bach and R. T. Harms (New York: 1968), pp. 91–122. For reasons of space I have not treated these views here. But some of my arguments that Donnellan's distinction is pragmatic apply against them also.

36. See pp. 177–178 above; also see note 10 above.

37. The term is Donnellan's. See "Putting Humpty Dumpty Together Again," p. 204, footnote 5.

38. I believe that when Donnellan heard the present paper, he too mentioned considerations of this kind. The cases are mentioned briefly in Donnellan's paper, "Putting Humpty Dumpty Together Again," *ibid*. Donnellan's paper "Speaker Reference, Descriptions and Anaphora" mentioned above also makes use of the existence of such incomplete descriptions but I do not find his arguments conclusive.

39. See the Santa Claus and Madagascar cases in "Naming and Necessity."

40. It seems likely that the considerations in this paper will also be relevant to the concept of a supposed " ± Specific" distinction for indefinite descriptions, as advocated by many linguists.

MERRIE BERGMANN

PRESUPPOSITION AND TWO-DIMENSIONAL LOGIC[1]

Mr. Strawson objects to my saying that 'the king of France is wise' is false if there is no king of France. He admits that the sentence is significant and not true, but not that it is false. . . . For my part, I find it more convenient to define the word 'false' so that every significant sentence is either true or false. This is a purely verbal question; and although I have no wish to claim the support of common usage, I do not think that he can claim it either.

B. Russell[2]

What we have here is the familiar philosophical situation of one party being attracted by one simplified, theoretical—or 'straightened out'—concept of truth and falsity, and the other by another. It might be asked: How does ordinary usage speak on the point? . . . But ordinary usage does not deliver a clear verdict for one party or the other. Why should it?

P. F. Strawson[3]

I

Despite their disagreements over the semantic treatment of sentences like

(1) The present king of France is wise,

Russell and Strawson agreed that appeal to ordinary intuitions is not sufficient to determine whether sentence (1) is false or neither true nor false.[4] Typically theoretical considerations are brought to bear when this question is addressed.

One such theoretical consideration involves the semantic concept of presupposition.[5] It *appears* to be the case that if we accept the semantic concept of presupposition, and if we believe that sentence (1) has nontrivial presuppositions (presuppositions which may fail to be true), then we must side with Strawson: sentence (1) is neither true nor false. This is because presuppositions are standardly defined in terms of languages with truth-value gaps. In this paper, however, I develop an alternative to this standard semantic account of presupposition, an alternative in which the presuppositions of a sentence are defined independently of the truth-conditions of that sentence. In doing so, I shall be challenging the link between presuppositions and truth-value gaps: presuppositions can be had in languages without truth-value gaps.

First, I'll explain how the concept of presupposition can be used to develop a semantic account of sentence (1). Although the issue of the truth-value of (1) is controversial, I believe that the following claims are not:

(a) Sentence (1) is nontrue (in 1980) in a way which differs from the nontruth of
   (2) The current U.S. President is a Republican.
   The nontruth of (1), but not that of (2), is due to failure of denotation.

(b) We can negate (1) in such a way that neither (1) nor the negation of (1) is true:
   (N1) The present king of France is not wise.
   This contrasts with
   (N2) The current U.S. President is not a Republican, which *is* true.

(c) Both (1) and (N1) bear a special relation to the sentence
   (E1) The present king of France exists.
   Namely, if either (1) or (N1) were true, (E1) would be true as well.

We may thus adopt the following minimal condition of adequacy for semantic accounts of (1): they should regiment, or account for, the data in (a)–(c). Trivalent semantics in which sentences can fail to be true or false meet this condition of adequacy as follows.[6]

Atomic sentences symbolizing sentences like (1)—subject-predicate sentences in which no logical particles occur—are assigned the value N when the subject term fails to denote (N for 'neither true nor false'). Otherwise, they may be assigned the value T (for 'true') or F (for 'false'). Negation $\sim$ is defined through the following matrix:[7]

A	$\sim A$
T	F
F	T
N	N

The trivalent concept of presupposition is defined as

A presupposes B = $_{df}$ whenever A is true or false, B is true.

Given the definition of $\sim$, this is equivalent to

A presupposes B iff, whenever A is true or $\sim A$ is true, B is true.

Making the reasonable assumption that a sentence *a exists* is true when *a* denotes, it follows according to this account that (1) presupposes

(E1) The present king of France exists,

as does

(N1) The present king of France is not wise.

That is, if either (1) or (N1) is true, then (E1) is true as well. This takes care of part (c) of the minimal condition of adequacy. But we have also taken care of (a) and (b): the nontruth of (1) differs from that of (2) insofar as the latter but not the former is false; and neither (1) nor (N1) is true.

Russell, as we know, also had his own way of regimenting the data in (a)–(c), without truth-value gaps. But the trivalent account of presupposition has a bonus. The trivalent definition of presupposition places no restrictions on the form of either *A* or *B*, the sentences standing in the presupposition relation; and the definition does not require that the value *N* be assigned only to sentences containing nondenoting singular terms. Two consequences follow. First, sentences having more complex forms than (1), (N1), and (E1) may bear the presupposition relation to one another. Second, sentences in which there is no problem of denotation failure, e.g., sentences containing factive verbs, may exhibit behavior similar to that recorded in claims (a)–(c). Thus the concept of presupposition is naturally extended to account for the vagaries of some sentences which do not contain nondenoting singular terms as well as the vagaries of those which do. Failure of presupposition is a phenomenon the scope of which extends well beyond the sort of case which gave rise to the disagreement between Russell and Strawson.

To the extent that semantic presupposition is identified with the concept defined in the trivalent account, the issue over whether to admit semantic truth-value gaps ceases to be a verbal one. The reason is well-known: semantic presupposition so characterized is a trivial relation in a language in which every sentence is evaluated as either true or false. In such a language each sentence stands in this relation to all *and only* the logically true sentences of the language. Evaluate every sentence as true or false, and there are no nontrivial semantic presuppositions.[8] Like Russell, I shall recognize only two truth-values and shall not admit gaps. Consequently, I will not explicate the concept of presupposition as trivalent theories do. The account I shall develop can be used to incorporate the core data concerning (1) by defining presupposition *independently* of truth-value, in terms of specific semantic aspects of sentences which induce presuppositions. The semantic distinctions I draw turn out to be finer than those typically drawn in three-valued or supervaluational semantics. Some surprising things happen when this is done, e.g., a sentence may both be true and have a false presupposition. And we can adopt various policies concerning the presuppositions of complex sentences without changing the truth-conditions of those sentences. Finally, this account generates the standard presuppositions for simple subject-predicate sentences and their negations.

II

The idea is this. Rather than evaluating sentences like sentence (1) as being neither true nor false, we shall evaluate the sentences as false while independently keeping track of occurrences of nondenoting singular terms. Hence, we shall be semantically evaluating sentences *twice*, that is, each sentence is assigned an ordered pair of values. The language thus generated will be a two-dimensional language in the sense of Herzberger[9] (to be discussed below). The first value indicates the truth-value of the sentence, and the second value registers what I shall call the *security-value* of the sentence. There are two truth-values: the first value of a sentence is 1 if the sentence is true, and 0 if the sentence is false. I hasten to add a caveat about my use of the word 'false': it does not affect the account if 'nontrue' is substituted for 'false' throughout. Whichever way it is read, we are still left with two truth-values; and every sentence will be assigned one of those two values. The work which is typically done by gaps in nonbivalent languages will be accomplished by the second semantic determinant, the security-value of a sentence.

There are two security-values, 1 and 0. A sentence is *secure* if its security value is 1, and *nonsecure* otherwise. In general, the role of the security-value assigned to a sentence is to keep track of information relevant to determining presuppositions. The sort of information which is used may be thought of as *semantic anomaly*, and in the case of existential presupposition the type of anomaly we are interested in concerns the presence of nondenoting singular terms. In this section we will judge a sentence to be nonsecure only if it contains a nondenoting singular term.[10] Why call a sentnce in which such a term occurs semantically anomalous? Here I hold a view which is widely accepted: the normal semantic function of singular terms is to refer. When they fail to refer, they fail to fulfill that function.[11]

The presuppositions of a sentence are then determined directly on the basis of conditions of semantic anomaly rather than in terms of truth-value. A sentence will be held to presuppose those sentences which are true whenever it is secure. Since I'm breaking tradition with nonbivalent accounts of presupposition, I'll introduce a new technical term: *preimplication*. Preimplication is a formal concept which we are to think of as a regimentation of the intuitive concept of presupposition:

A preimplies B = $_{df}$ whenever A is secure, B is true.

Now we'll see how the minimal condition of adequacy is met. The truth-value of a sentence *a is P* (where *P* is noncomplex and does not make an explicit attribution of existence) is 1 if *a is P* is true, and is 0 otherwise. The security-value of *a is P* is 1 if *a* has a denotation and 0 otherwise. Hence the value $\langle 0, 0 \rangle$ is assigned to

(1) The present king of France is wise.

and the value $\langle 0, 1 \rangle$ is assigned to

(2) The current U.S. President is a Republican.

We have now recorded a semantic distinction between the two sentences: (2) is secure and (1) is not. Second, the negation operation $\sim$ will make the following mappings:

$\langle 0, 1 \rangle \rightarrow \langle 1, 1 \rangle$,

$\langle 0, 0 \rangle \rightarrow \langle 0, 0 \rangle$.

(It will map the other two pairs of values as well; this will be discussed below.) So (N1) has the value $\langle 0, 0 \rangle$—it is nontrue and nonsecure (semantically anomalous), while (N2) has the value $\langle 1, 1 \rangle$—it is true and secure. Third, the first value of a sentence *a exists* is 1 if *a* denotes, and is 0 otherwise. The second value of *a exists* is always 1. Thus whenever a sentence *a is P* is secure, the sentence *a exists* is true. Finally, it follows that both *a is P* and $\sim$ (*a is P*) preimply *a exists*, and to this extent preimplication is our formal regimentation of presupposition.

I shall now introduce the full sentential language *L* which provides a framework for implementing the above ideas. Throughout, I shall explain the intuitive and formal motivations for the allotment of truth-values and security-values, and I shall state various presuppositional policies—policies concerning the presupposition relation[12]—which have been incorporated. Some of the policies will be familiar from trivalent semantics, and some will not.

The atomic sentences of *L* are sentences of the form *a is P* and *a exists*, where '*a*' and '*P*' range over distinct denumerable sets: '*a*' over lower case subscripted letters and '*P*' over upper case subscripted letters. The connectives are unary $\sim$, *T*, and γ and binary $\vee$, &, and $\supset$. Sentences are defined as usual. A valuation of *L* assigns to each atomic sentence a member of $\{\langle 1, 1 \rangle$, $\langle 0, 1 \rangle$, $\langle 1, 0 \rangle$, $\langle 0, 0 \rangle\}$. By convention, the angle brackets and commas in the expressions denoting ordered pairs will be dropped, e.g., '$\langle 1, 0 \rangle$' will be written as '10'. The *admissible valuations* are those valuations which assign one of the values 11, 01 to a sentence *a is P* only if the value 11 is assigned to *a exists*, and which never assign the value 10, 00 to sentences of the form *a exists*. In what follows I assume that we have restricted our attention to admissible valuations. The admissible valuations incorporate two presuppositional policies:

(A) Each sentence *a is P* presupposes *a exists*.

(B) A sentence *a exists* has no nontrivial presuppositions, i.e., it has no presuppositions which can be false.

That is, if only admissible valuations are admitted in the definition of preimplication, then *a is P* preimplies *a exists*; and, since *a exists* is always secure, no sentence preimplied by *a exists* can fail to be true. A sentence *a exists* is treated as always secure by the admissible valuations because in this case the nondenotation of *a* does not make for semantic anomaly. If it did, then such a sentence would be nonanomalous only if true.

The full matrix for the negation ∼ is:

A	$\sim A$
11	01
01	11
10	00
00	00

A sentence ∼A is secure just in case A is secure, and true only if A is both false and secure. The distribution of truth-values in the full matrix results from generalizing on the distinction between negating 'The king of France is wise' and negating 'The current U.S. President is a Republican': the negation ∼ takes any sentence containing a nondenoting term into a false one—regardless of the truth-value of the sentence negated. We may think of this negation along Russellian lines, as the semantic counterpart of "forcing" singular terms (definite descriptions) into primary occurrence. A sentence in which a singular term has primary occurrence is true *only if* the singular term denotes. Whereas Russell captured the semantics of a negation which yields falsehood when applied to sentences containing nondenoting terms by syntactic parsing in a quantified language, the use of two dimensions allows us to construct the semantics directly without disturbing the syntax. The negation (∼) of a nonsecure sentence is false, whether or not the sentence negated is false; the nonsecurity clinches the truth-value.[13]

As a consequence of the distribution of security-values in the matrix for ∼, we have implemented the presuppositional policy

(C) For each sentence A, A and ∼ A presuppose exactly the same sentences.[14]

The policy is typically implemented in trivalent semantics as well, since the matrix for $\sim$ there takes the value N, and only the value N, into the value N (where $\sim$ is choice negation).

The matrices for the three binary connectives are

$A \vee B$	11	01	10	00
11	11	11	10	10
01	11	01	10	00
10	10	10	10	10
00	10	00	10	00

$A \& B$	11	01	10	00
11	11	01	10	00
01	01	01	00	00
10	10	00	10	00
00	00	00	00	00

$A \supset B$	11	01	10	00
11	11	01	10	00
01	11	11	10	10
10	10	00	10	00
00	10	10	10	10

According to these matrices, the truth-value of a sentence governed by one of the binary connectives is determined classically, e.g., a disjunction is true just in case one of its disjuncts is true, and it is false otherwise. Nonsecurity is contagious: a sentence governed by one of the binary connectives is secure only of both of its immediate components are secure. And as a consequence of the distribution of security-values we have implemented the presuppositional policy:

(D) Each of $A \vee B$, $A \& B$, and $A \supset B$ presupposes all sentences which are presupposed either by A or by B.

Two features of the language L are brought out particularly clearly through consideration of the matrices for the binary connectives. The first feature concerns the role of the security-value, which in general is used to signify semantic anomaly (in our present case, the occurrence of a nondenoting term). The distinction between truth-value and security-value has a particular payoff here; consider the sentence:

(3) Either the present king of France is wise or the current U.S. President is a Democrat.

According to the matrices for L, this sentence is both true and nonsecure if its disjuncts respectively have the values 00 and 11. It is true in virtue of the truth of the second disjunct, and nonsecure because of the occurrence of a nondenoting term in the first disjunct. But consider what might be the case in a trivalent treatment of (3), where the disjuncts are assigned the values N and T. If we adopt Bochvar's internal matrix for disjunction:[15]

$A \lor B$	T	F	N
T	T	T	N
F	T	F	N
N	N	N	N

then sentence (3) is assigned the value N. On the other hand, (3) is assigned the value T if we adopt Kleene's strong matrix for disjunction:[16]

$A \lor B$	T	F	N
T	T	T	T
F	T	F	N
N	T	N	N

There is a problem in deciding between the two matrices, if we interpret the value N as signifying both nontruth and semantic anomaly. A Bochvarian might argue, in support of the first matrix, that (3) is anomalous; a Kleenean might argue, in support of the second matrix, that (3) is true. In L, we can and indeed do have it both ways because truth-conditions and security-conditions are separated: sentence (3) is both true and nonsecure.

The second feature concerns the definition of preimplication in terms of security-conditions. In trivalent semantics, a true sentence cannot have false presuppositions. In L, a true sentence may preimply a false one, as does (3). In general the truth—or falsehood—of a sentence is independent of the truth-values of its preimplications. (There are exceptions, as in the case of the negation $\sim$.) And the way this is accomplished is by computing preimplications directly in terms of sources of semantic anomaly—e.g., nondenoting terms— rather than through the route of truth-values.[17] Moreover, because security-values and truth-values may be computed independently, we may choose to implement alternative presuppositional policies without affecting truth-conditions, by computing security-values in different ways. For instance, we may choose to make security rather then nonsecurity contagious in the case of sentences formed from binary connectives. Policy (D) would then be violated, e.g., (3) would not preimply either

(E1) The present king of France exists.

or

(E2) The current U.S. President exists.[18]

But the way in which truth-values are determined need not be changed in order to accommodate this change in presuppositional policy. In favor of the matrices I have chosen for the three binary connectives, it should be noted that they support one generalization from the data concerning core cases like

(1): the presuppositions of a sentence are sentences whose nontruth signals semantic anomaly in the presupposing sentence.

The remaining unary connectives yield certain degrees of semantic closure in L. The connective T, which may be read as 'it is true that', has the following matrix:

A	TA
11	11
01	01
10	11
00	01

The sentence TA is true just in case A is, and is always secure. The latter is a reflection of the "metalinguistic" character of the truth-connective. Sentences formed with this connective involve some sort of semantic ascent; the sentence TA is *about* the sentence A or, if you wish, *about* the proposition expressed by A.[19] In semantically ascending, we isolate or block the anomalousness of sentences over which we ascend, in the sense that the sentence used to ascend does not share the anomalousness. Thus 'It is true that the king of France is wise' does not purport to be about the king but rather about a sentence or a proposition;[20] the singular term is not in this case *used* to perform its normal semantic function. Since TA is always secure, it will never have any false presuppositions. Thus we have the policy

(E) For each sentence A, there is a sentence which is true exactly when A is and which is always secure, i.e., which never has false presuppositions.

Do note that although A and TA are equivalent in the weak sense of having identical truth-conditions, they are not in general equivalent in the stronger sense of having identical security-conditions as well.

The connective γ also involves semantic ascent, and it has the matrix

A	γA
11	11
01	11
10	01
00	01

The connective forms from A a sentence which is true just in case A is secure. We may read γA as: A is secure, or: A is not semantically anomalous, or: A has no false presuppositions. Introducing this connective in L gives us the presuppositional policy

(F) For each sentence A, there is a sentence which is true exactly when A is secure.

Indeed, we have the stronger policy

(G) For each sentence A there is a sentence which is true exactly when A is secure and which is itself always secure, i.e., which never has false presuppositions.

Three comments will round out my discussion of the language L before turning to the first-order language in the next section. First, L is *not* functionally complete; there are functions on the four values of L which are not expressible in L. The reason is easy to see: every nonsecure sentence must have at least one nonsecure component. Intuitively, then, the connectives of L are never themselves responsible for semantic anomaly and never induce presuppositions.

Second, we can now define a variety of other connectives in L. For example, we may define a second negation   (e.g., as $\sim A \vee \sim TA$):

A	A
11	01
01	11
10	00
00	10

Insecurity is contagious here; and truth-values are defined classically. Sentences governed by the connectives   , $\vee$, and $\supset$ are thus classical in the sense that their truth-values are determined from the truth-values of their immediate components just as in the classical truth-tables for those connectives. Hence any classical tautologies formed from these connectives (with their usual interpretations) remain tautologies in L, i.e., they are always true.

We may say also define stronger versions of the binary connectives, stronger in the sense that a sentence governed by one of these connectives is true only if its immediate components are secure. As in the case of the negation $\sim$, such connectives could be thought of as forming sentences in which the connectives fall within the scope of singular terms. So, for example, we can define

$$A \wedge B =_{df} \sim \sim (A \ \& \ B).$$

Since $\sim \sim A$ is true only if A is both true and secure, $A \wedge B$ will be true only if secure. Indeed, we may think of $\sim \sim$ as a 'strong' assertion operator: $\sim \sim A$ is equivalent (in the strong sense) to $A \ \& \ \gamma A$. (Note that if we take the negation   as primitive, the the negation $\sim$ is definable in terms of   and γ:

$\sim A =_{\mathrm{df}} \neg A \mathbin{\&} \gamma A.$

That is, $\sim A$ is true just in case A is both false (first conjunct) and secure (second conjunct), and secure just in case A is secure).

Third, I mentioned earlier that L is a "two-dimensional" language. Herzberger describes two-dimensional languages as follows:

> Two-dimensional languages are a special kind of four-valued language, whose sentences are subject to two separate valuations, one on each "dimension" of a semantic space. Intuitively, the two component valuations can be thought of as registering two distinct aspects of the meaning of sentences of the language. Thus each sentence of such a language will have associated with it an ordered pair of classical two-valued propositions, somewhat in the manner of Post's construction of 'higher-dimensional propositions'. . . . This provides a way of implementing the Fregean notion that sentences can bear at least two distinct semantic relations to propositions: each sentence can be thought of as *expressing* one proposition, and as *presupposing* another.[21]

Using this idea, we may identify the proposition expressed by a sentence with the set of valuations on which it is true, and the proposition presupposed by a sentence with the set of valuations on which it is secure. (And in Section III, substitute 'model' for 'valuation'.) The proposition presupposed by A is then expressible by one of A's preimplications, namely, γA.[22] Viewing the two-dimensional approach in this way leads to a natural "translation" of L into a bivalent language L^*, with the same syntax, as follows.

Since γA expresses the proposition presupposed by A—a proposition that is true exactly when A is secure—we may view the two-dimensional valuations as implicitly evaluating *two* sentences at a time, A and the corresponding γA, rather than as evaluating the same sentence twice. Thus we may replace each two-dimensional valuation v of L with a bivalent valuation v^* of L^* which assigns a truth-value to each atomic sentence A and to its corresponding γA:

$v^*(A) = T$ iff $v(A) \in \{11, 10\}$ (i.e., iff A is true on v); $v^*(A) = F$ otherwise.

$v^*(\gamma A) = T$ iff $v(A) \in \{11, 01\}$ (i.e., iff A is secure on v); $v^*(\gamma A) = F$ otherwise.

The values for the rest of the pairs of sentences C, γC of the language are inductively defined on the basis of the valuation v^*:

(i)   (a) $v^*(\sim A) = T$ iff $v^*(A) = F$ and $v^*(\gamma A) = T$,
      (b) $v^*(\gamma \sim A) = T$ iff $v^*(\gamma A) = T$;

(ii)   (a) $v^*(A \vee B) = T$ iff $v^*(A) = T$ or $v^*(B) = T$,
      (b) $v^*(\gamma(A \vee B)) = T$ iff $v^*(\gamma A) = v^*(\gamma B) = T$;

(iii)   (a) $v^*(A \& B) = T$ iff $v^*(A) = v^*(B) = T$,
      (b) $v^*(\gamma(A \& B)) = T$ iff $v^*(\gamma A) = v^*(\gamma B) = T$;

(iv)   (a) $v^*(A \supset B) = T$ iff $v^*(A) = F$ or $v^*(B) = T$,
      (b) $v^*(\gamma(A \supset B)) = T$ iff $v^*(\gamma A) = v^*(\gamma B) = T$;·

(v)   (a) $v^*(TA) = T$ iff $v^*(A) = T$,
     (b) $v^*(\gamma TA) = T$.

(It is understood that a sentence receives the value F if it doesn't receive the value T.) And we add a clause for the case where two occurrences of γ are piled up:

(vi) $v^*(\gamma\gamma A) = T$.

It is a straightforward matter to prove that for every valuation v of L and every sentence A, $v(A)$ is true (is a member of $\{11, 10\}$ if and only if $v^*(A) = T$. Whereas in L, the truth-value of a sentence is sometimes affected by the security-values of its components, in L^* the truth-value of a sentence is sometimes affected by the truth-values of sentences closely associated with its components (sentences governed by γ). Thus, for example, the truth-value of $\sim A$ is a function of the truth-value of A *and* that of γA.[23]

III

The first-order language L_1 has the following vocabulary:[24]

N-place predicates P_1^n, P_2^n, P_3^n, . . . for each finite number n;

Individual constants: $c_1, c_2, c_3 \ldots$;

Individual variables: $x_1, x_2, x_3, \ldots$;

Logical consonants and punctuation: $\sim, \vee, \&, \supset, T, \gamma, \forall, i, \hat{\ }, E!, =, (\,,), [,]$.

The individual consonants and individual variables are (primitive) *terms*. Complex expressions of L_1 are defined as follows:

1a. If F is an n-place predicate and $t_1, \ldots, t_n$ are terms then $Ft_1 \ldots t_n$ is a formula.

1b. If t_1 and t_2 are terms than $E!t_1$ and $t_1 = t_2$ are formulas.

1c. If A and B are formulas, then $\sim A$, TA, γA, $(A \vee B)$, $(A \mathbin{\&} B)$ and $(A \supset B)$ are formulas.

1d. If A and B are formulas and w is an individual variable, then $[\forall w A]B$ is a formula.

2. If A is a formula and w is an individual variable, then iwA is a term.

3. If A is a formula and $w_1, \ldots, w_n$ are individual variables, then $\hat{w}_1 \ldots \hat{w}_n(A)$ is an n-ary predicate.

An individual variable w is *bound* in a formula A iff each occurrence of w occurs either as part of a term iwA, or as part of a predicate $\hat{w}_1 \ldots \hat{w}_n A$ where w is some w_1, $1 \leq i \leq n$, or as part of a formula of the form $[\forall w A]B$. A *sentence* of L_1 is a formula in which every individual variable is bound.

Before introducing the semantics I will explain informally the motivation for some of its unusual aspects. As in the case of L, each sentence of L_1 will be evaluated twice. But here we can look more closely at the semantic effects of nondenoting terms on sentences in which they occur. First, a nondenoting term may occur within a complex predicate like 'either loves or loathes the present king of France'. In such a position the nondenoting term may affect security conditions of sentences. Thus the treatment of complex predicates. Second, the quantifiers are restricted in the sense that in evaluating a sentence governed by a quantifier we may not be looking at the entire domain. Unrestricted quantification is then definable in L_1 in terms of restricted quantifiers. Restricted quantification is introduced so that we can treat a sentence of the form *All Fs are Gs* as presupposing *There are Fs*, and nevertheless treat *All Fs are Gs* as true even when there are no *Fs*. As in the case of L, it is possible for a sentence which is true to have false presuppositions. So, for example, 'All John's children are asleep' may be true and yet falsely presuppose that John has children. Third, we may quantify into terms. Doing so, we may treat sentences like 'Mortimore detests every country in which the ruling party is elitist' as presupposing not only that there are countries, but also that every country has a ruling party. Again, the falsehood of the presupposition will not guarantee the falsehood of the presupposing sentence.

A *model* M for L_1 is an ordered pair $\langle D, I \rangle$ where D (the domain) is a nonempty set and I (the interpretation) is a function which makes the following assignments. For each individual constant a, either a member of D is assigned to a by I or $I(a)$ is undefined. I assigns to each primitive n-ary predicate of L_1 a set of n-tuples of members of D.

A *variable assignment* s on a model M is a function which assigns to each individual variable of L_1 a member of D. For any variable assignment s, $s[d_1/w_1, \ldots, d_n/w_n]$ is the variable assignment which is like s except that it assigns d_i to w_i, $1 \leqslant i \leqslant n$. A *valuation* V_s on M *induced* by the variable assignment s is a pair of functions v_s, p_s which assign values to the terms, predicates, and formulas of L_1 as follows:

(i)   If w is an individual variable, then
    (a) $v_s(w) = s(w)$,
    (b) $p_s(w) = 1$.

(ii)   If a is an individual constant, then
    (a) $v_s(a) = I(a)$ if $I(a)$ is defined; $v_s(a)$ is undefined otherwise,
    (b) $p_s(a) = 1$ if $I(a)$ is defined; $p_s(a) = 0$ otherwise.

(iii)   If F is an n-ary primitive predicate, then
    (a) $v_s(F) = I(F)$,
    (b) $p_s(F) = 1$.

(iv)   If A is a formula of the form $Ft_1 \ldots t_n$, where F is a primitive predicate and $t_1, \ldots, t_n$ are terms, then
    (a) $v_s(A) = 1$ if $v_s(t_1), \ldots, v_s(t_n)$ are defined and $\langle v_s(t_1), \ldots, v_s(t_n) \rangle \ \varepsilon v_s\ (F)$; $v_s(A) = 0$ otherwise,
    (b) $p_s(A) = 1$ if $p_s(t_1) = \ldots = p_s(t_n) = 1$; $p_s(A) = 0$ otherwise.

(v)   If A is a formula of the form $E!t$, then
    (a) $v_s(A) = 1$ if $v_s(t)$ is defined; $v_s(A) = 0$ otherwise,
    (b) $p_s(A) = 1$.

(vi)   If A is a formula of the form $t_1 = t_2$, then
    (a) $v_s(A) = 1$ if $v_s(t_1)$ and $v_s(t_2)$ are both defined and $v_s(t_1) = v_s(t_2)$; $v_s(A) = 0$ otherwise,
    (b) $p_s(A) = 1$ if $p_s(t_1) = p_s(t_2) = 1$; $p_s(A) = 0$ otherwise.

(vii)   If A is a formula of the form $\hat{w}_1 \ldots \hat{w}_n B t_1 \ldots t_n$, then
    (a) $v_s(A) = 1$ if $v_s(t_1), \ldots, v_s(t_n)$ are all defined and $\langle v_s(t_1), \ldots, v_s(t_n) \rangle \in v_s(\hat{w}_1 \ldots \hat{w}_n B)$; $v_s(A) = 0$ otherwise,
    (b) $p_s(A) = 1$ if $p_s(t_1) = \ldots = p_s(t_n) = 1$ and $p_{s[v_s(t_1)/w_1, \ldots, v_s(t_n)/w_n]}(B) = 1$; $p_s(A) = 0$ otherwise.

(viii) If A is a formula of the form $\sim B$, then
    (a) $v_s(A) = 1$ if $v_s(B) = 0$ and $p_s(B) = 1$; $v_s(A) = 0$ otherwise,
    (b) $p_s(A) = p_s(B)$.

(ix)   If A is a formula of the form $(B \lor C)$, then
    (a) $v_s(A) = 1$ if either $v_s(B) = 1$ or $v_s(C) = 1$; $v_s(A) = 0$ otherwise,
    (b) $p_s(A) = 1$ if $p_s(B) = p_s(C) = 1$; $p_s(A) = 0$ otherwise.

(x)   If A is a formula of the form $(B \mathbin{\&} C)$, then
      (a) $v_s(A) = 1$ if $v_s(B) = v_s(C) = 1$; $v_s(A) = 0$ otherwise,
      (b) $p_s(A) = 1$ if $p_s(B) = p_s(C) = 1$; $p_s(A) = 0$ otherwise.

(xi)   If A is a formula of the form $(B \supset C)$, then
      (a) $v_s(A) = 1$ if either $v_s(B) = 0$ or $v_s(C) = 1$; $v_s(A) = 0$
      otherwise,
      (b) $p_s(A) = 1$ if $p_s(B) = p_s(C) = 1$; $p_s(A) = 0$ otherwise.

(xii) If A is a formula of the form TB, then
      (a) $v_s(A) = v_s(B)$,
      (b) $p_s(A) = 1$.

(xiii) If A is a formula of the form γB, then
      (a) $v_s(A) = p_s(B)$,
      (b) $p_s(A) = 1$.

(xiv) If A is a formula of the form $[\forall w B]\, C$, then
      (a) $v_s(A) = 1$ if for every $d \in D$ such that $v_{s[d/w]}(B) = 1$,
      $v_{s[d/w]}(C) = 1$; $v_s(A) = 0$ otherwise,
      (b) $p_s(A) = 1$ if there is some $d \in D$ such that $v_{s[d/w]}(B) = 1$
      and for every $d \in D$ such that $v_{s[d/w]}(B) = 1$, $p_{s[d/w]}$
      $(B) = p_{s[d/w]}(C) = 1$; $p_s(A) = 0$ otherwise.

(xv) If iwA is a term, then
      (a) if there is exactly one $d \in D$ such that $v_{s[d/w]}(A) = 1$
      then $v_s(iwA) = d$; $v_s(iwA)$ is undefined otherwise,
      (b) $p_s(iwA) = 1$ if $v_s(iwA)$ is defined and $p_{s[d/w]}(A) = 1$
      where $d = v_s(iwA)$; $p_s(iwA) = 0$ otherwise.

(xvi) If $\hat{w}_1 \ldots \hat{w}_n(A)$ is an n-ary predicate, then
      (a) $v_s(\hat{w}_1 \ldots \hat{w}_n(A)) = \{\langle d_1, \ldots, d_n \rangle \in D^n :$
      $v_{s[d_1/w_1, \ldots, d_n/w_n]}(A) = 1\}$,
      (b) $p_s(\hat{w}_1 \ldots \hat{w}_n(A)) = p_s(A)$.

Finally, a sentence A is true/false on M if $v_s(A) = 1/0$ for every variable assignment s on M, and A is secure/nonsecure on M if $p_s(A) = 1/0$ for every variable assignment s on M.

A sentence of L_1 is *logically true* just in case it is secure on every model, and *logically secure* just in case it is secure on every model. A set Γ of sentences of L_1 *logically entails* the sentence B just in case B is true on every model on which every member of Γ is true; and A *preimplies* B just in case B is true on every model on which A is secure. Sentences A and B are *weakly equivalent* just in case there is no model on which A and B have different truth-values, and A and B are *strongly equivalent* just in case they are weakly equivalent and there is no model on which A and B have different security-values.

Now for some examples. Consider the following English subject-predicate sentence in which the predicate is complex:

(6) Emma is either the mother of Harry or a sister of Joan,

symbolized as

(6a) $\hat{x}(x = iyMyh \lor Sxj)e$.[25]

By clause (vii), (6a) is false on a model in which $I(e)$ is undefined. However, it need not be false if $I(e)$ is defined but one of $I(h)$, $I(j)$ isn't defined. If $I(e)$ and $I(j)$ are both defined and $\langle I(e), I(j) \rangle \in I(s)$, then (6a) will be true. And if $I(e)$ and $I(e)$ are both defined, and if $I(e)$ is the only $d \in D$ such that $\langle d, I(h) \rangle \in I(M)$, then (6a) will be true. As far as presupposition is concerned, (6a) preimplies '$E!e$', '$E!h$', $E!j$', and '$E!iyMyh$' (as well as infinitely many other sentences). Of these four sentences, the unit set of (6a) logically entails only '$E!e$'. It does, in addition, logically detail '$E!j \lor E!iyMyh$'.

The device of forming complex predicates to parse English sentences should be used with caution, for it is not always the case that sentences $\hat{w}_1 \ldots \hat{w}_n Bt_1 \ldots t_n$ and $B(t_1/w_1, \ldots, t_n/w_n)$[26] are weakly equivalent. For example compare

(7a) $Meh \lor Mjl$,

and

(7b) $\hat{x}(Mxh \lor Mjl)e$.

On a model in which $I(j)$ and $I(l)$ are defined, $I(e)$ and $I(h)$ are undefined, and $\langle I(j), I(l) \rangle \in I(M)$, sentence (7a) will be true and (7b) false.[27] On the other hand, in virtue of (b) of clause (vii), the sentences (7a) and (7b) are either both secure or both nonsecure on any given model.[28]

Next, consider the sentence

(8) All John's children are asleep,

symbolized as

(8a) $[\forall x Cxj]Ax$.

On a model on which $I(j)$ is defined and $\{d \in D: \langle d, I(j) \rangle \in I(C)\}$ is empty (John has no children), (8a) is true and nonsecure. It is true according to (a) of clause (xiv), since there is no variable assignment s and $d \in D$ such that $v_{s[d/x]}(Cxj) = 1$. It is nonsecure according to (b) of clause (xiv) *for the same reason*.

To substantiate the claim that according to L_1, (8), presupposes

(9) John has children,

it will be convenient to define some new expressions. First, the unrestricted universal quantifier:

$$(\wedge w)B =_{df} [\forall w \; w = w] \, B.$$

This definition yields

(xvii) If A is a formula of the form $(\wedge w)B$, then
  (a) $v_s(A) = 1$ if for every $d \in D$, $v_{s[d/w]}(B) = 1$; $v_s(A) = 0$ otherwise,
  (b) $p_s(A) = 1$ if for every $d \in D$, $p_{s[d/w]}(B) = 1$; $p_s(A) = 0$ otherwise.

Second, the negation $\rceil$:

$$\rceil A =_{df} \sim A \vee \sim TA,$$

which yields

(xviii) If A is a formula of the form $\rceil B$, then
  (a) $v_s(A) = 1$ if $v_s(B) = 0$; $v_s(A) = 0$ otherwise,
  (b) $p_s(A) = p_s(B)$.

Third, the unrestricted existential quantifier:[29]

$$(\vee w)B =_{df} \rceil(\wedge w)\rceil B,$$

which yields

(xix) If A is a formula of the form $(\vee w)B$, then
  (a) $v_s(A) = 1$ if for some $d \in D$, $v_{s[d/w]}(B) = 1$;
      $v_s(A) = 0$ otherwise,
  (b) $p_s(A) = 1$ if for every $d \in D$, $p_{s[d/w]}(B) = 1$;
      $p_s(A) = 0$ otherwise.

The sentence (8a) preimplies the symbolization

(9a) $(\vee x)Cxj$

of (9). More generally, we have the policy

(H) Each sentence $[\forall wB]C$ preimplies $(\vee w)B$.

Finally, consider the sentence

(10) Mortimore detests every country in which the ruling party is elitist,

symbolized as

(10a) $\hat{w}[\forall x Cx]$ $(EiyRyx \supset Dwx)m$

(which has the same *security* conditions as '$[\forall x Cx](EiyRyx \supset Dmx)$'). This sentence is nonsecure on any model which meets one of the following three conditions:

$I(m)$ is undefined;
$I(C)$ is empty;
$I(C)$ is nonempty but there is some $d \in I(C)$ such that there is not a unique $d' \in D$ for which $\langle d', d \rangle \in I(R)$.

Thus (10a) preimplies at least the three sentences

(11a) $E!m$;

(12a) $(\forall x)Cx$;

(13a) $[\forall x Cx]E!iyRyx$.

That is, parsing (10) as in (10a), (10) presupposes at least

(11)   Mortimore exists.

(12)   Some countries exist.

(13)   Every country has exactly one ruling party.

Here again, the way in which an English sentence is parsed *does* make a difference. Sentence (10a) is not strongly equivalent to

(14a) $\hat{w}(\wedge x)((Cx \ \& \ EiyRyx) \supset Dwx)m$,

or to

(15a) $\hat{w}([\forall x(Cx \ \& \ EiyRyx)]Dwx)m$.

Sentence (14a) does not preimply (12a); and (14a) preimplies some sentences which (10a) does not preimply, e.g.,

(16a) $(\wedge x)E!iyRyx$

(everything has exactly one ruling party). Sentence (15a) does not preimply (13a).

However, (15a) has no preimplications which are not shared by (10a). What is making the difference between these ways of parsing (10) is essentially the restrictions in the respective quantifiers: is the sentence (10) 'about' all countries as in (10a), 'about' everything as in (14a), or 'about' all countries in which there is a unique ruling party as in (15a)? The restrictions determine presuppositions in two ways: first, it is presupposed that something *meets* the restriction; second, it is presupposed that terms which are quantified into are 'satisfied' with respect to the restricted, rather than the entire, domain of the model. Despite all of this, each sentence of the form $[\forall wB]C$ is weakly equivalent to the corresponding $(\wedge w)(B \supset C)$; it is only strong equivalence that can fail.

Finally, some general comments about L_1. First, a sentence of the form $E!t$ is weakly equivalent to the corresponding $(\vee w)w = t$. But the two sentences are not in general *strongly* equivalent, because one of the two sentences is logically secure while the other may not be. For any model in which t has no denotation, the sentence $(\vee w)w = t$ is nonsecure. Second, if two sentences are weakly equivalent but fail of strong equivalence, they are not everywhere substitutable one for the other *salva veritate*. This is most easily seen by considering what happens when each sentence is prefixed with γ. And just as for L, TA and A are weakly but not always strongly equivalent; hence they are not in general substitutable one for the other *salva veritate*.

Third, a sentence may be logically true but not logically secure, e.g., '$Pa \supset Pa$'. Do note, however, that '$(\forall x)(Px \supset Px)$' is both logically true and logically secure. The fourth comment is that a sentence of L_1 is logically secure if it contains no constants and no occurrences of i, and if its only quantifiers are nonrestricted ones. Put another way, the constants, definite descriptions, and restricted quantifiers are the inducers of nontrivial presuppositions in L_1.

IV

What of Russell's and Strawson's disagreement over the truth-value of "The present king of France is wise"? If it is an objection to Russell that we can't have nontrivial presupposition in a language without truth-value gaps, I hope I have shown that this objection is wrong. The systems L and L_1 show that we *can* regiment the intuitive concept of presupposition in such a language. Taking security-values into account, of course, the languages are four-valued. But the four values do not arise through admitting truth-values other than *true* and *false*. Rather, they result from the semantic assessment of sentences with respect to anomaly as well as with respect to truth-values. And L_1, like L, can be compressed into a bivalent language.

It should be noted, moreover, that the language L can be used to characterize presuppositional phenomena other than the existential variety. For example, the security-value can be used to represent the truth-values of factive complements, or the sortal compatibility of terms co-occurring in sentences.[30] What I referred to, in Section I, as a 'bonus' of the trivalent account of presupposition thus applies to the two-dimensional account as well: sentences of any form can have preimplications, and the framework itself places no constraints on the grounds for nonsecurity, i.e., it places no constraints on the semantic aspects of sentences which are responsible for inducing presuppositions.

NOTES

1. The research for this paper was partially supported by a Faculty Fellowship from Dartmouth College.

2. Russell (1975, p. 179).

3. Strawson (1964, p. 104).

4. This point has been stressed recently in Herzberger (1978) and in Martin (1979). Both of these papers have helped me a great deal in straightening out my own thoughts on the topic of presupposition.

5. There is a large body of literature on presupposition, and lately the term 'presupposition' has been used to describe pragmatic as well as semantic phenomena. See Stalnaker (1973) and Martin (1979). In this paper, I restrict discussion to presupposition as a semantic concept.

6. Supervaluational semantics can also be used to develop a nonbivalent theory of presupposition. See, for example, van Fraassen (1966).

7. I adopt the policy of using the connectives of formal languages as their own names.

8. See Herzberger (1978).

9. See Herzberger (1973).

10. In Section III I shall introduce a first-order language in which phrases like 'every unicorn' may also be responsible for nonsecurity.

11. See Strawson (1956, p. 35), and Quine (1960, p. 90).

12. A presuppositional policy may do one of two things. First, it may restrict the sets of presuppositions of certain sorts of sentences. Policy (C) below, which states that for each sentence A, A and ~ A have exactly the same presuppositions, is an example of a policy of this sort. Second, it may state that the language has a certain degree of semantic closure. Policy (F) below is a policy of this sort. See Herzberger (1976) on semantic closure and presuppositional policies. My use of the term 'presuppositional policy' in this paper is broader than that of Herzberger (1976); Herzberger's policies are concerned only with semantic closure conditions.

13. Thus where A is 'The present king of France is wise', ~ A is something like 'The present king of France is such that he is not wise' or 'The present king of France exists and is not wise'. The value 00 is mapped into 00. What about the mapping of 10? An example of a sentence which is both true and nonsecure is introduced immediately below in the text: 'Either the present king of France is wise or the current U.S. President is a Democrat'. In the case of this sentence, as well as the simpler one, the negation operates semantically as if it is forcing the singular terms into primary position: 'The present King of France and the current U.S. President are such that neither the first is wise nor the second is a Democrat'. This sentence is true only if both singular terms denote (and is secure only if both denote).

See Russell (1905) for the concept of primary occurrence. There is a qualification which should be added to what I say here about ~ and scope distinction, but I leave it for below where the qualification is relevant—when the connectives T and γ are introduced. (See Note 19.) I shall also introduce another negation below, which corresponds to giving negation wider scope than singular terms. This second negation uniformly takes false sentences into true ones, and vice versa; it will take 'The present king of France is wise' into a true sentence.

14. Checking such claims is a fairly routine matter; consequently proofs will generally be omitted. In the present case it is necessary to establish that for each sentence A, A and ~ A preimply exactly the same sentences. So first assume that A preimplies B. If ~ A is secure, than A is also secure and hence B is true. Therefore ~ A preimplies B as well. Proof of the converse is similar.

15. Bochvar (1938).

16. Kleene (1952).

17. Part of a debate between two nonexistent philosophers reported in Herzberger (1978) bears on the present issue:

Strawman reasons in this way:

I have a criterion for semantic presuppositions in terms of truth and falsity. These are intuitive notions, and I can examine a language such as English to see whether or not in particular cases sentences are related presuppositionally.

Rustler reasons in this way:

It is an illusion to suppose that you have a criterion for presupposition in terms of truth and falsity, Strawman, any more or any less than you have a criterion for truth and falsity in terms of presuppositions. Within your framework a sentence which is clearly nontrue may be evaluated as False or Gap [MB: neither true nor false], depending on nothing other than the source of its nontruth—whether it is nontrue on account of denotation failure and the like, or on some other ground.

Rustler's position may be a little hard to grasp on first acquaintance, especially since it's characteristically overstated. . . . as I understand Rustler's position, the identification of semantic presuppositions is a question involving theoretical explanations at least as much as intuitions of truth-value. (p. 7)

18. This would result in the implementation of a presuppositional policy to the effect that a sentence governed by a binary connective preimplies every disjunction in which the first disjunct is presupposed by one immediate component of the sentence and the second is presupposed by the other immediate component.

19. See Quine (1960, p. 271 ff.), and Herzberger (1970) for two accounts of semantic ascent.

20. See the discussion in Woodruff (1970). In connection with the caveat in Note 11, viewing the situation in Russellian terms, the effect of prefixing a sentence with an ascending connective is to *block* singular terms from moving to primary occurrence in any sentence containing the sentence thus formed.

21. Herzberger (1975, p. 430).

22. Thus policy (F) gives us an important degree of semantic closure, which rules out 'inexpressible presuppositions' in the following sense. (This is an adaptation of the concept of inexpressible presupposition found in Herzberger (1976).) Let $p(A)$ be the collection of valuations on which A is secure $- p(A)$ is the proposition presupposed by A. Policy F states that $p(A)$ is expressible for every A.

Actually, I like to think of $p(A)$ not as *the* proposition presupposed by A but as the *maximal* proposition presupposed by A. Let $t(A)$ be the set of valuations on which A is true. Then we may identify the following set of propositions presupposed by a sentence B. $P(B) = \{t(A): B$ preimplies $A\}$. The proposition $p(A)$ is then maximal for A in the sense that $p(A)$ is included in every member of $P(B)$.

23. Similar ways of interpreting nonbivalent valuations through bivalent ones were suggested many years ago by Post (1921) and, more recently, by Scott (1973). Concerning the method, Scott says: "One way to describe the process . . . is to say that we have replaced many *values* by many *valuations*." (p. 268.) Karttunen and Peters (1979) have proposed an extension of Montague grammar in which ordered pairs of formal expressions are associated with English phrases so that each sentence generated will have two formal expressions associated with it: the first gives the truth-conditions of the sentence; the second the truth-conditions of certain implicatures and presuppositions.

24. The method of forming complex predicates and definite descriptions along with the truth-conditions for sentences containing such expressions are inspired by Stalnaker (1977). Concerning the definite descriptions, Stalnaker writes:

... to the extent that a divergence between logical and grammatical form is essential to Russell's analysis, this description theory is essentially different from Russell's. If it is an objection to Russell's theory that there is this divergence between logical and grammatical form, then there is an objection to Russell's analysis which does not apply to the proposed theory. (p. 337)

Nor, thanks to Stalnaker, to the present theory. This is important, as one objection to Russell's treatment of sentences like (1) as *false* is that he depends on the distinction between logical and grammatical form.

25. For perspicuity, I am using symbols for variables, constants, and predicates which are not contained in L_1. I also drop outermost parentheses and redundant parentheses in formulas.

26. Where $B(t_1/w_1, \ldots, t_n/w_n)$ is the expression obtained from B by the simultaneous substitution of t_1 for all free occurrences of w_1 in $B, \ldots, t_n$ for all free occurrences of w_n in B.

27. That different ways of parsing should have an effect on truth-conditions is nothing new. In looking at sentences of English, it may take considerations involving context of utterance to decide how the sentences should be parsed. See also the discussion of the concept of topic in Strawson (1964).

28. Note that (b) of clause (xvi) is really doing no work in the semantics. I have added it for simplicity so that every expression considered gets evaluated twice. It is doing no work insofar as the clause which evaluates formulas just formed from complex predicater and terms—clause (vii)—does not make use of (xvi) (b). When a term occurring in B contains a free variable which is bound in $\hat{w}_1 \ldots \hat{w}_n Bt_1 \ldots t_n$, whether that term is defined in $\hat{w}_1 \ldots \hat{w}_n Bt_1 \ldots t_n$ will depend on the values assigned (or lack thereof) to $t_1, \ldots, t_n$.

29. We can also define a restricted existential quantifier:

$$[\exists wB] \; C =_{df} \quad [\forall wB] \quad C$$

which gives clause

(xx) If A is a formula of the form $[\exists wB] \; C$, then
    (a) $v_s(A) = 1$ iff for some $d \in D$, $v_{s[d/w]}(B) = v_{s[d/w]} \; (C) = 1$; $v_s(A) = 0$ otherwise,
    (b) $p_s(A) = 1$ iff there is some $d \in D$ such that $v_{s[d/w]}(B) = 1$ and for every $d \in D$ such that $v_{s[d/w]}(B) = 1$, $p_{s[d/w]})(B) = p_{s[d/w]}(C) = 1$; $p_s(A) = 0$ otherwise.

Thus $[\exists wB] \; C$ and $[\forall wB] \; C$ have the same security conditions and share the same preimplications. Anticipating example (10) below, a treatment of

Mortimore detests some country in which the ruling party is elitist.

as

$[\exists xCx] \; (EiyRyx \; \& \; Dmx),$

yields (11), (12), and (13) as presuppositions of the sentence.

30. See Bergmann (1977). Although the language L_c developed there is not two-dimensional, it can be used to generate a two-dimensional language in virtue of the presence of the connective γ, by the converse to the method of compression presented at the end of Section

II in this paper. With respect to each valuation v of L_c, we associate with each sentence A a pair of values in which the first member is 1 iff $v(A) = T$ and the second member is 1 iff $v(\gamma A) = T$. The matrices thus generated for the connectives $\sim$, &, $\supset$, $\rceil$, T, and γ of L_c correspond to the matrices for those connectives in L in the present paper.

REFERENCES

Bergmann, Merrie, 'Logic and sortal incorrectness', *The Review of Metaphysics* 30 (1977), 61–69.

Bochvar, D. A. 'On a three-valued logical calculus and its application to the analysis of contradictions', *Matematicheskii Sbornik n.s.* 4 (1938), 287–308.

Herzberger, Hans G., *Truth and Modality in Semantically Closed Languages*, in R. L. Martin (ed.), *The Paradox of the Liar*, Yale, New Haven, pp. 25–46, 1980.

Herzberger, Hans G., 'Dimensions of truth', *Journal of Philosophical Logic* 2 (1973), 536–556.

Herzberger, Hans G., 'Supervaluations in two dimensions', *Proceedings of the International Symposium on Multiple-Valued Logic*, Indiana University Linguistics Club, Bloomington, pp. 429–435, 1975.

Herzberger, Hans G., 'Presuppositional Policies', in A. Kasher (ed.), *Language in Focus*, Reidel, Dordrecht, Holland, pp. 140–163, 1976.

Herzberger, Hans G., *True, False, Etc.*, Unpublished typescript, University of Toronto, 1978.

Karttunen, Lauri, and Peters, Stanley, 'Conventional implicature', in C.-K. Oh and D. A. Dineen (eds.), *Syntax and Semantics*, v. 11, Academic Press, New York, pp. 1–56, (1979).

Kleene, Stephen C., *Introduction to Metamathematics*. D. van Nostrand, Toronto, 1952.

Martin, John N., *Some Misconceptions in the Critique of Semantic Presupposition*, Indiana University Linguistics Club, Bloomington, 1979.

Post, Emil, 'Introduction to a general theory of elementary propositions'. *American Journal of Mathematics* 43 (1921), 265–283.

Quine, Willard V. O., *Word and Object*, M.I.T., Cambridge, Mass., 1960.

Russell, Bertrand A. W. 'On denoting', *Mind n.s.* 14 (1905), 479–493.

Russell, Bertrand, A. W., *My Philosophical Development*, Unwin, London, 1975.

Scott, Dana S., 'Background to formalization', in H. LeBlanc (ed.), *Truth, Syntax, and Modality*, North-Holland, Amsterdam, pp. 244–273, 1973.

Stalnaker, Robert C., 'Presuppositions', *Journal of Philosophical Logic* 2 (1973), 447–457.

Stalnaker, Robert C., 'Complex predicates', *The Monist* 60 (1977), 327–339.

Strawson, P. F., 'On referring', in A. Flew (ed.), *Essays in Conceptual Analysis*, St. Martin's, New York, pp. 21–52, 1956.

Strawson, P. F., 'Identifying reference and truth-values', *Theoria* 30 (1964), 96–118.

van Fraassen, Bas C., 'Singular terms, truth-value gaps, and free logic', *Journal of Philosophy* 63 (1966), 481–495.

Woodruff, Peter W., 'Logic and truth value gaps' in K. Lambert (ed.), *Philosophical Problems in Logic*, Reidel, Dordrecht, Holland, pp. 121–142, 1970.

DAVID KAPLAN

DTHAT

Donnellan, in "Reference and Definite Descriptions" says, "Using a definite description referentially a speaker may say something true even though the description correctly applies to nothing."[1] His example—taken from Linsky[2]—has someone saying of a spinster:

Her husband is kind to her

after having had Mr. Jones—actually the spinster's brother—misintroduced as the spinster's husband. And—to fill it out—having noticed Jones' solicitous attention to his sister. The speaker used the nondenoting description "Her husband" to refer to Mr. Jones. And so, what he said was true.

There are a lot of entities associated with the utterance of "Her husband is kind to her" which are commonly said to have been said: tokens, types, sentences, propositions, statements, etc. The something-true-said, Donnellan calls a *statement*.

On the other hand, "If . . . the speaker has just met the lady and, noticing her cheerfulness and radiant good health, made his remark from his conviction that these attributes are always the result of having good husbands, he would be using the definite description attributively."[3]

After pointing out that "in general, whether or not a definite description is used referentially or attributively is a function of the speaker's intentions

Do not partake of this article before reading the following Warning: This paper was prepared for and read at the 1970 Stanford Workshop on Grammar and Semantics. Peter Cole has persuaded me—against my better judgment—that it has aged long enough to be digestible. The paper has not been revised other than to remove the subtitle comment "[Stream of Consciousness Draft: Errors, confusions, and disorganizations are not to be taken seriously]." That injunction must still be strictly obeyed. Some parts of this ramble are straightened out in the excessive refinements of "Bob and Carol and Ted and Alice" (which appeared in the proceedings for which this was destined). A more direct presentation of the resulting theory along with some of its applications is to be found in my *Demonstratives* An intermediate progress report occurs in "On the Logic of Demonstratives." "DTHAT" is pronounced as a single syllable.

in a particular case,"[4] he mentions that according to Russell's theory of descriptions, the use of *the* φ might be thought of as involving reference "in a very weak sense . . . to *whatever* is the one and only one φ, if there is any such."[5] Donnellan then concludes:

Now this is something we might well say about the attributive use of definite descriptions. . . . But this lack of particularity is absent from the referential use of definite descriptions precisely because the description is here merely a device for getting one's audience to pick out or think of the thing to be spoken about, a device which may serve its function even if the description is incorrect. More importantly perhaps, in the referential use as opposed to the attributive, there is a right thing to be picked out by the audience, and its being the right thing is not simply a function of its fitting the description.[6]

Donnellan develops his theory by adducing a series of quite plausible examples to help him answer certain theoretical questions, e.g., are there sentences in which the contained definite description can only be used referentially (or only attributively)? Can reference fail when a definite description is used referentially?, etc.

In my own reading and rereading of Donnellan's article I always find it both fascinating and maddening. Fascinating, because the fundamental distinction so clearly reflects an accurate insight into language use, and maddening, because: first, the examples seem to me to alternate between at least two clearly discriminable concepts of *referential use*; second, the notion of *having someone in mind* is not analyzed but used; and third, the connections with the developed body of knowledge concerning intensional logics—their syntax and semantics—are not explicitly made, so we cannot immediately see what Donnellan and intensional logic have to offer each other, if anything.

As one of the body developers, I find this last snub especially inexcusable. This is not a divergent perception for those of my ilk. Hintikka remarks (plaintively?), "The only thing I miss in Donnellan's excellent paper is a clear realization that the distinction he is talking about is only operative in contexts governed by propositional attitudes or other modal terms."[7]

Hintikka's remark is at first surprising, since none of Donnellan's examples seem to have this form. But the remark falls into place when we recognize that Donnellan is concerned essentially with a given speaker who is *asserting* something, *asking* something, or *commanding* something. And thus if we pull back and focus our attention on the sentence *describing* the speech act;

John asserted that Mary's husband is kind to her

the intensional operator appears.

Probably Hintikka wanted to argue that the sentence:

Her husband is kind to her

is not itself ambiguous in the way that, say:

Every boy kissed a girl

is. The fact that an ambiguous sentence is produced by embedding φ in some sentential context (for example, an intensional or temporal operator) should not be construed to indicate an ambiguity in φ. For were it so, (almost?) all sentences would be ambiguous.

Donnellan's distinction is a contribution to the redevelopment of an old and commonsensical theory about language which—at least in the philosophical literature—has rather been in a decline during the ascendency of semantics over epistemology of the 1930s, '40s, and '50s. The commonsense theory is one that Russell wrestled with in *The Principles of Mathematics*[8] but seemed to reject in "On Denoting."[9] This theory asserts roughly that the correct analysis of a typical speech act, for example,

John is tall

distinguishes *who* is being talked about, i.e. the individual under consideration—here, John—from *how* he is being characterized—here, as tall.

Russell's analysis of the proposition expressed by

John is tall

provides it with two components: the property expressed by the predicate is tall, and the individual John. That's right, John himself, right there, trapped in a proposition.

During the Golden Age of Pure Semantics we were developing a nice homogeneous theory, with language, meanings, and entities of the world each properly segregated and related one to another in rather smooth and comfortable ways. This development probably came to its peak in Carnap's *Meaning and Necessity*.[10] Each *designator* has both an intension and an extension. Sentences have truth-values as extensions and propositions as intentions, predicates have classes as extensions and properties as intensions, terms have individuals as extensions and *individual concepts* as intensions, and so on. The intension of a compound is a function of the intensions of the parts and similarly the extension (except when intensional operators appear). There is great beauty and power in this theory.

But there remained some nagging doubts: proper names, demonstratives, and quantification into intensional contexts.

Proper names may be practical convenience in our mundane transactions, but they are a theoretician's nightmare. They are like bicycles. Everyone easily learns to ride, but no one can correctly explain how he does it. Completely new theories have been proposed within the last few years, in spite of the fact that the subject has received intense attention throughout this century, and in some portions of Tibet people have had proper names for even longer than that.

The main difficulty has to do, I believe, with the special intimate relationship between a proper name and its bearer. Russell said that in contrast with a common noun, like "unicorn," a proper name *means* what it names. And if it names nothing, it means nothing. In the case of "unicorn" we have a meaning, perhaps better a *descriptive meaning*, which we make use of in looking for such things. But in the case of the name "Moravcsik" there is just Moravcsik. There is no basis on which to ask whether Moravcsik exists. Such a question is—for Russell—meaningless. But people persist in asking this question. Maybe not this very question, but analogous ones like:

Does Santa Claus exist?

There were other apparent difficulties in Russell's theory. The astronomical discovery that Hesperus was identical with Phosphorus became a triviality. The sentence expressing it expressed the same proposition as "Hesperus is identical with Hesperus." Furthermore, although the bearer of a given proper name is the be-all and end-all of the name's semantic relata, almost every proper name has dozens of bearers.

And then there are the unforgivable distortions of the minimal descriptive content of proper names. We all know of butchers named "Baker" and dogs named "Sir Walter." The ultimate in such perversity occurs in titles of the top administrative officers at UCLA. We have four vice-chancellors at UCLA, one of whom has the title "The Vice-Chancellor."

All in all, proper names are a mess and if it weren't for the problem of how to get the kids to come in for dinner, I'd be inclined to just junk them.

At any rate, the attempt during the Golden Age was to whip proper names into line. In fact into the line of common nouns. People do ask:

Does Santa Claus exist?

So that must mean something like:

Does a unicorn exist?

They do ask:

Is Hesperus identical with Phosphorus?

So that must mean something like:

Are bachelors identical with college graduates?

Thus was waged a war of attrition against proper names. Many were unmasked as disguised descriptions, e.g. "Aristotle" means *the student of Plato and teacher of Alexander who. . . .*—not an unreasonable proposal.

However, some of these exposés did seem a bit oppressive, e.g. Russell's suggestion that:

Scott is Sir Walter

really means:

The person named "Scott" is the person named "Sir Walter"

followed by his nonchalant remark: "This is a way in which names are frequently used in practice, and there will, as a rule, be nothing in the phraseology to show whether they are being used in this way or as names."[11] But at least they isolated the few real troublemakers—who turned out not to be our good old proper names at all but a handful of determined outside demonstratives: "this," "that," etc.

In summary, the technique was first to expose a proper name as a disguised description (sometimes on tenuous and unreliable evidence) and then ruthlessly to eliminate it.

We thus reduce the exciting uncertainties of:

Socrates is a man

to the banality of:

All men are mortal

The demonstratives were still there, but they were so gross they could be ignored.

Lately, under the pressure of the new interest in singular propositions generated by intensional logic, the verities of the Golden Age are breaking down. Once logicians became interested in formalizing a logic of necessity, belief, knowledge, assertion, etc., traditional syntactical ways quickly led to formulas like

John asserted that x is a spy

with free 'x' and then with 'x' bound to an anterior operator. Under what circumstances does a given individual, taken as value of 'x', satisfy this formula? Answer: If the appropriate singular proposition was the content of John's assertive utterance.

It seems that in at least certain speech acts, what I am trying to express can't quite be put into words. It is that proposition of Russell's with John trapped in it.

The property of being tall is exactly expressed by "is tall," and the concept of the unique spy who is shorter than all other spies is exactly expressed by "the shortest spy"; but no expression exactly expresses John. An expression may express a concept or property that, in reality, only John satisifes. There are many such distinct concepts; none of which is John himself.

I would like to distinguish between the kind of propositions which were considered by Aristotle (*all S is P, some S is not P*, etc.) and the kind of proposition considered by the early Russell. I call the former *general propositions* and the latter *singular propositions*. Suppose, just for definiteness, that we fix attention on sentences of simple subject-predicate form. The following are examples:

(1) A spy is suspicious.

(2) Every spy is suspicious.

(3) The spy is suspicious.

(4) John is suspicious.

Now let us think of the proposition associated with each sentence as having two components. Corresponding to the predicate we have the property of being suspicious; and corresponding to the subject we have either what Russell in 1903 called a *denoting concept* or an individual. Let us take the proposition to be the ordered couple of these two components.

Again, to fix ideas, let us provide a possible-world style of interpretation for these notions. We think of each total or complete possible state of affairs as a possible world. The possible worlds are each continuants through time and may in fact overlap at certain times. For example, a possible world may agree with the actual world up to the time at which some individual made a particular decision; the possible world may then represent an outcome of a decision other than the one actually taken. (In science fiction, such cases are called *alternate time lines*.)

Within this framework we can attempt to represent a number of the semantic notions in question. We might represent the property of *being suspicious* by that function P which assigns to each possible world w and each time t the set of all those individuals of w which, in w, are suspicious at t. We might represent the denoting concepts expressed by the denoting phrases 'A spy', 'Every spy', and 'The spy' as, say, the ordered couples: $\langle$'A',$S\rangle$, $\langle$'Every',$S\rangle$, $\langle$'The',$S\rangle$ where S is the property (represented as above) of *being a spy*.[12] The fact that the logical words 'A', 'Every', and 'The' are just carried along reflects our treatment of them as *syncategorematic*, i.e. as having no independent meaning but as indicators of how to combine the meaning-bearing parts (here "spy" and the predicate) in determining the meaning of the whole. For (1), (2), and (3) the corresponding propositions are now represented by:

(5) $\langle\langle$'A',$S\rangle P\rangle$

(6) $\langle\langle$'Every',$S\rangle P\rangle$

(7) $\langle\langle$'The',$S\rangle P\rangle$

It should be clear that each of (5)–(7) will determine a function which assigns to each possible world w and time t a truth value. And in fact the truth value so assigned to any w and t will be exactly the truth value in w at t of the corresponding sentence. For example: (6) determines that function which assigns truth to a given w and t if and only if every member of $S(w,t)$ is a member of $P(w,t)$. Notice that the function so determined by (6) also correctly assigns to each w and t the truth value in w at t of (2). (For the purpose of (7), let us take * to be a "truth value" which is assigned to w and t when $S(w,t)$ contains other than a single member.)

The proposition corresponding to (4) would be:

(8) $\langle$John,$P\rangle$

not $\langle$'John',$P\rangle$ mind you, but $\langle$John,$P\rangle$. And (8) will determine that function F which assigns Truth to w and t if and only if John is a member of $P(w,t)$. If John is an individual of w at the time t (i.e. John exists in w and is alive at t) but is not a member of $P(w,t)$, then $F(w,t)$ is falsehood; and if John is not an individual of w at the time t, then $F(w,t)$ is *.

This brief excursion into possible-world semantics is only to fix ideas in a simple way within that framework (I will later make further use of the framework) and is not put forward as an ideal (in any sense: generalizability, elegance, etc.) representation of the semantic notions of property, proposition, denoting concept, etc. My main motivation is to present a representation which will clearly distinguish singular and general propositions.

It would, of course, have been possible to supply a representation of the proposition expressed by (4) which is, in a sense, formally equivalent to (8) and which blurs the distinction I wish to emphasize. I do it now lest anyone think that the possibility is a relevant refutation of my later remarks. Let us clearly depart from Russell by associating a denoting concept:

(9) $\langle$'Proper Name',$J\rangle$

where J is what we might call *John's essence*, the property of *being John*, namely, that function which assigns to each possible world w and time t the set {John} if John is an individual of w and is alive in w at t and the empty set otherwise. The analogue to (8) is now

(10) $\langle\langle$'Proper Name',$J\rangle P\rangle$

It will be noted that we have now treated the proper name "John" rather like the definite description "The John," in which the proper name plays the role of a common noun. Accordingly the function from possible worlds and times to truth values which is determined by (10) is identical with that determined by:

(11) $\langle\langle$'The',$J\rangle I\rangle$

There are certainly other representations of these propositions which ally various subgroups. In fact, once any formal structure is established, the production of isomorphic structures satisfying specified "internal" conditions is largely a matter of logical ingenuity of the "pure" kind.[13]

To return to the point, I have represented propositions in a way which emphasizes the singular–general distinction, because I want to revive a view of language alternate to that of the Golden Age. The view of the Golden Age is, I believe, undoubtedly correct for a large portion of language behavior, in particular, communication by means of general propositions. But the alternate view accounts for a portion of language behavior not accommodated by the view of the Golden Age.

The alternate view is: *that some or all of the denoting phrases used in an utterance should not be considered part of the content of what is said but should rather be thought of as contextual factors which help us interpret the actual physical utterance as having a certain content.* The most typical of such contextual factors is the fact that the speaker's utterance is to be taken as an utterance of some specific language, say, English. When I utter "yes," which means *yes* in English and *no* in Knoh, you must know I am speaking Knoh to know I have said *no*. It is no *part* of what I have said that I am speaking Knoh, though Knoh being a complete tongue, I could add that by uttering "I am speaking English." Such an utterance is of doubtful utility in itself; but, fortunately, there are other means by which this fact can be ascertained by my auditor, e.g. by my general physical appearance, or, if I am not a native Knoh, by my pointing to Knoh on a celestial globe. A homelier example has a haberdasher utter to a banker, "I am out of checks." Whether the utterance takes place in the store or at the bank will help the banker determine what the haberdasher has said. In either case it is no *part* of what was said that the haberdasher used "checks" to mean bank checks rather than suits with a checkered pattern. Of course the haberdasher could go on, if he desired, to so comment on his past performance, but that would be to say something else. Still closer to home is my wife's utterance: "It's up to you to punish Jordan for what happened today." It is by means of various subtle contextual clues that I understand her to be charging me to administer discipline to our son and not to be calling on me to act where the United Nations has failed. Again, should I exhibit momentary confusion she might, by a comment, a gesture, or simply some more discourse on the relevant naughtiness, assist me in properly decoding her first utterance so that I could understand what she was, in fact, saying. There are other ways—more controversial than the intentional resolution of the reference of a proper name among the many persons so dubbed—in which contextual factors determine the content of an utterance containing a proper name; but I am reserving all but the most blatantly obvious remarks for later.

Now let us narrow our attention to utterances containing *singular denoting phrases* (i.e. denoting phrases which purport to stand for a unique individual, such as "the spy," "John", "$\sqrt{2}$," etc.).[14]

How can contextual factors determine that part of the content of an utterance which corresponds to a singular denoting phrase? Two ways have already been mentioned: by determining what language is being spoken and by determining which of the many persons so dubbed a proper name stands for. But the most striking way in which such contextual factors enter is in connection with *demonstratives:* "this," "this spy," "that book," etc. In at least some typical uses of these phrases, it is required that the utterance be accompanied by a *demonstration*—paradigmatically, a pointing—which indicates the object for which the phrase stands.[15] I will speak of a *demonstrative use* of a singular denoting phrase when the speaker intends that the object for which the phrase stands be designated by an associated demonstration.[16]

Now we can add another example of a subject-predicate sentence to those of (1)–(4):

(12) He [the speaker points at John] is suspicious.

I am adopting the convention of enclosing a description of the relevant demonstration in square brackets immediately following each denoting phrase which is used demonstratively.[17]

What shall we take as the proposition corresponding to (12) (which I also call the *content* of the *utterance* (12))? In line with our program of studying contextual factors which are not *part* of what is said but whose role is rather to help us interpret the utterance as *having* a certain content, we shall take the component of the proposition which corresponds to the demonstrative to be the individual demonstrated. Thus the varying *forms* which such a demonstration can take are not reflected in the content of the utterance (i.e. the proposition). The demonstration "gives us" the element of the proposition corresponding to the demonstrative. But *how* the demonstration gives that individual to us is here treated as irrelevant to the content of the utterance; just as the different *ways* by which I might have come to understand which Jordan was relevant to my wife's utterance, or the different *ways* by which one might come to understand that a speaker is speaking Knoh rather than English, do not alter the content of those utterances. Thus, for example, the utterances (in English):

(13) He [the speaker points at John, as John stands on the demonstration platform nude, clean shaven, and bathed in light] is suspicious.

(14) He [the speaker points at John, as John lurks in shadows wearing a trenchcoat, bearded, with his hat pulled down over his face] is suspicious.

are taken, along with other refinements of (12), as expressing the same proposition, namely:

(15) ⟨John,*P*⟩.

It should immediately be apparent that we are in store for some delightful anomalies. Erroneous beliefs may lead a speaker to put on a demonstration which does not demonstrate what he thinks it does, with the result that he will be under a misapprehension as to *what* he has said. Utterances of identity sentences containing one or more demonstratives may express necessary propositions, though neither the speaker nor his auditors are aware of it. In fact, we get extreme cases in which linguistic competence is simply insufficient to completely determine the content of what is said. Of course this was already established by the case of the Knoh-English translation problem, but the situation is more dramatic using the demonstratives.

The present treatment is not inevitable. An alternative is to incorporate the demonstration in the proposition. We would argue as follows: Frege's *sense and denotation* distinction[18] can be extended to all kinds of indicative devices. In each case we have the object indicated (the "denotation") and the manner of indication (the "sense"). It is interesting to note that (at least in Feigl's translation) Frege wrote of "the sense (connotation, meaning) of the sign in which is contained the *manner and context* of presentation of the denotation of the sign."[19] I think it reasonable to interpret Frege as saying that the sense of a sign is what is grasped by the linguistically competent auditor, and it seems natural to generalize and say that it is the "sense" of the demonstration that is grasped by the competent auditor of utterances containing demonstratives. Thus we see how the drawn-out English utterance:

(16) That [the speaker points at Phosphorus in early morning] is the same planet as that [the speaker points at Hesperus in the early evening].

could be both informative and true.

Let us call the preceding a *Fregean treatment of demonstratives*. It is worth developing (which means primarily working on the ontology (metaphysics?) of demonstrations and the semantics of demonstration descriptions) but, I believe, will ultimately be unsatisfactory. For now I'll just outline some of the reasons. The demonstrative use of demonstratives plays an important role in language learning, in general, in the learning and use of proper names, in our misty use of *de re* modalities, in our better grounded use of what Quine calls the *relational* senses of epistemic verbs (i.e. the senses of those intensional verbs that permit quantification in).[20] And, in general, I believe that we can sharpen our epistemological insights in a number of areas by taking account of what I call the demonstrative use of expression. Such uses are far more widespread than one imagined.

I earlier called the Fregean treatment of demonstratives "unsatisfactory." I would be more cautious in saying that it was wrong. (However I do think an empirical argument from linguistic behavior could be developed to show that it is wrong. I take Donnellan's study of the phenomenology of what he calls referential use to be an excellent start in that direction.) What I am confident of is that if we force all phenomena that suggest a special *demonstrative* use of language, along with what I regard as a corresponding feature— a special *singular* form of proposition—into the Fregean mold of linguistic elements with a sense and a denotation, the sense being the element which appears in the proposition (thus leaving us with only general propositions), then important insights will be lost. I don't deny that on a phenomenon-by-phenomenon basis we can (in some sense) keep stretching Frege's brilliant insights to cover. With a little ingenuity I think we *can* do that. But we shouldn't.

Now let me offer a slightly different and somewhat a priori justification for studying the phenomena of demonstrative uses of expressions and singular propositions. I leave aside the question whether we have correctly analyzed any actual linguistic behavior, whether concerned with the so-called demonstrative *phrases* or otherwise.

Having explained so clearly and precisely what such a use of language would amount to, in terms of a possible-world semantics, I can simply resolve to so use the word "that" in the future. At a minimum I could introduce the new word "dthat" for the demonstrative use of "that." Couldn't I? I can, and I will. In fact, I do.

I like this intentional (i.e. stipulative) way of looking at the use of "dthat" because I believe that in many cases where there are competing Fregean and demonstrative analyses of some utterances or class of utterances the matter

DAVID KAPLAN • 223

can be resolved simply by the intentions of the speaker (appropriately conveyed to the auditor?). Thus in the case of proper names (to which I will return below) I might simply resolve to use them demonstratively (i.e. as demonstrating the individual whom they are a name *of* in the nomenclature of an earlier paper[21]) on certain occasions and in a Fregean way[22] on other occasions. Of course one who did not have a clear understanding of the alternatives might have difficulty in characterizing his own use, but once we have explored each choice there is nothing to prevent us from choosing either, "unnatural" though the choice may be.

It should probably be noted that despite the accessibility of the semantics of "dthat" our *grasp* of the singular propositions so expressed is, in John Perry's apt phrase, a bit of *knowledge by description* as compared with our rather more direct acquaintance with the general propositions expressed by nondemonstrative utterances.

Armed with "dthat" we can now explore and possibly even extend the frontiers of demonstrations.

When we considered the Fregean analysis of demonstrations, we attempted to establish parallels between demonstrations and descriptions.[23] Insofar as this aspect of the Fregean program is successful, it suggests the possibility of a demonstrative analysis of descriptions. *If pointing can be taken as a form of describing, why not take describing as a form of pointing?* Note that our demonstrative analysis of demonstrations need not, indeed should not, deny or even ignore the fact that demonstrations have both a sense and a demonstratum. It is just that according to the demonstrative analysis the sense of the demonstration does not appear in the proposition. Instead the sense is used only to fix the demonstratum which itself appears directly in the proposition. I propose now to do the same for descriptions. Instead of taking the sense of the description as subject of the proposition, we use the sense only to fix the denotation which we then take directly as subject component of the proposition. I now take the utterance of the description as a demonstration and describe it with the usual quotation devices, thus:

(17) Dthat ["the spy"] is suspicious.

For fixity of ideas, let us suppose, what is surely false, that in fact, actuality, and reality there is one and only one spy, and John is he. We might express this so:

(18) "the spy" denotes John.[24]

In the light of (18), (17) expresses:

(19) $\langle John, P \rangle$

(also known as '(8)' and '(15)').

Recollecting and collecting we have:

(3) The spy is suspicious.

(4) John is suspicious.

(7) ⟨⟨'The',S⟩ P⟩

(12) He [the speaker points at John] is suspicious.

or as we might now write (12):

(20) Dhe [the speaker points at John] is suspicious.[25]

Earlier we said that an utterance of (3) expresses (7), and only an utterance of (12) [i.e. (20)] or possibly (4) expresses (19). I have already suggested that an utterance of (4) may sometimes be taken in a Fregean way to express something like (7), and now I want to point out that for want of "dthat" some speakers may be driven to utter (3) when they intend what is expressed by (17).

If an utterance of (3) may indeed sometimes express (19), then Donnellan was essentially correct in describing his referential and attributive uses of definite descriptions as a "duality of function." And it might even be correct to describe this duality as an *ambiguity* in the sentence type (3). I should note right here that my demonstrative use is not quite Donnellan's referential use— a deviation that I will expatiate on below—but it is close enough for present purposes.

The ambiguity in question here is of a rather special kind. For under no circumstances could the choice of disambiguation for an utterance of (3) affect the truth-value. Still there are two distinct propositions involved, and even two distinct functions from possible worlds and times to truth-values, determined by the two propositions.

Before continuing with the ambiguity in (3), it would be well to interject some remarks on sentence types and sentence tokens (of which utterances are one kind) especially as they relate to demonstratives.

Sentence types vary considerably in the degree to which they contain implicit and explicit references to features of the context of utterance. The references I have in mind here are those that affect the truth-value of the sentence type on a particular occasion of utterance. At one extreme stand what Quine (in *Word and Object*) called *eternal sentences*: those in which the feature linguists call *tense* does not really reflect a perspective from some point in time, which contain no *indexicals* such as "now," "here," "I," etc., and whose component names and definite descriptions are not understood to require contextual determination as did the "Jordan" of our earlier example. Quine describes such sentences as "those whose truth value stays fixed through time and from speaker to speaker."[26] But I prefer my own vaguer formulation: *those sentences which do not express a perspective from within space-time.* Quine and I would both count "In 1970 American women exceed American men in wealth" as eternal; he would (presumably) also count "The UCLA football team always has, does, and will continue to outclass the Stanford football team" as eternal, I would not.

Truth values are awarded directly to eternal sentences without any relativization to time, place, etc.[27] But for the fugitive sentence no stable truth value can be awarded. Let us consider first tensed sentences, e.g.:

(21) American men will come to exceed American women in intelligence.

Without disputing the facts, if (21) were true at one time, it would fail to be true at some later time. (Since one doesn't come to exceed what one already exceeds.)

Now let's dredge up the possible worlds. We associated with (21) a function which assigns to each possible world and time a truth value. Such a function seems to represent, for reasons which have been much discussed, at least part of the meaning of (21) or part of what we grasp when we understand (21).[28] There is another kind of "content" associated with a fugitive sentence like (21), namely, the content of a particular utterance of (21). In a sense, any particular utterance (token) of a fugitive sentence (type) is an *eternalization* of the fugitive sentence. The relativization to time is fixed by the time of utterance. We can associate with each utterance of a fugitive sentence the same kind of function from possible worlds to truth values that we associate directly with eternal sentences.

Before becoming completely lost in a vague nomenclature, let me make some stipulations. I will call the function which assigns to a time and a possible world the truth value of a given fugitive sentence (type) at that time in that world the *meaning* of the given sentence. The meaning of a sentence is what a person who is linguistically competent grasps, it is common to all utterances of the sentence, and it is one of the components which goes into determining the *content* of any particular utterance of the sentence. The *content* of an utterance is that function which assigns to each possible world the truth value which the utterance would take if it were evaluated with respect to that world. There is some unfortunate slack in the preceding characterizations, which I will try to reduce.[29]

Let ϕ be a fugitive sentence like (21); let $\overline{\phi}$ be the meaning of ϕ, let W be the set of possible worlds; let T be the set of times (I assume that all possible worlds have the same temporal structure and, in fact, the very same times, i.e. a given time in one world has a unique counterpart in all others); let U be the set of possible utterances; for $u \epsilon U$ let $S(u)$ be the sentence uttered in u; let $T(u)$ be the time of u (when only $S(u)$ and $T(u)$ are relevant; we might identify u with $\langle S(u), T(u) \rangle$ and let $\overline{u}$ be the content of u. The relation between the meaning of a sentence (whose only fugitive aspect is its temporality) and the content of one of its possible utterances can now be concisely expressed as follows:

(22) $Au\varepsilon\ UAw\varepsilon\ W(\bar{u}(w) = \overline{S(u)}\ (T(u),w))$

or, identifying u with $\langle S(u),\ T(u)\rangle$:

(23) $Aw\varepsilon WAt\varepsilon T\ (\overline{\langle\varphi,t\rangle}(w) = \bar{\varphi}(t,w))$

To put it another way, an utterance of φ fixes a time, and the content of the utterance takes account of the truth value of φ in all possible worlds but *only at that time*.

From (22) and (23) it would appear that the notions of meaning and content are interdefinable. Therefore, since we already have begun developing the theory of meaning for fugitive sentences (see especially the work of Montague),[30] why devote any special attention to the theory of content? Is it not simply a subtheory of a definitional extension of the theory of meaning? I think not. But the reasons go beyond simple examples like (21) and take us, hopefully, back to the main track of this paper. It is worth looking more deeply into the structure of utterances than a *simple* definition of that notion within the theory of meaning would suggest. (I stress *simple* because I have not yet really investigated sophisticated definitions.)

First we have problems about the counterfactual status of possible utterances: Are utterances *in* worlds, are they assumed to occur in worlds in which their content is being evaluated, or are they extraworldly, with their content evaluated independent of their occurrence? Consider the infamous 'I am here now', or perhaps more simply:

(24) An utterance is occurring.

Is the meaning of (24) to assign to a time and world the truth-value which an utterance of (24) *would* take *were* it to occur in that world at that time? Or does it assign simply the truth value of (24), in that world at that time? Presumably the latter. But this is to assume that utterances come complete, with the value of all their contextually determined features filled in (otherwise the utterance alone—without being set in a world—would not have a content). I do not want to make this assumption since I am particularly interested in the *way* in which a demonstration, for example, picks out its demonstratum.

And now we are back to the ambiguity in (3). I would like to count my *verbal* demonstration, as in (17), as part of the sentence type. Then it seems that an utterance of such a sentence either must include a world, or else, what is more plausible, must be in a world. I guess what I want to say, what I should have said, is that an utterance has to occur *somewhere*, in some world, and the world in which it occurs is a crucial factor in determining what the content is. This really says something about how (I think) I want to treat (possible) demonstrations. I want the same (possible) demonstrations (e.g. ["the spy"]) to determine different demonstrata in different worlds (or possibly even at different times in the same world). Now I see why I was so taken with the Fregean treatment of demonstrations. We should be able to represent demonstrations as something like functions from worlds, times, etc., to demonstrata. Thus, *just like the meaning of a definite description!* The difference lies in how the content of a particular utterance is computed.

I realize that the foregoing is mildly inconsistent, but let us push on. Let u be an utterance of (17) in w at t, and let u' be an utterance of (3) in w at t. Let's not worry, for now, about the possibility of a clash of utterances. If we look at the content of u and the content of u' we will see that they differ—though they will always agree in w. The content of u' is like what I earlier called a singular proposition (except that I should have fixed the time), whereas the content of u' is like that I earlier called a general proposition. For the content of u to assign truth to a given world w', the individual who must be supicious in w' at t is not the denotation of "the spy" in w' at t, but rather the denotation of "the spy" in w at t. The *relevant individual* is determined in the world in which the utterance takes place, and then that same individual is checked for suspicion in all other worlds, whereas for the content of u', we determine a (possibly) new relevant individual in each world.[31]

What is especially interesting is that these two contents must agree in the world w, the world in which the utterance took place.

Now note that the verbal form of (3) might have been adopted by one who lacked "dthat" to express what is expressed by (17). We seem to have here a kind of *de dicto–de re* ambiguity in the verbal form of (3) and without benefit of any intensional operator. No question of an utterer's intentions has been brought into play. *There is no question of an analysis in terms of scope, since there is no operator.* The two sentence types (3) and (17) are such that when uttered in the same context they have different contents but always the same truth value where uttered. Donnellan vindicated! (Contrary to my own earlier expectations.)

I am beginning to suspect that I bungled things even worse than I thought in talking about meanings, contents, etc. The meaning of a sentence type should probably be a function from utterances to *contents* rather than from something like utterances to truth values. If this correction were made, then we could properly say that (13) and (17) differ in meaning.

It would also give a more satisfactory analysis of a sentence type like:

(25) Dthat ['the morning star'] is identical with dthat ['the evening star'].

Although (25) expresses a true content on some possible occasions of use and a false content on others, it is not simply contingent, since on all possible occasions its content is either necessary or impossible. (I am assuming that distinct individuals don't merge.) Even one who grasped the meaning of (25) would not of course know its truth value simply on witnessing an utterance.

Thus we answer the question how an utterance of an identity sentence can be informative though *necessary!*

Another example on the question of necessity. Suppose I now utter:

(26) I am more than thirty-six years old.

What I have said is true. Is it necessary? This may be arguable. (*Could* I be younger than I am at this very same time?) But the fact that the sentence, if uttered at an earlier time or by another person, could express something false is certainly irrelevant. The point is: simply to look at the spectrum of *truth-values* of different utterances of (25) and (26) and not at the spectrum of *contents* of different utterances of (25) and (26) is to miss something interesting and important.

I earlier said that my demonstrative use is not quite Donnellan's referential use, and I want now to return to that point. When a speaker uses an expression demonstratively he *usually* has in mind—so to speak—an intended demonstratum, and the demonstration is thus *teleological*. Donnellan and I disagree on how to bring the intended demonstratum into the picture. To put it crudely, Donnellan believes that for most purposes we should take the demonstratum to be the intended demonstratum. I believe that these are different notions that may well involve different objects.

From my point of view the situation is interesting precisely because we have a case here in which a person can fail to say what he intended to say, and the failure is not a linguistic error (such as using the wrong word) but a factual one. It seems to me that such a situation can arise only in the demonstrative mode.

Suppose that without turning and looking I point to the place on my wall which has long been occupied by a picture of Rudolf Carnap and I say:

(27) Dthat [I point as above] is a picture of one of the greatest philosophers of the twentieth century.

But, unbeknownst to me, someone has replaced my picture of Carnap with one of Spiro Agnew. I think it would simply be wrong to argue an "ambiguity" in the demonstration, so great that it can be bent to my intended demonstratum. I have said of a picture of Spiro Agnew that it pictures one of the greatest philosophers of the twentieth century. And my speech and demonstration suggest no other natural interpretation to the linguistically competent public observer.

Still, it would be perhaps equally wrong not to pursue the notion of the intended demonstratum. Let me give three reasons for that pursuit:

1. The notion is epistemologically interesting in itself.

2. It may well happen—as Donnellan has pointed out—that we succeed in communicating what we intended to say in spite of our failure to say it.

(E.g. the mischievous fellow who switched pictures on me would understand full well what I was intending to say.)

3. There are situations where the demonstration is sufficiently ill-structured in itself so that we would regularly take account of the intended demonstratum as, *within limits*, a legitimate disambiguating or vagueness-removing device.

I have two kinds of examples for this third point. First, there are the cases of vague demonstrations by a casual wave of the hand. I suppose that ordinarily we would allow that a demonstration had been successful if the intended object were *roughly* where the speaker pointed. That is, we would not bring out surveying equipment to help determine the content of the speaker's assertion; much more relevant is what he intended to point at. Second, whenever I point at something, from the surveyor's point of view I point at many things. When I point at my son (and say "I love dthat"), I may also be pointing at a book he is holding, his jacket, a button on his jacket, his skin, his heart, and his dog standing behind him—from the surveyor's point of view. *My* point is that if I intended to point at my son and it is true that I love him, then what I said is true. And the fact that I do not love his jacket does not make it equally false. There are, of course, limits to what can be accomplished by intentions (even the best of them). No matter how hard I intend Carnap's picture, in the earlier described case, I do not think it reasonable to call the content of my utterance true.

Another example where I would simply distinguish the content asserted and the content intended is in the use of "I."[32] A person might utter:

(28) I am a general.

intending—that is "having in mind"—de Gaulle, and being under the delusion that he himself was de Gaulle. But the linguistic constraints on the possible demonstrata of "I" will not allow anyone other than de Gaulle to so demonstrate de Gaulle, no matter how hard they try.

All this familiarity with demonstratives has led me to believe that I was mistaken in "Quantifying In" in thinking that the most fundamental cases of what I might now describe as a person having a propositional attitude (believing, asserting, etc.) toward a singular proposition required that the person be *en rapport* with the subject of the proposition. It is now clear that I can assert *of* the first child to be born in the twenty-first century that *he* will be bald, simply by assertively uttering,

(29) Dthat ['the first child to be born in the twenty-first century'] will be bald.

I do not now see exactly how the requirement of being *en rapport* with the subject of a singular proposition fits in. Are there two kinds of singular propositions? Or are there just two different ways to know them?

EXCITING FUTURE EPISODES

1. Making sense out of the foregoing.

2. Showing how nicely (3) and (17) illustrate an early point about the possibility of incorporating contextual factors (here, a demonstration) as part of the content of the utterance. Another example compares uses of 'the person at whom I am pointing' as demonstration and as subject.

3. Justifying calling (17) a *de re* form by showing how it can be used to explicate the notion of modality *de re* without depending on scope.

4. Extending the demonstrative notion to *in*definite descriptions to see if it is possible to so explicate the ± specific idea. (It isn't.)

5. Improving (by starting all over) the analysis of the relation between Montague's treatment of indexicals and my treatment of demonstratives.

6. Showing how the treatment of proper names in the Kripke-Kaplan-Donnellan way (if there is such) is akin (?) to demonstratives.

7. Discussing the role of common noun phrases in connection with demonstratives, as in:

(30) Dthat coat [the speaker points at a boy wearing a coat] is dirty.

8. Quine's contention that the content of any utterance can also be expressed by an eternal sentence. Is it true?

9. Much more to say about the phenomenology of intending to demonstrate *x*, and also about the truth-conditions of '*y* intends to demonstrate *x*'.

10. Demonstratives, dubbings, definitions, and other forms of language learning. Common nouns: what they mean and how we learn it. This section will include such pontifications as the following:

It is a mistake to believe that normal communication takes place through the encoding and decoding of general propositions, by means of our grasp of *meanings*. It is a more serious mistake, because more pernicious, to believe that other aspects of communication can be accounted for by a vague reference to "contextual features" of the utterance. Indeed, we first learn the meanings of almost all parts of our language by means quite different from those of the formal definitions studied in metamathematics; and the means used for first teaching the meanings of words, rather than withering away, are regularly and perhaps even essentially employed thereafter in all forms of communication.

ACKNOWLEDGMENTS

This work was supported by the National Science Foundation.

NOTES

1. Keith S. Donnellan, "Reference and Definite Descriptions," *The Philosophical Review*, 75 (1966): 298.
2. Leonard Linsky, "Reference and Referents," in *Philosophy and Ordinary Language*, ed. C. Caton (Urbana: 1963).
3. Donnellan, "Reference and Definite Descriptions," p. 299.
4. *Ibid.*, p. 297.
5. *Ibid.*, p. 303.
6. *Ibid.*
7. Jaakko Hintikka, "Individual, Possible Worlds, and Epistemic Logic," *Noûs*, 1 (1967): 47.
8. Bertrand Russell, *The Principles of Mathematics* (Cambridge, England: 1903).
9. Bertrand Russell, "On Denoting," *Mind*, 14 (1905): 479–93.
10. Rudolf Carnap, *Meaning and Necessity* (Chicago: 1947).
11. Bertrand Russell, *Introduction to Mathematical Philosophy* (London: 1920), p. 174.
12. Both 'denoting concept' and 'denoting phrase' are Russell's terms used in Russell's way.
13. An example is the possibility of producing set theoretical representations of the system of natural numbers which make all even numbers alike in certain set theoretical features (distinct from such numerical features as divisibility by two) and all odd numbers alike in other set theoretical features, or which provide simple and elegant definitions (i.e. representations) of certain basic numerical operations and relations such as *less than* or *plus*, etc.
14. It is not too easy to single out such phrases without the help of some theory about logical form or some semantical theory. I suppose what I am after is what linguists call syntactical criteria. But I have had difficulty in finding one which will not let in phrases like "a spy." Another difficulty is concerned with phrases like "John's brother" which seem to vary in their uniqueness suppositions. "John's brother is the man in dark glasses" carries, for me, the supposition that John has just one brother; whereas "The man in dark glasses is John's brother" does not. In fact the latter seems the most natural formulation when suppositions about the number of John's brothers are completely absent, since both "The man in dark glasses is one of John's brothers" and "The man in dark glasses is a brother of John" suppose, for me, that John has more than one brother.
15. The question whether all uses of demonstratives are accompanied by demonstrations depends on a number of factors, some empirical, some stipulative, and some in the twilight zone of theoretical ingenuity. The stipulative question is whether we use 'demonstrative' to describe certain phrases which might also be described by enumeration or some such syntactical device, e.g. all phrases beginning with either "this" or "that" and followed by a common noun phrase; or whether we use 'demonstrative' to describe a certain characteristic *use* of such phrases. In the latter case it may be stipulatively true that an utterance containing a demonstrative must be accompanied by a demonstration. In the former case, the question turns both on how people in fact speak and on how clever our theoretician is in producing *recherché* demonstrations to account for apparent counterexamples.
16. This formulation probably needs sharpening. Don't take it as a definition.
17. It should not be supposed that my practice indicates any confidence as to the nature and structure of what I call *demonstrations* or the proper form for a *demonstration-description* to take. Indeed, these are difficult and important questions which arise repeatedly in what follows.

18. Gottlob Frege, "Ueber Sinn und Bedeutung," *Zeitschrift Fur Philosophie und Philosophische Kritik.* Translated (by Feigl) in *Readings in Philosophical Analysis*, eds. H. Feigl and W. Sellars (New York: 1949). Also translated (by Black) in *Translations from the Writings of Gottlob Frege*, eds. P. Geach and M. Black (Oxford: 1966).

19. *Ibid.*, emphasis added.

20. W. V. Quine, "Quantifiers and Propositional Attitudes." *Journal of Philosophy*, 53 (1955): 177–87.

21. David Kaplan, "Quantifying In," *Synthese*, 19 (1968): 178–214. I will attempt later to press the case that this use of proper names, which involves no waving of hands or fixing of glance, may be assimilated to the more traditional forms of demonstrative use.

22. "In the case of genuinely proper names like 'Aristotle' opinions as regards their sense may diverge. As such may, e.g., be suggested: Plato's disciple and the teacher of Alexander the Great. Whoever accepts this sense will interpret the meaning of the statement 'Aristotle was born in Stagira' differently from one who interpreted the sense of 'Aristotle' as the Stagirite teacher of Alexander the Great" (from Feigl's translation of Frege's "Ueber Sinn und Bedeutung").

23. A third kind of indicative device is the picture. Consideration of pictures, which to me lie somewhere between pointing and describing, may help drive home the parallels—in terms of the distinction between the object indicated and the manner of indication—between description, depiction, and demonstration.

24. That all utterances are in English is a general and implicit assumption except where it is explicitly called into question.

25. "Dhe" is really a combination of the demonstrative with a common noun phrase. It stands for "dthat male." More on such combinations later.

26. W. V. Quine, *Word and Object* (Cambridge, Mass.: 1960), p. 193.

27. There are, of course, two hidden relativizations involved even for eternal sentences. One is to a *language*, i.e. an association of meanings with words. The Knoh-English example was meant to dramatize this relativization. The other is to a possible world. There is always the implicit reference to the actual world when we use just the expression 'true'. If the analogy between moments of time and possible worlds holds—as some philosophers think—then maybe we should begin our classification of sentences not with explicitly dated eternal sentences like "in 1970 . . ." but with 'perfect' sentences like "In the possible world Charlie in 1970 . . .".

28. Rather than talking directly to these functions, I should really talk of entities like ⟨⟨'The',S⟩P⟩ and only derivatively of the functions.

29. This is aside from the inadequacy mentioned in the previous note, which continues to bother me.

30. The most relevant works are "Pragmatics" (1968) and "Pragmatics and Intensional Logic" (1970), both reprinted in Richard Montague, *Formal Philosophy* (New Haven, 1974).

31. I am still bothered by the notion of an utterance at t in w, where there is no utterance at t in w.

32. "I" is, of course, a demonstrative; as opposed, e.g. to "the person who is uttering this utterance," which contains only the demonstrative 'this utterance'. Let us compare utterances of:

(i) I am exhausted

(ii) The person who is uttering this utterance is exhausted

both uttered by s on the same occasion (!): To find the truth value of the content of (ii) in w' we must first locate the same utterance in w' (if it exists there at all) and see who, if anyone, is uttering it. Since s could well be exhausted silently in w', the two contents are not the same.

BIBLIOGRAPHIC POSTSCRIPT

This paper was written (if that is the right word for it) in early 1970. Since that time I have written (really written, and even published) several papers in which the ideas of the present work are expounded and developed. These works are:

"On the Logic of Demonstratives" *The Journal of Philosophical Logic* 8 (1979) pp. 81–98; reprinted in this volume.

"Demonstratives: An Essay on the Semantics, Logic, Metaphysics, and Epistemology of Demonstratives and other Indexicals" in Almog, Perry, and Wettstein (editors), *Themes From Kaplan* (Oxford University Press 1989), pp. 481–563.

"Afterthoughts" in Almog, Perry, and Wettstein (editors), *Themes From Kaplan* (Oxford University Press 1989), pp. 565–614.

And to some extent:

"Bob and Carol and Ted and Alice" in J. Hintikka *et al.* (editors) *Approaches to Natural Language* (Reidel 1973) pp. 490–518.

"How to Russell a Frege-Church" *The Journal of Philosophy* LXXII (1975) pp. 716–729; reprinted in M. Loux (editor) *The Possible and the Actual: Readings in the Metaphysics of Modality* (Cornell 1979).

"Opacity" in L. Hahn (editor), *The Philosophy of W.V. Quine*, The Library of Living Philosophers (Open Court, 1986) pp. 229–289, especially section VII.

DAVID KAPLAN

ON THE LOGIC OF DEMONSTRATIVES[1]

In this paper, I propose to outline briefly a few results of my investigations into the theory of demonstratives: words and phrases whose *in*tension is determined by the contexts of their use. Familiar examples of demonstratives are the nouns 'I', 'you', 'here', 'now', 'that', and the adjectives 'actual' and 'present'. It is, of course, clear that the *ex*tension of 'I' is determined by the context—if you and I both say 'I' we refer to different persons. But I would now claim that the intension is also so determined. The intension of an 'eternal' term (like 'The Queen of England in 1973') has generally been taken to be represented by a function which assigns to each possible world the Queen of England in 1973 of that world. Such functions would have been called *individual concepts* by Carnap. It has been thought by some—myself among others—that by analogy, the intension of 'I' could be represented by a function from speakers to individuals (in fact, the identity function). And, similarly, that the intensions of 'here' and 'now' would be represented by (identity) functions on places and times. The role of contextual factors in determining the extension (with respect to such factors) of a demonstrative was thought of as analogous to that of a possible world in determining the extension of 'the Queen of England in 1973' (with respect to that possible world). Thus an enlarged view of an intension was derived. The intension of an expression was to be represented by a function from certain factors to the extension of an expression (with respect to those factors). Originally such factors were simply possible worlds, but as it was noticed that the so-called tense operators exhibited a structure highly analogous to that of the modal operators, the factors with respect to which extension was to be determined were enlarged to include moments of time. When it was noticed that contextual factors were required to determine the extension of sentences containing demonstratives, a still more general notion was developed and called an 'index'. The extension of an expression was to be determined with respect to an index. The intension of an expression was that function which assigned to every index the extension at that index. Here is a typical passage.

The above example supplies us with a statement whose truth-value is not constant but varies as a function of $i \in I$. This situation is easily appreciated in the context of time-dependent statements; that is, in the case where I represents the instants of time. Obviously the same statement can be true at one moment and false at another. For more general situations one must not think of the $i \in I$ as anything as simple as instants of time or even possible worlds. In general we will have

$$i = (w, t, p, a, \ldots)$$

where the index i has many *coordinates*: for example, w is a *world*, t is a *time*, $p = (x,y,z)$ is a (3-dimensional) *position* in the world, a is an *agent*, etc. All these coordinates can be varied, possibly independently, and thus affect the truth values of statements which have indirect reference to these coordinates. (From the Advice of a prominent logician.)

A sentence ϕ was taken to be logically true if true at every index (in every 'structure'), and $\Box\ \phi$ was taken to be true at a given index (in a given structure) just in case ϕ was true at every index (in that structure). (Or possibly just in case ϕ was true at every index *which differed from the given index only in possible world coordinate*.) Thus the familiar principle of modal generalization: if $\models \phi$, then $\models \Box\ \phi$, is validated.

This view, in its treatment of demonstratives, now seems to me to have been technically wrong (though perhaps correctable by minor modification) and, more importantly, conceptually misguided.

Consider the sentence

(1) I am here now.

It is obvious that for many choices of index—i.e. for many quadruples $\langle w, x, p, t \rangle$ where w is a possible world, x is a person, p is a place, and t is a time—(1) will be false. In fact, (1) is true only with respect to those indices $\langle w, x, p, t \rangle$ which are such that in the world w, x is located at p at the time t. Thus (1) fares about on a par with

(2) David Kaplan is in Los Angeles on 21 April 1973.

(2) is contingent, and so is (1).

But here we have missed something essential to our understanding of demonstratives. Intuitively, (1) is deeply, and in some sense universally, true. One need only understand the meaning of (1) to know that it cannot be uttered falsely. No such guarantees apply to (2). *A Logic of Demonstratives* which does not reflect this intuitive difference between (1) and (2) has by-passed something essential to the logic of demonstratives.

Here is a proposed correction. Let the class of indices be narrowed to include only the *proper* ones—namely, those $\langle w, x, p, t \rangle$ such that in the world w, x *is* located at p at the time t. Such a move may have been intended originally since improper indices are like impossible worlds; no such contexts

236 · ON DESCRIPTIONS

could exist and thus there is no interest in evaluating the extensions of expressions with respect to them. Our reform has the consequence that (1) comes out, correctly, to be logically true. Now consider

(3) □ I am here now.

Since the contained sentence (namely (1)) is true at every proper index, (3) also is true at every proper index and thus also is logically true. (As would be expected by the aforementioned principle of modal generalization.)

But (3) should not be *logically* true, since it is false. It is certainly *not* necessary that I be here now. But for several contingencies I would be working in my garden now, or even writing this in a location outside of Los Angeles.

Perhaps enough has now been said to indicate that there are difficulties in the attempt to assimilate the role of a *context* in a logic of demonstratives to that of a *possible world* in the familiar modal logics or a *moment of time* in the familiar tense logics.

I believe that the source of the difficulty lies in a conceptual confusion between two kinds of meaning. Ramifying Frege's distinction between sense and denotation, I would add two varieties of sense: content and character. The content of an expression is always taken *with respect to* a given context of use. Thus when I say

(4) I was insulted yesterday

a specific content—*what I said*—is expressed. Your utterance of the same sentence, or mine on another day, would not express the same content. What is important to note is that it is not just the truth value that may change; what is said is itself different. Speaking today, my utterance of (4) will have a content roughly equivalent to that which

(5) David Kaplan is insulted on 20 April 1973

would have spoken by you or anyone at any time. Since (5) contains no demonstratives, its content is the same with respect to all contexts. This content is what Carnap called an 'intension' and what, I believe, has been often referred to as a 'proposition'. So my theory is that different contexts for (4) produce not just different truth values, but different propositions.

Turning now to character, I call that component of the sense of an expression which determines how the content is determined by the context the 'character' of an expression. Just as contents (or intensions) can be represented by functions from possible worlds to extensions, so characters can be represented by functions from contexts to contents. The character of 'I' would then be represented by *the function (or rule, if you prefer) which assigns to each context that content which is represented by the constant function from possible words to the agent of the context*. The latter function has been called an 'individual concept'. Note that the character of 'I' is represented by a function from contexts to individual *concepts*, not from contexts to individuals. It was the idea that a function from contexts to individuals could represent the intension of 'I' which led to the difficulties discussed earlier.

Now what is it that a competent speaker of English knows about the world 'I'? Is it the content with respect to some particular occasion of use? No. It is the character of 'I': the rule italicized above. Competent speakers recognize that the proper use of 'I' is—loosely speaking—to refer to the speaker. Thus, that component of sense which I call 'character' is best identified with what might naturally be called 'meaning'.

To return, for a moment, to (1). The character (meaning) of (1) determines each of the following:

(*a*) In different contexts, an utterance of (1) expresses different contents (propositions).

(*b*) In most (if not all) contexts, an utterance of (1) expresses a contingent proposition.

(*c*) In all contexts, an utterance of (1) expresses a true proposition (i.e. a proposition which is true at the world of the context).

On the basis of (*c*), we might claim that (1) is analytic (i.e. it is true solely in virtue of its meaning). Although as we see from (*b*), (1) rarely or never expresses a necessary proposition. This separation of analyticity and necessity is made possible—even, I hope, plausible—by distinguishing the kinds of entities of which 'is analytic' and 'is necessary' are properly predicated: characters (meanings) are analytic, contents (propositions) are necessary.

The distinction between character and content was unlikely to be noticed before demonstratives came under consideration, because demonstrative-free expressions have a constant character, that is they express the same content in every context. Thus, character becomes an uninteresting complication in the theory.

Though I have spoken above of contexts of utterance, my primary theoretical notion of *content with respect to a context* does not require that the agent of the context utter the expression in question. I believe that there are good reasons for taking this more general notion as fundamental.

I believe that my distinction between character and content can be used to throw light on Kripke's distinction between the *a-priori* and the necessary. Although my distinction lies more purely within logic and semantics, and Kripke's distinction is of a more general epistemic metaphysical character,[2] both seem to me to be of the same *structure*. (I leave this remark in a rather cryptic state.)

The distinction between content and character and the related analysis of demonstratives have certainly been foreshadowed in the literature (though they are original-with-me, in the sense that I did not consciously extract them from prior sources). But to my knowledge they have not previously been cultivated to meet the standards for logical and semantical theories which currently prevail. In particular, Strawson's distinction between the significance (meaningfulness) of a sentence and the statement (proposition) which is expressed in a given use is clearly related.[3] Strawson recognizes that such sentences as 'The *present* King of France is *now* bald' may express different propositions in different utterances, and he identifies the meaningfulness of the sentence with its potential for expressing a true or false proposition in some possible utterance. Though he does not explicitly discuss *the* meaning of the sentence, it is clear that he would not identify such a meaning with any of the propositions expressed by particular utterances. Unfortunately Strawson seems to regard the fact that sentences containing demonstratives can be used to express different propositions as immunizing such sentences against treatment by 'the logician'.

In order to convince myself that it is possible to carry out a consistent analysis of the semantics of demonstratives along the above lines, I have attempted to carry through the program for a version of first-order predicate logic. The result is the following Logic of Demonstratives.

If my views are correct, the introduction of demonstratives into intensional logics will require more extensive reformulation than was thought to be the case.

THE LOGIC OF DEMONSTRATIVES

The *Language* LD is based on first-order predicate logic with identity and descriptions. We deviate slightly from standard formulations in using two sorts of variables, one sort for positions and a second sort for individuals other than positions (hereafter called simply 'individuals').

Primitive Symbols for Two Sorted Predicate Logic

0. Punctuation: (,)

1. (i) An infinite set of individual variables: $\mathcal{V}_i$
   (ii) An infinite set of position variables: $\mathcal{V}_p$

2. (i) An infinite number of m-n-place predicates, for all natural numbers m, n
   (ii) The 1-0-place predicate: Exist
   (iii) The 1-1-place predicate: Located

3. (i) An infinite number of m-n-place i-functors (functors which form terms denoting individuals)
   (ii) An infinite number of m-n-place p-functors (functors which form terms denoting positions)

4. Sentential Connectives: $\land$, $\lor$, $\lnot$, $\rightarrow$, $\leftrightarrow$

5. Quantifiers: ∀, ∃

6. Definite Description Operator: the

7. Identity: =

Primitive Symbols for Model and Tense Logic
8. Modal Operators: □, ◇

9. Tense Operators: F (it will be the case that)
P (it has been the case that)
G (one day ago, it was the case that)

Primitive Symbols for the Logic of Demonstratives
10. Three one place sentential operators:
N (it is now the case that)
A (it is actually the case that)
Y (yesterday, it was the case that)

11. A one place functor: dthat

12. An individual constant (0-0-place i-functor): I

13. A position constant (0-0-place p-functor): Here

The *well-formed expressions* are of three kinds: formulas, position terms (p-terms), and individual terms (i-terms).

1. (i) If $\alpha \in \mathcal{V}_i$, then α is an i-term.
(ii) If $\alpha \in \mathcal{V}_p$, then α is a p-term.

2. If π is an m-n-place predicate, $\alpha_1 \ldots \alpha_m$ are i-terms, and $\beta_1 \ldots \beta_n$ are p-terms, then $\pi\alpha_1 \ldots \alpha_m\beta_1 \ldots \beta_n$ is a formula.

3. (i) If η is an m-n-place i-functor, $\alpha_1 \ldots \alpha_m, \beta_1 \ldots \beta_n$ as in 2, then $\eta\alpha_1 \ldots \alpha_m\beta_1 \ldots \beta_n$ is an i-term.
(ii) If η is an m-n-place p-functor, $\alpha_1 \ldots \alpha_m, \beta_1 \ldots \beta_n$ as in 2, then $\eta\alpha_1 \ldots \alpha_m\beta_1 \ldots \beta_n$ is a p-term.

4. If ϕ, ψ are formulas, then $(\phi \wedge \psi)$, $(\phi \vee \psi)$, $\neg \phi$, $(\phi \rightarrow \psi)$, $(\phi \leftrightarrow \psi)$ are formulas.

5. If ϕ is a formula and $\alpha \in \mathcal{V}_i \cup \mathcal{V}_p$, then $\forall\alpha\phi$, $\exists\alpha\phi$ are formulas.

6. If ϕ is a formula, then
(i) if $\alpha \in \mathcal{V}_i$, then   the α ϕ is an i-term.
(ii) if $\alpha \in \mathcal{V}_p$, then   the α ϕ is a p-term.

7. If both α, β are either i-terms or p-terms, then $\alpha = \beta$ is a formula.

8. If ϕ is a formula, then $\square\phi$, $\diamond\phi$ are formulas.

9. If ϕ is a formula, then $F\phi$, $P\phi$, $G\phi$ are formulas.

10. If ϕ is a formula, then $N\phi$, $A\phi$, $Y\phi$ are formulas.

11. (i) If α is an i-term, then dthat α is an i-term.
    (ii) If α is a p-term, then dthat α is a p-term.

Semantics for LD

DEFINITION. $\mathfrak{A}$ *is an LD Structure* iff there are $\mathscr{CWUPTI}$ such that

1. $\mathfrak{A} = \langle\mathscr{CWUPTI}\rangle$.

2. $\mathscr{C}$ is a non-empty set (the set of *contexts*, see 10 below).

3. If $c \in \mathscr{C}$, then (i) $c_A \in \mathscr{U}$ (the *agent* of c).
   (ii) $c_T \in \mathscr{T}$ (the *time* of c).
   (iii) $c_P \in \mathscr{P}$ (the *position* of c).
   (iv) $c_w \in \mathscr{W}$ (the *world* of c).

4. $\mathscr{W}$ is a non-empty set (the set of *worlds*).

5. $\mathscr{U}$ is a non-empty set (the set of all *individuals*, see 9 below).

6. $\mathscr{P}$ is a non-empty set (the set of *positions*; common to all worlds).

7. $\mathscr{T}$ is the set of integers (thought of as the *times*; common to all worlds).

8. $\mathscr{I}$ is a function which assigns to each predicate and functor an appropriate *intension* as follows:
   (i) if π is an m-n-place predicate, $\mathscr{I}_\pi$ is a function such that for each $t \in \mathscr{T}$ and $w\in \mathscr{W}$, $\mathscr{I}_\pi(tw) \subseteq (\mathscr{U}^m \times \mathscr{P}^n)$.
   (ii) If η is an m-n-place i-functor, $\mathscr{I}_\eta$ is a function such that that for each $t \in \mathscr{T}$ and $w \in \mathscr{W}$,
   $$\mathscr{I}_\eta(tw) \in (\mathscr{U} \cup\{\dagger\})^{(\mathscr{U}^m \times \mathscr{P}^n)}.$$
   (*Note:* $\dagger$ is a completely alien entity, in neither $\mathscr{U}$ nor $\mathscr{P}$, which represents an 'undefined' value of the function. In a normal set theory we can take $\dagger$ to be $\{\mathscr{U}, \mathscr{P}\}$.)
   (iii) If η is an m-n-place p-functor, $\mathscr{I}_\eta$ is a function such that for each $t \in \mathscr{T}$ and $w \in \mathscr{W}$, $\mathscr{I}_\eta(tw) \in (\mathscr{P} \cup \{\dagger\})^{(\mathscr{U}^m \times \mathscr{P}^n)}$.

9. $i \in \mathscr{U}$ iff $\exists t \in \mathscr{T} \exists w\in \mathscr{W} \langle i\rangle \in \mathscr{I}_{\text{Exists}}(tw)$.

10. If $c \in \mathscr{C}$, then $\langle c_A c_P\rangle \in \mathscr{I}_{\text{Located}}(c_T c_w)$.

11. If $\langle i\ p\rangle \in \mathscr{I}_{\text{Located}}(tw)$, then $\langle i\rangle \in \mathscr{I}_{\text{Exists}}(tw)$.

Truth and Denotation in a Context

We write: $\underset{cftw}{\overset{\mathfrak{A}}{\models}} \phi$ for ϕ when taken in the context c (under the assignment f and in the structure $\mathfrak{A}$) *is true with respect to* the time t and the world w.

We write: $\mid \alpha \mid^{\mathfrak{A}}_{cftw}$ for *The denotation of* α when taken in the context c (under the assignment f and in the structure $\mathfrak{A}$) *with respect to* the time t and the world w.

In general we will omit the superscript '$\mathfrak{A}$', and we will assume that the structure $\mathfrak{A}$ is $\langle \mathscr{C}\mathscr{W}\mathscr{U}\mathscr{P}\mathscr{T}\mathscr{I} \rangle$.

DEFINITION. *f is an assignment* (with respect to
$$\langle \mathscr{C}\mathscr{W}\mathscr{U}\mathscr{P}\mathscr{T}\mathscr{I} \rangle) \text{ iff}$$
$$\exists f_1 f_2 (f_1 \in \mathscr{U}^{\mathscr{V}_i} \& f_2 \in \mathscr{P}^{\mathscr{V}_p} \& f = f_1 \cup f_2).$$

DEFINITION. $f^{\alpha}_x = (f \sim \{\langle \alpha f(\alpha) \rangle\}) \cup \{\langle \alpha x \rangle\}$ (i.e. the assignment which is just like f except that it assigns x to α).

For the following recursive definitions, assume that $c \in \mathscr{C}$, f is an assignment, $t \in \mathscr{T}$, and $w \in \mathscr{W}$.

1. If α is a variable, $|\alpha|_{cftw} = f(\alpha)$.

2. $\underset{cftw}{\models} \pi\alpha_1 \ldots \alpha_m\beta_1 \ldots \beta_n$ iff
   $\langle \mid \alpha_1 \mid_{cftw} \ldots \mid \beta_n \mid_{cftw} \rangle \in \mathscr{I}\pi(tw)$.

3. If η is neither I nor Here (see 12, 13 below), then $\mid \eta\alpha_1 \ldots \alpha_m\beta_1 \ldots \beta_n \mid_{cftw}$
   $$= \begin{cases} \mathscr{I}_\eta(tw)(\langle \mid \alpha_1 \mid_{cftw} \ldots \mid \beta_n \mid_{cftw} \rangle), \text{ if none of} \\ \quad \mid \alpha_j \mid_{cftw} \mid \beta_k \mid_{cftw} \text{ are } \dagger \\ \dagger, \text{ otherwise.} \end{cases}$$

4. (i) $\underset{cftw}{\models} (\phi \wedge \psi)$ iff $\underset{cftw}{\models} \phi \& \underset{cftw}{\models} \psi$.
   (ii) $\underset{cftw}{\models} \phi$ iff $\sim \underset{cftw}{\models} \phi$.
   etc.

5. (i) If $\alpha \in \mathscr{V}_i$, then $\underset{cftw}{\models} \forall\alpha\phi$ iff $\forall_i \in \mathscr{U}\underset{cf^{\alpha}_i tw}{\models} \phi$.
   (ii) If $\alpha \in \mathscr{V}_p$, then $\underset{cftw}{\models} \forall\alpha\phi$ iff $\forall_p \in \mathscr{P}\underset{cf^{\alpha}_p tw}{\models} \phi$.
   Similarly for $\exists\alpha\phi$.

6. (i) If $\alpha \in \mathscr{V}_i$, then $\mid \text{the } \alpha \ \phi \mid_{cftw}$
   $$= \begin{cases} \text{the unique } i \in \mathscr{U} \text{ such that } \underset{cf^{\alpha}_i tw}{\models} \phi, \text{ if there is such.} \\ \dagger, \text{ otherwise.} \end{cases}$$
   (ii) Similarly for $\alpha \in \mathscr{V}_p$.

7. $\quad \underset{cftw}{\models} \alpha = \beta \quad$ iff $\quad | \alpha |_{cftw} = | \beta |_{cftw}.$

8.   (i) $\quad \underset{cftw}{\models} \square \phi \quad$ iff $\quad \forall w' \in \mathscr{W} \underset{cftw'}{\models} \phi.$

    (ii) $\quad \underset{cftw}{\models} \Diamond \phi \quad$ iff $\quad \exists w' \in \mathscr{W} \underset{cftw'}{\models} \phi.$

9.   (i) $\quad \underset{cftw}{\models} F\phi \quad$ iff $\quad \exists t' \in \mathscr{T}$ such that $t' > t$ and $\underset{cft'w}{\models} \phi.$

    (ii) $\quad \underset{cftw}{\models} P\phi \quad$ iff $\quad \exists t' \in \mathscr{T}$ such that $t' < t$ and $\underset{cft'w}{\models} \phi.$

    (iii) $\quad \underset{cftw}{\models} G\phi \quad$ iff $\quad \underset{cf(t-1)w}{\models} \phi.$

10.   (i) $\quad \underset{cftw}{\models} N\phi \quad$ iff $\quad \underset{cfc_T w}{\models} \phi.$

    (ii) $\quad \underset{cftw}{\models} A\phi \quad$ iff $\quad \underset{cfc_w}{\models} \phi.$

    (iii) $\quad \underset{cftw}{\models} Y\phi \quad$ iff $\quad \underset{cf(c_T-1)w}{\models} \phi.$

11. $\quad | \text{ dthat } \alpha |_{cftw} = | \alpha |_{cfc_Tc_W}.$

12. $\quad | \text{ I} |_{cftw} = c_A.$

13. $\quad | \text{ Here} |_{cftw} = c_P.$

Remark 1. Expressions containing demonstratives will, in general, express different concepts in different contexts. We call the concept expressed in a given context the *Content* of the expression in that context. The Content of a sentence in a context is, roughly, the proposition the sentence would express if uttered in that context. This description is not quite accurate on two counts. First, it is important to distinguish an *utterance* from a *sentence-in-a-context*. The former notion is from the theory of speech acts, the latter from semantics. Utterances take time, and utterances of distinct sentences cannot be simultaneous (i.e. in the same context). But in order to develop a logic of demonstratives it seems most natural to be able to evaluate several premises and a conclusion all in the same context. Thus, the notion of ϕ being true in c and $\mathfrak{A}$ does not require an utterance of ϕ. In particular, c_A need not be uttering ϕ in c_w at c_r. Second, the truth of a proposition is not usually thought of as dependent on a time as well as a possible world. The time is thought of as fixed by the context. If ϕ is a sentence, the more usual notion of the proposition expressed by ϕ-in-c is what is here called the Content of $N\phi$ in c.

Where Γ is either a term or a formula, we write: $\{\Gamma\}^{\mathfrak{A}}_{cf}$ for the Content of Γ in the context c (under the assignment f and in the structure $\mathfrak{A}$).

DEFINITION. (i) If ϕ is a formula, $\{\phi\}_{cf}$ = that function which assigns to each $t \in \mathscr{T}$ and $w \in \mathscr{W}$, Truth if $\underset{cftw}{\overset{\mathfrak{A}}{\models}} \phi$, and Falsehood otherwise.

    (ii) If α is a term, $\{\alpha\}_{cf}$ = that function which assigns to each $t \in \mathscr{T}$ and $w \in \mathscr{W}$, $| \alpha |^{\mathfrak{A}}_{cftw}$

Remark 2. $\underset{cftw}{\overset{\mathfrak{A}}{\models}} \phi$ iff $\{\phi\}^{\mathfrak{A}}_{cf} (tw)$ = Truth. Roughly speaking, the sentence ϕ taken in the context c is *true with respect to* t and w iff the proposition expressed by φ-in-the-context-c would be true at the time t if w were the actual world. In the formal development of pages 195 through 197 it was smoother to ignore the conceptual break marked by the notion of *Content in a context* and to directly define *truth in a context with respect to a possible time and world*. The important conceptual role of the notion of Content is partially indicated by the following two definitions.

DEFINITION. φ *is true in the context* c (in the structure $\mathfrak{A}$) iff for every assignment f, $\{\phi\}_{cf}^{\mathfrak{A}}(c_T, c_W) = $ Truth.

DEFINITION. φ is valid in LD ($\models \phi$) iff for every LD structure $\mathfrak{A}$, and every context c of $\mathfrak{A}$, φ is true in c (in $\mathfrak{A}$).

Remark 3. $\models (\alpha = $ dthat α), $\models$ N (Located I, Here), $\models$ Exist I, $\sim \models \Box$ ($\alpha = $ dthat α), $\sim \models \Box$N(Located I, Here), $\sim \models \Box$ (Exist I). In the converse direction we have the usual results in view of the fact that $\models (\Box \phi \rightarrow \phi)$.

DEFINITION. If $\alpha_1 \ldots \alpha_n$ are all the free variables of φ in alphabetical order, then *the closure of* φ $= $ AN$\forall \alpha_1 \ldots \alpha_n \phi$.

DEFINITION. φ *is closed* iff φ is equivalent to its closure (in the sense of *Remark* 12, below).

Remark 4. If φ is closed, then φ is true in c (and $\mathfrak{A}$) iff for every assignment f, time t, and world w $\models_{cftw}^{\mathfrak{A}}$ φ.

DEFINITION. Where Γ is either a term or a formula, *the Content of* Γ *in the context* c (*in the structure* $\mathfrak{A}$) *is stable* iff for every assignment f, $\{\Gamma\}_{cf}^{\mathfrak{A}}$ is a constant function. (i.e. $\{\Gamma\}_{cf}^{\mathfrak{A}}(tw) = \{\Gamma\}_{cf}^{\mathfrak{A}}(t'w')$, for all t, t', w, w', in $\mathfrak{A}$).

Remark 5. Where φ is a formula, α is a term, and β is a variable each of the following has a stable Content in every context (in every structure): $AN\phi$, dthat α, β, I, Here.

If we were to extend the notion of Content to apply to operators, we would see that all demonstratives have a stable Content in every context. The same is true of the familiar logical constants, although it does not hold for the modal and tense operators (not, at least, according to the foregoing development)

Remark 6. That aspect of the meaning of an expression which determines what its Content will be in each context, we call the *Character* of the expression. Although a lack of knowledge about the context (or perhaps about the structure) may cause one to mistake the Content of a given utterance, the

Character of each well formed expression is determined by rules of the language (such as 1–13, pages 196–197 above) which are presumably known to all competent speakers. Our notation '$\{\phi\}^{\mathfrak{A}}_{cf}$' for the Content of an expression gives a natural notation for the Character of an expression, namely '$\{\phi\}$'.

DEFINITION. Where Γ is either a term or a formula the *Character of Γ* is that function which assigns to each structure $\mathfrak{A}$, assignment f, and context c of $\mathfrak{A}$, $\{\Gamma\}^{\mathfrak{A}}_{cf}$.

DEFINITION. Where Γ is either a term or a formula, *the Character of Γ is stable* iff for every structure $\mathfrak{A}$, and assignment f the Character of Γ (under f in $\mathfrak{A}$) is a constant function. (i.e. $\{\Gamma\}^{\mathfrak{A}}_{cf} = \{\Gamma\}^{\mathfrak{A}}_{c'f}$ for all c, c' in $\mathfrak{A}$).

Remark 7. A formula or term has a stable Character iff it has the same Content in every context (for each $\mathfrak{A}$, f).

Remark 8. A formula or term has a stable Character iff it contains no essential occurrence of a demonstrative.

Remark 9. The logic of demonstratives determines a sub-logic of those formulas of LD which contain no demonstratives. These formulas (and their equivalents which contain inessential occurrences of demonstratives) are exactly the formulas with a stable Character. The logic of demonstratives brings a new perspective even to formulas such as these. The sub-logic of LD which concerns only formulas of stable Character is not identical with traditional logic. Even for such formulas, the familiar Principle of Necessitation: if $\models \phi$, then $\models \Box \phi$, fails. And so does its tense logic counterpart: if $\models \phi$, then $\models (\neg P \neg \phi \wedge \neg F \neg \phi \wedge \phi)$. From the perspective of LD, validity is truth in every possible *context*. For traditional logic, validity is truth in every possible *circumstance*. Each possible context determines a possible circumstance, but it is not the case that each possible circumstance is part of a possible context. In particular, the fact that each possible context has an agent implies that any possible circumstance in which no individuals exist will not form a part of any possible context. Within LD, a possible context is represented by $\langle \mathfrak{A}, c \rangle$ and a possible circumstance by $\langle \mathfrak{A}, t, w \rangle$. To any $\langle \mathfrak{A}, c \rangle$, there corresponds $\langle \mathfrak{A}, c_T, c_W \rangle$. But it is not the case that to every $\langle \mathfrak{A}, t, w \rangle$ there exists a context c of $\mathfrak{A}$ such that $t = c_T$ and $w = c_W$. The result is that in LD such sentences as $\exists x \text{ Exist } x$ and $\exists x \exists p \text{ Located } x, p$ are valid, although they would not be so regarded in traditional logic. At least not in the neo-traditional logic that countenances empty worlds. Using the semantical developments of pages 240–242, we can define this traditional sense of validity (for formulas which do not contain demonstratives) as follows. First note that by *Remark 7*, if ϕ has a stable Character

$\overset{\mathfrak{A}}{\underset{c\,ftw}{\vDash}}$ φ iff $\overset{\mathfrak{A}}{\underset{c'ftw}{\vDash}}$ φ.

Thus for such formulas we can define,

φ *is true at tw* (*in* $\mathfrak{A}$) iff for every assignment f and every context c

$$\overset{\mathfrak{A}}{\underset{c\,ftw}{\vDash}}\ φ.$$

The neo-traditional sense of validity is not definable as follows:
$\underset{T}{\vDash}$ φ iff for all structures $\mathfrak{A}$, times t, and worlds w, φ is true at tw (in $\mathfrak{A}$). (Properly speaking, what I have called the neo-traditinal sense of validity is the notion of validity now common for a quantified S5 modal tense logic with individual variables ranging over possible individuals and a predicate of existence.) Adding the subscript 'LD' for explicitness, we can now state some results.

(i) If φ contains no demonstratives, if $\underset{T}{\vDash}$ φ, then $\underset{LD}{\vDash}$ φ.

(ii) $\underset{LD}{\vDash}$ ∃x Exist x, but ~ $\underset{T}{\vDash}$ ∃x Exist x.

Of course $\square$∃x Exist x is not valid even in LD. Nor are its counterparts, $\ulcorner F \urcorner$∃x Exist x and $\ulcorner P \urcorner$∃x Exist x.

This suggests that we can transcend the context-oriented perspective of LD by generalizing over times and worlds so as to capture those possible circumstances $\langle\mathfrak{A}, t, w\rangle$ which do not correspond to any possible contexts $\langle\mathfrak{A}, c\rangle$. We have the following result:

(iii) If φ cntains no demonstratives
$\underset{T}{\vDash}$ φ iff $\vDash_{LD}\square($ P φ ∧ F φ ∧ φ).

Although our definition of the neo-traditional sense of validity was motivated by consideration of demonstrative-free formulas, we could apply it also to formulas containing essential occurrences of demonstratives. To do so would nullify the most interesting features of the logic of demonstratives. But it raises the question: can we express our new sense of validity in terms of the neo-traditional sense? This can be done:

(iv) $\underset{LD}{\vDash}$ φ iff $\underset{T}{\vDash}$ANφ.

Remark 10. Rigid designators (in the sense of Kripke) are terms with a stable Content. Since Kripke does not discuss demonstratives, his examples all have, in addition, a stable Character (by *Remark 8*). Kripke claims that for proper names α, β it may happen that α = β, though not *a-priori*, is nevertheless necessary. This, in spite of the fact that the names α, β may be introduced by means of descriptions α′, β′ for which α′ = β′ is not necessary. An analogous situation holds in LD. Let α′, β′ be definite descriptions (without free variables) such that $\alpha' = \beta'$ is not *a-priori*, and consider the rigid terms dthat α' and dthat β' which are formed from them. We know that $\models (\text{dthat } \alpha' = \text{dthat}\beta' \leftrightarrow \alpha' = \beta')$. Thus, if $\alpha' = \beta'$ is not *a-priori*, neither is dthat$\alpha' = $ dthat β'. But, since $\models [\text{dthat } \alpha' = \text{dthat}\beta' \rightarrow \Box(\text{dthat}\alpha' = \text{dthat}\beta')]$, it may happen that dthat$\alpha' = $ dthatβ' is necessary. The converse situation can also be illustrated in LD. Since $(\alpha' = \text{dthat}\alpha')$ is valid (see *Remark 3*), it is surely capable of being known *a-priori*. But if α' lacks a stable Content (in some context c), $\Box\,(\alpha' = \text{dthat}\alpha')$ will be false.

Remark 11. Our *o-o*-place *i*-functors are not proper names, in the sense of Kripke, since they do not have a stable Content. But they can easily be converted by means of the stabilizing influence of dthat. Even dthat α lacks a stable Character. The process by which such expressions are converted into expressions with a stable Character is 'dubbing'—a form of definition in which context may play an essential role. The means to deal with such context indexed definitions is not available in our object language.

There would, of course, be no difficulty in supplementing our language with a syntactically distinctive set of *o-o*-place *i*-functors whose semantics requires them to have both a stable Character and a stable Content in every context. Variables already behave this way; what is wanted is a class of constants that behave, in these respects, like variables.

The difficulty comes in expressing the definition. My thought is that when a name, like 'Bozo', is introduced by someone saying, in some context c^*, 'Let's call the Governor, "Bozo" ', we have a context indexed definition of the form: $A = {}_{c^*}\alpha$, where A is a new constant (here, 'Bozo') and α is some term whose denotation depends on context (here, 'the Governor'). The intention of such a dubbing is, presumably, to induce the semantical clause: for all c, $\{A\}_{cf}^{\mathfrak{A}} = \{\alpha\}_{c^*f}^{\mathfrak{A}}$. Such a clause gives A a stable Character. The context indexing is required by the fact that the Content of α (the 'definiens') may vary from context to context. Thus the same semantical clause is not induced by taking either $A = \alpha$ or even $A = $ dthat α as an axiom.

I think it likely that such definitions play a practically (and perhaps theoretically) indispensable role in the growth of language, allowing us to introduce a vast stock of names on the basis of a meagre stock of demonstratives and some ingenuity in the staging of demonstrations.

Perhaps such introductions should not be called 'definitions' at all, since they essentially enrich the expressive power of the language. What a nameless man may express by 'I am hungry' may be inexpressible in remote contexts. But once he says 'Let's call me "Bozo" ' his Content is accessible to us all.

Remark 12. The strongest form of logical equivalence between two formulas ϕ and ϕ' is sameness of Character, $\{\phi\} = \{\phi'\}$. This form of synonymy is expressible in terms of validity:

$\{\varphi\} = \{\varphi'\}$ iff $\models \Box[$ P $(\varphi \leftrightarrow \varphi') \wedge$ F $(\varphi \leftrightarrow \varphi') \wedge (\varphi \leftrightarrow \varphi')]$.
[Using *Remark 9* (iii) and dropping the condition, which was stated only to express the intended range of applicability of $\models_{\overline{T}}$, we have: $\{\varphi\} = \{\varphi'\}$ iff $\models_{\overline{T}} (\varphi \leftrightarrow \varphi')$.] Since definitions of the usual kind (as opposed to dubbings) are intended to introduce a short expression as a mere abbreviation of a longer one, the Character of the defined sign should be the same as the Character of the definiens. Thus, with LD, definitional axioms must take the form indicated above.

Remark 13. If β is a variable of the same sort as the term α but is not free in α, then $\{$dthat $\alpha\} = \{$the β $AN(\beta = \alpha)\}$. Thus for every formula φ, there can be constructed a formula φ' such that φ' contains no occurrence of dthat and $\{\varphi\} = \{\varphi'\}$.

Remark 14. Y (yesterday) and G (one day ago) superficially resemble one another in view of the fact that $\models (Y\varphi \leftrightarrow G\varphi)$. But the former is a demonstrative whereas the latter is an iterative temporal operator. 'One day ago it was the case that one day ago it was the case that John yawned' means that John yawned the day before yesterday. But 'Yesterday it was the case that yesterday it was the case that John yawned' is only a stutter.

POSSIBLE REFINEMENTS

(1) The primitive predicates and functors of first-order predicate logic are all taken to be extensional. Alternatives are possible.
(2) Many conditions might be added on $\mathscr{P}$; many alternatives might be chosen for $\mathscr{T}$. If the elements of $\mathscr{T}$ do not have a natural relation to play the role of $<$, such a relation must be added to the structure.
(3) When K is a set of LD formulas, $K \models \varphi$ is easily defined in any of the usual ways.
(4) Aspects of the contexts other than c_A, c_P, c_T, and c_W would be used if new demonstratives (e.g. pointings, 'You', etc.) were added to the language. (Note that the subscripts A, P, T, W are external parameters. They may be thought of as functions applying to contexts, with c_A being the value of A for the context c.)
(5) Special continuity conditions through time might be added for the predicate Exists.
(6) If individuals lacking positions are admitted as agents of contexts, 3(iii) of page 195 should be weakened to $c_P \in \mathscr{P} \cup \{\dagger\}$. It would no longer be the case that $\models$ Located I, Here. If individuals also lacking temporal location (disembodied minds?) are admitted as agents of contexts, a similar weakening is required of 3(ii). In any case it would still be true that $\models$ Exist I.

NOTES

1. This paper was originally composed in two parts. The formal 'Logic of Demonstratives' was first presented at the Irvine Summer Institute on the Philosophy of Language in 1971. It was expanded in 1973. The initial discursive material was written on 20 April 1973, as part of a research proposal. This paper was intended as a companion piece to and progress report on the material in 'Dthat'. (D. Kaplan, 'Dthat' in Peter Cole (ed.), *Syntax and Semantics*, 9, *Pragmatics* (Academic Press: New York, 1978), 221–43. Also reprinted in P. French *et. al.* (eds), *Contemporary Perspectives in the Philosophy of Language* (Minneapolis: University of Minnesota Press, 1979), pp. 383–400.) A more extensive presentation occurs in my manuscript 'Demonstratives', in J. Almog. J. Perry, and H. Wettstein (eds.), *Themes from Kaplan* (Oxford University Press, forthcoming). This work was supported by the National Science Foundation.

2. S. Kripke, 'Naming and Necessity', in Donald Davidson and Gilbert Harman (eds.), *Semantics of Natural Language* (Dordrecht: Reidel, 1972) 253–355; Addenda, pp. 763–769.

3. P. Strawson, *Introduction to Logical Theory*, (New York: John Wiley & Sons, 1952).

PART THREE

ON TARSKI

INTRODUCTION

This section is about the theory of meaning, although its title may hardly seem to indicate that. But Davidson's influential paper is an argument to the effect that a theory of truth, in the manner of Tarski, is a theory of linguistic meaning; moreover, he argues, it is a confusion to expect more.

Davidson objects to the Fregean theory of the compositionality of meaning that inspires much of the work collected in this volume, and represented in the first two sections. His argument against it is an instance of what Barwise and Perry (1985) call the Slingshot. Recall that on Frege's theory any two sentences with the same truth-value have the same nominatum (Bedeutung). This is a result that Frege welcomed, for he took the reference of a sentence to be just its truth-value; so all true sentences refer to the same thing. This did not prevent him from distinguishing semantically between true sentences, since overall semantic meaning consists of both nominatum and sense. For a strictly referential semantics, however, the Slingshot has the unwelcome consequence that all true sentences (and all false ones) mean the same thing. Reference just is meaning according to such theories. Hence, if the sense component of meaning can be undermined—if a theory of meaning can be constructed making use only of reference—Fregean compositionality must go.

Davidson and his followers argue that nonreferential meanings are obscure in that they are intensional (infra.) For a variety of programmatic, metaphysical, and epistemological reasons, they conclude that intensions, senses, and their ilk have no place in a suitably scientific theory of linguistic meaning. Referential meanings, according to the Slingshot, reduce to two—truth and falsity—clearly not enough to distinguish between the semantic values of all of the infinitely many sentences of a language. Davidson proposes then to abandon meaning altogether, to give up the project of discovering for every sentence, s, and meaning, m, of a given language, whether s means m. Semantics, he argues, is properly concerned with that other great semantic notion, Truth, and Tarski has shown the way to a theory of truth for a given language. If a truth-theory for a natural language can be provided, he argues, there remains no role for a misguided theory of meaning.

Hartry Field's essay pushes the Davidsoninan critique of semantics one step further, asking whether Tarski's definition makes even the concept of truth respectable, much less that of meaning. Is it a legitimate scientific concept, he asks, or can it be reduced via definition to legitimate scientific concepts? To make his point that Tarski does not define truth in nonsemantic terms, Field sketches a Tarski-style definition of truth for a fake language, *L*. This is an extremely useful two-page sketch for those coming new to formal semantics in that it is both clear and typical of the way semantics is written for many differest kinds of formal languages. This outline shows that truth is defined in terms of primitive denotation, that the truth of the sentences of *L* depends on what their names and variables denote. So one does not exit from the semantic circle, denotation being as much a semantic notion as that of truth.

On p. 274 Field returns to the point raised by Tarski's restriction on his own heuristic language, *L*, viz., that "the sense of every expression is unambiguously determined by its form." This is precisely the problem that Davidson considers at the end of his essay. Natural languages such as English are full of ambiguous expressions and, perhaps worse, demonstratives and indexicals such as "this" and "you" whose denotation shifts from one utterance token or instance to another. Yet the major semantic properties such as truth and meaning are ascribed to sentence or utterance types. One doesn't want to worry about every individual writing or saying of the sentence "snow is white." Yet this is what ambiguity and indexicality seem to force one to do. (This is discussed in the last section of this book, and also of course in this copy, this token of this book, but luckily we do not have to say both things.)

Field's essay illustrates how complex and language-dependent is the meaning of "true." Defined as Tarski originally defined it its meaning would change every time a new primitive word was introduced. Field shows how to avoid this possibly unwelcome consequence, but the large lesson of the Tarskian movement in semantics is nonetheless that to know what "true" or "wahr" or "dorost" means is to know a great deal about the structure of English or German or Parsee.

Field's main concern is, however, the compatibility of semantics with the program of physicalism. He describes the latter as a high-level empirical hypothesis that says semantic, mental, chemical, and biological phenomena "are all explicable (in principle) in terms of physical facts" (p. 279ff). This is big stuff. One route to the "physicalization" of semantics goes through psychology. If linguistic meanings are in the head, *contra* Putnam (1975), and the head contains only molecules, atoms, and electrons, then the hypothesis is true. But if meanings are such intensions as propositions, whether Fregean

Gedanken or sets of possible worlds, then the hypothesis is not true. In either case, whether true or false, semantics, unlike syntax, lacks autonomy. Yet the Tarskian program seems to pursue the subject in blithe or purposeful ignorance of this. Field first reduces truth by definition to the primitive denotation of terms and predicates, e.g., "the moon" denotes the moon and "is round" denotes the set of round things, so the composed sentence will be true if and only if the denotation of the first belongs to the denotation of the second. Field then works to provide a similar reduction of the semantic relation of denotation.

John McDowell takes issue with Field's main thesis—that Tarski's account of truth fails from a physicalistic standpoint on the grounds that Tarski has not defined truth in strictly physical terms. He reviews Field's two versions, T1 and T2, of Tarski's definition and raises questions as to the superiority of T1 over T2. McDowell's concern is to understand just exactly what a physicalistic reduction of semantic phenomena—truth, satisfaction, primitive denotation—means. McDowell proposes instead a compatibilist doctrine that holds that intentional explanations of the phenomena of semantics are consistent with physics having explanatory dominion over all events. In the course of articulating his alternative, he provides a helpful reprise of Tarski's great conceptual artifact.

This small selection of essays demonstrates amply Tarski's enormous influence on semantics and the philosophy of language. It by no means exhausts the issues Tarski raises. The theory of truth is an ongoing domain of exciting research. We hope here to have introduced the semantic program Tarski's theory of truth most directly inspires, and to have indicated a few of the more central questions it raises.

DONALD DAVIDSON

TRUTH AND MEANING

It is conceded by most philosophers of language, and recently by some linguists, that a satisfactory theory of meaning must give an account of how the meanings of sentences depend upon the meanings of words. Unless such an account could be supplied for a particular language, it is argued, there would be no explaining the fact that we can learn the language: no explaining the fact that, on mastering a finite vocabulary and a finitely stated set of rules, we are prepared to produce and to understand any of a potential infinitude of sentences. I do not dispute these vague claims, in which I sense more than a kernel of truth. Instead I want to ask what it is for a theory to give an account of the kind adumbrated.

One proposal is to begin by assigning some entity as meaning to each word (or other significant syntactical feature) of the sentence: thus we might assign Theaetetus to 'Theaetetus' and the property of flying to 'flies' in the sentence 'Theaetetus flies'. The problem then arises how the meaning of the sentence is generated from these meanings. Viewing concatenation as a significant piece of syntax, we may assign to it the relation of participating in or instantiating; however, it is obvious that we have here the start of an infinite regress. Frege sought to avoid the regress by saying that the entities corresponding to predicates (for example) are 'unsaturated' or 'incomplete' in contrast to the entities that correspond to names, but this doctrine seems to label a difficulty rather than solve it.

The point will emerge if we think for a moment of complex singular terms, to which Frege's theory applies along with sentences. Consider the expression 'the father of Annette': how does the meaning of the whole depend on the meaning of the parts? The answer would seem to be that the meaning of 'the father of' is such that when this expression is prefixed to a singular term the result refers to the father of the person to whom the singular term refers. What part is played, in this account, by the unsaturated or incomplete entity for which 'the father of' stands? All we can think to say is that this entity 'yields' or 'gives' the father of x as value when the argument is x, or perhaps that this entity maps people on to their fathers. It may not be clear whether the entity for which 'the father of' is said to stand performs any genuine explanatory function as long as we stick to individual expressions; so think instead of the infinite class of expressions formed by writing 'the father of' zero or more times in front of 'Annette'. It is easy to supply a theory that tells, for an arbitrary one of these singular terms, what it refers to: if the term is 'Annette' it refers to Annette, while if the term is complex, consisting of 'the father of' prefixed to a singular term t, then it refers to the father of the person to whom t refers. It is obvious that no entity corresponding to 'the father of' is, or needs to be, mentioned in stating this theory.

It would be inappropriate to complain that this little theory *uses* the words 'the father of' in giving the reference of expressions containing those words. For the task was to give the meaning of all expressions in a certain infinite set on the basis of the meaning of the parts; it was not in the bargain also to give the meanings of the atomic parts. On the other hand, it is now evident that a satisfactory theory of the meanings of complex expressions may not require entities as meanings of all the parts. It behooves us then to rephrase our demand on a satisfactory theory of meaning so as not to suggest that individual words must have meanings at all, in any sense that transcends the fact that they have a systematic effect on the meanings of the sentences in which they occur. Actually, for the case at hand we can do better still in stating the criterion of success: what we wanted, and what we got, is a theory that entails every sentence of the form 't refers to x' where 't' is replaced by a structural description[1] of a singular term, and 'x' is replaced by that term itself. Further, our theory accomplishes this without appeal to any semantical concepts beyond the basic 'refers to'. Finally, the theory clearly suggests an effective procedure for determining, for any singular term in its universe, what that term refers to.

A theory with such evident merits deserves wider application. The device proposed by Frege to this end has a brilliant simplicity: count predicates as a special case of functional expressions, and sentences as a special case of complex singular terms. Now, however, a difficulty looms if we want to continue in our present (implicit) course of identifying the meanings of a singular term with its reference. The difficulty follows upon making two reasonable assumptions: that logically equivalent singular terms have the same reference, and that a singular term does not change its reference if a contained singular term is replaced by another with the same reference. But now suppose that 'R' and 'S' abbreviate any two sentences alike in truth value. Then the following four sentences have the same reference:

(1) R
(2) $\hat{x}(x = x.R) = \hat{x}(x = x)$

(3) $\hat{x}(x = x.S) = \hat{x}(x = x)$
(4) S

For (1) and (2) are logically equivalent, as are (3) and (4), while (3) differs from (2) only in containing the singular term '$\hat{x}(x = x.S)$' where (2) contains '$\hat{x}(x = x.R)$' and these refer to the same thing if S and R are alike in truth value. Hence any two sentences have the same reference if they have the same truth value.[2] And if the meaning of a sentence is what it refers to, all sentences alike in truth value must be synonymous—an intolerable result.

Apparently we must abandon the present approach as leading to a theory of meaning. This is the natural point at which to turn for help to the distinction between meaning and reference. The trouble, we are told, is that questions of reference are, in general, settled by extra-linguistic facts, questions of meaning not, and the facts can conflate the references of expressions that are not synonymous. If we want a theory that gives the meaning (as distinct from reference) of each sentence, we must start with the meaning (as distinct from reference) of the parts.

Up to here we have been following in Frege's footsteps; thanks to him, the path is well known and even well worn. But now, I would like to suggest, we have reached an impasse: the switch from reference to meaning leads to no useful account of how the meanings of sentences depend upon the meanings of the words (or other structural features) that compose them. Ask, for example, for the meaning of 'Theaetetus flies'. A Fregean answer might go something like this: given the meaning of 'Theaetetus' as argument, the meaning of 'flies' yields the meaning of 'Theaetetus flies' as value. The vacuity of this answer is obvious. We wanted to know what the meaning of 'Theaetetus flies' is; it is no progress to be told that it is the meaning of 'Theaetetus flies'. This much we knew before any theory was in sight. In the bogus account just given, talk of the structure of the sentence and of the meanings of words was idle, for it played no role in producing the given description of the meaning of the sentence.

The contrast here between a real and pretended account will be plainer still if we ask for a theory, analogous to the minature theory of reference of singular terms just sketched, but different in dealing with meanings in place of references. What analogy demands is a theory that has as consequences all sentences of the form 's means m' where 's' is replaced by a structrual description of a sentence and 'm' is replaced by a singular term that refers to the meaning of that sentence: a theory, moreover, that provides an effective method for arriving at the meaning of an arbitrary sentence structurally described. Clearly some more articulate way of referring to meanings than any we have seen is essential if these criteria are to be met.[3] Meanings as entities, or the related concept of synonymy, allow us to formulate the following rule relating sentences and their parts: sentences are synonymous whose corresponding parts are synonymous ('corresponding' here needs spelling out of course). And meanings as entities may, in theories such as Frege's, do duty, on occasion, as references, thus losing their status as entities distinct from references. Paradoxically, the one thing meanings do not seem to do is oil the wheels of a theory of meaning at least as long as we require of such a theory that it non-trivially give the meaning of every sentence in the language. My objection to meanings in the theory of meaning is not that they are abstract or that their identity conditions are obscure, but that they have no demonstrated use.

This is the place to scotch another hopeful thought. Suppose we have a satisfactory theory of syntax for our language, consisting of an effective method of telling, for an arbitrary expression, whether or not it is independently meaningful (i.e. a sentence), and assume as usual that this involves viewing each sentence as composed, in allowable ways, out of elements drawn from a fixed finite stock of atomic syntactical elements (roughly, words). The hopeful thought is that syntax, so conceived, will yield semantics when a dictionary giving the meaning of each syntactic atom is added. Hopes will be dashed, however, if semantics is to comprise a theory of meaning in our sense, for knowledge of the structural characteristics that make for meaningfulness in a sentence, plus knowledge of the meanings of the ultimate parts, does not add up to knowledge of what a sentence means. The point is easily illustrated by belief sentences. Their syntax is relatively unproblematic. Yet, adding a dictionary does not touch the standard semantic problem, which is that we cannot account for even as much as the truth conditions of such sentences on the basis of what we know of the meanings of the words in them. The situation is not radically altered by refining the dictionary to indicate which meaning or meanings an ambiguous expression bears in each of its possible contexts: the problem of belief sentences persists after ambiguities are resolved.

The fact that recursive syntax with dictionary added is not necessarily recursive semantics has been obscured in some recent writing on linguistics by the intrusion of semantic criteria into the discussion of purportedly syntactic theories. The matter would boil down to a harmless difference over terminology if the semantic criteria were clear; but they are not. While there is agreement that it is the central task of semantics to give the semantic interpretation (the meaning) of every sentence in the language, nowhere in the linguistic literature will one find, so far as I know, a straightforward account of how a theory performs this task, or how to tell when it has been accomplished. The contrast with syntax is striking. The main job of a modest syntax is to characterize *meaningfulness* (or sentencehood). We may have as much confidence in the correctness sentencehood. We may have as much confidence in the correctness of such a characterization as we have in the representativeness of our sample and our ability to say when particular expressions are meaningful (sentences). What clear and analogous task and test exist for semantics?[4]

We decided a while back not to assume that parts of sentences have meanings except in the ontologically neutral sense of making a systematic contribution to the meaning of the sentences in which they occur. Since postulating meanings has netted nothing, let us return to that insight. One direction in which it points is a certain holistic view of meaning. If sentences depend for their meaning on their structure, and we understand the meaning of each item in the structure only as an abstraction from the totality of sentences in which it features, then we can give the meaning of any sentence (or word) only by giving the meaning of every sentence (and word) in the language. Frege said that only in the context of a sentence does a word have meaning; in the same vein he might have added that only in the context of the language does a sentence (and therefore a word) have meaning.

This degree of holism was already implicit in the suggestion that an adequate theory of meaning must entail *all* sentences of the form '*s* means *m*'. But now, having found no more help in meanings of sentences than in meanings of words, let us ask whether we can get rid of the troublesome singular terms supposed to replace '*m*' and to refer to meanings. In a way, nothing could be easier: just write '*s* means that *p*', and imagine '*p*' replaced by a sentence. Sentences, as we have seen, cannot name meanings, and sentences with 'that' prefixed are not names at all, unless we decide so. It looks as though we are in trouble on another count, however, for it is reasonable to expect that in wrestling with the logic of the apparently nonextensional 'means that' we will encounter problems as hard as, or perhaps identical with, the problems our theory is out to solve.

The only way I know to deal with this difficulty is simple, and radical. Anxiety that we are enmeshed in the intensional springs from using the words 'means that' as filling between description of sentence and sentence, but it may be that the success of our venture depends not on the filling but on what it fills. The theory will have done its work if it provides, for every sentence *s* in the language under study, a matching sentence (to replace '*p*') that, in some way yet to be made clear, 'gives the meaning' of *s*. One obvious candidate for matching sentence is just *s* itself, if the object language is contained in the metalanguage; otherwise a translation of *s* in the metalanguage. As a final bold step, let us try treating the position occupied by '*p*' extensionally: to implement this, sweep away the obscure 'means that', provide the sentence that replaces '*p*' with a proper sentential connective, and supply the description that replaces '*s*' with its own predicate. The plausible result is

(*T*) *s* is *T* if and only if *p*.

What we require of a theory of meaning for a language L is that without appeal to any (further) semantical notions it place enough restrictions on the predicate 'is T' to entail all sentences got from schema T when 's' is replaced by a structural description of a sentence of L and 'p' by that sentence.

Any two predicates satisfying this condition have the same extension,[5] so if the metalanguage is rich enough, nothing stands in the way of putting what I am calling a theory of meaning into the form of an explicit definition of a predicate 'is T'. But whether explicitly defined or recursively characterized, it is clear that the sentences to which the predicate 'is T' applies will be just the true sentences of L, for the condition we have placed on satisfactory theories of meaning is in essence Tarski's Convention T that tests the adequacy of a formal semantical definition of truth.[6]

The path to this point has been tortuous, but the conclusion may be stated simply: a theory of meaning for a language L shows 'how the meanings of sentences depend upon the meanings of words' if it contains a (recursive) definition of truth-in-L. And, so far at least, we have no other idea how to turn the trick. It is worth emphasizing that the concept of truth played no ostensible role in stating our original problem. That problem, upon refinement, led to the view that an adequate theory of meaning must characterize a predicate meeting certain conditions. It was in the nature of a discovery that such a predicate would apply exactly to the true sentences. I hope that what I am saying may be described in part as defending the philosophical importance of Tarski's semantical concept of truth. But my defence is only distantly related, if at all, to the question whether the concept Tarski has shown how to define is the (or a) philosophically interesting conception of truth or the question whether Tarski has cast any light on the ordinary use of such words as 'true' and 'truth'. It is a misfortune that dust from futile and confused battles over these questions has prevented those with a theoretical interest in language—philosophers, logicians, psychologists, and linguists alike—from seeing in the semantical concept of truth (under whatever name) the sophisticated and powerful foundation of a competent theory of meaning.

There is no need to suppress, of course, the obvious connection between a definition of truth of the kind Tarski has shown how to construct, and the concept of meaning. It is this: the definition works by giving necessary and sufficient conditions for the truth of every sentence, and to give truth conditions is a way of giving the meaning of a sentence. To know the semantic concept of truth for a language is to know what it is for a sentence—any sentence—to be true, and this amounts, in one good sense we can give to the phrase, to understanding the language. This at any rate is my excuse for a feature of the present discussion that is apt to shock old hands; my free-wheeling use of the word 'meaning', for what I call a theory of meaning has after all turned out to make no use of meanings, whether of sentences or of words. Indeed, since a Tarski-type truth definition supplies all we have asked so far of a theory of meaning, it is clear that such a theory falls comfortably within what Quine terms the 'theory of reference' as distinguished from what he terms the 'theory of meaning'. So much to the good for what I call a theory of meaning, and so much, perhaps, against my so calling it.[7]

A theory of meaning (in my mildly perverse sense) is an empirical theory, and its ambition is to account for the workings of a natural language. Like any theory, it may be tested by comparing some of its consequences with the facts. In the present case this is easy, for the theory has been characterized as issuing in an infinite flood of sentences each giving the truth conditions of a sentence; we only need to ask, in sample cases, whether what the theory avers to be the truth conditions for a sentence really are. A typical test case might involve deciding whether the sentence 'Snow is white' *is* true if and only if snow is white. Not all cases will be so simple (for reasons to be sketched), but it is evident that this sort of test does not invite counting noses. A sharp conception of what constitutes a theory in this domain furnishes an exciting context for raising deep questions about when a theory of language is correct and how it is to be tried. But the difficulties are theoretical, not practical. In application, the trouble is to get a theory that comes close to working; anyone can tell whether it is right.[8] One can see why this is so. The theory reveals nothing new about the conditions under which an individual sentence is true; it does not make those conditions any clearer than the sentence itself does. The work of the theory is in relating the known truth conditions of each sentence to those aspects ('words') of the sentence that recur in other sentences, and can be assigned identical roles in other sentences. Empirical power in such a theory depends on success in recovering the structure of a very complicated ability—the ability to speak and understand a language. We can tell easily enough when particular pronouncements of the theory comport with our understanding of the language; this is consistent with a feeble insight into the design of the machinery of our linguistic accomplishments.

The remarks of the last paragraph apply directly only to the special case where it is assumed that the langauge for which truth is being characterized is part of the language used and understood by the characterizer. Under these circumstances, the framer of a theory will as a matter of course avail himself when he can of the built-in convenience of a metalanguage with a sentence guaranteed equivalent to each sentence in the object language. Still, this fact ought not to con us into thinking a theory any more correct that entails ' "Snow is white" is true if and only if snow is white' than one that entails instead:

(S) 'Snow is white' is true if and only if grass is green,

provided, of course, we are as sure of the truth of (S) as we are of that of its more celebrated predecessor. Yet (S) may not encourage the same confidence that a theory that entails it deserves to be called a theory of meaning.

The threatened failure of nerve may be counteracted as follows. The grotesqueness of (S) is in itself nothing against a theory of which it is a consequence, provided the theory gives the correct results for every sentence (on the basis of its structure, there being no other way). It is not easy to see how (S) could be party to such an enterprise, but if it were—if, that is, (S) followed from a characterization of the predicate 'is true' that led to the invariable pairing of truths with truths and falsehoods with falsehoods then there would not, I think, be anything essential to the idea of meaning that remained to be captured.[9]

What appears to the right of the biconditional in sentences of the form 's is true if and only if p' when such sentences are consequences of a theory of truth plays its role in determining the meaning of s not by pretending synonymy but by adding one more brush-stroke to the picture which, taken as a whole, tells what there is to know of the meaning of s; this stroke is added by virtue of the fact that the sentence that replaces 'p' is true if and only if s is.

It may help to reflect that (S) is acceptable, if it is, because we are independently sure of the truth of 'Snow is white' and 'Grass is green'; but in cases where we are unsure of the truth of a sentence, we can have confidence in a characterization of the truth predicate only if it pairs that sentence with one we have good reason to believe equivalent. It would be ill advised for someone who had any doubts about the colour of snow or grass to accept a theory that yielded (S), even if his doubts were of equal degree, unless he thought the colour of the one was tied to the colour of the other.[10] Omniscience can obviously afford more bizzare theories of meaning than ignorance; but then, omniscience has less need of communication.

It must be possible, of course, for the speaker of one language to construct a theory of meaning for the speaker of another, though in this case the empirical test of the correctness of the theory will no longer be trivial. As before, the aim of theory will be an infinite correlation of sentences alike in truth. But this time the theory-builder must not be assumed to have direct insight into likely equivalences between his own tongue and the alien. What he must do is find out, however he can, what sentences the alien holds true in his own tongue (or better, to what degree he holds them true). The linguist then will attempt to construct a characterization of truth-for-the-alien which yields, so far as possible, a mapping of sentences held true (or false) by the alien on to sentences held true (or false) by the linguist. Supposing no perfect fit is found, the residue of sentences held true translated by sentences held false (and vice versa) is the margin for error (foreign or domestic). Charity in interpreting the words and thoughts of others is unavoidable in another direction as well: just as we must maximize agreement, or risk not making sense of what the alien is talking about, so we must maximize the self-consistency we attribute to him, on pain of not understanding *him*. No single principle of optimum charity emerges; the constraints therefore determine no single theory. In a theory of radical translation (as Quine calls it) there is no completely disentangling questions of what the alien means from questions of what he believes. We do not know what someone means unless we know what he believes; we do not know what someone believes unless we know what he means. In radical interpretation we are able to break into this circle, if only incompletely, because we can sometimes tell that a person accedes to a sentence we do not understand.[11]

In the past few pages I have been asking how a theory of meaning that takes the form of a truth definition can be empirically tested, and have blithely ignored the prior question whether there is any serious chance such a theory can be given for a natural language. What are the prospects for a formal semantical theory of a natural language? Very poor, according to Tarski; and I believe most logicians, philosophers of language, and linguists agree.[12] Let me do what I can to dispel the pessimism. What I can in a general and programmatic way, of course, for here the proof of the pudding will certainly be in the proof of the right theorems.

Tarski concludes the first section of his classic essay on the concept of truth in formalized languages with the following remarks, which he italicizes:

. . . *The very possibility of a consistent use of the expression 'true sentence' which is in harmony with the laws of logic and the spirit of everyday language seems to be very questionable, and consequently the same doubt attaches to the possibility of constructing a correct definition of this expression.* (165)

Late in the same essay, he returns to the subject:

. . . the concept of truth (as well as other semantical concepts) when applied to colloquial language in conjunction with the normal laws of logic leads inevitably to confusions and contradictions. Whoever wishes, in spite of all difficulties, to pursue the semantics of colloquial language with the help of exact methods will be driven first to undertake the thankless task of a reform of this language. He will find it necessary to define its structure, to overcome the ambiguity of the terms which occur in it, and finally to split the language into a series of languages of greater and greater extent, each of which stands in the same relation to the next in which a formalized language stands to its metalanguage. It may, however be doubted whether the language of everyday life, after being 'rationalized' in this way, would still preserve its naturalness and whether it would not rather take on the characteristic features of the formalized languages. (267)

Two themes emerge: that the universal character of natural languages leads to contradiction (the semantic paradoxes), and that natural languages are too confused and amorphous to permit the direct application of formal methods. The first point deserves a serious answer, and I wish I had one. As it is, I will say only why I think we are justified in carrying on without having disinfected this particular source of conceptual anxiety. The semantic paradoxes arise when the range of the quantifiers in the object language is too generous in certain ways. But it is not really clear how unfair to Urdu or to Wendish it would be to view the range of their quantifiers as insufficient to yield an explicit definition of 'true-in-Urdu' or 'true-in-Wendish'. Or, to put the matter in another, if not more serious way, there may in the nature of the case always be something we grasp in understanding the language of another (the concept of truth) that we cannot communicate to him. In any case, most of the problems of general philosophical interest arise within a fragment of the relevant natural language that may be conceived as containing very little set theory. Of course these comments do not meet the claim that natural languages are universal. But it seems to me that this claim, now that we know such universality leads to paradox, is suspect.

Tarski's second point is that we would have to reform a natural language out of all recognition before we could apply formal semantical methods. If this is true, it is fatal to my project, for the task of a theory of meaning as I conceive it is not to change, improve, or reform a language, but to describe and understand it. Let us look at the positive side. Tarski has shown the way to giving a theory for interpreted formal languages of various kinds; pick one as much like English as possible. Since this new language has been explained in English and contains much English we not only may, but I think must, view it as part of English for those who understand it. For this fragment of English we have, *ex hypothesi*, a theory of the required sort. Not only that, but in interpreting this adjunct of English in old English we necessarily gave hints connecting old and new. Wherever there are sentences of old English with the same truth conditions as sentences in the adjunct we may extend the theory to cover them. Much of what is called for is to mechanize as far as possible what we now do by art when we put ordinary English into one or another canonical notation. The point is not that canonical notation is better than the rough original idiom, but rather that if we know what idiom the canonical notation is canonical *for*, we have as good a theory for the idiom as for its kept companion.

Philosophers have long been at the hard work of applying theory to ordinary language by the device of matching sentences in the vernacular with sentences for which they have a theory. Frege's massive contribution was to show how 'all', 'some', 'every', 'each', 'none', and associated pronouns, in some of their uses, could be tamed; for the first time, it was possible to dream of a formal semantics for a significant part of a natural language. This dream came true in a sharp way with the work of Tarski. It would be a shame to miss the fact that as a result of these two magnificent achievements, Frege's and Tarski's, we have gained a deep insight into the structure of our mother tongues. Philosophers of a logical bent have tended to start where the theory was and work out towards the complications of natural language. Contemporary linguists, with an aim that cannot easily be seen to be different, start with the ordinary and work toward a general theory. If either party is successful, there must be a meeting. Recent work by Chomsky and others is doing much to bring the complexities of natural languages within the scope of serious theory. To give an example: suppose success in giving the truth conditions for some significant range of sentences in the active voice. Then with a formal procedure for transforming each such sentence into a corresponding sentence in the passive voice, the theory of truth could be extended in an obvious way to this new set of sentences.[13]

One problem touched on in passing by Tarski does not, at least in all its manifestations, have to be solved to get ahead with theory: the existence in natural languages of 'ambiguous terms'. As long as ambiguity does not affect grammatical form, and can be translated, ambiguity for ambiguity, into the metalanguage, a truth definition will not tell us any lies. The chief trouble, for systematic semantics, with the phrase 'believes that' in English lies not in its vagueness, ambiguity, or unsuitability for incorporation in a serious science: let our metalanguage be English, and all *these* problems will be carried without loss or gain into the metalanguage. But the central problem of the logical grammar of 'believes that' will remain to haunt us.

The example is suited to illustrating another, and related, point, for the discussion of belief sentences has been plagued by failure to observe a fundamental distinction between tasks: uncovering the logical grammar or form of sentences (which is in the province of a theory of meaning as I construe it), and the analysis of individual words or expressions (which are treated as primitive by the theory). Thus Carnap, in the first edition of *Meaning and Necessity*, suggested we render 'John believes that the earth is round' as 'John responds affirmatively to "the earth is round" as an English sentence'. He gave this up when Mates pointed out that John might respond affirmatively to one sentence and not to another no matter how close the meaning.[14] But there is a confusion here from the start. The semantic structure of a belief sentence, according to this idea of Carnap's, is given by a three-place predicate with places reserved for expressions referring to a person, a sentence, and a language. It is a different sort of problem entirely to attempt an analysis of this predicate, perhaps along behaviouristic lines. Not least among the merits of Tarski's conception of a theory of truth is that the purity of method it demands of us follows from the formulation of the problem itself, not from the self-imposed restraint of some adventitious philosophical puritanism.

I think it is hard to exaggerate the advantages to philosophy of language of bearing in mind this distinction between questions of logical form or grammar, and the analysis of individual concepts. Another example may help advertise the point.

If we suppose questions of logical grammar settled, sentences like 'Bardot is good' raise no special problems for a truth definition. The deep differences between descriptive and evaluative (emotive, expressive, etc.) terms do not show here. Even if we hold there is some important sense in which moral or evaluative sentences do not have a truth value (for example, because they cannot be verified), we ought not to boggle at ' "Bardot is good" is true if and only if Bardot is good'; in a theory of truth, this consequence should follow with the rest, keeping track, as must be done, of the semantic location of such sentences in the language as a whole—of their relation to generalizations, their role in such compound sentences as 'Bardot is good and Bardot is foolish', and so on. What is special to evaluative words is simply not touched: the mystery is transferred from the word 'good' in the object language to its translation in the metalanguage.

But 'good' as it features in 'Bardot is a good actress' is another matter. The problem is not that the translation of this sentence is not in the metalanguage—let us suppose it is. The problem is to frame a truth definition such that ' "Bardot is a good actress" is true if and only if Bardot is a good actress'— and all other sentences like it—are consequences. Obviously 'good actress' does not mean 'good and an actress'. We might think of taking 'is a good actress' as an unanalysed predicate. This would obliterate all connection between 'is a good actress' and 'is a good mother', and it would give us no excuse to think of 'good', in these uses, as a word or semantic element. But worse, it would bar us from framing a truth definition at all, for there is no end to the predicates we would have to treat as logically simple (and hence accommodate in separate clauses in the definition of satisfaction): 'is a good companion to dogs', 'is a good 28-years old conversationalist', and so forth. The problem is not peculiar to the case: it is the problem of attributive adjectives generally.

It is consistent with the attitude taken here to deem it usually a strategic error to undertake philosophical analysis of words or expressions which is not preceded by or at any rate accompanied by the attempt to get the logical grammar straight. For how can we have any confidence in our analyses of words like 'right', 'ought', 'can', and 'obliged', or the phrases we use to talk of actions, events, and causes, when we do not know what (logical, semantical) parts of speech we have to deal with? I would say much the same about studies of the 'logic' of these and other words, and the sentences containing them. Whether the effort and ingenuity that have gone into the study of deontic logics, modal logics, imperative and erotetic logics have been largely futile or not cannot be known until we have acceptable semantic analyses of the sentences such systems purport to treat. Philosophers and logicians sometimes talk or work as if they were free to choose between, say, the truth-functional conditional and others, or free to introduce non-truth-functional sentential operators like 'Let it be the case that' or 'It ought to be the case that'. But in fact the decision is crucial. When we depart from idioms we can accommodate in a truth definition, we lapse into (or create) language for which we have no coherent semantical account—that is, no account at all of how such talk can be integrated into the language as a whole.

To return to our main theme: we have recognized that a theory of the kind proposed leaves the whole matter of what individual words mean exactly where it was. Even when the metalanguage is different from the object language, the theory exerts no pressure for improvement, clarification, or analysis of individual words, except when, by accident of vocabulary, straightforward translation fails. Just as synonymy, as between expressions, goes generally untreated, so also synonymy of sentences, and analyticity. Even such sentences as 'A vixen is a female fox' bear no special tag unless it is our pleasure to provide it. A truth definition does not distinguish between analytic sentences and others, except for sentences that owe their truth to the presence alone of the constants that give the theory its grip on structure: the theory entails not only that these sentences are true but that they will remain true under all significant rewritings of their non-logical parts. A notion of logical truth thus given limited application, related notions of logical equivalence and entailment will tag along. It is hard to imagine how a theory of meaning could fail to read a logic into its object language to this degree; and to the extent that it does, our intuitions of logical truth, equivalence, and entailment may be called upon in constructing and testing the theory.

I turn now to one more, and very large, fly in the ointment: the fact that the same sentence may at one time or in one mouth be true and at another time or in another mouth be false. Both logicians and those critical of formal methods here seem largely (though by no means universally) agreed that formal semantics and logic are incompetent to deal with the disturbances caused by demonstratives. Logicians have often reacted by downgrading natural language and trying to show how to get along without demonstratives; their critics react by downgrading logic and formal semantics. None of this can make me happy: clearly demonstratives cannot be eliminated from a natural language without loss or radical change, so there is no choice but to accommodate theory to them.

No logical errors result if we simply treat demonstratives as constants;[15] neither do any problems arise for giving a semantic truth definition. ' "I am wise" is true if and only if I am wise', with its bland ignoring of the demonstrative element in 'I' comes off the assembly line along with ' "Socrates is wise" is true if and only if Socrates is wise' with *its* bland indifference to the demonstrative element in 'is wise' (the tense).

What suffers in this treatment of demonstratives is not the definition of a truth predicate, but the plausibility of the claim that what has been defined is truth. For this claim is acceptable only if the speaker and circumstances of utterance of each sentence mentioned in the definition is matched by the speaker and circumstances of utterance of the truth definition itself. It could also be fairly pointed out that part of understanding demonstratives is knowing the rules by which they adjust their reference to circumstance; assimilating demonstratives to constant terms obliterates this feature. These complaints can be met, I think, though only by a fairly far-reaching revision in the theory of truth. I shall barely suggest how this could be done, but bare suggestion is all that is needed: the idea is technically trivial, and in line with work being done on the logic of the tenses.[16]

We could take truth to be a property, not of sentences, but of utterances, or speech acts, or ordered triples of sentences, times, and persons; but it is simplest just to view truth as a relation between a sentence, a person, and a time. Under such treatment, ordinary logic as now read applies as usual, but only to sets of sentences relativized to the same speaker and time; further logical relations between sentences spoken at different times and by different speakers may be articulated by new axioms. Such is not my concern. The theory of meaning undergoes a systematic but not puzzling change; corresponding to each expression with a demonstrative element there must in the theory be a phrase that relates the truth conditions of sentences in which the expression occurs to changing times and speakers. Thus the theory will entail sentences like the following:[17]

'I am tired' is true as (potentially) spoken by p at t if and only if p is tired at t.

'That book was stolen' is true as (potentially) spoken by p at t if and only if the book demonstrated by p at t is stolen prior to t.

Plainly, this course does not show how to eliminate demonstratives; for example, there is no suggestion that 'the book demonstrated by the speaker' can be substituted ubiquitously for 'that book' *salva veritate*. The fact that demonstratives are amenable to formal treatment ought greatly to improve hopes for a serious semantics of natural language, for it is likely that many outstanding puzzles, such as the analysis of quotations or sentences about propositional attitudes, can be solved if we recognize a concealed demonstrative construction.

Now that we have relativized truth to times and speakers, it is appropriate to glance back at the problem of empirically testing a theory of meaning for an alien tongue. The essence of the method was, it will be remembered, to correlate held-true sentences with held-true sentences by way of a truth definition, and within the bounds of intelligible error. Now the picture must be elaborated to allow for the fact that sentences are true, and held true, only relative to a speaker and a time. Sentences with demonstratives obviously yield a very sensitive test of the correctness of a theory of meaning, and constitute the most direct link between language and the recurrent macro-scopic objects of human interest and attention.[18]

In this paper I have assumed that the speakers of a language can effec-tively determine the meaning or meanings of an arbitrary expression (if it has a meaning), and that it is the central task of a theory of meaning to show how this is possible. I have argued that a characterization of a truth predicate describes the required kind of structure, and provides a clear and testable criterion of an adequate semantics for a natural language. No doubt there are other reasonable demands that may be put on a theory of meaning. But a theory that does no more than define truth for a language comes far closer to constituting a complete theory of meaning than superficial analysis might suggest; so, at least, I have urged.

Since I think there is no alternative, I have taken an optimistic and programmatic view of the possibilities for a formal characterization of a truth predicate for a natural language. But it must be allowed that a staggering list of difficulties and conundrums remains. To name a few: we do not know the logical form of counterfactual or subjunctive sentences; nor of sentences about probabilities and about causal relations; we have no good idea what the logical role of adverbs is, nor the role of attributive adjectives; we have no theory for mass terms like 'fire', 'water', and 'snow', nor for sentences about belief, perception, and intention, nor for verbs of action that imply purpose. And finally, there are all the sentences that seem not to have truth values at all: the imperative, optatives, interrogatives, and a host more. A comprehensive theory of meaning for a natural language must cope successfully with each of these problems.[19]

NOTES

1. A 'structural description' of an expression describes the expression as a concatenation of elements drawn from a fixed finite list (for example of words or letters).

2. The argument derives from Frege. See A. Church, *Introduction to Mathematical Logic*, 24 5. It is perhaps worth mentioning that the argument does not depend on any particular identification of the entities to which sentences are supposed to refer.

3. It may be thought that Church, in 'A Formulation of the Logic of Sense and Denotation', has given a theory of meaning that makes essential use of meanings as entities. But this is not the case: Church's logics of sense and denotation are interpreted as being about meanings, but they do not mention expressions and so cannot of course be theories of meaning in the sense now under discussion.

4. For a recent statement of the role of semantics in linguistics, see Noam Chomsky, 'Topics in the Theory of Generative Grammar'. In this article, Chomsky (1) emphasizes the central importance of semantics in linguistic theory, (2) argues for the superiority of transformational grammars over phrase-structure grammars largely on the grounds that, although phrase-structure grammars may be adequate to define sentencehood for (at least) some natural languages. They

are inadequate as a foundation for semantics, and (3) comments repeatedly on the 'rather primitive state' of the concepts of semantics and remarks that the notion of semantic interpretation 'still resists any deep analysis'.

5. Assuming, of course, that the extension of these predicates is limited to the sentences of *I*.

6. A. Tarski, "The Concept of Truth in Formalized Languages".

7. But Quine may be quoted in support of my usage, '. . . in point of *meaning* . . . a word may be said to be determined to whatever extent the truth or falsehood of its contexts is determined.' ('Truth by Convention', 82.) Since a truth definition determines the truth value of every sentence in the object language (relative to a sentence in the metalanguage), it determines the meaning of every word and sentence. This would seem to justify the title Theory of Meaning.

8. To give a single example: it is clearly a count in favour of a theory that it entails ' "Snow is white" is true if and only if snow is white'. But to contrive a theory that entails this (and works for all related sentences) is not trivial. I do not know a wholly satisfactory theory that succeeds with this very case (the problem of 'mass terms').

9. Critics have often failed to notice the essential proviso mentioned in this paragraph. The point is that (*S*) could not belong to any reasonably simple theory that also gave the right truth conditions for 'That is snow' and 'This is white'. (See the discussion of indexical expressions below.) [Footnote added in 1982.]

10. This paragraph is confused. What it should say is that sentences of the theory are empirical generalizations about speakers, and so must not only be true but also lawlike. (*S*) presumably is not a law, since it does not support appropriate counterfactuals. It's also important that the evidence for accepting the (time and speaker relativized) truth conditions for 'That is snow' is based on the causal connection between a speaker's assent to the sentence and the demonstrative presentation of snow. For further discussion see Essay 12. [Footnote added in 1982.]

11. This sketch of how a theory of meaning for an alien tongue can be tested obviously owes it inspiration to Quine's account of radical translation in Chapter 11 of *Word and Object*. In suggesting that an acceptable theory of radical translation take the form of a recursive characterization of truth, I go beyond Quine. Toward the end of this paper, in the discussion of demonstratives, another strong point of agreement will turn up.

12. So far as I am aware, there has been very little discussion of whether a formal truth definition can be given for a natural language. But in a more general vein, several people have urged that the concepts of formal semantics be applied to natural language. See, for example, the contributions of Yehoshua Bar-Hillel and Evert Beth to *The Philosophy of Rudolph Carnap*, and Bar-Hillel's 'Logical Syntax and Semantics'.

13. The *rapprochement* I prospectively imagine between transformational grammar and a sound theory of meaning has been much advanced by a recent change in the conception of transformational grammar described by Chomsky in the article referred to above (note 5). The structures generated by the phrase-structure part of the grammar, it has been realized for some time, are those suited to semantic interpretation; but this view is inconsistent with the idea, held by Chomsky until recently, that recursive operations are introduced only by the transformation rules. Chomsky now believes the phrase-structure rules are recursive. Since languages to which formal semantic methods directly and naturally apply are ones for which a (recursive) phrase-structure grammar is appropriate, it is clear that Chomsky's present picture of the relation between the structures generated by the phrase-structure part of the grammar, and the sentences of the language, is very much like the picture many logicians and philosophers have had of the relation between the richer formalized languages and ordinary language. (In these remarks I am indebted to Bruce Vermazen.)

14. B. Mates, 'Synonymity'.

15. See W. V. Quine, *Methods of Logic*, 8.

16. This claim has turned out to be naïvely optimistic. For some serious work on the subject, see S. Weinstein, 'Truth and Demonstratives'. [Note added in 1982.]

17. There is more than an intimation of this approach to demonstratives and truth in J. L. Austin, 'Truth'.

18. These remarks derive from Quine's idea that 'occasion sentences' (those with a demonstrative element) must play a central role in constructing a translation manual.

19. For attempted solutions to some of these problems see Essays 6–10 of *Essays on Actions & Events*, and Essays 6–8 of *Inquiries into Truth and Interpretation*. There is further discussion in Essays 3, 4, 9, and 10 and reference to some progress in section 1 of Essay 9.

HARTRY FIELD

TARSKI'S THEORY OF TRUTH[1]

In the early 1930s there was prevalent, among scientifically minded philosophers, the view that semantic notions such as the notions of truth and
denotation were illegitimate: that they could not or should not be incorporated
into a scientific conception of the world. But when Tarski's work on truth
became known, all this changed. 'As a result of Tarski's teaching, I no longer
hesitate to speak of "truth" and "falsity",'[2] wrote Popper, and Popper's
reaction was widely shared.[3]

A philosopher who shared Popper's reaction to Tarski's discoveries would
presumably argue as follows. 'What Tarski did was to define the term "true",
using in his definitions only terms that are clearly acceptable. In particular,
he did not employ any undefined semantic terms in his definitions. So Tarski's
work should make the term "true" acceptable even to someone who is initially
suspicious of semantic terms.'

This contention has an initial plausibility, but I will argue that it is radically wrong. My contrary claim will be that Tarski succeeded in reducing the
notion of truth *to certain other semantic notions*; but that he did not in any
way explicate these other notions, so that his results ought to make the word
'true' acceptable only to someone who already regarded these other semantic
notions as acceptable.

By claiming that Tarski merely reduced truth to other semantic notions,
I don't mean to suggest that his results on truth are trivial. On the contrary,
I think that they are extremely important, and have applications not only to
mathematics but also to linguistics and to more directly philosophical problems
about realism and objectivity. I think, however, that the real value of Tarski's
discoveries for linguistics and philosophy is widely misunderstood, and I hope
to eradicate the most central misunderstandings by clarifying and defending
the claim that Tarski merely reduced truth to other semantic notions.

I

I believe that Tarski presented his semantic theory in a very misleading way, one which has encouraged the misinterpretations just alluded to. In this section I will present Tarski's theory as I think he should have presented it. However, I do not expect instant agreement that this new way is better than the old, and so I will use the name 'Tarski*' for a logician who gave the sort of semantic theory I will now sketch. Later in the paper I will compare Tarski*'s semantics to the semantics that the real Tarski actually gave; by doing this I will cast light on the issues raised in my introductory paragraphs.

In sketching Tarski*'s theory, I will focus my attention on a particular object language L. The language L that I choose will be a quantificational language, with names ('c_1', 'c_2', . . .), one-place function symbols ('f_1', 'f_2', . . .), and one-place predicates ('p_1', 'p_2', . . .). The language of course cannot be viewed as an 'uninterpreted' language, i.e. as just a bunch of strings of meaningless marks, for then there would be no truth to worry about. Instead, the language should be regarded as something that people actually speak or write; and it is because the speakers speak or write the way they do that the words of the language have the meaning they have.[4]

Initially I will follow Tarski in supposing that in L 'the sense of every expression is unambiguously determined by its form',[5] i.e., that whenever two speakers use the same name (or one speaker uses it on two occasions) they are referring to the same thing; that whenever two speakers use the same sentence either both are saying something true or neither is, etc. In these circumstances it makes sense to speak of the names of the language denoting things (a name denotes whatever the users of the name refer to) and the sentences being true or false (true when speakers who use it say something true by so doing). The more general situation, in which there are expressions whose 'sense' is not determined wholly by their form will be dealt with later. (We'll see that it is one of the advantages of Tarski*'s semantics that it can easily handle this more general situation.)

The syntax of L can be given by two recursive definitions: first we define the *singular terms* by saying that all names and variables are singular terms, and a function symbol followed by a singular term is a singular term; then we define the *formulas* by saying that a predicate followed by a singular term is a formula, as is the negation of a formula, the conjunction of two formulas, and the universal qualification of a formula with any variable. The *sentences*, or *closed formulas*, are then singled out in the usual way.

Now we can proceed to Tarski*'s semantics. Rather than characterize truth directly, we characterize it relative to some assignment of objects to the variables, say s_k to 'x_k'. The idea is going to be to treat the variables, or at least the free variables, as sort of 'temporary names' for the objects assigned to them. So we proceed by fixing a sequence $s = \langle s_1, s_2, . . .\rangle$ of objects, to be assigned to 'x_1', 'x_2', . . . , respectively; and we want to say what it is for a formula to be true$_s$, i.e. true relative to the assignment s. As a preliminary we say what it is for a term to denote an object, i.e. to denote it relative to the assignment s. The denotation of 'x_k' relative to s is evidently s_k, for this is the object assigned to 'x_k'. But what is the denotation relative to s of 'c_k'? Evidently what objects are assigned to the variables here is irrelevant, and the denotation$_s$ of 'c_k' is some fixed object that users of the language refer to when they use the name 'c_k'. Just what this object is depends on facts we have not yet been given about the use of 'c_k'. Similarly there are facts we have not yet been given about the use of 'p_k' and 'f_k' which we need in order to fix the truth value of sentences containing them. For 'p_k' the relevant facts concern the extension of the predicate—what objects the predicate *applies to*—for it is this which affects the truth value of all utterances containing 'p_k'. For 'f_k', the relevant facts concern what pairs of objects *fulfil* that function symbol—in the sense that the pair ⟨John Adams, John Quincy Adams⟩ and every other father-son pair fulfil the function symbol 'father of'.

With these points in mind it is now easy to give an inductive characterization of denotation$_s$:

T1 (A) 1 'x_k' denotes$_s$ s_k.
      2 'c_k' denotes$_s$ what it denotes.
      3 ⌜$f_k(e)$⌝ denotes$_s$ an object a if and only if
            (i) there is an object b that e denotes$_s$
      and (ii) 'f_k' is fulfilled by ⟨a,b⟩.

(Here 'e' is a variable ranging over expressions of L.) Similarly we define 'true$_s$' for formulas—what Tarski calls satisfaction of a formula—by s:

    (B) 1 ⌜$p_k(e)$⌝ is true$_s$ if and only if
            (i) there is an object a that e denotes$_s$
      and (ii) 'p_k' applies to a.
      2 ⌜$\sim e$⌝ is true$_s$ if and only if e is not true$_s$.
      3 ⌜$e_1 \wedge e_2$⌝ is true$_s$ if and only if e_1 is true$_s$ and so is e_2.
      4 ⌜$\forall x_k(e)$⌝ is true$_s$ if and only if for each sequence s^* that differs from s at the kth place at most, e is true$_{s^*}$.

This completes the characterization of truth relative to an assignment of objects to the variables. In the case of sentences it is easily seen that we get the same results whatever such assignment we pick; we can say

(C) A sentence is true if and only if it is true$_s$ for some (or all) s.

This completes my elaboration of Tarski*'s 'truth definition' T1 for L—or his truth characterization (TC), as I prefer to call it. What is its philosophical significance? The obvious answer, and the correct one, I think, is that the

TC reduces one semantic notion to three others. It explains what it is for a sentence to be true in terms of certain semantic features of the primitive components of the sentence: in terms of what it is for a name to denote something, what it is for a predicate to apply to something, and what it is for a function symbol to be fulfilled by some pair of things. It is convenient to introduce the expression 'primitively denotes' as follows: every name *primitively denotes* what it denotes; every predicate and every function symbol *primitively denotes* what it applies to or is fulfilled by; and no complex expression primitively denotes anything. In this terminology, what T1 does is to explain truth in terms of primitive denotation. Similarly we can explain denotation for arbitrary closed singular terms [such as '$f_1(c_1)$'] in terms of primitive denotation, i.e. in terms of the semantic features of the names and function symbols from which the complex singular term is composed—we merely say that a closed singular term denotes an object a if it denotes$_s$ a for some (or all) s, where denotation$_s$ is defined as before. We see then that *Tarski*'s semantics explains the semantic properties of complex expressions* (e.g., truth value for sentences, denotation for complex singular terms) *in terms of semantic properties of their primitive components.*

To explain truth in terms of primitive denotation is, I think, an important task. It certainly doesn't answer *every* question that anyone would ever want answered about truth, but for many purposes it is precisely what we need. For instance, in model theory we are interested in such questions as: given a set Γ of sentences, is there any way to choose the denotations of the primitives of the language so that every sentence of Γ will come out true given the usual semantics for the logical connectives?[6] For questions such as this, what we need to know is how the truth value of a whole sentence depends on the denotations of its primitive nonlogical parts, and that is precisely what T1 tells us. So *at least for model-theoretic purposes*, Tarski*'s TC is precisely the kind of explication of truth we need.

I want now to return to a point I mentioned earlier, about Tarski's restriction to languages in which 'the sense of every expression is unambiguously determined by its form'. Natural languages are full of expressions that do not meet this requirement. For instance, different tokens of 'John takes grass' can differ in 'sense'—e.g., one token may be uttered in saying that John Smith smokes marijuana, and another may be uttered in saying that John Jones steals lawn material, and these differences may give rise to differences of truth value in the tokens. (I say that a complete[7] token of a sentence is true if the person who spoke or wrote that token said something true by so doing; I also say that a name token denotes an object if the person who spoke or wrote the token referred to the object by so doing.) The prevalence of such examples in natural languages raises the question of whether Tarski's type of semantic theory is applicable to languages in which the sense is *not* determined by the form; for if the answer is no, then Davidson's very worthwhile project[8] of giving truth characterizations for natural languages seems doomed from the start.

It seems clear that if we stick to the kind of TC that Tarski actually gave (see next section), there is no remotely palatable way of extending TCs to sentences like 'John takes grass'. But if we use TCs like T1 there is no difficulty at all. The only point about languages containing 'John' or 'grass' or 'I' or 'you' is that for such languages 'true', 'denotes' and other semantic terms make no clear sense as applied to expression types; they make sense only as applied to tokens. For this reason we have to interpret clause (B)2 of T1 as meaning

A token of $\ulcorner \sim e \urcorner$ is true$_s$ if and only if the token of e that it contains is not true$_s$

and similarly for the other clauses. Once we interpret our TC in this way in terms of tokens, i.e. individual occasions of utterance, that TC works perfectly: someone who utters 'John is sick' (or 'I am sick') says something true if and only if his token of 'sick' applies to the person he refers to by 'John' (or by 'I'); and the fact that other speakers (or this speaker on other occasions) sometimes refer to different things when they use 'John' (or 'I') is beside the point.

This analysis leaves entirely out of account the ways in which 'I' and 'John' differ: it leaves out of account, for instance, the fact that a token of 'I' always denotes the speaker who produced it. But that is no objection to the analysis, for the analysis purports merely to explain truth in terms of primitive denotation; it does not purport to say anything about primitive denotation, and the differences between 'I' and 'John' (or their analogues in a language like L) are purely differences of how they denote. (The word 'I' denotes according to the simple rule mentioned two sentences back; 'John' denotes according to much more complex rules that I have no idea how to formulate.)

Of course, the fact that a theory of denotation for a word like 'I' is so simple and obvious, makes it possible to alter the TC so that the theory of denotation for such a word is built into the TC itself—such a course is adopted, for instance, by Davidson at the end of 'Truth and Meaning'. I myself prefer to preserve the analogies of the word 'I' to words that function less systematically, e.g., 'we', 'she' and 'John'. How one treats 'I' is more or less a matter of taste; but the less systematic words I've just mentioned cannot be handled in the way that Davidson handles 'I', and the only reasonable way I can see to handle them is the way I have suggested: use a truth characterization like T1 (except stated in terms of tokens rather than types), and leave it to a separate theory of primitive denotation to explain the relevant differences between tokens of 'John' that denote John Adams and tokens of 'John' that denote John Lennon, and between tokens of 'bank' that apply to things along rivers and tokens of 'bank' that apply to the Chase Manhattan.[9]

There are other advantages to T1 besides its ability to handle ambiguous sentences, i.e. sentences for which the sense is not determined by the form. For instance, Tarski required that the vocabulary of the language be fixed once and for all; but if we decide to give truth characterizations of type T1, this is unnecessary: all that is required is that the general structure of the language be fixed, e.g. that the semantic categories[10] (name, one-place predicate, etc.) be held constant. In other words, if a language already contained proper names, the invention of a new name to baptize an object will not invalidate the old TC; though introduction of a name into a hitherto nameless language will.

To show this, we have merely to reformulate the given TC so that it does not rely on the actual vocabulary that the language contains at a given time, but works also for sentences containing new names, one-place predicates, etc., that speakers of the language might later introduce. To do this is trivial: we define denotation$_s$ by

1 The kth variable denotes$_s$ s_k.
2 If e_1 is a name, it denotes$_s$ what it denotes.
3 If e_1 is a singular term and e_2 is a function symbol, then $\ulcorner e_2(e_1) \urcorner$ denotes$_s$ a if and only if
      (i) as before,
and (ii) e_2 is fulfilled by $\langle a,b \rangle$].

And we can generalize the definition of truth$_s$ in a similar manner.[11] This shows that, in giving a TC, there is no need to utilize the particular vocabulary used at one temporal stage of a language, for we can instead give a more general TC which can be incorporated into a diachronic theory of the language (and can also be applied directly to other languages of a similar structure). *If*, that is, we accept the modification of Tarski proposed in this section.

II

The kind of truth characterization advocated in the previous section differs from the kind of TC Tarski offered in one important respect. Tarski stated the policy 'I shall not make use of any semantical concept if I am not able previously to reduce it to other concepts' (CTFL 152/3), and this policy is flagrantly violated by T1: T1 utilizes unreduced notions of proper names denoting things, predicates applying to things, and function symbols being fulfilled by things.

Tarski's truth characterizations, unlike T1, accorded with his stated policy: they did not contain any semantic terms like 'applies to' or 'denotes'. How did Tarski achieve this result? Very simply: first, he translated every name, predicate, and function symbol of L into English; then he utilized these translations in order to reformulate clauses 2 and 3(ii) of part (A) of the definition and clause 1(ii) of part (B). For simplicity, let's use '$\bar{c}_1$', '$\bar{c}_2$', etc. as abbreviations for the English expressions that are the translations of the words 'c_1', 'c_2', . . . of L: e.g., if L is simplified German and 'c_1' is 'Deutschland', then '$\bar{c}_1$' is an abbreviation for 'Germany'. Similarly, let '$\bar{f}_1$' abbreviate the translation into English of the word 'f_1' of L, and let '$\bar{p}_1$' abbreviate the translation of 'p_1' into English. Then Tarski's reformulated truth definition will read as follows:

T2 (A) 1 as before
      2 'c_k' denotes$_s$ $\bar{c}_k$
      3 $\ulcorner f_k(e)\urcorner$ denotes$_s$ a if and only if
        (i) as before
        (ii) a is $\bar{f}_k(b)$
  (B) 1 $\ulcorner p_k(e)\urcorner$ is true$_s$ if and only if
        (i) as before
        (ii) $\bar{p}_k(a)$
    2–4 as before
  (C) as before

What T2 is like depends of course on the precise character of the translations of the primitives that are utilized. For instance, if we translate 'c_1' as 'the denotation of "c_1" ', translate 'p_1' as 'is something that "p_1" applies to', etc., then T2 becomes identical with T1. This of course is *not* what Tarski intended. What Tarski intended is that T2 not contain unexplicated semantic terms, and if we are to get this result we must not employ any semantic terms in our translations.[12]

But other restrictions on translations are also necessary: if we were to translate 'Deutschland' as 'Bertrand Russell', a truth characterization T2 that was based on this translation would grossly misrepresent L. In order to state the matter more generally, I introduce the term 'coreferential': two singular terms are coreferential if they denote the same thing; two predicative expressions are coreferential if they have the same extension, i.e., if they apply to the same things; and two functional expressions are coreferential if they are fulfilled by the same pairs. It is then easily seen that any departure from coreferentiality in translation will bring errors into T2. For instance, suppose we translate the foreign predicate 'glub' as 'yellow', and suppose 'glub' and yellow are not *precisely* coreferential; then clause (B)$_1$ will say falsely that 'glub(x)' is true of just those objects which are yellow.

Let us say, then, that

(1) An adequate translation of a primitive e_1 of L into English is an expression e_2 of English such that

(i) e_1 and e_2 are coreferential, and
(ii) e_2 contains no semantic terms.

This notion of an adequate translation is of course a semantic notion that Tarski did not reduce to non-semantic terms. But that is no objection to his characterization T2 (at least, it isn't obviously an objection), for the notion of an adequate translation is never built into the truth characterization and is not, properly speaking, part of a theory of truth. On Tarski's view we need to adequately translate the object language into the metalanguage in order to give an adequate theory of truth for the object language; this means that the notion of an adequate translation is employed in the methodology of giving truth theories, but it is not employed in the truth theories themselves.

In what follows I shall assume that the language L with which we are dealing is so related to English that all its primitives *can* be adequately translated into English, according to the standards of adequacy set forth in (1). (This is another restriction that we avoid if we give TCs of the type T1; quite a significant restriction, I think.) If we then suppose that the translation given ('$\bar{c}_1$' for 'c_1', etc.) is one of the adequate translations, then T2, like T1, is a correct recursive characterization of truth for the language L. There is, of course, a simple procedure for transforming recursive characterizations such as these into explicit characterizations. To carry the procedure through in these cases would be pretty complicated, but it could be done; so we could regard T1 (or T2) as implicitly specifying a metalinguistic formula '$A_1(e)$' (or '$A_2(e)$'), and saying that an utterance e of L is true if and only if $A_1(e)$ (or $A_2(e)$). If we regard T1 and T2 as written in this form, then the key difference between them is that '$A_1(e)$' *contains semantic terms and* '$A_2(e)$' *does not.* The question then arises: is the fact that '$A_2(e)$' does not contain semantic terms an advantage of T2 over T1? If so, then *why* is it an advantage?

In order to discuss the possible advantages of T2 over T1, I think we have to go beyond mathematical considerations and focus instead on linguistic and other 'philosophical' matters. It is not enough to say that T2 *defines* truth without utilizing semantic terms, whereas T1 defines it only in other semantic terms; this is not enough until we say something more about the purpose of definition. If the purpose of giving a 'definition' of truth is to enable you to do model theory, then the elimination of semantic terms from T1 gives no advantage. For what purpose do we want definitions for which the elimination of semantic terms is useful?

One purpose to which definitions are sometimes put is in explaining the meaning of a word. This of course is very vague, but I think it is clear enough to enable us to recognize that neither T1 nor T2 has very much to do with explaining the meaning of the word 'true'. This is especially obvious for T2: a T2-type truth definition works for a single language only, and so if it 'explains the meaning of' the word 'true' as applied to that language, then for *any* two languages L_1 and L_2, the word 'true' means something different when applied to utterances of L_1 than it means when applied to utterances of L_2! I make this point not in criticism of T2, but in criticism of the idea that the significance of T2 can be explained by saying that it 'gives the meaning of' the word 'true'.

We still need to know what purpose a truth characterization like T1 or T2 could serve that would give someone reason to think that a TC without unexplicated semantic terms would be better than a TC with unexplicated semantic terms. Tarski hints at such a purpose in one place in his writings, where he is discussing the importance of being able to define the word 'true', as opposed to merely introducing axioms to establish the basic properties of truth. If a definition of semantic notions such as truth could not be given, Tarski writes, 'it would then be difficult to bring [semantics] into harmony with the postulates of the unity of science and of physicalism (since the concepts of semantics would be neither logical nor physical concepts)'.[13] This remark seems to me to be of utmost importance in evaluating the philosophical significance of Tarski's work, and so I will now say something about the general philosophical issues it raises. When this is done we will be in a better position to understand Tarski's choice of T2 over T1.

III

In the early 1930s many philosophers believed that the notion of truth could not be incorporated into a scientific conception of the world. I think that the main rationale for this view is hinted at in the remark of Tarski's that I quoted at the end of the last section, and what I want to do now is to elaborate a bit on Tarski's hint.

In the remark I have quoted, Tarski put a heavy stress on the doctrine of physicalism: the doctrine that chemical facts, biological facts, psychological facts and semantical facts are all explicable (in principle) in terms of physical facts. The doctrine of physicalism functions as a high-level empirical hypothesis, a hypothesis that no small number of experiments can force us to give up. It functions, in other words, in much the same way as the doctrine of mechanism (that all facts are explicable in terms of *mechanical* facts) once functioned: this latter doctrine has now been universally rejected, but it was given up only by the development of a well-accepted theory (Maxwell's) which described phenomena (electromagnetic radiation and the electromagnetic field) that were very difficult to account for mechanically, and by amassing a great deal of experiment and theory that together made it quite conclusive that mechanical explanations of these phenomena (e.g., by positing 'the ether') would never get off the ground. Mechanism has been empirically refuted; its heir is physicalism, which allows as 'basic' not only facts about mechanics, but facts about other branches of physics as well.[14] I believe that physicists a hundred years ago were justified in accepting mechanism, and that, similarly, physicalism should be accepted until we have convincing evidence that there is a realm of phenomena it leaves out of account. Even if there *does* turn out to be such a realm of phenomena, the only way we'll ever come to know that there is, is by repeated efforts and repeated failures to explain these phenomena in physical terms.

That's my view, anyway, but there are philosophers who think that it is in order to reject physicalism now. One way of rejecting physicalism is called 'vitalism': it is the view that there are irreducibly biological facts, i.e. biological facts that aren't explicable in nonbiological terms (and hence, not in physical terms). Physicalism and vitalism are incompatible, and it is because of this incompatibility that the doctrine of physicalism has the methodological importance it has for biology. Suppose, for instance, that a certain woman has two sons, one haemophilic and one not. Then, according to standard genetic accounts of haemophilia, the ovum from which one of these sons was produced must have contained a gene for haemophilia, and the ovum from which the other son was produced must not have contained such a gene. But now the doctrine of physicalism tells us that there must have been a *physical* difference between the two ova that explains why the first son had haemophilia and the second one didn't, if the standard genetic account is to be accepted. We should not rest content with a special biological predicate 'has-a-haemophilic-gene'—rather, we should look for nonbiological facts (chemical facts; and ultimately, physical facts) that underlie the correct application of this predicate. That at least is what the principle of physicalism tells us, and it can hardly be doubted that this principle has motivated a great deal of very profitable research into the chemical foundations of genetics.

So much for vitalism; now let us turn to other irreducibility doctrines that are opposed to physicalism. One such irreducibility doctrine is Cartesianism: it is the doctrine that there are irreducibly mental facts. Another irreducibility doctrine has received much less attention than either vitalism or Cartesianism, but it is central to our present concerns: this doctrine, which might be called 'semanticalism', is the doctrine that there are irreducibly semantic facts. The semanticalist claims, in other words, that semantic phenomena (such as the fact that 'Schnee' refers to snow) must be accepted as primitive, in precisely the way that electromagnetic phenomena are accepted as primitive (by those who accept Maxwell's equations and reject the ether); and in precisely the way that biological phenomena and mental phenomena are accepted as primitive by vitalists and Cartesians. Semanticalism, like Cartesianism and vitalism, posits nonphysical primitives, and as a physicalist I believe that all three doctrines must be rejected.

There are two general sorts of strategy that can be taken in rejecting semanticalism, or Cartesianism, or vitalism. One strategy, illustrated two paragraphs back in discussing vitalism, is to try to explicate the terms of a biological theory in nonbiological terms. But there is another possible strategy, which is to argue that the biological terms are illegitimate. The second strategy seems reasonable to adopt in dealing with the following predicate of (reincarnationist) biology: 'x has the same soul as y'. A physicalist would never try to find physical or chemical facts that underlie reincarnation; rather, he would reject reincarnation as a myth.

Since biological theory is as well developed as it is, we usually have a pretty good idea which biological terms require explication and which require elimination. When we turn to psychology and semantics, however, it is often not so obvious which strategy is the more promising. Thus in semantics, physicalists agree that all *legitimate* semantic terms must be explicable non-semantically—they think in other words that there are no irreducibly semantic facts—but they disagree as to which semantic terms are legitimate. That disagreement has become fairly clear in recent years in the theory of meaning, with the work of Quine: the disagreement is between those physicalists who would look for a nonsemantic basis for terms in the theory of meaning, and those who would follow Quine in simply throwing out those terms. Our concern, however, is not with the theory of meaning, but with the theory of reference, and here the disagreement has been less clear, since there haven't been many physicalists who openly advocate getting rid of terms like 'true' and 'denotes'. There were such physicalists in the early 1930s; part of the importance of Tarski's work was to persuade them that they were on the wrong track, to persuade them that we should explicate notions in the theory of reference nonsemantically rather than simply get rid of them.

The view that we should just stop using semantic terms (here and in the rest of this paper, I mean terms in the theory of reference, such as 'true' and 'denotes' and 'applies to') draws its plausibility from the apparent difficulty of explicating these terms nonsemantically. People utter the sounds 'Electrons have rest mass but photons don't', or 'Schnee ist weiss und Gras ist grün', and we apply the word 'true' to their utterances. We don't want to say that it is a primitive and inexplicable fact about these utterances that they are true, a fact that cannot be explicated in nonsemantic terms; this is as unattractive to a physicalist as supposing that it is a primitive and inexplicable fact about an organism at a certain time that it is in pain. But how could we ever explicate in nonsemantic terms the alleged fact that these utterances are true? *Part* of the explication of the truth of 'Schnee ist weiss und Gras ist grün', presumably, would be that snow is white and grass is green. But this would only be part of the explanation, for still missing is the connection between snow being white and grass being green on the one hand, and the German utterance being true on the other hand. It is this connection that seems so difficult to explicate in a way that would satisfy a physicalist, i.e. in a way that does not involve the use of semantic terms.

If, in face of these difficulties, we were ever to conclude that it was *impossible* to explicate the notions of truth and denotation in nonsemantic terms, we would have either to give up these semantic terms or else to reject physicalism. It seems to me that that is essentially what Tarski is saying in the quotation at the end of the last section, and I have tried to make it plausible by sketching analogies to areas other than semantics. Tarski's view, however, was that, for certain languages at least, semantic terms *are* explicable nonsemantically, and that truth definitions like T2 provide the required explication. It is understandable that as far as *philosophical* purposes go Tarski should think that T1 leaves something to be desired: after all, it merely explicates truth in terms of other semantic concepts; but what good does that do if those other concepts can't be explicated nonsemantically? T2, then, has a strong *prima facie* advantage over T1. In the next section I will show that it is not a genuine advantage.

IV

The apparent advantage of T2 over T1, I have stressed, is that it appears to reduce truth to nonsemantic terms; and I *think* this is why Tarski wanted to give a truth definition like T2 rather than like T1. This interpretation makes sense of Tarski's remark about physicalism, and it also explains why someone who was certainly not interested in 'meaning analysis' as that is usually conceived would have wanted to give 'definitions' of truth and would emphasize that, in these 'definitions', 'I will not make use of any semantical concept if I am not able previously to reduce it to other concepts'. In any case, the problem of reducing truth is a very important problem, one which T1 and T2 provide a partial solution to, and one which T2 *might* be thought to provide a full solution to; and it is not at all clear what *other* interesting problems T2 could be thought to solve better than T1.

In Tarski's own exposition of his theory of truth, Tarski put very little stress on the problem of reduction or on any other problem with a clear philosophical or mathematical motivation; instead, he set up a formal criterion of adequacy for theories of truth without any serious discussion of whether or why this formal criterion is reasonable. Roughly, the criterion was this:[15]

(M) Any condition of the form
$$(2) \qquad (\forall e) \, [e \text{ is true} \equiv B(e)]$$
should be accepted as an adequate definition of truth if and only if it is correct and '$B(e)$' is a well-formed formula containing no semantic terms. (The quantifiers are to be taken as ranging over expressions of one particular language only.)

The 'only if' part of condition M is not something I will contest. It rules out the possibility of T1 *by itself* being an adequate truth definition; and it is right to do so, if the task of a truth definition is to reduce truth to nonsemantic terms, for T1 provides only a *partial* reduction. (To complete the reduction we need to reduce primitive denotation to nonsemantic terms.) T2, on the other hand, meets condition M; so either T2 is superior to T1 as a reduction, or else condition M is too weak and the 'if' part of it must be rejected. My own diagnosis is the latter, but the other possibility seems initially reasonable. After all, how could condition M be strengthened? We might try requiring that '$B(e)$' be not only *extensionally* equivalent to 'e is true', but *intensionally* equivalent to it; but this clearly won't do, for even if we grant that there is an intelligible notion of intensional equivalence, our concern is not with analysing the meaning of the word 'true' but with performing a reduction. A clear and useful standard of equivalence that is stronger than extensional equivalence but not so strong as to rule out acceptable reductions is unknown at the present time, so I know no way to improve on condition M. My view is that we have a rough but useful concept of reduction which we are unable to formulate precisely; but I must admit that the alternate view, that extensional equivalence is adequate, has an initial appeal.

A closer look, however, will reveal quite conclusively that extensional equivalence is not a sufficient standard of reduction. This can be seen by looking at the concept of valence. The valence of a chemical element is an integer that is associated with that element, which represents the sort of chemical combinations that the element will enter into. What I mean by the last phrase is that it is possible—roughly, at least—to characterize which elements will combine with which others, and in what proportions they will combine, merely in terms of their valences. Because of this fact, the concept of valence is a physically important concept, and so if physicalism is correct it ought to be possible to explicate this concept in physical terms—e.g., it ought to be possible to find structural properties of the atoms of each element that determine what the valence of that element will be. Early in the twentieth century (long after the notion of valence had proved its value in enabling chemists to predict what chemical combinations there would be) this reduction of the concept of valence to the physical properties of atoms was established; the notion of valence was thus shown to be a physicalistically acceptable notion.

Now, it would have been easy for a chemist, late in the last century, to have given a 'valence definition' of the following form:

(3) $(\forall E)(\forall n)$ (E has valence $n \equiv E$ is potassium and n is $+1$, or . . . or E is sulphur and n is -2)

where in the blanks go a list of similar clauses, one for each element. But, though this is an extensionally correct definition of valence, it would not have been an acceptable reduction; and had it turned out that nothing else was possible—had all efforts to explain valence in terms of the structural properties of atoms proved futile—scientists would have eventually had to decide either

(a) to give up valence theory, or else (b) to replace the hypothesis of physicalism by another hypothesis (chemicalism?). It is part of scientific methodology to resist doing (b); and I also think it is part of scientific methodology to resist doing (a) as long as the notion of valence is serving the purposes for which it was designed (i.e. as long as it is proving useful in helping us characterize chemical compounds in terms of their valences). But the methodology is not to resist (a) and (b) by giving lists like (3); the methodology is to look for a real reduction. This is a methodology that has proved extremely fruitful in science, and I think we'd be crazy to give it up in linguistics. *And I think we are giving up this fruitful methodology, unless we realize that we need to add theories of primitive reference to T1 or T2 if we are to establish the notion of truth as a physicalistically acceptable notion.*

I certainly haven't yet given much argument for this last claim. I *have* argued that the standard of extensional equivalence doesn't guarantee an acceptable reduction; but T2 is obviously not trivial to the extent that (3) is. What *is* true, however, is roughly that T2 minus T1 is as trivial as (3) is. One way in which this last claim can be made more precise is by remembering that really we often apply the term 'valence' not only to elements, but also to configurations of elements (at least to stable configurations that are not compounds, i.e. to radicals). Thus, if we abstract from certain physical limitations on the size of possible configurations of elements (as, in linguistics, we usually abstract from the limitations that memory, etc., impose on the lengths of possible utterances), there is an infinite number of entities to which the term 'valence' is applied. But it is an important fact about valence that the valence of a configuration of elements is determined from the valences of the elements that make it up, and from the way they're put together. Because of this, we might try to give a recursive characterization of valence. First of all, we would try to characterize all the different *structures* that configurations of elements can have (much as we try to characterize all the different grammatical structures before we give a truth definition like T1 or T2). We would then try to find rules that would enable us to determine what the valence of a complicated configuration would be, given the valences of certain less complicated configurations that make it up and the way they're put together. If we had enough such rules, we could determine the valence of a given configuration given only its structure and the valences of the elements that make it up. And if we like, we can transform our recursive characterization of valence into an explicit characterization, getting

V1 $(\forall c)(\forall n)$ (c has valence $n \equiv B(c,n)$)

The formula '$B(c,n)$' here employed will still contain the term 'valence', but it will contain that term only as applied to elements, not as applied to configurations. Thus our 'valence definition' V1 would characterize the valence of the complex *in terms of the valences of the simple*.

It would now be possible to eliminate the term 'valence' from '$B(c,n)$', in either of two ways. One way would be to employ a genuine reduction of the notion of valence for elements to the structural properties of atoms. The other way would be to employ the pseudo-reduction (3). It is clear that we could use (3) to give a trivial reformulation V2 of V1, which would have precisely the 'advantages' as a reduction that T2 has over T1. (V2, incidentally, would also have one of the disadvantages over V1 that T2 has over T1: V1 does not need to be overhauled when you discover or synthesize new elements, whereas V2 does.)

That is a sketch of one way that the remark I made two paragraphs back about 'T2 minus T1' could be made more precise. But it is somewhat more fruitful to develop the point slightly differently: dong this will enable me to make clearer that there is unlikely to be *any* purpose that T2 serves better than T1 (not merely that T2 is no better at reduction).

To get this result I'll go back to my original use of the term 'valence', where it applies to elements only and not to configurations. And what I will do is compare (3) not to Tarski's theory of *truth*, but to Tarski's theory of *denotation* for names; the effect of this on his theory of truth will then be considered. Tarski states his theory of denotation for names in a footnote, as follows ('CTFL', p. 194):

To say that the name x denotes a given object a is the same as to stipulate that the object a . . . satisfies a sentential function of a particular type. In colloquial language it would be a function which consists of three parts in the following order: a variable, the word 'is' and the given name x.

This is actually only part of the theory, the part that defines denotation in terms of satisfaction; to see what the theory looks like when all semantic terms are eliminated, we must see how satisfaction is defined. The definition is given by the (A) and (B) clauses of T2, for, as I've remarked, 'satisfaction' is Tarski's name for what I've called 'truth$_s$'. What Tarski's definition of satisfaction tells us is this: for any name N, an object a satisfies the sentential function $\ulcorner x_1$ is $N \urcorner$ if and only if a is France and N is 'France' or . . . or a is Germany and N is 'Germany'. Combining this definition of satisfaction (for sentential functions of form $\ulcorner x_1$ is $N \urcorner$) with the earlier account of denotation in terms of satisfaction, we get:

(DE): To say that the name N denotes a given object a is the same as to stipulate that either a is France and N is 'France', or . . . or a is Germany and N is 'Germany'.

This is Tarski's account of denotation for English proper names. For foreign proper names, the definition of denotation in terms of satisfaction needs no modification (except that the 'is' must be replaced by a name of a foreign word, say 'ist' for German). Combining this with the definition (again given by T2) of satisfaction for foreign sentential functions like $\ulcorner x_1$ ist $N\urcorner$, we get:

(DG): To say that the name N denotes a given object a is the same as to stipulate that either a is France and N is 'Frankreich', or . . . or a is Germany and N is 'Deutschland'.

DE and DG have not received much attention in commentaries on Tarski, but in fact they play a key role in his semantic theory; and it was no aberration on Tarski's part that he offered them as theories of denotation for English and German names, for *they satisfy criteria of adequacy exactly analogous to the criteria of adequacy that Tarski accepted for theories of truth*.[16] Nevertheless, it seems clear that DE and DG do not really reduce denotation to nonsemantic terms, any more than (3) reduces valence to nonchemical terms. What would a real explication of denotation in nonsemantic terms be like? The 'classical' answer to this question (Russell's) is that a name like 'Cicero' is 'analytically linked' to a certain description (such as 'the denouncer of Catiline'); so to explain how the name 'Cicero' denotes what it does you merely have to explain

(i) the process by which it is linked to the description (presumably you bring in facts about how it was learned by its user, or facts about what is going on in the user's brain at the time of the using) and
(ii) how the description refers to what it does.

Because of (ii), of course, the project threatens circularity: the project is to explain how names refer in terms of how descriptions refer; but the natural way to explain how descriptions refer is in terms of how they're built up from their significant parts,[17] and how those significant parts refer (or apply, or are fulfilled), and those significant parts will usually include names. But Russell recognized this threat of circularity, and carefully avoided it: he assumed that the primitives of the language were to be partially ordered by a relation of 'basicness', and that each name except a most basic ('logically proper') name was to be analytically linked to a formula containing only primitives more basic than it. The most basic primitives were to be linked to the world without the intervention of other words, by the relation of acquaintance.

This classical view of how names (and other primitives) latch onto their denotations is extremely implausible in many ways (e.g., it says you can refer only to things that are definable from 'logically proper' primitives; it requires that there be certain statements, such as 'If Cicero existed then Cicero denounced Catiline', which are analytic in the sense that they are guaranteed by linguistic rules and are immune to revision by future discoveries). I conjecture that it is because of the difficulties with this classical theory, which was the only theory available at the time that Tarski wrote, that Tarski's pseudo-theories DE and DG seemed reasonable—they weren't exciting, but if you wanted something exciting you got logically proper names. The diagnosis that any attempt to explain the relation between words and the things they are about must inevitably lead to either a wildly implausible theory (like Russell's) or a trivial theory (like Tarski's) seems to be widely accepted still; but I think that the diagnosis has become less plausible in recent years through the development of *causal* theories of denotation by Saul Kripke[18] and others. According to such theories, the facts that 'Cicero' denotes Cicero and that 'muon' applies to muons are to be explained in terms of certain kinds of causal networks between Cicero (muons) and our uses of 'Cicero' ('muon'): causal connections both of a social sort (the passing of the word 'Cicero' down to us from the original users of the name, or the passing of the word 'muon' to laymen from physicists) and of other sorts (the evidential causal connections that gave the original users of the name 'access' to Cicero and give physicists 'access' to muons). I don't think that Kripke or anyone else thinks that *purely* causal theories of primitive denotation can be developed (even for proper names of past physical objects and for natural-kind predicates); this however should not blind us to the fact that he has suggested a kind of factor involved in denotation that gives new hope to the idea of explaining the connection between language and the things it is about. It seems to me that the possibility of *some such* theory of denotation (to be deliberately very vague) is essential to the joint acceptability of physicalism and the semantic term 'denotes', and that denotation definitions like DE and DG merely obscure the need for this.

It might be objected that the purpose of DE and DG was not reduction; but what was their purpose? One answer might be that (DE) and (DG) enable us to eliminate the word 'denote' whenever it occurs. ('To explain is to show how to eliminate.') For instance,

(4) No German name now in use denotes something that does not yet exist.

would become

(4') For any name N now in use, if N is 'Frankreich' then France already exists, and . . . , and if N is 'Deutschland' then Germany already exists.

provided that (DG) is a correct and complete list of the denotations of all those German proper names that have denotations. It seems reasonably clear that we could specify a detailed procedure for transforming sentences like (4) into materially equivalent sentences like (4'). A similar claim could be made for the 'valence definition' (3). Such a valence definition makes it possible to eliminate the word 'valence' from a large class of sentences containing it, and in a uniform way. For instance,

(5) For any elements A and B, if one atom of A combines with two of B, then the valence of A is -2 times that of B.

is materially equivalent to

(5') For any elements A and B, if one atom of A combines with two of B, then either A is sodium and B is sodium and $+1 = -2(+1)$, or . . . , A is sulphur and B is sodium and $-2 = -2(+1)$, or. . . .

provided that (3) is a correct and complete list of valences. So if anyone ever wants to eliminate the word 'denote' or the word 'valence' from a large class of English sentences by a uniform procedure, denotation definitions and valence definitions are just the thing he needs. There are, however, sentences from which these words are not eliminable by the sketched procedure. For instance, in semantics and possibly in chemistry there are problems with counterfactuals; e.g., 'If "Germany" had been used to denote France, then . . .'. Moreover, there are special problems affecting the case of semantics, arising from the facts

(i) that the elimination procedure works only for languages in which nothing is denoted that cannot be denoted (without using semantic terms) in one's own language,

(ii) that it works only for languages that contain no ambiguous names,

and

(iii) that the denotation definitions provide no procedure for eliminating 'denote' from sentences where it is applied to more than one language; e.g., it gives no way of handling sentences like ' "Glub" denotes different things in different languages.'

But, subject to these three qualifications (plus perhaps that involving counterfactuals), the elimination procedure for 'denote' is every bit as good as that for 'valence'!

What value did Tarski attach to such transformations? Unfortunately he did not discuss the one about valences, but he did discuss the one that transforms 'Smith used a proper name to denote Germany' into something logically equivalent to 'Smith uttered "Deutschland".' And it is clear that to this definition he attached great philosophical importance. After defining semantics as 'the totality of considerations concerning those concepts which, roughly speaking, express certain connexions between the expressions of a language and the objects and states of affairs referred to by those expressions' ('ESS', p. 401), he says that with his definitions, 'the problem of establishing semantics on a scientific basis is completely solved' ('ESS', p. 407). In other places his claims are almost as extravagant. For instance, the remark about physicalism that I quoted at the end of section II is intended to apply to denotation as well as to truth: if definitions of denotation like DE and DG could not be given, 'it would . . . be impossible to bring [semantics] into harmony with . . . physicalism' ('ESS', p. 406); but because of these definitions, the compatibility of the semantic concept of denotation with physicalism is established. By similar standards of reduction, one might prove that witchcraft is compatible with physicalism, as long as witches cast only a finite number of spells: for then 'cast a spell' can be defined without use of any of the terms of witchcraft theory, merely by listing all the witch-and-victim pairs.

In other places Tarski makes quite different claims for the value of his denotation definitions. For example:[19]

We desire semantic terms (referring to the object language) to be introduced into the meta-language only by definition. For, if this postulate is satisfied, the definition of truth, or of any other semantic concept [including denotation, which Tarski had already specifically mentioned to be definable], will fulfil what we intuitively expect from every definition; that is, it will explain the meaning of the term being defined in terms whose meaning appears to be completely clear and unequivocal.

But it is no more plausible that DE 'explains the meaning of' 'denote' as applied to English, or that DG 'explains the meaning of' 'denote' as applied to German, than that (3) 'explains the meaning of' 'valence'—considerably *less* so in fact, since for 'valence' there is no analogue to the conclusions that 'denote' means something different when applied to English than it means when applied to German. In fact, it seems pretty clear that denotation definitions like DE and DG have no philosophical interest whatever. But what conclusions can we draw from this about Tarski's *truth* definitions like T2? I think the conclusion to draw is that *T2 has no philosophical interest whatever that is not shared by T1*. How this follows I will now explain.

We have seen that Tarski advocated theories of denotation for names that had the form of mere lists: examples of his denotation definitions were DE and DG, and for language L his denotation definition would take the following form:

D2 $(\forall e)(\forall a)$ [e is a name that denotes $a \equiv$ (e is 'c_1' and a is $\bar{c}_1$) or (e is 'c_2' and a is $\bar{c}_2$) or . . .]

where into the dots go analogous clauses for every name of L. Similarly, we can come up with definitions of application and fulfilment which are acceptable according to Tarski's standards, and which also have the form of mere lists. The definition of application runs:

A2 $(\forall e)(\forall a)$ [e is a predicate that applies to $a \equiv (e$ is 'p_1' and $\bar{p}_1(a))$ or (e is 'p_2' and $\bar{p}_2(a))$ or . . .].

Similarly, we can formulate a list-like characterization F2 of fulfilment for the function symbols. Clearly neither A2 nor F2 is of any more theoretical interest than D2.

Tarski, I have stressed, accepted D2 as part of his semantic theory, and would also have accepted A2 and F2; and this fact is quite important, since D2, A2, and F2 together with T2 imply T1. In other words, T1 is simply a weaker version of Tarski's semantic theory; it is a logical consequence of Tarski's theory. Now, an interesting question is what you have to add to T1 to get the rest of Tarski's semantic theory. Suppose we can find a formula R that we can argue to be of no interest whatever, such that Tarski's semantic theory (T2 $\wedge$ D2 $\wedge$ A2 $\wedge$ F2) is logically equivalent to T1 $\wedge$ R. It will then follow that the whole interest of Tarski's semantic theory lies in T1—the rest of his semantic theory results simply by adding to it the formula R, which (I have assumed) has no interest whatever. And if there is nothing of interest in the conjunction T2 $\wedge$ D2 $\wedge$ A2 $\wedge$ F2 beyond T1, certainly there can be nothing of interest in T2 alone beyond T1.

An example of such a formula R is D2 $\wedge$ A2 $\wedge$ F2: it is obvious that Tarski's semantic theory is logically equivalent to T1 $\wedge$ D2 $\wedge$ A2 $\wedge$ F2. Because of this, *any interest in Tarski's semantic theory over T1 must be due to an interest in* D2 *or* A2 *or* F2 *(or to confusion): in this sense* D2 $\wedge$ A2 $\wedge$ F2 *is* T2 *minus* T1'. But I've already argued that D2, A2, and F2 have no theoretical interest whatever, and so that establishes that T2 has no theoretical interest whatever that is not shared by T1.

V

Much of what I've said in this paper gains plausibility by being put in a wider perspective, and so I now want to say a little bit about why we want a notion of truth. The notion of truth serves a great many purposes, but I suspect that its original purpose—the purpose for which it was first developed—was to aid us in utilizing the utterances of others in drawing conclusions about the world. To take an extremely simple example, suppose that a friend reports that he's just come back from Alabama and that there was a foot of snow on the ground there. Were it not for his report we would have considered it extremely unlikely that there was a foot of snow on the ground in Alabama— but the friend knows snow when he sees it and is not prone to telling us lies for no apparent reason, and so after brief deliberation we conclude that probably there *was* a foot of snow in Alabama. What we did here was first to use our evidence about the person and his situation to decide that he probably said something true when he made a certain utterance, and then to draw a conclusion from the truth of his utterance to the existence of snow in Alabama. In order to make such inferences, we have to have a pretty good grasp of (i) the circumstances under which what another says is likely to be true, and (ii) how to get from a belief in the truth of what he says to a belief about the extralinguistic world.

If this idea is right, then two features of truth that are intimately bound up with the purposes to which the notion of truth are put are (I) the role that the attempt to tell the truth and the success in doing so play in social institutions, and (II) the fact that normally one is in a position to assert of a sentence that it is true in just those cases where one is in a position to assert the sentence or a paraphrase of it. It would then be natural to expect that what is involved in communicating the meaning of the word 'true' to a child or to a philosopher is getting across to him the sorts of facts listed under (I) and (II); for those are the facts that it is essential for him to have an awareness of if he is to put the notion of truth to its primary use (child) or if he is to get a clear grasp of what its primary use is (philosopher).

I think that this natural expectation is correct; and that it gives more insight than was given in sections II and IV into why it is that neither T1 nor T2 can reasonably be said to explain the meaning of the term 'true'—even when a theory of primitive reference is added to them. First consider (I). The need of understanding the sort of thing alluded to in (I), if we are to grasp the notion of truth, has been presented quite forcefully in Michael Dummett's article 'Truth',[20] in his analogy between speaking the truth and winning at a game. It is obvious that T1 and T2 don't explain anything like this (and in fact Dummett's fourth paragraph, on Frege-style truth definitions, can be carried over directly to T1 and T2).

The matter might perhaps be expressed in terms of assertibility conditions that one learns in learning to use the word 'true': part of what we learn, in learning to use this word, is that in cases like that involving the friend from Alabama there is some *prima facie* weight to be attached to the claim that the other person is saying something true. But there are also *other* assertibility conditions that one learns in learning the word 'true', assertibility conditions which have received considerable attention in the philosophical literature on truth. To begin with, let's note one obvious fact about how the word 'true' is standardly learned: we learn how to apply it to utterances of our own language first, and when we later learn to apply it to other languages it is by conceiving the utterances of another language more or less on the model of utterances of our own language. The obvious model of the first stage of this process is that we learn to accept all instances of the schema

(T) X is true if and only if p.

where 'X' is replaced by a quotation-mark name of an English sentence S and 'p' is replaced by S. This must be complicated to deal with ambiguous and truth-value-less sentences, but let's ignore them. Also let's ignore the fact that certain pathological instances of (T)—the Epimenides-type paradoxical sentences—are logically refutable. Then there is a sense in which the instances of (T) that we've learned to accept determine a unique extension for the predicate 'true' as applied to sentences of our own language.[21] Our views about what English sentences belong to this unique extension may be altered, but as long as we stick to the instances of (T) they cannot consistently be altered without also altering our beliefs in what those sentences express. This fact is extremely important to the functions that the word 'true' serves (as the Alabama example illustrates).

In stressing the assertibility conditions for simple sentences containing the word 'true', I have followed Quine;[22] for, like him, I believe that such assertibility conditions are enough to make the term 'true' reasonably clear. But now it might be asked, 'Then why do we need causal (etc.) theories of reference? The words "true" and "denotes" are made perfectly clear by schemas like (T). To ask for more than these schemas—to ask for causal theories of reference to nail language to reality—is to fail to recognize that we are at sea on Neurath's boat: we have to work *within* our conceptual scheme, we can't glue it to reality from the outside.'

I suspect that this would be Quine's diagnosis—it is strongly suggested by secion 6 of *Word and Object*, especially when that is taken in conjunction with some of Quine's remarks about the inscrutability of reference and truth value, the underdetermination of theories and the relativity of ontology. It seems to me, however, that the diagnosis is quite wrong. In looking for a theory of truth and a theory of primitive reference we *are* trying to explain the connection between language and (extralinguistic) reality, but we are *not* trying to step outside of our theories of the world in order to do so. Our accounts of primitive reference and of truth are not to be thought of as something that could be given by philosophical reflection prior to scientific information—on the contrary, it seems likely that such things as psychological models of human beings and investigations of neurophysiology will be very relevant to discovering the mechanisms involved in reference. *The reason why accounts of truth and primitive reference are needed is not to tack our conceptual scheme on to reality from the outside; the reason, rather, is that without such accounts our conceptual scheme breaks down from the inside.* On our theory of the world it would be extremely surprising if there were some nonphysical connection between words and things. Thus if we could argue from our theory of the world that the notion of an utterer's saying something true, or referring to a particular thing, cannot be made sense of in physicalist terms (say, by arguing that any semantic notion that makes physicalistic sense *can* be explicated in Skinnerian terms, and that the notions of truth and reference *can't* be explicated in Skinnerian terms), then to the extent that such an argument is convincing we ought to be led to conclude that, if we are to remain physicalists, the notions of truth and reference must be abandoned. No amount of pointing out the clarity of these terms helps enable us to escape this conclusion: 'valence' and 'gene' were perfectly clear long before anyone succeeded in reducing them, but it was their reducibility and not their clarity before reduction that showed them to be compatible with physicalism.

The clarity of 'valence' and 'gene' before reduction—and even more, their *utility* before reduction—did provide physicalists with substantial reason to think that a reduction of these terms was possible, and, as I remarked earlier, a great deal of fruitful work in physical chemistry and chemical genetics was motivated by the fact. Similarly, in so far as semantic notions like 'true' are useful, we have every reason to suspect that they will be reducible to nonsemantic terms, and it is likely that progress in linguistic theory will come by looking for such reductions. (In fact, the fruitfulness of Tarski's work in aiding us to understand language is already some sign of this, even though it represents only a partial reduction.) Of course, this sort of argument for the prospects of reducing semantic notions is only as powerful as our arguments for the utility of semantic terms; and it is clear that the question of the utility of the term 'true'—the purposes it serves, and the extent to which those purposes could be served by less pretentious notions such as warranted assertibility—needs much closer investigation.

All these remarks require one important qualification. The notion of valence, it must be admitted, is *not* reducible to nonchemical terms on the *strictest* standards of reduction, but is only *approximately* reducible; yet, in spite of this, we don't want to get rid of the notion, since it is still extremely useful in those contexts where its approximate character isn't too likely to get in the way and where if we did not approximate we'd get into quantum-mechanical problems far too complex for anyone to solve. (Moreover, considerations about the purposes of the notion of valence were sufficient to show that the notion of valence would only be approximately reducible: for the utility of the notion of valence is that it aids us in approximately characterizing which elements will combine with which and in what proportions; yet it is obvious that no such *precise* characterization is possible.)

Similarly, it may well be that a detailed investigation into the purposes of the notion of truth might show that these purposes require only an approximate reduction of the notion of truth. Still, to require an approximate reduction is to require quite a bit; after all, 'is a reincarnation of' isn't even approximately reducible to respectable biology, and 'electromagnetic field' is not approximately reducible to mechanics. Obviously the notion of approximate reduction needs to be made more precise (as in fact does the notion of strict, or nonapproximate, reduction); but even without making it so, I think we can see that T2 is no more of an approximate reduction than is V2, since D2 $\wedge$ A2 $\wedge$ F2 is no more of an approximate reduction than is (3). In other words, the main point of the paper survives when we replace the ideal of strict reduction by the ideal of approximate reduction.

It should be kept carefully in mind that the Quinean view that all we need do is clarify the term 'true', in the sense that this term is clarified by schema T (or by schema T plus a theory of translation to handle foreign languages; or by schema T plus the sort of thing alluded to in connection with Dummett), is *not* Tarski's view. Tarski's view is that we have to provide a truth characterization like T2 (which, when we choose as our object language L a 'nice' fragment of our own language, can be shown correct merely by assuming that all instances of schema T are valid—cf. n.14); and such a truth characterization does much more than schema T does. It does not do everything that Tarski ever claimed for it, for Tarski attached much too much importance to the pseudo-theories D2, A2, and F2; but even when we 'subtract' such trivialities from his truth characterization T2, we still get the very interesting and important truth characterization T1. T1, I believe, adequately represents Tarski's real contribution to the theory of truth, and in doing this it has a number of positive advantages over T2 (in addition to the important negative advantage I've been stressing, of preventing extravagant claims based on the fact that T2 contains no semantic terms). First of all, T1, unlike T2, is applicable to languages that contain ambiguities and languages that contain terms not adequately translatable into English. Second, T1, unlike T2, can be used in diachronic linguistics: it doesn't need overhauling as you add new words to the language, provided those new words belong to the same semantic category as words already in the language. Third, I think that the reason why Tarski's theory of truth T2 has seemed so uninteresting to so many people is that it contains the vacuous semantic theories D2, A2, and F2 for the primitives of the language. By expressing the really important features of Tarski's results on truth, and leaving out the inessential and uninteresting 'theories' of the semantics of the primitives, T1 should make the philosophical importance of Tarski's work more universally recognized.

NOTES

1. This paper grew out of a talk I gave at Princeton in the fall of 1970, where I defended T1 over T2. Donald Davidson and Gilbert Harman—and later, in private conversation, John Wallace—all came to the defence of T2, and their remarks have all been of help to me in writing the paper. I have also benefited from advice given by Michael Devitt, Paul Benacerraf, and especially David Hills.

2. K. Popper, *Logic of Scientific Discovery* (New York, Basic Books, 1968), p. 274.

3. Cf. Carnap's 'Autobiography', in P. A. Schilpp, ed., *The Philosophy of Rudolf Carnap* (Lasalle, Ill., Open Court, 1963), p. 61.

4. It is sometimes claimed that Tarski was interested in languages considered in abstraction from all speakers and writers of the language; that the languages he was dealing with are abstract

entities to be specified by giving their rules. This seems incorrect: Tarski was interested in giving the semantics of languages that mathematicians had been writing for years; and only as a result of Tarski's work was it then possible for philosophers like Carnap to propose that the clauses of a Tarski-type truth definition for such languages be called rules of the languages and be used in defining the languages as abstract entities.

5. A. Tarski, 'The Concept of Truth in Formalized Languages' ('CTFL'), in *Logic, Semantics, Metamathematics (LSM)* (New York, Oxford University Press, 1956), p. 166.

6. Actually in model theory we are interested in allowing a slightly unusual semantics for the quantifiers: we are willing to allow that the quantifier not range over everything. We could build this generalization into our truth definition, by stipulating that in addition to the denotations of the nonlogical symbols we specify a universe U, and then reformulating clause (B)4 by requiring that the kth member of s^* belong to U. If we did this, then it would be the range of the quantifiers as well as the denotations of the nonlogical primitives that we would have explained truth in terms of.

7. An *incomplete* sentence token is a sentence token which [like the occurrence of '2 + 2 = 4' inside '~ (2 + 2 = 4)'] is part of a larger sentence token.

8. D. Davidson, 'Truth and Meaning', *Synthèse*, vol. XVII, no. 3 (September 1967), pp. 314–15.

9. Note that the claims I've been making are intended to apply only to cases where different tokens have different semantic features; they are not intended to apply to cases of indeterminacy, i.e., to cases where a particular name token or predicate token has no determinate denotation or extension. To deal with indeterminacy requires more complex devices than I employ in this paper.

10. The notion of a semantic category is Tarski's: cf. 'CTFL', p. 215.

11. To do so in the obvious way requires that we introduce semantic categories of negation symbol, conjunction symbol, and universal-quantification symbol; though by utilizing some ideas of Frege it could be shown that there is really no need of a separate semantic category for each logical operator. The use of semantic categories in the generalized truth characterization raises important problems which I have had to suppress for lack of space in this paper.

12. For simplicity, I have assumed that L itself contains no semantic terms.

13. A. Tarski, 'The Establishment of Scientific Semantics' ('ESS') in *LSM*, p. 406.

14. This, of course, is very vague, but most attempts to explicate the doctrine of physicalism more precisely result in doctrines that are very hard to take seriously [e.g., the doctrine that for every acceptable predicate '$P(x)$' there is a formula '$B(x)$' containing only terminology from physics, such that '$\forall x(P(x) \equiv B(x))$' is true]. Physicalism should be understood as the doctrine (however precisely it is to be characterized) that guides science in the way I describe.

15. Tarski actually gives a different formulation, the famous Convention T, evidently because he does not think that the word 'correct' ought to be employed in stating a criterion of adequacy. First of all Tarski writes ('ESS', p. 404):

we shall accept as valid every sentence of the form

[T] the sentence x is true if and only p

where 'p' is to be replaced by any sentence of the language under investigation and 'x' by any individual name of that sentence provided this name occurs in the metalanguage.

Is Tarski's policy of accepting these sentences as 'valid' (i.e., true) legitimate? It seems to me that it is, in a certain special case. The special case is where

I The object language is a proper part of the metalanguage (here, English).

II The object language contains no paradoxical or ambiguous or truth-value-less sentences.

In this special case—and it was the case that Tarski was primarily concerned with—I think it will be generally agreed that all instances of Schema T hold. From this, together with the fact that only grammatical sentences are true, we can argue that, if a necessary and sufficient condition of form (2) has the following consequences:

(a) Every instance of Schema T

(b) The sentence '$(\forall x)$ (x is true $\supset$ $S(x)$)', where '$S(x)$' formulates (correct) conditions for an utterance of L to be a sentence

then that necessary and sufficient condition is correct. Let's say that a 'truth definition' for L (a necessary and sufficient condition of truth in L) *satisfies Convention T* if it has all the consequences listed under (a) and (b). Then, restating: when L is a language for which I and II hold, then any truth definition satisfying Convention T is correct; and since only quite uncontroversial assumptions about truth are used in getting this result, anyone will admit to the correctness of a truth characterization satisfying Convention T. If we use the term 'formally correct definition' for a sentence of form (2) in which '$B(e)$' contains no semantic terms, this means that a formally correct definition that satisfies Convention T is bound to satisfy Condition M (when the language L satisfies I and II). As far as I can see, this is the only motivation for Convention T; if so, we can discredit Convention T by discrediting condition M.

Tarski sometimes states a more general form of Convention T, which applies to languages that do not meet restriction I: it is what results when one allows as instances of Schema T the results of replacing 'p' by a *correct translation* of the sentence that the name substituted for 'x' denotes (in some sense of 'correct translation' in which correctness requires preservation of truth value). But then the advantage of the ungeneralized form of Convention T (viz., that anything satisfying it wears its correctness on its face, or more accurately, on the faces of its logical consequences) is lost.

16. A sentence of the form '$(\forall N)$ $(\forall x)$ [N denotes $x \equiv B(N,x)$]' *satisfies convention D* if it has as consequences every instance of the schema 'y denotes z', in which 'y' is to be replaced by a quotation-mark name for a name N, and 'z' is to be replaced by (an adequate translation of N into English, i.e.) a singular term of English that contains no semantic terms and that denotes the same thing that N denotes. Clearly DE and DG are not only extensionally correct, they also satisfy Convention D. Presumably philosophers who are especially impressed with Convention T will be equally impressed with this fact, but they owe us a reason why satisfying Convention D is of any interest.

17. For example, by extending our definition of denotation$_s$ to descriptions by:

⌜$ix_k(e)$⌝ denotes$_s$ a if and only if [for each sequence s^* which differs from s at the kth place at most, e is true$_s$*if and only if the kth member of s^* is a].

and then defining denotation in terms of denotation$_s$ by stipulating that a closed term denotes an object if and only if it denotes$_s$ that object for some (or all) s.

18. Some of Kripke's work on names is published in Davidson and Harman, eds., *Semantics of Natural Language* (Dordrecht: Reidel, 1971). What I've said about Russell's view is influenced by some of Kripke's lectures on which his paper there is based.

19. A. Tarski, 'The Semantic Conception of Truth and the Foundations of Semantics', *Philosophy and Phenomenological Research*, vol. IV, no. 3 (March 1944), p. 351.

20. Michael Dummett, 'Truth', *Proceedings of the Aristotelian Society*, vol. LIX (1958–59), pp. 141–62.

21. Cf. W. V. Quine, *From a Logical Point of View* (New York, Harper & Row, 1961), p. 136.

22. Ibid., p. 138.

JOHN McDOWELL

PHYSICALISM AND PRIMITIVE DENOTATION: FIELD ON TARSKI[1]

I

In this paper I want to discuss a contention made by Hartry Field, in his influential article 'Tarski's Theory of Truth' (*Journal of Philosophy*, vol. 59 (1972), p. 347). Tarski claimed that his work on truth ('The Concept of Truth in Formalized Languages', in *Logic, Semantics, Metamathematics* (Clarendon Press, Oxford 1956): henceforth 'CTFL') made semantics respectable from a physicalist standpoint ('The Establishment of Scientific Semantics', in *Logic, Semantics, Metamathematics*—henceforth 'ESS'—at p. 406). Field's contention is that Tarski thereby misrepresented what he had done, because of an erroneous belief that he had shown how truth (for formalized languages of finite order) can be interestingly defined without using prior semantic notions. What Tarski in fact did, according to Field, was to show how truth (for those languages) can be characterized in terms of a small number of primitive semantic notions. Physicalism requires something more, which Tarski did not offer: namely explication of those primitive notions in physical terms.

I believe Field is right about Tarski's view of the relation between physicalism and his work on truth. I believe also that, given the physicalism he espouses (which is probably Tarski's doctrine too), Field is right to regard Tarski's claim as overblown. (This is not to suggest that Field depreciates the magnitude of Tarski's formal contribution; that is not affected if Tarski's somewhat incidental claims about physicalism are rejected.) What I want to dispute is how semantics and physics are related, which Field aims to motivate by these considerations about Tarski.

II

I shall begin by setting out the contrast between what Tarski allegedly should have done and what he actually did, on which Field's argument turns.

We are to consider a simple first-order language L, with names (c_1, c_2, and so on to the appropriate last subscript; we use 'c_k' as a variable to range over the names); one-place function symbols $(f_1, f_2, \ldots$; variable 'f_k'); one-place predicates $(p_1, p_2, \ldots$; variable 'p_k'); variables $(x_1, x_2,$ and so on indefinitely; variable 'x_k'); connectives $\sim$ and $\wedge$; and a quantifier $\forall$.[2] L's singular terms are: the names, the variables, and the result of writing any function symbol followed by any singular term. L's atomic well-formed formulae (wffs) are: the result of writing any predicate followed by any singular term. The wffs are: the atomic wffs, the negation of any wff, the conjunction of any two wffs, and the universal quantification of any wff with respect to any variable. Sentences are, as usual, closed wffs.

In the case of languages whose only complex sentences are formed by truth-functional compounding, it is straightforward to characterize truth for complex sentences in terms of truth for simple sentences. With quantification, the straightforward procedure is blocked, since the constituents of complex sentences are no longer necessarily sentences. Tarski saw that the obstacle can be circumvented with the concept of satisfaction. In the truth-functional case, the semantic impact of sentence-forming operations is captured in a recursive characterization of truth itself; when sentence-forming operations operate on open as well as closed sentences, their semantic impact is captured instead in a recursive characterization of satisfaction, in terms of which truth can then be directly defined. Satisfaction (of open or closed sentences, by sequences of objects) is, as the above might suggest, something of which truth can be regarded as a limiting case. For a closed sentence to be satisfied by any sequence whatever simply is for it to be true; for an open sentence to be satisfied by a sequence is for it to be true, so to speak, on the fiction that its free variables denote the corresponding members of the sequence. Field aptly describes the idea as being to treat free variables as 'temporary names', and, in place of satisfaction by a sequence, speaks of truth relative to a sequence.

In more detail: the construction has three components. Working backwards:

(i) Truth *tout court* is defined as satisfaction by, or truth relative to, any sequence whatever.

(ii) Truth relative to a sequence, for complex wffs, is recursively characterized in terms of the truth, relative to that sequence, of their simpler constituents. Obvious clauses handle the connectives:

(a) $\sim A$ is true$_s$ iff A is not true$_s$;[3]
(b) $(A \wedge B)$ is true$_s$ iff A is true$_s$ and B is true$_s$;
and the clause for the quantifier is only slightly less obvious:

(c) $\forall x_k A$ is true$_s$ iff, for every sequence s' different from s in at most the kth place, A is true$_{s'}$.

Using these clauses, we could, for any complex wff of L, determine conditions under which it would be true relative to a sequence, in terms of the truth or not, relative to that sequence, of its atomic wffs. What, then, are we to say about the base case: sequence-relative truth for atomic wffs? A *closed* atomic wff is true (*tout court*) just in case its predicate *applies* to what its name *denotes* (as 'is wise' applies to what 'Socrates' denotes, given that Socrates is wise); and we want it to be true relative to any sequence whatever in just those circumstances ((i) above). An *open* atomic wff is satisfied by a sequence just in case a corresponding closed wff, with the variable replaced by a name of the relevant member of the sequence, would be true (see above). Neatness recommends introducing the notion of sequence-relative denotation; then truth relative to a sequence, for atomic wffs open or closed, can be explained as a function of the predicate's application-conditions and the open or closed singular term's denotation relative to that sequence:

(d) $p_k t$ is true$_s$ iff there is something y which t denotes$_s$ and p_k applies to y.

(iii) Now we need an account of denotation relative to a sequence for singular terms. With closed singular terms, the relativity to a sequence is idle; thus, for names:

(a) c_k denote$_s$ what c_k denotes.

What a variable denotes, relative to a sequence, has already been fixed:

(b) x_k denotes$_s$ the kth member of s.

And obviously, with function symbols:

(c) $f_k t$ denotes$_s$ y iff there is something z which t denotes$_s$ and f_k is *fulfilled* by $\langle y, z \rangle$

(as 'the capital of' is fulfilled by $\langle$London, Great Britain$\rangle$ in virtue of the fact that London is the capital of Great Britain).

That completes the truth characterization, T1, which, according to Field, Tarski should have given for L.

Truth is defined in terms of the auxiliary semantic notion of truth relative to a sequence, or satisfaction. In the truth characterization as it stands, the extension of the satisfaction relation is fixed only recursively; so we cannot simply write down, from the characterization, a formula coextensive with the truth-predicate from which the terminology of sequence-relative truth is absent. With sufficient set theory, we could convert the recursive characterization of the auxiliary notion into a 'normal' or eliminative definition ('CTFL', p. 193, n. 1). That would enable us to eliminate the terminology of sequence-relative truth from the definition of truth; but the resulting formula would still contain the subsidiary semantic terminology of sequence-relative denotation. The recursive characterization of sequence-relative denotation could similarly be converted into an eliminative definition, yielding an eliminative definition of truth free from the sequence-relative semantic terminology. But the result would still contain, in a way which T1 yields no suggestions for eliminating, the evidently semantic terminology 'applies to', 'denotes', and 'is fulfilled by'.

T2, a truth characterization which Tarski might actually have given for L, differs in just that respect. The difference is achieved by the following modifications:

(i) Instead of the general clause ((ii)(d) above) about sequence-relative truth of atomic wffs, each predicate has sequence-relative truth-conditions, for atomic wffs which contain it, spelled out individually. Thus, say:

(a) $p_1 t$ is true$_s$ iff there is something y which t denotes$_s$ and y is a country;
(b) $p_2 t$ is true$_s$ iff there is something y which t denotes$_s$ and y is a city;

and so on, one clause for each predicate; or they could all be collected in a disjunction.

(ii) Similarly, instead of the general clause about sequence-relative denotation of names ((iii)(a) above), the denotation of each name, relative to any sequence whatever, is specified individually. Thus, say:

(a) c_1 denotes$_s$ Germany;
(b) c_2 denotes$_s$ France;

and so on, one clause for each name, or a disjunction as before.

(iii) Correspondingly for function symbols; instead of the general clause ((iii)(c) above), T2 has, say:

(a) $f_1 t$ denotes$_s$ y iff there is something z which t denotes$_s$ and y is the capital of z;
(b) $f_2 t$ denotes$_s$ y iff there is something z which t denotes$_s$ and y is the president of z;

and so on, one clause for each function symbol, or a disjunction as before.

In T2, explicit employments of the semantic notions of application, denotation, and fulfilment disappear in favour of piecemeal specifications of (what are in fact) application-conditions, denotations, and fulfilment-conditions. The specifications are effected by using, for each simple object-language expression, a coextensive expression of the metalanguage. These metalanguage expressions are free from semantic terminology; obviously the trick would not be turned if they were expressions on the pattern of 'is applied to by p_1', 'what c_1 denotes', or 'the first member of an ordered pair which fulfils f_1 and whose second member is'. If we had a complete T2 for L, with a clause for every simple expression, and converted the recursive characterizations as before, the result would be a formula coextensive with the truth-predicate and, this time, entirely free from semantic terminology.

Notice that the masterstroke of approaching truth indirectly, using the notion of satisfaction to circumvent the problem posed by non-sequential sentence-components, is common to both T1 and T2. That is why Field's favouring of the only partially Tarskian T1 over the Tarskian T2 is compatible with a proper respect for Tarski's technical achievement.

III

There are three incidental points on which Field claims superiority for T1-style truth characterizations over those in the style of T2.

(i) L may fail to conform to Tarski's condition that 'the sense of every expression is unambiguously determined by its form' ('CTFL', p. 166). For instance, a name may have more than one bearer. If the expressions mentioned are taken to be tokens, T1 is unaffected; whereas Field claims that 'there is no remotely palatable way of extending' T2-style truth characterizations to cope with such languages.

(ii) If L is enriched, then provided only that the additions belong to semantic categories already represented, T1 needs no alteration; whereas T2 needs new clauses.

(iii) T2-style truth characterizations can be given only in metalanguages with vocabularies which match, extension for extension, those of the object languages; whereas T1-style truth characterizations are subject to no such restriction.

How solid these points are, as advantages for T1, is open to question. Point (i) is vulnerable to the production of palatable treatments, in the style of T2, for, say, languages with promiscuous names.[4] That point (ii) tells in favour of T1 is a thesis which is not really independent of Field's central contention, to be discussed shortly (see the end of section IV and the end of section VI). And from a certain perspective, to be sketched below, point (iii) simply disappears (see the end of section V). Field's main interest, however, is different, and I shall not devote further attention, except in passing, to the three points listed above.

IV

Field's main concern is with the difference emphasized in my exposition of T1 and T2, namely that T2 does, whereas T1 does not, permit construction of a formula coextensive with the truth-predicate and containing no semantic vocabulary.

The difference means that T1, Field's favoured candidate, is in violation of one of Tarski's ground rules. Tarski announced: 'I shall not make use of any semantical concept if I am not able previously to reduce it to other concepts' ('CTFL', pp. 152–153).

Field argues plausibly that the motivation for that ground rule was the aspiration (expressed at 'ESS', p. 406, mentioned in section I above) of making the notion of truth respectable from the standpoint of physicalism. Field's version of physicalism (probably close to Tarski's, in view of Tarski's talk, in the 'ESS' passage, of the unity of science) is this: 'the doctrine that chemical facts, biological facts, psychological facts, and semantical facts, are all explicable (in principle) in terms of physical facts'. If a physicalist found the notion of truth, and hence putative facts in whose formulation it figures, in some way suspect, he would hardly be content with other semantic notions: in particular those of denotation, fulfilment and application, which Field collectively labels 'primitive denotation'. So T1 leaves the job of rehabilitating truth (for L) at best incompletely executed; whereas if one obeyed the ground rule which T1 violates, one might hope to perform the task all at once. In Field's view, however, T2, for all its obedience to the ground rule, does not fulfil the hope.

Obviously a lot depends on what it takes to make the notion of truth acceptable to a physicalist. Consider, for instance, a claim of Tarski's as to what is shown by the possibility of constructing T2-style theories for formalized languages of finite order: he says ('CTFL', p. 265) he has demonstrated that for each such language

a formally correct and materially adequate definition of true sentence can be constructed in the metalanguage, making use only of expressions of a general logical character, expressions of the language itself [he is speaking of the case in which metalanguage includes object language] as well as terms belonging to the morphology of language, i.e. names of linguistic expressions and of the structural relations existing between them.

If a T2-style theory for L, in a metalanguage which included L (so that the theory could use, in those of its clauses which effect T2's distinctive trick, the very expressions which the clauses deal with), had its recursive characterizations converted as before, and if we agreed for present purposes to count expressions of set theory as 'expressions of a general logical character', the result would exactly conform to Tarski's description. Now suppose a physicalist is satisfied with the physical credentials of logic, set theory, and the morphology of language, and those of the non-logical vocabulary of L (which could not leave him unsatisfied, if we moved to the case in which metalanguage does not include object language, with the physical credentials of translations of that vocabulary in the metalanguage). Why could he not allay any doubts about 'true' by reflecting on the availability of the long-winded substitute which Tarski showed he could construct?

Different languages would need different substitutes, even if the languages differed only in that, say, one contained a predicate which the other did not contain (cf. section III, (ii)). But why should that matter? What Tarski promises is a set of physicalistically acceptable formulae containing a formula coextensive with 'true' in its application to the sentences of each language of the relevant sort. To insist that what is needed, if a semantic predicate is to be respectable, is a physicalistically acceptable formula coextensive with it in all its applications, even across the boundaries between languages, could be justified on the basis of a physicalism that requires a single physical equivalent for every decent predicate; but that is something Field explicitly rejects.

Field's reason for being unimpressed by a defence of T2 on the above lines comes out very clearly in his use of an analogy from chemistry.

We might have a theory which enabled us to determine the valences of chemical compounds on the basis of the valences of the elements out of which they are compounded. We could write it in this form:

$(c)(n)(c$ has valence n iff $B(c, n))$;

where we fix the extension of the valence relation, as it holds between compounds and numbers, in terms of a formula '$B(c, n)$' which would contain the term 'valence' as applied to elements. Then we could go on to specify the valence of each element, on these lines:

$(e)(n)(e$ has valence n iff e is potassium and n is $+1$, or . . . or e is sulphur and n is $-2)$.

Substituting the right-hand side of this for occurrences of the predicate 'ξ has valence ζ' in the formula '$B(c, n)$' would yield an open sentence, coextensive with the valence relation as it holds between compounds and numbers, in which 'valence' did not appear. But such a construction would compare unfavourably with what we would have if we eliminated 'valence' from '$B(c, n)$' by means of a *reduction* of the valence relation, as it holds between elements and numbers, to structural (physical) properties of atoms. The 'valence'-free open sentence constructed in the first way would be revealed by the comparison as a pseudo-reduction of the concept of the valence of a compound.

What Field suggests is that T2's way of eliminating 'denotes', 'is fulfilled by', and 'applies to' from the definition of truth parallels that pseudo-reduction. Parallel to what the pseudo-reduction is unfavourably compared with would be a theory like T1, but supplemented with genuine explications of the primitive-denotation relations in physical terms: something which does not merely, like T2, specify the extensions of those relations as far as L is concerned, but describes physical relations between expressions and things on which the semantic relations depend, and from whose description, together with suitable physical facts, the extensions of the semantic relations could be determined.[5]

The idea is, then, that T2 is merely T1 plus bogus reductions of the concepts of primitive denotation. By not purporting complete reduction, T1 advertises the fact that we do not yet have genuine explications of those concepts; T2 simply papers over that gap. Tarski's genuine achievement, reflected in T1, involves seeing how to specify the semantic properties of complex expressions in terms of those of simple expressions. T2 gives the appearance of going further, and eliminating the semantic properties of simple expressions. But the appearance is deceptive: we are told nothing interesting—in fact, nothing at all—by T2 about what it is for a simple expression to have one of the appropriate semantic properties, any more than we are told, by a list of the valences of elements, what it is for an element to have a particular valence.

Chemical concepts applied to compounds are reasonably conceived as relating indirectly to the physical facts on which their applicability depends, by way of the application of chemical concepts to elements; it is at the level of elements and their properties that we expect chemistry to be revealed as, so to speak, adhering to the physical facts. Field's picture of semantics is parallel: the semantic properties of complex expressions, in particular truth, relate to the physical facts about those expressions by way of the semantic properties of simple expressions, and it is at that level—the level of the *axioms* of a truth-characterization—that we must seek to reveal the adherence of semantics to the physical facts.

Given the chemical parallel, the vacuity of what is peculiar to T2, as against T1, seems undeniable. From that perspective, moreover, the differences between T2-style theories for different languages, even with the same semantic structure (see section III, (ii)), look like a symptom of how bogus the explication effected is. Differences between languages, in the extensions of the primitive denotation relations, should be capable of being displayed as consequences of different instantiations of those general physical relations between expressions and things on which primitive denotation depends; not represented as brute differences, as at first glance they seem to be in T2-style theories, where the concepts of primitive denotation disappear in favour of, precisely, specifications of their extensions. (But see the end of section VI below.)

A contrasting view about the point of contact between semantical facts and the underlying physical facts is possible. In order to sketch it, I shall begin (in section V) by rescuing Tarski's 'Convention T' (*Kriterium W*) from the contumelious treatment to which Field subjects it.

V

According to Field, Tarski's 'formal criterion of adequacy for theories of truth' was 'roughly' this:

(M) Any condition of the form

$$(2) \quad (e)(e \text{ is true iff } B(e))$$

should be accepted as an adequate definition of truth if and only if it is correct and '$B(e)$' is a well-formed formula containing no semantic terms.

Field remarks in a footnote that 'Tarski actually gives a different formulation, the famous Convention T, evidently because he does not think that the word "correct" ought to be employed in stating a condition of adequacy.'

Is there not something in that thought? In fact it is a travesty to represent Convention T as merely 'a different formulation' of Convention M; for Convention M's 'if and only if it is correct' begs the very question which Convention T is meant to settle. Convention T, as is well known, requires a truth characterization to entail, for each object-language sentence, an instance of the schema 's is true iff p', where 's' is replaced by a designation of the object-language sentence and 'p' by that very sentence, if the object language is included in the metalanguage; otherwise by a translation thereof ('CTFL', pp. 187–188). Conformity with the requirement is a sufficient condition for the predicate characterized by a theory to have in its extension all and only the true sentences of the object language; that is, precisely, for the truth characterization to be, in Field's term, correct.

Tarski has *two* prerequisites for acceptability in a truth characterization: formal correctness and material adequacy (see e.g., 'CTFL', p. 265, quoted in section IV above). Convention T is his condition of *material adequacy* (Field's 'correctness'). Convention M does not address the question of material adequacy, but, with its insistence on an eliminative definition free of semantic terms, expresses a view of Tarski's about *formal correctness*. The second is detachable from the first: a truth characterization could conform to Convention T while being, because of sparseness of set theory, incurably recursive in its account of satisfaction, and hence failing to conform to Convention M.

If we want a recipe for constructing truth theories for languages in general (at least those amenable to Tarski's methods), we cannot evade the question when a truth theory is correct (materially adequate). Nothing Field says supersedes Convention T (or some version of it: see section VI below) as a general test of correctness. But T1 as it stands yields no nonsemantical truth-conditions for sentences, and so cannot be subjected to any such test. T1 yields assignments of truth-conditions like this (a simple case for illustration):

p_1c_1 is true iff there is something y which c_1 denotes and p_1 applies to y.

One might suppose that that could not be false, so that Convention T is trivially met. But in a real case, we could not be confident of so much as the categorization of the expressions as a predicate and a name, in advance of checking assignments of truth-conditions which result from specific interpretations of them as such—that is, the sort of thing a T2-style truth characterization would give.

Something in the spirit of Field's contrast can still be drawn, even between theories amenable for subjecting to Convention T. The modified contrast would be between:

(a) T2-style theories, which tell us nothing about the concepts of primitive denotation over and above fixing their extensions for the language dealt with; and

(b) a modified version of T1-style theories: theories which, unlike T1 as it stands, do fix the extensions of the primitive-denotation relations (so that they entail specific assignments of truth-conditions, which can be tested against Convention T); but which, unlike T2-style theories, represent the information as derived from the application, to physical facts about particular expressions, of those explications of the primitive-denotation concepts with which Field seeks to supplement T1.

Note, incidentally, that any truth characterization, of either of the two sorts distinguished in the modified contrast, will have to employ, in its specifications of primitive denotation, metalanguage expressions which aim at coextensiveness with the object-language expressions dealt with. (Conformity to Convention T would indicate success in the aim.) If the metalanguage does not, in advance of construction of the truth characterization, contain expressions with suitable extensions, it must be enriched so as to do so (perhaps—the easiest way—by borrowing from the object language). So once we take seriously the assessment of truth characterizations for correctness, there seems no substance to the idea that it is a merit of T1-style theories not to require object-language vocabulary to be suitably matched in the metalanguage (cf. section III, (iii)).[6]

VI

Once we appreciate the need for a test of material adequacy, we can see the possibility of inverting Field's conception of the point of contact between semantic theories and the physical facts.

Consider what would be involved in the interpretation, from scratch, of a foreign language. To simplify, suppose the language is used only to make assertions and that there is no indexicality.[7] Our interpretative needs would be met by a theory which entailed, for any sentence which might be uttered in the foreign language, a theorem of the (highly schematic) form '$s \ldots p$'; where 's' is replaced by a suitable designation of the object-language sentence, and 'p' by a sentence of ours such that, if a foreign speaker utters the object-language sentence, we can acceptably report what he says by using that sentence of ours. If we had a theory which met the requirement, replacements for '*p*' in its theorems would translate the sentences designated by the corresponding replacements for '*s*'. So if our requirement-meeting theory worked by characterizing a predicate, 'ϕ', so that the gap between replacements for '*s*' and replacements for '*p*' was filled by 'is ϕ iff', then, by virtue of the theory's conforming to Convention T, the extension of 'ϕ' would be the extension of 'true'. A sufficient condition of correctness, then, in a truth characterization for the language in question, would be the possibility of putting it to interpretative use in the way described above; that is, treating it as if its theorems were of the form '*s* can be used to say that *p*'.[8]

We can picture ourselves equipped with all the physically formulable facts about language use in the community, and aiming to construct, via interpretation as above, a truth characterization for their language. Two interlocking requirements would govern the fit between the truth characterization and the physical facts.

(i) The first requirement is one of *system*. We want to see the content we attribute to foreign sayings as determined by the contributions of distinguishable parts of aspects of foreign utterances, each of which may occur, making the same contribution, in a multiplicity of utterance. This is secured by having the theorems deducible, as in T2-style truth characterizations, from axioms which deal with simple expressions and figure as premisses in the deduction of the appropriate theorems for any sentences in which their expressions occur. For the theorems to be so deducible, utterances must be identifiable in terms of structures and constituents assigned to them by a systematic syntax; and it must be possible to match up those structures (if necessary obliquely, through transformations) with configurations observable in physical utterance-events.

(ii) The second requirement is one of *psychological adequacy*. Used as an interpretative theory, the truth characterization is to serve up, in the systematic way sketched under (i), specifications of the content of assertions which we can take speakers to be making. Not just any piece of physically described behaviour can be reasonably redescribed as a saying with a specific content. Whether such redescriptions are acceptable turns on whether the behaviour, as redescribed, is intelligible. That requires the possibility of locating it suitably against a background of propositional attitudes—centrally beliefs and desires—in terms of which the behaviour seems to make sense. Ascription of propositional attitudes, in turn, is constrained in complex ways by the physical facts about behaviour, the environment, and their interconnections; also (circling back) by the possibilities of interpreting linguistic behaviour in comformity with requirement (i). Interpretation can be pictured as the superimposition, on all that is available in physical terms about language use, of the content-specifying mode of discourse: ascriptions of sayings, beliefs, and desires. Partly because requirement (i) demands ramified interdependencies between interpretations of different utterances, and partly for general reasons stemming from the character of intentional discourse, the superimposition has to be in principle holistic (which is not, of course, to deny that in practical theory-construction one would need to proceed by way of piecemeal hypotheses).

The hard physical facts, then, which constrain the construction of a truth characterization for a language actually spoken, are (i) the structural properties of physical utterance-events which permit the language to be given a syntactic description; and (ii) the complex relations between behaviour and the environment which permit (some of) the behaviour to be described and understood in intentional terms.

Now it is at the level of its *theorems* that a truth characterization, on this account, makes contact with those hard physical facts. If the theorems are to be systematically deducible so that requirement (i) is met in the way described above, then replacements for 's' must characterize utterances in terms of structures and constituents; so that the relation of match or transformational accessibility, which, according to requirement (i), must hold between the structures assigned to sentences by the syntax with which the theory operates, on the one hand, and configurations observable in physical utterance-events, on the other, is revealed or not at the theorem level. Moreover, interpretations of parts of utterances can be subjected to requirement (ii) only through interpretations of whole utterances; an assignment of denotation, for instance, is tested by whether assignments of truth-conditions derivable from it facilitate ascriptions of sayings which are for the most part intelligible; and of course it is the theorems which record interpretations of whole utterances. So requirement (i) makes itself felt, not only directly, in connection with the match between theoretical syntax and actual utterance-events, but in another way too: we can conceive the deductive shape which the theory assumes, in order to meet requirement (i), as setting up a complex of channels by which the impact of requirement (ii), bearing in the first instance on interpretations of whole utterances, is transmitted backwards, through the derivations of theorems licensed by the theory, to the premisses of those derivations, in which the theory says what it does about sentence-components and modes of sentence-construction.

Describing, on the lines of requirements (i) and (ii), the nature of the fit between an acceptable truth characterization's theorems and the physical facts can be regarded as spelling out what Convention T comes to, in a case in which what translates what cannot be taken (as it could in the cases Tarski considered) to be simply given or up for stipulation.

According to this picture, a truth characterization fits the underlying physical facts from the theorems upward; not, as in Field's conception, from the axioms downward. The deductive apparatus used in deriving the theorems needs no anchoring in the physical facts, independently of the overall acceptability of the derived assignments of truth-conditions.[9] The relations between language and extra-linguistic reality which a truth characterization describes hold in the first instance between simple expressions and things, and only mediately, via the laws of semantic combination set out in the truth characterization, between complex expressions and the world.[10] But from its being at the level of primitive denotation that relations between words and the world are set up *within* a semantic theory, it does not follow—nor, according to the inverted picture, is it true—that it is at the level that the primary connection should be sought between the semantic theory *itself* and the physical facts on which its acceptability depends.

A T2-style truth characterization specifies what are in fact denotations, fulfilment-conditions, and application-conditions. (It does not matter that the primitive-denotation concepts are not explicitly expressed in the T2-style theory sketched above: see below.) Now the axioms dealing with names, function symbols, and predicates play roles which are distinctively parallel within each of the three classes, and dissimilar between them, in the derivations of assignments of truth-conditions which the truth characterization licenses. According to the view which inverts Field's picture, there is nothing to the specific primitive-denotation concepts over and above those distinctive deductive powers. To give an account of one of the modes of primitive denotation, what we should do is (a) spell out, on the lines of requirements (i) and (ii), what it is for a truth characterization's assignments of truth-conditions to be acceptable; and (b) describe the relevant distinctive deductive capacity, so that the empirical content which (a) confers on the notion of truth can be channelled backwards through the licensed derivations into the relevant sort of premiss. (Clearly the various modes of primitive denotation will not, on this view, be separately explicable; that is as it should be.)

If it is at the level of its theorems that a truth characterization makes contact, obeying a version of Convention T glossed by requirements (i) and (ii), with the physical facts, then it does not matter a scrap whether the truth characterization yields an eliminative truth-definition free of semantic vocabulary. What matters is the possibility of eliminating semantic terms from the right-hand sides of the theorems (unless the object language contains semantic vocabulary, so that semantic terms can properly occur in reports of what is, on occasion, said by its speakers). That elimination is possible even if we leave the characterization of satisfaction, in a T2-style theory, in its recursive form, so that the concept of satisfaction is still present in any equivalent which the theory yields for the truth-definition. From this viewpoint, then, there is nothing to favour a direct truth-definition over an axiomatic truth characterization, so long as the latter yields acceptable theorems.

Similarly, the absence from a T2-style theory of explicit expression of the primitive-denotation concepts is not in itself a virtue. We could construct a trivial variant of the T2-style truth characterization partly sketched above, which would explicitly assign denotations, fulfilment-conditions and application-conditions, labelled as such, so that the theory would lack that putative virtue; that would not matter, since the semantic terminology could still be made to disappear in deriving the final assignments of truth-conditions.

Eliminative 'definitions' of the primitive-denotation concepts through specifications of their extensions, such as T2 yields, are not to be conceived as purporting to say what it is for one of those relations to hold; that task is discharged, rather, by the combination of (a) and (b) above. This should alleviate concern over how T2-style truth characterizations would vary from language to language (section III, (ii)). What is said under (a) would be, details aside, common to anything recognizable as a language; and if there is any point in carrying over a specific batch of primitive-denotation concepts from one language to another, that would show up in similarities in what would be sayable about the deductive powers of the relevant sets of axioms, under (b). So the inter-language variations between T2-style theories would leave invariant that about them which contributes to the task of saying what it is for the relations to hold If someone supposed that we were freed from obligations to look for further explications of the primitive-denotation concepts solely by virtue of the fact that the concepts were not explicitly expressed in eliminative definitions constructed from T2-style theories, then it would be reasonable to be perturbed by variation in the materials of those eliminative definitions (cf. the end of section IV). But the absence of explicit employment of the concepts is not rightly taken in that way. (Notice that it is not in a T2-style theory itself that, on this view, we find accounts of what it is for the primitive-denotation relations to hold; (a) and (b) would be metatheoretical remarks about T2-style theories.)

Tarski's own insistence on eliminative truth-definitions free of semantic terms, justified as it is by a mention of physicalism ('ESS', p. 406), suggests that he himself conceived the virtues of T2-style theories, from a physicalist standpoint, in a way justly parodied by Field's chemical example. But we can accept Tarski's favoured style of truth characterization without needing to agree with everything he thought about its merits.

VII

Not only is there no need to look for physical underpinnings for the deductive apparatus of truth-theories, over and above their output. There is no reason to expect that the search would turn up anything interesting.

On the view sketched above, superimposition of a semantic theory on the physical facts about a language-using community is a subtask in the superimposition of a way of describing and understanding their behaviour in content-specifying terms. For all its extensionality, the truth characterization has its relation to the realm of the physical governed by the conditions which govern the relation of intentional to physical discourse. Now the nature of those conditions makes it quite implausible that the relation of semantics to physics should be anything like the relation of chemistry to physics.

When we shift from chemical to physical explanation, we shift to a style of explanation which, though at a deeper level, is still of the same general kind: a kind in which events are displayed as unsurprising because of the way the world works.[11] If we are physicalists, we hold that physics can in principle give a complete account of all events, so far as that mode of explanation is concerned. So if there is any substance in chemical explanations of compounding behaviour, then, since those explanations purport to reveal events as unsurprising *qua* instances of the world's workings, the laws which, in those explanations, state how the world is said to work should, law by law, have physical credentials. And that is how it turns out: the chemical laws which (roughly) determine the compounding behaviour of composite substances on the basis of that of elements are, by way of the (approximate) reduction of element valences to physical properties of atoms, (approximately) mirrored in physical laws which govern compounding transactions described in terms of atomic and molecular structure.

But the difference between physical explanation and that mode of explanation which is largely constitutive of the network of intentional concepts is not a difference within a broadly homogeneous kind. Intentional explanation makes an action unsurprising, not as an instance of the way the world works (though of course it does not follow that an action is *not* that), but as something which the agent can be understood to have seen some point in going in for.[12] An intentional explanation of an event does not, like a chemical explanation, offer, so to speak, to fill the same explanatory space as a physical explanation would. So we can go on claiming, as physicalists, that physics can completely fill that explanatory space, without requiring that, on pain of seeing intentional explanations as substanceless, we must be able to ground the details of those explanations, detail by detail, in physical counterparts.

Explanations of the semantic properties of complex expressions in terms of the semantic properties of simple expressions, appealing as they do to semantic laws whose formulation is part of the move from the physical to the intentional, should be of a piece with intentional explanations, in respect of their relation to the physical; because of the different explanatory pretensions of the intentional, there is no threat to the completeness of physics, as far as the appropriate kind of explanation is concerned, if those semantic laws and their special conceptual content cannot be physically mirrored in the way exemplified in the chemical case. Physicalism, construed as the doctrine that physics is in principle competent to yield an explanation of that kind for all that happens, affords no reason for insisting that such mirroring be available if semantics is to be other than empty; that is (given the assumption that semantics is not empty) for expecting that such mirroring will be found.

If intentional concepts are largely constituted by their role in a special kind of explanation, which does not compete with the kind which physics yields but offers a different species of comprehension, then we need not expect to be able, even approximately, to reduce those concepts to physical terms. The distinctive point of the intentional concepts makes it intelligible that there should be a kind of incommensurability between them and physical concepts.[13] And if the intentional concepts are not reducible to physical terms, then it is, if anything, still less to be expected that reductions should be available for the concepts of primitive denotation, whose conceptual identity, according to the position sketched in section VI, consists solely in their impact on a semantic property of complex expressions—truth-conditions—the concept of which we can explain only in terms of requirements for the applicability of intentional notions.

Field seeks to motivate the contrary thought that we must look for physicalist explanations of the concepts of primitive denotation by arguing that 'without such accounts our conceptual scheme [as physicalists] breaks down from the inside. On our theory of the world it would be extremely surprising if there were some non-physical connection between words and things'. This remark needs careful consideration.

It is not claimed, on behalf of the position Field opposes, that there are no physical connections between words and things (which would certainly be surprising). Assignments of truth-conditions are partly controlled by, for instance, the possibilities of belief-ascription, and belief-ascription is governed in part by principles about how the content of beliefs is sensitive to the causal impact of their subject matter. That, and similar features in a fuller account of acceptability in assignments of truth-conditions, require the presence of causal, no doubt ultimately physical, connections between the world and words at the level of whole utterances, construed as (in our example) voicings of belief. Such causal connections presumably reflect, in ways corresponding to the derivability of assignments of truth-conditions from specifications of primitive denotation, causal connections between occurrences of simple expressions and physically describable circumstances. The position Field opposes is quite compatible with the thesis that whenever a name, say, occurs in an utterance-event, the event is suitably related, in physically describable ways, with events or circumstances involving the name's denotation.

What need not be true is a corresponding thesis with a quantifier shift: that there is some one physically describable relation which obtains between any occurrence of any name and its denotation. This denial is not just the reflection of a needlessly strict view of when we have a single relation. According to the thesis allowed at the end of the last paragraph, any instance of the denotation relation will have what we might call a physical realization. The physical realizations will differ from instance to instance, but that is not the issue; it is not necessarily Pickwickian to classify as a physical relation one which holds just in case some one of a set of physical relations holds.

The question is about the principle on which the members of the set are collected. If the point of the grouping cannot be given in purely physical terms, but consists simply in the fact that those physical relations are the ones which obtain when the denotation relation, explicated on the lines suggested in section VI, obtains, then there is no justification for claiming that a reduction has been effected.[14]

It seems right to conclude that denotation, on this view, is a non-physical relation; and similar considerations apply to the other primitive-denotation concepts. Now just how surprising is it that there should be such relations between words and things?

Semantic relations, on this view, are indeed not like chemical relations; if explicability in terms of physical facts, which is what Field's physicalism demands of all facts worthy of the name, requires the sort of grounding, in physical facts, of the facts into which genuine relations enter that is exemplified in the chemical case, then the idea that semantic relations might be as here suggested is either offensive to physicalism or a condemnation of semantics. But perhaps we should look sceptically at Field's formulation of physicalism. Certainly his assimilation of the thesis of semantical irreducibility to such anti-materialistic theses as Cartesianism is unfair.

A doctrine with some claim to be called 'physicalism' is this: (i) all events are physical events, that is, have physical descriptions; (ii) under their physical descriptions, all events are susceptible of total explanations, of the kind paradigmatically afforded by physics, in terms of physical laws and other physically described events. Field's version of physicalism excludes any thesis according to which there are facts irreducible to physical facts—'semanticalism' and Cartesianism alike. But the version just given discriminates; it allows some irreducibility theses but rejects others. Cartesianism, as standardly understood, is still excluded; for according to it, mental events have no physical descriptions, in violation of (i), and some physically describable events (for instance limb movements) have such events in their causal ancestry, in violation of (ii). However, 'semanticalism'—the irreducibility thesis outlined above—is compatible with physicalism in the revised formulation. The events which comprise linguistic behaviour have physical descriptions, as required by (i). There is no reason to deny that under those descriptions they are explicable as instances of the way the world works, and if physics delivers on its claim to saturate the relevant explanatory space, it must be possible to put the explanations which reveal them as such, ultimately, into physical shape, as required by (ii). The irreducibility thesis turns on the idea that formulation of a truth characterization subserves the compiling of a way of talking whose point lies in a kind of understanding, of those and other events, quite different from that which physics might afford; so, as emphasized above, it poses no threat to the ambitions of physics to be complete in its own sphere. Cartesianism holds, by contrast, that there are questions of the sort physics purports to be able to handle, to which the answers are stubbornly non-physical.[15]

In a common usage of 'science', the scope of science is taken to cover just such questions; if physicalism is good scientific methodology—which certainly seems plausible on that understanding of what science is—then doctrines like Cartesianism are unscientific. But it is a different matter to refuse to accept that all questions fall within the province of science so understood. We can agree that semantics, on the view here taken, is not in that sense scientific (though there is plenty to justify its claim to be scientific in some more relaxed sense) without thereby agreeing that it is *un*scientific. A discipline can be both rigorous and illuminating without being related to physics in the way Field wants semantics to be; the strong physicalism which denies that seems to me to be, as Field says about a version he himself rejects, hard to take seriously.

NOTES

1. First published in *Erkenntnis*, vol. 13 (1978), pp. 131–52. I read an earlier version of this paper to an Oxford seminar in 1973. It should be obvious that my debts to Donald Davidson's writings far outrun those signalled in the notes. Gareth Evans and Colin McGinn helped with an intermediate revision, and more recently I have had aid and comfort from Hilary Putnam's 1976 John Locke Lectures.

2. I treat 'c_i', etc., as names (in the metalanguage) of L's names, etc., which might be 'Deutschland', etc.; this involves notational divergence from Field. '∀' is the name of L's quantifier, rather than a quantifier of the metalanguage; later in the paper I rewrite some of Field's formula with the bracket notation for universal quantification.

3. Concatenations of metalanguage names of object-language expressions denote corresponding concatenations of the named expressions. In such structural descriptions names may give way to variables. Open sentences are to be read as universally quantified (thus the present formula should be understood with quantifiers binding 'A' and 's'). Brackets round designations of conjunctions (as in (b) below) are a scope-marking convention.

4. I believe we can get such a thing out of an account of names on the lines of Tyler Burge, 'Reference and Proper Names', *Journal of Philosophy*, vol. 70 (1973), p. 425.

5. Field ('Tarski's Theory of Truth', p. 99) cites Saul Kripke's work as a beginning on the task of giving the required explications. I prefer to take seriously Kripke's denial that he intended to produce a theory of denotation for names (see pp. 280, 300–303, of 'Naming and Necessity', in Donald Davidson and Gilbert Harman, eds, *Semantics of Natural Language*, Dordrecht, Reidel, 1972). Construed as correcting an alternative picture, rather than giving a substantive account of denotation, Kripke's work is quite compatible with the view of semantics, divergent from Field's, to be sketched in sections VI and VII below.

6. If truth characterizations have to be got into a form in which they can be subjected to the test of Convention T (or some version of it), then it must be possible to circumvent problems posed by indexicality (cf. section III, (i)). But I shall ignore the complications of doing so.

7. Not making these suppositions would complicate the exposition, but (I believe) introduce no new issues of principle.

8. Cf. D. Davidson, 'Truth and Meaning', *Synthèse*, vol. 17 (1967), p. 304; and the first section of my 'Truth Conditions, Bivalence, and Verificationism', in Gareth Evans and John McDowell, eds, *Truth and Meaning* (Oxford, Clarendon Press, 1976).

9. Cf. D. Davidson, 'In Defense of Convention T', in H. Leblanc, ed., *Truth, Syntax, and Modality* (Amsterdam, North-Holland, 1973), at p. 84.

10. This is a very important fact about Tarskian truth characterizations. We are potentially liberated from much bad philosophy about truth by seeing that sentences need no special extra-linguistics items of their own (states of affairs, facts, or whatever) to be related to. (Talk of facts in this paper is, I hope, only a *façon de parler*.) See D. Davidson, 'True to the Facts', *Journal of Philosophy*, vol. 66 (1969), p. 748.

11. This is not meant to be more than a crude intuitive gesture in the direction of an account of the kind of explanation in question.

12. Again, this is intended only as a gesture.

13. For the claim of irreducibility, see W. V. Quine, *Word and Object* (Cambridge, Mass., MIT Press, 1960), section 45 (note the references to other authors). On the ground of the irreducibility, see D. Davidson, 'Mental Events', in Lawrence Foster and J. W. Swanson, eds, *Experience and Theory* (Amherst, University of Massachusetts, 1970).

14. This is relevant to Michael Friedman's remarks about weak reduction, in 'Physicalism and the Indeterminacy of Translation', *Noûs*, vol. 9 (1975), p. 353.

15. Similarly vitalism, which Field also cites ('Tarski's Theory of Truth', p. 92).

INTENSIONALITY

PART FOUR

INTENSIONALITY

INTRODUCTION

Philosophers and linguists refer to such psychological states as belief, hope, fear, and others that have propositions as their contents and can be attributed using verbs that take "that . . . clauses" as their complements ("believes that . . . ," "hopes that . . ." *etc.*) as *propositional attitudes*. Sentences that attribute these attitudes ("John believes that bats fly," "Carmen hopes that the boy next door will stop bothering her") have odd semantic properties. One can't substitute codesignating terms for one another within the sentence embedded in the "that . . ." clause. The semantic value of the whole sentence seems strangely independent of the truth-value of the embedded sentence, but exquisitely sensitive to the choice of words in which the sentence is embedded. New ambiguities arise that appear to call for semantic distinctions (such as the *de dicto–de re* distinction) that have surprising import for the philosophy of mind. This semantic anomaly was noted early on, as is evident in the essays of Frege and Russell above. Frege argued that the appearance of such verbs called for a systematic shift of reference from customary nominatum to customary sense within the oblique or content clauses they controlled. Thus, if one wished to describe Othello's belief that Desdemona loved Cassio, the expressions used to designate Desdemona and Cassio would instead designate the senses of the two names rather than their bearers. However one is to understand just exactly what this Fregean doctrine means, there is no doubt as to the justice of his semantic observation. One cannot simply take "Desdemona" and "Cassio" as designating their bearers, for they are not replaceable by expressions that codesignate those two characters, e.g., "his faithful wife" and "his faithless lieutenant." Othello emphatically did *not* believe the proposition that his faithful wife loved his faithless lieutenant, and so these substitutions make a true sentence false (though—as noted above—there is a reading of his attribution sentence on which it is true—despite the fact that the embedded sentence is not in any obvious way ambiguous. Such contexts in which substitutivity of codesignating expressions *salva veritate* fails (and in which certain other apparently unproblematic logical operations have problematic consequences) have generally been called, following Quine's usage, "opaque."

Quine carries this semantic insight a step further in the essay reprinted here. Not only do the verbs of propositional attitude affect singular designators, he argues, but they affect general designators as well. When one ascribes a hope or belief that is about unicorns, or spies, or yachts, generality of the sort that the symbolism of logic is designed to capture occurs. This symbolism represents sentences with "some," "all," "a," or "the" attached to common nouns by the use of operator symbols whose scope is clearly marked with parenthesized open sentences whose variables mark the reach of the operator that binds the variables. The closest analogue to these variables in a natural language are nondemonstrative or anaphoric pronouns whose antecedent is not a proper name but rather a common noun phrase. In the sentence "I bought a car and it broke down," the indefinite article is symbolized by the existential quantifier, $(\exists x)(x$ is a car & I bought x & x broke down). The problems that Quine's deservedly much discussed essay initiated turn on the semantics of these hidden bound variables that appear in propositional attitude sentences. If belief affects names, then unsurprisingly it will also affect bound variables that stand where names stand. But how? This is the question taken up by the remaining essays in this section.

This question becomes especially troubling when one notes that there is, e.g., a great difference between believing something general and generalizing a thing believed. It is one thing to believe that there is a sloop in the slip, and quite another to believe of a particular sloop that it is in the slip; one thing to believe that all spies are short, and another to believe of each and every spy that s/he is short. One can quantify within the belief-clause or quantify into it. This distinction that Quine mobilizes and that David Kaplan takes as the point of departure for his "Quantifying In," an essay we sorrowfully cannot reprint, predicts and explains a common semantic intuition that finds voice in the comedian's two lines. "I've got a suit for every day of the year . . . (sadly) and this is it." The distinction between wanting one sloop in particular and just wanting a sloop can be represented as the distinction between treating the "a"-quantifier as binding the variable from outside the desire or from within. Quine labels these two senses of desire (etc.) as respectively relational and notional, a distinction that probably coincides with Russell's distinction above between primary and secondary occurrence of denoting phrases.

Quine does not stay with this distinction, however. Or better, he shows a different way of construing it. That way draws distinctions in the objects of belief rather than beliefs themselves. One can either believe a proposition, *tout court,* or believe an attribute (to be true) of some ordered sequence of the appropriate length. These intensions are named by intensional abstracts and any term that falls within one is ipso facto referentially opaque, and cannot be exported to a generalizable position. If George IV wondered whether the attribute of writing *Waverley* was true of Scott, he also wondered whether it was true of the author of *Waverley* and of someone. But if his wonder was propositional, the substitution is blocked. Belief and other propositional attitudes are now conceived as some sort of mental relation that relates minds either to propositions or to attributes and those sequences of things the attribute is thought or hoped to be true of. Whether one can think of these intensions as words and their intensional abstraction as quotation Quine ponders at the essay's end. It is fascinating, however, to note the ways in which the semantic problems posed by propositional attitude locutions lead one straightaway into metaphysical and epistemological problems in the philosophy of mind. This proclivity of the attitudes to lead one into metaphysics will also be amply evident in the next section of this book.

Donald Davidson's essay purports to undertake a metaphysically more modest subject, viz., speech rather than belief. Natural languages the world over report both speech and belief with similar grammatical constructions, a dependent clause abstracted from a sentence, as in the English "that . . ." construction. Further, Hintikka reports that at least for European languages the history of this construction—an evolution of a paratactic "we all believe this: he once lived here" to a hypotactic "we all believe he once lived here"— is the same. Davidson proposes a return to the antique construction, thus avoiding both Intensionalism and Quotationalism. The hypotactic or subordinate clause need then be regarded as neither an indirect quotation nor an intensional abstract. His task, of course, is to say what the demonstrative pronoun is demonstrating without falling back into either of the other two positions.

While both Quine and Davidson respond to the Fregean problems about the composition of apparently intensional constituents by attempting nonintensional reinterpretations of them, other in the neo-Fregean tradition have responded by developing precise formal theories of intensional semantics. Steven Weiseler lays out and explains the doctrines of the most thoroughgoing intensionalist of them all, Richard Montague. Montague took his theoretical responsibilities very seriously and developed an articulated philosophical theory of the logic and semantics of natural language that takes as its central motivation the explanation of intensionality and the development of a mathematical theory of semantic and syntactic composition. Nor did he harbor suspicions that intensional entities were, to paraphrase Quine, creatures of individuative darkness. Where there is a logic, its universe of discourse cannot be too blameworthy, and there is an intensional logic. Montague develops a grammar for English (or more accurately for a fragment of English) that maps English sentences first into an intensional logic capable of representing such constructions as the propositional attitude sentences, and their various readings, and then into a semantics that allows for the composition both of sense and reference in a way that reflects Frege's intuitions about compositionality, including those regarding the accommodations that must be made for opaque contexts. Montague's semantic program has been enormously influential, and virtually all contemporary programs of formal natural language semantics reflect Montague's pioneering work, either in virtue of being recognizable variants (as is Cresswell's selection) or in virtue of being self-consciously alternative to it.

One thing that these otherwise diverse treatments of scope and opacity have in common is that they treat opacity as a single phenomenon for which a single theory is to be offered. Murray Kiteley, on the other hand, is impressed with the variety or motleyness of opacity and ambiguity of scope. He argues that they are far from all being cases of indirect discourse or prositional attitude, which raises questions about the aptness of a uniform Intensionalist or Quotationalist treatment. He proposes instead an account that turns on the machinery of reference rather than on its kinds. This essay hence nicely anticipates the discussions that occupy the next section.

W. V. O. QUINE

QUANTIFIERS AND PROPOSITIONAL ATTITUDES

I

The incorrectness of rendering 'Ctesias is hunting unicorns' in the fashion:

$(\exists x)$ (x is a unicorn · Ctesias is hunting x)

is conveniently attested by the nonexistence of unicorns, but is not due simply to that zoological lacuna. It would be equally incorrect to render "Ernest is hunting lions" as:

    (1) $(\exists x)$ (x is a lion · Ernest is hunting x),

where Ernest is a sportsman in Africa. The force of (1) is rather that there is some individual lion (or several) which Ernest is hunting; stray circus property, for example.

The contrast recurs in "I want a sloop." The version:

    (2) $(\exists x)$ (x is a sloop · I want x)

is suitable insofar only as there may be said to be a certain sloop that I want. If what I seek is mere relief from slooplessness, then (2) gives the wrong idea.

The contrast is that between what may be called the *relational* sense of lion-hunting of sloop-wanting, viz., (1)–(2), and the likelier or *notional* sense. Appreciation of the difference is evinced in Latin and Romance languages by a distinction of mood in subordinate clauses; thus *"Procuro un perro que habla"* has the relational sense:

$(\exists x)$ (x is a dog · x talks · I seek x)

as against the notional *"Procuro un perro que hable"*:

I strive that $(\exists x)$ (x is a dog · x talks · I find x).

Pending considerations to the contrary in later pages, we may represent the contrast strikingly in terms of permutations of components. Thus (1) and (2) may be expanded (with some violence to both logic and grammar) as follows:

(3) $(\exists x)$ (x is a lion · Ernest strives that Ernest finds x).

(4) $(\exists x)$ (x is a sloop · I wish that I have x).

whereas "Ernest is hunting lions" and "I want a sloop" in their notional senses may be rendered rather thus:

(5) Ernest strives that $(\exists x)$ (x is a lion · Ernest finds x),

(6) I wish that $(\exists x)$ (x is a sloop · I have x).

The contrasting versions (3)–(6) have been wrought by so paraphrasing "hunt" and "want" as to uncover the locutions "strive that" and "wish that," expressive of what Russell has called *propsitional attitudes*. Now of all examples of propositional attitudes, the first and foremost is *belief*; and, true to form, this example can be used to point up the contrast between relational and notional senses still better than (3)–(6) do. Consider the relational and notional senses of believing in spies:

(7) $(\exists x)$ (Ralph believes that x is a spy),

(8) Ralph believes that $(\exists x)$ (x is a spy).

Both may perhaps be ambiguously phrased as "Ralph believes that someone is a spy," but they may be unambiguously phrased respectively as "There is someone whom Ralph believes to be a spy" and "Ralph believes there are spies." The difference is vast; indeed, if Ralph is like most of us, (8) is true and (7) is false.

In moving over to propositional attitudes, as we did in (3)–(6), we gain not only the graphic structural contrast between (3)–(4) and (5)–(6) but also a certain generality. For we can now multiply examples of striving and wishing, unrelated to hunting and wanting. Thus we get the relational and notional senses of wishing for a president:

(9) $(\exists x)$ (Witold wishes that x is president),

(10) Witold wishes that $(\exists x)$ (x is president).

According to (9), Witold has his candidate; according to (10) he merely wishes the appropriate form of government were in force. Also we open other propositional attitudes to similar consideration—as witness (7)–(8).

However, the suggested formulations of the relational senses—viz., (3), (4), (7), and (9)—all involve quantifying into a propositional-attitude idiom from outside. This is a dubious business, as may be seen from the following example.

There is a certain man in a brown hat whom Ralph has glimpsed several times under questionable circumstances on which we need not enter here: suffice it to say that Ralph suspects he is a spy. Also there is a gray-haired man, vaguely known to Ralph as rather a pillar of the community, whom Ralph is not aware of having seen except once at the beach. Now Ralph does not know it, but the men are one and the same. Can we say of this *man* (Bernard J. Ortcutt, to give him a name) that Ralph believes him to be a spy? If so, we find ourselves accepting a conjunction of the type:

(11) *w* sincerely denies '. . .' · *w* believes that . . .

as true, with one and the same sentence in both blanks. For, Ralph is ready enough to say, in all sincerity, "Bernard J. Ortcutt is no spy." If, on the other hand, with a view to disallowing situations of the type (11), we rule simultaneously that

(12) Ralph believes that the man in the brown hat is a spy,

(13) Ralph does not believe that the man seen at the beach is a spy,

then we cease to affirm any relationship between Ralph and any man at all. Both of the component "that"-clauses are indeed about the man Ortcutt; but the "that" must be viewed in (12) and (13) as sealing those clauses off, thereby rendering (12) and (13) compatible because not, as wholes, about Ortcutt at all. It then becomes improper to quantify as in (7); "believes that" becomes, in a word, referentially opaque.[1]

No question arises over (8); it exhibits only a quantification *within* the "believes that" context, not a quantification *into* it. What goes by the board, when we rule (12) and (13) both true, is just (7). Yet we are scarcely prepared to sacrifice the relational construction. "There is someone whom Ralph believes to be a spy," which (7) as against (8) was supposed to reproduce.

The obvious next move is to try to make the best of our dilemma by distinguishing two senses of belief: *belief*$_1$, which disallows (11), and *belief*$_2$, which tolerates (11) but makes sense of (7). For belief$_1$, accordingly, we sustain (12)–(13) and ban (7) as nonsense. For belief$_2$, on the other hand, we sustain (7); and for *this* sense of belief we must reject (13) and acquiesce in the conclusion that Ralph believes$_2$ that the man at the beach is a spy even though he *also* believes$_2$ (and believes$_1$) that the man at the beach is not a spy.

II

But there is a more suggestive treatment. Beginning with a single sense of belief, viz., belief$_1$ above, let us think of this at first as a relation between the believer and a certain *intension*, named by the "that"-clause. Intentions are creatures of darkness, and I shall rejoice with the reader when they are exorcised, but first I want to make certain points with the help of them. Now intensions named thus by "that"-clauses, without free variables, I shall speak of more specifically as intensions of degree 0, or propositions. In addition I shall (for the moment) recognize intensions of degree 1, or attributes. These are to be named by prefixing a variable to a sentence in which it occurs free; thus $z(z$ is a spy) is spyhood. Similarly we may specify intensions of higher degrees by prefixing multiple variables.

Now just as we have recognized a dyadic relation of belief between a believer and a proposition, thus:

(14) Ralph believes that Ortcutt is a spy,

so we may recognize also a triadic relation of belief among a believer, an object, and an attribute, thus:

(15) Ralph believes $z(z$ is a spy) of Ortcutt.

For reasons which will appear, this is to be viewed not as dyadic belief between Ralph and the proposition *that* Ortcutt has $z(z$ is a spy), but rather as an irreducibly triadic relation among the three things Ralph, $z(z$ is a spy), and Ortcutt. Similarly there is tetradic belief:

(16) Tom believes $yz(y$ denounced $z)$ of Cicero and Catiline,

and so on.

Now we can clap on a hard and fast rule against quantifying into propositional-attitude idioms; but we give it the form now of a rule against quantifying into names of intensions. Thus, though (7) as it stands becomes unallowable, we can meet the needs which prompted (7) by quantifying rather into the triadic belief construction, thus:

(17) $(\exists x)$ (Ralph believes $z(z$ is a spy) of x).

Here then, in place of (7), is our new way of saying that there is someone whom Ralph believes to be a spy.

Belief$_1$ was belief so construed that a proposition might be believed when an object was specified in it in one way, and yet not believed when the same object was specified in another way; witness (12)–(13). Hereafter we can adhere uniformly to this narrow sense of belief, both for the dyadic case and for triadic and higher; in each case the term which names the intension (whether proposition or attribute or intension of higher degree) is to be looked on as referentially opaque.

The situation (11) is thus excluded. At the same time the effect of belief$_2$ can be gained, simply by ascending from dyadic to triadic belief as in (15). For (15) does relate the men Ralph and Ortcutt precisely as belief$_2$ was intended ot do. (15) does remain true of Ortcutt under any designation; and hence the legitimacy of (17).

Similarly, whereas from:

Tom believes that Cicero denounced Catiline

we cannot conclude:

Tom believes that Tully denounced Catiline.

on the other hand we can conclude from:

Tom believes $y(y$ denounced Catiline) of Cicero

that

Tom believes $y(y$ denounced Catiline) of Tully,

and also that

(18) $(\exists x)$(Tom believes $y(y$ denounced Catiline) of x).

From (16), similarly, we may infer that

(19) $(\exists w)(\exists x)($ Tom believes $zy(y$ denounced $z)$ of w and x).

Such quantifications as:

$(\exists x)$ (Tom believes that x denounced Catiline).
$(\exists x)$ (Tom believes $y(y$ denounced $x)$ of Cicero)

still count as nonsense, along with (7); but such legitimate purposes as these might have served are served by (17)–(19) and the like. Our names of intensions, and these only, are what count as referentially opaque.

Let us sum up our findings concerning the seven numbered statements about Ralph. (7) is now counted as nonsense, (8) as true, (12)–(13) as true, (14) as false, and (15) and (17) as true. Another that is true is:

(20) Ralph believes that the man seen at the beach is not a spy,

which of course must not be confused with (13).

The kind of exportation which leads from (14) to (15) should doubtless be viewed in general as implicative. Under the terms of our illustrative story, (14) happens to be false; but (20) is true, and it leads by exportation to:

(21) Ralph believes $z(z$ is not a spy) of the man seen at the beach.

The man at the beach, hence Ortcutt, does not receive reference in (20), because of referential opacity; but he does in (21), so we may conclude from (21) that

(22) Ralph believes $z(z$ is not a spy) of Ortcutt.

Thus (15) and (22) both count as true. This is not, however, to charge Ralph with contradictory beliefs. Such a charge might reasonably be read into:

(23) Ralph believes $z(z$ is a spy-z is not a spy) of Ortcutt,

but this merely goes to show that it is undesirable to look upon (15) and (22) as implying (23).

It hardly needs be said that the barbarous usage illustrated in (15)–(19) and (21)–(23) is not urged as a practical reform. It is put forward by way of straightening out a theoretical difficulty, which, summed up, was as follows: Belief contexts are referentially opaque; therefore it is prima facie meaningless to quantify into them; how then to provide for those indispensable relational statements of belief, like "There is someone whom Ralph believes to be a spy"?

Let it not be supposed that the theory which we have been examining is just a matter of allowing unbridled quantification into belief contexts after all, with a legalistic change of notation. On the contrary, the crucial choice recurs at each point: quantify if you will, but pay the price of accepting near-contraries like (15) and (22) at each point at which you choose to quantify. In other words: distinguish as you please between referential and non-referential positions, but keep track, so as to treat each kind appropriately. The notation of intensions, of degree one and higher, is in effect a device for inking in a boundary between referential and nonreferential occurrences of terms.

III

Striving and wishing, like believing, are propositional attitudes and referentially opaque. (3) and (4) are objectionable in the same way as (7), and our recent treatment of belief can be repeated for these propositional attitudes. Thus, just as (7) gave way to (17), so (3) and (4) give way to:

(24) $(\exists x)$ (x is a lion · Ernest strives z(Ernest finds z) of x),

(25) $(\exists x)$ (x is a sloop · I wish z(I have z) of x,

a certain breach of idiom being allowed for the sake of analogy in the case of "strives."

These examples came from a study of hunting and wanting. Observing in (3)–(4) the quantification into opaque contexts, then, we might have retreated to (1)–(2) and foreborne to paraphrase them into terms of striving and wishing. For (1)–(2) were quite straightforward renderings of lion-hunting and sloop-wanting in their relational senses; it was only the notional senses that really needed the breakdown into terms of striving and wishing, (5)–(6).

Actually, though, it would be myopic to leave the relational senses of lion-hunting and sloop-wanting at the unanalyzed stage (1)–(2). For, whether or not we choose to put these over into terms of wishing and striving, there are other relational cases of wishing and striving which require our consideration anyway—as witness (9). The untenable formulations (3)–(4) may indeed be either corrected as (24)–(25) or condensed back into (1)–(2); on the other hand we have no choice but to correct the untenable (9) on the pattern of (24)–(25), viz., as:

$(\exists x)$ (Witold wishes $y(y$ is president) of x).

The untenable versions (3)–(4) and (9) all had to do with wishing and striving in the relational sense. We see in contrast that (5)–(6) and (10), on the notional side of wishing and striving, are innocent of any illicit quantification into opaque contexts from outside. But now notice that exactly the same trouble begins also on the notional side, as soon as we try to say not just that Ernest hunts lions and I want a sloop, but that someone hunts lions or wants a sloop. This move carries us, ostensibly, from (5)–(6) to:

(26) $(\exists w)$ (w strives that $(\exists x)$ (x is a lion $\cdot w$ finds x)),

(27) $(\exists w)$ (w wishes that $(\exists x)$ (x is a sloop $\cdot$ w has x)),

and these do quantify unallowably into opaque contexts.

We know how, with help of the attribute apparatus, to put (26)–(27) in order; the pattern, indeed, in substantially before us in (24)–(25). Admissible versions are:

$(\exists w)$ (w strives $y(\exists x)$ (x is a lion $\cdot$ y finds x) of w),
$(\exists w)$ (w wishes $y(\exists x)$ (x is a sloop $\cdot$ y has x) of w),

or briefly:

(28) $(\exists w)$ (w strives $y(y$ finds a lion) of w),
(29) $(\exists w)$ (w wishes $y(y$ has a sloop) of w).

Such quantification of the subject of the propositional attitude can of course occur in belief as well; and, if the subject is mentioned in the belief itself, the above pattern is the one to use. Thus "Someone believes he is Napoleon" must be rendered:

$(\exists w)$ (w believes $y(y =$ Napoleon) of w).

For concreteness I have been discussing belief primarily, and two other propositional attitudes secondarily: striving and wishing. The treatment is, we see, closely parallel for the three; and it will pretty evidently carry over to other propositional attitudes as well—e.g., hope, fear, surprise. In all cases my concern is, of course, with a special technical aspect of the propositional attitudes: the problem of quantifying in.

IV

There are good reasons for being discontent with an analysis that leaves us with propositions, attributes, and the rest of the intensions. Intensions are less economical than extensions (truth values, classes, relations), in that they are more narrowly individuated. The principle of their individuation, more-over, is obscure.

Commonly logical equivalence is adopted as the principle of individuation of intensions. More explicitly: if S and S' are any two sentences with n ($\geqq$ 0) free variables, the same in each, then the respective intensions which we name by putting the n variables (or "that," if $n = 0$) before S and S' shall be one and the same intension if and only if S and S' are logically equivalent. But the relevant concept of logical equivalence raises serious questions in turn.[2] The intensions are at best a pretty obscure lot.

Yet it is evident enough that we cannot, in the foregoing treatment of propositional attitudes, drop the intensions in favor of the corresponding extensions. Thus, to take a trivial example, consider "w is hunting uniforms." On the analogy of (28), it becomes:

w strives $y(y$ finds a unicorn) of w.

Correspondingly for the hunting of griffins. Hence, if anyone w is to hunt unicorns without hunting griffins, the attributes

$y(y$ finds a unicorn),
$y(y$ finds a griffin),

must be distinct. But the corresponding classes are identical, being empty. So it is indeed the attributes, and not the classes, that were needed in our formulation. The same moral could be drawn, though less briefly, without appeal to empty cases.

But there is a way of dodging the intensions which merits serious consideration. Instead of speaking of intensions we can speak of sentences, naming these by quotation. Instead of:

w believes that . . .

we may say:

w believes-true '. . .'.

Instead of:

(30) *w* believes *y*(. . . *y* . . .) of *x*

we may say:

(31) *w* believes '. . . *y* . . .' satisfied by *x*.

The words "believes satisfied by" here, like "believe of" before, would be viewed as an irreducibly triadic predicate. A similar shift can be made in the case of the other propositional attitudes, of course, and in the tetradic and higher cases.

This semantical reformulation is not, of course, intended to suggest that the subject of the propositional attitude speaks the language of the quotation, or any language. We may treat a mouse's fear of a cat as his fearing true a certain English sentence. This is unnantural without being therefore wrong. It is a little like describing a prehistoric ocean current as clockwise.

How, where, and on what grounds to draw a boundary between those who believe or wish or strive that *p*, and those who do not quite believe or wish or strive that *p*, is undeniably a vague and obscure affair. However, if anyone does approve of speaking of belief of a proposition at all and of speaking of a proposition in turn as meant by a sentence, then certainly he cannot object to our semantical reformulation "*w* believes-true *S*" on any special grounds of obscurity; for "*w* believes-true *S*" is explicitly definable in *his* terms as "*w* believes the proposition meant by *S*." Similarly for the semantical reformulation (31) of (30); similarly for the tetradic and higher cases; and similarly for wishing, striving, and other propositional attitudes.

Our semantical versions do involve a relativity to language, however, which must be made explicit. When we say that *w* believes-true *S*, we need to be able to say what language the sentence *S* is thought of as belonging to; not because *w* needs to understand *S*, but because *S* might by coincidence exist (as a linguistic form) with very different meanings in two languages.[3] Strictly, therefore, we should think of the dyadic "believes-true *S*" as expanded to a triadic "*w* believes-true *S* in *L*"; and correspondingly for (31) and its suite.

As noted two paragraphs back, the semantical form of expression:

(32) *w* believes-true '. . .' in *L*

can be explained in intensional terms, for persons who favor them, as:

(33) *w* believes the proposition meant by '. . .' in *L*,

thus leaving no cause for protest on the score of relative clarity. Protest may still be heard, however, on a different score: (32) and (33), though equivalent to each other, are not strictly equivalent to the "*w* believes that . . ." which is our real concern. For, it is argued, in order to infer (33) we need not only the information about *w* which "*w* believes that . . ." provides, but also some extraneous information about the language *L*. Church[4] brings the point out by appeal to translations, substantially as follows. The respective statements:

w believes that there are unicorns,
w believes the proposition meant by "There are unicorns" in English

go into German as:

(34) *w* glaubt, dass es Einhöƌne gibt,
(35) *w* glaubt diejenige Aussage, die "There are unicorns" *auf Englisch bedeutet,*

and clearly (34) does not provide enough information to enable a German ignorant of English to infer (35).

The same reasoning can be used to show that "There are unicorns" is not strictly or analytically equivalent to:

"There are unicorns" is true in English.

Nor, indeed, was Tarski's truth paradigm intended to assert analytic equivalence. Similarly, then, for (32) in relation to "*w* believes that . . ."; a systematic agreement in truth value can be claimed, and no more. This limitation will prove of little moment to persons who share my skepticism about analyticity.

What I find more disturbing about the semantical versions, such as (32), is the need of dragging in the language concept at all. What is a language? What degree of fixity is supposed? When do we have one language and not two? The propositional attitudes are dim affairs to begin with, and it is a pity to have to add obscurity to obscurity by bringing in language variables too. Only let it not be supposed that any clarity is gained by restituting the intensions.

NOTES

1. See *From a Logical Point of View* (Cambridge, Mass.: Harvard University Press; 1953, 2d ed., 1961), pp. 142–159; also "Three grades of modal involvement," Essay 13 of *Ways of Paradox* (Random House, New York: 1966).

2. See my "Two dogmas of empiricism," in *From a Logical Point of View*, op. cit.; also "Carnap and logical truth," Essay 10 in *Ways of Paradox*, op. cit.

3. This point is made by Church, "On Carnap's analysis of statements of assertion and belief," *Analysis*, 10 (1950), 97–99.

4. Ibid., with an acknowledgment to Langford.

DONALD DAVIDSON

ON SAYING THAT

"I wish I had said that," said Oscar Wilde in applauding one of Whistler's witticisms. Whistler, who took a dim view of Wilde's originality, retorted, "You will, Oscar; you will." The function of this tale (from Holbrook Jackson's *The Eighteen-Nineties*) is to remind us that an expression like "Whistler said that" may on occasion serve as a grammatically complete sentence. Here we have, I suggest, the key to a correct analysis of indirect discourse, an analysis that opens a lead to an analysis of psychological sentences generally (sentences about propositional attitudes, so-called), and even, though this looks beyond anything to be discussed in the present paper, a clue to what distinguishes psychological concepts from others.

But let us begin with sentences usually deemed more representative of *oratio obliqua*, for example "Galileo said that the earth moves" or "Scott said that Venus is an inferior planet." One trouble with such sentence is that we do not know their logical form. And to admit this is to admit that, whatever else we may know about them, we do not know the first thing. If we accept surface grammar as guide to logical form, we will see "Galileo said that the earth moves" as containing the sentence "the earth moves," and this sentence in turn as consisting of the singular term 'the earth', and a predicate, 'moves'. But if 'the earth' is, in this context, a singular term, it can be replaced, so far as the truth or falsity of the containing sentence is concerned, by any other singular term that refers to the same thing.

The notorious apparent invalidity of this rule can only be apparent, for the rule no more than spells out what is involved in the idea of a (logically) singular term. Only two lines of explanation, then, are open: we are wrong about the logical form, or we are wrong about the reference of the singular term.

What seems anomalous behavior on the part of what seem singular terms dramatizes the problem of giving an orderly account of indirect discourse, but the problem is more pervasive. For what touches singular terms touches what they touch, and that is everything: quantifiers, variables, predicates, connectives. Singular terms refer, or pretend to refer, to the entities over which the variables of quantification range, and it is these entities of which the predicates are or are not true. So it should not surprise us that if we can make trouble for the sentence "Scott said that Venus is an inferior planet" by substituting "the Evening Star" for "Venus," we can equally make trouble by substituting "is identical with Venus or with Mercury" for the coextensive "is an inferior planet." The difficulties with indirect discourse cannot be solved simply by abolishing singular terms.

What should we ask of an adequate account of the logical form of a sentence? Above all, I would say, such an account must lead us to see the semantic character of the sentence—its truth or falsity—as owed to how it is composed, by a finite number of applications of some of a finite number of devices that suffice for the language as a whole, out of elements drawn from a finite stock (the vocabulary) that suffices for the language as a whole. To see a sentence in this light is to see it in the light of a theory for its language, a theory that gives the form of every sentence in that language. A way to provide such a theory is by recursively characterizing a truth-predicate, along the lines suggested by Tarski, that satisfies this criterion: the theory entails, for each sentence s (when described in a standardized way), that the truth-predicate holds of s if and only if _____ .—Here the blank is to be filled by a sentence in the metalanguage that is true if and only if s is true in the object language.[1] If we accept Tarski's further requirement that no undefined semantical notions be used in characterizing a truth-predicate, then no theory can satisfy the criterion except by describing every sentence in terms of a semantically significant structure.

A satisfactory theory of meaning for a language must, then, give an explicit account of the truth-conditions of every sentence, and this can be done by giving a theory that satisfies Tarski's criteria; nothing less should count as showing how the meaning of every sentence depends on its structure.[2] Two closely linked considerations support the idea that the structure with which a sentence is endowed by a theory of truth in Tarski's style deserves to be called the logical form of the sentence. By giving such a theory, we domonstrate in a persuasive way that the language, though it consists in an indefinitely large number of sentences, can be comprehended by a creature with finite powers. A theory of truth may be said to supply an effective explanation of the semantic role of each significant expression in any of its appearances. Armed with the theory, we can always answer the question, "What are these familiar words doing here?" by saying how they contribute to the truth-conditions of the sentence. (This is not to assign a 'meaning', much less a reference, to every significant expression.)

The study of the logical form of sentences is often seen in the light of another interest, that of expediting inference. From this point of view, to give the logical form of a sentence is to catalogue the features relevant to its place on the logical scene, the features that determine what sentences it is a logical consequence of, and what sentences it has as logical consequences. A canonical notation graphically encodes the relevant information, making theory of inference simple, and practice mechanical where possible.

Obviously the two approaches to logical form cannot yield wholly independent results, for logical consequence is defined in terms of truth. To say a second sentence is a logical consequence of a first is to say, roughly, that the second is true if the first is no matter how the nonlogical constants are interpreted. Since what we count as a logical constant can vary independently of the set of truths, it is clear that the two versions of logical form, though related, need not be identical. The relation, in brief, seems this. Any theory of truth that satisfies Tarski's criteria must take account of all truth-affecting iterative devices in the language. In the familiar languages for which we know how to define truth the basic iterative devices are reducible to the sentential connectives, the apparatus of quantification, and the desecription operator if it is primitive. Where one sentence is a logical consequence of another on the basis of quantificational structure alone, a theory of truth will therefore entail that if the first sentence is true, the second is. There is no point, then, in not including the expressions that determine quantificational structure among the logical constants, for when we have characterized truth, on which any account of logical consequence depends, we have already committed ourselves to all that calling such expressions logical constants could commit us. Adding to this list of logical constants will increase the inventory of logical truths and consequence-relations beyond anything a truth definition demands, and will therefore yield richer versions of logical form. For the purposes of the present paper, however, we can cleave to the most austere interpretations of logical consequence and logical form, those that are forced on us when we give a theory of truth.

We are now in a position to explain our aporia over indirect discourse: what happens is that the relation between truth and consequence just sketched appears to break down. In a sentence like "Galileo said that the earth moves" the eye and mind perceive familiar structure in the words "the earth moves." And structure there must be if we are to have a theory of truth at all, for an infinite number of sentences (all sentences in the indicative, apart from some trouble over tense) yield sense when plugged into the slot in "Galileo said that _____ ." So if we are to give conditions of truth for all the sentences so generated, we cannot do it sentence by sentence, but only by discovering an articulate structure that permits us to treat each sentence as composed of a finite number of devices that make a stated contribution to its truth conditions. As soon as we assign familiar structure, however, we must allow the consequences of that assignment to flow, and these, as we know, are in the case of indirect discourse consequences we refuse to buy. In a way, the case is even stranger than that. Not only do familiar consequences fail to flow from what looks to be familiar structure, but our common sense of language feels little assurance in any inferences based on the words that follow the 'said that' of indirect discourse (there are exceptions).

So the paradox is this: on the one hand, intuition suggests, and theory demands, that we discover semantically significant structure in the 'content-sentences' of indirect discourse (as I shall call sentences following "said that"). On the other hand, the failure of consequence-relations invites us to treat contained sentences as semantically inert. Yet logical form and consequence relations cannot be divorced in this way.

One proposal at this point is to view the words that succeed the "said that" as operating within concealed quotation marks, their sole function being to help refer to a sentence, and their semantic inertness, explained by the usual account of quotation. One drawback of this proposal is that no usual account of quotation is acceptable, even by the minimal standards we have set for an account of logical form. For according to most stories, quotations are singular terms without significant semantic structure, and since there must be an infinite number of different quotations, no language that contains them can have a recursively defined truth-predicate. This may be taken to show that the received accounts of quotation must be mistaken—I think it does. But then we can hardly pretend that we have solved the problem of indirect discourse by appeal to quotation.[3]

Perhaps it is not hard to invent a theory of quotation that will serve: the following theory is all but explicit in Quine. Simply view quotations as abbreviations for what you get if you follow these instructions; to the right of the first letter that has opening quotation marks on its left write right-hand quotation marks, then the sign for concatenation, and then left-hand quotation marks, in that order; do this after each letter (treating punctuation signs as letters) until you reach the terminating right-hand quotation marks. What you now have is a complex singular term that gives what Tarski calls a structural description of an expression. There is a modest addition to vocabulary: names of letters and of punctuation signs, and the sign for concatenation. There is a corresponding addition to ontology: letters and punctuation signs. And finally, if we carry out the application to sentences in indirect discourse, there will be the logical consequences that the new structure dictates. For two examples, each of the following will be entailed by "Galileo said that the earth moves":

$(\exists x)$ (Galileo said that "the ea" $- x -$ "th moves")

and (with the premise "r = the 18th letter in the alphabet"):

Galileo said that "the ea" - the 18th letter in the alphabet - "th moves"

(I have clung to abbreviations as far as possible.) These inferences are not meant in themselves as criticism of the theory of quotation; they merely illuminate it.

Quine discusses the quotational approach to indirect discourse in *Word and Object*,[4] and abandons it for what seems, to me, a wrong reason. Not that there is not a good reason; but to appreciate *it* is to be next door to a solution, as I shall try to show.

Let us follow Quine through the steps that lead him to reject the quotational approach. The version of the theory he considers is not the one once proposed by Carnap to the effect that "said that" is a two-place predicate true of ordered pairs of people and sentences.[5] The trouble with this idea is not that it forces us to assimilate indirect discourse to direct, for it does not. The "said that" of indirect discourse, like the "said" of direct, may relate persons and sentences, but be a different relation; the former, unlike the latter, may be true of a person, and a sentence he never spoke in a language he never knew. The trouble lies rather in the chance that the same sentence may have different meanings in different languages—not too long a chance either if we count ideolects as languages.

Not that it is impossible to find words (as written or sounded) which express "Empedokles liebt" do fairly well as a German or an English sentence, in one case saying what Empedokles loved and in the other telling us what he did from the top of Etna. We can scoff at the notion that if we analyze "Galileo said that the earth moves" as asserting a relation between Galileo and the sentence "The earth moves" we must assume Galileo spoke English, but we cannot afford to scoff at the assumption that on this analysis the words of the content-sentence are to be understood as an English sentence.[6]

Calling the relativity to English an assumption may be misleading; perhaps the reference to English is explicit, as follows. A long-winded version of our favorite sentence might be "Galileo spoke a sentence that meant in his language what 'The earth moves' means in English." Since in this version it takes everything save "Galileo" and "The earth moves" to do the work of "said that," we must count the reference to English as explicit in the "said that." To see how odd this is, however, it is only necessary to reflect that the English words "said that," with their built-in reference to English, would no longer translate (by even the roughest extensional standards) the French "dit que."

We can shift the difficulty over translation away from the "said that" or "dit que" by taking these expressions as three-place predicates relating a speaker, a sentence, and a language, the reference to a language to be supplied either by our (in practice nearly infallible) knowledge of the language to which the quoted material is to be taken as belonging, or by a demonstrative reference to the language of the entire sentence. Each of these suggestions has its own appeal, but neither leads to an analysis that will pass the translation test. To take the demonstrative proposal, translation into French will carry "said that" into "dit que," the demonstrative reference will automatically, and hence perhaps still within the bounds of strict translation, shift from English to French. But when we translate the final singular term, which names an English sentence, we produce a palpably false result.

These exercises help bring out important features of the quotational approach. But now it is time to remark that there would be an anomaly in a position, like the one under consideration, that abjured reference to propositions in favor of reference to languages. For languages (as Quine remarks in a similar context in *Word and Object*) are at least as badly individuated, and for much the same reasons, as propositions. Indeed, an obvious proposal linking them is this: languages are identical when identical sentences express identical propositions. We see, then, that quotational theories of indirect discourse, those we have discussed anyway, cannot claim an advantage over theories that frankly introduce intensional entities from the start; so let us briefly consider theories of the latter sort.

It might be thought, and perhaps often is, that if we are willing to welcome intensional entities without stint—properties, propositions, individual concepts, and whatever else—then no further difficulties stand in the way of giving an account of the logical form of sentences in *oratio obliqua*. This is not so. Neither the languages Frege suggests as models for natural languages nor the languages described by Church are amenable to theory in the sense of a truth-definition meeting Tarski's standards.[7] What stands in the way in Frege's case is that every referring expression has an infinite number of entitites it may refer to, depending on the context, and there is no rule that gives the reference in more complex contexts on the basis of the reference in simpler ones. In Church's languages, there is an infinite number of primitive expressions; this directly blocks the possibility of recursively characterizing a truth-predicate satisfying Tarski's requirements.

Things might be patched up by following a leading idea of Carnap's *Meaning and Necessity* and limiting the semantic levels to two: extensions and (first-level) intensions.[8] An attractive strategy might then be to turn Frege, thus simplified, upside down by letting each singular term refer to its sense or intension, and providing a reality function (similar to Church's delta function) to map intensions onto extensions. Under such treatment our sample sentence would emerge like this: "The reality of Galileo said that the earth moves." Here we must suppose that "the earth" names an individual concept which the function referred to by "moves" maps onto the proposition that the earth moves; the function referred to by "said that" in turn maps Galileo and the proposition that the earth moves onto a truth value. Finally, the name, "Galileo" refers to an individual concept which is mapped, by the function referred to by "the reality of" onto Galileo. With ingenuity, this theory can accommodate quantifiers that bind variables both inside and outside contexts created by verbs like "said" and "believes." There is no special problem about defining truth for such a language: everything is on the up and up, purely extensional save in ontology. This seems to be a theory that might do all we have asked. Apart from nominalistic qualms, why not accept it?

My reasons against this course are essentially Quine's. Finding right words of my own to communicate another's saying is a problem in translation (216–217). The words I use in the particular case may be viewed as products of my total theory (however vague and subject to correction) of what the originating speaker means by anything he says: such a theory is indistinguishable from a characterization of a truth-predicate, with his language as object language and mine as metalanguage. The crucial point is that within limits there is no choosing between alternative theories which differ in assigning clearly nonsynonymous sentences of mine as translations of his same utterance. This is Quine's thesis of the indeterminacy of translation (218–221).[9] An example will help bring out the fact that the thesis applies not only to translation between speakers of conspicuously different languages, but also to cases nearer home.

Let someone say (and now discourse is direct). "There's a hippopotamus in the refrigerator"; am I necessarily right in reporting him as having said that there is a hippopotamus in the refrigerator? Perhaps; but under questioning he goes on, "It's roundish, has a wrinkled skin, does not mind being touched. It has a pleasant taste, at least the juice, and it costs a dime. I squeeze two or three for breakfast." After some finite amount of such talk we slip over the line where it is plausible or even possible to say correctly that he said there was a hippopotamus in the refrigerator, for it becomes clear he means something else by at least some of his words than I do. The simplest hypothesis so far is that my word "hippopotamus" no longer translates his word "hippopotamus"; my word "orange" might do better. But in any case, long before we reach the point where homophonic translation must be abandoned, charity invites departures. Hesitation over whether to translate a saying of another by one or another of various nonsynonymous sentences of mine does not necessarily reflect a lack of information: it is just that beyond a point there is no deciding, even in principle, between the view that the Other has used words as we do but has more or less weird beliefs, and the view that we have translated him wrong. Torn between the need to make sense of a speaker's words and the need to make sense of the pattern of his beliefs, the best we can do is choose a theory of translation that maximizes agreement. Surely there is no future in supposing that in earnestly uttering the words "There's a hippopotamus in the refrigerator" the Other has disagreed with us about what can be in the refrigerator if we also must then find ourselves disagreeing with him about the size, shape, color, manufacturer, horsepower, and wheel-base of hippopotami.

None of this shows there is no such thing as correct reporting, through indirect discourse, what another said. All that the indeterminacy shows is that if there is one way of getting it right there are other ways that differ substantially in that nonsynonymous sentences are used after "said that." And this is enough to justify our feeling that there is something bogus about the sharpness questions of meaning must in principle have if meanings are entities.

The lesson was implicit in a discussion started some years ago by Benson Mates. Mates claimed that the sentence "Nobody doubts that whoever believes that the seventh consulate of Marius lasted less than a fortnight believes that the seventh consulate of Marius lasted less than a fortnight" is true and yet might well become false if the last word were replaced by the (supposed synonymous) words "period of fourteen days," and that this could happen no matter what standards of synonymy we adopt short of the question-begging "substitutable everywhere *salva veritate*."[10] Church and Sellars responded by saying the difficulty could be resolved by firmly distinguishing between substitutions based on the speaker's use of language and substitutions colored by the use attributed to others.[11] But this is a solution only if we think there is some way of telling, in what another says, what is owed to the meanings he gives his words and what to his beliefs about the world. According to Quine, this is a distinction not there to be drawn.

The detour has been lengthy; I return now to Quine's discussion of the quotational approach in *Word and Object*. As reported above, Quine rejects relativization to a language on the grounds that the principle of the individuation of languages is obscure, and the issue when languages are identical irrelevant to indirect discourse (214). He now suggests that instead of interpreting the content-sentence of indirect discourse as occurring in a language, we interpret it as voiced by a speaker at a time. The speaker and time relative to which the content-sentence needs understanding is, of course, the speaker of that sentence, who is thereby indirectly attributing a saying to another. So now, "Galileo said that the earth moves" comes to mean something like "Galileo spoke a sentence that in his mouth meant what 'The earth moves' now means in mine." Quine makes no objection to this proposal because he thinks he has something simpler and at least as good in reserve. But in my opinion the present proposal deserves more serious consideration, for I think it is nearly right, while Quine's preferred alternatives are seriously defective.

The first of these alternatives is Scheffler's inscriptional theory.[12] Scheffler suggests that sentences in indirect discourse relate a speaker and an utterance: the role of the content-sentence is to help convey what sort of utterance it was. What we get this way is, "Galileo spoke a that-the-earth-moves utterance." The predicate "x is-a-that-the-earth-moves-utterance" has, so far as theory of truth and of inference are concerned, the form of an unstructured one-place predicate. Quine does not put the matter quite this way, and he may resist my appropriation of the terms 'logical form' and 'structure' for purposes that exclude application to Scheffler's predicate. Quine calls the predicate "compound" and describes it as composed of an operator and a sentence (214, 215). These are matters of terminology; the substance, about which there may be no disagreement, is that on Scheffler's theory sentences in *oratio obliqua* have no logical relations that depend on structure in the predicate, and a truth-predicate that applies to all such sentences cannot be characterized in Tarski's style. The reason is plain: there is an infinite number of predicates with the syntax "x is-a-_____ -utterance" each of which is, in the eyes of semantic theory, unrelated to the rest.

Quine has seized one horn of the dilemma. Since attributing semantic structure to content-sentences in indirect discourse apparently forces us to endorse logical relations we do not want, Quine gives up the structure. The result is that another desideratum of theory is neglected, that truth be defined.

Consistent with his policy of renouncing structure that supports no inferences worth their keep, Quine contemplates one further step: he says, ". . . a final alternative that I find as appealing as any is simply to dispense with the objects of the propositional attitudes" (216). Where Scheffler still saw "said that" as a two-place predicate relating speakers and utterances, though welding content-sentences into one-piece one-place predicates true of utterances, Quine now envisions content-sentence and "said that" welded directly to form the one-place predicate "x said-that-the-earth-moves," true of persons. Of course some inferences inherent in Scheffler's scheme now fall away: we can no longer infer "Galileo said something" from our sample sentence, nor can we infer from it and "Someone denied that the earth moves" the sentence "Someone denied what Galileo said." Yet as Quine reminds us, inferences like these may fail on Scheffler's analysis too when the analysis is extended along the obvious line to belief and other propositional attitudes, since needed utterances may fail to materialize (215). The advantages of Scheffler's theory over Quine's "final alternative" are therefore few and uncertain; this is why Quine concludes that the view that invites the fewest inferences is "as appealing as any."

This way of eliminating unwanted inferences unfortunately abolishes most of the structure needed by the theory of truth. So it is worth returning for another look at the earlier proposal to analyze indirect discourse in terms of a predicate relating an originating speaker, a sentence, and the present speaker of the sentence in indirect discourse. For that proposal did not cut off any of the simple entailments we have been discussing, and it alone of recent suggestions promised, when coupled with a workable theory of quotation, to yield to standard semantic methods. But there is a subtle flaw.

We tried to bring out the flavor of the analysis to which we have returned by rewording our favorite sentence as "Galileo uttered a sentence that meant in his mouth what 'The earth moves' means now in mine." We should not think ill of this verbose version of "Galileo said that the earth moves" because of apparent reference to a meaning ("what 'The earth moves' means"); this expression is not treated as a singular term in the theory. We are indeed asked to make sense of a judgment of synonymy between utterances, but not as the foundation of a theory of language, merely as an unanalyzed part of the content of the familiar idiom of indirect discourse. The idea that underlies our awkward paraphrase is that of *samesaying*: when I say that Galileo said that the earth moves, I represent Galileo and myself as samesayers.

And now the flaw is this. If I merely *say* we are samesayers, Galileo and I, I have yet to *make* us so; and how am I to do this? Obviously, by saying what he said; not by using his words (necessarily), but by using words the same in import here and now as his then and there. Yet this is just what, on the theory, I cannot do. For the theory brings the content-sentence into the act sealed in quotation marks, and on any standard theory of quotation, this means the content-sentence is mentioned and not used. In uttering the words "The earth moves" I do not, according to this account, say anything remotely like what Galileo is claimed to have said; I do not, in fact, say anything. My words in the frame provided by "Galileo said that _____" merely help refer to a sentence. There will be no missing the point if we expand quotation in the style we recently considered. Any intimation that Galileo and I are samesayers vanishes in this version:

Galileo said that 'T' 'h' 'e' '' 'e' 'a' 'r' 't' 'h' '' 'm' 'o' 'v' 'e' 's'

We seem to have been taken in by a notational accident, a way of referring to expressions that when abbreviated produces framed pictures of the very words referred to. The difficulty is odd; let's see if we can circumvent it. Imagine an altered case. Galileo utters his words "Eppur si muove," I utter my words, "The earth moves." There is no problem yet in recognizing that we are samesayers: an utterance of mine matches an utterance of his in purport. I am not now using my words to help refer to a sentence; I speak for myself, and my words refer in their usual way to the earth and to its movement. If Galileo's utterance "Eppur si muove" made us samesayers, then some utterance or other of Galileo's made us samesayers. The form "$(\exists x)$ (Galileo's utterance x and my utterance y makes us samesayers)" is thus a way of attributing any saying I please to Galileo provided I find a way of replacing 'y' by a word or phrase that refers to an appropriate utterance of mine. And surely there is a way I can do this: I need only produce the required utterance and replace 'y' by a reference to it. Here goes:

The earth moves.
$(\exists x)$ (Galileo's utterance x and my last utterance make us samesayers).

Definitional abbreviation is all that is needed to bring this little skit down to:

The earth moves.
Galileo said that.

Here the "that" is a demonstrative singular term referring to an utterance (not a sentence).

This form has a small drawback in that it leaves the hearer up in the air about the purpose served by saying "The earth moves" until the act has been performed. As if, say, I were first to tell a story and then add, "That's how it was once upon a time." There's some fun to be had this way, and in any case no amount of telling what the illocutionary force of our utterances is is going to insure that they have that force. But in the present case nothing stands in the way of reversing the order of things, thus:

Galileo said that.
The earth moves.

Perhaps it is now safe to allow a tiny orthographic change, a change without semantic significance, but suggesting to the eye the relation of introducer and introduced: we may suppress the stop after "that" and the consequent capitalization:

Galileo said that the earth moves.

Perhaps it should come as no surprise to learn that the form of psychological sentences in English apparently evolved through about the stages our ruminations have just carried us. According to the *Oxford English Dictionary*,

The use of *that* is generally held to have arisen out of the demonstrative pronoun pointing to the clause which it introduces. Cf. (1) He once lived here: we all know *that*; (2) *That* (now *this*) we all know: he once lived here; (3) We all know *that* (or *this*): he once lived here; (4) We all know *that* he once lived here . . .[13]

The proposal then is this: sentences in indirect discourse, as it happens, wear their logical form on their sleeves (except for one small point). They consist of an expression referring to a speaker, the two-place predicate "said," and a demonstrative referring to an utterance. Period. What follows gives the content of the subject's saying, but has no logical or semantic connection with the original attribution of a saying. This last point is no doubt the novel one, and upon it everything depends: from a semantic point of view the content-sentence in indirect discourse is not contained in the sentence whose truth counts.

We would do better, in coping with this subject, to talk of inscriptions and utterances and speech acts, and avoid reference to sentences.[14] For what an utterance of "Galileo said that" does is announce a further utterance. Like any utterance, this first may be serious or silly, assertive or playful; but if it is true, it must be followed by an utterance synonymous with some other. The second utterance, the introduced act, may also be true or false, done in the mode of assertion or of play. But if it is as announced, it must serve at least the purpose of conveying the content of what someone said. The role of the introducing utterance is not unfamiliar: we do the same with words like "This is a joke," "This is an order," "He commanded that," "Now hear this." Such expressions might be called performatives, for they are used to usher in performances on the part of the speaker. A certain interesting reflexive effect sets in when performatives occur in the first-person present tense, for then the speaker utters words which if true are made so exclusively by the content and mode of the performance that follows, and the mode of this performance may well be in part determined by that same performative introduction. Here is an example that will also provide the occasion for a final comment on indirect discourse.

"Jones asserted that Entebbe is equatorial" would, if we parallel the analysis of indirect discourse, come to mean something like, "An utterance of Jones' in the assertive mode had the content of this utterance of mine. Entebbe is equatorial." The analysis does not founder because the modes of utterance of the two speakers may differ; all that the truth of the performative requires is that my second utterance, in whatever mode (assertive or not) match in content an assertive utterance of Jones. Whether such an asymmetry is appropriate in indirect discourse depends on how much of assertion we read into saying. Now suppose I try: "I assert that Entebbe is equatorial." Of course by saying this I may not assert anything; mood of words cannot guarantee mode of utterance. But if my utterance of the performative is true, then I do say something in the assertive mode that has the content of my second utterance—I do, that is, assert that Entebbe is equatorial. If I do assert it, an element in my success is no doubt my utterance of the performative, which announces an assertion; thus performatives tend to be self-fulfilling. Perhaps it is this feature of performatives that has misled some philosophers into thinking that performatives, or their utterances, are neither true nor false.

On the analysis of indirect discourse just proposed, standard problems seem to find a just solution. The appearance of failure of the laws of extensional substitution is explained as due to our mistaking what are really two sentences for one: we make substitutions in one sentence, but it is the other (the utterance of) which changes in truth. Since an utterance of "Galileo said that" and any utterance following it are semantically independent, there is no reason to predict, on grounds of form alone, any *particular* effect on the truth of the first from a change in the second. On the other hand, if the second utterance had been different in any way at all, the first utterance *might* have had a different truth value, for the reference of the "that" would have changed.

The paradox, that sentences (utterances) in *oratio obliqua* do not have the logical consequences they should if truth is to be defined, is resolved. What follows the verb "said" has only the structure of a singular term, usually the demonstrative "that." Assuming the "that" refers, we can infer that Galileo said something from "Galileo said that"; but this is welcome. The familiar words coming in the train of the performative of indirect discourse do, on my account, have structure, but it is familiar structure and poses no problem for theory of truth not there before indirect discourse was the theme.

Since Frege, philosophers have become hardened to the idea that content-sentences in talk about propositional attitudes may strangely refer to such entities as intensions, propositions, sentences, utterances and inscriptions. What is strange is not the entities, which are all right in their place (if they have one), but the notion that ordinary words for planets, people, tables and hippopotami in indirect discourse may give up these pedestrian references for the exotica. If we could recover our pre-Fregean semantic innocence, I think it would seem to us plainly incredible that the words "The earth moves," uttered after the words "Galileo said that," mean anything different, or refer to anything else, than is their wont when they come in other environments. No doubt their role in *oratio obliqua* is in some sense special; but that is another story. Language is the instrument it is because the same expression, with semantic features (meaning) unchanged, can serve countless purposes. I have tried to show how our understanding of indirect discourse does not strain this basic insight.

ACKNOWLEDGMENTS

I am indebted to W. V. Quine and John Wallace for suggestions and criticisms. My research was in part supported by the National Science Foundation.

NOTES

1. Alfred Tarski, "The Concept of Truth in Formalized Languages," in *Logic, Semantics, Metamathematics* (Oxford: 1956), pp. 152–278 . The criterion is roughly Tarski's Convention *T* that defines the concept of a truth-predicate.
2. The view that a characterization of a truth-predicate meeting Tarski's criteria is the core of a theory of meaning is defended in my "Truth and Meaning," *Synthèse* 17 (1967) 304–323.
3. For documentation and details see my "Theories of Meaning and Learnable Languages,"

in *Logic, Methodology and Philosophy of Science, Proceedings of the 1964 International Congress*, ed. Yehoshua Bar-Hillel (Amsterdam: 1965), pp. 388–390.

4. *Word and Object* (Cambridge, Mass.: 1960) chapter VI. Hereafter numerals in parentheses refer to pages of this book.

5. R. Carnap, *The Logical Syntax of Language* (London: 1937), p. 248. The same was in effect proposed by P. T. Geach, *Mental Acts* (London: 1957).

6. The point is due to A. Church, "On Carnap's Analysis of Statements of Assertion and Belief." *Analysis* 10 (1950) 97–99.

7. G. Frege, "On Sense and Reference," in *Philosophical Writings*, ed. P. Geach and M. Black (Oxford: 1952) and A. Church, "A Formulation of the Logic of Sense and Denotation," in *Structure, Method, and Meaning: Essays in Honor of H. M. Shetter* ed. Henie, Kallen and Langer (New York: 1951).

8. R. Carnap, *Meaning and Necessity* (Chicago: 1947). The idea of an essentially Fregean approach limited to two semantic levels has also been suggested by Michael Dummett (in an unpublished manuscript). Neither of these proposals is in detail entirely satisfactory in the light of present concerns, for neither leads to a language for which a truth-predicate can be characterized.

9. My assimilation of a translation manual to a theory of truth is not in Quine. For more on this, see the article in reference 2.

10. B. Mates, "Synonymity," in *Meaning and Interpretation* (Berkeley: 1950), pp. 201–226. The example is Church's.

11. A Church, "Intensional Isomorophism and Identity of Belief." *Philosophical Studies* 5 (1954) 65–73; W. Sellars, "Putnam on Synonymity and Belief." *Analysis* 15 (1955) 117–20.

12. I. Scheffler, "An Inscriptional Approach to Indirect Quotation." *Analysis* 14 (1954) 83–90.

13. J. A. H. Murray et al., eds., *The Oxford English Dictionary* (Oxford: 1933) vol. XI, p. 253. Cf. C. T. Onions, *An Advanced English Syntax* (New York: 1929), pp. 154–156. I first learned that "that" in such contexts evolved from an explicit demonstrative in J. Hintikka, *Knowledge and Belief* (Ithaca: 1962), p. 13. Hintikka remarks that a similar development has taken place in German and Finnish. I owe the reference to the *O.E.D.* to Eric Stiezel.

14. I assume that a theory of truth for a language containing demonstratives must strictly apply to utterances and not to sentences, or will treat truth as a relation between sentences, speakers, and times. The point is discussed in "Truth and Meaning." (see note. 2).

STEVEN WEISLER

AN OVERVIEW
OF MONTAGUE SEMANTICS

Although some logicians consider human languages too vague and ambiguous to yield to logical analysis, others have attempted to modify and to extend their techniques in order to explore the system of meaning and patterns of deduction in natural languages. One such logician is Richard Montague, whose article "The Proper Treatment of Quantification in Ordinary English" (PTQ) has had a tremendous impact on the direction of semantic theory since its publication in 1973. In this essay I attempt to convey some of the importance, scope, and direction of Montague's approach to the semantics of English. I will proceed by identifying and describing some of the problems addressed in PTQ, and then by characterizing the principles and analyses developed in Montague's quite technical work.[1] Often, before considering Montague's proposals directly, I first discuss more standard analyses upon which Montague seeks to improve. The problems are divided into three major sections: Reference, Truth-Conditions, and Inference.

REFERENCE

Montague's grammar is, among other things, an attempt to provide an explicit account of meaning. Consequently, we begin by considering what a theory of meaning (a *semantic theory*) ought to accomplish, and, more basically, what sort of thing a meaning is. This extremely vexed question has received a number of different answers. Meanings have been variously treated as concepts, entities in a Platonic heaven, objects, and behaviors. Some philosophers have even come to the conclusion that it does not make sense to talk about meanings, *per se* (Austin, 1962).

As a starting assumption, language is construed as a symbolic system in which forms of expression stand for (or *refer* to) things. Suppose, furthermore, that what an expression refers to—its *semantic value*—is its meaning.[2] This tack is perhaps most intuitive in the case of names; it is natural to say that the name "Churchill" refers to Churchill and that this exhausts its meaning.[3]

The approach can be extended to other parts of the language as well. One-place predicates, for example, intransitive verbs such as "smoked," would have as their semantic value a set of individuals, in this case, {individuals who smoked}.[4] Since sets can also be represented by enumerating their members, the set may also be represented as "{Churchill, Groucho Marx, George Burns, . . .}."

Montague's own treatment of the interpretation of verbs (and other one-place predicates) incorporates the insight captured by the set-theoretic approach in a somewhat different manner. His analysis, which has the advantage of rendering the computation of the meanings of complex expressions easier, takes the semantic value of an intransitive verb to be a characteristic function rather than a set.[5] A characteristic function is a relation between individuals[6] and the truth-values "True" and "False." Intuitively, for a given verb, those individuals who "have" the property expressed by the verb will be mapped into "True," and those that do not will be mapped into "False." The function assigned to "smoked" can be (partially) represented as follows.

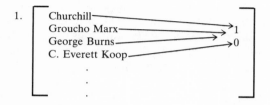

"1" is the abbreviation Montague uses for "True," and "0" stands for "False." Notice that the individuals who are mapped into "1" by the function are precisely those individuals who are members of the set of those who smoked. Furthermore, anyone who hasn't smoked—the complement of this set—is mapped into "0." A characteristic function, then, partitions the domain of individuals into two sets. On this view, knowing the meaning of "smoked" amounts to being able to distinguish those who have smoked from those who have not.[7]

Having determined the semantic value of "Churchill" and of "smoked," it remains to consider the semantic value of the sentence "Churchill smoked." Following Frege's suggestion, Montague adopts the principle that the semantic value of a (simple) sentence is a truth-value (i.e., "True" or "False"). Furthermore, Montague also incorporates Frege's insight that semantic interpretation must be *compositional*. That is, the semantic value of a sentence must be calculable on the basis of the semantic values of the parts of the sentence. In the case at hand, we can determine the truth value of "Churchill smoked" by applying the function denoted by the verb to the individual denoted by the subject. This involves evaluating the function in (1) for the argument for which "Churchill" stands (namely, Churchill). The result is "True," just as we would suspect.[8]

The goal, in this calculation, is to formalize the notion of semantic value by characterizing the relationship between expressions in a language (in this case, English) and the world. However, formal semantic theories (and PTQ, in particular) do not characterize the fit between English and the actual world directly.[9] Instead, Montague adopts a *model-theoretic* approach to meaning which specifies the meaning of a sentence by describing the way the world must be for a given sentence to be true. This description of the world is rendered by detailing which individuals have which properties. In the course of assigning an interpretation to a sentence in the fragment, the grammar of PTQ establishes which of the descriptions of the world are consistent with the truth of that sentence, and which are not.

Let us, then, provisionally accept the claim that to know the meaning of a word involves knowing what it can properly be used to refer to, and that the reference, or semantic value, of a term is the object or function that it picks out, like Churchill for "Churchill"[10] or the function (partially) described in (1) for "smoked." There remain a range of classical problems, many of which were noted by Frege (1892), that complicates this attempt to recruit an account of reference as a theory of meaning. PTQ addresses many of these problems, often deploying neo-Fregean solutions by adopting and formalizing some of Frege's most basic assumptions and distinctions.

Cognitive Value

The first question to be considered concerns the proper relationship between a theory of reference and a theory of meaning. Consider the following pairs of examples:

2a. Churchill
2b. The PM of England during WWII

3a. Nixon is Nixon.
3b. Nixon is the only U.S. president to have resigned.

Notice that the members of each of these pairs differ in meaning in as much as they have a different *cognitive value*—they express different information. Consequently, a theory of meaning must be able to distinguish the interpretation of each member of the pair from the other. Unfortunately, as long as we identify reference (semantic value) and meaning, we will be unable to do so. In the case of (2), for example, while each expression refers to Churchill, only (2a) does so by naming him. (2b), by contrast, is a description, whose rather different meaning in presumably constructed from the meanings of its parts. Furthermore, whereas the name "Churchill" necessarily picks out Churchill, the description in (2b) only *happens to be true* of Churchill. It could have been, for instance, that Chamberlain retained that office. Thus, although both expressions refer to the same individual, they do not characterize that individual in the same way. If we adopt a style of semantic analysis that fails to distinguish meaning from reference, we will not account for the possibility that coreferential expressions can differ in meaning.

Sentences (3a) and (3b) make this point in a slightly different way. (3a) is a logical, or a necessary, truth; it is impossible for it to be false. (3b), however, while also true, is true not in virtue of the laws of logic, but rather in virtue of the facts of history. It could have been otherwise; for instance, if the burglars hadn't been caught, or if the tapes had been burned, etc. This difference in logical status ought to be reflected by a difference in the meaning of the two sentences, despite their agreement in truth-value, and despite the fact that the description in (3b) picks out exactly the same individual as the name it replaces in (3b). In particular, our semantic theory must be consistent with the fact that (3a) is a *necessary truth*, while (3b) is only a happenstance, or *contingent truth*.

Seeing how Montague approaches these problems requires a digression to explore some of the basic underpinnings of the PTQ grammar. We begin with Frege's famous distinction between *sense* and reference, drawn precisely to challenge the position that meaning is reference. The idea of sense is less concrete than that of reference. It is the aspect of the meaning of a word in virtue of which you understand it, and in virtue of which it succeeds in picking out its referent. For a sentence, the sense is the way it describes the world, which, if accurate, makes it true, and, if inaccurate, makes it false. Sense is therefore the feature of a linguistic expression that *determines* its reference, and it is *what the mind grasps* when it understands an expression. The key to the solution of the puzzles in (2) and (3), Frege argued, lies in the introduction of sense as the meaning of linguistic expressions.

It follows from these considerations that the sense of a sentence is not its truth-value, but rather *what makes the sentence true or false*. Similarly, the sense of a predicate expression is not the function to which it refers, but rather *what makes the predicate expression refer to that function*. The sense of a sentence is a characterization of what the world must be like if the sentence were true, and the sense of a predicate expression is the property that a thing would have to have in order to be in the set described by that predicate.

To incorporate these ideas, Montague formalizes a distinction between *intension* and *extension* that is parallel to and inspired by Frege's sense/reference distinction. Part of the reason for the terminological change is that for Montague (but not for Frege), the construct of a possible world plays a crucial role in characterizing these notions. Consequently, to understand Montague's intensions, we must first understand his conception of a possible world. A (logically) possible world is any way the world might have been, consistent with logic. The PTQ model includes these *counterfactual* descriptions of the world, in addition to descriptions of how it, in fact, is. With this enrichment of the model, we can account for sentences making reference to possibility or necessity. For example, one way of construing "Nixon could have remained in office" would be "There is a possible world in which Nixon remained in office."

We can formalize intensions by developing the rough and ready notions of sense sketched a few paragraphs ago more carefully using possible worlds. To begin with, let us consider the intensions of names. The semantic function of a name is to pick out an individual. "Nixon," for instance, picks out Nixon. Since we want to be able to interpret sentences like "It was possible for Nixon to burn the tapes." by describing its meaning in terms of possible worlds, we must be able to find a reference (an extension) for "Nixon" at randomly chosen possible worlds. Furthermore, to guarantee that we are making counterfactual claims about *Nixon*, "Nixon" must have Nixon as its extension at each of these worlds. Proper names of this sort, (sometimes called *rigid designators*) designate the same individual at all possible worlds. Thus, the intension of such a name is the constant function which picks out its bearer at each world.[11] It is this function, rather than merely the relation between "Nixon" and Nixon in the actual world, that must be grasped by anyone who knows what "Nixon" means.

We consider the intensions of predicate expressions, next. The intension of a predicate expression is called a *property*, a usage which accords pretty much with our ordinary language meaning of the world "property." Recall that understanding a word like "smokes" requires that I understand *what it is to smoke*. Using possible worlds semantics, this amounts to what it takes to qualify for membership in the set of smokers in any possible world. More precisely, the intension associated with a predicate is a function from each possible world and time to the characteristic function corresponding to the set of things "in" the reference of that predicate expression at that world and time. The intension of "smokes" specifies, for the actual world, a characteristic function corresponding to the set of actual smokers, and, in another world, one corresponding to the set of smokers in that world, etc.

Finally, let us consider the intension of a sentence, also called a *proposition*. Following Frege, Montague develops a compositional analysis of propositions. That is, the intension of a sentence is composed out of the intension of the subject of the sentence and the intension of the predicate of the sentence. As in the case of the semantic value (the extension) of a sentence, this combination can be accomplished by applying functions to arguments (*functional application*).[12] Once composed, a proposition is a function from possible worlds to truth values which describes the set of worlds in which the sentence is true. Accordingly, grasping the meaning of a sentence involves knowing its intension, and knowing the intension requires being able to determine the truth-value of the sentence in any circumstance (possible world).

It is intension (rather than reference) that specifies the interpretation of a sentence. Although it may seem strange at first to identify the interpretation of a sentence with (a function that describes) a set of possible worlds, this amounts to the claim that when someone asserts a sentence, such as "Grass is green," for that sentence to be true is for this world (the *actual world*) to be in the set of worlds in which grass is green. If they had said, "Grass is purple," we would have understood that sentence, and known it to be false, because the actual world is not in the set of purple-grassed worlds. The important thing to see is that although this sentence is false, we know what it would be for that sentence to be true, viz., for one of the possible worlds with purple grass to be the actual one.

To sum up, on Montague's account, when we understand the meaning of an expression we grasp not its reference, but rather its intension. The intension of an expression, together with the way the world is, determines its extension. We can now return to our problematic pairs of sentences, and consider the basis of Montague's solution.

2a. Churchill
2b. The PM of England during WWII

3a. Nixon is Nixon.
3b. Nixon is the only U.S. president to have resigned.

First, recall that although each expression in (2) picks out Churchill, only (2a) does so by naming him. (2b), by contrast, is a description that characterizes him from a particular perspective. Furthermore, unlike the former, the latter only *happens* to describe Churchill. Montague's account of the differences in these examples turns on the observation that each expression has a different way of designating its referent. "Churchill" refers to Churchill, as does "the PM of England during WWII," but on Montague's analysis, the intension of "Churchill" will pick out Churchill at every possible world, while the semantic value of "the PM of England during WWII" will pick out, at each world, whoever happens to hold that office. In the actual world, these intensions determine the same reference, explaining the truth of "Churchill was the PM of England during WWII." But our intuition that this fact is merely happenstance is accounted for by the ways in which the values of the two intensions diverge across possible worlds. Although in the *actual* world, being the PM was one of Churchill's properties, it is not so at all possible worlds. In other worlds, it is *possible* that Churchill was not PM during WWII. In this way, we explain both the sameness of reference of these expressions (Churchill) and their difference in intension (Churchill at all worlds vs. whoever, at each world, is PM of England during WWII, at that world).

Turning now to (3a), notice that both occurrences of "Nixon" pick out Nixon at every world. So, taking "is" to require identity between its two arguments, it follows that (3a) is true at all possible worlds and times. Furthermore, the identity is guaranteed as a point of logic, explaining the necessity of the proposition. In contrast, although the intension of "Nixon" picks Nixon out at all worlds, the intention of "the only U.S. president to have resigned" picks out different individuals at different worlds. Moreover, worlds in which the latter intension picks out an individual distinct from Nixon are those in which (3b) is false, establishing that the truth-value of (3b) depends on the way the world happens to be. In this fashion, we can explain how these two sentences express different propositions, both true, but one true necessarily, and one merely contingently.

Indexicality

A second problem concerns expressions that appear to vary in reference depending on the context of use. In such cases, it is not clear how to capture the relationship between a term and its semantic value, since the latter seems to fluctuate. Terms in natural languages that display this property, including 'I,' "you," "now," and "here," are said to be indexical because they refer to different entities at different times when used by different speakers in different situations. When I use 'I,' I refer to myself; when you use it, you refer to yourself. "Now" refers to *this* moment, now, but a different one when used at different times. The account of the interpretation of such expressions and of sentences that contain them requires a specification of how to fix the reference of these expressions depending upon these situational variables.

Montague does not provide a complete account of indexicality in PTQ, but does include a partial analysis of one indexical aspect of English, tense. Like certain pronouns and adverbials, the interpretation of tensed sentences requires establishing a temporal point of reference. For example, "Churchill smoked," a simple past-tense assertion, is true only when spoken at times after he acquired the habit. It was not true at his birth, nor at any time prior to that event. More generally, sentences of natural languages can only be evaluated for truth or falsity relative to a moment of utterance and with respect to a time frame.

In order to address these matters of tense and time, Montague incorporates the future and past operators "H" and "W" into his logical system, as well as an interpretation procedure which evaluates an expression relative to a time index. In effect, these operators function as sentence modifying adverbs (e.g., "heretofore") by adjusting the time frame in which an assertion must describe the world in order for the sentence to be true. Montague formalizes this interpretation of tense markers by again appealing to the notion of a possible world.

Previously we saw that a possible worlds model includes, but is not exhausted by, a description of the actual world at a given moment of utterance.

To incorporate the interpretation of tensed sentences, the model must now specify not only the way the world is, and the present counterfactual alternatives, but also all the ways it might have been and all the ways it might well be. This specification will include, of course, all the actual ways the world was, and all the actual ways it will turn out to be. On this view, we can determine that "Churchill smoked," uttered at high noon on January 2, 1985, was true provided that at some moment of time prior to the moment of utterance the world was such that the sentence "Churchill smokes." was true. "It is possible that Churchill didn't drink" is true if there is some possible world prior to the moment of utterance and consistent with the laws of logic in which the sentence "Churchill drinks." is *false*.[13]

Function Words and Connectives

Another problem confronting any attempt to equate reference with meaning concerns the interpretation of non-nominal, non-verbal expressions which lack any obvious referent. Function words, for example, the conjunctions "and" and "or," (and certain other logical expressions) are cases in point. If we take the referent of an expression to be its meaning, then such expressions would apparently count as meaningless. One standard approach involves interpreting these logical words *syncategorematically*. That is, instead of assigning each expression to some general syntactic category and associating it with whatever type of interpretation members of that category receive, we assign these expressions a special interpretation. One way of accomplishing this employs truth tables. For example, the table for conjunction looks like this:

4. *and*

P	Q	P&Q
T	T	T
T	F	F
F	T	F
F	F	F

This table indicates that if "P" and "Q" are any two sentences, and "P&Q" is their conjunction, the latter will be true if and only if both of the former are.

In Montague's grammar, these logical expressions are interpreted in an equivalent, syncategorematic manner using a series of biconditional statements that establish the way in which the interpretations of complex sentences depend on the interpretations of their constituitive sentences. These statements have the general flavor of the subordinate clause in last sentence of the previous paragraph.[14]

Quantifiers and the FOPC

In addition to the function words just considered, there are several type of nominal expressions not obviously susceptible to a referential analysis. For instance, it is not clear what individual it might be that the subject noun phrase "Nothing" refers to in (5).

5. Nothing eats.

Once again, the apparent problem is that there *is* no individual for *nothing* to refer to. If we take a word's meaning to be its referent, and reference is a relation between words and things in the world, then we would expect the subject of this sentence to be meaningless, which of course it is not.

One way of providing a systematic interpretation of this data involves deploying the first order predicate calculus (FOPC).[15] By translating a sentence of English into FOPC we reveal its *logical form* for the purpose of clarifying the structure and interpretation of its meaningful constituents. The FOPC representation of (5) will be:

6. $(\forall x)[\sim x \text{ eats}]$

or equivalently,

7. $\sim(\exists x) [x \text{ eats}]$

"$(\forall x)$," the universal quantifier, is read as "for all x. . . .," "$(\exists x)$," the existential quantifier, as "there exists an x such that . . . ," and "$\sim$" (negation) as "it is not the case that. . . ." A universal quantifier also appears in the first order translation of (8).

8. Everything eats $=> (\forall x)[x \text{ eats}]$

An existential quantifier would appear in prenex position (i.e., before the brackets) in the following case:

9. Something eats $=> (\exists x)[x \text{ eats}]$

English expressions involving quantification, which seem not to have any obviously referential interpretation, can often be represented in this fashion. Notice, however, that by merely translating expressions in English into expressions in the FOPC, we have not actual interpreted (i.e., provided the meaning for) the English expressions. Rather, we have only established an equivalence between the English expressions and corresponding expressions in a logical system. A full semantic theory, however, must accomplish more than mere translation.[16]

To complete the analysis, we must provide interpretation procedures for logical forms. Informally,[17] the rules of interpretation for (9) will, among other things, have us check for at least one individual in the world who eats. The existence of such an individual is required for the truth of the expression.

Similarly, after translating (5) into the predicate calculus, we require rules of interpretation for the expressions in (6), or (7). The method of interpretation for examples such as (6) involves considering each thing in a given possible world in turn, and checking whether it is mapped to true by the function corresponding to "eats." If none are, (6) is true, and so is (5), since we are taking the former to represent the meaning of the latter. Such procedures for interpreting the predicate calculus account for the meaning of an expressions in the sense that they reveal the conditions under which the expression would be true (its *truth-conditions*).

Although Montague Grammar is a *truth-conditional semantics*, and it incorporates an analysis of quantification, Montague departs from the standard FOPC analysis to remedy certain inadequacies of this system in representing meanings. In this regard, Montague develops a complicated logical system called IL-Intensional Logic. Every sentence in the fragment of English analyzed in PTQ is translated into a formula of IL, and it is the latter that is interpreted in the model. Semantic values and intensions are assigned to expressions in IL, and are therefore only indirectly associated with the corresponding English expressions by the translation relation. For example, the verb "smokes" translates into the IL expression "smoke'," and the semantic value of "smoke' " will be the appropriate characteristic function.[18]

In many cases, expressions in IL can be translated into equivalent, simpler expressions in the first order system. However, there is a residue of interesting cases, some of which we turn to now, in which the more complex representations of IL seem to be required.

Uniformity

Among the issues Montague addresses in PTQ is the matter of how to assign meanings to syntactically complex phrases systematically. In this regard, the FOPC is problematic in that it violates the principle that there should be a uniform interpretation procedure available for all (possibly structurally distinct) members of a single syntactic category. This is a theoretical premise which Montague adopts in the interest of achieving generality in the interpretation procedure, as well as the closest possible fit between the syntactic and semantic rules of the grammar.

Unfortunately, were we to adopt the proposed account of noun phrases, we would run afoul of Montague's principle of uniformity. Although both "Churchill" and "everything" are syntactic noun phrases, each receives a different type of interpretation in the FOPC. The former expression, a proper name, is taken to refer to an individual, and the latter, a quantificational expression, is analyzed along the lines of (8), above. Consequently, in order to honor his principles of uniformity, Montague is forced to reconsider the analysis of proper names as well as that of quantificational expressions.

He begins by calling into question our simple initial assumption to the effect that the semantic values of names are simply their bearers, and the corresponding claim that intensions of proper names are functions that pick out their bearer in each possible world. This must be modified, Montague argues, if we are to achieve a uniform analysis of noun phrases. Montague's solution involves assigning a function which picks out *not* the named individual, but rather *the set of his/her/its/properties* as the semantic value of a proper name. In other words, proper names are treated as abbreviations for the bundle of properties possessed by the named individual. The corresponding intension is a function from worlds and times to property sets.[19] In the case of "Churchill," the intension tells us what Churchill might have been like in any logically possible world.

Although this reanalysis of proper names may seem intuitively farfetched, recall that the motivation for considering it was to see if it can be applied to quantificational expressions (as well as to proper names). Indeed, as Montague demonstrates, this interpretive maneuver can be so generalized. Rather than taking a quantified noun phrase like "every book" to be represented by universal quantification in a FOPC formula, we can take its semantic value to be the set of properties that every book has. The intension of "every book" will be a function from possible worlds to the set of properties common to every book in each world. Thus, both quantificational expressions and proper names can be taken to denote bundles of properties and to express the corresponding intensions allowing us to maintain a single type of interpretation for all noun phrases.

This analysis of quantifiers also has an additional advantage over the FOPC in that it allows us to identify a separate, well-formed, coherent semantic value for determiners such as "every" and "some." "Every," for example, will stand for a function that applies to the interpretation[20] of a common noun (the characteristic function corresponding to the set of books in the case of "book") to yield a function which combines with the interpretation of a predicate expression to yield the semantic value of a sentence (its truth-value). In other words, determiners are construed as functors which combine with the interpretation of the common noun they modify and that of a predicate expression, to form the interpretation of a sentence. Thus, not only does Montague's reanalysis of quantificational expressions render them consistent with his principle of interpretational uniformity across a syntactic category, but, unlike the FOPC analysis of quantifiers, it also observes compositionality.[21]

Opacity

Yet another problem with the FOPC analysis of quantificational expressions, and arguably the most important one dealt with in PTQ, concerns the interpretation of these expressions in certain linguistic contexts called *opaque contexts*. Opaque contexts are generally introduced by certain verbs and prep-

ositions, most notoriously by those verbs which introduce propositional attitudes. Such contexts have three defining properties: (1) expressions within
them are subject to nonspecific interpretations, (2) certain existential commitments normally set up by referring expressions are canceled, and (3) substitutions of coreferential expressions do not necessarily preserve truth-value.
Let us restrict our attention to nonspecificity and existential entailment, for
now, since the third characteristic is best treated in the section on deduction.

Quine has pointed out, in sentences such as (10),

10. I want a sloop.

the (informal) first-order representation in (11)

11. $\exists x$ [x is a sloop & I want x]

". . . is suitable in so far only as there may be said to be a certain sloop that
I want. If what I seek is mere relief from slooplessness, then [(11)] gives the
wrong idea." (Quine [1956]). Quine calls the two interpretations (10) *notional*
and *relational*, respectively, but they are more commonly referred to as *de
re* (= relational) and *de dicto* (= notional). The hallmark of interpretation *de
dicto* is a kind of non-specific interpretation which attaches to expressions
such as "a sloop" in (10). That is, for (10) to be true, there need be no
particular sloop that I desire. Unfortunately the standard interpretation in
(11) requires that there be such a sloop, suggesting, as Quine notes, that it
is an inadequate representation of the *de dicto* reading of (10).

One of the interesting features of PTQ is that Montague treats sentences
admitting of a *de re ≠ de dicto* ambiguity as *syntactically* ambiguous. For example, in the case of (10), the *de re* reading is derived syntactically by combining "a sloop" with "John seeks it," yielding "John seeks a sloop" with an
interpretation equivalent to "A sloop is such that John seeks it." Thus, although there are some additional complications involved, Montague's analysis
of the *de re* interpretation of examples such as (10) pretty much follows the
outlines of Quine's proposed analysis.[22]

In the case of interpretation *de dicto*, the syntactic analysis is more conventional, with the direct object being directly incorporated into the verb
phrase by a rule forming predicates out of verbs and objects. Montague's
semantic analysis of these constructions again follows the work of Frege.
Frege argued that within contexts which manifest opacity, an expression fails
to denote its normal reference, taking on instead an *indirect reference*. For
example, although the sentence "Albany is the capital of New York" normally
designates the value "True," obviously it is contributing more than its truth-
value to the interpretation of the sentence "Jean believes Albany is the capital
of New York." Jean does not merely believe a true thing, but rather a particular true thing, viz., the proposition that Albany is the capital of New York.
Frege concludes that the indirect reference of an expression is its normal

sense, thereby explaining how it is that the object of Jean's belief is a proposition instead of a truth-value.[23]

Although Montague adopts the core of this strategy, he is not able to selectively incorporate Frege's distinction between direct and indirect reference on pain of violating the uniformity principle requiring every member of a single syntactic category to receive the same type of interpretation (see above). Therefore, Montague incorporates the translation of *every* term into composed expressions of IL as if it established indirect reference, requiring a reduction to the normal case in nonopaque contexts (in which direct reference is achieved) by other principles and conventions. He achieves this composition by a principle known as *intensional functional application* under which functions (e.g., the semantic values of one-place predicates) take as arguments the intensions, rather than the semantic values, of incorporated expressions. Somewhat counterintuitively, then, Montague treats every occurrence of a noun-phrase argument[24] as a potentially opaque occurrence.

In the of (10), for example, Montague forms the semantic value of "wants a sloop" by combining the intension of "a sloop" with the semantic value of "wants" to form the property of wanting a sloop. Since the intension of "a sloop" is (roughly) the property of being a sloop, the object of my desire will be modeled as a complex function (from possible worlds to bundles of sloop properties at each world) rather than as any individual sloop, doing justice to the nonspecific, *de dicto* interpretation we are after. Thus, when the interpretation of the subject is incorporated, the sentence will be true if and only if the property of seeking some sloop (or other) is among my properties in the actual world.[25]

This analysis also explains why the truth of (10) on its *de dicto* interpretation does not require the existence of a sloop. The absence of existential entailment may be brought out by considering the *de dicto* interpretation of (10′).

10′. John wants a unicorn.

In this case, it is clear that John may be truly said to want a unicorn despite the fact that none exist (compare "John kicked a unicorn," which does require that one exist). Montague explains this quality of interpretation *de dicto* by construing the semantic value of "a sloop" in (10′), and in (10), as an intensional function rather than as an object. Of course this function will fail to pick out any unicorn properties in the actual world (in consequence of the lack of unicorns), and in other possible worlds it will pick out the relevant sets of properties, but what John wants is independent of the zoological fact of the matter. His desire is a relation to what we may loosely call the concept of a unicorn, leaving open the question of whether or not there is any such thing.

Montague applies this intensional analysis to other opaque contexts, as well, including those introduced by verbs taking sentential complements (e.g., "believes"), verbs taking infinitival complements (e.g., "try"), and intensional prepositions (e.g., "about"). Consequently, in all of the following examples Montague accounts for the possibility of both the *de re* and the *de dicto* interpretations of "a fish."

11. John believes that a fish walks.

12. John tries to find a fish.

13. John talks about a fish.

Finally, Montague is also able to account for *de dicto* interpretations of pronouns, as in the following example.

14. John wishes to catch a fish and eat it.

In additional to the *de re* reading on which John has a certain fish in mind which he wants to catch and eat, there is a second, *de dicto* interpretation on which any fish will serve. In this case, "it" does not refer to any particular fish, which Montague accounts for by translating it into an expression in IL that designates a set of properties rather than as a variable that ranges over individuals.

Truth-Conditions

One of the central principles developed in PTQ is that to know the meaning of a sentence is to know the conditions under which it is true, or, alternatively, to know what makes it true, or how the world would have to be for it to be true. In this spirit, we have seen that PTQ involves the systematic translation of sentences of a natural language (English) into a logical language, taken together with an interpretation procedure for the latter that assigns truth-conditions to the logical formulae. This truth conditional approach to semantics is combined in PTQ with another crucial assumption—compositionality, viz., that the meanings of sentences and other constituents are built up out of the meanings of their parts.

Before examining the composition of interpretations in PTQ, let us see how truth-conditions are composed in a first order language by considering the following example:

15. Churchill smokes $=>$ smoke (Churchill).

What are the semantic values of the constituent expressions? In the case of the argument, Churchill, the semantic value is the WWII prime minister of Great Britain. We write this as:

16. ⟦Churchill⟧ = Winston Churchill

reading the "⟦ . . . ⟧" notation as "the semantic value of . . . ," and taking the expression on the right hand side of the " = " to denote the man. What, then, does "smoke" have as its semantic value? Putting aside the matter of the tense (or time frame) of the verb, we have analyzed the semantic value of intransitive verbs as characteristic functions, in this case,

17. ⟦smoke⟧ =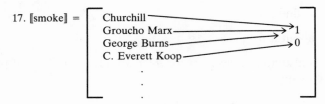

Given that ⟦Churchill⟧ is Winston Churchill, and ⟦smoke⟧ is the function given in (17), it remains to calculate the semantic value of the sentence as a whole, bringing together the ideas of compositionality and truth-conditionality. Inasmuch as the semantic value of the subject of this sentence is an individual, and the semantic value of the predicate is a characteristic function, we can compose these semantic values to get the semantic value of the sentence (e.g., "True" or "False") by applying the function to the argument. The truth value of a sentence such as (15), then, can be computed by applying the rule in (18).

18. If a formula $\mathcal{F}$ has the structure $\ulcorner \beta(\propto) \urcorner$ where β is a one-place predicate and $\propto$ is a term, then $⟦\mathcal{F}⟧ = 1$ iff $⟦\beta⟧\,(⟦\propto⟧ = 1$.

In the case of (15), this amounts to asking whether

19. ⟦smoke⟧ (⟦Churchill⟧) = 1

which, of course, it does.

The analysis in PTQ, however, requires a different pattern of composition, owing to the rather different assumptions about the type of interpretation assigned to noun-phrases. That is, since noun-phrases are treated as denoting functions from properties to truth values, Montague treats the semantic value of the subject noun phrase as a functor and the semantic value of the predicate expression as the argument. Furthermore, since Montague uses intensional functional application to compose complex semantic values, the function corresponding to the subject will take the *intension* of the predicate expression as its argument, rather than the semantic value of the predicate, itself. The composition that Montague adopts is roughly like that in (20).

20. If a sentence φ has the structure $\ulcorner \beta\alpha \urcorner$ where β is a noun-phrase and α is an intransitive verb-phrase, then $⟦\varphi⟧ = 1$ iff $⟦\beta'\,(^\wedge\alpha')⟧ = 1$.

The single quotation mark means "the translation in IL of. . . ," so that "β' " stands for the translation of "β" (the subject of the sentence) into IL. The "$\wedge$" stands for "the intension of. . . ." Thus, the expression "$\wedge\alpha'$ " stands for the intension of the IL translation of "α," which is the predicate, in this case. In turn, $[\![\beta'(\wedge\alpha')]\!]$ will be "True" if the result of applying the function corresponding to the translation of the subject ($[\![$Churchill$']\!]$) to the intension of the translation of the predicate ($[\![\wedge$smoke$']\!]$) is the value "1," as indicated in (21).

21. $[\![$Churchill smokes$]\!]$ = 1 iff $[\![$Churchill$']\!]([\![\wedge$smoke$']\!])$ = 1

Since the semantic value of Churchill$'$ will be Churchill's property set, and since this set contains the property of smoking, "Churchill smokes," comes out true, as we would expect.

Notice that in the case of (21), the intensionality of "$\wedge$smoke$'$ " is "absorbed" in the functional composition. That is, since the semantic value of "Churchill$'$ " is a function from intensions (i.e., properties) to "True" or "False," the semantic value assigned to "$[\![$Churchill$']\!]([\![\wedge$smoke$']\!])$" will be a truth value rather than a proposition. Consequently, (21) is not treated as involving an opaque context, and its interpretation is quite similar to that rendered by the FOPC.

Nevertheless, Montague also exploits the technique of intensional functional application to compose the interpretations of phrasal constituents that do manifest opacity. For example, the composition of verbs with their complements and prepositions with their objects is accomplished in this way. In the case of the *de dicto* interpreteation of (10$'$), for example, the composition of the translation into IL will have the following structure.[26]

22. John$'(\wedge$want$'(\wedge$a unicorn$'))$

Again in this case, the semantic value of the whole sentence will be a truth value since "John$'$ " stands for a function from properties (e.g., the property of wanting a unicorn) to truth-values. It is the second intensionality operator introducing "a unicorn$'$ " that accounts for the intensional interpretation of the direct object. Since the want relation in (22) is a relation-in-intension rather than a relation to an object, it does not place John in the want relation to a particular unicorn. His desire may be more general yet still be consistent with the truth of (22). In this way, the *de dicto* character of (10$'$) is accounted for as a consequence of Montague's system of translation and interpretation.

Scope Ambiguities

Another famous puzzle Montague treats involves the interpretation of quantificationally ambiguous sentences. In the following examples, the sentences each have two different interpretations.

23a. Blik is not available in all areas.

23b. Someone voted for everyone.

Sentence (23a) can be used both to assert that the product is available only in some areas, or that it is available in none. (23b) means either that someone voted multiple times until he or she cast votes for everyone, or that no one failed to receive a vote (with the votes coming from potentially different voters). Part of the interest in these examples lies in the fact that their ambiguity does not appear to derive from ambiguities in word meaning.

Montague concludes that there must be two different ways of combining the interpretations of its constituent parts to produce the interpretations of a complete sentence. In the case of (23a), for example, the crucial issue is *when* we factor the interpretation of negation into the interpretation of the sentence. In other words, (23a) can be construed as asserting either (24) or (25).

24. It is not the case that [Blik is available in all areas]

25. For all areas, it is not the case that [Blik is available in them]

Notice that in (24), the negation qualifies the quantifier "all," whereas in (25) it applies only to the constituent sentence "Blik is available in them." There are two ways of assigning relative *scope* to the negation operator and the quantifier. In (24), negation has *wide scope* over the quantifier "all," because the quantifier occurs inside the range of negation (i.e., within the brackets); in (25), the quantifier has wide scope, because it occurs outside of the range of the negation.

We can see that there is a similar scope contest at work, this time between two quantifiers, in (23b). Its two interpretations may be represented in the first order predicate calculus as (28) and (29), where the former reading describes voter fraud, and the latter, the usual state of affairs.

28. $(\exists x)\,(\forall y)\,(x$ voted for $y)$

29. $(\forall y)\,(\exists x)\,(x$ voted for $y)$

As in the case of the scope of negation, Montague treats the problem of relative quantifier scope as a consequence of when the interpretation of each quantifier is factored in to the composition of the interpretation of the whole sentence. To accomplish this, Montague takes sentences like (23) to be *syntactically* ambiguous, just as in the case of sentences manifesting the *de re de dicto* distinction. For example, on the reading captured in (28), (23) would be built up syntactically out of the subject "Someone"[27] and the predicate "voted for every candidate," parallel to the cases of interpretation *de dicto*, discussed above.[28] In the case of the reading represented in (29), (23) is built up out of "everyone" and the open sentence "Someone voted for him" (cf.

"Everyone is such that someone voted for him"). This is reminiscent of the composition we observed earlier in the derivation of *de re* interpretations. The systematic interpretation of the logical forms produced from these two types of syntactic derivations capitalizes the difference in composition to account for the two alternative scope interpretations.

INFERENCE

One of the challenges to any formal semantic theory is to provide an account of natural deduction. For example, our native ability to reason tells us that it is legitimate to infer (30c) if (30a) and (30b) (which we call the premises of the argument) are true.

30a. Johnny is a whale

30b. All whales are mammals

Therefore

30c. Johnny is a mammal

but that the conclusion in (31c) does not follow from (31a) and (31b).

31a. Johnny is a mammal

31b. All whales are mammals

Therefore

31c. Johnny is a whale

Logicians have traditionally investigated the logical structure of arguments such as these to determine how to distinguish valid arguments (i.e., those arguments whose conclusions *must* be true if their premises are true) from invalid arguments (those arguments the truth of whose conclusion is not entailed by the truth of their premises).

One standard approach to categorizing valid arguments involves translating the sentences which represent them into the first-order predicate calculus, and seeing whether or not the conclusion of a given argument can be proven on the basis of the premises along with certain axioms and rules of deduction. In the case of the argument given in (30), above, the representation of the argument would be as follows.

32a. $W(j)$
32b. $\forall x[W(x) \supset M(x)]$[29]

Therefore

32c. $M(j)$

Our goal is to prove (32c) from (32a–b) and the axioms and rules of deduction. In this case, we begin by using a rule called Universal Instantiation to infer (32d) from (32b).

(32d. W(j)⊃M(j)

Applied to (32b), what Universal Instantiation guarantees is that if everything that is W is M, then surely if j is W, it will be M. In other words, it allows us to infer a specific case from a general premise.

The second rule of inference which applies in this case is *Modus Ponens*, which has the following form:

33. If P implies Q (is true)
and P (is true)
then Q (follows)

Along with (32a) and (32d), *Modus Ponens* allows us to infer (32c), proving that (30) is a valid argument.

Substitutivity

Montague was interested in certain argument forms that, although not valid, could not be distinguished from other valid argument forms using the resources of the first order predicate calculus coupled with a theory of natural deduction. For example, although (34) is a valid argument, (35) is not.

34a. John is Bill. (cf. Samuel Clemens is Mark Twain.)
34b. John smiles.
34c. (Therefore) Bill smiles.

35a. The temperature is ninety.
35b. The temperature rises.
35c. (Therefore) Ninety rises.

In the case of (34), (34c) comes from (34a–b) by a rule known as substitutivity of identicals. In a predicate calculus representation, the argument would look like this:

36a. j = b
36b. S(j)
36c. (Therefore) S(b)

The rule of substitutivity allows that two expressions that are equal—that have the same semantic value—may be intersubstituted *salva veritate* (preserving truth-value). Unfortunately, Montague notes that while (35) would seem to require the same type of representation,[30] (35c) does not follow from (35a–b). He is, therefore, obliged to provide different analyses of these two types of arguments in his framework.

In the first case, each of the two names will pick out the property set associated with the bearer of the name. As was mentioned earlier, proper names are rigid designators in PTQ. That is to say, they pick out a property set corresponding to the *same individual* in each possible world. Consequently, "Bill" and "John" name the same individual in the actual world, and the semantic values of each name will be identical, and since "smiles" is a property of individuals, free intersubstitutivity is justified. In the second case, although "ninety" rigidly designates the same number in every possible world, "the temperature" corresponds to different numbers in different worlds. Furthermore, Montague treats "rises" (actually, "rise' ") as a property of *individual concepts*[31] rather than of individuals (e.g., numbers). To assert (35b), on this analysis, is to claim that the function that picks out the number that is the temperature in a given possible world is such that the values it returns in other worlds (e.g., temporally later worlds) are progressively higher.[32] "The temperature," then, corresponds to different individuals than "ninety" does in many possible worlds, and since "rise' " sensitive to these differences in interpretation, we would not expect "ninety" and "the temperature" to substitute for one another *salva veritate*.

Substitutivity and Opacity

Another problem concerning inferential reasoning addressed in Montague's PTQ concerns deduction in opaque contexts. Consider the following pair of sentences.

37a. Carmen is a bat.
37b. Carmen is a winged mammal.

Sentences (37a) and (37b) are both true. But Fred, who can always recognize a bat when he sees one, and knows Carmen well, believes that bats are birds. So, (38a) is true, while (38b) is false:

38a. Fred believes that Carmen is a bat.
38b. Fred believes that Carmen is a winged mammal.

Montague's semantic theory seeks to explain how this is possible[33] despite the sameness in semantic value of "bat," and "winged mammal," and of (37a) and (37b), coupled with the fact that (38a) and (38b) are alike in all respects except for the substitution of expressions that don't differ in ordinary reference. We have another apparent failure of substitutivity: the principle that coextensional expressions may be inter-substituted without affecting the interpretation of sentence. To address this problem, Montague again appeals to his account of intensionality.

How does taking intensionality into account solve the problem of substitutivity in (37)–(38)? First, note that the intentions of "a bat" and "a winged mammal" are different functions. Although every bat is a winged mammal in the actual world (and vice versa), this is not necessarily so—in some possible worlds, the extensions diverge. Consequently, the intention associated with each expression is a different function (from possible worlds and times to characteristic functions). Finally, since their intensions are different, and the semantic values of the two expressions *are* their respective intensions (since they appear in an opaque context),[34] their semantic values are different. This explains why these terms are not intersubstitutable in (38). The principle that semantically identical terms are intersubstitutable is maintained, but "a bat" and "a winged mammal" are judged not to be identical because their intensions diverge.

In Montague's system, this is accomplished since the semantic value of an expression in an opaque contexts is equivalent to its normal intension. Indeed, as we pointed out earlier, it is a consequence of Montague's scheme of translation that *every* phrasal expression functioning as an argument contributes its intension to the interpretation, ultimately requiring a special analysis for the *transparent* (i.e., non-opaque) contexts.

Central to this explanation are some crucial assumptions about sentences such as (38), which involve the attribution of belief. Belief states, and other related states, sometimes called *propositional attitudes*, are treated in PTQ as connecting persons to *propositions*. This is as opposed to the semantic values of the sentences they believe (truth values, on the current analysis), or to the things referred to by the constituents of those sentences (objects and functions).

We can exploit this analysis to explain how Fred can maintain the belief expressed by (38a) without simultaneously holding that expressed by (38b). In this case, the semantic value (i.e., the intension) of "Carmen" picks Carmen's property set out in every world, and the intensions of "a bat" and of "a winged mammal" pick out property bundles that correspond to some bat and some winged mammal, respectively, at each world. Now, at this world, those are the same functions, and if what Fred believed was related in some simple way just to the extension of either (37a), (37b), or of any of the normal extensions of their constituents, we would not be able to account for how it is that (38a) and (38b) differ in truth value. But by taking the object of Fred's belief to be a proposition composed out of the intensions of the constitutive parts, we can observe that there are plenty of *possible* worlds in which {bats} does not equal {winged mammals}. Fred simply takes the actual world to be one of those in which Carmen, while a member of {bats}, is not a member of {winged mammals}. Since the intensions (i.e., the semantic values) associated with "a bat" and "a winged mammal" contain characteristic functions that pick out different sets in *some* possible worlds, we have a sufficiently rich apparatus to describe Fred's (mistaken) beliefs about where the functions diverge. So long as belief is a relation between believers and intensional objects, rather than the extensions of the sentences that express them, or to the extensions of their constituents, we can distinguish (38a) from (38b).

SUMMATION

Montague's PTQ provides a precise analysis of a number of semantic puzzles, many of which have resisted solution in less powerful frameworks. By combining the resources of intensions, tense logic, model theory, quantification theory, and more, he was able to approach the semantics of quantifiers, propositional attitude constructions, pronouns, names, the copula, and various modifiers in a systematic framework that forms the point of departure for much recent work on natural language semantics. Furthermore, as a formalization of many of Frege's original insights, Montague's work contributes to the investigations of neo-Fregean semantics, which are central to the current discourse in philosophy of language. Even as the letter of Montague's proposals invites critical scrutiny, undergoes adaptations, and catalyzes alternatives, the importance of his outstanding work is assured. For perhaps more than any other logician, he has shown the way to revealing the logic of natural linguistic systems.

NOTES

1. The goal is not to put the reader in a position to read Montague's work but merely to introduce the main ideas behind it. For one thing, some of the detail of Montague's analysis is often ignored so as not to obscure the main point. There is, moreover, no discussion of the system of categorial syntax that Montague employs. The reader who wishes to tackle PTQ is advised to consult Partee (1975), and Dowty, Wall, and Peters (1981).

2. Below meaning will be distinguished from semantic value, but for now they can be considered equivalent.

3. Cf. Mill (1849), this volume, p. 8, for example.

4. We postpone a discussion of the tense (or time frame) of the verb. The "0" notation is the usual notation from set theory for a set.

5. It also makes different commitments about the nature of meanings and what it is to grasp a meaning. For example, knowing how to compute a characteristic function is different from knowing which members of the domain are mapped to "True" by that function.

6. Actually, the domain of these characteristic functions is somewhat different in PTQ for reasons having to do with opacity. See below.

7. Specifying precisely the sense in which competent speakers know how to do this, however, is problematic. See Partee (1981) for discussion.

8. For reasons we consider below, in PTQ, Montague adopts a different pattern of composition.

9. Actually, in two senses. Below we consider the second issue concerning translation into the logical language, IL.

10. In PTQ, Montague adopts a more complicated analysis of names and other referring expressions. We return to this point below.

11. For all we have said so far, we could take the function to map from possible worlds

and times to the bearer of the name in each world and time. However, Montague takes the function to map into property sets of individuals, for reason discussed below.

12. We consider the details in the section on truth-conditions, below.

13. Here and elsewhere I use "possible worlds" as a shorthand for "possible worlds and times."

14. Montague also considers the interpretation of certain nonsentential conjunctions and disjunctions (e.g., "the man or the woman" and "runs and talks"), which requires a more complicated analysis. Other nonlogical function words, for example, prepositions, require a rather different tack involving complex functions. The determiners "the," "a," and "every," discussed separately in the next section on quantification, receive another sort of syncategorematic analysis. Finally, Montague addresses the interpretation of various kinds of adverbs, which are also treated as standing for particular kinds of complex functions. For all these matters, see Dowty, Wall, and Peters (1981).

15. See Dowty, Wall,and Peters (1981), among many other sources, for details.

16. In fact, Montague believed that translations into a logical language were a matter of convenience rather than of necessity, and that direct interpretations of English expressions could be provided at the cost of some complication of his analysis. For an example, see Montague (1970).

17. See Dowty, Wall, and Peters (1981) for the details.

18. Not all of the translations into IL look so much like English expressions, and so this example is a bit misleading. Verbs, with the exception of the copula, do however, systematically translate into primed uninflected cognates in IL. The prime notation is also used in an attributive sense by Montague to mean "the translation of . . . ," *whatever it may be*. For instance, whatever the IL expression that translates "about" is, "about' " is a shorthand way of referring to that translation. In order to avoid the details of IL, we will frequently use the prime notation in this second manner to talk about expressions in IL. See Dowty, Wall, and Peters (1981) for more details.

19. Put functionally, the intension will be a function from possible worlds to functions from properties to truth values.

20. Actually, Montague combines it with the *intension* of the common noun in the interest of generalizing his analysis of opacity. See below (and Dowty, Wall and Peters (1981) for more details).

21. Montague also takes up the issue of the interpretational uniformity of the verb "to be," arguing that the "is" of predication and the "is" of identity are essentially the same. See Dowty, Wall, and Peters (1981) for details.

22. That is, although Montague initially translates quantificational expressions as expressions that denote property sets (see above), in the case of *de re* interpretation these can be reduced to formulae that are virtually equivalent to a first-order representation. See Dowty, Wall, and Peters (1981) for details.

23. See the discussion of substitutivity in opaque contexts, below, for further discussion of this point.

24. In fact, *every* argument is treated in this way so that every expression in an opaque context has the possibility of indirect reference.

25. Extensional verbs, such as "kicks," "eats," etc., do not allow a *de dicto* interpretation (compare "I kicked a sloop" to (10), above). To handle such cases, Montague reduces "potential" *de dicto* interpretations to *de re* interpretations by establishing restrictions on the model known as *meaning postulates*. The postulates require that each member of the set of worlds consistent with the truth of a sentence lacking a *de dicto* interpretation is also consistent with the corresponding *de re* interpretation. See Dowty, Wall, and Peters (1981) for details.

26. Montague treats the interpretation of transitive verbs such as "wants" as combining with intensions of noun phrases to form intransitive verb-*phrase* interpretations. In other words,

after "wants' " combines with (the intension of) its direct object, the function associated with the composed predicate is the same type as that associated with an intransitive verb. That is because after a transitive verb is saturated with a direct object, it acts like a derived one-place predicate. The resulting verb phrase interpretation will always involve a *relation-in-intension* since the intension of the direct object serves as the argument to the verb interpretation. It is this general appeal to intensional functional application that requires a special reduction in the case of extension verbs that do not support intensional interpretations. See note 25 and Dowty, Wall, and Peters (1981) for further discussion.

27. Actually, Montague only treats quantified noun-phrases with lexical nouns (e.g., "some fish") in PTQ but the extension is straightforward.

28. This doesn't mean that (23) receives a *de dicto* interpretation, but only that Montague is able to use the same technique of composition to account for quantifier/quantifier ambiguities that he uses to account for *de re ≠ de dicto* ambiguities.

29. The "⊃" symbol stands for implication—the logical connective meaning "if . . . then." Thus, (32b) is read "For all things x, if x is W then x is M."

30. Except for the difference that "The temperature" is a quantifier expression. This difference is independent of the problem with the rule of substitution at issue. See notes 31 and 32, below.

31. Individual concepts are functions from possible worlds to individuals. These are not to be confused with the semantic values associated with proper names (i.e., functions from possible worlds to functions from properties to truth values).

32. More specifically, Montague analyzes "the temperature" as a quantificational expression in which the bound variable ranges over functions from worlds and times to individuals. It is satisfied by the number that is the temperature at each world and time (clearly different numbers in different worlds).

33. Although Montague does not discuss this particular example (since there is no analysis of adjectives in PTQ), he considers others of this sort.

34. See the discussion of opacity, above.

MURRAY KITELEY

SUBJECTIVITY'S BAILIWICK:
and the person of its bailiff

I have just broken a convention of scope. Titles should not trespass into texts, as this title does. This rule perhaps explains the convention that places a peer's given names before, and therefore outside, his title. Bertrand Arthur Willian Third Earl Russell is properly said or written thus, *de re*; only a younger son's title or an honorary one is given *de dicto*, as in Lord Jeffery Amherst. Primogeniture forbids exportation.

The scope of titles is of little importance to semantics and less to philosophy. But that is not true of scope in general. The unmarked scope of quantifier noun-phrases in "everyone loves someone," and the resultant ambiguity, requires the machinery of the predicate calculus for its unraveling; and the idea that the verbs of propositional attitude affect the semantics of their content clauses is just the idea that these clauses are within their semantic scope.

The kind of scope in question here, then, is broadly semantic: it is that sort of semantic dependency between the parts of a sentence or between the sentences themselves that can affect their meaning and truth. When the scope is uncertain, so also is the meaning and truth. It is not syntactic scope, not, e.g., the sort that governs wh-movement. ("What did she ask for" rather than "she asked for what.") It is rather that piquant uncertainty as to which modifier has superior scope over which in the phrase, "the little used bookstore," and in Russell's sentence, "I thought your yacht was much larger than it is," (above) an uncertainty that infects their meaning. Is the store, its books, or its custom little? Are the books new or used? Is the size of the yacht thought to be other than it is? Or is it thought to be other than it is thought to be? In contrast, the conventional order of Russell's names and his title, or of adjectives in a noun-phrase—"big round red ball" rather than "red round big ball"—lacks semantic significance.

This is not to say that how titles work in the language is not linguistically significant. The title line of Dylan Thomas's poem, "A Solitary Mister in the

Park," uses the titular noun "mister" in a purposefully unconventional way. The convention that is violated by this figure of speech is one of language even if not clearly one of meaning.

The topics of opacity, scope, and compositionality, in a word, intensionality, can be pursued in either of two directions, for either of two different ends, one purely semantic, one psychostructural.

But first a word on what they are.

The ancient Babylonians discovered that the evening star is the morning star, but they already knew that the evening star was the evening star (see Frege and Russell above). The two descriptions describe the same heavenly body. Why should it matter to the meaning or the truth of the sentence how Venus is described? That it does matter means that the sentence is opaque (Quine) to coreferential substitution. Such normally unaffecting substitutions here affect meaning and truth.

The Latin word "nihil" means nothing, yet it does mean something. This apparently contradictory state of affairs results from the uncertain scope of the operator expressed by "nothing." If its scope is wide, saying that there is nothing that "nihil" means, we get a falsehood; if it is narrow, saying "nihil" means nothing, we get a true translation. If one were to build up the meaning of "the little used bookstore" by first putting together the meanings of "little" and "store" rather than by first combining "little" and "used," the meaning of the phrase would come out very differently. Scope thus gives the order in which compound meanings are to be composed, and if this order is not indicated, as it is not in Aristotle's "a man can walk while sitting" (*On Sophistical Refutations*, 166a22–30), then structural ambiguity or amphiboly occurs. (The conjunction of walking and sitting is not possible, but one can conjoin the possibility of walking with sitting.)

These phenomena have played a prominent role in twentieth-century semantics by initiating two broad lines of investigation. One line follows Russell in seeing intensionality as a clue to the logical form of mental representation at the level of belief and the other propositional attitudes. The other follows Frege in seeing it as an obstacle to simple referential (Bedeutungs) compositionality. The distinction Russell draws [in "On Denoting" reprinted in this volume] between the primary and secondary occurrence of a denoting phrase that appears in a propositional attitude sentence is one of scope, and this connects to substitutivity. George IV wondered whether Scott was the author of *Waverley*. If the authorial description is outside the scope of his wonder, it is fair and true to say he wondered whether Scott was Scott. Otherwise not. The substitution preserves the meaning and truth of the original sentence when the term substituted has primary occurrence, i.e., wide scope. Otherwise not. It thus seemed fair to think that human subjectivity as we report it in speech draws within its boundaries designating expressions that have only secondary, intensional, or opaque meaning. Quine observed [in the essay reprinted in this volume] that opacity interacts also with generalization. Generalization (quantification) reaches out over positions in a sentence that are sometimes indicated by pronouns: "All snakes are oviparous and *they* are also cold-blooded." Scope thus is integral both to the expression of propositional attitudes and to quantification into and within them. Their mixture, picturesquely called quantifying-in and exporting-out (David Kaplan), is, unsurprisingly, troublesome.

These semantic phenomena, these ills of meaning, however, have a much wider occurrence than just in the reports of propositional attitudes and the intentions to act, as the examples above suggest. They appear across the semantic landscape. This was first observed by Quine and made a prime explanandum of Montague's semantics (see Weisler). I shall argue that although their causes are various, many having nothing to do with modality or mentality, the most apt general description of them is impurity. It is not that these unsubstitutable, ungeneralizable, unexportable expressions have some other kind of meaning that calls for an intensional semantics, it is rather that they do more than simply designate their extensions.

I shall nonetheless follow custom and use the word "intensionality" as a catchall for them, on the weak classificatory grounds that they succumb to a treatment that translates the language of their expression into intensional logic (see Weisler in this volume). It is plain that intensional phenomena are not simply those involved in the expression of human cognition, nor even those that further turn on modalities such as the one expressed by Aristotle's "can" above.

If the phenomena of intensionality are seen as semantic ills, or at least as anomalies, cures, or explanations are needed, and two have been advanced. One is Quotationalism and the other is Intensionalism. They both postulate an odd kind of context-imposed lexical ambiguity. Both go back to Frege, but the second more obviously than the first. Intensionalism, having supposed two kinds of meaning, intensional and extensional, says that oblique or propositional attitude contexts operate on their content clauses to call forth the former kind of meaning. Thus substitution on the grounds of coextensionality is fallacious where only intensional meaning is operative and where only cointensionality is relevant. Granted, e.g., that "the evening star" and "the morning star" have the same extension, granted they both designate Venus, the discovery that the evening star is the morning star must not be collapsed via coextensional substitution into the discovery that the evening star is the evening star. Both Quotationalism and Intensionalism prevent this collapse. The words designating Venus are very different and so are the intensions or senses of those words. But note that this means the discovery was not about a heavenly body.

Quotationalism hypothesizes that every opaque or nonsubstitutional context is either an overt or a covert quotation in which the words appear as a syntactic device for naming themselves rather than what they ordinarily name. In indirect discourse the words quoted belong to the language of the tongue, but in beliefs they belong to the language of the mind.[1]

A consequence of both Intensionalism and Quotationalism is the doctrine that all expressions are potentially ambiguous, even such determiners or model-theoretic expressions as "a," "some," and "most." They mean one thing when within the scope of a report of someone's speech or subjectivity and possibly another thing outside such a scope. In designing a model, e.g., for a language both with the determiner "most" and a subjectivity operator, one would need subjective as well as objective finite domains to serve as "most"-measures. Truth-conditions for the sentence "I hope most of the people voted that we canvased" will differ depending on whether it is understood *de re* or *de dicto*, depending, i.e., on whether the meaning of "most" is measured objectively or *de re* against the number of the assumed population, say the 200 who were canvased, or whether it is measured subjectively or *de dicto* against the number the speaker mistakenly has in mind, say 100. Most would be 150 or more in the first case, and 75 or more in the second.

There is a further uncertainty. The count got by using the appropriate subjective measure for "most" may vary depending on how well the speaker's criteria of voter individuation match those of the local political machine. Does the speaker, for example, naively think that all voters must be alive? The count, thus, as well as the measure may be subjective.

A way of describing half of this amphiboly or structural ambiguity is as a contest in scope between "most" and "hope." The subjective or *de dicto* reading gives "hope" superior scope over "most", thus quantifying *within* the hoped for content; the objective or *de re* does the opposite, thus quantifying *into* what is hoped. The additional opaque and transparent readings add a further semantic option and thus a new layer of subjective ambiguity. But what is the cash value of superiority of scope? How does it alter meaning? According to Intensionalism, the meaning of an expression within the scope of an intensionalizing operator is its intension; outside the meaning is its extension. Quotationalism is analogous: Within the quotha operator the expression refers to itself or its mentalese counterpart, but outside it refers as usual.

Intensionalism and Quotationalism are both wrong. Neither gives the right account of why one cannot substitute another coreferential description, such as "my ward boss" for "my plumber" in "my plumber overcharges for his services." It is hardly plausible that the economic predicate sets a context in which these two noun-phrases come to designate themselves, their mentalese counterparts or their intensions. They still designate my plumber even if that is not all they do, even if in addition they impurely help to determine which services are in question.

Impure uses of the parts of speech, uses in which the expression does more than purely or simply designate its extension, vary widely. Compare the three opaque sentences "Giorgione (= Barbarelli) is so-called for his size," "$2/6$ (= $1/3$) is more than $2/7$ and it has an even denominator," and "the author of *Waverley* (= the author of *Marmion*) denines he wrote it." These three sentences and the resultant ones got by the indicated substitution have nothing in common except their opacity or intensionality, which raises doubts about the naturalness of this semantic natural kind. Their opaque designators do three different things in addition to their primary job of designating the painter, the ratio, and the author: self-reference in the first, reference to a divisor that with the appropriate dividend yields the quotient/ratio, and in the third, provision of an antecedent for the *it* Scott wrote.

This doctrine I espouse, the doctrine that (almost) every time a designator designates impurely, every time it, so to speak, hyper-designates, it also designates in the ordinary nonintensional way, needs a trivial qualification and supports a nontrivial implication. The qualification is for ordinary quotation as distinct from the putative obliquity of belief and also for fictional designation that fails for reasons other than its impurity: in the sentence "Mrs. Malaprop was so-called for her solecisms," the lady's name is nonreferential not because it is impurely used to aid in the reference to itself, but because it is fictional. The nontrivial implication has to do with scope, with the *de re–de dicto* distinction. If all intensionality is a matter of impure designation, and if all impure designation is a combination of ordinary and hyper-designation, then the scope distinction between wide scope *de re* occurrences of a designator and narrow scope *de dicto* occurrences collapses. All occurrences are in part *de re* in that their dictive and hyper-designative layer is simply added. The distinction can, however, be rehabilitated as a distinction between pure and impure occurrences of a designator; and only those occurrences that are pure are substitutable. One can, e.g., substitute "$1/3$" for $2/6$" when it is used purely to pick out the ratio, as it is so used in "$2/6$ is more than $2/7$."[2]

The semantic programs of Intensionalism and Quotationalism have usually been restricted to the content-sentences of propositional attitudes, and the sentences in which a modal operator appears. Such sentences admittedly provide striking examples of scope amphiboly. Quine's "the number of planets might have been even" and George IV's curiosity regarding the authorship of *Waverley* as recorded by Russell tug us both ways in the structural ambiguity. It is not possible that nine should have been even (wide scope), but certainly there might have been eight planets (narrow scope).

The one thing common to all these phenomena is scope amphiboly. Opacity is a partial exception, in that some failures of the substitutivity of identicals arise from causes other than a substitution-induced change in scope-valence, e.g., $2/6$ (= $1/3$) has an even denominator.

The scope, however, need not be that of a subjectifying or intensional-izing operator outside of which terms may stand *de re*, having been, to use the movement metaphor, exported.

II. DEPICTING SCOPE

Parentheses and brackets are used in logic and arithmetic to indicate the scope of arithmetical and logical operations. Without them "2 + 7 − 3 · 8" and "*p* & *q* or *r*" are amphibolous. Parentheses tell in which order the operations are to be applied to the operands. The great variety of relations of scope in a natural language do not submit to this simple system, e.g., "the little used bookstore" and "the number of planets might have been even."

Let me, then, introduce a simple notation for indicating relative scope that is more generally applicable. This would not be needed if the herculean task of translating all sentences of English (or any other natural language) into the formalisms of logic were done; parentheses then would suffice. But that is music of the future. In the two cases above, Russell showed us how to make the planets-sentence into a sentence of predicate logic with the proper positions for parenthesized bound variables. The bookstore phrase, however, cannot simply be logicized into "*x* is a store and *x* is for books and *x* is little and *x* is used." To mention only one obstacle, in one of its meanings "little" is an adverbial modifier of "used."

I propose, then, a system of semantic scope markings that does not need to cast the containing sentence into logical form. The notation simply lists, Polish style, the expressions that affect the meaning of other parts of the sentence in the order of their precedence. I shall enclose them within the pointed brackets that show order. If *a* is listed before *b* for the meaning of a sentence *S*, viz., ⟨*a, b*⟩ [*S*], this tells one to figure out the meaning that *b* contributes to the meaning of the sentence before doing the same for *a*. Relative superiority of scope affects the meaning of a sentence when the result of applying *a* to *b* has a different semantic effect from the reverse, as in Quine's sentence about the planets. If the possibility expressed by the modal auxiliary "might" is applied to "the number of planets" giving it wide scope, then the sentence contemplates various solar histories one of which resulted in an even number of planets. If, on the other hand, "might" narrowly and inferiorly is applied just to the number got by counting our actual planets, then nine is incredibly conjectured to be even. The two options are repre-sented thus: ⟨*the number of planets, might*⟩ [*S*], which applies possible evenness to the actual number of planets, vs. ⟨*might, the number of plants*⟩ [*S*], which applies evenness to a possible number of planets.

C. S. Pierce's classic amphiboly, "Everyone loves someone" is construed in the "lucky guy" or cynosure reading by ⟨*someone, everyone*⟩ [*everyone loves someone*], and the reverse in the ordinary case where it means that

everyone loves someone or other. Pierce further saw that the effect of reversing the quantifiers is tantamount to substituting a conjunction of disjuncts
for a disjunction of conjuncts, the one saying that everyone loves either this
one person or that and the other saying that there is one or the other someone
for everyone.[3]

The square brackets indicate a function that yields the semantic value or
extension of the words within them. And the parts of this evaluative function
are to be composed, this notation says, in the historical order that matches
their written order.

Quine demonstrated the centrality of scope in distinguishing between an
indefinite and a definite object of desire. In wanting a sloop, any sloop may
satisfy one, or only one very definite and particular sloop. The former gives
superior scope to the desire, the latter gives superior scope to the object of
desire. If one represents the indefinite article, "a," by the existential quantifier, "$\exists x$," the two distinct meanings are shown by whether the quantified
phrase precedes the verb "want" or follows it. The simple notation I am
suggesting, however, does not require translation into the scope-explicit predicate calculus. The indefinite or relief-from-slooplessness reading simply goes:
⟨*want, a sloop*⟩ [I want a sloop]. This notation is thus not tied to just those
cases where at least one of the operators is a truth function or quantifier.
And of course it is good for any number of operators and for the disambiguation of amphiboly of any degree, to wit Kripke's, "necessarily the number
of planets might have been even" (above). Another of his much discussed
examples has one reading as follow: ⟨*London, thinks*⟩ [Pierre thinks London
is ugly].[4]

Kripke's doubly modal sentence about the planets has three interacting
operators. I think it is doubtful that the sentence is uncertain as to which of
the two modal operators takes precedence, but if that were the case the
sentence would enjoy a remarkable six way amphiboly. My representation
of his sentence about Pierre allows "London" to designate the city Pierre
finds ugly, even though "Londres est joli" expresses one of his beliefs.

What Feinberg and Davidson call the accordion effect in the ascription
of complex actions may be seen as the flexible scope of a covert verb or adverb
of conation, such as "will," "intend," and "intentionally."[5] "He (intentionally) switched on the light and alerted the burglar," can be understood *de re*
so that the narrow scope of "intentionally" does not extend to the alerting
of the burglar. When so read this is structurally just like questions of distribution in the predicate calculus and modal logic: Did the homeowner's intention distributes into conjunction, as it would when read wide relative to
"and," or did the superiority of conjunction to intention spare him the charge
of cowardly avoidance.

To say that necessity distribute into conjunction, is to say in the present
notion ⟨*nec, and*⟩ [necessarily p and q] iff ⟨*and, nec*⟩ [necessarily p and nec-

essarily q]. The distribution of conjunction into disjunction is more subtle: $\langle and, or \rangle$ [p and q or r] iff $\langle or, and \rangle$ [p and q or p and r]. Since conjunction and necessity appear twice in the distributed form, the notation strictly should index them and have them appear twice in their sequences, viz., $\langle and, nec1, nec2 \rangle$.

This is all well and good but how, one may wonder, does it relate to the topic of intensionality? The fact that some instances of unmarked relative scope are so in relation to intensional operators, such as desire, belief, necessity, and conation is of no great moment. Scope, however, relates more particularly and more importantly to opacity and substitutivity in that some coextensional substitutions alter what might be called scope valence. One clear case is that of substituting the numeral "9" for the description "the number of planets" in either Quine's original sentence of Kripke's iterated version of it. The numeral unlike the description always forces itself to the front of the scope cue; it is a rigid designator (Kripke) in the sense that alternative possibilities do not alter the number it picks out.

There is a slightly different way in which anaphoric scope blocks codesignative substitution. This sentence illustrates it. "The person who is sitting near the front and coughing is doing it to annoy me." The meaning of the anaphor "doing it" (here a pro-participle rather than a pro-noun) depends on how much (if any) of the relative clause is consulted in determining its meaning. There is thus an indeterminacy as to how much if any of the description is being applied to "doing it" in order to fill out the predicate. Where "doing it" works either as a demonstrative or as an anaphor for a previous piece of the discourse, no part of the description determines its meaning. This three- or four-way amphiboly does not then strictly speaking arise from uncertainty regarding the relative superiority in scope of *sitting near the front, coughing,* or *sitting near the front and coughing.* It is not the order or superiority of application that counts here, but rather whether or not they are applied at all. This is not a case where a function is applied to the result of another function's application which is for that reason construed as being inferior in scope to it; it is instead simply a yes-no question of application. Letting "S," "C" and "S and C" abbreviate the three operators, C [the person, etc.] shows the reading in which only the coughing is being said to be advertent. One could write in the other two operators inferior to C, but since they are not applied to the anaphor at all, so to do would be misleadingly otiose.

The resulting opacity nonetheless is broadly the result of changing the antecedent of the anaphor, which is a relation of scope. To do this alters that part of the sentence's overall semantics I shall call its complete reference. The complete reference (CR) of a sentence is the set of all things mentioned in the sentence that are being said to satisfy the main predicate, where that is understood to be the attribute that is expresseed by the highest VP in the parsing tree that then is purged of all lower NPs. But more of this below.

Another kind of case discussed by Donnellan [in this volume] raises an awkward contention of Stich, Chastain, and Wilson.[6] If I say something about "the man drinking a martini" and he is drinking water with an olive in it, the description may be taken either referentially or attributively. In the referential use it picks the man out as a subject of conversation even though it attributively misdescribes him. Stich and company say that indefinite noun-phrases enjoy a similar ambiguity between designating one thing in particular, of the indicated kind, or designating at least one but anyone. So, indefinite NPs, whether or not they appear in potential interaction with desire or some other propositional attitude, may have either a referential or an attributive meaning. The *de re–de dicto* distinction, this says, is not a distinction of scope but rather a distinction between two different lexical meanings of the indefinite pronoun "a": it is ambiguity rather than amphiboly. Thus, only the attributive use of an "a"-phrase is correctly represented by the existential quantifier. This doctrine unhappily extracts all humor from the report of Jean Harlow's command, "Don't give me a book for my birthday; I have a book." She simply chose, if these authors are right, one meaning of "a" rather than the other. It also leaves unexplained why "I want a sloop" or "I owe him a sloop" are amphibolous while "I bought a sloop" is not; the evidence that this is so is that "one in particular" is otiose in the latter but not in the former sentences.

It must be said, however, that the distinction between structural ambiguity and lexical ambiguity is no firmer than the distinction between word and structure. In many of these cases one can find a word denoting an operator's scope whose absence causes the semantic uncertainty. One might say, e.g., that the null lexeme that occupies the position of "both" in "both p or q and r" when the marker 'both' is missing is the bearer of the ambiguity. And certainly in the oracle's ambiguous advice to Phyrrus, "Aio te Romanos vincere posse," one can locate the amphiboly in the like declension of "te" and "Romanos." Since they are both accusative in this oblique construction they fail to tell us whether the scope of *Romanos* is superior to that of *te*, or vice versa. The uninflected English "I say that you can conquer Rome" cannot bear the meaning that Rome will conquer you.

A figure of speech that hinges on semantic scope in a different way is zeugma.

The following two paragraphs on scope and zeugma are not directly relevant to the present enterprise. The kind of semantic scope illustrated by zeugma does not lead either to opacity or failure of compositionality. It is a figure not a fault of speech, but nonetheless interesting and important even if safely neglected by the purposeful reader.

An example of it is Alexander Pope's "She sometimes counsel took and sometimes tea." Its effect results from competing and conflicting scope of the verb *to take*. The yoking of "tea" and "counsel" into a compound direct

object of the verb *to take* results in an irresolvable conflict of semantic juris-
dictions. Counsel is taken differently than is tea; it is an internal accusative
rather than an internalized one, an accusative cognate rather than an accusative bibulate. To depict such occluded meanings the difference between a
VP-construction with a cognate or internal accusative and one with an external
accusative has to be shown, since the composition of the evaluation of the
VP "take counsel" is not the same as that of the VP "take tea." The material
mode shape of this intuition is the distinction between taking a thing and
taking thought. Not only is the semantics of the VP determined, as it should
be, by that of its constituents, but the semantics of one constituent, the verb
to take, is jointly and incompatibly determined by that of the two others,
counsel and *tea*.

My notation for scope is designed to show by the order of operators
which operations precede which. The zeugma effect, however, unlike scope
amphiboly, is one in which a word is forced simultaneously to express two
conflicting meanings owing to the fact that its syntax does not allow the parts
of its compound noun-phrase separately to determine meaning. A single
occurrence of the verb lies within the conflicting scope of both NPs and it
does not matter in which order they are applied for *take* cannot at the same
time have both meanings. Zeugma neither results from nor is removable by
substitution; but it is susceptible to paraphrase. If one follows Frege in letting
sentences have extensions, then a truth-preserving paraphrase *is* a coextensional substitution and it does not preserve zeugma.

These examples show both how various are the relations of scope and
how divergent are the means for marking them. It makes me think of G. E.
Moore's charming imputation of chicanery to the structure of English. "It
seems to me very curious that language . . . should have grown up just as if
it were expressly designed to mislead philosophers; and I do not know why
it should have."

The illustrations, however, would be idle were the phenomena they illustrate not connected to opacity and compositionality; but they are so connected. Substitution of one codesignator for another can alter scope relations
within a sentence and its semantics without. Substituting "nine" for "the
number of planets" in one of Quine's sentence and "a particular sloop" for
"a sloop"[7] in the other changes what might be called the semantic quantity
of the sentence, i.e., how many meanings it expresses. The theoretical importance of such voice reduction via mere syntactic alteration can be seen in
the passive transformation of "everyone loves someone." The amphiboly of
the active voice disappears in the passive: "Someone is loved by everyone"
has only the cynosure reading. One feels this ought not to happen, that
syntactic change as trifling as this should not change meaning. Nor should
mere syntactic substitution of one coreferential word for another, alter the

semantics of the containing sentence. That it does happen testifies to the fact that words and even structures are often made to do more than their primary job.

The semantics of natural languages lacks purity. This is the lesson to be drawn from opacity and amphiboly of scope. The words and phrases of sentences do more than merely or purely designate their extensions.[8] It is no surprise that different codesignators may have a different psychological or, more narrowly, cognitive effect, but that they should make a different compositional contribution to the semantics of a sentence is surprising. The mere syntactic undoing of Pope's sentence, the unloosening of his yoked predicate, "She took counsel and she took tea," surprisingly removes the semantic zeugma. This is because "counsel" and "tea" do more semantically than designate their extensions. They affect the meaning of the verb *to take*.

Undetermined relative scope stems, then, from optional but unranked parameters of evaluation. Substitutivity fails when the substitution affects what might be called the scope-valence of the sentence, and thereby its voice- or meaning-quantity. This sentence, e.g., is ambiguous: "The sister of Sheila (= Sally) says she wasn't there"; but it loses its ambiguity when "Sally" is substituted for "the sister of Sheila."

III. THE MANY SOURCES OF OPACITY

Opacity arises from more than one cause. The set of counterexamples to the principle of Substitutivity lack causal kinship. They are motley. The fact that the antecedent of that principle which simply requires that the substituting expressions name the same thing can be strengthened in stages, each stage eliminating more opaque sentences shows that how the substitution changes the truth-value is various. The intuition that motivates Substitutivity is that if one simply replaces one expression with another which means the same thing, this should not change meaning nor the truth that depends on it. The motleyness of the failure of this principle is shown by the fact that as one makes its "if"-clause stronger, more counterexamples are eliminated. The conditions stated in that principle's "if"-clause thus work as filters whose decreasing mesh size excludes ever larger sets of counterexamples to it. Differing mesh sizes differentiate substitutions that alter truth-value by different mechanisms.

The principle states two conditions for maintaining truth through substitution: the first requires that the substituting expressions codesignate, have the same extension, and second that they occupy the same syntactic position, such as a node in a tree depicting the sentence's phrase structure. To these I added two more. To state these conditions I need two new semantic notions, those of what might be called the total logical subject and the purged logical predicate of the sentence. The opaque sentence "The author of *Waverley* denies he wrote it" shows why. That description is codesignative with "the author of *Marmion*"; they both designate Scott, but they also, auxiliary to so designating, name two different works of his, which an anaphor in the predicate picks up. So even though the main designators both refer to Scott, the replacement of one by the other alters the complete reference of the sentence and the satisfaction of the open predicate "x denies x wrote y." The two-ordered triples ⟨Scott, Scott, *Waverley*⟩ and ⟨Scott, Scott, *Marmion*⟩ respectively satisfy and fail to satisfy that predicate. So the condition of co-designation is met for the subject NP but not for the total NP, something I have called in an earlier paper the complete reference of the sentence (CR). The other notion, the attribute expressed by the main VP of the sentence when purged of subordinate NPs I called the sentence's pure sense. This is not too happy a term in light of Frege's very different use of "Sinn." I shall simply call it the sentence's PS.

The CR of a sentence is, with qualification, the ordered n-tuple of all the things designated by its NPs. The PS is that property or relation expressed by the sentence's predicate that has been purged of all those designata that are in the CR. A sentence is true thus just in case its CR satisifies its PS, or, alternatively, when that attribute-PS is thought of as a set say of ordered triples, the sentence is true just when CR *belongs* to the PS. In order to make these two ideas workable some very difficult things must be done. But let me first use them to explicate opacity.

I now think that the baffling fractions sentence does not mention the ratio; it speaks of the process of dividing 2 by 6, not the result of so doing. The utility of the idea of CR is nonetheless shown by the semantic effects of this substitution. Substituting "⅓" for "²⁄₆" alters the sentence's CR. The divisional processes are different because the divisors and dividends are different even if the quotient is the same. The number 3 belongs to it now, whereas 6 did before. If, on the other hand, "⅓" means the *result* rather than the operation of dividing 1 by 3, the description is like "the author of *Waverley*" in that the references to 3 and *Waverley* are part of the CR quite independently of what the predicate says.

The degree of the attribute and the length of the CR must either be the same or the first less than the second. With a nod to Frege, I shall call this the rule of Full Saturation. The CRs of the two sentences "Daphne loves Chloe" and "Narcissus admires himself" are ⟨Daphne, Chloe⟩, and ⟨Narcissus, Narcissus⟩. Each has a length of two, which matches the polyadicity of their attributes or PSs.

I write a sentence's PS with a lambda abstract, but I intend this notation to tolerate attributes either as sets of thing (or pairs, etc.) that have the attribute, or, as in the Montague way, functions to such sets from various global possibilities. Since these functions are intensions, I may seem to be weakening my resolve against Intensionalism, but I only dislike intensions as explainers of the opacity of opaque and intensional contexts.

The PSs of the sentences above are then $\Lambda xy(x$ loves $y)$ and $\Lambda x(x$ admires x.) As said, I allow these two abstracts to represent either the actual extensions of "loves" and "admires" or a set of such extensions, one per possible world. The abstract nouns, "love" and "self-admiration," serve just about as well. The polyadicity of the PS, however, can be read off the lambda abstracts simply by counting variable occurrences.

The Narcissus example points to a cluster of apparent exceptions to full Saturation: Some will say that the semantic model for this sentence must be an intensional one. For it may be true (*de re*) that Narcissus admires Narcissus, but, his being ignorant of the phenomenon of reflection, be false (*de dicto*) that Narcissus admires himself. (The so-called *de se* phenomenon.) In an Intensionalist model, the CR of this sentence is a set of sequences rather than a single one, the set crafted by Narcissus's subjectivity. If he is not narcissistic, only ignorant, then there is no satisfying sequence ⟨Narcissus, Narcissus⟩ though there is a nonsubstitutable one ⟨Narcissus, the person Narcissus sees before him⟩.

The same exception to Full Saturation appears to occur in the case of general sentences that contain quantifier NPs, such as "Some pawns are in front of a rook." Their CR is, according to one view, a set of sequences rather than a single one, and that set is at least as large as the Cartesian product of the language's domain with itself. To make it simple suppose this sentence belongs to a language that is just that fragment of English which describes the initial position of pieces on a chess board. The PS, Λxy (x is a pawn and y is a rook and x is in front of y), has two places, so sequences that satisfy it must be at least that long. But there are many of them, even in so simple a language as this whose domain consists only of thirty-two chess pieces, thirty-two squared in fact. The length of each sequence, however, will match the degree of the PS.

The rule for the CR, then, is this. It is that sequence or ordered n-tuple that is at least as long as the polyadicity of the PS, each element of which is the designation of an NP in the sentence's parsing tree, which elements are to be ordered by the sense of that attribute which is the sentence's PS. If the NP is a singular designator, the element is an individual from the domain. If the NP is a general NP, the element is a set.[9]

It is easier to allow idle and excess elements in the CR over and above the satisfaction size of the PS than not to. *Waverley* needs to belong to the CR of "The author of *Waverley* denies he wrote it" but need not belong to "The author of *Waverley* is a Scott." So I put it in both, order the sequence according to position in the parsing tree, and say the sentence is true when the initial segment of its CR (which could be all of it) satisfies its PS.

This still will not do, however, as a general definition of truth or satisfaction in terms of CR and PS. If part of the CR is general, as in "most of the voters canvased voted," the kind of generality involved will determine what sort of satisfaction clause is needed, roughly whether all, some, most, or none of the relevant set in the sequence are needed to satisfy the predicate.

I will for the remainder of this section turn aside from these complications and let ⟨Daphne, Chloe⟩ stand as CR of its sentence, and let its satisfaction clause say that it is true iff its CR satisfies or belongs to its PS. The CR of the amphibolous "Everyone loves someone" I will write either as "⟨everyone, someone⟩" for one meaning, or as "⟨someone, everyone⟩" for the other; so doing I adopt Kaplan's practise (above) of letting the QNP stand in for the appropriate set of individuals from the domain and the appropriate form of the satisfaction clause in the truth definition.

The point of all this is that substitutions of codesignative expressions, one for another, even though they do not and cannot change what the sentence talks about in respect of those designata, can nonetheless change what the sentence talks about. Such substitutions can change CR. They can also change the PS.

The two conditions added to Substitutivity are, then, that the substitution change neither the CR of the sentence nor its PS. Substituting "Barbarelli" for "Giorgione" in Quine's example changes the CR of "Giorgione is so-called for his size" from Giorgione and his nickname, to wit ⟨Giorgione, "Giorgione"⟩, to Giorgione and his given name, viz., ⟨Giorgione, "Barbarelli"⟩, thus changing the extension or truth-value as well.

An example whose substitution changes the pure attribute (PS) is the following: "The man who is yawning is doing so reluctantly." If it is also correct to describe this man as the one who is listening to Mozart, and if this is an activity he relishes, then the substitution would not preserve the truth of the sentence. This substitution, however, does not preserve the sentence's PS, since it changes the expressed attribute from that of reluctantly yawning to that of reluctantly listening to Mozart. (In this example it also changes the CR by the addition of Mozart to the listener.) The two filters one can make with the ideas of Cr and PS enable one to sift opaque sentences into two piles according to whether their substitutions change the one or the other. (I ignore the parenthesized possibility above.)

I have introduced these two concepts, CR and PS, to show how it is that codesignative substitutions can nonetheless alter the meaning of a sentence by changing what it talks about. They also can be used to define grades of opacity and its opposite transparency. Opacity is defined by the principle of the substitutivity *salva veritate* of coreferential expressions. One can express the coreferentiality of "Saki" and "H. H. Munro" by an identity statement: Saki = H. H. Munro. A sentence can be more or less opaque relative to different principles, to principles of different selectivity. After substitution, the reference of its substituting terms may remain the same, or its CR may remain the same, or its PS may remain the same. Letting "= R," "= CR," and "= PS" abbreviate the three conditions of coreference, co-complete-reference, and co-pure-sense, the Giorgione sentence is opaque according to Sub(= R) but not so according to Sub(= R & = CR): the reference of "Giorgione" and "Barbarelli" are the same but not so the CR of the sentences that contain them. The sentence above about the reluctant yawner meets the conditions both of reference and CR, but in failing the condition that its predicate express the same attribute whichever description is used for the subject it is only transparent relative to Sub(= R, = CR & = PS).

Sentences that meet all three transparency tests are perfectly transparent and extensional. This hypothesis, I should think, removes a significant part of the stigma of folk psychology from ordinary ascriptions of belief. They are no worse in their semantics than is talk of fractions.[10]

Let me be tedious with further illustration of the ideas of CR and PS. A reason for this tedium is that I here give a fragment of a theory of natural language designation, not a full theory of a fragment, as is usual. The examples of these ills of meaning are too various syntactically to admit of collection into a fragment.

The *Waverley-Marmion* sentence illustrates how the CR of a sentence can vary from one semantic theory to another and still serve to classify opaque sentences. The CR given above for the *Waverley* sentence treats the description as a complex designator rather than as a fragment of a complex quantified sentence, à la Russell. If one were to Russell the CR and the PS of the above sentence, its PS would be Λxyz (x wrote y and if z wrote y then $z = x$ and x denies x wrote y). The CR is this: ⟨someone1, *Waverley,* anyone2, *Waverley,* one2, one1, one1, one1, *Waverley*⟩, where the word "one" with the appended number functions like a variable bound by "someone" or "everyone." The loglish sentence goes: "Someone wrote W and if anyone else wrote W, that person is the same person, and he denies he wrote it." All these complications, even if forced by other semantic considerations, result in a CR that does no more to show the change wrought by substitution than does the simpler one: they both differ in containing the novel rather than the poem.

Barbara Partee's famous example, the temperature (= ninety degrees) is rising (see Weisler), belongs to a semantically difficult group of sentences whose descriptions describe functions, but do so in such a way that the operation rather than its result is designated. Unlike "the square root of nine," that designates the unique value or result of the extraction, her sentence describes a course of values over an indeterminate set of temporal indices applied to some one or other measurement function. (Or maybe it just refers metonymously to a column of mercury!) The example involves vagueness and indexicality in addition to the kind of vulgar function talk illustrated by the fractions sentence discussed above and also by "of two the square is four, of three *it* is nine." The anaphor, "it" cannot refer to the square of two, because

MURRAY KITELEY · 387

that is four not nine, so it must refer just to the operation of squaring, as applied in one case to two and the other to three. "My plumber (= my ward boss) overcharges for his services" is the same, insofar as occupation nouns imply a function or service; and so, too, is "an hour ago the time was four, now *it* is five" (substitute "four" for "the time").

The latter of these two sentences is like the inverted sentence: "Of two, the square is four, of three, *it* is nine." It is wrong to substitute "four" for "the square" and "it" despite the identity that the sentence appears to assert between four and the value of the square function. It is not the square that equals four, but the square of two that does so. The anaphor "it" oddly picks up its designation from only part of the antecedent phrase, from just "the time" and "the square" and not from "the time an hour ago" and "the square of two." In so doing "it" becomes a functor anaphor that has to supply its own word for the argument to which the function is applied, "now" in the first example and "three" in the second. (Why this construction only works in inverted form, but not as "the square of two is four, it of three is nine" is a puzzle for the syntax of English.)

Vagueness and indexicality are problems for any semantic theory, not just for the notion of CR, as are also the vagaries and varieties of the uses of "the"-phrases.

These cases are instructive examples of impure designation. Although the substituens for the descriptions "my plumber," "the time an hour ago" and "the square of two" certainly do codesignate, they alter the semantics of the functor anaphors for which they become the new antecedents. His services are a very different thing if he is described as a ward boss rather than a plumber; so too does "it" tell a different time when it appears in "the time an hour ago was four, now *it* is five" rather than in "the time an hour ago was four, and *it* seemed a decade coming."

The semantic interdependencies of natural languages are such that co-referential substitutions alter CR and PS; they change either the whole set of things a sentence takes about, or they change what it says about the whole set.

In this way CR and PS reveal the springs of opacity. They also explain what the transparent paraphrases of opaque sentences have in common. Transparent paraphrases eliminate CR-affecting or the PS-affecting impurity of the substituting expressions. In fact, as I say below, there is a universally available transparent paraphrase for all opaque sentences. It is CR(S) satisfies PS(S).

There are various ways, despite their utility, that the ideas of CR and PS may seem conceptually itchy. To a degree they live off the semantics of the natural language to which they are applied and would therefore vary according to whether, e.g., it were an intensionalist or an extensionalist semantics. It is not unreasonable to think, nonetheless, that even though CR and PS may vary from theory to theory, that this variation will not detract from their explanatory value. I will in fact illustrate this point below when I set out an impure model of the NPs of English.

IV. WHAT THE MOTLEYNESS OF OPACITY TEACHES

What lessons are to be learned from these examples of how substitution affects the complete reference (CR) and the pure attribute (PS) of sentences?

Compositionality lies in shreds. This is the first and mośt obvious lesson. If the extension of the whole is solely the product of the extension of the parts, then replacing one part with another having the same extension should make no difference in truth-value, as it unmistakably does in these examples.

To restore compositionality, to restore the doctrine that the semantics of the whole is built up from the semantics of the parts, the composing parts must be broadly conceived. They must comprise not only the semantics of the words and phrases of the sentence, but the semantic relations between them that affect the CR and the PS, relations that, in effect, work as parameters of evaluation.

A pure designator is one that stands in no such evaluation-affecting relations *in a given sentence.* "⅔" occurs impurely in "⅔ has an even denominator," but it occurs purely in "⅔ is less than ⅖." The purity of a designator will thus come and go from sentence to sentence. It is the semantic structure of these containing sentences that must be fixed to avoid scope amphiboly and other forms of opacity. Intensionalism and Quotationalism, laudable as they are for recognizing the importance of compositionality and the challenge opacity poses for it, are both wrong in saying that the reference of the designator in opaque or intensional contexts changes: that "⅔" refers to an intension or to itself in the first sentence and to the ratio in the second.

Purity and impurity of designation, or more broadly of having an extension, are not intrinsic features of the expression's semantics. They depend on what the rest of the sentence says. They are thus completely unlike referential rigidity (or flaccidity), or directness. A numeral rigidly designates its number in every possible world irrespective of what its sentence says, but "⅔" may designate purely or impurely from sentence to sentence.

Thus an impure designator may be rigid, as "Giorgione" is in the example above, and a non rigid designator may be pure, as the description is in "The number of planets is odd." This same description, can, however, appear impurely, as it does in "The number of planets in the cardinal of their set," construing nine's set as its unit set and not its von Neuman set, viz., {0,1,2 . . . 8}. This is because impure designation is a relational property that relates the designator to the semantics of other parts of the sentence in a way that sensitizes meaning and truth-value to the presence of one rather than another of a coreferring designator set.

Intensional and quotational abstracts, "that"-clauses and quotations, distort designation. "He thinks/says someone came" may report either the thought/utterance that John came or that someone came.

One of the functions of the individual variables of logic is to turn sentences into predicates: the sentence "Nine is a number" becomes the predicate "x is a number." This predicate may be returned to sentencehood by binding the variable with a quantifier; but it can also be turned into a namelike thing called an abstract. One can either abstract the set of numbers from the predicate (its extension) or the property of being a number (its intension.) The familiar brackets of set theory, $\{x|x$ is a number$\}$, do the former and the lambda notation does the latter, although it can be used to do both. These are the formal analogues of the abstract suffixes of English. Number-*hood* is the property and number-*dom* the set. Is the "that" of "believes that the moon is round" also an abstractor? Does it turn a sentence into a name of a proposition that is the sentence's intension? Or is it just a form of quotation, indirect quotation? In the essays above, Quine explores both possibilities and Davidson defends the latter.

There are two ways to think of these sentential intensional abstracts. One is that they are semantically like direct or indirect quotation. The words within them do only one thing and that is to make a contribution to the abstract's overall reference. The other is to think of them solely as marking the scope or reach of an intensional operator, e.g., *says* or *believes*. In the former case they will have independent semantic effects on the expressions within; in the latter they will only mark where the effects of the operators work.

There is evidence that the latter is the correct view. Coextensional substitution does not fail for intensional abstracts in the "true that" or "fact that" environments. The propositional abstracts introduced by "true" and "fact" are not as such opaque or intensional. They are so only when they mark the reach of an opacity-inducing operator, such as those of modality and propositional attitude. This is a simpler explanation than one that makes the abstracts opaque or intensional and then postulates some sort of deintensionalizing operator that is part of the meaning of "true" and "fact." But more than this, the idea that intensional or quotational abstracts are the source of opacity runs aground on all the examples outside of such abstracts. It is much more plausible that the verbs *believe* and *say* along with a variety of other constructions cause semantic impurity.

An advantage an Impurity Explanation of the tropes of designation has over an Intensional Explanation is the greater simplicity of the referential and quantificational apparatus needed. But perhaps even more impelling is this. It protects the sound conviction that the terms occurring in an opaque or *de dicto* sentence designate their extensions, even if they do not do so solely or purely.

This is the last lesson I draw from the motleyness of opacity. Opaque or impure designation is still designation, and ordinary or *gerade* designation at that: "Giorgione" designates Giorgione even if it also contributes to the designation of his nickname. Whether this is also so for the ascription of beliefs and intentions is a vexed question the answer to which doubtlessly depends on the nature of the cause of their opacity. What makes it so sorely vexing is the conflict of intuition and theory. Intuition tells us that insofar as Oedipus thought it would be good to marry Jocasta he thought about Jocasta, even where this is an opaque report of a *de dicto* belief. Wittgenstein reinforces this intuition in an efficient refutation of unqualified Fregeanism in section 444 of the *Investigations*: "One may have the feeling that in the sentence 'I expect he is coming' one is using the words 'he is coming' in a different sense than the one they have in the assertion 'He is coming'. But if this were so how could I say that my expectations were fulfilled."

If attitudinative contexts merely cause their NPs to designate impurely, as in the cases above, but do not cause them obliquely to designate their intension, rather than their extension, then their opacity will not interfere with their designating their ordinary designata. This, however, cannot be said of the failure of objectual, existential generalization (EG) into such contexts. Impure designation invalidates objectually understood EG even where the parallel inference understood substitutionally succeeds. There exists a verifying substituend of "x" in "x is so-called because of his size," or in "x is a fraction with an even denominator," but no such objectual value. This last sentence, note, is a comment on substitutional quantification not an instance of it.

Objectual existential generalization does not, however, fail for opaque sentences if they are put in the following canonical form. Let 'CR(S)' represent the complete reference of the sentence, S. Let 'PS(S)' represent the sentence's pure sense. Even where S is opaque, so long as it is true, there objectually is a value of CR(S) that satisfies PS(S). Objectual existential generalization holds; and the canonical form, though a metaphrase, is in an extensional language.

This form of E.G. is valid even in those motley cases where opacity interferes with designation, viz., quotation. The CR of " 'Cicero' has six letters" is a name not an orator, and if the orator is thought to have been mentioned as a means of designating his name, then as suggested in the next section the man can be nested in the sequence with his name. This sort of tactic is mentioned next.

V. IMPURE QUANTIFICATION

Since opacity causes trouble with designation it also causes trouble with the generalization over the position of the opaque designator. This trouble can be avoided if not cured either by the use of substitutionally understood quantifiers, or by rewriting the sentence in a canonical way. The first uses a substitutional model of general designation, and the second effects a translation into a transparent language. This latter can be done in the "CR(S)" way described above. A more outré method is first to reduce singular designators to descriptions in the fashion of Quine's "the pegasizer," and then obey Russell's injunction against substitutions for such "incomplote symbols." But this is an even more high-handed procedure than an Intensionalist doctrine that such expressions do not designate what we know in our hearts they do designate.

The generalization of "the man sitting near the front and coughing is doing it to annoy me," viz., "$(\exists x)(x$ is doing it to annoy me)," would come out true according to a substitutional model that contained in its substitution set "the man sitting near the front and coughing," but false for one that contained just "the man sitting near the front."

Various regular systems of translation or paraphrase, are, as just indicated, possible.

Might there not, however, be another way? Might not a way be found, a model be constructed, that would allow for the vagaries of impure designation without eliminating via paraphrase the offending sentence?

The substitutional model of course does this for quantifier noun phrases and it could be extended to names by means of Quine's device for turning "Pegasus" into "the x such that x = Pegasus," which description is then Russelled. I am uneasy with this solution to the semantics of impurity because the power of substitutional quantification makes it insensitive to the various sources of impurity.

What I wonder is whether one might not construct an objectual model for the referential apparatus of natural languages that would not founder on opaque or impure designation.

Such an impure model would not simply assign an object or sequence of objects from the domain as the satisfaction set of an opaque sentence, open or closed. For opaquely occurring designators do more than designate their objects. So the interpretation function of the model must do this as well; it must supply not only the sequence of so to speak pure objects but the impure semantic contribution as well. The sentence about Scott—let me simplify it to "the author of *Waverley* denies writing it"—would, e.g., be judged true in such an impure model only if it itself or the description within it, were assigned both Scott and *Waverley*. Its PS, $\Lambda x,y$ (x denies writing y), has two places, so its CR has to be at least that long. Yet, on the simple designator view of descriptions, this sentence's CR is just $\langle$Scott$\rangle$. An impure model, thus, would allow the description to designate without losing the reference to *Waverley*, thus enjoying some of the virtues of both quantifier (Russell's) and designator theories of descriptions. The qualification is needed because as Bergmann shows above means are needed to account for the presupposition of descriptions on a designator account.

I think it is simpler to allow excess designation, designation beyond that needed to satisfy the PS. The CR of "the author of *Waverley*, who is from Scotland, denies writing it" is ⟨Scott, *Waverley*, Scotland⟩ only the first two elements of which are relevant to its two-place PS. There is trouble for the order of the CR if the subordinate supernumerary name in the description appears before the essential one, e.g., "Scotland" before "*Waverley*." The first two elements of the CR would then not satisfy the PS and the sentence would be judged false. But the sentence is arguably ambiguous any way—anaphorically uncertain. So one of its meanings is false.

Here is a sketch of a working out of my idea for an impure semantics. First how to get the CR of a sentence.

Suppose we know how to parse English and our categories are the usual Chomskian ones. Parsing will single out the arguments to which the model's interpretation function, [. . .], is applied. The trouble with a straightforward application of this program is that it would result in interpretations such as this: [("the author of *Waverley*")NP] = Scott, where what is wanted depends on whether the occurrence is pure or not, being ⟨Scott⟩ in one case and ⟨Scott, *Waverley*⟩ in the other. The application of the interpretation function must be made contingent on the PS of that sentence in which the interpreted part of speech occurs. If the PS calls for two NPs, two must be found, even if this entails searching lower nodes in a parsing tree.

A considerable surface simplification of the clauses of the truth definition within such impure or CR models can be got by adopting a Barwise-Cooper interpretation of all NPs as generalized quantifiers. The general form of the definition says that a sentence is true iff its CR satisfies its PS. Barwise and Cooper turn this around. According to them satisfaction consists in the PS belonging to the family of sets designated by the quantifier NP, and, as said, every NP, even names, are construed to be such.[11]

To illustrate, let "*S*" abbreviate "the author of *Waverley* is a Scot." According to their account, if a description describes exactly one thing, then it designates the family of all supersets of the descriptum. Otherwise it is undefined. If we let this be *S*'s CR, ignoring for the moment *Waverley*, and understand the PS to be the set of all Scots, then the sentence will be true iff the set of all Scots belongs to the set of all supersets of Sir Walter.

According to Barwise-Cooper every NP (including proper names) may be construed as a family of sets. The classical quantifier NPs, such as "all men" and "no Greeks" either designate sets of supersets or null or non-null intersects. What belongs to the supersets and intersects is determined by the application of functions that are the meaning of "all" and "no" to sets named by common nouns such as "Greeks": applying the function ["no"] to

["Greeks"] = the set of all null intersects with the set of Greeks. This entails reversing the order of the truth definition for noncompound sentences. Instead of S is true iff its [NP] satisfies its [VP], it will say that S is true iff [VP] belongs to [NP].

How does this fit with CR and PS?

First CR is a sequence of the semantic values of all the sentence's NPs. PS also is not just [VP], but rather the semantic value of a purged VP, a VP with subordinate NPs replaced by lambda-abstracted variables. My version of Barwise-Cooper, then, says that a (simple) sentence is true iff its PS belongs to its CR. The trouble is that for the authorship-eschewing sentence this has a set of sequences of authorship eschewers and their eschewed writings, the PS, belonging to—what?—all the supersets of the pair, Scott, and *Waverley*?

It is not, as a matter of fact, perfectly clear how Barwise and Cooper intended to treat relational predication, especially ones like Pierce's old amphiboly, "Everyone loves someone." Like Henry James of the clerihew, they are not always too deuced/lucid. In L(GQ) they make all one-place predicates set terms, but many-place ones are formulae and become set terms only by set abstraction. Barwise and Cooper's semantics calls for just two kinds of subsentence expressions: set terms or one-place predicates and quantifiers. Quantifiers are made by applying a determiner, such as "a," "most," or "all," to a set term. The "loves someone" of Pierce's sentence is by their lights neither fish nor fowl, neither a set term nor purely a quantifier NP.

The solution, which I owe to Tom Tymoczko, seems to be this. Satisfaction consists in the predicate belonging to the subject; and this means that the semantic value of a one-place predicate, that set, belongs to the family of sets that is the quantifier, i.e., to the semantic value of the subject NP. So Pierce's sentence is true iff [loves someone] belongs to [everyone], where the brackets stand for a function that gives the semantic value of the expression within them.

But this won't do, for two reasons. We don't yet know how to make [loves someone] out of [loves] and [someone], and being amphibolous the sentence must have two distinct satisfaction clauses.

The answer is that Barwise and Cooper countenance open set-terms such as "the set of those y such that x loves y", ("lambda y (x loves y)") or "the set of those x such that x loves y", (lambda x (x loves y), designating respectively the set of the beloveds of x and the set of lovers of y. The open set of the loved, if it is subjected to the quantifier [someone], gives us the open set of some who are loved. If we now close this sentence with set or lambda abstraction, the truth of the sentence turns on whether or not this set belongs to [everyone], i.e., whether or not this sentence belongs to the set of supersets of people. This is the reading where the scope of [everyone] is superior to the scope of [someone], meaning that everyone loves someone or other. The other reading is got by constructing the open set of everyone who loves (lambda x (x loves y), and construing the sentence as asserting this set to belong to [someone].

My representation of the two meanings of this sentence are as follows. The first is CR(S) = ⟨everyone, someone⟩ and PS(S) = lambda xy (x loves y). The second is CR(S) = ⟨someone, everyone⟩ and PS(S) = lambda xy (x loves y). And I suggest the spelling out of these semantic representations in the manner of Barwise and Cooper. How, then, fares exportation?

To infer *de re* from *de dicto*, it has been the argument of this essay, it is necessary only to reduplicate that form of designator impurity that results from a change in scope valence caused by the appearance of different co-designators. Here is an easy case. To substitute "or" for "either" . . . or" in sentences of the form "either p and q or r" is to cause amphiboly by substitution. The interpretation function, [. . .], of the impure model structure that I have been sketching is to have the effect of preventing amphiboly by so to speak rigidifying "or." It will give it the wide scope lost by the loss of the scope-indicator—the quasi-bracket—"either." But we do not want "or" always to have wide scope relative to other truth functions. So the interpretation function must "know" the inferential source of "p and q or r." And this may be too much to expect of it: the trade off between syntax and semantics has been loaded too much on the side of semantics.

V. CONCLUSION

In an old paper of mine, in which I sought to make all opaque attitudinative sentences transparent, I suggested the use of a local vigilante purifier. It was to be the attitudinative counterpart of a rigidifier like Kaplan's "d-that" or the English "actual." Such scope-pegging functions in the area of subjectivity we might call representifiers. Rigidifiers and representifiers undo locally for adjacent NPs what outriding modal or attitudinative operators do generally for all NPs within their bailiwicks.[12]

With an impure model none of these syntactic devices are necessary. And further, such a model structure takes care of all opacity, not just that induced by subjectivity and modality.

Why then is there the air about it of a cheap trick? I think it is because what we want to know about subjectivity is how it distorts designation, not just that it does and that a certain sort of semantics will cope with that. To know that, I suggest, is to know an algorithm for an impure interpretation function.

NOTES

1. William of Ockham, *Summa Totius Logicae*; Wilfrid Sellars, in many of his essays, e.g., "Reply to Quine," *Synthese* 26 (1973); William G. Lycan, *Logical Form in Natural Language* (Cambridge, MA, 1984).

2. The opaque fractions sentence gives the *coup de grace* to Intensionalism. It instructs us to take the fractional numerals as designating their intensions rather than their extensions, but this does not remove the opacity, since the same ratio is designated in every possible world. For numerals there is no difference between intension and extension; numerals are thus unlike a number designation such as "the number of planets" that designates different numbers at different possible worlds. And this is so even if "⅔" is a description to the effect "the result of dividing two by six."

I have worried myself and many others about this sentence ever since Quine suggested it to me years ago, for it is tempting to read the fraction as a function description, "the result of dividing 2 by six." But the result does not have an even denominator. I now think the proper functional expansion is "the *process* of dividing 2 by 6 has an even denominator."

3. In *The Development of Logic*, (Oxford at the Clarendon Press, 1962) p. 323, the Kneales give the citation and explain Pierce's notation.

4. "A Puzzle about Belief," *Meaning and Use*, ed. by Avashai Margalit (Dordrecht, Holland, 1979), pp. 239ff.

5. Joel Feinberg, "Action and Responsibility," in *Philosophy in America*, ed. by Max Black (Ithaca, NY, 1965) and discussed in Donald Davidson's "Agency," *Essays on Actions and Events* (Oxford, 1980).

6. E.g., George Wilson, "On Definite and Indefinite Descriptions," *Philosophical Review* 87 (Jan., 1978): 48–76.

7. This example might be objected to on the grounds that the two expressions not being designators cannot be codesignators. There is, however, a way of doing the semantics of quantifier noun-phrases in which they are construed as designating families of sets, viz., Barwise and Cooper, "Generalized Quantifiers."

8. Tom Tymoczko chides me for my wording here, since in many cases the impure designator is more being done to than doing, e.g., "Giorgione." Let me then take this opportunity to remark my indebtedness over the years to the members of Herbert Heidelberger's Propositional Attitudes Task Force, and not least of all its much missed founder.

9. In a categorial grammar the PS is expressed by an intransitive verb, i.e., that which a name makes into a sentence. But here no definite number of designators can be listed for the purged predicate until its polyadicity is known. The grammatical analogue of PS might then look like this, using "N" for designator and "S" for sentence. $\langle\langle N1, N2, \ldots Nn\rangle, S\rangle$.

10. For stigmatizers, see Churchland (1982, 1984) and Stich (1983) and for stigmata removers, Jay Garfield's *Belief in Psychology* (1988) and L. R. Baker, *Saving Belief* (1987).

11. They are motivated by the need for a semantics of determiners such as "most," "more than half," as well as the standard ones, which they show classical logic unable to handle. Jon Barwise and Robin Cooper, "Generalized Quantifier," 1981.

12. M. Kiteley, 1968.

THE STRUCTURE OF MEANING

INTRODUCTION

The essays collected in this section offer distinct proposals regarding the manner in which meanings are represented and composed in order that to compute of the meaning of a sentence on the basis of the meanings of its parts. Many of the difficulties that lie in the way of this computation have been surveyed in earlier sections of this collection, and a number of specific proposals for surmounting them have been considered. Quite a few (those discussed by Frege, Russell, Bergmann, Kaplan, Weisler, and Kiteley) implicitly or explicitly argue that the assignment of meaning to a sentence involves representing its logical form, and that semantics requires some account of the relationship between surface structure and logical form. Such an account must explain such phenomena as scope ambiguity, the *de dicto/de re* distinction and the curious ability of sentences of *prima facie* distinct surface forms nonetheless to say the same thing. These are the central puzzles that the essays in this section address.

Norbert Hornstein's "Two Types of Quantifiers" (from his *Logic as Grammar*) classifies natural language quantifier noun phrases (QNPs) according to their scope possibilities relative to other operators—according to whether or not they can take either wide or narrow scope. It has been recognized for some time that proper names and numerals unlike descriptions always take wide scope. "The number of planets might have been even" has both a true and a false reading depending on the relative scope of the description and the modal "might," but "Nine might have been even" is simply false.

Hornstein works within a theoretical approach called the Government Binding framework which is an extension of the Chomskian Extended Standard Theory or transformational grammar. This theory postulates a hierarchy of structures that explain (or constitute, depending on one's interpretation of the theory) a speaker's linguistic competence. That part of the competence that accounts for our ability to grasp meaning and truth rests on a structure called logical form (LF), an old friend noticed or invented by Russell 80 years ago. In the essay by Russell reprinted above he distinguishes primary from secondary uses of denoting phrases (QNPs) a distinction of scope. When such scope is unmarked in a sentence, a species of structural ambiguity or amphiboly occurs, an amphiboly that reflects the fact that the surface structure can be mapped onto two distinct structures at LF, structures having distinct interpretations.

Does scope amphiboly arise owing to the lexical ambiguity of the quantifiers in QNPs, or because the sentences in which they appear are not marked for scope, not parenthesized, so to speak? Kiteley and perhaps Russell take the latter view. Hornstein takes the former position as indicated by his speaking of different types of quantifiers rather than differently marked QNPs. His evidence turns on the notion that scope amphiboly can be construed as an instance of a movement rule called quantifier raising (QR). He argues that from the fact that QNPs of the form "a certain N" do not move ("Everyone loves someone" is amphibolous; "Everyone loves a certain person" is not) it follows that the consequent interpretative independence of such phrases is not a feature of the syntax of the sentence's logical form.

He argues the same thing for "any"-QNPs. Quine observed in "Logic as a Source of Syntactical Insights" (in *The Ways of Paradox*), that "I do not know every poem" is scope amphibolous, whereas "I do not know any poem" is not. Hornstein admits the datum but denies that it is a matter of scope. "Any N" is not like "a particular N" or like names that always take wide scope, as if they carried in their deep structure outriding parentheses analogous to the "either . . . or." The evidence that it is not, is that in a sentence such as "someone doesn't like anyone" "any" 's scope is narrower than that of "someone."

Ivan Sag, in "A Logical Theory of Verb Phrase Deletion," seeks a rule (VPD) that determines when verb phrases may be deleted rather than repeated, as in "this phrase may be deleted but this one may not." The rule that he proposes supposes that sentences have a logical form expressible in the language of the predicate calculus with the addition of an untyped lambda operator. This operator binds the postulated free variable(s) that stand in for the subject or object of a verb phrase. What results from this binding is however not a quantified sentence but the name of an attribute: the operation is hence analogous to that represented by definite descriptions or by functional abstraction.

The rule Sag proposes is roughly that a VP may be deleted that otherwise would have to be repeated *iff* its lambda abstract is an alphabetic variant of the lambda abstract of another VP. The letters of the alphabet that are allowed to vary serve as variables that are bound either by the lambda operator or by a standard quantifier. (He does, however, also allow nonstandard wh-operators.) Alphabetic variation is a device used by logicians to gain a certain kind of formal generality in stating theorems. E.g., "$\forall x(x = x)$" is the same theorem as its alphabetic variant, "$\forall y(y = y)$."

The first of the two chapters we have selected from Max Cresswell's book, *Structured Meanings*, starts with an admirably clear and non-technical description of the compositional element in compositional semantics. Frege said (above) that the meaning of the whole is a function of the meaning of the parts. Since meaning comes in two species for Frege, there must be two kinds of compositionality. Frege used his two kinds of meaning to explain the semantics of the "that"-clauses of belief and other propositional attitudes. The expressions in these oblique constructions fail to hew to Leibniz' law which states that the substitution of expressions with the same meaning or nominatum should not change truth-value (substitution *salva veritate*). The failure of substitutivity is, *prima facie*, tantamount to the failure of compositionality, for if word and phrase meanings compose into a sentence's meaning and truth, mere verbal substitutions that leave these meanings the same should not change the truth or meaning of the sentence.

Quine has shown and Kiteley elaborates the many failures of this "law" outside the sentence of belief and indirect discourse. Cresswell, however, restricts his attention to sentences of the latter two sorts and argues for an account of *de re* attitude ascriptions that is reminiscent of Russell's account in *The Problems of Philosophy* and Quine's account of the relational sense of belief above. But Cresswell's account is importantly different. Russell suggested that the belief in Helen's belief that $5 + 7 = 12$ relates her to $(5 + 7)$, 12 and the relation of being equal to. This, however, is the same as its relating her to 12, 12, and identity, which allows one to infer that her belief that $5 + 7 = 12$ is the belief that $12 = 12$. And we expect a theory of the logical form of sentences to account exactly for the fact that Helen can perfectly well believe the latter while being unfortunately ignorant of the former.

Cresswell revamps Frege's distinction between sense and reference to avoid this unhappy consequence. The reference of the original "that"-clause is that $12 = 12$, but the sense of the sentence "$5 + 7 = 12$" is quite different. It is not, e.g., a composite of Frege's "modes of presentation" of "5," "7," etc. It is also not a proposition in the sense of Stalnaker above. It is rather a structure or ordered triple the first element of which is an ordered triple: $\langle\langle 5,7, +\rangle, 12, =\rangle$. Unlike Russell's account in which belief is a relation that relates various numbers of terms depending on the complexity of its "that"-clause, Cresswell's makes it a two-place relation between the believer and structures of varying degrees of complexity, corresponding to the different possible readings of the sentence, each representing a distinct manner of composing the meanings of the parts to yield a meaning for the whole.

Cresswell takes the "that" of "that"-clauses very seriously, but not the way Davidson does. It is not a demonstrative but rather the mark of a function, but not as is usual a function from sentences to names, but rather one whose input is the reference of the sentence it precedes and whose output is the structure that is the sense of the clause itself.

This diversity of approaches to understanding the logical form of English sentences by no means exhausts the field. It should, however, indicate the flavor of the debates surrounding this issue, and of the principal lines of inquiry.

NORBERT HORNSTEIN

TWO TYPES OF QUANTIFIERS

will argue that there are basically three types of quantificational NP expressions, which can be described roughly as follows:

I. a set of NP expressions whose interpretive scope domain is always wide;
II. a set whose interpretive scope domain is restricted to the clause in which the quantified NP is situated;
III. a set whose scope domain is unbounded if originating in some syntactic positions but sententially bound when originating from others.

Each kind of quantified NP expressions has other properties as well. The aim of the next several chapters will be, first, to describe these distinct kinds of quantifiers more carefully and, second, to show how these properties follow from a version of the general principles—the *binding principles*—currently being developed within a version of the Extended Standard theory (EST) called the Government-Binding framework (GB).

Within this version of EST, the theory of quantifier structure is seen as one aspect of a more general theory of logical form. Within EST, the problem of defining the logical structure of quantified expressions in natural language (partially) translates into the question of how to derive the logical syntax of quantified expressions *step by step* from a level of representation known as S-structure. In other words, given a grammar organized as in (1), what sorts of rules are needed to yield a structure appropriate to the interpretation of quantified sentences?

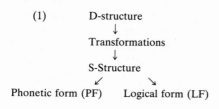

(1) D-structure
  ↓
  Transformations
  ↓
  S-Structure
  ↙ ↘
Phonetic form (PF) Logical form (LF)

In this grammar, organized according to the views of GB theory, D-structure is analogous to the deep structure of earlier interpretive theories. It is a level of representation that is input to the syntactic transformational component but *not* to semantic interpretation. The representation of a sentence that is relevant to semantic interpretation is its S-structure, a string with syntactic labeled bracketings that is the output of the transformational component. This S-structure is input to the rules of LF. LF rules operate on S-structures to yield structures that represent certain aspects of the "meanings" of sentences, called their *logical form*.[1] To determine just *which* aspects of natural language that we would pretheoretically see as relating to meaning are to be represented at LF, and *how* they are to be represented, is the task of a theory of linguistic semantics. In particular, what are the properties of LF representations and what is the nature of the rules that transform S-structures into structures representing logical form?

This problem is by no means trivial. Many logically possible solutions are excluded because although the rules invoked are observationally adequate (i.e., they describe the data correctly), they do not comport with the general restrictions on rule types that linguistic theory must impose if it is to achieve its main research goal of providing a solution to the logical problem of language acquisition. I will argue that by embedding questions concerning the logical form of quantified expressions within a model of language of the sort advocated within EST, one can gain considerable insight into how such information is actually expressed within natural language.

This belief has a more general and a more specific expression. The general view is that seeing semantic competence as responsible to the same poverty-of-stimulus considerations that motivate much current work in syntax will allow us to bring comparatively refined empirical considerations to bear on competing proposals concerning the logical syntax of natural language. As characterized in chapter 1, current linguistic theory views the process of language acquisition essentially as the fixing, on the basis of the primary linguistic data, of certain open parameters of a deductively organized innate language schematism. This view leads one to look for linguistic interdependencies, clusterings of phenomena that result from a parameter's being set one way or another. When cast against the background of the acquisition problem, many of the traditional philosophical analyses of LF can be a fertile source of specific proposals concerning the nature of the innate schematism and its parameters. Furthermore, by reinterpreting various philosophical proposals concerning LF as a subpart of a general theory of linguistic competence, responsible to the same set of considerations as other aspects of grammatical theorizing, we are able to sharpen aspects of these proposals in several ways and so better appreciate their differences. In particular, "capturing" the phenomena in some logical notation yields to explaining why the phenomena pattern as they do. Hopefully these skeletal remarks will gain flesh as we consider specific issues regarding natural language quantification.

The more specific application of this viewpoint is that many of the theoretical devices that have been developed within EST can be used to probe the features of LF in natural languages. I will make crucial use of the idea that rules relating S-structure to LF are of the same kind that operate in the syntax (i.e., Move-α), and that the Empty Category Principle (ECP) is a condition on LF and thus can be used to probe the features of logical form in natural language. Different theories of quantifier structure interact with these independently motivated devices in different ways. Thus, at least in principle, it is possible to exploit these grammatical constraints in assessing the relative empirical merits of different proposals concerning the logical syntax of quantified expressions in natural language.

I thus hope to show that by embedding versions of familiar philosophical theories about logical form within the framework of current linguistic theorizing, one can turn many questions of a logical or philosophical flavor into empirical questions associated with quite definite debits and credits; a sort of cost accounting that can be used to assess the empirical value of competing approaches to logical form in natural language.

In this chapter, I will concentrate on the distinction (developed in Hornstein 1981) between type I and type II quantifiers. In the next, I will trace the implications of the results developed here for an analysis of definite descriptions and 'belief'-sentences with quantified expressions in the content clause—the embedded 'that'-sentence of a 'believe-that' construction. In chapter 4 of *Logic & Grammar* I turn to the properties of type II and type III quantifiers, arguing that the special clause-bounded features of each can be explained. In chapter 5, I will deal with certain puzzles that arise from treating quantified NPs in the way I have proposed. This will lead to developing certain grammatical mechanisms that can fruitfully be used to explain other interpretive phenomena. I will close this section of the book with a brief review of the results and a discussion of what they show about a theory of natural language interpretation.

MOVED AND UNMOVED QUANTIFIERS: TYPES I AND II

The standard logical treatments of quantified sentences in natural language construe them as having a logical syntax of operator-variable form, i.e., $\ulcorner(Ox)(P(x))\urcorner$.[2] Currently, in EST, the logical form of quantified sentences is derived via a rule of quantifier raising (QR)[3] that Chomsky-adjoins the operators to the most proximate sentential node (S node), yielding a structure like (2b) from a structure like (2a)(in matrix clauses):

(2) a. $\left[_{\bar{s}}\left[_{s} \ldots Qx \ldots \right]\right]$

   b. $\left[_{\bar{s}}\left[_{s} Qx\left[_{s} \ldots x \ldots \right]\right]\right]$

QR is a "movement" rule—it moves a constituent from one position in the phrase marker to another position. Moreover, it is conceived to be an instantiation in the LF component, of the more general movement rule operative in the transformational component, the rule Move-α. Given that QR applies at LF, the effects of its application cannot be detected by inspecting the linear order of the string at surface structure. Some evidence for such abstract movement comes from considering the interpretation of certain multiply quantified sentences. The standard scope ambiguities apparent in such simple sentences can be represented in a standard disambiguated format via the repeated application of this rule. For example, consider a sentence like (3):

   (3) Everybody loves somebody

(3) is ambiguous with either the universal quantifier 'everybody' or the existential quantifier 'somebody' enjoying wide scope. The free, unordered application of QR will in fact yield two separate representations of (3):

   (4) a. $\left[_{\bar{s}}\left[_{s} \text{everybody}_{x} \left[_{s} \text{somebody}_{y} \left[_{s} x \text{ loves } y\right]\right]\right]\right]$

   b. $\left[_{\bar{s}}\left[_{s} \text{somebody}_{y} \left[_{s} \text{everybody}_{x} \left[_{s} x \text{ loves } y\right]\right]\right]\right]$

In (4a) QR applied to 'everybody' before applying to 'somebody', resulting in a structure in which 'everybody' dominates or c-commands 'somebody'; in (4b) it applied in the opposite order, with the result that 'somebody' dominates or c-commands 'everybody'.[4] On the assumptions that 'everybody' and 'somebody' are quantified expressions that are moved in LF by QR and that scope relations are determined in LF by c-command relations, Move-α can be used to generate the scope ambiguities of a sentence like (3).

   These interpretive features of a simple example like (3) are not strong evidence in favor of a rule of QR. They are at most suggestive. However, we will see that construing the relative scope interactions of quantifiers as being dependent on the application of a rule like QR has very rich consequences. To take just one example, we will expect certain kinds of scope interactions to be impossible given the limited way in which QR applies, namely, by adjoining a quantified phrase (QP) to the most proximate S node. At any rate, we will expect QPs whose scope domains are determined by the application of QR to have rather intricate and interesting properties. In what follows, we will assume that quantified phrases subject to QR exist and that phrases such as 'everyone', 'someone',[5] 'every man', 'a woman' are noun phrase (NP) expressions of this kind—*type II quantifiers*.

   In the literature on logic, quantified expressions have traditionally been contrasted with names. Names, unlike quantified phrases, do not form operator-variable structures. Their logical form can be represented as ⌜P(a)⌝ ('a' stands for a name, 'P' for a predicate). Translated into the terms of the above discussion, names and namelike expressions are not subject to QR. What, however, is a name or a namelike expression? NPs like 'John', 'Mary', 'Susan' are paradigmatic instances. However, I would like to suggest that many other phrases fall into this category as well; in particular, quantified expressions involving 'any' and 'a certain'. Phrases such as 'anyone', 'a certain woman', 'any gift', 'a certain toy', I would like to argue, have a logical syntax like that of names. Specifically, they are not subject to QR and do not form operator-variable structures in LF. Interestingly, these kinds of quantified expressons— the type I quantifiers—are the ones usually characterized as having wide scope interpretation in relation to other logical entities such as quantified NP ne-gation and modals (see Evans 1977). For example, consider a sentence like (5):

(5) Everyone loves a certain woman

Unlike (3), (5) is not ambiguous. Rather, it has only the interpretation as-sociated with representation (4b); that is, the NP 'a certain woman' has wide scope over the universally quantified expression. However, if it is namelike, 'a certain woman' is not movd by QR and has the LF structure shown in (6):

(6) $[_s[_s$ everyone$_x$ $[x$ loves a certain woman$]]]$

In short, type I quantifiers do not form operator-variable structures and are generally interpreted as having wide scope.

In what follows, we will consider evidence concerning the behavior of type I and type II quantifiers and show that the distinction is empirically well motivated. Given even the brief description of these two kinds of quantifiers above, we should expect to find important differences in their linguistic be-havior. Since the phrase marker representing the logical forms of the sentences that contain type I quantifiers is derived via the movement rule QR, we should expect these quantifiers to be sensitive to conditions or principles constraining movement rules. On the other hand, type II quantifiers, which do not move, should not be affected by such conditions or principles. Moreover, we can expect the two types to differ in their interpretive properties. In fact, we would expect type I quantifiers to act in many respects like ordinary names, particularly where the behavior of names and variables diverges in natural language. Variables are the entities that type II quantifiers leave behind and bind or coindex as a result of QR (see note 2). Last, and most important, we will expect these properties to cluster. That is, wherever a QP is insensitive to movement, we will expect its interpretation to be namelike in certain respects, and vice versa. In short, the distinction between type I and type II quantifiers predicts in a principled manner, in the context of current gram-matical theory, rather specific kind of behavior dependencies. From the point of view of a theory of interpretation, such dependencies are particularly interesting. If they cut a wide enough empirical swath, we can expect the analyses to support just the sorts of features that should be characteristic of a program for which poverty-of-stimulus considerations are central. I will return to this point after considering the empirical data.

THE DATA

Let us look at the behavior of the type II quantifiers 'every', 'a'/'someone' and the type I quantifiers 'any', 'a certain'.[6]

Pronouns as Bound Variables
Consider sentences (7a–g):

(7) a. *John likes every dog$_i$ and it$_i$ likes him
    b. *If John owes every man$_i$ money then Sam pays him$_i$
    c. *Every soldier kissed someone$_i$ if she$_i$ said hello
    d. *Every soldier loves a gun$_i$ because it$_i$ never jams
    e. *John likes every dog$_i$ and Sam feeds it$_i$
    f. *If a/some large man$_i$ loves every woman, then Sally loves him$_i$
    g. *That every wooden house$_i$ is highly inflammable makes it$_i$ expensive to insure

In these sentences, the indexed pronoun cannot be bound by the coindexed quantifier. That is, the interpretation of the pronoun is not determined by the coindexed NP. This is as expected if QR applies as indicated in (2), adjoining the operator to the most proximate S. In (7a), for example, the rule will adjoin the QP 'every dog' to the most proximate S, yielding a structure like (8):

(8) $[_S[_S$ every dog$_i$ $[_S$ John likes $x_i]]$ and $[_S$ it$_i$ likes him$]]$

For a pronoun to be interpreted as a bound variable of a type II QP, it must be c-commanded by that expression in LF.[7] Therefore, in a structure like (8) since 'it' is not c-commanded by and hence not in the scope of the quantified expression 'every dog', it cannot be construed as a bound variable. By claiming that 'every' is a subject to the movement rule QR—that it is a type II quantifier—we can account both for its behavior in such cases and for the unacceptability of the sentence interpreted as in (7a). Similar considerations hold for the other examples in (7).

Contrast this with the sentences in (9):

(9) a. If John likes any man$_i$, then Sam lends him$_i$ money
    b. Every knight loves a certain sword$_i$ because it$_i$ cannot break

    c. John likes a certain dog$_i$ but it$_i$ only likes Sam

    d. Take any number$_i$ and divide it$_i$ by two

    e. That any wooden house$_i$ might be highly inflammable makes it$_i$ expensive to insure

In these sentences, coindexing is possible. This could not be explained if the quantifiers were moved by QR and treated as in (7). What is happening here? If these quantifiers were type I quantified NPs, their logical form would parallel the logical form of names in simple sentences. Thus, it would not be surprising if they had the same coindexing properties as names. Consider sentences (10a–e):

(10) a. If John likes Fred$_i$, then Sam lends him$_i$ money

      b. Every knight loves Excalibur$_i$ because it$_i$ cannot break

      c. John likes Fido$_i$ but he$_i$ only likes Sam

      d. Take four$_i$ and divide it$_i$ by two

      e. That Buckingham Palace$_i$ might be highly inflammable makes it$_i$ expensive to insure

The sentences in (10) are just those in (9) with names in place of the quantifiers. Clearly, these sentences allow coindexing. As is well known, the coindexing possibilities for names are not governed by the same c-command conditions that operate in the case of type II quantified NPs. In particular, coindexing can occur between a name and a pronoun, even if the name does not c-command the pronoun. Indeed, generally speaking, coindexing is impossible between a name and a pronoun if and only if the pronoun c-commands the name. Otherwise it is possible. (See chapter 4 for discussion.) In short, by treating 'any' and 'a certain' as type I quantifiers, we can explain the similar behavior of the sentences in (9) and (10) by citing a common logical form. In other words, we can explain the binding properties displayed by 'any' and 'a certain' by claiming that as far as coindexing is concerned, logical form is the relevant determinant and by treating the logical form of sentences with type I quantifiers in a manner parallel to those with names.

The parallel between names and quantifiers like 'any' and 'a certain' in fact extends beyond sentence grammar. Names can be coindexed with pronouns even across a discourse:

(11) a. Everyone likes Fido$_i$. John sees him$_i$ on the way to work every day.

      b. Take four$_i$ for example. If you multiply it$_i$ by two, the product is even.

If 'any' and 'a certain' are type I quantifiers, we would expect them to act in a similar fashion:

(12) a. Everyone likes a certain dog$_i$. John sees it$_i$ on the way to work every day.

b. Take any number$_i$. If you multiply it$_i$ by two, the product is even.

The behavior of 'any' in examples like (12b) makes it very difficult to interpret it as a type II quantifier of any kind. I mention this because it has often been suggested that 'any' should be treated, in at least some cases, as a wide scope universal quantifier, that is, as a wide scope version of 'every' (see Quine 1960, Hintikka 1976a,b). There are problems with such an approach, however, one of which is relevant here. Briefly, the problem is that the notion of scope relevant to explaining the behavior of universal quantifiers like 'every' is different from the one needed to account for 'any'. The facts in (12) indicate that a non-sentence-bound notion of scope is needed to account for the behavior of 'any', since here its coindexing possibilities appear to extend beyond the sentence. In example (13), however, a narrower sentence-bound notion of scope is crucially utilized to explain the phenomena.

(13) *Everyone$_i$ bought a beer. He$_i$ drank it quickly.

Thus, even though 'every' can have *sententially* wide scope in (13), coindexing across a discourse with the indicated pronouns is not possible because of the sentence-bound nature of this scope. Taken together, these observations seem to indicate that treating 'any' as a wide scope version of 'every' will simply not suffice to predict the full range of its behavior. The relevant notion of scope in the two cases is just not the same.

The Leftness Condition

Chomsky 1976 and Higginbotham 1980 point out that a variable cannot be coindexed with a pronoun to its left. In other words, variables in natural language appear to obey a Leftness Condition with regard to their coindexing possibilities:

(14) a. *That he$_i$ might be sent to the front doesn't bother every good soldier$_i$

b. *That he$_i$ might be sent to fight doesn't bother someone$_i$/a good soldier$_i$[8]

c. *His$_i$ being sent to the front doesn't bother every good soldier$_i$

d. *His$_i$ being sent to the front doesn't bother a good soldier$_i$/someone$_i$

e. *Who$_i$ doesn't his$_i$ being sent to the front bother x_i

In LF these sentences have the structure shown in (15):

(15) $[_s[_s$ every good soldier$_i$ $[_s$ that $[_s$ he$_i$ might be sent to fight doesn't bother $x_i]]]]$

Note that in (15) the quantified NP 'every good soldier' c-commands the pronoun 'he$_i$'. Therefore, (14a) cannot be ruled unacceptable for the same reason as (7 a–g). In the case of (15), the quantifier has full sentential scope. Instead, (14a) is unacceptable because the coindexing violates the Leftness Condition. Similar considerations hold for the other sentences in (14).

The Leftness Condition does not apply to unstressed names,[9] which can be coindexed with pronouns to their left:

(16) a. That he$_i$ might be sent to the front doesn't bother Bill$_i$
     b. His$_i$ being sent to the front doesn't bother Bill$_i$

Thus, the behavior of proper names and variables diverges with regard to the Leftness Condition: the former can violate it, but not the latter. This being so, the Leftness Condition can be used as a diagnostic for whether some position is occupied by a variable or a namelike expression. The issue will turn on whether an expression can coindex a pronoun to its left.[10] Given the analysis of 'any' and 'a certain' as type I quantifiers, we would expect them to behave like names with regard to the Leftness Condition. This prediction is borne out:

(17) a. That he$_i$ might be sent to fight doesn't bother any good soldier$_i$
     b. His$_i$ being sent to the front doesn't bother any good soldier$_i$
     c. That he$_i$ might be sent to fight doesn't bother a certain good soldier$_i$
     d. His$_i$ being sent to the front doesn't bother a certain good soldier$_i$

The Relative Scope of Quantifiers

So far I have discussed some aspects of quantifier "scope" in natural language by focusing on the pronoun binding behavior of various English quantifiers. In this section, I will consider another feature of the interpretation of quantifiers that has traditionally been discussed in terms of scope: the interpretation of multiply quantified sentences. In multiply quantified sentences the different semantic interpretations of the sentence have been analyzed in terms of differences in the relative scopes of the quantifiers in logical form.

In this discussion, I will make two major points. The first is an observation: certain kinds of quantifiers have a property that I will call *interpretative independence*. By this I mean that certain quantifiers are relatively insensitive to their logical environments as far as their interpretations are concerned.[11] This observation is by no means novel. It simply renames a feature of the interpretation of certain quantifiers that has often been discussed in terms of scope considerations. Thus, for example, it has often been claimed that 'any' is a universal quantifier that always takes wide sentential scope. As my remarks indicate, I think it is wrong to describe this feature in terms of a formal notion like scope. However, I will discuss the phenomenon itself, under the name of *interpretative independence*.

Second, I will suggest that this phenomenon of relative interpretive independence correlates with a more formal feature of quantifiers: whether the quantifier is moved by QR to form an operator-variable structure. In effect, lack of QR is a necessary condition for this sort of interpretation in natural language. Although I will discuss in passing how the interpretation of non moved quantifiers should be approached theoretically, this correlation between wide scope interpretation and lack of movement is the point I wish to emphasize.

Let us first consider the interpretation of 'a certain', with the aid of the following sentences:

(18) a. A man/Someone likes every woman
     b. Every man likes a woman/someone
     c. A certain man likes every woman
     d. Every woman likes a certain man

(18a,b) are ambiguous. Either the universal or the existential quantifier can be regarded as having wide scope. Thus, for example, (18b) can be represented as having the structure (19a) if QR applies to 'a woman'/'someone' after it applies to 'every man', or (19b) if the order of application is reversed.

(19) a. $[_s$ every man$_x$ $[_s$ a woman$_y$/someone$_y$ $[_s$ x likes $y]]]$
     b. $[_s$ a woman$_y$/someone$_y$ $[_s$ every man$_x$ $[x$ likes $y]]]$

(19b) corresponds to the interpretation where there is a single woman whom every man likes. (19a) says that for every man there is some woman that he likes; for example, it is true if Bill likes Sally, Fred Ann, and Max Golda.

For (18c,d), however, only the interpretation corresponding to (19b) is available. In other words, the reading of 'a certain man' is interpretively independent of the information provided by the universally quantified phrase 'every woman'.

The interpretation of 'a certain' also tends to be independent of the interpretation of other logical elements such as modals and negations:

(20) a. John didn't kiss a woman/someone at the party
     b. John didn't kiss a certain woman at the party
     c. John must kiss a woman/someone to get in
     d. John must kiss a certain woman to get in

The favored interpretation of (20a,c) corresponds to a structure where the existentially quantified phrase lies within the negation or the modal:

(21) a. not [a woman at the party$_x$ [John kissed x]]
     b. must [a woman$_x$ [John kiss x to get in]]

In (20b,d), however, there is a different interpretation. In these cases the existentially quantified phrase is interpreted as having "wide scope" over the negative and the modal. These sentences would have interpretations parallel to those represented in (22):

(22) a. a woman$_x$ [not [John kiss $_x$]]
 b. a woman$_x$ [must [John kiss x to get in]]

In other words, phenomenally speaking, the interpretation of a quantified noun phrase involving 'a certain' can proceed without regard for the interpretation of other logical elements such as negations, modals, or quantifiers in the phrase.

How should these facts about 'a certain' be incorporated within a theory of meaning for natural language? One way would be to treat them as scope facts, scope being a syntactic property of formal configurations. On such a view, 'a certain' is a quantifier that is mandatorily moved by QR to the widest possible scope position. This would in effect assimilate the behavior of quantified phrases with 'a certain' to standard quantifiers with 'a' or 'every' by appending an additional proviso to QR in the case of 'a certain', namely, that 'a certain' must be moved to widest possible scope position.

There are several problems with such an approach. First, I have already provided evidence that quantifiers like 'a certain' are not moved by QR at all. If this is correct, the property of interpretive independence that they appear to have should not be traced to syntactic features of the logical forms of the sentences in which they occur. However, a scope analysis involves just such a suggestion. On such an approach the ambiguity is related to the specifics of the logical syntax of such sentences yielded by the LF rule of QR.

A second problem is that it does not seem right to treat the interaction of negatives and quantifiers as scope facts, as such a QR analysis of 'a certain' suggests. A scope approach claims that the lack of ambiguity in sentences like (20b) arises from QR assigning mandatory wide scope to 'a certain', i.e., a scope wider than the scope of the negation. However, QR in general seems unable to do this. Thus, sentences like (23) are unambiguous, 'every' being *mandatorily* interpreted as lying within the scope of the negation 'not':

(23) John didn't kiss every woman at the party

If the reason that 'a certain' is not interpreted as within the scope of 'not' in (20b) is that QR mandatorily assigns it wide scope, why can't 'every' *optionally* have wide scope over 'not' when QR optionally assigns it wide scope as in (19a)? Accepting that a scope mechanism of the sort QR embodies is responsible for the interpretation of 'a certain', but also as it applies to 'every' in examples like (23). Given that such complications exact a cost with respect to the acquisition of such rules, this type of approach is not highly favored.

Another set of facts also suggests dealing with the interpretive properties of 'a certain' independently of any mechanism of syntactic scope. QR encodes the observation that the scope of quantifiers like 'every' and 'a'/'someone' is generally limited to their minimal sentential domain. This accounts for the lack of quantifier ambiguities in sentences like (24a,b):

(24) a. Everyone believes that a pretty woman loves him
b. Someone believes that everyone ate well

Given QR as described in (2), the lack of ambiguity in (24) follows. (24b) will have only the logical form (25), where the universal quantifier 'everyone' is in the scope of the existential quantifier 'someone':

(25) $[_s$ someone$_i$ $[x_i$ believes]$[$that $[$everyone$_j$ $[x_j$ ate well]]]]

Now consider (26):

(26) Everyone believes that a certain pretty woman is here

In (26) there is a single pretty woman of whom all have the same belief. If 'a certain' were subject to QR, it would have to be moved beyond the minimal S that contains it so that it would have wide scope over 'everyone'. This would be a further complication of Qr for the case of 'a certain'. Even worse, as we shall see in the next section, structures of the sort that QR would yield in this case are, in general, ill formed. Thus, not only would QR have to be complicated, but the very acceptability of (26) would be difficult to account for given the illicit nature of the structure underlying it.

In light of these considerations it seems worthwhile to divorce the interpretive independence of 'a certain' from a syntactic scope mechanism embodied in a rule like QR. More positively, it is interesting to note that interpretive independence is shared by names. Consider sentences like (27a–d):

(27) a. John likes everyone
b. Everyone likes John
c. Sam doesn't like John
d. Everyone must kiss John

In (27) the behavior of 'John' is quite parallel to that of 'a certain'. Its interpretation is independent of its logical environment. Thus, for example, as Kripke and others have stressed, names are rigid with respect to modal interpretation. The same is true of the interaction of names with negations and quantifiers. The interpretation of names is by and large oblivious to the interpretation of other elements in the clause. In short, names and 'a certain' seem to have many interpretive similarities. We have seen that they also share a significant number of pronoun binding properties. Why not deal with the interpretive behavior of 'a certain' in much the same way that we dealt with its pronoun binding properties—by assimilating the interpretive properties of quantifiers like 'a certain' to those of names? More specifically, let us say that *all* noun phrases not forming operator-variable structures (i.e., all phrases, not only names, that are not moved by QR) are interpreted in a manner functionally independent of the interpretation of other logical operators in the clause.[12] This proposal amounts to saying that the rules of interpretation make a distinction between rules for the interpretation of unmoved elements and rules for the interpretation of moved ones. In particular, these two kinds of rules cannot monitor each other; hence, each is insensitive to the values that the other assigns. On such an account, names and quantifiers like 'a certain' are cases of unmoved elements, and this fact, together with the above suggestion concerning interpretation procedures, accounts for their interpretive independence.

This suggestion regarding interpretation is related to the claim that branching quantification of the sort that Hintikka has suggested occurs in natural languages. Given that on this proposal such phrases are not moved, they do not in fact form branching structures. Still, these phrases act as if they were represented in a branching structure, and we find interpretive effects analogous to those a branching account would imply. The suggestion here is that there are two fundamentally disjoint classes of interpretive rules that are clearly linked with certain syntactic features of operators, i.e., their movability. In earlier proposals such as Hintikka's, quantifiers were treated as a single class. In sum, the present proposal has the interpretive effects of these earlier ones but differs from them considerably in detail by divorcing certain aspects of interpretation from structural features like syntactic scope. I will have more to say on this topic when I discuss the interpretation of 'any'.

A similar, though more complex and interesting, version of the phenomenon of interpretive independence occurs in the case of 'any'. Consider the following sentences:

(28) a. John doesn't like any woman
     b. John doesn't like every woman
     c. John will be richer than any man here
     d. John will be richer than every man here

In (28a,c) the 'any' phrase is interpreted independently of the interpretation of the negation or the modal, as can be seen by comparing these sentences with the corresponding 'every' sentences in (28b,d). This interpretive independence has often been explained by glossing 'any' as a wide scope universal quantifier. On such an approach sentences (28a,c) are given the structures in (29):

(29) a. for all men here$_x$ [not [John like x]]
     b. for all men here$_x$ [will [John more rich than x]]

Thus, under this analysis of 'any', what I have been calling interpretive independence is linked to a special feature pertaining to its scope possibilities in the syntactic sense of scope. As in the case of 'a certain', this approach seems to me beset with many difficulties.

First, I will show in the next section that a scope treatment of 'any' in terms of QR would yield structures that are generally unacceptable. Second, as with 'a certain', there is evidence that 'any' is not moved by QR and does not form operator-variable structures. Scope is a property of syntactic configurations, the scope of an operator being a feature of that operator in a given formal configuration. In a situation where QR does not take place, this syntactic concept cannot apply, and it is therefore not clear how it can be relevant. The problem is this: what sense is there to talking about the scope of an operator where there is no difference at the level of logical syntax between names and quantifiers like 'any'? What is clearly needed is not the notion of scope but its interpretive analogue; something like Kripke's notion of rigidity, for example, or some other notion specifying what interpretive independence amounts to. In any event, the previous two sections have provided evidence against adopting the standard scope treatment of 'any' as an account of how it functions within a natural language like English.

In light of these two considerations, I do not think it would be fruitful to explicate the various aspects of the interpretation of 'any' in terms of a scope mechanism like QR. Rather, it seems more promising to divorce this semantic property of interpretive independence, trying instead to extend the observation concerning names and 'a certain' to the case of 'any'; that is, interpretive independence is a feature of NP elements that are not moved by QR. As in the case of names and 'a certain', the rules for the interpretation of 'any' will be disjoint from other interpretive rules; hence their lack of interaction with the modal and negation in (28).

This said, interpretive independence in the case of 'any' is much more complex than in the case of 'a certain'. In what follows I will briefly consider some of these peculiar interpretive properties and touch on some of the proposals that have been advanced to deal with them.

Linguists and philosophers have adopted two approaches to the treatment of the interpretation of 'any'. One approach postulates two homophonic 'any's'. One of these lexical items receives a reading related to those of existential quantifiers and found when the 'any' resides in a negative polarity environment, for example, in the vicinity of 'not' or 'nobody'. The other 'any'—called *free choice 'any'* by Linebarger 1980—has an interpretation related to universal quantification and is found for example in modal environments. As a concrete example, consider how such a dual approach would interpret the sentences (28a,b). (28a) would have an interpretation analogous to that of (30a):

(30) a. not $[\exists x \ [\text{John like } x]]$
    b. $\forall x \ [\text{will } [\text{more } [\text{John rich than } x]]]$

(28c), on the other hand, would be treated as having an interpretation parallel to that of (30b).

The second approach gives 'any' a uniform interpretation. Both negative 'any' and free choice 'any' are treated like universal quantifiers. The existential import of negative sentences such as (28a) comes from treating 'any' like a wide scope quantifier and exploiting the logical equivalence between "for all x not . . ." and "it's not the case that there exists an x such that . . ." And since sentences like (28c) appear to have no existential import,[13] it is clear that a uniform approach to the interpretation of 'any' would have to select the universal reading.

In what follows I will consider how certain facts concerning the interpretation of 'any' and the proposal concerning the logical syntax of 'any' both bear on these two approaches.

Consider the following sentences:[14]

(31) a. Someone doesn't like anyone
    b. Someone likes every woman
    c. Someone doesn't like every woman

In (31a) the interpretation of the existential phrase 'someone' is not affected by the interpretation of the 'any'-phrase. In other words, whereas (31b,c) are ambiguous with either the universal or the existential enjoying wide scope, in (31a) 'someone' is construed as unambiguously taking wider scope; significantly, this means that 'any' appears *not* to be taking wide scope.

Consider what this means for the two approaches to 'any'. For the two 'any's' theory this is in some sense expected. Thus, for example, Linebarger's theory (1980) holds that 'any' must be interpreted as being in the immediate scope of the negation if there is one—a provision called the *Immediate Scope Condition*.[15] Thus, (31a) would have an interpretation corresponding to the logical form (32):

(32) $\text{someone}_x \ [\text{not } [\text{someone}_y \ [x \text{ likes } y]]]$

Given that quantifiers in subject positions are generally not interpreted as being in the scope of a negation in VP position, and given the Immediate Scope Condition that Linebarger motivates, the correct interpretation of (31a) follows.

What about the single 'any' thesis? In and of itself (31a) poses no problem for treating 'any' as a universal quantifier. What it does show, however, is that the scope properties of 'any' are unusual; it takes interpretive precedence over a negative or a modal but not over other quantifiers in the clause. In other words, though 'any' is a wide scope quantifier, it is not a widest scope quantifier. What this means, I believe, is one of two things: either 'any' has the property that it takes wide scope over at most one logical operator—in (31a) the negation but not the existential quantifier—or it is an operator that takes wide scope but is interpreted in a branching manner. Let us consider these possibilities.

If we wished to treat 'any' in a unified manner as a special type of universal quantifier, we could account for (31a) by saying that 'any' takes wide scope over at most one operator, in this case the negation. This proposal would amount to reformulating the Immediate Scope Condition to read, in the case of 'any', that the negation must appear in the immediate scope of 'any'. The interpretation of (31a) would then parallel the interpretation of a sentence with the logical form (33):

(33) someone$_x$ [everyone$_y$ [not [x likes y]]]

However, based on our discussion of 'a certain', a more attractive solution presents itself—the second alternative above—which allows us to maintain the claim that 'any' has wide scope in (31a) despite the interpretation of 'someone' noted. As discussed in the case of 'a certain', the interpretation of unmoved elements is functionally independent of the interpretations of the moved quantified NPs. If this idea were extended to the case of 'any', the interpretation of (31a) would be parallel to the *interpretion* (but would not have the *form*) of structures like (34):

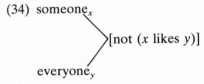

(34) someone$_x$

[not (x likes y)]

everyone$_y$

If the interpretation of sentences with 'any' is parallel to those represented in (34), then the interpretation noted for (31a) follows. In structures like (34) the quantifiers in different arms of a branching structure are interpreted independently of one another. Thus, the interpretation of (34) will be equivalent to the interpretation of (35):

(35) some$_x$ [every$_y$ [not [x likes y]]]

The structure represented in (35) correctly accounts for the interpretation that (31a) in fact has. Thus, by accepting this branching view of the interpretation of unmoved elements, of which 'any' is one, we can maintain an analysis of 'any' as a wide scope universal quantifer.[16]

Others (most notably Hintikka) have suggested that natural languages do in fact have interpretations involving branching quantification. My suggestion, though compatible with theirs, nonetheless differs from it. What I have considered above (and throughout this study, following the EST paradigm) is a question concerning the format of certain mental representations: should the interpretation of sentences having quantifiers like 'any' be represented as involving branching interpretation procedures? In Hintikka's discussion of the branching quantifiers (1974, 1976b) the argument is that in certain rather complex sentences involving four quantifiers—two universal and two existential in ∀ ∃ ∀ ∃ linear order—interpretations of the quantifiers arise that a nonbranching theory would forbid. Such interpretations hang on the informational independence of the two sets of ∀ ∃ quantifiers. As Hintikka observes, one way of neatly representing this sort of informational independence is to claim that the interpretation of such sentences involves branching rules. However, by itself Hintikka's argument does not force the conclusion that the theory of *grammar* should allow branching quantification. An obvious alternative would trace the interpretation of such sentences to considerations of processing rather than grammar. We might claim that the rules of grammar yield linear interpretive formats but that because of the complexity of the sentences involved, processing limitations lead to interpreting the pairs of quantifiers independently of one another. In this way the effects of branching quantification in *complex* constructions could be obtained even if the actual representation of the sentences in the grammar involved only linearly ordered interpretation procedures for quantifiers.

In the cases discussed here, however, a branching format for the interpretation rules seems more clearly implicated. (31a) is not particularly complex, so that processing limitations do not seem very relevant. Moreover, the cases involving 'any' *only* allow a reading in which the quantifiers are interpreted independently, even though such sentences are no more complex than sentences involving 'every', where ambiguity is possible.

(36) a. Someone at the party likes anyone who was invited
     b. Someone at the party likes everyone who was invited

(36a) has an interpretation parallel to (37a), whereas (36b) can also be interpreted as in (37b):

(37) a. Some y [every x [[x likes y]]]
     b. every x [some y [x likes y]]

The general conclusion is that in dealing with the grammar of natural language, one must distinguish acceptability from grammaticality. The latter is a theoretical notion relating to the actual rules characterizing the mental representation of linguistic entities. The former is a far less theoretically loaded concept. Significantly, sentences that are not grammatical may still be acceptable, though their acceptability will be due to *extragrammatical* factors such as processing.[17] My remarks on branching differ from Hintikka's in trying to keep these different possible sources of acceptability in focus and in suggesting that, in the case of 'any', a grammatical approach is the most reasonable one to pursue.

A second important difference is that under Hintikka's proposal sentences like (31a) form branching structures, whereas under mine they do not. To be more precise, if Hintikka's proposal were taken literally and embedded within the assumptions adopted here, it would suggest that type I quantifiers *do* move, though the positions to which they move branch with respect to the other linearly ordered elements. In other words, the interpretive independence of 'any'-phrases is due to their having structures like (34). On my account, 'any'-phrases do not move. They do not form syntactic structures like (34) in LF. Rather, I associate a certain kind of interpretive rule with unmoved NPs. Since Hintikka's own discussion of branching does not proceed within the assumptions adopted here, it would be fair to see my proposal as only a slight modification of his. Still, if we are to explain the phenomena of earlier sections, it is important to keep this modification of Hintikka's proposal in mind.

Of the two approaches to a uniform treatment of the interpretation of 'any', I prefer the branching analysis. Despite some difficulties, such an analysis seems worth pursing, since it allows 'any' and 'a certain' to be treated alike. However, either uniform treatment of 'any' seems preferable to the dual interpretation homophonic theory. To support this belief, I offer the following indirect suggestive evidence: namely, that regardless of whether one gets the existential reading ((38b,d,f)) or the universal reading ((38a,c,e)), 'any' acts uniformly with regard to the Leftness Condition, pronoun coindexing, and cross-discourse reference.[18]

      Leftness Condition
(38) a. That he$_i$ might get shot would bother anyone$_i$
      b. That he$_i$ might get shot didn't bother any soldier$_i$
      Pronoun Coindexing
      c. Sam will hit anyone$_i$ if he$_i$ wins
      d. If anyone$_i$ wins, Sam will hit him$_i$
      Cross-Discourse Reference
      e. Take any number$_i$. Divide it$_i$ by two.
      f. John$_j$ didn't kiss any woman$_i$ at the party. Why? Because she$_i$ would have hit him$_j$ if he$_j$ had.

In other words, as far as these interpretive procedures go, the distinctions that a dual approach would make between existential and free choice 'any' disappear. One could retain the dual analysis despite these facts, concluding that 'any' is a single element in the syntax of LF and nonetheless interpretively ambiguous. However, such an approach would be less favored than one that treated 'any' as interpretively singular in both LF and interpretation.

In this section I have briefly discussed some aspects of 'any' interpretation and have hesitantly opted for a treatment of 'any' and 'a certain' that involves branching interpretation procedures, though not a branching syntactic form at LF. More important, however, are the two basic facts (a) that both elements have relative interpetive independence and (b) that both act as if they are not moved by QR to form operator-variable structures. The main goal of the discussion was to suggest that these two facts should be seen as correlating as a matter of grammatical principle. It is a principle of Universal Grammar that unmoved elements are interpretively independent and moved elements interpretively dependent.

The Empty Category Principle

In this section I will focus on the fact that QR is a *movement* rule.

Kayne 1979, Aoun, Hornstein, and Sportiche 1980, and Chomsky 1981 have argued that all movement rules, including those in the LF component of the grammar, of which QR is one are subject to a condition called the *Empty Category Principle* (ECP).[19] This condition prohibits "long" movement of the quantifier phrase from the subject position of tensed clauses. As a result of ECP violations, the following sentences are marked unacceptable:

(39) a. *Jean n'exige que personne aime le gâteau
        'John doesn't demand that anyone like the cake.'
     b. *Who believes that who left the party

A sentence like (39a) would have the structure in (40):

(40) $[_s$ personne$_x$ $[_s$ Jean n'exige $[_{\bar{s}}$ que $[_s$ x aime le gâteau$]]]]$

In a structure like (40) the quantifier 'personne' controls the variable 'x' in a nonlocal manner from outside the clause within which the variable resides. It is binding of this sort between a moved element and its trace left in the subject position of a tensed sentence that the ECP prohibits.

Importantly, the ECP is a condition on the residue of *movement* rules (i.e., the empty categories such rules leave behind) and thus can be used to distinguish elements that move from those that do not. Given the analysis I have proposed, we should expect the latter—type I quantified NPs—never to lead to ECP violations despite a "wide scope" interpretation. We should also expect the former to be subject to the ECP and so possibly violate it. In English, the second hypothesis is harder to test, since type II quantifiers are generally assigned scope in their minimal sentential domains, thus, no "long" movement takes place and no ECP violations result. However, cases of this sort do occur in French, as (39a) indicates. The scope of 'personne' is determined by the position of 'ne'. It will have scope over the clause of which 'ne' is an element. In (39a) 'personne' is moved to the matrix clause—as shown in (40)—by QR. However, since the variable in the most embedded S is now not locally bound, an ECP violation occurs and the sentence is unacceptable.

That the ECP holds in English is attested to by (39b).[20] The ECP forbids interpreting (39b) as a double question of the following form:

(41) (For which x, which y) (x believes that y left the party)

Since the rule Move-α is involved in the formation of the structure that underlies sentences of this sort, the same "long" movement prohibitions are in force.

As we have seen, both 'any' and 'a certain' are generally construed as having widest possible scope:

(42) a. Everyone believes that *a certain pretty woman* is here
     b. Sam doesn't believe that *anyone* came to the party

The fact that (42a,b) are fully acceptable corroborates the argument given in the previous section that such sentences are not derived from structures where QR has moved the indicated phrases. If QR were involved, we would expect the same unacceptability noted in (39), for here too the ECP would be violated.[21] However, by treating 'any' and 'a certain' as type I quantifiers not subject to a movement rule like QR, we have no more reason to expect unacceptability in (42) than in (43):

(43) John believes that Harry is here

A Cluster of Effects

We have seen that there are two distinct *kinds* of quantifiers in English. On the one hand there are type II quantifiers, which are moved by QR. As a result of being subect to a movement rule like this one, these expressions obey the Leftness Condition, have restricted scope and coindexing properties, are subject to the ECP, and have interpretive rules that are sensitive to the interpretation of other quantifiers.

On the other hand there are type I quantifiers, which in many respects act like names. These are not moved by QR. Thus, they are interpreted in a branching manner, have extensive coindexing properties, and are subject neither to the Leftness Condition nor to the ECP.

In a word, my proposal is that the two kinds of quantifiers are distinguished by whether or not they are subject to QR, that is, whether or not they form operator-variable structures. Moreover, by explaining the coincidence of properties noted above by reference to the *single* fact of whether the quantifiers do or do not undergo QR, we predict that the phenomena will appear together.[22] This prediction is borne out. Let us consider in more detail the French quantifier 'ne . . .personne':

(44) *Jean n'exige que personne aime le gâteau

The scope of 'personne' is determined by the position of 'ne'. It is moved by QR, which adjoins it to the clause that 'ne' inhabits. The unacceptability of (44) is due to ECP violation. The proposed analysis thus predicts that 'ne . . . personne' is a type II quantifier and that it will pattern accordingly. It does:

(45) a. *Qu'il$_i$ soit arrêté par la police n'a jamais empêché personne$_i$ de voler (Leftness Condition)
'That he would be arrested never deterred anyone from stealing.'

b. *Si personne$_i$ n'est arrêté par la police, il$_i$ continuera à voler (limited coindexing)
'If anyone is not arrested by the police, he will continue to steal.'

c. *Personne$_i$. n'aime quelqu'un. Il$_i$ aime seulement les gâteaux. (no cross-discourse coindexing)
'Nobody likes anyone. He only likes cakes.'

Thus, 'ne . . . personne' not only falls under the ECP but also has limited scope and coindexing possibilites, obeys the Leftness Condition, and cannot coindex across a discourse. As predicted, the properties cluster together.

That this should be the case is particularly interesting evidence in favor of the analysis presented here. It predicts an interdependence of phenomena that is by no means obvious or logically necessary.[23]

These 'ne . . . personne' facts support the analysis in a more subtle way as well. In providing the relevant explanations, the above account focuses on the *formal* property of whether quantifiers are moved by QR to form operator-variable structures rather than on the interpretation of the quantifiers. The French facts corroborate this focus because, although the two expressions pattern very differently with respect to the relevant formal phenomena, 'ne . . . personne' and 'any' are virtually synonymous. For most purposes, the best English translation of a sentence with 'ne . . . personne' is almost always a sentence with 'any'. By locating the difference between quantifiers in a difference in their logical syntax, we allow for the possibility that their interpretive procedures will be similar. Comparing 'any' and 'ne . . . personne' vividly shows that these two features—interpretation and logical syntax—must be kept distinct. If the interpretation and thelogical form of an expression co-varied, we would expect items with similar interpretive properties to behave similarly in all cases. But, as we have seen, this is not the case.

ACQUIRING QUANTIFICATIONAL COMPETENCE

Before we continue, it is worthwhile pausing a moment to see how the logical problem of acquisition drives the arguments presented above.

I have argued that bifurcating the class of quantifiers and representing them as either type I or type II allows a *principled* explanation for a broad and interesting range of linguistic phenomena. I have *not* argued that it is impossible to treat 'any', 'every', 'a', 'someone', 'a certain' in a unitary fashion. It is indeed possible to capture or represent the relevant phenomena in a theory exclusively exploiting an operator-variable approach. Pronoun binding and relative quantifier scope could be accounted for simply by adjusting QR so that it moved 'any' and 'a certain' to their proper places in the course of applying. The facts pertaining to the Leftness Condition, cross-sentential coindexing, and the ECP could always be accommodated by special devices distinguishing QR as it applies to 'any'/'a certain' and 'every'/'a'/'someone'. Although these alternatives may be inelegant, they will suffice if the goal is simply to cover the data. However, if the goal is to explain how a child could acquire these rules, such approaches lead to insurmountable problems. What could lead a child to treat these quantifiers differently, especially given the often close similarity in meaning, for example, between 'any' and 'every' or even more strikingly between 'any' and 'ne . . . personne'? Why shouldn't the child bring these quantifiers together under one generalization? One might answer that the evidence cited above is surely what forces the child to treat these quantifiers differently. But how reasonable is this? Is it really reasonable to believe that sentences bearing on the Leftness Condition, such as (15)–(17), abound or even exist in the primary linguistic data? Would anyone ever use the unacceptable sentences in (14)? If not (as seems most likely, given their unacceptability), what evidence could force the distinctions noted? Even if relevant data are available, is it reasonable to think the child pays attention to them? How likely is it that the facts concerning the ECP can be winnowed from the primary linguisitic data? In English, neither 'every' nor 'any' violates the ECP, so they appear to act alike. However, this similarity is mere coincidence arising from the local nature of QR, as the French facts and the double-'wh' facts cited in (39) show. Is it plausible that English speakers refer to French data in constructing their grammars and vice versa? Why does the child learning French not treat 'ne . . . personne' in the same way that the English child treat 'any'? The meanings are very similar. Moreover, why do the phenomena cluster as they do? Why does 'ne . . . personne' not act like 'every' with respect to pronoun coindexing and the ECP but like 'any' with respect to the Leftness Condition?

The answers seem obvious. There is no reason to believe that the different patterns of phenomena can be explained by citing features of the primary linguistic data. As this is what a uniform treatment implies when viewed in relation to the logical problem of acquisition, such an approach appears untenable. Though it can "cover" the data, the difficulties that confront a uniform approach when viewed as an explanation for the acquisition of quantifier competence demonstrate its empirical inadequacy.

An account that bifurcates the class of natural language quantifiers does not face these difficulties. The quantifiers behave differently because they are different kinds of quantifiers in Universal Grammar. The different patterns of behavior can be traced back to a single difference encoded in Universal Grammar: whether or not the quantifier forms operator-variable structures. That there are two types of quantifiers and that they have their associated properties and features of Universal Grammar and, as such, are innate. Thus, the fact that different quantifiers exemplify different paradigms of behavior can be accounted for without invoking the shaping effects of the primary linguistic data. Moreover, the child can accomplish the (simpler) task of *classification* quite easily on the basis of evidence from the linguistic environment. For example, from hearing sentences like (18a,b), the child gains evidence that 'every' and 'a'/'someone' are type II quantifiers. From hearing sentences like those in (9) and (28) and discourses like those in (11) and (12), the child learns that 'any' and 'a certain' are type I quantifiers. To classify the quantifiers, given that the classification scheme is itself innate, the child can rely exclusively on the positive data available in these kinds of simple sentences. Contrary to what happens in the other scenario, the child is not dependent on the kinds of data available only from complex sentences involving the ECP or even more exotic ones involving the Leftness Condition. Furthermore, the child needs no negative data, i.e., data to the effect that certain sentence types are unacceptable. From the perspective of the logical problem of acquisition, a theory of this kind makes far fewer demands on the language learner. The child need only decide whether a given quantifier is type I or type II, a manageable task since all the relevant information is contained in simple sentences of the kind noted above. Everything else follows from the child's innate grammatical endowment.

To be empirically adequate, any account will have to deal with the central fact that language acquisition proceeds despite an extremely poor data base. Embedding semantic questions like the nature of quantifier structure within the larger concerns of current linguistic theory forces one to hypotheses compatible with this most prominent of linguistic facts. In effect, it highlights a set of empirical costs and benefits that can be used to evaluate the relative merits of competing proposals about the logical structure of natural language. Judged by these costs and benefits, a bifurcated theory of quantifiers in natural language seems clearly superior to a unitary treatment.

CONCLUSION

The arguments of this chapter have shown that there exist two fundamentally different kinds of quantifiers. To put it more accurately, understanding the semantic aspects of natural language quantifiers requires distinguishing two axes that until now have generally been merged: an *interpretive* axis and a *logical syntax* axis. The interpretive axis is what philosophers have by and large concentrated on. 'Any', 'every', 'a'/'someone', 'a certain' do share important similarities when contrasted with names. Unlike names, none of them is a denoting expression. There is no anyman or anywoman. Rather, these expressions are interpreted relative to a given domain of entities.[24] Moreover, 'any' and 'every' both have general interpretations; 'a'/'someone' and 'a certain' do not.

The nature of the logical syntax axis should be clear; some phrases are of operator-variable form and some are not. Traditional logical analyses have treated all phrases that are quantifiers on the interpretive axis as also having operator-variable form. The above considerations show that this conflation is incorrect for natural language. More precisely, call elements having the interpretive properties noted above *quantifiers*, and those not having them *names*. Call NP elements moved by QR and so forming operator-variable structures *operators*, and those not so moved *terms*. The discussion above can be seen as claiming that not all quantifiers are operators and that some terms are quantifiers. An NP element has two axes relevant to predicting its semantic behavior; it can be [±:operator] ([−operator] = term) and [±quantifier] ([−quantifier] = name). Type I quantifiers such as 'any' and 'a certain' are [+quantifier, −operator]. Type II quantifiers such as 'every', and 'a' are [+quantifier, +operator]. Both features are relevant in explaining how what are pretheoretically called quantifiers behave semantically in natural language. In particular, distinguishing these two axes makes it possible to capture the namelike properties of certain kinds of quantifiers.

Furthermore, this typology of quantifiers is an aspect of Universal Grammar, an innate feature of the language faculty. There is simply not enough evidence to presuppose that the typology itself could be acquired on the basis of primary linguistic data. However, there is no a priori basis for expecting *in general* that a quantifier will fall into one or another class. Which element falls into which class is clearly a parameter set by the primary linguistic data. In short, the parameter [±operator] is innate. The specific value accorded a particular expression is a function of the linguistic environment.

NOTES

1. Too much should not be made of this use of words. *Logical form*, in this context, is not intended to carry any of the metaphysical or ontological import that the term carries in the philosophical literature.

2. Variables in EST are defined as empty NP categories, i.e., [$_{NP}$ e], which are coindexed with operators. Variables are found in argument positions (A-positions). These positions include subject, object, indirect object, and object of a preposition. Operators are found in Ā-positions, e.g., in complementizer position or adjoined positions. For a full discussion, see Chomsky 1981.

3. QR, see Chomsky 1976 and May 1977. On the local nature of QR—i.e., that type II QPs are adjoined to the most proximate S-node—see chapter 4 of *Logical Grammar* and Aoun and Hornstein (forthcoming).

4. An element A c-commands an element B if and only if the first branching category dominating A also dominates B. For example, consider structure (i):

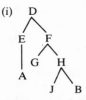

(i)

In (i) the first category dominating A is E. However, the first *branching* category dominating A is D. D in turn dominates B. Thus, A c-commands B. A also c-commands G,F, H, and J. Of these, only F c-commands A. See Reinhart 1976 for a full discussion of c-command.

5. 'Someone' is a type II QP, as are 'somewhere', 'something', 'somebody', 'sometime', etc. However, quantified NPs whose quantifier is 'some', such as 'some woman', 'some man', are not type II QPs. The latter expressions appear to function in some dialects more like type I QPs than type II QPs. In fact, 'some N' seems to function in such dialects quite similarly to 'a certain N'. I will discuss this later in the text.

6. The 'a' to be discussed here is the nongeneric, existential 'a'. Isolating this 'a' can be tricky. One way to make sure one is dealing with the existential 'a' is to embed it in the scope of a universal quantifier. For a discussion of generics, see chapter 5.

7. See Chomsky 1976 and Higginbothan 1980 for discussion of pronoun binding.

8. The judgments indicated here are for the existential 'a', not the generic 'a'. See note 6.

9. Stressed names—indeed, stressed elements in general—are subject to a rule of Focus. This rule moves the stressed element, by QR, to an Ā-position. In effect, stress creates structures of operator-variable form. See Chomsky 1976 for discussion, as well as note 23.

10. The Leftness Condition has recently been analyzed as a special instance of the Bijection Principle in Koopman and Sportiche 1981. I consider their analysis and its relationship to the issues discussed here in chapter 4 of Logical Grammar.

11. I say "relatively" insensitive because it appears that unstressed 'any' may interact with other operators in certain complex constructions. See Hintikka 1976a,b for discussion of some of these issues, as well as note 16.

12. In standard semantical approaches, the noninteraction of names with quantifiers is attributed to a uniqueness condition on names. In the account given here, a focus on the termlike nature of names is what allows the explanation for names to be extended to operators more generally, even those whose interpretation is not subject to uniqueness conditions. This does not mean that uniqueness is not sufficient to allow free scope permutations without affecting interpretation. Rather, it is not necessary. Operators that do not form operator-variable structures, but are not subject to uniqueness conditions, can nonetheless be regarded as branching,

or freely permutable with respect to all other operators. The point made here is that this is true for all terms (elements not forming operator-variable structures), and not just names or definite descriptions. See chapter 3 of Logical Grammar for further discussion of the relationship between uniqueness and termhood in definite descriptions.

13. There is one kind of sentence that appears to require an existential treatment of 'any':

(i) Is anyone home?

(i) is roughly paraphrased as (ii) rather than (iii), where '?' is the operator involved in yes/no questions:

(ii) ? ∃x (x home)
(iii) ∀x ? (x home)

One way around such cases is to note that '?' is a trigger for a negative polarity item (Linebarger 1980). For regular negations like 'not', 'not ∃x' is equivalent to '∀x not'. What if we extended such equivalence to '?'? We could then treat 'any' as having wide scope and explain its existential import by noting that 'any ?' is equivalent to '? ∃x'. In short, the yes/no question operator decomposes into two parts: a question operator and a hidden negation. The latter, like negation in general, permits the above equivalences and hence the existential reading in (i).

14. Similar data are discussed in Linebarger 1980.

15. This presentation of the Immediate Scope Condition (ISC) is adapted from Linebarger 1980. Her account treats the ISC as a condition on logical form rather than interpretation procedures. She thus interprets the scope part of the ISC syntactically. As I have argued, this notion cannot apply to 'any'-phrases, since they do not have operator-variable form in LF. I have therefore reinterpreted the ISC as a condition on interpretation procedures rather than LF.

16. If a branching account were to be pursued, the standard accounts would have to be altered in important ways. For example, branching would not be symmetrical. In standard accounts, if a quantifier A branches with respect to B, then B also branches with respect to A (see (34)). However, in English, if a branching account of 'any' is correct, then this is not the case.

(i) John didn't give anyone a present

Here the existential phrase is conditioned by the interpretation of 'anyone'; thus, its interpretation cannot branch with respect to 'anyone'. In (ii), however, 'anyone' does not condition the interpretation of the existential.

(ii) Someone doesn't like anyone

Note that in (ii), but not (i), the existential c-commands 'any'. Perhaps, then, A branches with respect to a type I QP B if and only if A c-commands B. This would account for the examples above.

17. For other examples of acceptable, yet ungrammatical, sentences, see Hornstein and Weinberg 1981.

18. Both types of 'any' are also immune to ECP violations, as discussed in the next section. Note that if different interpretive procedures are required to account for these two kinds of 'any', the main point will still be valid: the different interpretive procedures for 'any' do not correspond to different representations at LF. Interpretive interaction, if it is found to be necessary, is not due to QR or other mechanisms of syntactic scope. Also see note 23.

19. The ECP is defined as follows:

(i) An empty category [ₐ e] must be properly governed.
(ii) An element α properly governs an element β iff α governs β and

a. β is a variable bound by an operator or
b. α is adjacent to β.
(iii) α governs β iff
a. α is a lexical category and
b. α and β c-command each other.

For further discussion and details, see Chomsky 1981:250ff.

20. As noted in Chomsky 1981:234, Kayne 1979 gives some plausible English violations of the ECP. See Aoun, Hornstein, and Sportiche 1980 for a more elaborate discussion of the ECP and the case of multiple questions.

21. Sentences like (42a,b) are discussed in chapter 4 of Chomsky 1981. The difficulties he notes are eliminated if 'any' is treated as a type I QP.

22. What appears to be pronoun binding can occur even if binding is not involved. These sorts of cases are discussed in Evans 1977. As Evans points out, there are important differences between his cases of E-type pronouns and regular binding. Most overtly, there are complex conditions on pronoun agreement in the case of E-type pronouns that do not exist in the case of binding:

(i) Everyone$_i$ saw his$_i$ mother
(ii) *If everyone$_i$ comes he$_i$ will have a good time
(iii) If everyone comes they will have a good time

(i) is a regular case of pronoun binding. In (ii), since 'everyone' is a type II QP, the indicated coindexing is disallowed. (iii), however, is fine with 'everyone' and 'they' coreferential; it is an instance of E-type binding. In this book, I have tried to control for E-type effects by concentrating on examples such as (i) and (ii).

As Evans notes, pronoun binding and E-type binding exhibit other differences as well, of an interpretive variety. The cases he discusses and the ones considered here appear to be interpretively and structurally distinct. To take one example:

(iv) Mary danced with many boys$_i$ and they$_i$ found her interesting.

(iv) does not mean 'Mary danced with many boys who found her interesting', which a bound pronoun approach would require. Similarly for (v):

(v) John likes $\left\{\begin{array}{l}\text{just any dog,}\\\text{every dog,}\end{array}\right\}$ and $\left\{\begin{array}{l}\text{*it,}\\\text{they,}\end{array}\right\}$ like(s) him

23. Consider one more case. The proposed theory predicts dependencies among the five properties discussed in the text. Thus, for example, if an NP obeys the Leftness Condition, it will act like a type II quantified expression more generally. Consider the case of 'any' found in "insult" sentences:

(i) If anybody can do it, John can.
(ii) John won't talk to (just) anybody.

In these cases 'any' carries intonational stress. Therefore, by the rule of Focus, discussed in Chomsky 1976, it is moved by QR; that is, it is treated like a type II QP. Note that in (i) 'any' is *within* the scope of the conditional. Similarly, in (ii) it is in the scope of the negation. This case of 'any' (call it *insult-'any'*) is not interpretively independent in the sense discussed earlier. Moreover, it does not allow cross-sentence or cross-discourse coindexing, and it obeys the Leftness Condition:

(iii) *His$_i$ being sent home didn't worry (just) anybody$_i$
(iv) *If (just) anybody$_i$ can win, he$_i$ can.
(v) *John likes any dog$_i$ (stressed intonation). He$_i$ only likes Sam.

Here, sentences with insult-'any' do not act like the sentences with 'any' discussed in the text. The rule of Focus, plus the distinction between type I and type II QPs, explains why this is so and predicts the properties in (i)–(v).

Note as well that insult-'any' has the import of a universal quantifier. This adds some weight to the account of 'any' as a *single* interpretive element, i.e., a universal quantifier. The unstressed counterparts of (i) and (ii) would require the existential reading of 'any'. Stress appears to change these to universal 'any'. Why stress should be able to do this if there are in fact two types of 'any' is unclear. However, the assumption that 'any' is always universal accounts straightforwardly for these sorts of examples.

24. These sorts of semantical notions will be discussed in chapter 7 of *Logical Grammar*.

IVAN A. SAG

A LOGICAL THEORY OF VERB-PHRASE DELETION[1]

It has been known for some time that mere identity of terminal strings is insufficient to guarantee recoverability of deletion. Lees (1960), for instance, cited examples like (1) to show that in order for deletion to apply, the deletion target and the deletion trigger must have identical constituent structure. (Lees actually argued for the stronger condition of identity of derivational history).

(1) *Drowning cats, which is against the law, are hard to rescue.

Similar arguments can be found scattered throughout the transformational literature of the last decade or so (see for instance Chomsky, (1965), (1968); Ross, (1967); Lakoff, (1968); and Hankamer, (1971). Ross and Lakoff both speculate that the necessary condition on deletion is identity of underlying structure. The standard examples are those in (2)—all involving Verb Phrase Deletion (VPD)—which are two, not four, ways ambiguous.

(2) (a) John likes flying planes, and Bill does too.
    (b) Betsy divulged when Bill promised to call me, and Sandy did, too.
    (c) The chickens are ready to eat, and the children are too.

Now Lakoff discusses (2) (c) in some detail. He notes in fact that on the "ready to be eaten" reading, (2) (c) presents a problem for the theory of identity of underlying structure as a necessary condition for deletion. The problem, *tout court*, is that on the standard view of these sentences, the trigger and target VP's correspond to non-identical entities in underlying structure. In an Aspects-type theory, for instance (which Lakoff was working on at the time), the underlying structure of (2) (c) on this "object-deletion" reading, would be as in (3).

(3)

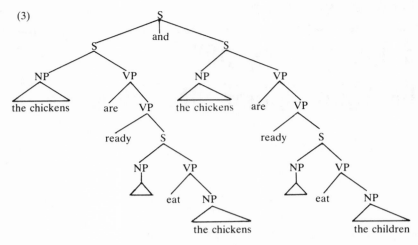

The circled VP's are non-identical (in fact no VP's are identical).

Lakoff suggested that "items that do not appear in the derived structure are completely irrelevant to the question of linguistically significant identity." This suggestion, though hardly explanatory, might conceivably handle the following cases as well.

(4) (a) Paul was hassled by the police, and Norma was too.
(b) Betsy seems to me to be unhappy, and Sandy does too.
(c) Peter is easy to talk to, and Betsy is too.

It is interesting to note, however, that Lakoff's suggestion fails to account for why these next examples are ungrammatical.

(5) (a) *The steak is ready to eat, and the chicken is ready to, also.
(b) *Peter is easy to talk to, and Betsy is easy to, also.

These have the same underlying structure and the same structure immediately prior to deletion (in all relevant respects) as (2) (c) and (3) (c), which are legitimate instances of VPD. Why should it be possible to delete the "higher" VP and not the embedded one, when the necessary identity holds between all the VP's in question. Note further that on the EQUI reading, similar sentences with *ready to* are perfectly acceptable:

(6) Peter is ready to give up, and Betsy $\begin{Bmatrix} \text{(a) is} \\ \text{(b) is ready to} \end{Bmatrix}$ also.

We will return to this curious state of affairs in a moment, but some further remarks are in order first.

In Lakoff (1970), the claim is made that VP-Deletability is a test for true ambiguity, rather than "vagueness" of meaning (see Sadock and Zwicky,

(1973), for further discussion of this matter). Now for reasons that I'll mention later, it's not completely clear that the level where the appropriate identity for deletion is determined is the same level where such matters as logical consequence are determinable (Lakoff's claim would appear to be tantamount to this). Nevertheless I would like to argue that there is a level of logical form (I mean level in the sense of Chomsky (1955)) where the applicability of deletion rules is determined. Moreover, I would like to suggest that logical forms are far less "abstract" than is frequently claimed, especially, say, by proponents of Generative Semantics.

By this I mean that the logical form of a sentence like "Betsy loves Peter" should not be as in (7) (many details omitted), as many philosophers and linguists (especially following McCawley, (1970) assume, but rather

(7) LOVE (BETSY, PETER)

should express the *grammatical* relation of subject-predicate overtly. Recent work in the framework of Montague Grammar, it seems, to me, (Montague, (1974); Partee, (1975); Thomason, (1974), has come much closer to positing the kind of logical forms that will allow us to give an adequate account of VPD (though I will not commit myself here to Montague's "proper treatment" of quantification).

The crucial device whose credibility I would like to establish (from the point of view of capturing linguistically significant generalizations) is the λ-calculus (Church, 1941). Suppose, essentially along with Montague, that every surface verb phrase corresponds to a λ-predicate in logical form. The logical form of "Betsy loves Peter" we will write as in (8)[2]

(8) Betsy, λx(love $(x$, Peter)) or simply
    Betsy, $\lambda x(x$ love Peter)

Very roughly, this is to be thought of intuitively as predicating a property of Betsy, namely, the property of loving Peter.

Now the λ-calculus allows us to do many things (this is hardly one of its virtues). One very nice feature of the λ-calculus however, is that it allows us to assign to a quantifier what is essentially VP-scope. The preferred reading of "someone loves everyone," then, we will write as (9)

(9) $(\text{E}x \ (x, \ \lambda y \ ((\forall z) \ (y \ \text{loves} \ z)))$

(intuitively, there exists some x, such that x has the property of loving everyone). Further speculations about the nature of logical forms will be offered in what follows.

One more notion that must be brought to the fore before proceeding is the standard notion of "alphabetic variance." Intuitively, two λ-expressions are alphabetic variants, if they differ only with regard to variable letters. The notion is not quite this simple, however. For two λ-expressions, $\lambda x(A)$ and

$\lambda y(B)$, to be alphabetic variants, every occurrence of x in A must have a corresponding instance of y in B, and vice versa. Also, any quantifier in A that binds variables in A must have a corresponding (identical) quantifier in B that binds variables in all the corresponding positions in B. However, if there are any variables in A that are bound by some quantifier outside of $\lambda x(A)$, then the corresponding variable in $\lambda y(B)$ must be bound by the same operator in order for alphabetic variance to obtain ($\lambda x(. . .)$ and $\lambda y(. . .)$ are alphabetic variants in ($\forall z$) ([John, $\lambda x(x$ loves $z)$] & [Bill, $\lambda y(y$ loves $z)$])). Crucially, if $\lambda x(A)$ contains a variable bound outside of $\lambda x(A)$ (for instance, z in ($\forall z$) (John, $\lambda x(x$ loves z))) and $\lambda y(B)$ contains a corresponding variable bound outside of $\lambda y(B)$ (even one bound by an analogous operator, for instance, w in ($\forall w$)(John, $\lambda y(y$ loves w))) the two λ-expressions are not alphabetic variants (though here the universally quantified expressions, considered as a whole, would be).[3]

By way of illustration, the following pairs of λ-expressions are alphabetic variants.

(10) (a) $\lambda x(x$ is happy) $= \lambda y(y$ is happy)
   (b) $\lambda w(w$ loves John) $= \lambda z(z$ loves John)
   (c) $\lambda w((\forall y) (w$ likes $y)) = \lambda z(\forall q(z$ likes $q))$
   (d) $\lambda w((Ez)(w$ ate $z)) = \lambda q((Er)(q$ ate $r))$
   (e) $\lambda x(x$ said (Mary, $\lambda y(y$ likes $x)))$
$$= \lambda z(z \text{ said (Mary, } \lambda w(w \text{ likes } z)))$$
   (f) $\lambda x(x$ loves $y) = \lambda z(z$ loves $y)$ as in
      ($\forall y$) ([John, $\lambda x(x$ loves $y)$] & [Bill, $\lambda z(z$ loves $y)$])

Conversely, the pairs of λ-expressions in (10) are not alphabetic variants.

(11) (a) $\lambda x(x$ is happy) $\neq \lambda y(y$ is sad)
   (b) $\lambda w(w$ loves John) $\neq \lambda z(z$ loves Mary)
   (c) $\lambda x(x$ likes $y) \neq \lambda w(w$ likes $z)$, as in (Ey)(John, $\lambda x(x$ likes $y))$
      & ($\forall z$)(Bill, $\lambda w(w$ likes z)), or in John, $\lambda y(y$ said(Mary, $\lambda x(x$
      likes $y)))$ & Bill, $\lambda z(z$ said(Mary, $\lambda w(w$ likes $z)))$

Now, assuming that logical forms bear a very close relation to the surface syntax (i.e. given that there is at the very least a definable correspondence between surface verb phrases and λ-expressions), we have the necessary apparatus to account for the intuition of McCawley (1967), who writes, "The only way I know of stating this transformation [= VPD-I.A.S.] is to say that the deletion may take place only in a structure whose semantic representation is of the form $f(x_1)$ & $f(x_2)$"[4]

I offer the following formulation of VPD.

(12) With respect to a sentence S, VPD can delete any VP in S^5 whose representation at the level of logical form is a λ-expression that is

an alphabetic variant of another λ-expression present in the logical form of S or in the logical form of some other sentence S', which precedes S in discourse.

In many cases, this theory makes the same predictions as a purely syntactic theory. Sentences like the following one, for instance, (where the possibility of deletion would be guaranteed by any purely syntactic theory) is a possible VPD environment because of its logical form, which is as indicated.

(13) ″Peter loves Betsy, and Sandy $\{{loves\ Betsy \atop does\ \emptyset}\}$ too.

(13)′ Peter, $\lambda x(x$ love Betsy) & Sandy, $\lambda y(y$ love Betsy)

In (13)′, $\lambda x(. . .)$ and $\lambda y(. . .)$ are alphabetic variants. This captures nicely the intuition that (13) is "saying the same thing" about Peter and Sandy, which is essentially McCawley's intuition.

Our theory makes some rather novel predictions also, many of which have escaped notice in the literature. The well known ambiguity of a sentence like "someone hit everyone" for instance, is accounted for by assigning it the two logical representations in (14)

(14) (a) $(Ex)\ (x, \lambda y((\forall z)\ (y$ hit $z)))$
     (b) $(\forall z)\ (Ex)\ (x, \lambda w(w$ hit $z))$

Now a sentence like "Bill hit everyone" will be assigned only one logical form, that in (15), because there is no scopal variation possible when only one quantifier word is present.

(15) Bill, $\lambda q((\forall p)\ (q$ hit $p))$

We therefore predict that in a sentence like the following one, the left conjunct is disambiguated.

(16) Someone hit everyone, and then Bill did.

That is, the left conjunct in (16) can be interpreted only as in (14)(a), where the existential quantifier has wide scope. $\lambda y(. . .)$ in (14)(a) is an alphabetic variant of $\lambda q\ (. . .)$ in (15). Deletion is impossible if the left conjunct of (16) is interpreted as in (14)(b) because the only λ-expression there $(\lambda w(. . .))$ is not an alphabetic variant of $\lambda q(. . .)$ in (15). This prediction seems to be correct. (16) allows only the interpretation where the existential quantifier has wide scope in the left conjunct.

Consider now (17).

(17) Betsy greeted everyone when Sandy did.

(17) has two readings, one which would be true, say, if Betsy and Sandy walked into a room full of people and said "Hello everybody" in two-part

harmony. (17) on this reading is derivable from (18) whose logical form is as indicated (details omitted, especially a precise treatment of *when*)

(18) Betsy greeted everyone when Sandy greeted everyone.

(18)′ (a) [Betsy, $\lambda x((\forall y)(x$ greet $y))$] when [Sandy, $\lambda w((\forall z)$ (w greet z))]

or perhaps,

(b) Betsy, $\lambda r([r, \lambda x((\forall y)$ (x greet y)] when [Sandy, $\lambda w((\forall z)$ (w greet z))])

In either formula, $\lambda x(. . .)$ and $\lambda w(. . .)$ are alphabetic variants.

Another reading of (17) is one it shares with (19).

(19) Betsy greeted everyone when Sandy greeted $\{{}^{\text{them}}_{\% \text{ him}}\}$.

Notice that (18) does not have this reading, and further that in (19), no two VP's are syntactically identical. Our claim is that logical, rather than syntactic identity is what determines deletability. Therefore (17) can be derived from (19) because in its logical form, (19)′ (in either rendition), $\lambda y(. . .)$ and $\lambda w(. . .)$ are alphabetic variants.

(19)′ (a) $(\forall x)$([Betsy, $\lambda y(y$ greet $x)$] when [Sandy, $\lambda w(w$ greet $x)$])

or

(b) Betsy, $\lambda q((\forall x)$([$q, \lambda y(y$ greet $x)$] when [Sandy, $\lambda w(w$ greet $x)$]))

Thus our theory is able to account for the ambiguity of (17), which, in a syntactic identity theory, is derivable only from (18).

Now consider the following discourse.

(20) (a) Speaker A: What was Harry able to take a picture of?
(b) Speaker B: A Gnu.
(c) Speaker A: *What was Tom $\emptyset$?

[$\emptyset$ = able to take a picture of].

The ungrammaticality of (20)(c) follows from our theory given the standard assumption that *wh*-words in questions are to be treated on a par with quantifiers, i.e. given the assumption that *wh*-words bind variables (see Hiż (1962), and many later references). That is, (20)(a) and (c) will have logical forms roughly as follows:

(20) (a)′ (for what x)(John, $\lambda y(y$ was able to take a picture of x))
(20) (c)′ (for what z)(Tom, $\lambda w(w$ was able to take a picture of z))

$\lambda w(. . .)$ and $\lambda y(. . .)$ are not alphabetic variants, because they each contain variables bound by different outside operators. (x and z are bound by different *wh* operators—see the preceding discussion.)

Similar behavior can be observed with pseudo-clefts, whose logical forms we might represent using Russell's iota operator (again we omit many details, including a proper treatment of tense).

(21) *What Betsy saw was *Topkapi*, and what Peter did ∅ was *South Pacific*

$$[∅ = \text{see}]$$
(21)' $ix(\text{Betsy}, \lambda y(y \text{ see } x)) = Topkapi \;\&$
$iz(\text{Peter}, \lambda w(w \text{ see } z)) = South\ Pacific$

$\lambda w(...)$ and $\lambda y(...)$ are also not alphabetic variants because of the diverse binding of the variables x and z contained within them. The deletion in (21) is therefore predicted to be impossible by our theory.

Moreover, this example should be compared with the following one, where deletion is in fact possible.

(22) What Betsy tried to see, but couldn't, is *Topkapi*.

(22)' $ix([\text{Betsy}, \lambda y(y \text{ tried } (y, \lambda r(r \text{ see } x)))]$ but COULD $[\text{Betsy}, \lambda z(z \text{ see } x)]) = Topkapi$

In the logical form of (22)' , $\lambda z(...)$ and $\lambda r(...)$ are indeed alphabetic variants, for they each contain a variable, i.e. x, bound by the same outside operator (1). Crucially, the last three examples have all involved constraints on the deletion of syntactically identical VP's. Our theory seems to be able to sort out precisely which ones are deletable, and which are not, in a way that no purely syntactic theory is able to.

We are now ready to return to the *ready* sentences we observed at the outset. The standard view of the derivation of sentences like "the steak is ready to eat" is essentially Lakoff's (see also Hankamer, 1971). That view is that these sentences are derived by deletion under identity from structures like the one we saw earlier (cf. (3) above).

Now there is something wrong with this view. Consider a sentence like (23). The source for this sentence would be identical to the one

(23) The steak which Harry sold to Sue is ready to eat.

underlying (24), whose derivation differs from that of (23) only in

(24) The steak which was sold to Sue by Harry is ready to eat.

that optional cyclic rules have applied. But if that source contains an identical NP as the underlying object of *eat*, what is to prevent optional cyclic rules from applying to the second relative clause, but not to the first one, creating non-identity at the level when the deletion rule is to apply? The result will be ungrammatical sequences like the following:[6]

(25) *The steak which Harry sold to Sue is ready to eat the steak which was sold to Sue by Harry.

One solution to this dilemma might be to treat the target of such deletion rules as a pronominal element. We might further speculate that such pronominal elements are always to be treated as bound variables, a speculation which receives further support from the existence of sentences like this next one:

(26) Everything is ready to eat.

That is, we would not want to derive this sentence from an underlying structure with two *everythings*, for we would not be able to capture the fact that the object of *eat* is to be treated logically as a bound variable (the argument is analogous to the by now standard arguments regarding EQUI).

Now the fact that the object of *eat* in such sentences must be interpreted as a bound variable is certainly a property of the *ready* class of predicates. We might therefore require the λ of the *ready* predicate also to bind the position of the embedded object pronoun. *ready for John to eat* would then correspond to the following λ-predicate.

(27) $\lambda x(x$ is ready for [John, $\lambda y(y$ eat $x)])$

Letting △ represent an unspecified subject, *ready to eat* would correspond to this λ-predicate:

(28) $\lambda x(x$ is ready for [△, $\lambda y(y$ eat $x)])$

We are now ready to explain the *ready* deletion facts we observed earlier. (29) would be assigned a logical form like that in (29)′ (on the "object-deletion" reading).

(29) The steak is ready to eat, and the chicken is ready to eat also.

(29)′ The steak, $\lambda x(x$ is ready for [△, $\lambda y(y$ eat $x)])$ &
the chicken, $\lambda w(w$ is ready for [△, $\lambda z(z$ eat $w)])$.

The VP: *ready to eat* in the second conjunct of (29) corresponds to $\lambda w(\ldots)$ in (29)′, which is an alphabetic variant of $\lambda x(\ldots)$. That VP is therefore deletable. The embedded VP: *eat*, on the other hand, corresponds to $\lambda z(\ldots)$, which has no alphabetic variant in (29)′ ($\lambda y(\ldots)$, the only reasonable candidate, has x where $\lambda z(\ldots)$ has w). Therefore only the higher VP is deletable in (29). This explains the contrast we noted above between (2) (c) and *(5) (b).[7]

Notice that since we have dispensed with a syntactic identity requirement on the rule of VPD, having relegated the recoverability of deletion to our theory of logical form, we can write VPD simply as in (30). Arguments that AUX must be mentioned in the SD of the rule

(30) X - AUX - VP - Y
$$\Downarrow$$
$$\emptyset$$

can be found in Bresnan (1976a) and Sag (forthcoming). We might further hypothesize that all deletion rules that can apply in discourse (see Sag and Hankamer, 1976, for a survey of these rules) are like (30) in not mentioning the deletion trigger.

This formulation of the rule allows us to account for the extremely problematic examples noted by Bouton (1970). Bouton observed that VPD can apply in sentences like the following, where the target VP is contained within the antecedent VP.

(31) I read everything you $\{{}^{\text{read}}_{\text{did } \emptyset}$

The problem of course is that the standard formulation of VPD (whose S.D. is something like: X - VP - Y - VP - Z) cannot apply to sentences like this, whose structure is something like that in (32) (after relativization).

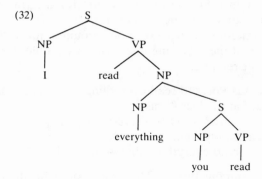

Notice, however, that these sentences will have a logical form something like the following (where $(\forall y$: you, $\lambda r(r$ read $y))$ represents a restricted quantifier. An alternative analysis is possible using conditionals):

(32)' I, $\lambda x((\forall y{:}\text{you}, \lambda r(r \text{ read } y))[x, \lambda z(z \text{ read } y)])$

Rule (30) can apply to (32). The deletion will be recoverable because in (32)', $\lambda z(\ldots)$ and $\lambda r(\ldots)$ are alphabetic variants.

Sentences like this have some further interesting properties. Consider the ambiguity of (33) for instance.

(33) Betsy wants Peter to read everything Alan wants him to read.

This sentence has an opaque reading which is paraphrasable as: *What Betsy wants is for Peter to read everything Alan wants him to read.* The other, transparent reading of (33) might be paraphrased (rather crudely) as: *Everything that Alan wants Peter to read is also such that Betsy wants Peter to read it.* Now we might represent this ambiguity as two different scopes of the universal quantifier. The opaque reading would be something like (34), and the transparent reading, as in (35).

(34) Betsy, $\lambda x(x$ want $[(\forall y{:}Alan, \lambda z(z$ want $[Peter, \lambda w(w$ read $y)]))$
　　　　[Peter, $\lambda q(q$ read $y)]])$

(35) Betsy, $\lambda x(\forall y{:}$ Alan, $\lambda z(z$ want $[Peter, \lambda w(w$ read $y)]))$
　　　　[x, $\lambda r(r$ want $[Peter, \lambda q(q$ read $y)])])$

The decision to represent this ambiguity scopally is the right one, I would claim, because it accounts for the fact that (36), which is the result of applying VPD to the VP: *wants him to read* in (33), has only the transparent reading.[8]

(36) Betsy wants Peter to read everything that Alan does.

Why is this so? Because the deleted VP corresponds to $\lambda z(. . .)$ in both (34) and (35), but only in (35), the representation for the transparent reading, does $\lambda z(. . .)$ have an alphabetic variant (i.e. $\lambda r(. . .)$).

There are numerous other facts to be accounted for in this domain. For example, only one of the following discourses is possible if the first sentence has the transparent reading:

(37) Betsy wants Peter to read everything that Alan wants him to read.
　　(a) Yea, Sandy does 0, also.
　　　　[0 = *want Peter to read everything* . . .]
　　(b) *Yea, Sandy wants him to 0, also.
　　　　[0 = read everything that Alan . . .]

This also follows from our theory. The logical forms for the two sentences in (37) is given in (38) ((38) (*ii*) is the logical form for the sentence underlying (37)(a) or (b) prior to deletion).

(38) (*i*) Betsy, $\lambda x((\forall y{:}Alan, \lambda z(z$ want $[Peter, \lambda w(w$ read $y)]))$
　　　　[x, $\lambda r(r$ want $[Peter, \lambda q(q$ read $y)])])$
　　(*ii*) Sandy, $\lambda m((\forall o{:}Alan, \lambda n(n$ want $[Peter, \lambda p(p$ read $o)]))$
　　　　[m, $\lambda s(s$ want $[Peter, \lambda t(t$ read $o)])])$

The higher VP, which is the one deleted in (37)(a), corresponds to $\lambda m(. . .)$, which is an alphabetic variant of $\lambda x(. . .)$ in the logical form of the preceding sentence. The embedded VP, however, which is the one deleted in (37)(b), corresponds to $\lambda t(. . .)$, which would be an alphabetic variant of $\lambda q(. . .)$ in the logical form of the previous sentence except for the diverse binding of the variables o and y. The facts of (37)(a) and *(37)(b) thus fall out of our theory nicely.

Comparatives work the same way, which would point to the correctness of treating them scopally. The important facts in that area are those like the following.

(39) Sam claimed he was taller than he was and Bill did too.

In this sentence, the two conjuncts can both have either the sensible (transparent) or the contradictory (opaque) reading (they must both have the same interpretation, of course). That much is easy to explain. Notice, however, that the following example, which is just like (39) except only the embedded VP: *taller than he was* has been deleted, allows only the contradictory reading in both conjuncts.

(40) Sam claimed he was taller than he was, and Bill claimed he was, too.

The explanation is quite parallel to the one just given for the facts of (37).

We can also explain an observation of Edwin Williams's, namely, that a sentence like (41)

(41) Mary's father told her to work harder than her boss did 0.

cannot have the (opaque) reading which is paraphrasable by: *what Mary's father told her was that she should work harder than her boss told her to work*. The explanation for this fact is about the same as the one we gave for the missing reading of (36) above.

As for sloppy identity, our theory of logical form will allow us to do essentially everything that Keenan's (1971) analysis does, but without having to posit two separate deletion rules, as Keenan does. All we need to assume is that pronouns in the VP that bear the same referential index as the subject of the sentence are optionally represented in logical form by variables bound by the λ-operator. Thus (42) would have two logical forms, which are sketched in (43).

(42) John$_i$ scratched his$_i$ arm.

(43)(a) John$_i$, $\lambda x(x$ scratched his$_i$ arm)
    (b) John$_i$, $\lambda x(x$ scratched x's arm)

I will not elaborate on this matter here (a detailed analysis is given in Sag, forthcoming) except to point out that there are some surprising facts in this area too which have escaped notice in the literature and which follow from the proposed analysis. Thus consider (44), which is ambiguous depending on whom Peter said Betsy hit, himself (sloppy), or Alan (non-sloppy).

(44) Alan$_i$ said Betsy hit him$_i$, and Peter did $\emptyset$ too.
    [$\emptyset$ = said Betsy hit him]

We account for the two readings of this deleted sentence by assigning its pre-deletion source the following two logical forms.

(44)′ Alan$_i$, $\lambda x(x$ said [Betsy, $\lambda y(y$ hit him$_i)])$
    & Peter$_j$, $\lambda w(w$ said [Betsy, $\lambda z(z$ hit him$_i)])$

(44)″ Alan$_i$, $\lambda x(x$ said [Betsy, $\lambda y(y$ hit $x)])$
    & Peter$_j$, $\lambda w(w$ said [Betsy, $\lambda z(z$ hit $w)])$

In either case, $\lambda x(...)$ and $\lambda w(...)$ are alphabetic variants predicting the possibility of the deletion in (44) on either reading.

(45), however, which differs from (44) only in that it was the embedded VP that got deleted, is unambiguously non-sloppy, i.e., it says that Peter said that Betsy hit Alan.

(45) Alan$_i$ said Betsy hit him$_i$, and Peter said she did, too.

The reason for this is the following: if this sentence has the sloppy reading, i.e., if it has the logical form in (44)″, then the VP that was deleted in (45) corresponds to $\lambda z(...)$. But $\lambda z(...)$ *contains the variable w* (bound from outside) where $\lambda y(...)$ contains x (also bound from outside). No alphabetic variance obtains, and VPD is impossible.

In this paper I have proposed a theory of VPD and sketched an outline of a theory of logical form that I think should go with it. We have seen cases where a sentence loses one of its readings after VPD has applied, and cases where deleted sentences seem to gain readings that their sources (in a purely syntactic deletion theory) do not have. The conclusion then at the very least is that overt syntactic identity is neither a necessary nor a sufficient condition for VP-deletability. I have claimed that these deletion facts provide evidence for a very surfacy and relatively compositional view of logical form. This is not to say that an explanation for the facts noted in this paper could not be found in a more abstract theory of logical form. I am only claiming that a coherent account of the facts can be given in a theory of the sort that I have sketched and that it is not at all obvious what an alternative account could look like in a more abstract framework.[9]

Let me conclude with two observations. First, if my hypothesis about logical form is correct, and if the logical form of a sentence is taken to be sufficient to determine its logical consequences, then examples like the following (which was discovered with the aid of Geoff Nunberg) are rather troublesome.

(46) They caned a student severely when I was a child, but not like Miss Grundy did ∅ yesterday.
   [∅ = cane a student]

Here the first clause can be interpreted generically at the same time that the deleted indefinite NP has a specific interpretation.[10] But the distinction between generic and specific interpretations of such sentences is clearly relevant for determining logical consequences. I do not at present know how to reconcile facts like this with the theory I have presented except to say that indefinite NP's are not represented scopally at the level of logical form.

Finally, the commonly held position that transparent versus opaque understandings of sentences containing proper names and definite descriptions should be treated as scope differences in logical form (the position is essentially due to Russell, 1905) would seem to be inconsistent with our theory. Assuming the correctness of that view, we would expect, on the transparent readings, only the deletions in (47)(a) and (48)(b) (where the higher VP has been deleted) and not those in (47)(b) and (48)(b) (where the embedded VP has been deleted).[11]

(47)(a) Alan wanted to talk to Betsy. Peter did also.
   (b) Alan wanted to talk to Betsy. Peter wanted to also.

(48)(a) Alan wanted to talk to the tallest man in Chicago. Betsy did also.
   (b) Alan wanted to talk to the tallest man in Chicago. Betsy wanted to also.

All four examples, however, seem perfectly acceptable.

NOTES

1. This paper is an attempt to summarize the main points made in Chapter Two of my forthcoming doctoral dissertation. All matters discussed here are treated in more detail there. My research has been supported in part by a grant from The National Institute of Mental Health (5 Po1 MH13390-09) to M.I.T. I have had many helpful discussions with Barbara Abbott, Noam Chomsky, Ken Hale, Larry Horn, Hans Kamp, Susumu Kuno, Geoff Nunberg, and Haj Ross. I am also indebted to Barbara Partee, whose 1974 Linguistic Institute course in Montague Grammar is probably what provided the starting point for all my thinking on these matters. Many of the fact observed here, and some of the proposed explanations for them, have been discovered independently by Edwin Williams, who draws different conclusions from them.

2. Unlike standard λ-calculi, I write arguments before their λ-predicates. I think there are some good reasons for this, actually (see Sag, forthcoming), but I will not develop those here.

Note further that since every surface VP corresponds to a λ-predicate, corresponding active and passive sentences will have different logical forms. These will be related either by logical equivalence (see for instance Bresnan, 1976b) or else by meaning postulate (as Thomason has suggested).

3. For a more formal discussion of this notion see van Fraassen (1971, pp. 102–104), Hughes

and Cresswell (1968), and Kalish and Montague (1964). λ functions just like ∀ or E, with respect to alphabetic variance.

4. Keenan (1971) has a similar intuition.

5. Subject to the backwards anaphora constraint, of course. See the discussion in Sag and Hankamer (1976).

6. This type of argument was pointed out to me by Geoff Pullum, who attributes it to Michael Brame.

7. On the EQUI reading, of course, there is no bound variable in the object position of the embedded VP. Therefore, either the higher VP or the lower VP is deletable.

8. (36) has another reading, which is unproblematic, namely, the one it shares with (*i*).

(*i*) Betsy wants Peter to read everything that Alan reads.

9. Notice for instance that lexical decomposition in general wreaks havoc with our theory:

(*i*) *John melted the copper, and the tin did $\emptyset$, too.
    [$\emptyset$ = melted]

10. Kuno (1974) observes similar cases with specific vs. non-specific indefinite NP's.

11. This problem could be solved within a scopal theory only if we allowed proper names and definite descriptions to have scope over more than one sentence in discourse. (47), for instance, would be unproblematic if the logical form of the two sentences in discourse was (*i*).

(*i*) (Betsy-x)([John, λy(y want (y, λz(z talk to x)))].
    [Peter, λw(w want (w, λs(s talk to x)))])

REFERENCES

Bouton, L. (1970). "Antecedent-contained Pro-forms," in *Papers from the Sixth Regional Meeting of the Chicago Linguistic Society*, Chicago: University of Chicago.

Bresnan, J. W. (1976a). "On the Form and Functioning of Transformations," *Linguistic Inquiry*, Vol. 7, No. 1.

———. (1976b). "Toward a Realistic Model of Transformational Grammar," paper presented at MIT-AT&T Convocation on Communications, M.I.T.

Chomsky, N. (1955). *The Logical Structure of Linguistic Theory*. M.I.T. microfilm (published in part by Plenum, New York, 1975).

———. (1965). *Aspects of the Theory of Syntax*. Cambridge, Mass: M.I.T. Press.

———. (1968). *Language and Mind* (enlarged edition). New York: Harcourt Brace Jovanovich.

Church, A. (1941). *The Calculi of Lambda-Conversion*. Princeton, NJ: Princeton University Press. [Reprinted by Kraus Reprint Corp., N.Y., 1965].

Hankamer, J. (1971). *Constraints on Deletion in Syntax*. Unpublished doctoral dissertation, Yale University.

Hiż, H. (1962). "Questions and Answers," *Journal of Philosophy*, Vol. 59.

Hughes, G., and Cresswell, M. (1968). *An Introduction to Modal Logic*. London: Methuen.

Kalish, D., and Montague, R. (1964). *Logic: Techniques of Formal Reasoning*. New York: Harcourt, Brace and World.

Keenan, E. (1971). "Names, Quantifiers, and the Sloppy Identity Problem," *Papers in Linguistics*, Vol. 4, No. 2.

Kleene, S. (1952). *Mathematical Logic*. New York: John Wiley and Sons.

Kuno, S. (1974). "Lexical and Contextual Meaning," *Linguistic Inquiry*, Vol. 5, No. 3.

Lakoff, G. (1968). "Deep and Surface Grammar." [Available from Indiana University Linguistics Club].

———. (1970). "A Note on Vagueness and Ambiguity," *Linguistic Inquiry*, Vol. I.

Lees, R. (1960), *The Grammar of English Nominalizations*, M.I.T. doctoral dissertation [published by Indiania Uniersity, Bloomington, Mouton, The Hague, 1968].

McCawley, J. (1967). "Meaning and the Description of Languages", *Kotoba no Uchū* 2.

———. (1970), "English as a VSO Language," *Language*, 46, No. 2.

Montague, R. (1974). *Formal Philosophy* (edited by R. Thomason). New Haven: Yale University Press.

Partee, B. (1975). "Montague Grammar and Transformational Grammar," *Linguistic Inquiry*, Vol. 6, No. 2.

Ross, J. R. (1967). *Constraints on Variables in Syntax*, unpublished MIT doctoral dissertation. [available from Indiana University Linguistics Club.]

Russell, B. (1905). "On Denoting," *Mind*, 14 [reprinted in Russell's *Logic and Knowledge*, London: Allen & Unwin, 1958].

Sadock, J., and Zwicky, A. (1973). "Ambiguity Tests and How to Fail Them," *Ohio State Working Papers in Linguistics*, No. 16.

Sag, I. A. (forthcoming). *Deletion and Logical Form*. Doctoral dissertation, M.I.T.

Sag, I. A. and Hankamer, Jr. (1976). "Deep and Surface Anaphora," *Linguistic Inquiry*, Vol. 7, No. 3.

Thomason, R. (1974). "Some Complement Constructions in Montague Grammer," in *Papers from the Tenth Regional Meeting of the Chicago Linguistic Society* (M. LaGaly et al., eds.). Chicago.

van Fraasen, B. C. (1971). *Formal Semantics and Logic*. New York: Macmillan.

MAX CRESSWELL

STRUCTURED MEANINGS

A theory of meaning should be *compositional*. That is, the meaning of any complex expression should be determined by the meanings of its simple expressions together with the structure of the expression. Usually the expression will be built up in several stages, with successively more complex expressions being embedded in even more complex ones until the level of the sentence itself is reached. But the theory of meaning envisaged so far has been not merely compositional but what might be called *functionally* compositional. Consider the example of 5 + 7. The idea was that the meaning of the expression '5 + 7' is the number associated in the list that is the meaning of + with the pair of numbers 5 and 7. Put more formally, the meaning of '5 + 7' is the result of letting the function that is the meaning of ' + ' (i.e., the operation of addition) operate on the two numbers 5 and 7 and deliver their sum. The sum is of course the number 12, and it is this number that is the meaning of '5 + 7'.

The problem with sentences about propositional attitudes is that the attitude verb seems sensitive to more than the meaning (in this sense of meaning) of the complement sentence. The *de re* solution claims that the attitude is sensitive to the meaning of the parts of the sentence, together with its structure. In the propositional solution, the attitude verb operates just on the meaning that results from the functional application of the parts.

The problem of propositional attitudes arises because, in a functionally compositional theory of meaning, distinct structures can turn out to have the same meaning. In this case '5 + 7' has the same meaning as '6 + 6', *viz* they both mean the number 12. The *de re* solution consists in having the propositional attitude relate, not to the meaning of '5 + 7' taken as a whole, but to the meaning of its parts taken separately. This is opposed to the propositional solution, in which the attitude relates to the meaning of '5 + 7' taken as a whole.

One attempt to amalgamate these approaches is to take the meaning of '5 + 7' to be not the number 12 (i.e., not the result of + operating on 5 and

7) but rather the initially given structure $\langle 5,7, + \rangle$ and to say that that *structure* is involved in the object of the attitude. Presumably the object of a belief that $5 + 7 = 12$ would be the structure $\langle \langle 5,7, + \rangle, 12, = \rangle$ or some such thing. From one point of view this is just a way of rewriting the *de re* analysis so that it has the form of the propositional analysis. However, there are some hidden snags.

The main problem is where 12 fits into all this. For if the meaning of '$5 + 7$' is just $\langle 5,7, + \rangle$, how is that supposed to be equal to 12? Obviously, that structure is not 12. There are two rather different kinds of solution here. The first is to take ' $=$ ' not as having identity as its meaning but rather as being a predicate that relates structures in such a way that '$s_1 = s_2$' is true iff the results of evaluating s_1 out according to its functional structure (e.g., by letting $+$ operate on 5 and 7 to get 12) and of evaluating s_2 out according to *its* structure are the same.

The second type of solution is to say that 12 is not strictly the *meaning* of '$7 + 5$'; rather, it is the number denoted by or referred to by that expression. Using a terminology derived from the views of Frege, we could say that the structure $\langle 5,7, + \rangle$ is the *sense* of the expression '$5 + 7$', whereas the number 12 is its *reference*. In fact, the *de re* solution has much in common with the Fregean solution, though it is importantly different in ways I shall describe later. First, however, I want to show why the first kind of solution, in which the meaning of ' $=$ ' is taken to be not identity but instead something laxer, will not do. As a way into the difficulties here, let us consider ' $+$ ' rather than ' $=$ ' and let us begin with the expression '$(5 + 7) + 2$'. If the meaning of '$5 + 7$' is just the number 12, then there is no problem. We recall from chapter 1 that the meaning of ' $+$ ' may be represented by an infinite list of triples of numbers in which the number in the third column is the sum of the numbers in the first two columns. To find the meaning of '$(5 + 7) + 2$', we first look up the number associated with 5 and 7 in this list. It is 12. We then look up the number associated with 12 and 2 in the same list and find that it is 14. No problem.

But suppose that the meaning of '$5 + 7$' is not the number 12 but is the triple $\langle 5,7, + \rangle$. Remember that we are considering a solution in which the meaning of an expression $\alpha + \beta$ is obtained by using the meaning of ' $+$ ' to operate on the meanings of α and β, and the meaning of ' $+$ ' is an infinite list of triples that associates the meaning of $\alpha + \beta$ with the meanings of α and β. But the meaning of '$5 + 7$' is now the triple $\langle 5,7, + \rangle$. And this means that one of the members of the list that is $+$ must be the list that is $+$. And one of *its* members must be that list. And so on. On this view it would seem that $+$ never could have a definite meaning.

Of course, all this has depended on the assumption that the compositionality is functional; for instance, we have assumed that the meaning of '$(5 + 7) + 2$' has been obtained by the meaning of ' $+$ ' (in the form of the infinite list) "operating" on the structure $\langle 5,7, + \rangle$, which has meant looking it up in the list. But what if we let the meaning of '$(5 + 7) + 2$' simply be the structure $\langle \langle 5,7, + \rangle, 2, + \rangle$? Then the problem is that it is no longer clear what the meaning of ' $+$ ' should be. Since we have abandoned the requirement that the compositionality be functional, there is no reason why it should be the kind of infinite list described above, or any other list. The reason for making that particular list the meaning of ' $+$ ' was that, among other things, when applied to 5 and 7, it delivers 12. But on the present, nonfunctional, view of meaning, the number 12 is not the meaning of $\langle 5,7, + \rangle$. Rather, it is the reference. And here we have a curious phenomenon. If we look at '$(5 + 7) + 2$', we see that the *reference* of this whole expression is determined from the references of '5', '7', and '2' by the function $+$. In this process the structure $\langle \langle 5,7, + \rangle, 2, + \rangle$ plays no role at all. In other words, the choice of $+$ in a *non*functional account of meaning is motivated because of its role in a functional account of reference. Otherwise, there is no motivation for the choice of meaning for ' $+$ ' or even for '5' and '7'. The argument for compositionality in the case of the arithmetical language has proceeded on the assumption that there is an intimate connection between meaning and reference. On Frege's view, the reference of a numerical expression like '5 + 7' would be a number, in this case 12, and the reference of an arithmetical sentence would be a truth value: T in the case of $5 + 7 = 12$ and F in the case of $5 + 7 = 11$.

In the introduction I argued for a very intimate connection between truth and meaning. Specifically, I argued that a crucial element in knowing the meaning of a sentence is knowing the difference between conditions under which the sentence would be true and conditions under which it would be false. Explaining this knowledge seems to me the most important single goal of a semantic theory, and I for one have not seen any semantic theory that explains this knowledge that is not functionally compositional.

Nonfunctional but compositional theories of meaning have certainly been advocated. One of the best known is that defended by Jerrold Katz. But Katz takes truth and reference to have no part in a semantic theory and so, whatever enterprise he is engaged in, it is not a semantical one as I understand the term. As far as I can understand it, Katz has in mind the construction of a formal language underlying English in which there are no ambiguous sentences and no semantically anomalous sentences and in which entailment relations between sentences are somehow syntactically displayed. (It is rather like the state modal logic was in before the work of Kripke.)

To say that compositionality must be functional does not of course mean that reference in general has to be as simple as it is in the arithmetical case. In particular, it is certainly not plausible to identify the meaning of an empirical sentence simply with a truth value. Obviously, knowing the meaning of a sentence is not the same as knowing whether it is true. In part II I shall deal with what the analogue of reference should be in such cases. In the rest of part I I shall still use the arithmetical example. In the case of this language the notion of reference does seem reasonably clear.

The situation then seems to be that truth-conditional semantics (applied to the arithmetical language) requires functional compositionality at the level of reference. And if we have functional compositionality at the level of reference, then it seems we do not need a separate level of meaning. But the point is that functional compositionality at the level of reference fails in the case of propositional attitudes. That is, the truth or falsity of a propositional attitude sentence depends on more than the reference of its complement sentence. It must, in addition, take note of the references of the parts of the complement sentence. Recall, too, that functional compositionality fails in the case of propositional attitude sentences *whatever* kinds of entities are the meanings of the complex expressions, provided only that distinct structures sometimes evaluate to the same meanings.

Our problem is the meaning of propositional attitude sentences. And one might say it is the problem of the *reference* of propositional attitude sentences. For even the truth value of a propositional attitude sentence can be affected by substituting an expression with the same reference. The examples in chapters 1 and 2 make exactly this point. Veronica's belief that $5 + 7 = 12$ is not a belief that $12 = 12$. In other words, the truth of a sentence reporting it is affected by replacing '5 + 7' with '12'. Consider, then, how we might analyze the sentence

(1) Helen believes that $5 + 7 = 12$.

If the above remarks are correct, an adequate account even of the reference of this sentence may relate Helen to what was called previously the *sense* of '$5 + 7 = 12$', that is, to the structure $\langle \langle 5,7, + \rangle,12 = \rangle$, in which 5, 7, and 12 are numbers, $+$ is the addition function, and $=$ is the identity predicate. (For the moment we do not know precisely what its values are except that '$x = y$' is to be true iff x and y are identical.) What is required if functional compositionality is to be preserved, therefore, is a device for converting the *sense* of the complement sentence into the *reference* of the complement taken as a whole. The easiest way to do this in English seems to be to take seriously the role of the word 'that'. Of course, 'that' is often omitted, particularly in colloquial spoken English, and an equivalent word may not exist in all languages. Nevertheless, if the claims I am making are right, there will have to be some mechanism for achieving the result that English achieves by the use of 'that', and I would hope that the structure of this mechanism will be sufficiently indicated in what follows.

The first point I want to make is a syntactic one—namely, that the verb 'believes' in (1) is just an ordinary two-place predicate of the same syntactic category, whatever that is, as 'kicks', 'types', or 'frightens'. To be sure, there are semantic differences. The kinds of things that it makes sense to speak of as being kicked or frightened are not the same kinds of things that can be believed, but there seems little syntactic distinction between the following pairs:

(2) a. Vladimir types what he has been told to type.
 b. Vladimir believes what he has been told to believe.

(3) a. Helen kicks the winning goal.
 b. Helen believes the winning answer.

(4) a. Imogen kicks something.
 b. Imogen believes something.

Since this is so, then the role of the word 'that' seems to be to turn a sentence into what is often called a *noun phrase* (or what I called in Cresswell (1973a) a *nominal*)—that is, into an expression of the same syntactic category as 'something', or 'the winning answer', or 'what he has been told to believe'. This feature of 'that' explains how we can deal with inferences of the following type:

(5) Rob told Bill on Monday that Derek was out of the Cabinet
 Bill believed what Rob told him
 Bill believed that Derek was out of the Cabinet.

An important goal of part III will be to show how to provide a formal semantical theory within which these inferences will be valid.

Among phrases like 'something' or 'the winning answer' are those like 'Humpty Dumpty' or 'Carthage' that are just names. Although we see in chapter 5 of Structured Meaning, that the issue is actually more complicated than that, yet, for many purposes, the semantic function of a name can be regarded as being simply to refer to something. Its reference, therefore, is just the thing it names. For the present, it seems plausible to regard that-clauses as names, and, at least in the case of complement sentences in the language of arithmetic, there even seems a possibility of saying what their references might be.

The analogy with ' + ' might suggest that the meaning of 'that' is the function that operates on the reference of '5 + 7 = 12' to get the reference of 'that 5 + 7 = 12'. However, the reference of '5 + 7 = 12' is the same as that of '12 = 12', and we know that the truth (reference) of (1) is affected by a change from '5 + 7' to '12'. So the meaning of 'that' will have to work rather differently.

Recall that the *de re* solution takes Helen's belief to be about the numbers 5 and 7 and how they are related to 12. If this belief has an object, then it does seem to be the structure $\langle \langle 5,7, + \rangle,12, = \rangle$. So the function that is the meaning of 'believe', by contrast with the meaning of + or =, *should* take as arguments complex structures. This is where 'that' comes in. We want the *reference* of the clause 'that $5 + 7 = 12$' to be the structure $\langle \langle 5,7, + \rangle, 12, = \rangle$. So we want the reference of the word 'that' to be a function that operates on the refernces of the parts of the complement sentence that follows it, and operates on them in such a way as to produce the structure $\langle \langle 5,7, + \rangle, 12, = \rangle$ as a value. If we call this latter structure the *sense* of '$5 + 7 = 12$', then we have a rather Fregean account in which the reference of the that-clause is the sense of the sentence that follows it. Of course, Frege's own theory did not identify sense with structure, as has been done here, but such an identification makes a plausible link with the *de re* account of propositional attitudes.

Thus, we let the meaning of 'that' be a function (infinite list) that operates, not on the sentence that follows it as a whole, but on its parts. Consider the following example:

(6) that $12 = 12$.

On the *de re* solution a belief, say, that $12 = 12$, could be a belief about 12 and 12 to the effect that they are identical. If the meaning of 'that' is a function, then it would be a set of quadruples, the first two terms of each quadruple being numbers, the third being a function from numbers to numbers, and the fourth being just the triple consisting of the first three columns of that row. In this case, the first two columns would be 12 and 12, the third column would be $=$ ($=$ would be the list of pairs $\langle x,x \rangle$ for every number x), and the fourth column would be $\langle 12,12, = \rangle$.

This solution makes the *reference* of 'that $12 = 12$' the same as the *sense* of '$12 = 12$'. But notice, strangely enough, that it does so without actually using the notion of sense. For the meaning of 'that', as described, operates on the *references* of '12', '12', and ' $=$ '. To be sure, it does not operate on the reference of '$12 = 12$' taken as a single sentence, and it has the effect of operating on what we have called the *sense* of that expression, but it does so in the unified functional way in which the meanings of all the other expressions work.

But one gets nothing for nothing, and there is a price to be paid. One price is that the sentence following 'that' is no longer a constituent of the that-clause. The constituents are the symbols taken separately. This immediately causes a rift between surface syntax and logical form. But such a rift may be inevitable. For if the objects of *de re* beliefs are not single propositions, but structures, then at some point this will have to be indicated. So at some point there will have to be a rift between surface syntax and logical form.

In what I have just said about 'that', I have assumed that the reference of a that-clause is the whole sense of the complement sentence. But sometimes the that-clause may be sensitive not to the whole sense of '$5 + 7$' but only to its reference. In the next chapter I shall argue for two things: first, that sentences of propositional attitude are ambiguous, and second, that the ambiguity is to be located in the word 'that' (or in whatever mechanism plays the equivalent structural role) and not in either the attitude verb or any part of the complement sentence.

MAX CRESSWELL

STRUCTURAL AMBIGUITY

We have seen how the *de re* solution to the problem of propositional attitudes may be incorporated into a functionally compositional semantics. The idea is that the reference of a that-clause can sometimes be the structure that is the sense of the sentence that follows it. The sense of a sentence is just the structure composed out of the references of its parts. In the case of our arithmetical language, the references of the numerals are just the numbers they conventionally denote, the meaning of ' + ' is a function (in the sense of an infinite list), and the meaning of other arithmetical operation signs is analogous. The other kind of symbol is a predicate like ' = '. What sort of thing is its meaning? Presumably the meaning of ' = ' is a function from x and y to the proposition that $x = y$. But what is this proposition? Propositions have often been held to be the objects of propositional attitudes. Why else indeed were the latter so called? Presumably not because of their size. But things are a little more complicated. For the present I would like to postpone the question of the nature of propositions. It will form the principal topic of part II. All I want to note here is the intimate connection between propositions (whatever they are) and truth and falsity. For I hold the most certain principle of semantics to be that any two sentences that differ in truth value differ also in the proposition they express.

I suggested that propositional attitude sentences are ambiguous. Here I want to amplify the arguments for this ambiguity, in a way that will support and extend the treatment of that-clauses outlined in the previous chapter.

In order to show this, I propose to consider the semantics of a variety of propositional attitude words. This will show that the problem is not really, as many philsophers have supposed, a problem about the nature of belief, but a rather more general one. Two important constraints will guide the discussion. I will insist that the kind of analysis offered for one attitude should be applicable to all. That is, the only difference allowed in the semantics of

(1) $x \phi$ that p

for different choices of ϕ will be that which arises from the meaning of ϕ. The other constraint is that ϕ be unambiguous. This constraint is linked with the first, in that an ambiguity postulated for one ϕ would have to be systematically repeated for every ϕ and therefore should be respresented not by an ambiguity in ϕ, but rather by an ambiguity in its complement. Part of the evidence for putting the ambiguity in the that-clause comes from the fact that parallel ambiguities appear in a variety of attitude verbs and it is undesirable to postulate a parallel system of ambiguities in a large range of words and phrases (particularly when a possible infinity of verb phrases may be involved) when one will do.

Suppose that I am reading a map in which sectional distances are given along a route my wife and I propose to travel. The map might look like this:

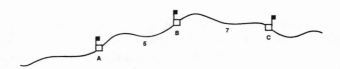

It is clear to me that the map indicates that it is 12 kilometers from A to C. Suppose now that my wife is driving and asks me how far it is from A to C. It seems to me that I might equally well give any of the following answers:

(2) Well, the map indicates that it is 12 kilometers from A to C.

(3) Well, the map indicates that it is 5 + 7 kilometers from A to C.

(4) Well, the map indicates that it is 7 + 5 kilometers from A to C.

I might utter (2) if I had done the addition; I might utter (3) if I had been reading the map from left to right; and I might utter (4) if I had been reading the map, against the direction of travel, from right to left. But the point is that they could all be equally true reports about what the map indicates. (I would argue that this is a case in which only the reference and not the sense of '5 + 7' and '7 + 5' is involved.)

Contrast this with a situation in which I am putting the map to a different kind of use. My wife wants to know whether the long stretch or the short stretch comes first, so she asks me to tell her what the map indicates about distances in the order in which we are driving. I again utter (3):

(3) Well, the map indicates that it is 5 + 7 kilometers from A to C.

In this situation I claim that (3) is true but (4) is false:

(4) Well, the map indicates that it is 7 + 5 kilometers from A to C.

The interpretation of (4) in which the relative order of 7 and 5 is important can be clinched by adding 'in that order':

(5) Well, the map indicates that it is 7 + 5 kilometers from A to C, in that order.

From these examples we can conclude, then, that (4) is ambiguous. We have to decide where the ambiguity should be located. Given the principle that we should not postulate an ambiguity in the attitude verb, in this case 'indicates' (there would seem to be no question of an ambiguity in the phrase 'the map'), the ambiguity must therefore be in the that-clause. How might that be? I suggest that the answer is found in the discussion of *de re* attitudes in chapters 1 and 2 of *Structured Meanings* which made it clear that there is no ambiguity in the complement sentence itself. Rather, ambiguity is in whether that sentence is evaluated as a whole unit, or whether the references of its parts are taken separately.

What has been said so far about *de re* attitudes suggests that, at the level of logical form, a variety of distinct symbols might underlie the one surface 'that', depending on how the complement sentence is to be evaluated. This means that (3) and (4) have different syntactic structures at the level of logical representation. An alternative solution would be to say that 'that' is a context-sensitive symbol, and that it is the duty of one of the contextual indices to tell it how to apply to the sentence that follows it. I do not myself find the latter alternative very plausible, but I do not think much turns on whether or not it is adopted. Either the structure of the sentence says 'Sometimes operate on the references of the parts and sometimes on the whole' or the context says to do this. (Even the first alternative will require principles of some kind to say which structure should be chosen to represent the sentence involved in some particular speech event. But they would not be strictly semantic principles in this case.)

In the formal language to be introduced in part III of *Structured Meanings*, the ambiguity will be accommodated by postulating a range of distinct lexical items underlying the one surface word 'that'. This seems to be the most appropriate device for the formal framework adopted there, but, details aside, the key feature is simply that the ambiguity in propositional attitude sentences should be located in the that-clause but not in the complement sentence.

In locating the ambiguity in propositional attitude setences in the that-clause rather than in the attitude verb, I do not of course want to suggest that each verb operates in the same way. Some verbs, like 'say' and (even more strikingly) 'giggle' and 'holler', seem to be sensitive even to the form of the complement sentence and to operate in a partly quotational manner. Some, at the other extreme, seem sensitive to nothing more than the reference of the embedded sentence. (Recall that I am using the term 'reference' to mean the proposition that is the semantic value of the complement sentence obtained in a function-and-argument way from the references of the words in the sentence. In part II of *Structured Meanings* I mention a pair of rather different notions of sense and reference. In the arithmetical language the reference can be identified with a truth value, but that is because of a peculiarity of that language.)

A verb expression that seems least sensitive to sense is the phrase 'is true'. (I shall treat this as a single phrase, though the fact that it is constructed using the adjective 'true' would eventually have to be accounted for along with the various uses of that adjective.) The phrase 'is true' can take not only that-clauses but also direct quotations as its arguments:

(6) '5 + 7 = 12' is true.

(7) That 5 + 7 = 12 is true.

The latter is often phrased as

(8) It is true that 5 + 7 = 12.

I am taking (8) to be a more elaborate version of (7) (presumably derived from it by extraposition).

Surprisingly, this very simple case causes problems. The problems arise because of our assumption that the attitude verbs are univocal. Applied to this case, it means that the phrase 'is true' in (6) and (7) must be the same. Unfortunately, it is known that the phrase 'is true' in (6) (via its negation 'is false') leads to semantic paradox in a language with the richness of English. Since this book is not about the semantic paradoxes, I shall say little more than that I favor some sort of levels of language theory in order to solve them. I will come back to this point later. At the moment note only that there will be problems in identifying 'is true' in (6) and (7) (because of the problems in the case of (6)).

What about (7) on its own? If we consider only a sentence like (7), there need be no problem, because 'is true' in (7) need operate only on the reference of the complement sentence. Remember that ambiguities in propositional attitude sentences are indicated by the meaning of 'that'. In the case of (7) we can take the meaning of 'that' to be simply the identity function, the function that operates on the reference of the complement sentence to give, as its value, the very same thing. This function is just the two-column list in which the same thing appears (in each row) in both columns. The "things" now are propositions, things whose nature we have as yet not specified. So the reference of a that-clause is just the same as the reference of the sentence that follows it. However, syntax prevents a that-clause from being a sentence. We need a predicate to turn it into one. One such predicate is 'is true', the predicate whose meaning is also the identity function, the very same list as the meaning of 'that'. As a result, (7) has the same reference as '5 + 7 = 12'. And in general 'it is true that α'' has the same reference as α. The fact that 'it is true that α'' means no more than α has led to what is called the *redundancy* of truth. It can be seen why this view is false. The word 'that' is independently needed because of other predicates besides 'is true', and the predicate 'is true' is needed because of other complement phrases, as in

(9) What Helen said is true.

It is only their combination that leads to redundancy.

A sentence like (9) is interesting because it does not seem to be clear whether the phrase 'is true' is the paradox-generating predicate of sentences or the innocuous predicate of propositions. Perhaps in this case we can (as I think most philosophers have supposed) just assume that until we know which 'is true' is involved, the meaning of (9) is just unclear.

But the situation is actually worse than that when we consider a that-clause that is sensitive to the parts of the embedded sentence. Let us call the 'that' in (7) 'that$_0$'. The meaning of 'that$_0$' is just the identity function operating on the reference of '5 + 7 = 12'. Now consider a 'that' of the kind discussed in chapter 3 that makes the reference of 'that 5 + 7 = 12' the structure $\langle\langle 5,7,+\rangle,12,=\rangle$, which is the sense of '5 + 7 = 12'. Call this 'that$_s$'. What happens if we try to predicate 'is true' of 'that$_s$ 5 + 7 = 12'? In this case the meaning of 'is true' cannot be the identity function, because $\langle\langle 5,7,+\rangle,12,=\rangle$ is not a proposition. What it should be is a funtion that in the case of this structure gives the proposition obtained by allowing + to operate on 5 and 7, and = to operate on the result and 12. In other words the reference of

(10) That$_s$ 5 + 7 = 12 is true

ought to be the very same proposition as the reference of '5 + 7 = 12'. Which of these functions should be the meaning of 'is true'? Two answers are possible, and unfortunately both lead to difficulties. One is that 'is true' is defined only to operate on propositions (i.e., defined only to operate on the references of complement sentences) and its meaning is then the identity function. (The predicate of sentences would then be a different 'is true'.) The other is to allow the meaning of 'is true' to be defined for all structures, but for its value to be the result of evaluating out those structures. Thus, for example, it would operate on $\langle\langle 5,7,+\rangle,12,=\rangle$ to get the proposition that is the reference of '5 + 7 = 12'. With sentences like (7) these two approaches seem to give equivalent results. On the first approach the surface sentence

(7) That 5 + 7 = 12 is true

would only have a meaning when interpreted as

(11) That$_0$ 5 + 7 = 12 is true.

On the second approach (7) could have the underlying form of either (10) or (11), but the semantics for 'is true' would give the same result in each case.

The problem with the first approach comes when 'is true' is applied to something when it is not a that-clause. Suppose that

(12) Mary said that$_s$ 5 + 7 = 12

is true but that

(13) Mary said that$_0$ 5 + 7 = 12

is not. This could easily happen because (13) is equivalent to

(14) Mary said that$_0$ 12 = 12,

and (14) could certainly be false while (12) is true. But if 'is true' only operates on that$_0$-clauses, then the following sentence would have to be false:

(15) Mary said something which is true.

This is because the only thing that Mary said is 'That$_s$ 7 + 5 = 12', and this is not even in the domain of the predicate 'is true' when construed as only applying to references. Yet it seems obvious that (15) ought to be true, because Mary did say something true. On this approach we would have to postulate not merely an ambiguity between 'is true' as a predicate of sentences and 'is true' as a predicate of that-clauses but also an ambiguity between 'is true' as a predicate of various kinds of that-clauses.

The second approach, in which 'is true' is a predicate of structures but in which the meaning of the whole phrase 'it is true that α' is just that of α, irrespective of what kind of 'that is involved, has difficulties of a rather different kind. These difficulties have been raised by Richmond Thomason as an objection to the whole idea of structured meanings, and they involve an application of Gödel's theorem on the incompleteness of arithmetic. Because I am trying to keep things as simple as I can at this stage, I will do little more than outline Thomason's proof. Yet it must be discussed because, if Thomason is right, it poses very serious questions for the views I have been advocating.

The difficulties arise in any language that is capable of expressing the truths of arithemtic. The language discussed so far is one of these. We also need to assume that such a language has been disambiguated and that there is an effective one-to-one correspondence between sentences and what I have called their *senses*. Further, since we may effectively number the sentences of arithmetic, there is an effective one-to-one correspondence between numbers and senses. By the techniques used in Gödel's theorem, this means that there is an expression *in the language* that may be read 'the sense with gödel number—'. This expression becomes the name of a sense when its argument place is supplied with a number.

Now suppose the language contains a predicate 'is true' when applied to all senses. This means that we can define a predicate T of numbers in the following way:

$T(n) =_{df}$ 'the sense with the gödel number n is true'.

(Strictly, we must distinguish between the number n and the numeral that represents it. The latter is usually written $\bar{n}$.)

Now, given any sentence α, we may suppose that its sense is the nth. This means that quite generally, where n is the gödel number of the sense of α,

(16) $T(n)$ iff α

is a truth of our semantical theory.

Using the techniques of Gödel's theorem, Thomason is able to show that there exists a sentence α that has two properties:

(i) The gödel number of the sense of α is n.

(ii) α is the sentence 'not $T(n)$'.

This means that from (16) we have the following as a truth of the semantical theory:

(17) $T(n)$ iff not $T(n)$.

And this of course means that the theory is inconsistent.

What are we to make of this? The question is whether these problems lie in the nature of semantics itself or are the consequences of an erroneous theory. My opinion is that they lie in the nature of semantics itself. In the first place I think, and have tried to show, that there are occasions when we refer to senses, though perhaps there are no occasions on which we want to refer to all senses. In the second place I think that there are arguments for identifying the semantic truth predicate and the indirect discourse truth predicate. These are arguments from the existence of sentences of the following kind:

(18) Jeremy believed that the sentence Miriam uttered and what Mary hinted were equally true.

If sentences like (18) are possible, then we are stuck with a paradox-generating truth predicate in any case and must take some steps to deal with it.

Thomason concedes that the inconsistency of such a truth predicate may not bother those who advocate a semantical view of the kind he is attacking. He is more worried by the fact that (following Montague's adaptation of Tarski) the same argument can be carried out for the predicate 'knows' when its second argument is a structured meaning. The paradox arises provided the phrase '*a* knows' obeys certain principles used in Hintikka's epistemic logic. Now Hintikka's epistemic logic only applies in a community of logically omniscient beings, and Thomason takes himself to have shown that such a community cannot exist if knowledge is taken that way. However, the real moral seems to me to be that in a community of logically omniscient beings every that-clause following a verb of knowing only involves a 'that$_0$' and therefore the second argument is just the reference of the embedded sentence. Hintikka's semantics shows what this reference might be and shows as well that no inconsistency arises.

PART SIX

POSSIBLE WORLDS

INTRODUCTION

Unlike syntax, semantics has one foot in the world outside of language—and indeed, as we shall see, not only in the actual world, but in the metaphysically luxurious universe of possible worlds (or at least in the possibly luxurious world of metaphysics). Meaning relates words to the world and truth cannot get on without it. Some truths are necessary and so are some falsehoods; others are merely possible while those we hearken to most often are actual. Rudolf Carnap in *Meaning and Necessity* revived Leibniz's idea of a compossible world in order to characterize most generally the truth conditions of sentences, including those with modal operators such as "possibly" and "necessarily." Leibniz's worlds in Carnap's more conservative hands become state-descriptions. A state description, for Carnap, is a maximally consistent set comprising every simple (or atomic) sentence or its negation. Modal truth is then definable in terms of occurrence or nonoccurrence in sets of state-descriptions. A possible truth is one that holds in in at least one state-description, i.e., "It would be true if the state description (that is, all sentences belong to it) were true" (p. 9). A necessary truth holds in all state-descriptions, and an actual truth holds in the state description which in fact characterizes the actual world.

Carnap hence understands possible worlds linguistically, perhaps even syntactically, since in formal languages an atomic sentence and hence a state description can be specified in terms of vocabulary. Not so, however, the contributors to this section. They are in different ways possible worlds realists (Lycan's critical contribution is to be excepted). There loom, because of this realism and the different forms it takes, deep and intransigent metaphysical controversies. Despite the desire of some to carve off the formal study of natural language from the suspicious domain of metaphysics, the questions raised here are theoretically central to the semantics of natural languages. For natural languages, as we have seen, are replete with at least *prima facie* ineliminable intensional and modal constructions. And the most promising lines of research regarding the semantics of expressions containing these constructions involve the use of models containing sets of possible worlds. If the postulation of worlds other than our own is required by semantic theory, semanticists cannot evade the task of characterizing those entities and defending their existence.

Robert Stalnaker expresses with great clarity the theoretical utility of possible worlds. The *extension* of an expression is a set: the individual or its unit set (singleton) if it is a name, the set or sequence of all those things the predicate is true of if it is a predicate and its truth-value if it is a sentence. The *intensions* of expressions, however, are function from possible worlds to those extensions. The proposition a sentence expresses, then, is a function to those worlds in which it is true. Or it may be thought of just as those worlds. This is a very different idea than is Carnap's. Stalnaker emphasizes this difference when he says that propositions so understood have none of "the extraneous structure of language." That is, they are not to be understood as syntactic entities, or as sets of such entities, but rather as the abstract entities that constitute the semantic values of such syntactically characterizable entities as sentences.

In this essay Stalnaker argues for the necessity of positing possible worlds in order to explain rational behavior. This has direct implications of their necessity for the semantics of natural languages. For rational behavior is behavior determined at least in part by such propositional attitudes as belief and desire. And, as we have seen, these are mental states with propositions as their objects. The sentences that attribute them hence have a semantics that reflects that propositional content, and hence, if Stalnaker is right, requires possible worlds in the model. There is a strong intuitive tug, certainly, to the idea that choice, say, contemplates various unrealized possibilities, possibilities that in the very least are fragments of possible worlds.

In the middle of his essay, Stalnaker heroically tackles what for this theory is the great awkwardness of necessary truth. According to the simplest (and perhaps standard) account of the possible worlds semantics for necessity, there is only one necessarily true proposition. So, counterintuitively, all sentences expressing necessary truths, on such a theory, come out meaning the same thing. Since a necessary truth is true at all possible worlds, or just is all possible worlds, there is no difference between the proposition that 3 is a prime and that 11 is a prime. Yet one feels that the first if believed is a belief about 3 while the second is about 11.

David Lewis introduces the notion of a possible world with an ingenious and ingenuous bit of vernacular, "ways things could have been." He then defends a robust modal realism as the only consistent position regarding the status of possible worlds. The modal idioms that are argued to necessitate modal realism are many, including such modal auxiliaries as "can" and "must"; their counterpart adverbs; contrary to fact subjunctive conditionals; perhaps even tense. (For are not the past and present other times if not other places?) Possible world semantics undercuts the venerable doctrine of the univocity of "exists." For on this account much that is nonexistent in fact exists in some sense—in other possible worlds. Or if we leave "exists" unambiguous a distinction has to be drawn between *actual* and *possible* existence. Lewis insists that possible worlds are as real as is our world. Why then do we call them possible and ours actual? "Actual," he says functions indexically; it just means *here*.

Once one has the idea of a possible world, questions arise. (If one believes in the intrinsic goodness of abstract questions, this is sufficient to justify their postulation.) One question that comes up is: What's in them? Possible objects or actual objects? Or both? Lewis addresses each of these central questions in a direct defense of his modal realism.

Alvin Plantinga describes the position articulated above of Stalnaker and Lewis as the Canonical Conception. He praises it for its utility but deprecates it for its ontological cost. That cost is an extravagant commitment to nonexistent objects. (Lewis allows there are such objects but demurs from their nonexistence; they are existent but nonactual.) He then proposes an alternative to the Canonical Conception that, he argues, has all its utility but does not incur the cost. It is called "Actualism" and in Plantinga's hands it articulates a conception of possible worlds and their contents that does not commit one to existent but nonactual things. He does not seek to reduce the concepts of proposition, state of affairs, and property to sets and functions from possible worlds; rather the reverse. He defines possible worlds in terms of those concepts, making them primitive or undefined. He says that a possible world is a complete or maximal state of affairs, thus returning, at least partially, and in a fashion, to Carnap.

The embarrassment discussed by Stalnaker that there is only one necessary proposition is extended to properties. If properties are functions from worlds to extensions, two properties necessarily true of the same thing, such as being the cube of 3 and being the square root of 81, are one and the same property. This may seem less embarrassing than the oneness of necessary truth, but we ought not enter into the very dense reasoning of Plantinga's essay. The main point is that he argues against the extravagant classism of the Canonical Conception: properties, relations and propositions, and worlds themselves, are all reduced to sets and sets of sets. Plantinga prefers to leave properties, relations, and propositions and the states of affairs they describe unreduced and make worlds from them. The title of William Lycan's essay sounds polemical. It sounds as if there is trouble not only with the Canonical Conception of possible worlds but with any conception of them. Proposed solutions for the troubles can be organized, Lycan suggests, around the single problem of making consistent the (Meinongian) formula $\exists x. - \exists y. x = y$," which says in apparent self-contradiction that there are nonexistent things. He surveys various ameliorations. One entails, making the existential quantifier ambiguous between a Meinongian and actualist sense. He spends, however, most energy on Lewis's position, nicely summarized and wittily described as relentless Meinongianism. It is the extremeness of Lewis's extreme realism, or complaints to that effect, that Lycan judiciously weighs.

We may appear to have wandered far from language and far into metaphysics. These metaphysical questions however, are issues in what Emmon Bach calls the metaphysics of natural languages. They are unavoidable if alternative explanations of the idioms of modality cannot be found and are forced by the positions now predominant in semantics and surveyed in this volume.

ROBERT STALNAKER

PROPOSITIONS

Propositions are things people express when they make predictions or promises, give orders or advice. They are also things people doubt, assume, believe to be very likely, and hope are true. What kind of thing are they? My aim is to present and discuss an account of propositions that appears to have great theoretical promise, but that also is faced with serious philosophical difficulties. I will first give a brief outline of the account I have in mind; then provide this account with some philosophical justification by tying it to an independently plausible account of propositional attitudes; and finally, raise and respond to some of the serious philosophical problems that the account faces. I cannot solve them, but I hope to indicate that they are not insurmountable problems and so are not reasons to reject the account out of hand.

The account of propositions that I have in mind is a byproduct of the semantical treatment of modal logic which defines necessity and possibility in terms of a structure of *possible worlds*. According to this kind of interpretation, the formulas of modal logic are assigned truth values not directly, but relative to possible worlds or possible states of the world. Exactly one possible world, or possible state of the world, is *actual*, and truth itself is just truth in this actual world.

Just as a domain of individuals must be specified in order to interpret sentences in first-order extensional logic, so a domain of possible worlds, each with its domain of individuals, must be specified in order to interpret first-order modal logic. This move allows for a natural interpretation of statements of necessity: "it is necessary that P" means that P is true in all possible worlds in the domain. It also allows for a natural distinction between the intensions and the extensions of singular terms, predicates, and sentences. The extension of an expression is given relative to a possible world; it is what is denoted by that expression in that possible world. The intension of an expression is the rule by which the extension is determined. Thus since the extension or denotation of a singular term is an individual, the intension is a function from possible worlds into individuals (an individual concept). Since the extension of a one-place predicate is a class of individuals, the intension of a predicate—the property it expresses—is a function from possible worlds into classes of individuals. And if one takes the extension of a sentence to be a truth value, then the intension of a sentence—the *proposition* it expresses—will be a function taking possible worlds into truth values. Equivalently, a proposition may be thought of as a set of possible worlds: the set of worlds in which the sentence expressing the proposition denotes the value true.

Intuitively, this account of propositions suggests that to *understand* what a sentence says is to know in what kinds of situations it would be true and in what kinds it would be false, or to know the rule for determining the truth value of what was said, given the facts. It also means that two sentences express the same proposition in a given context relative to a set of possible worlds just in case they are true together and false together in each of those possible worlds.

Now if propositions are to be the objects of speech acts and propositional attitudes, why should they be understood in this way? Part of the justification requested by this question can be given by pointing to the technical success of the theory of possible worlds in resolving paradoxes concerning referential opacity, in finding and analyzing subtle scope ambiguities, and in providing a formally elegant framework for the representation of the structure of intensional concepts. But a more general philosophical justification for this account can, I believe, be given. This justification rests on an assumption shared by some philosophers who reject the possible-world approach, and it has, I think, independent plausibility.

The assumption is that beliefs, presumptions, and presuppositions, as well as wants, hopes, and desires, are functional states of a rational agent. A functional state is a state which is defined or individuated by its role in determining the behavior of the object said to be in the state. In the case of propositional-attitude concepts, the objects are rational agents, and the relevant kind of behavior is rational behavior. Thus the notions of believing, wanting, and intending, on the assumption I am making, belong to a theory of rationality—a theory which is intended to explain how rational creatures operate when they deliberate, investigate, and communicate; that is, to answer questions about why their actions and reactions are appropriate when they are. A simple theory of this kind goes back at least to Aristotle and is taken for granted by common sense explanations of behavior. Its most basic concepts are belief and desire (where desire is taken broadly to include long-range dispassionate ends as well as attitudes more naturally called desires). To explain why a person did something, we show that by doing it, he could satisfy his desires in a world in which his beliefs are true. For example, I explain why Sam is turning cartwheels on the front lawn by pointing out that he wants to impress Alice and believes that Alice will be impressed if he turns cartwheels on the front lawn. The notions of belief and desire used in the explanation are correlative dispositions that jointly determine action.

Now if what is *essential* to belief is that it plays this kind of role in determining action, what is essential to the objects of belief? I shall argue that what is essential is given by the possible-world account of propositions sketched above.

First, the functional account, as a theory of rational action, already contains implicitly an intuitive notion of alternative possible courses of events. The picture of a rational agent deliberating is a picture of a man who considers various alternative possible futures, knowing that the one to become actual depends in part on his choice of action. The function of desire is simply to divide these alternative courses of events into the ones to be sought and the ones to be avoided, or in more sophisticated versions of the theory, to provide an ordering or measure of the alternative possibilities with respect to their desirability. The function of belief is simply to determine which are the relevant alternative possible situations, or in more sophisticated versions of the theory, to rank them with respect to their probability under various conditions of becoming actual.

If this is right, then the identity conditions for the objects of desire and belief are correctly determined by the possible-world account of propositions. That is, two sentences P and Q express the same proposition from the point of view of the possible-world theory if and only if a belief or desire that P necessarily functions exactly like a belief or desire that Q in the determination of any rational action. Suppose P and Q express the same proposition in the sense that they are true together and false together in all possible courses of events conceivable to some agent. If any of his attitudes toward the content of P were to differ from his attitudes toward the content of Q, then no coherent division or ranking of the alternative possibilities would be determined, and no straightforward rational explanation of any action could be given. An attitude toward P will be functionally equivalent to the same attitude toward Q, and in a functional theory, functional equivalents should be identified.

Now suppose that P and Q express different propositions in the sense that there is some possible course of events in which they differ in truth value. Then one can always imagine a coherent context of deliberation—one in which the agent's attitudes toward the possibilities that distinguish the two propositions are crucial. In such a context, he will have different attitudes toward P than he has toward Q.

A second reason that the possible-world theory provides a concept of propositions which is appropriate for the functional account of propositional attitudes is that it defines propositions independently of language. If desires and beliefs are to be understood in terms of their role in the rational determination of action, then their objects have nothing essential to do with language. It is conceivable (whether or not it is true) that there are rational creatures who have beliefs and desires, but who do not use language, and who have no internal representations of their attitudes which have a linguistic form. I think this is true of many animals—even some rather stupid ones—but there might be clearer cases. Imagine that we discovered living creatures—perhaps on some other planet—who did not communicate, but whose behavior was predictable, for the most part, on the hypothesis that they engaged in highly sophisticated theoretical deliberation. Imagine further that we had this indirect evidence supporting our hypothesis: that the beliefs that our hypothesis attributed to these creatures could be causally explained, in many cases, in terms of their sensory inputs; and that the desires attributed to them by the hypothesis were correlated appropriately, for the most part, with the physical requirements for their survival. Finally, imagine that we test the hypothesis by manipulating the environments of these creatures, say by feeding them misleading "evidence" and by satisfying or frustrating some of their alleged desires. If they continued to behave as predicted, I think we would be tempted to attribute to these creatures not just belief and desire analogues, but beliefs and desires themselves. We would not, however, have any reason to hypothesize that they thought in a mental language, or in any language at all.

It is plausible to think that if such creatures were intelligent and adaptable enough, it would almost certainly be in their interest, and within their power, to develop ways of communicating their beliefs and desires. Hence, a community of such sophisticated by inarticulate rational agents would be surprising. But it is not an incoherent hypothesis that there are such creatures, and in any case, on the functional account, the development and use of language is viewed as one pattern of rational behavior among others, and not as something on which the concept of rational behavior is itself dependent. For this reason an account of propositions that treats them as linguistic items of some kind would be inappropriate.

Even if we are concerned only with the behavior of real, language-using rational creatures, we should not treat the objects of propositional attitudes as essentially linguistic. There is no reason, according to the functional theory, a person cannot have a belief that goes beyond the expressive power of the language he speaks or that can be expressed only imperfectly in his language. For example, I may believe of a certain person I saw last week that he is a spy. I may not know his name, or even remember that I saw him last week; I just remember *him*, and I believe that he is a spy. You may attribute the belief to me (for example, by saying, "Stalnaker believes that Ortcott is a spy") in the course of explaining my behavior toward Ortcott without attributing to me either the language in which you express my belief or any translation of it. It should be clear that I may have the belief even if I know of no name or accurate unique description of the person whom my belief concerns. But it would be gratuitous to suppose that in this case there is a private inexpressible name which occurs in my belief. Such a supposition would be required by an account which treated propositions as linguistic things.

There are, of course, several essential features of the objects of propositional attitudes which are also essential features of linguistic items such as statements. Both can be true and false, and can stand in logical relations like implication, independence, and incompatibility. The possible-world account attributes these logical features to propositions without any of the extraneous structure of language. Propositions, according to this account, have no syntax, no "exact words" or word order, no subjects, predicates, or adverbial phrases; nor do they contain semantical analogues to these notions. This accords with the functional account, which assigns no role to such grammatical notions in the explanation of behavior. It also accords with intuitive ideas about belief and other propositional attitudes. We do naturally talk about true and false, incompatible and independent beliefs. But we do not normally talk about the first word, or the subordinate clause in a belief. For these reasons, it seems plausible to maintain that while beliefs resemble statements in some ways and are often expressible in statements, they are not, as statements are, composed of linguistic elements.

Before looking at the problems with this account that I find difficult, let me dismiss two that I think are not. First, some people find that the possible-world theory troubles their ontological consciences. Since there really are no such things as possible worlds, how can we take seriously a theory that says there are? Second—a closely related worry—some people claim not to understand the notion of a possible world. They say it has no useful intuitive content, and so it cannot play an essential role in an adequate explanation of propositional attitudes.

The first objection seems to me not to be distinct from a general objection that the theory as a whole is not fruitful. If the possible-world theory is useful in clarifying relationships among actions and attitudes, or among the contents of statements and beliefs, and if the basic notions of that theory cannot be analyzed away, then we have as good a reason as we could want for saying that possible worlds *do* exist, at least insofar as it is a consequence of the theory that they do. A simple denial of existence is not a good reason to reject a theory. Rather, one has reason to deny the existence of some alleged theoretical entity only if one has independent reason to reject the theory.

Philosophers with strict ontological scruples often justify their skepticism about some alleged entity by claiming not to understand it. Some people claim just not to know what a possible world could be, not to be able to recognize one or tell that one is different from another. One aim of drawing the connection between the possible-world theory and the functional account of propositional attitudes is to help such people understand possible worlds— to support the claim that the notion does have intuitive content, and to identify one of its sources. The connection suggests that we need at least a rudimentary notion of alternative possible situations in order to understand such notions as belief and rational deliberation. If this is right, then a notion of possible worlds is deeply involved in our ordinary ways of regarding some of our most familiar experiences.

This intuitive notion of an alternative possible state of affairs or course of events is a very abstract, unstructured one, but that is as it should be. The notion of rationality, as explained by the functional theory, involves a notion of alternative possibilities, but it does not impose any structure on those possibilities. That is, it is no part of the idea of rational deliberation that the agent regard the possible outcomes of his available alternative actions in any particular way. The kind of structure attributed to possible worlds will depend on the application of the theory to a particular kind of rational agent in a particular kind of context.

While the possible-world theory itself is neutral with respect to the form of individual possible worlds, one philosophical application of the theory is as a framework for the articulation of metaphysical theories which may impose some structure on them. One may think of possible worlds as quantities of some undifferentiated matter distributed in alternative ways in a single space-time continuum, or as alternative sets of concrete particular substances dressed in full sets of properties, or as a structure of platonic universals participating together in alternative ways. Those whose inclinations are anti-metaphysical may think of possible worlds simply as representations of alternative states of some limited subject matter relevant to some specific deliberation, inquiry, or discussion.

I have not really answered either the ontological skeptic or the philosopher who does not understand what possible worlds are. Rather, I have suggested that these people present not specific objections, but expressions of general skepticism about whether the theory of possible worlds has any fruitful application. A full answer can be given only by developing the theory and by applying it to particular problems.

Let me go on to a more specific and troublesome problem with the possible-world theory as applied to propositional attitudes. The problem is this: if two statements are logically equivalent, then no matter how complex a procedure is necessary to show them equivalent, they express the same proposition. Hence, if propositions are the objects of propositional attitudes, then any set of attitudes which an agent has toward the content of the one statement must be the same as the set of attitudes which he has toward the content of the other. But this is not plausible. If a person does not realize that two statements must have the same truth value, he may believe what the one says while disbelieving what the other says. And in many cases, it may be unrealistic and unreasonable to expect an agent to realize that two statements are equivalent.

The natural first reaction to this problem would be to try to develop finer identity conditions for propositions; that is, to develop a concept of proposition according to which logically equivalent statements sometimes may say different things. But if the intuitive account of propositional attitudes that we are using is right, then this reaction is a mistake. We have previously argued that the identity conditions that our theory imposes on propositions are exactly right from the point of view of the role of beliefs and desires in the rational determination of action. Hence the paradoxical consequence about logically equivalent statements is not just an unfortunate technical consequence of possible-world semantics which demands a technical solution. Rather, it is a consequence of the intuitive picture of belief and desire as determinants of action. In terms of this picture, it is not at all clear what it would mean to say that a person believed that P while disbelieving Q where P and Q are logically equivalent. There is no pattern of behavior, rational or irrational, that the hypothesis could explain. So, because I find this intuitive picture of belief and desire persuasive, I shall not respond to the problem in this way. Instead, I will take the heroic course: embrace the paradoxical consequence and try to make it palatable.

The usual way to make the consequence palatable is to admit that the functional theory of attitudes is an idealization which fits the real world only imperfectly. The ideal notions of belief and desire apply literally only to logically omniscient rational intelligences—agents whose behavior conforms strictly to a certain kind of coherent pattern. Of course no mere mortal rational agent can be expected to have a pattern of behavior which is fully coherent in every detail. The theory cannot plausibly be applied unless certain actions are set aside as actions to be explained not as consequences of some rational process, but in terms of some breakdown or limitation in the rational powers of the agent.

This admission is, I believe, correct, and it is relevant to explaining the possibility of irrational action. But it will not avoid or make palatable the paradoxical consequence for at least two reasons. First, while one might explain the *appearance* of incompatible beliefs, or the failure to believe all the equivalents of one's beliefs, in this way, one could never accept the appearance as reality. No matter how confused or irrational a person may be, one cannot consistently describe his state of mind by saying that he believes that P but fails to believe that Q where P and Q are logically equivalent, since in that case, the proposition expressed by P just *is* the proposition expressed by Q. A person can be so incoherent in his behavior that one hesitates to apply the notions of belief and desire to him at all, but his incoherence can never justify applying these notions to him in an inconsistent way.

The second reason is that this explanation of the paradoxical consequence seems to rule out too much as a "deviation from the norm." One cannot treat a mathematician's failure to see all the deductive relationships among the propositions that interest him in this way without setting aside all of mathematical inquiry as a deviation from rationality. But this would be absurd. Mathematical inquiry is a paradigm of rational activity, and a theory of rationality which excluded it from consideration would have no plausibility.

Let us look more closely at the paradoxical consequence, which I have expressed in a way that ignores use-mention distinctions. It is that if a person believes that P, then if P is logically equivalent to Q, he believes that Q. In this formulation, the expression "that P" is a schema for a nominalized sentence, which denotes some proposition. The statement "P is logically equivalent to Q," however, is a schema for a claim about the relation between two *sentences*. Hence the letters P and Q here stand in for expressions that denote things that *express* the proposition that P. Now once this is recognized, it should be clear that it is not part of the allegedly paradoxical consequence that a person must know or believe that P is equivalent to Q whenever P *is* equivalent to Q. When a person believes that P but fails to realize that the sentence P is logically equivalent to the sentence Q, he may fail to realize that he believes that Q. That is, he may fail to realize that one of the propositions he believes is expressed by that sentence. In this case, he will still believe that Q, but will not himself express it that way.

Because items of belief and doubt lack grammatical structure, while the formulations asserted and assented to by an agent in expressing his beliefs and doubts have such a structure, there is an inevitable gap between propositions and their expressions. Wherever the structure of sentences is complicated, there will be nontrivial questions about the relation between sentences and the propositions they express, and so there will be room for reasonable doubt about what proposition is expressed by a given sentence. This will happen in any account of propositions which treats them as anything other than sentences or close copies of sentences.

Now if mathematical truths are all necessary, there is no room for doubt about the propositions themselves. There are only two mathematical propositions, the necessarily true one and the necessarily false one, and we all know that the first is true and the second false. But the functions that determine which of the two propositions is expressed by a given mathematical statement are just the kind that are sufficiently complex to give rise to reasonable doubt about which proposition is expressed by a statement. Hence it seems reasonable to take the objects of belief and doubt in mathematics to be propositions about the relation between statements and what they say.

This suggestion is prima facie more plausible in some cases than in others. To take an easy case, if I do not recognize some complicated truth-functional compound to be a tautology, and so doubt whether what it says is true, this is obviously to be explained by doubt or error about what the sentence says. But in branches of mathematics other than logic it seems less plausible to take the objects of study to be sentences. For these cases we might take the objects of beliefs and doubts to be a common structure shared by many, but not all, of the formulations which express the necessarily true proposition. This common structure would be a kind of intermediate entity between the particular sentences of mathematics and the single, unstructured necessary proposition. In this kind of case, doubt about a mathematical statement would be doubt about whether the statements having a certain structure express the true proposition.

This suggestion for explaining mathematical ignorance and error implies that where a person fails to know some mathematical truth, there is a non actual possible world compatible with his knowledge in which the mathematical statement says something different from what it says in this world. To develop this suggestion, one would of course have to say much more about what these nonactual possible worlds are like for particular mathematical contexts. Such a development would be a part of a theory of mathematical knowledge. I have no such account in mind, and I do not know if an account that is both plausible and consistent could be constructed. My only aim in presenting the suggestion is to show that there is at least a possibility of reconciling a possible-world theory of propositions and propositional attitudes with the rationality of mathematical inquiry.

There is a closely related problem with a parallel solution. The problem arises for those of us who have been convinced by Saul Kripke's arguments that there are necessary truths that can be known only a posteriori. That is, there are statements such that empirical evidence is required in order to know that they are true, but nevertheless they are necessarily true, and so true in all possible worlds. The best examples (although not the only ones) are identity statements containing two proper names like "Hesperus is identical to Phosphorus." It is obvious that empirical evidence is required to know that this statement is true, and it is also obvious that the relevant evidence consists of astronomical facts, and not, say, facts about meanings of words or linguistic usage. On the other hand, to see that the proposition is necessary, consider what it could mean to suppose, contrary to fact, that it were false. How could Hesperus not have been Phosphorus? It might have been that other planets—says Mars and Jupiter—were *called* Hesperus and Phosphorus, but this is not relevant. It also might have been that a different planet was seen in a certain place in the evening where Hesperus is in fact seen. But to suppose this is not to suppose that a different planet *was* Hesperus, but to suppose that it was not Hesperus which was seen in the evening. If we mean to suppose, quite literally, that Hesperus itself is distinct from Phosphorus itself, then we are just not supposing anything coherent. The planet could not have been distinct from itself.

My point is not to defend this conclusion, which is adequately done elsewhere, but to reconcile it with the thesis that propositions in the sense explained are the objects of propositional attitudes. The reason reconciliation is needed is this: consider any necessary truth which can be known only a posteriori. Since knowledge of it depends on empirical evidence which one might not have, it is possible for a person—even an ideally rational, logically omniscient person—to be ignorant of that truth. But in the possible-world account of propositional attitudes, this means that there might be a possible world compatible with the person's knowledge in which the proposition is false. But this is impossible, since the proposition is necessary, and hence true in all possible worlds. Thus it would seem that the existence of necessary but a posteriori truths is incompatible with a possible-world account of knowledge.

Let us consider what happens when a person comes to know that Hesperus is identical to Phosphorus after first being in doubt about it. If the possible-world analysis of knowledge is right, then one ought to be able to understand this change in the person's state of knowledge as the elimination of certain epistemically possible worlds. Initially, certain possible worlds are compatible with the subject's knowledge; that is, initially, they are among the worlds which the person cannot distinguish from the actual world. Then, after the discovery, these worlds are no longer compatible with the subject's knowledge. What would such possible worlds be like? If we can give a clear answer to this question, then we will have found a *contingent* proposition, which is what astronomers learned when they learned that Hesperus was identical to Phosphorus.

If we are right about the necessity of the proposition that Hesperus is identical to Phosphorus, then the possible worlds ruled out in the discovery will not be possible worlds in which Hesperus is distinct from Phosphorus, since there are none of those. Nevertheless, there are some perfectly clear and coherent possible worlds which are compatible with the initial state of knowledge but incompatible with the new one. They are worlds in which the person in question exists (since presumably he knows that he exists), and in which the proposition he would express in *that* world with the sentence "Hesperus is identical to Phosphorus" is false. That proposition will be different from the one expressed by the sentence in the actual world, since it is a contingent fact that the name "Hesperus" picks out the planet that it does pick out. Moreover, a person using the name properly might be in doubt or mistaken about this fact. In such a case, the same sentence, with the same rules of references which determine its content, will express different propositions in different possible worlds compatible with his knowledge. It is a contingent fact that the proposition expressed is necessarily true, and it is this contingent fact which astronomers discovered.

If this is right, then the relevant object of knowledge or doubt is a proposition—a set of possible worlds—but a different one from the one that is necessarily true. There are two propositions involved, the necessary one and a contingent one. The second is a function of the rules which determine the first.

Now if the person, after finding out that Hesperus is identical to Phosphorus, were to announce his discovery by *asserting* that Hesperus is identical to Phosphorus, what would he be saying? If his assertion is really announcing his discovery, if what he is saying is what he has just come to believe, then it is the contingent proposition that he is asserting. There is generally no point in asserting the necessary proposition, although there is often a point in saying that what some statement says is necessarily true.

I will conclude my defense of the possible-world definition of propositions by summarizing three points that I have tried to make. First, I argued that this theory is motivated not just by the mathematical elegance of the model-theoretic framework, but by a familiar intuitive picture of propositional attitudes. I suggested that this picture in part explains the heuristic power and intuitive content of the notion of a possible world. Second, I argued that the philosophical problems that this theory faces are deep ones; that is, they spring from essential features of the intuitive picture of propositional attitudes, and not from accidental and removable features of possible-world semantics. Any account of propositional attitudes which explains them in terms of their role in the determination of rational action, and any account which treats the objects of these attitudes neither as linguistic items nor as close copies of linguistic items, will be faced with these or similar problems. Finally, I suggested that there is at least a hope of solving the problems without giving up the basic tenets of the theory if we recognize and exploit the gap between propositions and the linguistic formulations which express them. Ignorance of the truth of statements which seem to express necessary propositions is to be explained as ignorance of the relation between the statement and the proposition. I have not carried out the explanation in the most difficult case of mathematical ignorance, but I hope I have shown that such an explanation might be possible.

DAVID LEWIS

POSSIBLE WORLDS

■ believe that there are possible worlds other than the one we happen to inhabit. If an argument is wanted, it is this. It is uncontroversially true that things might be otherwise than they are. I believe, and so do you, that things could have been different in countless ways. But what does this mean? Ordinary language permits the paraphrase: there are many ways things could have been besides the way they actually are. On the face of it, this sentence is an existential quantification. It says that there exist many entities of a certain description, to wit 'ways things could have been'. I believe that things could have been different in countless ways; I believe permissible paraphrases of what I believe; taking the paraphrase at its face value, I therefore believe in the existence of entities that might be called 'ways things could have been'. I prefer to call them 'possible worlds'.

I do not make it an inviolable principle to take seeming existential quantifications in ordinary language at their face value. But I do recognize a presumption in favor of taking sentences at their face value, unless (1) taking them at face value is known to lead to trouble, and (2) taking them some other way is known not to. In this case, neither condition is met. I do not know any successful argument that my realism about possible worlds leads to trouble, unless you beg the question by saying that it already *is* trouble. (I shall shortly consider some unsuccessful arguments.) All the alternatives I know, on the other hand, do lead to trouble.

If our modal idioms are not quantifiers over possible worlds, then what else are they? (1) We might take them as unanalyzed primitives; this is not an alternative theory at all, but an abstinence from theorizing. (2) We might take them as metalinguistic predicates analyzable in terms of consistency: '*Possibly φ*' means that ϕ is a consistent sentence. But what is consistency? If a consistent sentence is one that could be true, or one that is not necessarily false, then the theory is circular; of course, one can be more artful than I have been in hiding the circularity. If a consistent sentence is one whose denial is not a theorem of some specified deductive system, then the theory is incorrect rather than circular: no falsehood of arithmetic is possibly true, but for any deductive system you care to specify either there are falsehoods among its theorems or there is some falsehood of arithmetic whose denial is not among its theorems. If a consistent sentence is one that comes out true under some assignment of extensions to the nonlogical vocabulary, then the theory is incorrect: some assignments of extensions are impossible, for instance one that assigns overlapping extensions to the English terms 'pig' and 'sheep'. If a consistent sentence is one that comes out true under some possible assignment of extensions, then the theory is again circular. (3) We might take them as quantifiers over so-called 'possible worlds' that are really some sort of respectable linguistic entities: say, maximal consistent sets of sentences of some language. (Or maximal consistent sets of atomic sentences, that is *state descriptions*; or maximal consistent sets of atomic sentences in the language as enriched by the addition of names for all the things there are, that is, *diagrammed models*.) We might call these things 'possible worlds', but hasten to reassure anyone who was worried that secretly we were talking about something else that he likes better. But again the theory would be either circular or incorrect, according as we explain consistency in modal terms or in deductive (or purely model-theoretic) terms.

I emphatically do not identify possible worlds in any way with respectable linguistic entities; I take them to be respectable entities in their own right. When I profess realism about possible worlds, I mean to be taken literally. Possible worlds are what they are, and not some other thing. If asked what sort of thing they are, I cannot give the kind of reply my questioner probably expects: that is, a proposal to reduce possible worlds to something else.

I can only ask him to admit that he knows what sort of thing our actual world is, and then explain that other worlds are more things of *that* sort, differing not in kind but only in what goes on at them. Our actual world is only one world among others. We call it alone actual not because it differs in kind from all the rest but because it is the world we inhabit. The inhabitants of other worlds may truly call their own worlds actual, if they mean by 'actual' what we do; for the meaning we give to 'actual' is such that it refers at any world i to that world i itself. 'Actual' is indexical, like 'I' or 'here', or 'now': it depends for its reference on the circumstances of utterance, to wit the world where the utterance is located.[1]

My indexical theory of actuality exactly mirrors a less controversial doctrine about time. Our present time is only one time among others. We call it alone present not because it differs in kind from all the rest, but because it is the time we inhabit. The inhabitants of other times may truly call their own times 'present', if they mean by 'present' what we do; for the meaning we give to 'present' is such that it is indexical, and refers at any time t to that time t itself.

I have already said that it would gain us nothing to identify possible worlds with sets of sentences (or the like), since we would need the notion of possibility otherwise understood to specify correctly which sets of sentences were to be identified with worlds. Not only would it gain nothing: given that the actual world does not differ in kind from the rest, it would lead to the conclusion that our actual world is a set of sentences. Since I cannot believe that I and all my surroundings are a set of sentences (though I have no argument that they are not), I cannot believe that other worlds are sets of sentences either.

What arguments can be given against realism about possible worlds? I have met with few arguments—incredulous stares are more common. But I shall try to answer those that I have heard.

It is said that realism about possible worlds is false because only our own world, and its contents, actually exist. But of course unactualized possible worlds and their unactualized inhabitants do not *actually* exist. To actually exist is to exist and to be located here at our actual world—at this world that we inhabit. Other worlds than ours are not our world, or inhabitants thereof. It does not follow that realism about possible worlds is false. Realism about unactualized possibles is exactly the thesis that there are more things than actually exist. Either the argument tacitly assumes what it purports to prove, that realism about possibles is false, or it proceeds by equivocation. Our idioms of existential quantification may be used to range over everything without exception, or they may be tacitly restricted in various ways. In particular, they may be restricted to our own world and things in it. Taking them as thus restricted, we can truly say that there exist nothing but our own world and its inhabitants; by removing the restriction we pass illegitimately from the truth to the conclusion that realism about possibles is false. It would be convenient if there were one idiom of quantification, say 'there are . . .', that was firmly reserved for unrestricted use and another, say 'there actually exist . . .', that was firmly reserved for the restricted use. Unfortunately, even these two idioms of quantification can be used either way; and thus one can pass indecisively from equivocating on one to equivocating on another. All the same, there are the two uses (unless realism about possibles is false, as has yet to be shown) and we need only keep track of them to see that the argument is fallacious.

Realism about possible worlds might be thought implausible on grounds of parsimony, though this could not be a decisive argument against it. Distinguish two kinds of parsimony, however: qualitative and quantitative. A doctrine is qualitatively parsimonious if it keeps down the number of fundamentally different *kinds* of entity: if it posits sets alone rather than sets and unreduced numbers, or particles alone rather than particles and fields, or bodies alone or spirits alone rather than both bodies and spirits. A doctrine is quantitatively parsimonious if it keeps down the number of instances of the kinds it posits; if it posits 10^{29} electrons rather than 10^{37}, or spirits only for people rather than spirits for all animals. I subscribe to the general view that qualitative parsimony is good in a philosophical or empirical hypothesis; but I recognize no presumption whatever in favor of quantitative parsimony. My realism about possible worlds is merely quantitatively, not qualitatively, unparsimonious. You believe in our actual world already. I ask you to believe in more things of that kind, not in things of some new kind.

Quine has complained that unactualized possibles are disorderly elements, well-nigh incorrigibly involved in mysteries of individuation.[2] That well may be true of any unactualized possibles who lead double lives, lounging in the doorways of two worlds at once. But I do not believe in any of those. The unactualized possibles, I do believe in, confined each to his own world and united only by ties of resemblance to their counterparts elsewhere do not pose any special problems of individuation. At least, they pose only such problems of individuation as might arise within a single world.

Perhaps some who dislike the use of possible worlds in philosophical analysis are bothered not because they think they have reason to doubt the existence of other worlds, but only because they wish to be told more about these supposed entities before they know what to think. How many are there? In what respects do they vary, and what is common to them all? Do they obey a nontrivial law of identity of indiscernibles? Here I am at a disadvantage compared to someone who pretends as a figure of speech to believe in possible worlds, but really does not. If worlds were creatures of my imagination, I could imagine them to be any way I liked, and I could tell you all you wish to hear simply by carrying on my imaginative creation. But as I believe that there really are other worlds, I am entitled to confess that there is much about them that I do not know, and that I do not know how to find out.

One comes to philosophy already endowed with a stock of opinions. It is not the business of philosophy either to undermine or to justify these preexisting opinions, to any great extent, but only to try to discover ways of expanding them into an orderly system. A metaphysician's analysis of mind is an attempt at systematizing our opinions about mind. It succeeds to the extent that (1) it is systematic, and (2) it respects those of our prephilosophical opinions to which we are firmly attached. Insofar as it does both better than any alternative we have thought of, we give it credence. There is some give-and-take, but not too much: some of us sometimes change our minds on some points of common opinion, if they conflict irremediably with a doctrine that commands our belief by its systematic beauty and its agreement with more important common opinions.

So it is throughout metaphysics; and so it is with my doctrine of realism about possible worlds. Among my common opinions that philosophy must respect (if it is to deserve credence) are not only my naive belief in tables and chairs, but also my naive belief that these tables and chairs might have been otherwise arranged. Realism about possible worlds is an attempt, the only successful attempt I know of, to systematize these preexisting modal opinions. To the extent that I am modally opinionated, independently of my philosophizing, I can distinguish between alternative versions of realism about possible worlds that conform to my opinions and versions that do not. Because I believe my opinions, I believe that the true version is one of the former. For instance, I believe that there are worlds where physics is different from the physics of our world, but none where logic and arithmetic are different from the logic and arithmetic of our world. This is nothing but the systematic expression of my naive, prephilosophical opinion that physics could be different, but not logic or arithmetic. I do not know of any noncircular argument that I could give in favor of that opinion; but so long as that *is* my firm opinion nevertheless, I must make a place for it when I do metaphysics. I have no more use for a philosophical doctrine that denies my firm, unjustified modal opinions than I have for one that denies my firm, unjustified belief in chairs and tables.

Unfortunately, though, I am not opinionated enough. There are too many versions of realism about worlds that would serve equally well to systematize my modal opinions. I do not know which to believe; unless I become more opinionated, or find unsuspected connections between my opinions I may never have any way to choose. But why should I think that I ought to be able to make up my mind on every question about possible worlds, when it seems clear that I may have no way whatever of finding out the answers to other questions about noncontingent matters—for instance, about the infinite cardinals?

Quine has suggested one way to seek fixation of belief about possible worlds by proposing that worlds might be put into correspondence with certain mathematical structures representing the distribution of matter in space and time.[3] Suppose, for simplicity, that we are concerned with worlds where space-time is Euclidean and four-dimensional, and where there is only one kind of matter and no fields. (Quine calls these *Democritean* worlds.) We can represent any such world by a mapping from all quadruples $\langle x, y, z, t \rangle$ of real numbers to the numbers 0 and 1. We are to think of the quadruples as coordinates, in some coordinate system, of space-time points; and we are to think of the quadruples mapped onto 0 as coordinates of points unoccupied by matter, and of quadruples mapped onto 1 as coordinates of points occupied by matter. Thus the entire mapping represents a possible distribution of uniform matter over Euclidean space-time. Since there are many different coordinate systems—differing in the location of the $\langle 0, 0, 0, 0 \rangle$ point, the length of the units of spatial and of temporal distance, and the directions of the spatial axes—there are many different mappings (differing by a transformation of coordinates) that we regard as representing the same distribution of matter. To overcome this dependence of the mapping on an arbitrary choice of coordinates, we take not the mappings themselves, but equivalence classes of mappings under transformations of coordinates. We get a perfectly well-defined, well-understood set of mathematical entities, exactly one for every different possible distribution of matter.

Of course, this is a simplified example. The construction must be generalized in several ways to cover possibilities so far overlooked. Space-time might be non-Euclidean; there might be scalar, vector, or tensor fields independent of the distribution of matter; there might be more than one kind of matter, or more or less density of matter, even in the small. We would have to go on generalizing as long as we could think of possibilities not yet taken into account. But generalizing Quine's simplified example is easy mathematical work. We can hope that soon we will reach the end of the generalizations required and permitted by our opinions about what is possible, and then we will have a well-defined set of mathematical entities of a familiar and well-understood sort, corresponding one-to-one in a specified way with the possible worlds.

I do not, of course, claim that these complicated mathematical entities *are* the possible worlds. I cannot believe (though I do not know why not) that our own world is a purely mathematical entity. Since I do not believe that other worlds are different in kinds from ours, I do not believe that they are either. What is interesting is not the reduction of worlds to mathematical entities, but rather the claim that the possible worlds stand in a certain one-to-one correspondence with certain mathematical entities. Call these *ersatz possible worlds*. Any credible correspondence claim would give us an excellent grip on the real possible worlds by their ersatz handles. It would answer most of our questions about what the possible worlds are like.[4]

We already have a good grip, in this way, on at least *some* of the possible worlds: those that correspond to mathematical ersatz worlds constructed at the highest level of generality that our modal opinions clearly require and permit. It is only because there may be higher levels of generality that we have failed to think of, and because our modal opinions are indecisive about whether there really are possibilities corresponding to some of the levels of generality we have thought of (what about letting the number of spatial dimensions vary? what about letting there be entities that are temporally but not spatially located? what about letting the distinction between space and time be local rather than global, like the distinction between up and down?), that we fail to have a good grip on all the worlds.

The mathematical construction of ersatz worlds may seem to depend too much on our current knowledge of physics. We know that we must generalize enough to include non-Euclidean worlds, for instance, just because the physicists have found reason to believe that we live in one. But physics is contingent. If we look to physics to tell us what is possible, will we get all possible worlds? Or only the physically possible worlds, according to current physics?

More, at least, than the latter. We will certainly construct ersatz worlds that disobey currently accepted physical laws; for instance, ersatz worlds where mass-energy is not conserved. Still, we cannot be sure of getting all possible worlds, since we cannot be sure that we have constructed our ersatz worlds at a high enough level of generality. If we knew only the physics of 1871, we would fail to cover some of the possibilities that we recognize today. Perhaps we fail today to cover possibilities that will be recognized in 2071. Our modal opinions do change, and physicists do a lot to change them. But this is *not* to say that we can argue from the contingent results of empirical investigation to conclusions about what possibilities there are. It is only to say that when we find it hard to locate our actual world among the possibilities that we recognize, we may reasonably be stimulated to reconsider our modal opinions. We may try to think of credible possibilities hitherto overlooked, and we may consider whether we are still as sure as we were about those of our modal opinions that have turned out to be restrictive. It is this reconsideration of modal opinions that may influence our construction of ersatz worlds, not the results of empirical investigation itself. We are concerned not with physics proper, but with the preliminary metaphysics done by physicists.

NOTES

1. For more on this theme, see my "Anselm and Actuality," *Noûs*, 4 (1970), 175–188.

2. W. V. O. Quine, "On What There Is," in *From a Logical Point of View* (Cambridge, Mass.; Harvard University Press, 1953), p. 4.

3. W. V. O. Quine, "Propositional Objects," in *Ontological Relativity and Other Essays* (New York: Columbia University Press, 1969), pp. 147–155.

4. Even the indefinite correspondence claim that *some* generalization of Quine's simplified example is right is enough to answer one important question about the possible worlds. How many are there? Answer: at least $]_2$, the infinite cardinal of the set of all subsets of the real numbers. It can easily be shown that this is the number of ersatz worlds in Quine's original construction. Indeed, it is the number of ersatz worlds at any level of generality that seems to me clearly called for. Here is another reason why possible worlds are not sets of sentences of a language. If we take 'language' at all literally, so that sentences are finite strings over a finite alphabet, there are not enough sets of sentences to go around. There are at most $]_1$, the infinite cardinal of the set of all real numbers.

ALVIN PLANTINGA

ACTUALISM AND POSSIBLE WORLDS

The idea of possible worlds has both promised and, I believe, delivered understanding and insight in a wide range of topics. Pre-eminent here, I think, is the topic of broadly logical possibility, both *de dicto* and *de re*. But there are others: the nature of propositions, properties, and sets; the function of proper names and definite descriptions; the nature of counterfactuals; time and temporal relations; causal determinism; in philosophical theology, the ontological argument, theological determinism; and the problem of evil (see [7], chapters IV–X). In one respect, however, the idea of possible worlds may seem to have contributed less to clarity than to confusion; for if we take this idea seriously, we may find ourselves committed to the dubious notion that there are or could have been things that do not exist. Let me explain.

I. THE CANONICAL CONCEPTION OF POSSIBLE WORLDS

The last quarter century has seen a series of increasingly impressive and successful attempts to provide a semantical understanding for modal logic and for interesting modal fragments of natural language (see, for example [4]; [5], p. 169; and [6]). These efforts suggest the following conception of possible worlds: call it 'the Canonical Conception'. Possible worlds themselves are typically 'taken as primitive', as the saying goes: but by way of informal explanation it may be said that a possible world is a *way things could have been—a total way*. Among these ways things could have been there is one—call it 'α'—that has the distinction of being actual; this is the way things actually are. α is the one possible world that obtains or is actual; the rest are merely possible. Associated with each possible world W, furthermore, is a set of individuals or objects: the *domain* of W, which we may call '$\psi(W)$'. The members of $\psi(W)$ are the objects that *exist in W*; and of course different objects may exist in different worlds. As Saul Kripke put it in [4], p. 65,

Intuitively, $\psi(W)$ is the set of all individuals existing in W. Notice, of course, that $\psi(W)$ need not be the same set for different arguments W, just as, intuitively, in worlds other than the real one, some actually existing individuals may be absent, while new individuals . . . may appear.[1]

Each possible world W, then, has its domain $\psi(W)$; but there is also the union—call it U—of the domains of all the worlds. This set contains the objects that exist in α, the actual world, together with those, if any, that do not exist in α but do exist in other possible worlds.

On the Canonical Conception, furthermore, *propositions* are thought of as set-theoretical entities—sets of possible worlds, perhaps, or functions from sets of worlds to truth and falsehood. If we think of propositions as sets of worlds, then a proposition is true in a given world W if W is a member of it. *Necessary* propositions are then the propositions true in every world; possible propositions are true in at least one world; impossible propositions are not true in any. Still further, the members of U are thought of as *having properties* and *standing in relations* in possible worlds. Properties and relations, like propositions, are set-theoretic entities: functions, perhaps, from possible worlds to sets of n-tuples of members of U. If, for simplicity, we ignore relations and stick with properties, we may ignore the n-tuples and say that a property is a function from worlds to sets of member of U. A property P, then, has an *extension* at a given world W: the set of objects that is the value of P for that world W. An object has a property P in a world W if it is in the extension of P for W; and of course an object may have different properties in different worlds. In the actual world, W. V. O. Quine is a distinguished philosopher; but in some other world he lacks that property and is instead, let us say, a distinguished politician. Modal properties of objects may now be explained as much like modal properties of propositions: an object x has a property P *accidentally* or *contingently* if it has P, but does not have P in every possible world; thus the property of being a philosopher is accidental to Quine. X has P *essentially* or *necessarily*, on the other hand, if x has P in every possible world. While *being a philosopher* is accidental to Quine, *being a person*, perhaps, is essential to him; perhaps there is no possible world in which he does not have that property.

Quantification with respect to a given possible world, furthermore, is over the domain of that world; such a proposition as

(1) $(\exists x)$ x is a purple cow

is true in a given world W only if $\psi(W)$, the domain of W, contains an object that has, in W, the property of being a purple cow. To put it a bit differently, (1) is true, in a world W, only if there is a member of U that is contained in the extension of *being a purple cow* for W and is also contained in $\psi(W)$; the fact, if it is a fact, that some member of U not contained in $\psi(W)$ has the property of being a purple cow in W is irrelevant. And now we can see how such propositions as

(2) $\Diamond (\exists x)$ x is a purple cow

and

(3) $(\exists x)$ $\Diamond$ x is a purple cow

are to be understood. (2) is true if there is a possible world in which (1) is true; it is therefore true if there is a member of U that is also a member of $\psi(W)$ for some world W in which it has the property of being a purple cow. (3), on the other hand, is true if and only if $\psi(\alpha)$, the domain of α, the actual world, contains an object that in some world W has the property of being a purple cow. (2), therefore, would be true and (3) false if no member of $\psi(\alpha)$ is a purple cow in any world, but some member of U exists in a world in which it is a purple cow; (3) would be true and (2) false if some member of $\psi(\alpha)$ is a purple cow in some world, but no member of U is a purple cow in any world in which it exists.

Now here we should pause to celebrate the sheer ingenuity of this scheme. Life is short, however; let us note simply that the Canonical Conception is indeed ingenious and that it has certainly contributed to our understanding of matters modal. In one regard, however, I think it yields confusion rather than clarity; for it suggests that there are things that do not exist. How, exactly, does the question of nonexistent objects rear its ugly head? Of course the Canonical Scheme does not as such tell us that there are some objects that do not exist; for perhaps $\psi(\alpha)$, the domain of the actual world coincides with U. That is, the Canonical Conception does not rule out the idea that among the possible worlds there are some in which exists everything that exists in any world; and for all the scheme tells us, α may be just such a world. There is, however, a very plausible proposition whose conjunction with the Canonical Conception entails that $\psi(\alpha) \neq U$. It is certainly plausible to suppose that there could have been an object distinct from each object that does in fact exist; i.e.,

(4) Possibly, there is an object distinct from each object that exists in α.

If (4) is true, then (on the Canonical Scheme) there is a possible world W in which there exists an object distinct from each of the things that exists in α. $\psi(W)$, therefore, contains an object that is not a member of $\psi(\alpha)$; hence the same can be said for U. Accordingly, U contains an object that does not exist in α; this object, then, does not exist in the actual world and hence does not exist. We are committed to the view that there are some things that don't exist, therefore, if we accept the Canonical Conception and consider that there could have been a thing distinct from each thing that does in fact exist.

And even if we reject (4), we shall still be committed, on the canonical scheme, to the idea that there *could have been* some nonexistent objects. For surely there are possible worlds in which you and I do not exist. These worlds are impoverished, no doubt, but not on that account impossible. There is, therefore, a possible world W in which you and I do not exist; but then $\psi(W) \neq U$. So if W had been actual, U, the set of possible objects, would have had some members that do not exist; there would have been some nonexistent objects. You and I, in fact, would have been just such objects. The canonical conception of possible worlds, therefore, is committed to the idea that there are or could have been nonexistent objects.

II. THE ACTUALIST CONCEPTION OF POSSIBLE WORLDS

I said that the canonical conception of possible worlds produces confusion with respect to the notion of nonexistent objects. I said this because I believe there neither are nor could have been things that do not exist; the very idea of a nonexistent object is a confusion, or at best a notion, like that of a square circle, whose exemplification is impossible. In the present context, however, this remark may beg some interesting questions. Let us say instead that the canonical conception of possible worlds exacts a substantial ontological toll. If the insight and understanding it undeniably provides can be achieved only at this price, then we have a reason for swallowing hard, and paying it—or perhaps a reason for rejecting the whole idea of possible worlds. What I shall argue, however, is that we can have the insight without paying the price. (Perhaps you will think that this procedure has, in the famous phrase, all the advantages of theft over honest toil; if so, I hope you are mistaken.) Suppose we follow Robert Adams ([1], p. 211) in using the name 'Actualism' to designate the view that there neither are nor could be any nonexistent objects. Possible worlds have sometimes been stigmatized as "illegitimate totalities of undefined objects"; from an actualist point of view this stigmatisation has real point. But suppose we try to remove the stimata; our project is to remain actualists while appropriating what the possible worlds scheme has to offer. I shall try to develop an actualist conception of possible worlds under the following five headings:

(1) worlds and books;

(2) properties;

(3) essences and the α-transform;

(4) domains and propositions;
and

(5) essences and truth conditions.

1. Worlds and Books

We begin with the notion of *states of affairs*. It is obvious, I think, that there are such things as states of affairs: for example, *Quine's being a distinguished philosopher*. Other examples are *Quine's being a distinguished politician, 9's being a prime number*, and the state of affairs consisting in all men's being mortal. Some states of affairs—*Quine's being a philosopher* and *7 + 5's being 12* for example—obtain or are actual. *Quine's being a politican*, however, is a state of affairs that is not actual and does not obtain. Of course it isn't my claim that this state of affairs *does not exist*, or that there simply is no such state of affairs; indeed there is such a state of affairs and it exists just as serenely as your most solidly actual state of affairs. But it does not obtain; it isn't actual. It *could have been* actual, however, and had things been appropriately different, it *would* have been actual; it is a *possible* state of affairs. *9's being prime*, on the other hand, is an impossible state of affairs that neither does nor could have obtained.

Now a possible world is a possible state of affairs. But not just any possible state of affairs is a possible world; to achieve this distinction, a state of affairs must be *complete* or *maximal*. We may explain this as follows. Let us say that a state of affairs S *includes* a state of affairs S* if it is not possible that S obtain and S* fail to obtain; and let us say that S *precludes* S* if it is not possible that both obtain. A maximal state of affairs, then, is one that for every state of affairs S, either includes or precludes S. And a possible world is a state of affairs that is both possible and maximal. As on the Canonical Conception, just one of these possible worlds—α—has the distinction of being such that every state of affairs it includes is actual; so α is the actual world. Each of the others *could have been* actual but in fact is not. A possible world, therefore, is a state of affairs, and is hence an abstract object. So α, the actual world, is an abstract object. It has no center of mass; it is neither a concrete object nor a mereological sum of concrete objects; indeed α, like *Ford's being ingenious*, has no spatial parts at all. Note also that we begin with the notions of possibility and actuality for states of affairs. Given this explanation of possible worlds, we couldn't sensibly go on to explain possibility as inclusion in some possible world, or actuality as inclusion in the actual world; the explanation must go the other way around.

It is also obvious, I believe, that there are such things as *propositions*—the things that are true or false, believed, asserted, denied, entertained, and the like. That there are such things is, I believe, undeniable; but questions may arise as to their nature. We might ask, for example, whether propositions are sentences, or utterances of sentences, or equivalence classes of sentences, or things of quite another sort. We might also ask whether they are *states of affairs*: are there really *two* sorts of things, propositions and states of affairs, or only one? I am inclined to the former view on the ground that propositions have a property—truth or falsehood—not had by states of affairs. But in any event there are propositions and there are states of affairs; and what I say will be true, I hope, even if propositions just are states of affairs.

We may concur with the Canonical Conception in holding that propositions are true or false *in* possible worlds. A proposition p is true in a state of affairs S if it is not possible that S be actual and p be false; thus

(5) Quine is a philosopher

is true in the state of affairs *Quine's being a distinguished philosopher*. A proposition p is true in a world W, then, if it is impossible that W obtain and p be false; and the propositions true-in-α, evidently, are just the true propositions. Here, of course, it is *truth* that is the basic notion. Truth is not to be explained in terms of truth-in-actual-world or truth-in-α; the explanation goes the other way around. Truth-in-α, for example, is to be defined in terms of truth plus modal notions. The set of propositions true in a given world W is the *book* on W. Books, like worlds, have a maximality property: for any proposition p and book B, either B contains p or B contains $\bar{p}$, the denial of p. The book on α, the actual world, is the set of true propositions. It is clear that some propositions are true in exactly one world;

(6) α is actual,

for example, is true in α and α alone. If we wish, therefore, we can take a book to be, not a set of propositions, but a proposition true in just one world.

2. *Properties*

On the canonical conception, objects have properties in worlds. As actualists we may endorse this sentiment: an object x has a property P in a world W if and only if x is such that W includes its having P. We *are* obliged, however, to reject the Canonical Conception of properties. On that conception, a property is a set-theoretical entity of some sort; perhaps a function from worlds to sets of individuals. This conception suffers from two deficiencies. In the first place, it entails that there are no distinct but necessarily coextensive properties—i.e., no distinct properties P and P^* such that there is no world W in which some object has P but not P^*. But surely there are. The property of being the square of 3 is necessarily coextensive with the property of being $\int_0^3 x^2 dx$; but surely these are not the very same properties. If the ontological argument is correct, the property of knowing that God does not exist is necessarily coextensive with that of being a square circle; but surely these are not the *same* property, even if that argument is correct.

The second deficiency is more important from the actualist point of view. Clearly enough the property of being a philosopher, for example, would have existed even if one of the things that *is* a philosopher—Quine, let's say—had not. But now consider the Canonical Conception: on this view, *being a phi-*

losopher is a function from possible worlds to sets of individuals; it is a set of ordered pairs whose first members are worlds and whose second members are sets of individuals. And this is in conflict with the truth just mentioned. For if Quine had not existed, neither would any set that contains him. Quine's singleton, for example, could not have existed if Quine had not. For from the actualist point of view, if Quine had not existed, there would have been no such thing as Quine at all, in which case there would have been nothing for Quine's singleton to contain; so if Quine had not existed, Quine's singleton, had it existed, would have been empty. But surely the set whose only member is Quine could not have existed but been empty; in those worlds where Quine does not exist, neither does his singleton. And of course the same holds for sets that contain Quine together with other objects. The set *S* of philosophers, for example—the set whose members are all the philosophers there are—would not have existed if Quine had not. Of course, if Quine had not existed, there would have been a set containing all the philosophers and nothing else; but *S*, the set that does in *fact* contain just the philosophers, would not have existed.

And here we come upon a crucial difference between sets and properties. No distinct sets have the same members; and no set could have lacked any member it has to had any it lacks. But a pair of distinct properties—*being cordate* and *being renate*, for example, or *being Plato's teacher* and *being the shortest Greek philosopher*—can have the same extension; and a property such as *being snubnosed* could have been exemplified by something that does not in fact exemplify it. We might put the difference this way: all sets but not all properties have their extensions essentially. If this is so, however, the actualist must not follow the canonical scheme in taking properties to be functions from worlds to sets of individuals. If no set containing Quine exists in any world where Quine does not, the same must be said for any set whose transitive closure contains him. So properties cannot be functions from worlds to sets of individuals; for if they were, then if Quine had not existed, neither would any of his properties; which is absurd.

As actualists, then, we must reject the canonical conception of properties; a property is not a function or indeed any set whose transitive closure contains contingent objects. We must agree with the canonical conception, however, in holding that properties are the sorts of things exemplified by objects, and exemplified by objects in possible worlds. An object x has a property P in a world W if x is such that W includes x's *having P*. Quine, for example, has the property of being a distinguished philosopher; since that is so he has that property in α, the actual world. No doubt he has it in many other worlds as well. Abstract objects as well as concrete objects have properites in worlds. The number 9 has the property of numbering the planets in α; but in some other worlds 9 lacks that property, having its complement instead. The proposition

(7) Quine is a distinguished philosopher

has the property *truth* in the actual world; in some other worlds it is false. A property *P* is *essential* to an object *x* if *x* has *P* in every world in which *x* exists; *x* has *P accidentally*, on the other hand, if it has *P*, but does not have it essentially. Thus Quine has the property of being a philsopher accidentally; but no doubt the property of being a person is essential to him. (7) has *truth* accidentally; but

(8) All distinguished philosophers are philosophers

has truth essentially. Indeed, a necessary proposition is just a proposition that has truth essentially; we may therefore see modality *de dicto* as a special case of modality *de re*. Some properties—truth, for example—are essential to some of the things that have them, but accidental to others. Some, like *self-identity*, are essential to all objects, and indeed *necessarily* essential to all objects; that is, the proposition

(9) Everything has self-identity essentially

is necessarily true. Others are essential to those objects that have them, but are had by only some objects; *being a member,* for example, or *being a person.*

Among the properties essential to all objects is *existence*. Some philosophers have argued that existence is not a property; these arguments, however, even when they are coherent, seem to show at most that existence is a special kind of property. And indeed it is special; like self-identity, existence is essential to each object, and necessarily so. For clearly enough, every object has existence in each world in which it exists. That is not to say, however, that every object is a *necessary being*. A necessary being is one that exists in every possible world; and only some objects—numbers, properties, pure sets, propositions, states of affairs, God—have this distinction. Many philosophers have thought there couldn't be a necessary being, that in no possible world is there a being that exists in every possible world. But from the present point of view this is a whopping error; surely there are as many necessary as contingent beings.

Among the necessary beings, furthermore, are states of affairs and hence possible worlds themselves. Now an object *x* exists in a world *W* if and only if it is not possible that *W* be actual and *x* fail to exist. It follows that every possible world exists in every possible world and hence in itself; *α*, for example, exists in *α*. This notion has engendered a certain amount of resistance, but not, so far as I can see, for anything like cogent reasons. A possible world *W* is a state of affairs; since it is not possible that *W* fail to exist, it it not possible that *W* be actual and *W* fail to exist. But that is just what it means to say that *W* exists in *W*. That *α* exists in *α* is thus, so far as I can see, totally unproblematic.

3. Essences and the α-transform

Among the properties essential to an object, there is one (or some) of particular significance; these are its *essences*, or individual natures, or, to use Scotus' word, its haecceities. I'll use 'essence'; it's easier. Scotus did not discover essences; they were recognized by Boethius, who put the matter thus:

For were it permitted to fabricate a name, I would call that certain quality, singular and incommunicable to any other subsistent, by its fabricated name, so that the form of what is proposed would become clearer. For let the incommunicable property of Plato be called 'Platonity'. For we can call this quality 'Platonity' by a fabricated word, in the way in which we call the quality of man 'humanity'. Therefore, this Platonity is one man's alone, and this not just anyone's, but Plato's. For 'Plato' points out a one and definite substance, and property, that cannot come together in another.[2]

So far as I know, this is the earliest explicit recognition of individual essences; accordingly we might let "Boethianism" name the view that there are such things. On the Boethian conception, an essence of Plato is a property he has essentially; it is, furthermore, "incommunicable to any other" in that there is no possible world in which there exists something distinct from him that has it. It is, we might say, essential to him and essentially unique to him. One such property, says Boethius, is the property of being Plato, or the property of being identical with Plato. Some people have displayed a certain reluctance to recognise such properties as this, but for reasons that are at best obscure. In any event it is trivially easy to state the conditions under which an object has Platonity; an object has it, clearly enough, if and only if that object is Plato.

But this is not the only essence of Plato. To see the others we must note that Plato has *world-indexed* properties. For any property P and world W, there is the world-indexed property P-in-W; and an object x exemplifies P-in-W if x is such that W includes x's having P. We have already encountered one world-indexed property: truth-in-α. Truth-in-α characterizes all the propositions that are in fact true. Furthermore it characterizes them in every possible world; there are worlds in which

(7) Quine is a distinguished philosopher

lacks truth, but none in which it lacks truth-in-α. (7) could have been false; but even if it *had* been, α would have included the truth of (7), so that (7) would have been true-in-α. Truth-in-α is *noncontingent*; every object has it, or its complement, essentially. But the same goes for every world-indexed property; if P is a world-indexed property, then no object has P, or its complement, accidentally.

Where P is a property, let's say that the world-indexed property P-in-α

(call it 'P_x') is the α-transform of P; and if P is a predicate expressing property P, its α-transform $\mathcal{P}_\alpha$ expresses P_α. And now consider any property Q that Quine alone has: *being the author of* Word and Object, for example, or *being born at P, T,* where P is the place and T the time at which he was born. Q is accidental to Quine; but its α-transform Q_α is essential to him. Indeed, Q_α is one of Quine's essences. To be an essence of Quine, we recall, a property E must be essential to him and such that there is no possible world in which there exists an object distinct from him that has E. Since Q_α is world-indexed, it satisfies the first condition. But it also satisfies the second. To see this, we must observe first that the property of being identical with Quine is essential to anything that has it: i.e.,

(10) Necessarily, anything identical with Quine has *being identical with Quine* essentially.

But then it follows that anything that has the complement of *identity-with-Quine*—that is, *diversity from Quine*—has that property essentially:

(11) Necessarily, anything diverse from Quine has diversity from Quine essentially.

We must also observe that

(12) Necessarily, an essence of an object x entails each property essential to x,

where a property P entails a property Q if it is not possible that P be exemplified by an object that lacks Q. And now suppose there is a world W in which there exists an object x that is distinct from Quine but has Q_α. Then there must be an essence E that is exemplified in W and entails (11) and (12), both *being distinct from Quine and* Q_α. Since E entails Q_α, E is exemplified in α—and exemplified by some object that is distinct from Quine and has Q. But by hypothesis there is nothing in α that is distinct from Quine and has Q; accordingly, Q α is an essence of Quine.

For any property P unique to Quine, therefore, P α, its α-transform, is one of his essences. So for any definite description (ιx) Fx that denotes Quine, there is a description (ιx) $F_\alpha x$ that *essentially* denotes him—singles him out by expressing one of his essences. Here we see an explanation of a phenomenon noted by Keith Donnellan [3]. A sentence containing a description, he says, can sometimes be used to express a proposition equivalent to that expressed by the result of supplanting the description by a proper name of what it denotes. Thus the sentence

(13) the author of *Word and Object. is ingenious*

can be used to express a proposition equivalent to

(14) Quine is ingenious.

The proposition expressed by (13) is true in a world W where not Quine but someone else—Gerald R. Ford, let's say—writes *Word and Object* if and only if it is *Quine* who is ingenious in W; Ford's ingenuity or lack thereof in W is irrelevant. We may see this phenomenon as an implicit application of the α-transform to 'the author of *Word and Object*', what (13) thus expresses can be put more explicitly as

(15) the (author of *Word and Object*)$_\alpha$ is ingenious,

a proposition true in the very same worlds as (14).

Now what Donnellan noted is that sentences containing *descriptions* display this phenomenon. For any predicate $\mathcal{P}$, however, there is its α-transform $\mathcal{P}_\alpha$. We should therefore expect to find Donnellan's phenomenon displayed in other contexts as well—by universal sentences for example. These expectations are not disappointed. Rising to address the Alpine Club, I say

(16) every member of the Alpine Club is a splendid climber!

Here, but for an untoward bit of prolixity, I might as well have gone through the membership roll, uttering a long conjunctive sentence of the form

(17) N_1 is a splendid climber & N_2 is a splendid climber & . . . & N_n is a splendid climber

where for each member of the Club there is a conjunct attaching 'is a splendid climber' to his name. If M_1 . . . M_n are the members of the Club, the proposition expressed by (16) is true, in a given world W, only if each of M_1 . . . M_n is a splendid climber in W; the fact, if it is a fact, that in W the Club contains some nonclimbers, or some unsplendid ones, is irrelevant. But then (16) can be put more explicitly as

(18) every (member of the Alpine Club)$_\alpha$ is a splendid climber.

We may state the point a big differently. Suppose 'S' is a name of the set of members of the Alpine Club; then (16), (17), and (18) express a proposition equivalent to

(19) every member of S is a splendid climber.

If we use (16) without implicitly applying the α-transform, of course, what we assert is not equivalent to (19); for what we then assert is true in a world W only if *in* W the Alpine Club contains none but splendid climbers.[3]

4. Domains and Propositions

But now back to our main concern. As actualists we reject the canonical conception of properties while agreeing that objects have properties in worlds and that some of their properties are essential to them; and among the properties essential to an object we have noted, in particular, its essences. But what about domains? On the Canonical Conception, each possible world has its domain: the set of objects that exist in it. Here I have two *caveats*. First, what are domains *for*? For quantifiers to range over, naturally enough. But now we must be careful. On the usual domain-and-variables account, quantification is understood as follows. Consider a universally quantified sentence such as

(20) All spotted dogs are friendly
    or
(20) (x (if x is a spotted dog, then x is friendly).

Here the quantifier is said to range over a set D of objects; and what (20) says is true if and only if every spotted dog in D is also friendly. But this seems fair enough; why must we be careful? Because it suggests that (20) expresses a proposition equivalent if not identical to

(21) every member of D is friendly, if a spotted dog

where D is the domain of the quantifier in (20). And this suggestion is clearly false. For consider a possible world where D and its members exist, the latter being, if spotted dogs, then friendly, but where there are other spotted dogs—dogs not in D—of a nasty and churlish disposition. What (21) expresses is true in that world; what (20) expresses, however, is flatly false therein. (20) and (21) are materially but not logically equivalent—both true or both false, but not true in the same worlds. We may say, if we wish, that in a sentence of the form '$(x)Fx$' the quantifier has a domain D; but propositions expressed by such a sentence will not in general be equivalent to the claim that every member of D has F.

And now for the second, and, in the present context, more relevant caveat. On the canonical scheme, each world W has a domain: the set of objects that exist in W. And though it is seldom stated, it is always taken for granted that a possible world W will domain $\psi(W)$ has *essentially* the property of having $\psi(W)$ as its domain. Having $\psi(\alpha)$ as domain is essential to α, had another world β been actual, other individuals might have existed, but $\psi(\alpha)$ would have been the domain of α. From an actualist point of view, however, this pair of claims, i.e.,

(22) for any world W there is a set $\psi(W)$ that contains just those objects that exist in W,
    and

(23) if D is the domain of W, then W has essentially the property of having D as its domain

leads to trouble. For a set, as we have already seen, can exist only in those worlds where all of its members exist. Hence $\psi(\alpha)$ would not have existed if any of its members had not. $\psi(\alpha)$, therefore, would not have existed had Socrates, let's say, failed to exist. But if, as (23) affirms, α has essentially the property of being such that $\psi(\alpha)$ is its domain, then α can exist only if $\psi(\alpha)$ does. Hence if Socrates had not existed, the same would have held for $\psi(\alpha)$ and α itself. If we accept both (22) and (23), we are burdened with the alarming consequence that possible worlds are not necessary beings; even the most insignificant pebble on the beach has the distinction of being such that if it had failed to exist, there would have been no such thing as α (or any other world whose domain includes that pebble) at all.

This difficulty induces another with respect to the Canonical Conception of propositions as set theoretical entities—sets of possible worlds, let's say. That conception must be rejected in any event; for it entails that there are no distinct but logically equivalent propositions. But clearly this is false.

(24) All bachelors are unmarried

and

(25) $\int_0^3 x^2 dx \rangle 7$

are equivalent. There are those, however, who believe the first without believing or even grasping the second. The first, therefore, has a property not had by the second and is, accordingly, distinct from it. But the principal difficulty with the Canonical Conception is due to the deplorable fragility of sets and domains—their deplorable liability to nonexistence in the worlds where some of their members do not exist. For consider any true proposition p; on the Canonical Conception p will be a set of worlds containing α. But now suppose some object—the Taj Mahal, let's say—had not existed; then neither would $\psi(\alpha)$, α, or p. So if the Taj Mahal had not existed, the same would have held for the truths that $7 + 5 = 12$ and that Socrates was wise; and this is absurd.. On the Canonical Conception, only necessarily false propositions together with such items as

(26) there are no contingent beings

turn out to be necessary beings. This is a distinction, surely, that they do not deserve.

How, then, shall we as actualists think of the domains of possible worlds? We may, if we wish, concur with the Canonical Conception that for each world W there is indeed the set $\psi(W)$ that contains just those objects that exist in W. On the actualist view, however, domains lose much of their significance; and they also display some anomalous properties. First of all, domains, as we have seen, are typically contingent beings. If Socrates had not existed, no set that includes him would have, so that $\psi(\alpha)$ would not have existed. Possible worlds, however, are necessary beings; hence worlds do not in general have their domains essentially. If Socrates had not existed, there would have been a set distinct from $\psi(\alpha)$ that would have been the domain of α, and if *no* contingent beings had existed, the domain of α would have contained only necessary beings. Secondly, the domain of any possible world W, from the actualist perspective, is a subset of $\psi(\alpha)$. Since there are no objects distinct from those that exist in α, $\psi(W)$ cannot contain an object distinct from each that exists in α. Of course the actualist will happily concede that there *could have been* an object distinct from any that exists in α. Hence there is a possible world W in which there exists an object distinct from any that actually exists. The actualist must hold, therefore, that $\psi(W)$ is a subset of $\psi(\alpha)$—despite the fact that W includes the existence of an object that does not exist in α. How can this be managed? How can the actualist understand

(27) There could have been an object distinct from each object that actually exists

if he holds that $\psi(W)$, for any W, is a subset of $\psi(\alpha)$?

5. Essences and Truth Conditions

Easily enough; he must appeal to essences. Socrates is a contingent being; his essence, however, is not. Properties, like propositions and possible worlds, are necessary beings. If Socrates had not existed, his essence would have been unexemplified, but not nonexistent. In worlds where Socrates exists, Socrateity is his essence; *exemplifying Socrateity* is essential to him. Socrateity, however, does not have essentially the property of being exemplified by Socrates; it is not exemplified by him in worlds where he does not exist. In those worlds, of course, it is not exemplified at all; so *being exemplified by Socrates if at all* is essential to Socrateity, while *being exemplified by Socrates* is accidental to it.

Associated with each possible world W, furthermore, is the set $\psi_E(W)$, the set of essences exemplified in W. $\psi_E(W)$ is the *essential* domain of W; and U_E, the union of $\psi_E(W)$ for all worlds W is the set of essences. Essential domains have virtues where domains have vices. Properties exist in every world; so, therefore, do sets of them; and hence essential domains are necessary beings. Furthermore, if $\psi_E(W)$ is the essential domain of a world W, then W has essentially the property of having $\psi_E(W)$ as its essential domain. And just as properties of other sorts are sometimes unexemplified, so there may be unexemplified essences. If Socrates had not existed, then Socrateity would have been an unexemplified essence. Very likely there are in fact some unexemplified essences; probably there is a world W whose essential domain

$\psi_E(W)$ contains an essence that is not in fact exemplified. U_E, therefore, no doubt contains some unexemplified essences.

We are now prepared to deal with (27). Before we do so, however, let us see how some simpler types of propositions are to be understood from the actualist perspective. Consider first.

(1) $(\exists x)$ x is a purple cow.

(1) is true if and only if some member of U_E is coexemplified with the property of being a purple cow; and (1) is true in a world W if $\psi_E(W)$ contains an essence that is coexemplified with that property in W.

(2) Possible $(\exists x)$ x is a purple cow

is true if there is a world in which (1) is true—if, that is, there is an essence that in some world is coexemplified with *being a purple cow*. (2) is therefore noncontingent—either necessarily true or necessarily false.

(3) $(\exists x)$ possibly x is a purple cow,

on the other hand, is true if some member of U_E is coexemplified with the property of possibly being a purple cow. So (3) is true if some exemplified essence is coexemplified in some possible world with the property *being a purple cow*. More generally, (3) is true in a possible world W if some member of $\psi_E(W)$ is coexemplified in some world W^* with *being a purple cow*. (3) entails (2); but if, as seems likely, it is possible that there be purple cows but also possible that there be no things that could have been purple cows, then (2) does not entail (3).

When we turn to singular propositions, it is evident that one like

(28) Ford is ingenuous

is true in a world W if and only if an essence of Ford is coexemplified with ingenuousness in W.

But what about

(29) Ford is not ingenuous?

The sentence (29) is in fact ambiguous, expressing two quite different propositions. On the one hand it expresses a proposition predicating a lack of ingenuousness of Ford, a proposition true in just those worlds where an essence of Ford is coexemplified with lack of ingenuousness. This proposition could be put more explicitly as

(29*) Ford is disingenuous;

i.e., Ford has the complement of ingenuousness. But (29) also expresses the denial of (28):

(29**) it is not the case that Ford is ingenuous.

(28) is clearly false in worlds where Ford does not exist; (29**), therefore, is true in those worlds. Indeed, a crucial difference between (29*) and (29**) is that the former but not the latter entails that Ford exists; (29**), unlike (29*), is true in worlds where Ford does not exist.

We may see the distinction between (29*) and (29**) as a *de re–de dicto* difference. (29*) predicates a property of Ford: disingenuousness. (29**), on the other hand, predicates falsehood of (28) but nothing of Ford. (29*) is true in those worlds where an essence of Ford is coexemplified with disingenuousness. Since there neither are nor could have been nonexistent objects, there neither are nor could have been nonexistent exemplifications of disingenuousness. (29*), therefore, entails that Ford exists. (29**), however, does not. It is true where (28) is false, and true in those worlds in which Ford neither exists nor has any properties.

We may see the ambivalence of the sentence (29) as due to scope ambiguity. In (29**) the sign for negation applies to a sentence and contains the name 'Ford' within its scope. In (29*), however, the sign for negation applies, not to a sentence, but to a predicate, yielding another predicate; and 'Ford' is not within its scope. Where 'Ford' has widest scope, as in (29*), the resulting sentence expresses a proposition that predicates a property of Ford and entails his existence; where the name has less than widest scope the proposition expressed may fail to predicate a property of Ford and may be true in worlds where he does not exist. This interplay between *de re–de dicto* distinctions and scope ambiguity is to be seen elsewhere. A sentence like

(30) If Socrates is wise, someone is wise

is ambiguous in the same way as (29). It can be read as predicating a property of Socrates: the property of being such that if he is wise, then someone is. What it expresses, so read, is put more explicitly as

(30*) Socrates is such that if he is wise, then someone is wise,

a proposition true in just those worlds where Socrates exists. But (30) can also express a proposition that predicates a relation of the propositions *Socrates is wise* and *someone is wise*. Since these propositions stand in that relation in every possible world, this proposition is necessarily true. Unlike (30*), therefore, it is true in worlds where Socrates does not exist. Similarly for

(31) If anything is identical with Socrates, then something is a person.

If we give 'Socrates' widest scope in (31), then what it expresses is a contingent proposition that predicates a property of Socrates and is true only in those worlds where he exists. If we give it narrow scope, however, (31) expresses a necessary proposition—provided, of course, that *being a person* is essential to Socrates.

What about singular existential propositions?

(32) Ford exists

is true in just those worlds where an essence of Ford is coexemplified with existence—the worlds where Ford exists.

(33) Ford does not exist,

however, is ambiguous in the very same way as (29); it may express either

(33*) Ford has nonexistence (the complement of existence)
    or
(33**) it is not the case that Ford exists.

(33**) is the negation of (32) and is true in just those worlds where (32) is false. (33*), however, is true in just those worlds where an essence of Ford is coexemplified with nonexistence. As actualists we insist that there neither are nor could have been things that don't exist; accordingly there is no world in which an essence is coexemplified with nonexistence; so (33*) is a necessary falsehood.

We may now return to

(27) there could have been an object distinct from each object that actually exists.

On the Canonical Conception, (27) is true only if there is a member x of U such that x does not exist in fact but does exist in some possible world distinct from α, (27), therefore, is true, on that conception, if and only if there are some things that don't exist but could have. On the actualist conception, however, there are no things that don't exist. How then shall we understand (27)? Easily enough; (27) is true if and only if there is a world where

(34) there is an object that does not exist in α

is true. But (34) is true in a world W if and only if there is an essence that is exemplified in W but not in α. (27) is true, therefore, if and only if there is at least one essence that is exemplified in some world but not exemplified in fact—if and only if, that is, there is an unexemplified essence. Hence (27) is very likely true. As actualists, therefore, we may state the matter thus:

(35) although there could have been some things that don't *in fact* exist, there are no things that don't exist but could have.

These, then, are the essentials of the actualist conception of possible worlds. It has the virtues but not the vices of the Canonical Conception; we may thus achieve the insights provided by the idea of possible worlds without supposing that there are or could have been things that don't exist.[4]

NOTES

1. For the sake of definiteness I substantially follow the semantics developed in this piece. The essentials of the canonical conception, however, are to be found not just here but in very many recent efforts to provide a semantics for modal logic or modal portions of natural language.

2. In *Librium de interpretatione editio secunda*, Pl. 64, 462d–464c. Quoted in [2], pp. 135–136.

3. The α-transform can also help us fathom the behavior of proper names; in particular it can help us bridge the gap between a broadly Fregean view and the anti-Fregean claims of Donnellan, Kaplan, Kripke, and others. See [8].

4. In "As Actualist Semantics for Modal Logic," Thomas Jager has developed and axiomatized a semantics for quantified modal logic that presupposes neither that things have properties in worlds in which they don't exist, nor that there are or could have been objects that do not exist. In the intended applied semantics, the domain of a model is taken to be a set of essences; and a proposition expressed by a sentence of the form $(\exists x)Fx$ is true in a world if and only if some essence is coexemplified, in that world, with the property expressed by F. Copies may be obtained from Professor Thomas Jager, Department of Mathematics, Calvin College, Grand Rapids, MI 49506, U.S.A.

REFERENCES

[1] Robert Adams, "Theories of Actuality," *Noûs*, 8 (1974), 211–231; Chapter 10 of this anthology.

[2] Hector-Neri Castañeda, "Individuation and Non-Identity: A New Look," *American Philosophical Quarterly*, 12 (1975), 131–140.

[3] Keith Donnellan, "Speaking of Nothing," *Philosophical Review*, 83 (1974), 3–31.

[4] Saul Krupke, "Semantical Considerations on Modal Logic," *Acta Philosophica Fennica*, 16 (1963), 83–94.

[5] David Lewis, "General Semantics," in *Semantics of Natural Language*, ed. by Gilbert Harman and Donald Davidson (Dordrecht: Reidel, 1972), pp. 169–218.

[6] Richard Montague, *Formal Philosophy*, ed. by Richmond Thomason (New Haven: Yale University Press, 1974).

[7] Alvin Plantinga, *The Nature of Necessity* (Oxford: Clarendon Press, 1974).

[8] Alvin Plantinga, "The Boethian Compromise," *American Philosophical Quarterly*, 15 (1978), 129–138.

WILLIAM LYCAN

THE TROUBLE
WITH POSSIBLE WORLDS

In what sense or senses, if any, should we admit that "there are" possible but nonexistent beings or possible but nonactual worlds? Sources of motivation for some such admission are powerful and various. By positing nonexistent individuals, it seems, we may understand true negative existentials and accommodate the intentionality of certain mental entities. By positing nonactual worlds or states of affairs, we may achieve our familiar but still remarkable reduction of the alethic modalities to quantifiers,[1] formulate Tarski-style semantics for propositional attitudes and hosts of other troublesome constructions, display the otherwise mysterious connection between Fregean senses and linguistic meaning,[2] illuminate the pragmatics of counterfactuals and other conditionals, and provide a rigorous format for the theoretical study of decision making.[3] Even ordinary ways of speaking encourage us to reify nonexistent possibles at every turn.

And yet many philosophers are uneasy about yielding to this encouragement; and many, despite all the foregoing, openly scorn the idea of a thing or world that has the property of being nonactual. What is striking is that for years now the dispute between the friends and the foes of mere possibilia has consisted largely of intuitive ventings, dogged repetition of slogans, mutual accusations of perverse or willful misunderstanding, bad jokes, and simple abuse. Only very recently have several philosophers tried thoughtfully and painstakingly to get to the bottom of the problem. I shall here correct some common misunderstandings of the issue, set it up in what I think is the neatest and most illuminating way, distinguish some fundamentally different approaches to the vindication of nonexistent possibles, attack several prominent recent instances of these approaches, survey further prospects, and point in the direction that seems to me most promising.

I. MEINONG VS. THE FORCES OF DECENCY

As I understand him, Alexius Meinong took it to be intuitively obvious or self-evident that there are nonexistent possibles and even nonexistent impossibles.[4] We refer to such things by means of names and descriptions; and they are the objects of thought, after all. Serious researchers doing science and philosophy concern themselves primarily with what is really true, of course; this is as it should be, but unfortunately it produces in them a bias toward the actual and a blindness toward the other sectors of our ontology.

Russell, and Quine a few decades later, expressed distaste for this way of looking at things.[5] Russell faulted Meinong's "sense of reality" and accused him of "doing a disservice to thought." Quine called Meinong's ("Wyman's") universe "overpopulated," "unlovely," "rank," a "slum," and "a breeding ground for disorderly elements." Russell and Quine thus found mere possibilia repugnant and wondered how Meinong could stomach them.

Meinong would not have been impressed by these gestures of distaste. He would simply have repeated his observation that philosophers who find nonexistent possibles aesthetically offensive have unhealthily (if understandably) restricted their diets to the actual.

Without doubt, metaphysics has to do with everything that exists. However, the totality of what exists, including what has existed and what will exist, is infinitely small in comparison with the totality of the Objects of knowledge. This fact easily goes unnoticed, probably because the lively interest in reality which is part of our nature tends to favour that exaggeration which finds the non-real a mere nothing—or, more precisely, which finds the non-real to be something for which science has no application at all or at least no application of any worth.[6]

Besides, Meinong would remind his critics, the ordinary person speaks quite familiarly and often of possible things that do not exist; this is as natural as breathing, and as palatable as beer. Russell and Quine have mongered the mystery, not he, and the cause of their doing so is their forgetting how such talk proceeds when the nature of the actual in particular is not what is specifically at issue.

A bit more can be said, however, about why Quine and Russell find mere possibilia so uncongenial. For one thing, notice that when in "A Theory of Objects" Meinong does try to spell out a vocabulary for talking about nonexistent possibles and impossibles, his discussion takes on a theoretical and moderately technical tone. Certainly an explanatory system is being envisioned and limned, though Meinong himself (I believe) regarded his work on Objects as purely descriptive;[7] and if Meinong's ontology is an explanatory system, it is the sort of thing that must be justified on grounds of elegance and coherence as well as by its explanatory power. Moreover, as soon as

Meinong does begin to talk a bit more technically, his apparatus raises questions whose answers are not obvious and which call for ad hoc ramifications on his part. For example: (1) Quine notoriously demands identity and individuation-conditions for mere possibilia. When have we one possible man and when have we two? When have we 8,003,746? (2) Meinong seems to assume that any (well-formed) superficial singular term refers either to an existent or to a nonexistent being, and he certainly believes that any nonexistent being has any property expressed by the matrix of any description used to refer to it.[8] This prompted Russell at one point[9] to ask whether *the existent round square* exists. Similarly, we might ask whether *the Object that has no Sosein* has a *Sosein*, and so on. (3) The same assumption requires that the city that is five miles north of Columbus and five miles south of Cleveland is five miles north of Columbus and five miles south of Cleveland. Does this not in turn entail that Columbus is ten miles south of Cleveland and so falsify Meinong's theory? (4) Meinong's Objects are indeterminate or *incomplete* in a well-known way: given virtually any nonexistent possible *O* there will be any number of properties *P* such that it is not a fact that *O* has *P* and not a fact that *O* lacks *P*. Now, how can there be, or even "be," a man who is tall but whose height does not fall into any specific range? (5) Meinong characteristically refers to his Objects by using *definite* descriptions, such as "the golden mountain." But on Meinong's own view there are many golden mountains, such as the one which has a beebleberry bush on top, the one which has no beebleberry bush on top, the one on which the Marines stage practice assaults, and the one on top of which Descartes wrote his *Meditations*. How can our phrase, "*the* golden mountain," then succeed in uniquely denoting a single Meinongian Object?

A partisan of possibilia can set about to answer questions like these easily enough. Any elaborate way of herding possible men etc. into full-fledged worlds will settle question (1) determinately (e.g., David Lewis'); Saul Kripke's or Nicholas Rescher's stipulative methods would work just as well. In answer to (2) we might impose a type theory on Meinong's ontology that would rule out such troublesome "descriptions" as ill-formed.[10] Richard Routeley responds to (3) by proposing a restriction on the assumption that generates the problem.[11] (4) may be handled by locating Objects within worlds, or by explicating their nature in such a way as to make their "incompleteness" familiar (as Hector-Neri Castañeda does). (5) leaves us any number of feasible alternatives. So Meinong need not be at all impressed by the fact that Quine and Russell can raise some trick questions for him. And there is some tendency in the recent literature to believe that Quine's objection to possibilia, at least, is based entirely on these trick questions. Any friend of possibilia who thinks this and who has answers to the questions will of course conclude that Quine need have no further quarrel with nonexistents. But such a person would miss the thrust of Quine's opposition entirely, as I shall now explain. The position I shall now ascribe to Quine never appears explicitly in his writings, but it falls trivially out of well-known views of his.

II. THE THEORETICAL STATUS OF NONEXISTENTS

We have conceded that questions such as (1)–(5) are readily answerable by the theorist. That is exactly the point: that a theorist is needed to answer them. Meinong's view has generated the questions without any help from Russell or Quine, and any answers to them will necessarily involve elaboration of a theoretical apparatus. Any such apparatus, along with the proclaimed nature of the possibilia it posits, will have to be justified on theoretical grounds and submit to evaluation of the sort to which any philosophical theory is subject.

One concern that we have about theories is that of parsimony. Most philosophers subscribe to Occam's principle or something like it; at least, few philosophers posit entities that they admit to be totally gratuitous for purposes of philosophical explanation. Now, consider Meinong's ontology. Quine accuses it of bloated unloveliness. But the problem here is even worse than Quine explicitly observes: If Meinong's ontology is bloated, it is bloated to the bursting point. In fact, it is bloated well *past* the bursting point; Meinong believes not only in all the things there could possibly be, but also in all the things there could not be. And the point is not just that Meinong has swallowed some indigestible entities. The problem is that it is now hard to retain any use for Occam's Razor at all. A Meinongian has *already* posited everything that could, or even could not, be; how, then, can any subsequent brandishing of the Razor be to the point? How can the Meinongian explain the continuing usefulness (some would say the indispensability) of parsimony principles in philosophy and in science?

We know how Meinong would respond: he would accuse us again of aiming our tunnel vision only at the actual. Everyone agrees that we must not posit entities *as existing* if they are not needed for purposes of explanation; Occam's Razor certainly applies to existents. But, Meinong would point out, his remaining Objects are *non*existents, and so they are unscathed by Occam's Razor or Occam's Stomach Pump or whatever.[12]

The suggestion is that we should posit possibilia, but not posit them as existing. Quine's reaction is classic:

Wyman, by the way, is one of those philosophers who have united in ruining the good old word 'exist.' Despite his espousal of unactualized possibles, he limits the word 'existence' to actuality—thus preserving an illusion of ontological agreement between himself and us who repudiate the rest of his bloated universe. . . . Wyman, in an ill-conceived effort to appear agreeable, genially grants us the nonexistence of Pegasus, and then, contrary to what *we* meant by nonexistence of Pegasus, insists that Pegasus *is*. Existence is one thing, he says, and subsistence is another. The only way I know of coping with this obfuscation of issues is to give Wyman the word 'exist'. I'll try not to use it again; I still have 'is'. So much for lexicography; let's get back to Wyman's ontology. ("On What There Is," p. 3)

The important point here is that Quine does not care which verbs we use to mark ontological distinctions. Meinong does not care which terms might be used to mark his ontological distinctions either; all he insists is that the distinctions are real. Quine may simply announce that he does not care about the distinctions and go on to repeat his charge of bloating. All Meinong can do in response is to repeat his answer to that charge: that we genuinely commit ourselves to, and thus need be parsimonious about, only the Objects that we claim to find in *this* world, and not those which are merely objects of thought— thought is free, after all, and talk is cheap.

    Contrary to what is suggested by the quoted passage, I believe Quine's real point has nothing to do with ordinary language: It is that anyone who actually makes theoretical use of a Meinongian apparatus in an appropriately regimented theory of modal semantics *quantifies over* nonexistent possibles in his official canonical idiom. Quine notoriously does not care what we say in casual speech; but the minute a semanticist such as Kripke or Richard Montague writes the backward E, the semanticist has got the nonexistents in his ontology and is stuck with them. Perhaps someone may find a way of doing modal semantics *without* genuinely (objectually) quantifying over mere possibilia; such a semantics would be welcome. But until it is produced, Quine contends, the modal theorist is committed to the presence of nonexistent possibles in his official ontology.

    So much the worse, Jaakko Hintikka has remarked,[13] for Quine's much-touted criterion of ontological commitment.

We have to distinguish between what we are committed to in the sense that we believe it to exist in the actual world or in some other possible world, and what we are committed to as a part of our ways of dealing with the world conceptually, committed to as a part of our conceptual system. The former constitute our ontology, the latter our 'ideology.' What I am suggesting is that the possible worlds we have to quantify over are a part of our ideology but not of our ontology. . . . Quantification over the members of one particular world is a measure of ontology, quantification that crosses possible worlds is often a measure of ideology. [Hintikka, "Semantics for Propositional Attitudes," p. 95]

Thus, an item's simply being the value of a bound variable is not sufficient for that item's being genuinely posited or for its being a member of our ontology. So, Hintikka concludes, Quine's criterion of ontological commitment should be rejected as incorrect and replaced by a suitably restricted criterion.

I believe this contention betrays a misunderstanding of Quine's use of the backward-E test as revealing a theorist's commitments. Hintikka maintains that Quine's view, or his usage, is *wrong* and needs to be revised. But, as I understand him,[14] Quine never intended his "criterion" to be in any way substantive or controversial. Insofar as he regards it as true, he takes it to be trivial: writing the backward E is the logician's way of making an existence claim and officially adding something to his ontology. That is just what a quantifier *is*, at least on its ordinary interpretation. Thus, if Hintikka wishes to continue in this vein, he will have to show Quine some other, nonstandard way of understanding the quantifiers, and that would be precisely to concede Quine's point. Let us therefore return to our consideration of possibilia and parsimony.

It might be complained that Quine's objections to possibilia are purely *aesthetic* in character; Occam's Razor itself is an aesthetic principle. But, according to Quine, this feature of his reason for rejecting Meinong's ontology is shared by virtually every reason anyone ever has for rejecting or accepting any theory of anything, particularly when the subject matter is highly abstract. Meinongian quantification must therefore be justified on the basis of its explanatory value.

Robert Stalnaker, M. J. Cresswell, and others[15] have appreciated this and argued that possible worlds and their denizens are rich in explanatory utility. In fact, it seems, we have no idea of how to go about doing modal semantics, decision theory, Montague Grammar, or any such thing without quantifying over possibilia; it is hard even to imagine what a competing approach would be like. For now, therefore (it is said), we *must* quantify over possibilia no matter what further aesthetic objections Quine has to them. And we do not violate Occam's principle in doing so, for that principle only forbids our positing entities *beyond* explanatory necessity.

Quine surely sees the force of this argument but refuses to grant the premise, for any number of fundamental reasons: (i) He believes that most of the "data" for modal and for propositional-attitude semantics are unreal or negligible (e.g., his philosophical skepticism about "necessity" is well known). (ii) He has argued tirelessly that syntax and "semantics" are indeterminate; he holds that linguistic semantics of the sort that is currently in favor is a pseudoscience and a pipe dream in any case.[16] (iii) He holds that "explanations" of the sort provided by possible-world explications of modalities are not explanations in any genuine sense. To say that "It is possible for there to be pink elephants" is true in virtue of there being some possible world in which there are pink elephants is to offer a pseudo or "dormitive virtue" explanation.[17]

Here we soon arrive at a set of basic methodological differences between Quine and the possibilia enthusiasts, having to do with the nature of science, the nature of explanation, and so on. Perhaps it is a fundamental impasse in this area that explains the intractability of the dispute between the friends and the foes of possibilia. And yet I do not think it is. I shall now argue that the real problem lies elsewhere and has little or nothing to do with Occam's Razor; in the rest of this essay, I shall try to make some progress toward its resolution.

III. THE REAL PROBLEM

It is maintained that, no matter how alien, ugly, and awkward nonexistent possibles may seem, they satisfy an aching theoretical need and that we have no real choice but to posit them as we have posited any other odd kind of abstract entities for explanatory purposes. I believe that this represents a bad misconception of the issue.

When we posited properties, some philosophers complained that properties were queer and obscure. When we posited sets, other philosophers complained that sets were queer and obscure; and the same for propositions, negative facts, and so on. But in each of these cases it was fairly clear what was being said, even if it was hard to imagine how an object could be non-spatiotemporal and yet be apprehended by a human mind or whatever; we understood the *quantificational* part of quantifying over abstract entities, even if we did not understand the nature of the entities themselves.[18] And this is what distinguishes nonexistent possibles from all the foregoing kinds of posited abstract entities: A first try at quantifying over "things that do not exist" yields

(A) $(\exists x) - (\exists y)(y = x)$

(cf. Meinong's "paradoxical" formulation, "The Theory of Objects," p. 83). And this formula is a *contradiction*. The crux is that, unlike the notion of a property or a proposition, the notion of a *nonexistent* thing or world is not merely queer or obscure or marginally intelligible, but is an apparent overt self-inconsistency.

Of course, no friend of possibilia intends his view to be understood in this absurd way. It is at this point that many different moves can be made. I suggest that the best way of organizing the whole issue is to see the various contemporary metaphysical theories of possibility as being partially or wholly conflicting ways of resolving the prima facie contradictoriness of (A). For this is the first job to be done; I cannot see that any further talk of theoretical utility is germane for now.

IV. CONTINUING HOSTILITIES

The obvious first move in this new direction is to disambiguate (A)'s quantifier. Meinong might therefore distinguish two different operators, one continuing to indicate actual existence and the other indicating some so far mysterious *secundum quid*. The former would be given the usual model-theoretic semantics; the latter would remain to be explained.

Meinong and other apologists for possibilia point out that this "mysterious" second operator already has a perfectly intelligible and straightforward English counterpart, viz., that which occurs in "There are things that don't exist," "There is a character in *Hamlet* who is smarter than anyone in our department," etc. Undeniably such constructions occur in English, and *almost* undeniably they occur in true sentences of English at that. The Meinongian may now say that insofar as we understand the casual use of such expressions, we can understand (A)'s leftmost quantifier—as a translation of this sort of thing. And this quantifier, introduced into our logical theory and into our semantical metalanguage for English, will bear the whole weight of our possiblistic apparatus. For our original, actuality-indicating quantifier can easily be defined in terms of our Meinongian quantifier, but not vice versa. "Actual" and "existent" figure as predicates in Meinongian English, and it is simple just to take this usage over into our logical theory. Thus, "There are things that don't exist" would be translated into Meinongian, not as (A), but as

$$(\exists x)_M - \text{Actual}(x)$$

or as

$$(\exists x)_M - (\exists y{:}\text{Actual}(y))(y = x),$$

neither of which is formally contradictory. And our original standard quantifier can now be introduced as a defined sign:

$$(\exists x)_A \ldots x \ldots \; =_{df} (\exists x)_M(\ldots x \ldots \& \text{Actual}(x));$$

or

$$=_{df} (\exists x{:}\text{Actual}(x))_M \ldots x \ldots .$$

(A), disambiguated accordingly, would be ruled satisfiable by whatever semantics the Meinongian intends to provide.

This last unspecific referring phrase was tokened in a smug and deprecating tone. It presupposes a demand on our part that the Meinongian search for, find, and offer "a semantics for" the quantifier "$(\exists x)_M$," and we have some fairly specific constraints in mind as to what is to be counted as success in this. In particular, what I am implicitly demanding is a *model-theoretic* semantics, done entirely in terms of actual objects and their properties—for what else *is there really?* I am allowing the Meinongian his funny operator only on the condition that he explain it to me in non-Meinongian terms.[19]

To this the Meinongian may reply that he will be happy to give us a model-theoretic semantics—one whose domains include nonactual objects, true enough, but that is all right, since *there are* nonactual objects, after all. And so it seems we have arrived at another impasse.

There is no formal circularity in this last Meinongian move. The Meinongian is explaining in the meta-metalanguage (English) how the expressions of his semantical metalanguage are to be understood, and so is not simply defining a linguistic item in terms of itself. But, clearly, anyone who *really needs* a semantics for "$(\exists x)_M$" (that is, anyone who needs a semantical explanation in order to understand "$(\exists x)_M$" *at all*) is not going to be relieved of his distress by an appeal to (or rather, by unexplained use of) a term of the meta-metalanguage of which it was introduced as a translation. The Meinongian evidently wants to take his "There is" *and* its canonical counterpart as *primitives* of their respective languages.

The difficulty that lies between Meinongians and philosophers who sport a "robust sense of reality" can thus be understood as being an intractable difference in what they are willing to take as primitives. Quine takes just his standard quantifier as primitive (and likewise talk of "existence," "actuality," etc. in English), and would seek some actualistic regimentation of Meinongian constructions in English. The point of such a regimentation would be to enable us to understand the Meinongian constructions, in terms of other constructions that we understand antecedently.[20] By contrast, the Meinongian takes his "There is" and $(\exists x)_M$" as primitive and explains the actualistic usage in terms of them. These two competing choices of primitives may engender a pair of mutually incomprehensible conceptual schemes.

It should be noticed that the impasse is slightly lopsided: Though each of the participants has so far run up just one unexplained primitive, the Meinongian is in fact stuck with a second, viz., the predicate "Actual." I see no way of explicating "Actual" in terms of "$(\exists x)_M$" plus notions accepted by both sides (that is, not without the use of further new primitives).[21] It is true that, so far as has been shown, attempts to explicate the Meinongian "There is" in terms of the actualistic notions already in play in reality-oriented semantical metalanguages may just fail and that we *may* therefore be forced to introduce a new primitive into the metalanguage amounting to a Meinongian quantifier. But that is what remains to be seen. The recent literature contains the seeds of a surprisingly various array of theories of possibility, which I shall now begin to distinguish.

V. APPROACHES TO POSSIBILITY

Again, I take the first task of any philosophical or semantical theory of possibility to be to resolve the prima facie contradictoriness of Meinongian formulations such as that translated by (A). I shall distinguish four basic approaches. They are not exclusive; some current views fall into more than one of the four categories. They may not turn out to be exhaustive either, though it is hard to imagine a further alternative.

1. The *Relentlessly Meinongian* approach. This is simply to leave our impasse as it is, embrace the Meinongian's two primitives, and dismiss Quinean-Russellian hostility as perverse. A Relentlessly Meinongian theory must be elaborated and ramified in something like the ways I have suggested in section I; such elaborations in fact have been carried out in some detail.[22]

2. The *Paraphrastic* approach. Some philosophers have believed that apparent reference to and "quantification over" nonexistent possibles could be eliminated by contextual definition, i.e., paraphrased away from whole sentences in which they occur. Possible individuals and possible worlds would then be treated as *façons de parler*.

3. The *Quantifier-Reinterpreting* approach. A practitioner of this method attempts to meet our Quinean challenge directly and provide a nonstandard semantics for the Meinongian quantifier which preserves its inferential properties but requires no nonactual entities.

4. The *Actualistic* approach. An actualist leaves his quantifiers standardly interpreted, but construes "possible worlds" etc. as being actual objects of some kind. The actualist ploy is to find some actual entities which are structurally analogous or isomorphic to an adequate system of possible objects and worlds, and which therefore can *do duty for* or *serve as* possibilia; he may then let his apparently Meinongian quantifiers range over these objects and define the Meinongian's "Actual" in terms of some property that some of them but not all of them have. Actualist positions differ, naturally, according to what objects they take as world-surrogates or "ersatz" worlds.

In the next two sections I shall return to Relentless Meinongianism and consider the well-developed theory of David Lewis as a leading example of an articulated view of this type. I shall offer some reasons why I think we should avoid following Lewis' lead in the direction of extreme realism concerning Meinong's Objects. I shall then turn to the Paraphrastic and the Quantifier-Reinterpreting approaches and sketch my reasons for thinking that neither method offers a promising start toward the explication of possibilistic talk. The remaining sections of this paper will be devoted to exploring some versions of actualism.

VI. LEWIS' "EXTREME" REALISM

Lewis' brand of Meinongianism is known for its distinctively extreme or radical air. In particular, he holds each of the following theses:

(i) The are nonactual possibles and possible worlds, and "there are" here needs no scare quotes; nonactual possibles and worlds exist, in exactly the same sense as that in which our world and its denizens exist.

(ii) Nonactual objects and worlds are of just the same respective *kinds* as are actual objects and the actual world. Nonactual tables are physical objects with physical uses; nonactual humans are made of flesh and blood, just as you and I are.

(iii) Nonactual objects and worlds are not *reducible* to items of less controversial sorts; worlds distinct from ours are not sets of sentences, or mental constructs of any sort, but blooming, buzzing *worlds*.

(iv) Quantifiers range over not all the actual individuals that there are but all the nonactual ones that there are as well, unless their ranges are explicitly or tacitly restricted in context.

(v) All individuals, actual or merely possible, are worldbound; there is no genuine identity across worlds. You and I are not world-lines, but merely have *counterparts* in other worlds who resemble us for certain purposes but are distinct individuals in their own right.

(vi) Expressions which distinguish actual individuals from among all the possible individuals, such as "real" and "actual," are really relational expressions holding between individuals and worlds; an individual *i* is actual only "at" or with respect to some world *w*. When we, in this (our) world, call some object "real" or "actual," these items are abbreviations for the indexical "real (actual) at *our* world"; every possible individual is real "at" the world it inhabits.

As Robert Stalnaker points out,[23] it is crucial to see that most of the foregoing claims are independent of one another and that the discriminating theorist might well accept some of them but disagree with Lewis over others. (v) and (vi) are perhaps the most obviously expendable; Stalnaker himself rejects (ii), while—interestingly—maintaining (iii).

On first hearing, in conversation anyway, philosophers have tended to respond with delighted horror and loud forebodings of incoherence. Not even Meinong dared to suggest that nonactual individuals *exist* in just the same way as you and I do, or that somewhere out in logical space there are flesh-and-blood counterparts of me who are leading admirable lives of their own, sharing all of my virtues and none of my faults. In short, Lewis' view seems just crazy (and unnecessarily so from the theoretician's point of view).

I believe this response is based on a misunderstanding (one which Lewis has rather charmingly avoided forestalling). The misunderstanding is a very natural one, for we have no easy way of saying just what the core claims (i) and (ii) come to. How should we express them in order to bring out the said *extremeness* or craziness of Lewis' "extreme" realism? "There *really are* possible worlds distinct from ours"? No. Lewis' other possible worlds exist but do not *really* exist. "Other worlds have *just the same ontological status* as ours"? No; our world is actual, while the others are not (although ontological status is an indexical matter for Lewis, our concern with individuals that inhabit the same world as *we* do is entirely natural and legitimate).

I suggest that Lewis' view in fact is just Meinong's view, smoothly elaborated in response to clever questions such as those raised in section I above. To see this, notice first that Lewis' (ii) falls right out of Meinong's doctrine of *Sosein*: just as (Meinong insists) the round square is both round and square, the golden mountain is a *mountain*, and not another thing. (Unlike Meinong's golden mountain, however, Lewis' individuals are not "incomplete" in the sense of section I; for Lewis there are (indenumerably) many golden mountains, each with its distinguishing maximally consistent set of properties.)

Second, notice that what shocks us the most about Lewis' formulation of Meinongian realism is precisely his use of the *word* "exist" in (i). Meinong (or his translators) had shied away from this, evidently fearing to create the same horrified reaction to which Lewis is suavely impervious. But is not the difference merely terminological? Meinong distinguishes between "existing" and merely "subsisting." Lewis between "being actual" and merely "existing." But in this respect their theories are notational variants of each other; Lewis has just abjured Meinong's euphemism, coopting "exists" and using it as his Meinongian quantifier. On this understanding, Meinong would accept Lewis' (i) as well as (ii).

(iii) seems to follow from (ii), and Meinong certainly would have accepted (iv). This leaves only (v) and (vi) as possible points of disagreement. I have already observed that (v) and (vi) are the least central or crucial components of Lewis' theory, in that they are less closely connected to the other four claims than those four claims are connected to each other. We cannot be sure exactly what attitude Meinong would have taken to (v) and (vi), since they concern worlds, and (so far as I am aware) Meinong did not think of grouping his Objects into worlds. The upshot is that, so far as we are able to say with confidence, Lewis' view is exactly as "extreme" as Meinong's own—no more so. Some readers will find Lewis' theory more palatable on this account; others will lose some of their naive tolerance of Meinong's view and come to regard *it* as radical or crazy.

Tom Richards and Susan Haack[24] have voiced the suspicion that Lewis actually is practicing a slightly more pernicious form of word magic. Haack writes,

Lewis thinks that [a] critic must either beg the question by equating 'exists' and 'actually exists,' or else equivocate on these two senses. The critic might justifiably wonder what makes Lewis confident that 'exists' and 'actually exists' *have* distinct senses. The trouble, to put it bluntly, is that by 'exists' Lewis means 'is possible,' and by 'actually exists' he means 'exists', so that when he says that ('other') possible worlds exist, though they don't actually exist, this amounts only to saying that they are possible, though they don't exist. [pp. 419–420]

(Haack goes on to bolster this suggestion a bit.) We would be shortsighted to understand her as making a claim about the uses of English words in ordinary speech (cf. my similar points about Quine and about Meinong in section II above). Haack could have made the same point against Lewis even if he had stuck with "subsist" and "exist" or used "bumble" and "stumble." And, as I understand it, that point is this: Lewis, she suspects, has merely taken ordinary talk of what is possible and worked a systematic but theoretically negligible orthographic permutation on it, just as if we were to translate it into Pig Latin. If this is so, then Lewis' view is even less "extreme," crazy, etc. than we have supposed. But it is also totally unilluminating; surely I would fail to illuminate or explain why physical bodies gravitationally attract each other by conjecturing that ysicalphay odiesbay avitationallygray attractay eachay otheray.

How might Lewis avoid this charge? He must show that his Meinongian quantification over "other" worlds is not just a trivial transcriptional exercise of this sort. By showing this he would not necessarily undercut the claim of his Meinongian explications to display the real truth-conditions of ordinary possibilistic talk (such is the lesson of the "Paradox of Analysis"). But if Lewis' Meinongian quantification is not just a respelling of ordinary alethic locutions, then we are correct in regarding him as bringing in novel theoretical appartus (and in taking its obscurity at face value); and so his claim to immediate naturalness and intuitiveness (like Meinong's) *is* undercut.

At the end of section IV above, we left the Relentless Meinongian and his reality-oriented opponent at an impasse regarding what they were respectively willing to take as primitives in philosophical discourse. Let us start again at this impasse and see what more might be said about it, now that we have distinguished Relentless Meinongianism from any softer or more tractable doctrine and hypothetically deprived ourselves of any tacit reparsings or reductive explications of quantification over nonexistent possibles.

I have to take my place among those who find *Relentlessly* (i.e., *genuinely* or *primitively*) Meinongian quantification simply unintelligible. However: in saying this, I am not using the term "unintelligible" in its sneering post-Wittgensteinian sense. So far as I am able to introspect, I am not expressing any tendentious philosophical *qualm*. (For this reason, my use of the term may be irrevocably misleading.) I mean that I really cannot understand Relentlessly Meinongian quantification at all; to me it is *literally* gibberish or mere noise.

Further, I hypothesize that most people who do profess to understand it are tacitly assuming that there *is* some paraphrastic program, some reinterpretation of the "Meinongian" quantifier, or possibly some actualist domain that will make sense of the quantifier. My evidence for this hypothesis is that professed Meinongians of my acquaintance, upon being pressed and confronted with suitably uncomprehending grimaces, typically are surprised that anyone would react in this way, infer that we must be talking past each other, and fall back on crude attempts at paraphrase or reinterpretation.

Yet I would quail at attributing any tacit assumption of this kind to Lewis himself. And, methodologically, I am not sure what argumentative force my unintelligibility claim has even if it is true for most people. For in some years' time a Relentlessly Meinongian scheme such as Lewis', or Richard Routley's and Valerie Routley's,[25] fully elaborated, may possibly have become quite fundamental to our semantical thinking, in such a way that younger philosohers will be taught it and work confidently within it without experiencing any difficulty of the sort I have forthrightly confessed to above. It may be that even I myself, if I follow developments and keep pace with the new generation, may come to share their linguistic facility and cease to have my now obdurate feeling of incomprehension. Should this prediction come true, how should we describe what it is that will have happened to me, or to the Meinongian quantifier, in the meantime?

It might be said (following Frege on the meaning of his term "sense") that during the interim the Meinongian quantifier will have taken on an indispensable role in the mechanics of a well-entrenched theory and that I will have come to grasp this role; this is why I will understand the quantifier then even though I genuinely do not understand it now. But this explanation will not do. For I already do grasp the explanatory role of the Meinongian quantifier, in the sense Frege intended: I already see and appreciate the functioning of the quantifier and its variables in semantical theories of the sort we all would like to bring to bear on the nasty philosophical problems they are designed to solve. So it is not understanding of the Meinongian quantifier's explanatory role that I lack now but will gradually acquire. Nor may we suppose that what I lack is knowledge of the real referents of the Meinongian variables, on the model of "gene" talk prior to the identification of "genes" as parts of DNA molecules: unreduced "gene" talk was understood (I presume) as placeholder talk, in that "gene" did duty for "whatever physical things play such-and-such a causal role in the mechanics of heredity"; but to treat "possible-world" talk similarly would be to envision (in fact, to demand) a reduction of "worlds" to actual objects, and thus to forswear Relentless Meinongianism and opt for some unspecified form of actualism instead. So if it is true that the Meinongian quantifier somehow will subtly acquire meaning for me within the foreseeable future, I cannot easily describe this hypothetical process or find a model or precedent for it.

In any case, suppose that the Relentless Meinongian continues to take the strong line suggested above, insisting that his quantifier *is* primitive, and that he does understand it even if I do not, and that no truth serum or searching psychoanalysis would reveal any hidden explicative program that mediates this understanding. I believe that even if we go along with this and try to regard Lewis' view as a competing theory which I just do not understand very well (rather than as gibberish), we will find some theoretical drawbacks that I believe suffice to motivate our seeking some other approach to possibility.[26]

VII. SOME DISADVANTAGES OF LEWIS' REALISM

Drawback 1: I have already pointed that the Relentless Meinongian is stuck with two primitives, while a practitioner of any of our other three approaches to modality deploys but one. This point is by no means decisive, but is not unimportant either. (It is closely connected to a more substantive theoretical problem that I shall bring out below.)

Drawback 2: The Relentless Meinongian leaves our impasse as it is, embraces the two primitives, and dismisses my Quinean hostility and incomprehension as slow-witted or perverse. This position may be tenable, but it does not illuminate what I have taken to be the fundamental problem. It resolves our contradiction (A), in effect, by announcing in a dramatic tone that the contradiction has been resolved and refusing further comment. (Compare the Cartesian Dualist on the subject of mind-body interaction.) Perhaps this is as it should be; perhaps Lewis' way of looking at things is on the whole a better way than any of the three more conciliatory ways, and perhaps I *am* being stupid and perverse in failing to see this and to understand the Meinongian quantifier. But it would be nice if this were not so and if there were some metaphysical theory of possibility that brought feelings of improved understanding to all concerned and did not instigate a wrenching cultural conflict.

Drawback 3: A Meinongian realism concerning worlds implies that other worlds contain individuals who are very different from me but who are in fact either identical with me or (as Lewis would have it) counterparts of me in their respective home worlds. And, since the Relentless Meinongian does not regard this consequence as metaphorical or as a *façon de parler*, he must suppose that there is some objective fact about these individuals in virtue of which they do bear this curiously intimate relation to me, that we can know there to be such a fact, and perhaps that we can come to know the fact itself by hypothetical inspection of the individuals and their properties, using an imaginary "telescope." It is this commitment on the realist's part that occasions all the traditional problems of transworld identity and their Lewisian counterparts concerning counterparts.[27] These problems, Kripke and Rescher have argued persuasively,[28] are pseudoproblems generated by the "telescope" view itself and not by anything in the actual nature of modality. It is possible for me to have been a purple chimpanzee with yellow spots; therefore, we are told, there is a nonactual world some inhabitant of which is a purple chimpanzee with yellow spots and is identical with (or is a counterpart of) me. Suppose this world contains many other chimpanzees of just the same type. Which one is, or is a counterpart of, me? The Relentless Meinongian must assume that there is a determinate, correct answer to this question rooted somewhere in transmundane reality. But, Kripke and Rescher point out, to accept this assumption is far less plausible than to say that worlds are something *we stipulate* in imagining ways in which *we* might have turned out differently and that one of the purple chimpanzees in the world I am imagining, to the exclusion of the other chimpanzees, is me or is my counterpart simply because I, who am doing the imagining, stipulate that it is and that the other chimpanzees are only its (my) casual acquaintances. So we should reject the "telescope" view, and therefore also the Meinongian realism that implies it.

Rescher and Richards have raised a closely related but more general epistemological point: How is it possible for us to know anything about other worlds, given that they are all "out there" independently of our mental activity and that they are causally and spatiotemporally inaccessible to us?

[Lewis'] truth-conditions are such that, for any given [modal] statement, it is impossible in general to determine whether they are met and hence whether the statement is true. There is, however, a certain measure of agreement between people about the truth-value of certain modal statements. Insofar as there is agreement one must assume that if it is not catechised into the populace without any understanding of any truth-conditions for these statements, then there is some other account of truth-conditions for these modal statements, and these truth-conditions are such that we may with some degree of confidence determine whether or not they are met. [Richards, "Worlds of David Lewis," p. 109]

Richards seems to be assuming that I cannot know a statement *S* without *first* knowing a statement T_S which expresses *S*'s truth-condition unless *S* has simply been "catechised" or drilled into me by rote. If "truth-condition" here means the fact in the world which ultimately makes *S* true, Richards' assumption is made doubtful by a number of standard cases of philosophical analysis. The *ordo cognoscendi*, contra "The Philosophy of Logical Atomism," need not coincide with the *ordo essendi*. But presumably Richards means "truth-condition" rather in the slightly different Davidsonian/Tarskian sense, in which a sentence's "truth-condition" is the core component of the sentence's locutionary *meaning*. Lewis intends his possible-world analyses of modal sentences to give those sentences' respective truth-conditions in this Davidsonian sense or something relevantly like it.[29] And it does seem we come to *know* a sentence in part by processing that sentence's Davidsonian truth-condition;[30]

it is not so obvious that the *ordo cognoscendi* is independent of the *ordo veritatis*. So I am inclined to think Richards is right in challenging Lewis to provide an account of how humans can know things about "other" physical worlds.

Of course, the only statements about other worlds that we need to know for semantical purposes are *general* statements. But how (Richards asks on page 110) do we know whether there is a world in which Saul Kripke is the son of Rudolf Carnap? We cannot tell by inspecting worlds. We must know (if we do) independently, on the basis of some test. Richards suggests that whatever test we do use constitutes the *real* truth-condition of "Saul Kripke might have been the son of Rudolf Carnap." This is overhasty, since we ought not to suppose that verification-conditions are truth-conditions (that way lies Analytical Behaviorism and its ilk). The point remains, though, that Lewis' knowledge of what possible worlds there are and of other general truths about worlds is posterior, not prior, to his knowledge of what things are possible and what things are impossible. This raises the question of why Lewis needs to posit Relentlessly Meinongian worlds, if they provide no epistemic advantage. Doubtless he would reply that he needs these worlds for ontological and for semantical purposes, since (according to him) no conciliatory metaphysics of modality will work. But he has not examined the question of what test we do ultimately use in deciding which possible worlds there are, and so he has not shown that that test, whatever it may be, does not yield a conciliatory metaphysics that is acceptable.[31] Further, how could we even in principle have any independent evidence for the existence of *physical* worlds of particular kinds or even for the existence of any "other" physical worlds at all? I do not see that Lewis has any choice but to immunize his view against criticism by supposing that things must be the way he says they are because they would have to be in order for his views to be correct. In itself this supposition would not be particularly vicious, if his views have proved (as they have) to have systematic utility. The point of the present complaint is that the particular criticisms to which Lewis would be immunizing himself, if I am right, would be directed against the part of his modal metaphysics which far outruns the *formal* structure of semantical explanatory tasks, so far that a demand for independent evidence seems justified. A view such as Kripke's or Rescher's, according to which worlds are the way we say they are because they are simply products of stipulations by us, has a considerable advantage over Lewis' here.

Drawback 4: Lewis' (ii) raises an awkward question.[32] It follows from his realism that just in virtue of the logical possibility of my having climbed Mt. Everest and proved Gödel's Theorem upon reaching the top, there is, somewhere out in logical space, a flesh-and-blood person who is just like me except for having accomplished this *tour de force*. Now, if this person and other various counterparts of mine in other worlds *are* all flesh-and-blood people who resemble me in certain important respects, it would be fascinating for me to be able to meet some of them personally and talk about the interesting things we have in common. What prevents me from traveling to another world and meeting my counterpart at that world and discussing life with him? Of course there cannot be a logical spaceship that allows me to traverse logical space in this way. But why not?

True, worlds are causally and spatiotemporally disjoint from each other and may even differ in their physical laws; this fact suffices to explain why my counterparts in other worlds are forever cut off from me and why my visiting them is impossible "in principle." But I would like to say that the idea of "visiting one of my counterparts," *so far as this idea is occasioned by the mere possibility of* my having climbed Mt. Everest, etc., is not a pleasure which is *denied* me by scientific or even metascientific obstacles, but is rather nonsense. The impossibility of crossing causal or spatiotemporal dislocations, admittedly a very high *grade* of impossibility (stronger than *physical*, though weaker than logical), fails to do justice to my more nibilistic intuition to the effect that the mere possibilities of everyday life do not or should not occasion even an intelligible scenario of the sort at issue.[33]

Drawback 5: Lewis' (ii), (v), and (vi) get him into trouble of a related kind, pointed out by Richards:

No criterion is provided for recognising [our] totality [of existents] as distinct from other totalities. The totalities are disjoint, but what divides them? Defining 'x actually exists' as 'x belongs to the same totality I do' presupposes an entirely unexplained principle of identity for these totalities. Their contents, for Lewis, are all equally real [*sic*] so 'our' world cannot be distinguished by appealing to a difference between existents and *possibilia*. ["Worlds of David Lewis," p. 107]

Richards and you and I are in our world @. Polonius is in another world w_N. The Wife of Bath is in still another world W_C, and so on. In virtue of what is Polonius in a world distinct from that enlivened by the Wife of Bath? In virtue of what is neither Polonius nor the Wife in *our* world? Since Lewis holds that all the worlds distinct from @ are physical and are out there independently of human imaginative or stipulative activity, he must seek some ontological ground for the grouping of possibilia into disjoint worlds. And there are not many possible sources (cf. the standard criticisms of Hume's "bundle" theory of the self). Richards pursues a couple of unpromising responses to this demand. Perhaps a more plausible suggestion, one that he does not address, is that possibilia are collected into worlds in virtue of causal or spatiotemporal interconnections; an object o_i iff o_i is causally or spatiotemporally reachable from o_j. But this criterion ignores nonphysical worlds of various kinds, worlds which themselves *contain* causal or spatiotemporal dislocations, and others.

The five drawbacks I have listed are neither individually nor jointly decisive against Lewis' position. I do not believe that it is possible to *refute* Lewis' position, unless the enormous cardinalities involved in a system of possible worlds should trigger some ingenious diagonal argument that is beyond my mathematical expertise to devise. I do think that the drawbacks are serious enough to provide strong motivation for seeking some alternative modal metaphysics. The remaining options are our three conciliatory ones: Paraphrastic, Quantifier-Reinterpreting, or Actualist.

VIII. THE MEINONGIAN QUANTIFIER AS NONOBJECTUAL

The Paraphrastic and the Quantifier-Reinterpreting approaches share a tenet: that our Meinongian quantifier "$(\exists x)_M$" is not what at first it appears to be. On the former approach, the "quantifier" functions only as part of an idiom or *façon de parler* and is not really a quantifier at all. On the latter, "$(\exists x)_M$" remains a quantifier at least in the minimal sense of preserving "$(\exists x)$"'s standard implicational relations and receiving its own base clause in a Tarskian truth theory for the Meinongian language, but the truth theory in question characterizes it in other than its usual objectual way.

An obvious instance of the Paraphrastic strategy is Russell's own treatment of possible objects in "On Denoting," which falls cleanly out of his Theory of Descriptions. This version has well-known disadvantages. One is that virtually all the sentences "about" possibilia that Meinong would regard as straightforwardly true come out false on Russell's proposal, precisely because of the nonexistence of the possibilia in question. Another is that Russell's method of handling problems of intensionality generally has not proved to be powerful enough to yield a satisfactory systematic treatment of those problems.[34] Finally, the method offers no obvious way of eliminating talk of possible *worlds* from modal semantics, which would be our main task.

A more promising Paraphrastic program would be to understand "possible-world" talk counterfactually, as Kripke has proposed.[35] This is quite a natural suggestion and does much to make talk of possible worlds more homey. An antic sentence such as "In some possible world distinct from our own, Richard Nixon is a Black Panther" might be paraphrased as "If things had been otherwise, Richard Nixon might have been a Black Panther," a sentence which we all more or less understand or at least would not balk at in ordinary conversation.

The counterfactual approach is inadequate in two serious ways, I think. First: It is not enough to provide a sample paraphrase or two. The counterfactual theorist would have to work out a systematic and rigorous *formula* for paraphrasing formal, model-theoretic sentences concerning possible worlds, and in such a way as to preserve all the theorems of our logical theory and all the advantages of each of the modal logics or modal semantics under analysis. It is hard to imagine how this would go.[36] The difficulty becomes critical when we note that any adequate modal semantics will require many *sets of* possible worlds, sets of sets of worlds, and so on.[37] Intuitively, the counterfactual approach leaves set abstraction on worlds undefined. (This seems to me to be a crucial point, one that I have never heard a Parpahrastic theorist address.) Even if we have provided a satisfactory system of eliminative contextual definitions for *quantification* over nonexistent possibles, this system would have to be extrapolated to cover set abstraction as well, and no way of doing this in terms of counterfactuals comes to mind. (We might try invoking "ways things might have been" and abstracting on them, but to do that would be to reify the *"ways"* and leave us with all the same problems we had before.)

My second complaint about the counterfactual approach, which I have made elsewhere,[38] is this: It is true that we "understand" counterfactuals in ordinary conversation, as I granted. But for purposes of serious philosophy they have proved to be among the most troublesome and elusive expressions there are. Their truth-conditions have remained genuinely (not just officially) mysterious; their well-known context-dependence has not been understood at all; and in a discussion or seminar on conditionals, people blank out or disagree even on very basic matters of data. Resting a philosophical theory on unexplicated counterfactuals is like hoping one may cross a freezing river by hopping across the heaving ice floes. Great progress has been made on the general understanding of counterfactuals in the last ten years, largely through the work of Stalnaker and Lewis; and the source of this progress is the considered, ingenious, and well-motivated use of possible-worlds semantics. Therefore we have extremely strong reason to analyze and understand counterfactuals in terms of possible worlds. But if we are to do so, we cannot without circularity turn back and paraphrase away talk of possible worlds in terms of unexplicated counterfactuals.[39]

I cannot say what other Paraphrastic programs might be devised concerning mere possibilia. But I think the kinds of considerations I have brought out so far give us substantial reason to look along still other lines. The same, I believe, can be said of the Quantifier-Reinterpreting approach, which has only one existing instance that I know of: Ruth Marcus has proposed[40] that Meinongian quantification be understood as *substitutional* quantification.

This suggestion has a good deal of intuitive appeal. It is quite plausible in the case of "There are things that don't exist": when I utter that sentence aloud, I feel a tendency to continue by listing *names* of things that don't exist (". . . you know, like the round square, Macbeth, the free lunch, and so on"). And there certainly is plenty of overt quantification in English that is substitutional. It might be thought that Marcus' proposal fails in the case of possible worlds on the grounds that worlds in general do not have names at all (the substitution class would be far too small); but we may easily generate a system of canonical names for possible worlds from existing resources: Each world, we may suppose, is correctly described by a maximally consistent set of sentences $[P, Q, R, \ldots]$; to obtain a name of a world in which $P, Q, R, \ldots$, simply form a definite description from the latter indefinite one: "$(iw)\text{In}_w(P \& Q \& R \& \ldots)$."

This proposal will inherit the usual sorts of problems that philosohers have raised for substitution interpretations of more familiar quantifiers. The most obvious of these is the "not enough names" problem: First, given that almost any real-valued physical magnitude characterizing our world will have nondenumerably many nonactual worlds corresponding to it, the cardinality of the set of all worlds (if this notion is not undefined or paradoxical) will be inconceivably high. But there are only denumerably many names of the sort exemplified above; thus, it seems, universal quantifications over worlds will be verified more easily than we would like.[41] Second, a number of philosophers have argued that the substitution interpretation somehow collapses into the standard interpretation when incorporated into a full-scale truth theory. Kripke has recently refuted at least the most salient versions of this charge,[42] though I have argued elsewhere that there is a further, somewhat related difficulty which impugns the usefulness of the substitution interpretation for the truth-conditional analysis of *natural* languages.[43]

The main problem for Marcus' proposal, as I see it, is the same that arose for the counterfactual approach: How will Marcus reinterpret set abstraction and all the other operations that will need to be applied to names of "worlds"? (Certainly there have been attempts at metalinguistic reinterpretations of set abstraction, but they have concentrated on reinterpreting the abstractor itself, not the variable it binds; that is, they have concentrated on detoxifying mention of the *sets* in question, not mention of the sets' members.)

If I am right in thinking that we should continue to look elsewhere for an understanding of possibilistic talk, only one option remains: to seek an actualist analysis.

IX. POTENTIAL WORLD-SURROGATES

The actualist's task is to find some system of actual objects that is structurally analogous or isomorphic to a system of possible worlds and therefore can *serve us* or *go proxy for* worlds. At least six sorts of systems come to mind:

Linguistic Entities

Historically, the most popular "ersatz" worlds have been sentences or sets of sentences. Carnap's "state descriptions" functioned as possible worlds. Hintikka followed a similar practice in *Knowledge and Belief*[44] (though he dropped this in later works). If a "world" is understood as being a set of sentences, then possibility may be understood as *consistency*, and "actuality" neatly reinterpreted as *truth*. (Note that the metalinguistic approach fits nicely with metalinguistic theories of the propositional attitudes and provides handy objects for the attitudes.)

Propositions

One might move to sets of language-independent propositions, i.e., sets of abstract (but actual) objects having sentencelike semantical properties. This approach is defended by Robert Adams and nicely elaborated by Alvin Plantinga.[45]

Properties

Castañeda, and subsequently Terry Parsons, have offered ways of construing Meinong's Objects as sets of properties.[46] Castañeda achieves a sort of fusing of Meinong with Frege and treats a number of semantical issues quite neatly without any appeal to genuinely nonexistent possibles. A drawback here is that the approach requires the introduction of several new primitives.

Combinatorial Constructs

Quine has suggested, and Max Cresswell has elaborated, the idea of taking "worlds" to be set-theoretic combinatorial rearrangements of the posited basic atoms of which our own world is composed.[47] I shall explain and discuss this view in more detail below.

Mental Items

An obvious but so far unattempted move would be to take mental entities of some sort as our "ersatz worlds." Rescher is tempted by this approach and points out a number of its advantages in *A Theory of Possibility*, but does not adopt it in the end (cf. pp. 216–217).

Ways Things Might Have Been

Stalnaker suggests taking "ways things might have been" as *sui generis* elements of our ontology,[48] thus, "ways things might have been" are actual abstract entities in their own right, not to be reduced to items of any more familiar kind. Stalnaker accepts Lewis' indexical analysis of "actual" (thesis (vi)), but regards it as metaphysically uninteresting, since there is only one *world* for entities to be actual "at."

I have argued that we have good reason to seek some such system of "ersatz worlds," giving up Lewis' Relentless Meinongianism but at least for now continuing to regard the Meinongian quantifier as a standard objectual one. And Actualism as a program has aesthetic attractions not unlike those of the analogous explications of number theory in terms of set theory. But any particular choice of a system of "ersatz worlds" may turn out to face philosophical difficulties of its own. For example, Lewis argues forcefully in *Counterfactuals* (p. 85) that the metalinguistic method of Carnap and Hintikka is circular, in that "consistency" of sentences cannot adequately be defined save in terms of possibility. In addition, more typically, a choice of a system of world-surrogates may be seen to be technically inadequate, in that the intended isomorphism between the system and the lattice of worlds for which it goes proxy falls short in some way that frustrates our purposes in using pseudo-Meinongian quantification in the first place. A mentalistic approach, for example, is daunted by the paucity of *actual* mental events: the entire history of the universe will quite probably contain only finitely many mental entities, and it is hard to see how these might be parlayed into a system of proxies for all the multiply uncountable sets of worlds that must be posited for purposes of modal logic.

To illustrate some of the philosophical and technical limitations to which particular actualist programs are subject, I shall discuss the Quine-Cresswell combinatorial approach in some detail. I shall then conclude by making a tentative prognosis and drawing a moral.

X. COMBINATORIALISM

To see the initial plausibility of combinatorialism, consider the familiar notion of a chess game. Many chess games have been played, but there are plenty of other chess games that never have actually been played, though they are permissible according to the rules of chess. We are little tempted, though, to assimilate unplayed chess games to the golden mountain or the present king of France. A *game* is quite naturally understood as being a sequence of moves. A *move* we may take to be a triple whose members are a chess piece, an initial square, and a destination square (castling would require a small refinement). *Pieces* and *squares* are types, which may be regarded as sets of tokens. A game is *played* when two people under appropriate circumstances make a series of physical motions using (physical) chessmen and a board, which series mimics the sequence of triples that *is* the game in question. Some allowable sequences are never in fact mimicked in this way, just as some grammatical sentences of English are never tokened. And there is nothing at all metaphysically mysterious about this, save perhaps to nominalists who have qualms about sets. Could we extrapolate our Actualist metaphysic of possible chess games to cover *all* "nonexistent" possibles, including "possible worlds"?

Suppose that there are some *metaphysically basic elements* out of which our universe is composed. Call them "atoms" (in the metaphysical rather than the chemical sense). Our world, we may say, consists of these atoms' being *arranged* in a certain fabulously complex way. The actual *arrangement* of the atoms could be taken to be, or to be represented by, a vastly complex *set* built up out of nothing but atoms and sets as members. Now let us construe "other possible worlds" as *alternative* arrangements of our atoms which mirror the ways our world might have been just as the actual arrangement mirrors the world as it is. These alternative arrangements are sets (actual entities), too, of course.

The "atoms" are the fundamental building blocks of our own world, whatever those may eventually be shown by science or philosophy to be. Hypothetically, we might take them to be little particles, or occupations of space-time points (Quine's preliminary choice), or Berkeleyan ideas, or whatever. As I shall now argue, however, our choice of "atoms" may ultimately affect the adequacy of our combinatorialist explication of nonactual worlds.

XI. PROBLEMS FOR COMBINATORIALISM

Lewis has pointed out[49] that certain choices of atoms (certain decisions as to which actual things we ought to count as being the fundamental building blocks of the universe) commit the combinatorialist to strong modal theses which would better be left as open questions. Schematically: Any combinatorialist will end up ruling out some apparently imaginable states of affairs as holding in no possible world, on the grounds that these states of affairs cannot be construed as being arrangements of that particular combinatorialist's chosen atoms. This means that any combinatorialist's choice of atoms places substantive constraints on what states of affairs are to count as possible states of affairs.

Lewis does not really elaborate this point, but we can give some trenchant examples of what he is talking about, and we can also work the point up into a principled argument against combinatorialism which will be hard to resist. The examples:

(a) It would seem to be possible that the world should have contained either more or less fundamental stuff. It is easy to envision an arrangement involving fewer atoms, or even one which would serve as the null world (presumably the null set). But how might we construct an arrangement corresponding to an increase in the amount of fundamental matter? (One might think of representing new "atoms" by artificial means, such as pairing existing atoms with real numbers. This would be an appropriately Actualistic strategy, but would constitute an abandoning of the *combinatorial* approach, since these new artificial "atoms" would not be the very sorts of things—atoms in the strict sense—that physical things would be *physically made of* in the alternate world. To put the point slightly differently: our hypothesis is that there might exist *atoms* that do not already exist in this world; and atoms are not arrangements of atoms and so cannot be represented as alternative arrangements of atoms.) It seems, then, that any choice of a stock of atoms commits the combinatorialist to the *necessary* nonexistence of any more atoms, since there will be no arrangement and hence no possible world in which there exists an atom that is not one of our prechosen stock; any such extraneous atoms would be nonactual, and so shunned by the combinatorialist.

(b) In making remark (a), I was thinking of alternative physical worlds. But our world contains abstract objects too. "Other" worlds might contain fewer abstract objects (no problem), or more (same problem as in (a)), or possibly even strange abstract objects not found here in @. How could we hit upon an arrangement mirroring a world that is mathematically deviant in this way? Here, perhaps, it *might* help to resort to artificial means (cf. Philip Wiener's construction of ordered pairs out of ordinary sets), since abstract objects, unlike atoms, are not noncomposite by defintion. But it is hard to imagine there being a way in which the abstract objects of this world might combine to form new composite abstract objects in another world, but in which they do *not* combine in this world.

(c) What about irreducibly spiritual objects? Very probably there are no ghosts, monads, or Cartesian egos in this world; but there could have been, at least if we are to take seriously the views of brilliant philosophers who have believed in them. What sort of arrangement of atoms and sets could mirror such a state of affairs?

(d) As Lewis points out, we want to leave open the possibility that our world could have operated according to an entirely different physics and even according to a radically different geometry. It follows that any combinatorialist who chooses either Euclidean space-time or Minkowskian space-time in which to locate his atoms will be oversimplifying at best. How might we allow for basic structural changes through worlds? It would be hard to motivate any further variegation of our procedures for forming wilder and more bizarre arrangements of the atoms of *this* world.

(e) I should think that *nonatomistic* worlds are also possible, such as one which consists of an undifferentiated miasma of Pure Spirit. A nonatomistic world can hardly be regarded as an arrangement of @'s stock of atoms.

Notice that in virtue of limitations such as (a)–(e), combinatorialism also constrains our accessibility relation in modal logic, and hence restricts the modal systems we may countenance.[50] For example, combinatorial accessibility will have to be asymmetric. A world having fewer atoms than @ is accessible from @, but @ cannot be accessible from it, since @ contains atoms that it does not contain and which therefore are nonactual relative to it. We are forced to conclude that S-5 is too strong a modal logic, since S-5 is based on a system of worlds whose accessibility relation is symmetric.

The obvious response for the combinatorialist to make to (a)–(e) is to bite the bullet and maintain that the apparent "possibilities" that I have imagined are simply *not* possible. But there are two crippling rejoinders to this. (1) When the combinatorialist says "not possible," he must mean this *in the strongest conceivable sense*. More atoms, spiritual objects, different physics, and so on must be impossible not merely in the physical sense, and *not merely in the metaphysical sense*, but in at least the sense in which overt contradictions are not possible. This is because otherwise there would have to be *logically* possible *worlds* in which such things obtained even if there were no physically or metaphysically possible worlds of that sort. And this is completely counterintuitive. It may be "impossible" for there to be Cartesian egos in some very strong sense or other, but not in as strong a sense as that in which it is impossible for 3 to be both prime and not prime. (2) Even if we collapse the distinctions between grades of possibility that I have just insisted on, the combinatorialist still cannot deny that bizarre situations of the kind we have been talking about are *believed in* by some people. Descartes, for example, believed that there were nonextended, irreducible egos. Now, one of the main functions of possible worlds is to provide semantics for propositional attitudes. E.g., *belief* is said to be a relation between a believer and a set of worlds (his doxastic alternatives). Thus, it should be true in each of Descartes' doxastic alternatives that there are nonextended egos—or else we shall have to rob the possible-worlds apparatus of much of its interest by finding a different semantics for propositional attitudes.[51]

A slightly more sophisticated combinatorialist ploy is that which Max Cresswell has taken in conversation.[52] This is to *refuse to make* a choice of particular items to serve as our atoms, and instead just to insist that there *are* basic objects in this world that play the modal role of atoms even though we shall never know or be able to say what they are. We are to find out what the atoms of our world are like by examining what is required to generate adequate modal semantics, and in no other way. This might seem to flout cherished principles of scientific realism, in that Cresswell's unspecifiable atoms are as inaccessible to physics as they are to the ordinary person, but Cresswell (I think) would respond that modal semantics *is* a science, and we are required by *it* to posit his unknowable atoms even if physics has no need of them and cannot discover them.

Further criticisms loom: (3) This Tractarian ploy is paradigmatically ad hoc. We posit the special, unknowable, subphysical atoms *solely* for the purpsoe of saving combinatorialism from refutation by entrenched modal intuitions. Accordingly, we render combinatorialism totally untestable. We also ignore the ineliminable *epistemic* possibility, given whatever objects are in fact the atoms. (4) The ploy gets by some of our previous objections only at the cost of substantive metaphysical commitments. Take (c). Cresswell would have us believe that bodies and Cartesian egos (in such worlds as contain both) are just different kinds of composites out of more basic metaphysical objects; he is committed to "neutral monism" as a theory of the mental.

Neutral monism might be true of minds and brains in this world, and it might be true even of Cartesian egos, but I doubt it, since *Cartesian* egos are supposed to be fundamentally different in kind from bodies. More to the point, we should not want our *semantics* to prejudge this venerable and complex metaphysical question if we can help it. (5) Cresswell's ploy fails even to address some of our objections, particularly (a) and (e). So if it helps at all, it does not help much.

A final criticism, one which applies to a number of other versions of actualism as well: In (a) and (b) above, I have mentioned the possibility of throwing together a system of set-theoretic objects that might *ape* the group of "nonactual" things or worlds we need, in the sense of being structurally isomorphic to that group of things (cf. again Wiener on ordered pairs). Suppose, to take another example, that our world contains only finitely many physical atoms out of which physical objects are made, but that we want to construct nonfinitely many physical variations on our world. We might easily allow for this by pairing existing atoms with numbers, or some such. The resulting set-theoretic objects might be quite arbitrarily chosen, and the objects themselves might well have nothing intuitively to do with the metaphysics of modality, even though they were carefully selected for their joint ability to play the desired combinatorial role. But why should we suppose that real *possibility* in this world has anything to do with pairs of atoms and numbers?

Frege would have rejected this question, and so do many of the intensional logicians who follow him on the methodology of positing abstract entities in semantics. ("*I* don't care what we let the quantifiers range over; the 'worlds' could be my dog, the Eiffel Tower, the real numbers, my grandmother's tricycle, and Bertrand Russell—just so long as the mathematics ends up dumping the right sentences into the right barrels.") This brings up Plantinga's distinction[53] between "pure semantics" and "applied semantics." A "pure" semantics does not interpret its quantifiers at all, and so does not commit itself to any particular domain. Its only adequacy-condition is that it predict the truth values of complex sentences given the truth and satisfaction values of their parts and that it capture the right sorts of felt implications. In effect, a "pure" semantics serves to axiomatize the predicate "valid modal formula" and nothing more. But any number of interpretations of such axiomatizations will be available, no one of them having any better claim to "correctness" than any other (compare now the alternative ways of reducing number theory to set theory). Plantinga points out that a "pure" semantics "does not give us a meaning for '□', or tell us under what condition a proposition is necessarily true, or what it is for an object to have a property essentially" (*Nature of Necessity*, p. 127; notice, incidentally, that the three tasks Plantinga mentions are mutually distinct). If our semantical theory is to *explain what it is* about our world that makes an alethic statement true in it, we must assign specific domains to its quantifiers, thus making it into an "applied" semantics.[54] (And if we are actualists, our domains must contain only actual objects.)

A serious qualification is needed here. Modal and intensional semantics have been employed in aid of many different sorts of jobs and projects, not just the few enterprises mentioned in the preceding paragraph. And many of these projects, though technically demanding, are not philosophically ambitious enough to require any very specific ontological choice of domains for the Meinongian quantifiers. A trivial and obvious example of a justifiably noncommittal appeal to "worlds" is the casual, everyday semantical computation we do in routinely checking the validity of complicated modal inferences in the process of carrying on philosophical arguments. Perhaps a less obvious example may be the use of "possible-worlds" semantics in obtaining consistency and completeness etc. results for modal systems.[55] Possibly we even learn something about the nature of necessity from "pure" semantics alone, though to articulate exactly what sort of illumination or understanding we gain here is much more difficult than most logicians admit. Then what uses of the "possible-worlds" apparatus do require a serious assignment of specific sorts of ranges to the Meinongian quantifiers?

I offer a paradigm case. Suppose someone were to argue as follows:[56] "Metaphysicians have always struggled with the problem of counterfactuals, wondering what fact it is in the world that makes a counterfactual true. Some have posited special dispositional facts; others have opted for what Quine calls an irresponsible metaphysic of unactualized potentials; still others have attempted deflationary but palpably inadequate metalinguistic accounts and such. Now, I can explain why metaphysicians have had such trouble with counterfactuals and have had to make such desperate lunges. The problem is that the metaphysicians have radically misconceived the issue: they have sought truth-makers[57] for counterfactuals *in the* (i.e., *this world*. A counterfactual's truth-maker is not in the single world at which the counterfactual is true, but is transmundance, involving lots of worlds distinct from this one all at once. Once we see this, we can make great progress on the metaphysical problem of counterfactuals."

This argument seems very compelling, and so do similar arguments concerning the metaphysics of possibility and necessity. But notice that its *mainspring* is the metaphysical claim that our world is not the only world and that other worlds and their histories figure just as crucially in determining the truth of a counterfactual "at" our world. This metaphysical claim, if it is genuinely to explain how earlier metaphysicians misconceived the problem of counterfactuals, must be understood in substance as well as in form—its proponent must be able to offer some account of what his "other worlds" are if it is to provide the kind of metaphysical illumination that is being claimed for it. (If we are actualists, of course, our "transmundane" facts will be reduced in turn to facts of our world; so for the actualist the foregoing account will not be literally correct, but will illuminate just in the way that a model does before it has been successfully demythologized.)

It is at this point that the arbitrariness of our choice among different methods of slapping together "arrangements" makes itself felt. No one way of pairing atoms or sets of atoms with real numbers is more intuitive or natural than all others, for example, and so none has a better claim than all others to tell us what fact it is that makes some counterfactual or alethic or doxastic statement true.

In fact, the arbitrariness goes a bit further down; we need not appeal to the indenumerability of worlds or to the need for bizarre worlds to be troubled by it. Take Quine's way of constructing "ersatz" worlds, in terms of occupations of space-time points. If a point is to be represented by a quadruple of numbers, what kind of set shall we choose to represent the occupation of a point? We might simply form the set of all the points that are occupied in a "world" and let that set be the "arrangement" that mirros that "world." Or we might pair our quadruples with 1 and with 0 alternatively, representing occupation or vacancy respectively. Or the other way around. Or we might use the letters "O" and "V," as suggested by the examples of restrooms on passenger trains. The alternatives are limitless.[58] In light of this it is hard to see how a combinatorial interpretation of modal semantics that has helped itself to artificial aids in this way could solve the problem of truth-makers even if it were technically adequate to lesser, merely computational tasks.

The case against combinatorialism seems serious. I have discussed it at such length partly just to illustrate the kinds of difficulties that an actualist can incur (for professed actualists often fail to notice these difficulties) and partly to urge combinatorialists to switch to some less troubled form of actualism. But to which one?

XII. PROGNOSIS

I believe that the only promising choice of actual entities to serve as "worlds" is that of sets of intensional objects. Thus, I would fall in either with Adams and Plantinga and construct worlds directly out of propositions, or with Castañeda and Parsons and construct possible objects out of properties and then group the objects into worlds on the basis of their stipulated inter-relations. My main reason for choosing familiar intensional entities is that actualist programs based on them do not seem to run into as serious difficulties of the kinds I have mentioned as do other actualist programs. I think this is largely because they are posits of *semantics* to begin with: so there are (or seem to be) enough of them; actuality can again be explained in terms of truth; set abstraction on worlds remains ordinary set abstraction; there is no arbitrariness problem of the sort raised in section XI, since properties and propositions are characteristically introduced as being the meanings of predicates and sentences in the first place; and for the same reason the connection between "possible worlds" and semantical notions and alethic notions becomes quite straightforward and intuitive. Plantinga in particular has proposed an actualist theory of this kind which seems to me quite promising and has defended it against a number of objections. I do not go along with all of Plantinga's choices of matters of detail,[59] nor with all of Adams', but I would like to work out an account along their lines.

I predict it will be fruitful to allow real individuals to be constituents of propositions; a simple atomic proposition might be said to consist of a paired object and property. This policy would provide an obvious basis for transworld identity and hence for quantifying in. It would also obviate the "telescope" problem faced by the Relentless Meinongian. (In keeping with the policy, no "nonexistent individual" which by stipulation is not identical with any real individual could be treated as a genuine individual. Such an "object" might be reconstrued as a set of properties *simpliciter* or as the intersection of a number of maximally consistent sets of properties; or else apparent references to it might be paraphrased away à la the Theory of Descriptions.[60] This would effectively prevent our allowing that such "individuals" can have *de re* modal properties or be the objects of *de re* psychological attitudes, but I believe these things ought not to be allowed in any case.[61])

A very significant virtue of an actualist account based on sets of propositions, in my opinion, is that it makes room for *impossible* worlds as well as possible ones. So far as I can see, we have just as great a theoretical need for Meinongian quantification over impossible objects and worlds as we do for admitting possible but nonactual ones. Further, I can think of no direct argument for "nonexistents" that does not support impossibilia by parity of reasoning, and I have never been impressed by any of the objections that have been raised against impossible objects but do not hold with equal force against nonexistents of any sort.[62] On the propositional account, an impossible world is simply an inconsistent set of propositions. (Impossible worlds, unlike possible ones, need not be closed under deduction.) The propositional account also explains something that would otherwise be a bit paradoxical,[63] viz., how it is possible for a self-contradictory proposition to be *true*, even "at" an impossible world: The account rejects Lewis' (vi) and does not analyze *truth* in terms of "truth at" our world. Rahter, it analyzes "truth at" a nonactual "world" simply as set membership. The self-contradictory proposition is a member of the set of propositions constituting the impossible "world" in question; hence it is "true at" it.

A few objections need to be dealt with. First: Does the propositional account not run into the same problem of "too much necessity" that I raised for the combinatorialist? For if we construct our "worlds" out of properties and propositions, how could we then represent nominalistic worlds containing no properties or propositions?[64] Reply: A world *in which* there are no properties or propositions, though, like any "nonactual world," is largely *made of* properties and propositions, is just a set of propositions one member of which is the proposition that there are no properties or propositions. A Carnapian state description theorist would likewise represent a world containing no sentences or other linguistic entities as a set of sentences containing the sentence, "There are no sentences or other linguistic entities." I can write a story about people who never write stories; there is no inconsistency here.

Second objection: Does the propositional account not take *consistency* and *mutual compatibility* of propositions as primitive, thus forfeiting the crucial benefit of explaining these notions in terms of *possibility* of worlds or simply in terms of *worlds* (if we join Lewis in abjuring impossible worlds)?[65] Replay: Yes. But this is no defect. What makes some propositions compatible or incompatible with others is no more mysterious, ultimately, than what makes some worlds possible and others not, or than what makes some stories describe segments of worlds and others not. Any metaphysics of possibility is going to have to take some one of these easily interdefinable notions as primitive, and I see no lasting conceptual superiority in any one of the three approaches over the other two on this point.

Third objection: What difference is there, in the end, between a *false proposition* and a *nonexistent state of affairs*? I have claimed the preferability of quantifying over the former to "quantifying over" the latter, but is the difference not merely terminological? Are nonexistent states of affairs not just as familiar as false propositions, belying my crucial argument in section III above?[66] Reply: (i) The argument of section III shows precisely why false propositions are preferable to "nonexistent" states of affairs. "There exist states of affairs that do not exist" has to be disambiguated, and my invocation of *falsity* achieves this, assuming we have an intuitive handle on what it is for a proposition to be false (or for a state of affairs not to *obtain*) that is prior to, or at least independent of, considerations of modal metaphysics. (ii) We do have such an intuitive handle, plus substantial grounds for expecting that it may be reinforced in a number of technical ways. For *falsity* is a familiar semantical property; and propositions (as they have traditionally been conceived) have *structures* relevant to the determination of their truth values. For example, a simple atomic proposition would be false if its individual constituent did not instantiate its property constituent. Falsity for more complex propositions might be explained in terms of a more elaborate picturing or mirroring relation,[67] or it might be recursively defined à la Tarski. (In either case, care would have to be taken to avoid the semantical paradoxes and other possible cardinality problems.) (iii) The question of whether a proposition *exists* is a substantive and interesting question quite independent of whether the proposition is *false*. A nominalist might admit that the sentence "Russell is a genius" expresses a true proposition rather than a false one *if* there *exists* any proposition at all for it to express; and we may debate whether (e.g.) the proposition that quadruplicity drinks procrastination exists without doubting that if it does exist it is false.

As usual, of course, we shall have to take the rough with the smooth; there is a further objection to the propositional account that does reveal a serious failing: the account sacrifices the wonderfully elegant practice of explicating properties, propositions, and other Fregean intensions as being functions from possible worlds to extensions. If we reduce "possible worlds" to sets of propositions, for example, we cannot then reduce propositions to functions from possible worlds to truth values. This is an unpleasant price to pay, but I think a small one when compared to the drawbacks that afflict other theories of modality. In any case, admittedly, more time will be needed to determine whether a program such as the one I have begun to sketch does not in fact face problems just as awful as those we have raised for its competitors.

XIII. POINTEDLY UNIRENIC MORAL

It is only recently that our four basic approaches to the metaphysics of modality, and their various versions and subversions, have become as visibly distinct as I hope I have brought out in this essay. The primary point to grasp, and my main contention, is that anyone who needs to traffic in "nonactual" possible and/or possible worlds and who is concerned to use these notions in a philosophically self-conscious and responsible way must (eventually) choose between our alternative approaches and *face the consequences*. I believe that much of the unconcern with which semanticists have countenanced possible-world talk has resulted from their having conflated two or more of our approaches and tacitly—but illicitly—helped themselves to the complementary advantages of each. (And perhaps some of the horror with which Quinean *anti*semanticists have reacted to intensional and modal semantics has resulted from their having conflated two or more of the approaches and likewise lumped together the *dis*advantages of each.) Logicians, who remain cautious in their explanatory claims, may put off the choice perhaps indefinitely; but it is time for philosophical semanticists and modal metaphysicians to get serious.

NOTES

1. The idea that when worlds are introduced as the values of variables, the apparently distinctive inferential properties of the alethic modalities fall right out of the familiar inferential properties of the quantifiers, and the concomitant identification of neccessity with truth in all possible worlds, are now so commonplace that we easily forget how stunning the idea is. It is almost universally credited to Leibniz, but I know of nowhere that it appears in Leibniz's standard

texts—despite casual allusions to the doctrine, and even some (specious) page references, by a number of commentators. The most suggestive passage I have been able to find is this one: "Hinc jam discimus alias esse propositiones quae pertinet ad Essentias, alias vero quae ad Existentias rerum; Essentiales nimirum sunt quae ex resolutione Terminorum possunt demonstrari; quae scilicet sunt necessariae, sive virtualiter contradictorium. Et hae sunt aeternae veritatis, nec tantum obtinebunt, dum stabit Mundas, sed etiam obtinuissent, si DEUS alia ratione Mundum creasset" (Couturat, *Opuscules*, PHIL., IV, 3, a, 1, p. 18). I am indebted to Michael Hooker and Robert Sleigh for the reference.

2. See David Lewis, "General Semantics," and Robert Stalnaker, "Pragmatics," in Donald Davidson and Gilbert Harman, eds., *Semantics of Natural Language* (Dordrecht: Reidel, 1973), pp. 169–218 and 380–397, for clear and well-motivated explications of this connection.

3. Cf. Jaakko Hintikka, "The Semantics of Modal Notions and the Indeterminacy of Ontology," in Davidson and Harman, eds., *Semantics of Natural Language*, n. 6.

4. He does not declare himself on the exact felt ground of his firm belief in possibilia. I believe that the intuitive irresistibility that his Objects had for him is best explained by ascribing the appropriate *semantical* views to him. The irresistibility in turn of a naive semantics for superficial singular terms is due to there having previously been no competing semantical theories such as Russell's to weigh against the naive account. (This is not to say that he would have gone on to accept Russell's account if he had thought of it.)

5. Bertrand Russell, "Descriptions," in *Logic and Knowledge*, ed. by R. C. Marsh (London: Routledge & Kegan Paul, 1956), and W. V. O. Quine, "On What There Is," in *From a Logical Point of View* (Cambridge, Mass.: Harvard University Press, 1953).

6. Alexius Meinong, "The Theory of Objects," in *Realism and the Background of Phenomenology*, ed. by Roderick Chisholm (Glencoe, Ill.: The Free Press, 1960), p. 79.

7. Daivd Lewis, probably the most notorious current defender of a strong form of Meinoagianism, begins his discussion of possible worlds (in *Counterfactual* [Cambridge, Mass.: Harvard University Press, 1973], sec. 4.1) with a brief paean to the hominess and familiarity of nonactual worlds. I shall argue below that his "natural as breathing" talk, like Meinong's, thinly masks a formidable theoretical apparatus which must be evaluated on theoretical grounds.

8. Meinong relies entirely on this principle in displaying the independence of *Sosein* from *Sein*: the round square, he says, must at least be round and be square.

9. "Critical Notice of Meinong (ed.), *Untersuchungen zur Gegenstandstheorie und Psychologie*," *Mind*, 14 (1905).

10. In fact, Richard Routley and Valerie Routley remind us in "Rehabilitating Meinong's Theory of Objects" (*Revue Internationale de Philosophie* [1973], fasc. 2–3) that Meinong did go on to impose a type theory of this sort.

11. Richard Routley proposes a solution to this problem in an unpublished paper.

12. What is to prevent our positing any crackpot kind of abstract entity we like and immunizing ourselves against criticism by adding that the entity is nonactual? For that matter, what is to prevent our positing lavish supplies of *physical* things such as unexplored planets and doing the same?

13. "Semantics for Propositional Attitudes," in Hintikka, *Models for Modalities* (Dordrecht: Reidel, 1969).

14. Cf. Gilbert Harman, "Quine on Meaning and Existence, II," *Review of Metaphysics* (1968), 348.

15. Stalnaker, "Propositions," in *Issues in the Philosophy of Language*, ed. by A. F. McKay and D. D. Merrill (New Haven: Yale University Press, 1976); Cresswell, "The World Is Everything That Is the Case," *Australasian Journal of Philosophy*, 50 (1972), 1–13.

16. See, e.g., "Methodological Reflections on Current Linguistic Theory," in Davidson and Harman, eds., *Semantics of Natural Language*, pp. 442–454. I discuss the impact of Quine's views on linguistics in "Reality and Semantic Representation," *Monist* 59 (1976), 424–440.

17. Cf. Gilbert Harman, "Quine on Meaning and Existence, I," *Review of Metaphysics* 21 (1967), 124–151, on the positing of intensional entities in semantics.

18. Of course, there are philsophers whose revulsion for intensional entities Platonistically understood is so great that they have tried to *reconstrue* such quantification as not having its normal meaning. Rudolf Carnap is one; Wilfrid Sellars is another.

19. In "On the Frame of Reference" (in Davidson and Harman, ed., *Semantics of Natural Language*, pp. 219–252), John Wallace seems to be proposing that we *can do no other* than to make such a demand vis-à-vis any canonical idiom if we are to understand that idiom.

20. I am here glossing over Quine's insistence that "regimentation" (the replacement of an awkward or troublesome locution in a natural language by a formal construction of some chosen canonical idiom for technical purposes) does not do anything that might properly be regarded as displaying or even illuminating the *meaning* of the original locution. This denial falls trivially out of Quine's indeterminacy doctrine. So he would balk at my talk of offering an actualistic "semantics for" the Meinongian quantifier in the going sense of the term (cf. note 16 above). For purposes of this paper I shall waive this issue and continue to take semantical theories to be genuine theories *about* their target locutions. I discuss Quine's indeterminacy doctrine in Chapter 9 of a book I am preparing on methodology in linguistics.

21. In unpublished address delivered at the 1978 Australasian Association of Philosophy Conference, Richard Routley and Valerie Routley criticized a number of analyses that might be suggested. They also worked toward a positive proposal of their own, though their idea is not yet fully enough developed to be evaluated.

22. Lewis, *Counterfactuals*, sec. 4.1, and elsewhere; Terence Parsons, "A Prolegomenon to a Meinongian Semantics," *Journal of Philosophy*, 71 (1974), 561–581; Routley and Routley, "Rehabilitating Meinong's Theory of Objects," and elsewhere.

23. "Possible Worlds," *Noûs*, 10 (1976), 65–75.

24. Richards, "The Worlds of David Lewis," *Australasian Journal of Philosophy*, 53 (1975), 105–118. Haack, "Lewis' Ontological Slum," *Review of Metaphysics*, 33 (1977), 415–429.

25. Richard Routley has kindly let me see a large body of unpublished material in which he and Valerie Routley refute a number of standard objections to Meinongianism outright and clean up Meinong's view considerably in response to more trenchant objections. Their work is unsettlingly convincing.

26. Lewis offers a positive argument for his view, besides the theoretical advantages he claims for it. I shall omit discussion of the argument here, since I have criticized it elsewhere (Steven Boer and William Lycan, review of *Counterfactuals* in *Foundations of Language*, 13 [1975], 145–151) and since several other commentators and reviewers have criticized it as well, some more effectively than I. (See Donald Nute, "David Lewis and the Analysis of Counterfactuals," *Noûs*, 10 (1976), 353–362; Richards, "The Worlds of David Lewis"; Haack, "Lewis' Ontological Slum"; and Stalnaker, "Possible Worlds."

27. See Roderick M. Chisholm, "Identity through Possible Worlds: Some Questions," *Noûs*, I (1967); and Fred Feldman, "Counterparts," *Journal of Philosophy*, 68 (1971), 406–409.

28. Saul Kripke, "Identity and Necessity," in *Identity and Individuation*, ed. by Milton Munitz (New York: New York University Press, 1971), pp. 135–164; Nicholas Rescher, *A Theory of Possibility* (Pittsburgh: University of Pittsburgh Press, 1975), chaps. 3 and 4.

29, "General Semantics."

30. I defend this claim in the manuscript cited in fn. 20 above.

31. Harman makes a related (though less specifically epistemological) point in "Logical Form" in Donald Davidson and Gilbert Harman, eds., *The Logic of Grammar* (Encino, Calif.: Dickenson, 1975), pp. 289–307.

32. I seem to remember that this point was suggested to me by Steven Boër.

33. Lewis himself has given a far more ingenious reply to the "logical spaceship" argument, in conversation. For fear of misrepresenting him I shall not try to reproduce it here in detail,

but the general idea is that the personal continuity required for the duration of intermundane travel in turn requires a sustaining causal chain, which in turn requires the truth of certain counterfactual statements about worlds, which statements turn out to be undefined in Lewis' semantics for counterfactuals. If all this is correct, then my talk of "visiting one of my counterparts" ultimately is undefined, and this explains its perceived nonsensicalness. My only objection to this line of reasoning is that, for antecedent and independent reasons, I believe that the counterfactuals in question ought *not* to be left undefined by an adequate semantics for counterfactuals. (On this last point, see also Richards, "Worlds of David Lewis," p. 108.)

34. A well-known attempt by A. F. Smullyan to extend Russell's theory in this way ("Modality and Description," *Journal of Symbolic Logic*, 13 [1948], 31–37) is criticized by Leonard Linsky in "Reference, Essentialism, and Modality," *Journal of Philosophy*, 66 (1968), 287–300. I have tried to push Russell's treatment in a slightly different way in sec. III of Steven Boër and William Lycan, "Knowing Who" (*Philosophical Studies*, 28 [1975]); in "Referential Opacity Explained Away" (in preparation) I go into the advantages and drawbacks of the Russell-Smullyan approach in considerable detail.

35. "Identity and Necessity"; "Naming and Necessity," in Harman and Davidson, eds., *Semantics of Natural Language*, pp. 253–355; and particularly in conversation. Nicholas Rescher shows considerable sympathy for the counterfactual approach (though he does not adopt it in the end) in *A Theory of Possibility*.

36. The point I am making here is very easily overlooked by philosophers seeking paraphrastic eliminations of the metaphysically dubious entities assumed by some formal and highly technical theory. Consider a simple (and mythical) example: It seems that sentences of the form "$x \in y(Fy)$" can be paraphrased simply as "Fx", as Quine has observed. Thus, some class abstracts may be regarded as *façons de parler*. A philosopher who lacked Quine's own mathematical sophistication might well come to think that nominalism had been achieved, in that Quine had hit upon a program whereby class abstraction and talk of classes could be paraphrased away. What this naive philosopher would be overlooking is that simple class abstraction is not the only technical operation that occurs essentially in set theory. In this case, as Quine points out, one would not even be able to explicate talk of classes of classes, since his "virtual class" device leaves undefined any construction in which a bound variable occurs immediately to the right of "$\in$." A nonmythical example of this optimistic sort of fallacy is some philsophers' reaction to Wilfrid Sellars' approach to abstract entities. Sellars, mobilizing his ingenious device of dot quotation, has offered some very plausible paraphrases for simple talk of properties, propositions, sets, and so on. Philosophers justly impressed by the cleverness and by the naturalness of these paraphrases have taken Sellars to have offered an acceptable nominalistic *theory of* abstract entities. But Sellars has given us no reason at all for thinking that the rarefied operations of (e.g.) graph theory, the integral calculus, or other areas of higher mathematics can be explicated in terms of dot quotation, since he has provided no directions in which his original paraphrases of simple and relatively nontechnical constructions are to be extrapolated. (Jeffrey Sicha has tried to provide at least one such direction in *A Metaphysics of Elementary Mathematics* [Amherst, Mass.: University of Massachusetts Press, 1974], but the mathematics he is able to treat is very elementary indeed.)

37. Perhaps the most elaborate set-theoretic world-encapsulating edifice to be found in the existing literature is that built up by M. J. Cresswell in *Logics and Languages* (London: Methuen, 1973).

38. William Lycan and Ronald Nusenoff, review of Milton Munitz, ed., *Identity and Individuation*, *Synthese*, 28 (1974), 553–559.

39. Kripke has replied to this criticism (in conversation) that he regards the circularity as a trade-off; he does not believe that any analysis of counterfactuals will be found that is more acceptable than a possible-worlds analysis and does believe that unreduced possible-worlds analyses are unacceptable for more or less Quinean reasons similar to those I have presented above.

40. "Dispensing with Possibilia," *Proceedings and Addresses of the American Philosophical Association*, 44 (1975–1976), 39–51. Another option may emerge from Rantala's "urn" semantics; see Veikko Rantala, "Urn Models: A New Kind of Non-Standard Model for First-Order Languages," and Hintikka, "Impossible Possible Worlds Vindicated"; both are found in *Journal of Philosophical Logic*, 4 (1975), 455–474 and 475–483.

41. Several philosophers have recently claimed that the "not enough names" problem is soluble for the usual sorts of subject matters such as arithmetic. See (e.g.) Sicha, *Metaphysics*, and R. D. Gallie, "A. N. Prior and Substitutional Quantification," *Analysis*, 34 (1974), 65–69. I have not seen these purported solutions adjudicated in the literature, so I cannot say whether they could correctly be extended to cover the cardinalities involved in a system of nonexistent possibles.

42. "Is There a Problem about Substitutional Quantification?" in Gareth Evans and John McDowell, eds., *Truth and Meaning* (Oxford: Oxford University Press, 1976).

43. "Semantic Competence and Funny Functors," forthcoming in *The Monist*.

44. Ithaca, N.Y.: Cornell University Press, 1962.

45. Adams, "Theories of Actuality," *Noûs*, 8 (1974), 211–231; Plantinga, *The Nature of Necessity* (Oxford: Clarendon Press, 1974). Plantinga actually talks of *states of affairs* which *obtain* or do not obtain and does not commit himself to identifying these respectively with true and false propositions (p. 45); I do not see that any fine distinctions here will be of importance to the metaphysics of modality.

46. Hector-Neri Castañeda, "Thinking and the Structure of the World," *Philosophia*, 4 (1974), 3–40; and Parsons, "A Prolegomenon to a Meinongian Semantics."

47. Quine, "Propositional Objects," in *Ontological Relativity and Other Essays* (New York: Columbia University Press, 1968); Cresswell, *Logics and Languages* and "The World Is Everything That Is the Case."

48. "Possible Worlds."

49. *Counterfactuals*, pp. 89–91.

50. I owe this point to Phil Quinn.

51. This point is somewhat weakened by the fact, already brought out and illuminatingly discussed by Gail Stine in "Essentialism, Possible Worlds, and Propositional Attitudes" (*Philosophical Review*, 82 [1973]. 471–482), that the failure of real people to be logical saints causes problems of this sort for possible-worlds semanticists in any case.

52. I am indebted to Cresswell for a number of helpful discussions on this topic.

53. *The Nature of Necessity*, chap. 7, sec. 4.

54. I do *not* believe a parallel argument would succeed regarding number theory and set theory. I have proposed an analysis of numerical terms that blocks it in William Lycan and George Pappas, "Quine's Materialism," *Philosophia*, 6 (1976), 109–110.

55. Thus, in no way am I suggesting that modal semanticists should interrupt their work and wait for our ontological problems to be solved to everyone's satisfaction. I am a bit more doubtful, though, about linguistic semanticists, who base their theories of *natural* language on intensional formal systems; at least, the type of illumination that such theories yield needs very careful examination and sorting out, which to my knowledge it has not yet received.

56. Something like this is suggested, though not expressly claimed, by Stalnaker in "A Theory of Conditionals," in *Studies in Logical Theory*, ed. by Nicholas Rescher, *American Philosophical Quarterly* Monograph Series, No. 2 (Oxford: Blackwell, 1968), 98–112.

57. I borrow this term from David Armstrong.

58. Quine himself would reject this criticism and would reject the spirit of Plantinga's "pure"/"applied" distinction. In "Ontological Relativity" he argues in effect that any choice of an interpretation for *any* quantifier is arbitrary in this way, or at least that it is relative to an arbitrarily prechosen *scheme* of interpretation. Thus, he finds Plantinga's and my demand inherently unreasonable. The important thing to see, though, is that if they are successful, Quine's arguments

for this indeterminacy of ontology also impugn the status of semantics as a science and the whole idea of giving determinate "truth-conditions" for modal sentences or any other sentences, not to mention the whole idea of any sentence's having a determinate "meaning." Quine is radically skeptical of all such enterprises (on this, see Harman's "Quine on Meaning and Existence, I, II," and my "Reality and Semantic Representation"). So appeal to Quine's doctrine of ontological relativity will not help the combinatorialist defend his own proposal for an applied semantics. Ironically, Quine himself (on page 149–152 of "Propositional Objects") expends a fair bit of energy in trying to remove arbitrariness of this sort which infects spatial and temporal dimensions, apparently in an effort to get at the *real* (nonarbitrary) members of his domain of arrangements. This seems conpletely uncharacteristic of Quine and remains for me an exegetical paradox. A further mystery is that Quine seemingly invokes his "ersatz worlds" only to model the propositional attitudes of nonverbal creatures and does not seem to notice that his apparatus potentially generates a stock of arrangements adequate to deal with modal semantics generally.

59. For example, I do not preserve Plantinga's distinction between *worlds* and "world-*books*." I employ only the world-books, or, as Adams calls them, world-stories.

60. Rescher has elaborated and defended the idea of "supernumerary" individuals of this kind in *A Theory of Possibility*, chap. 3.

61. Cf. Robert Kraut, "Attitudes and Their Objects," *Journal of Philosophical Logic*, forthcoming.

62. For further defense of impossibilia see Richard and Valerie Routley, "Rehabilitating Meinong's Theory of Objects," p. 230; also Richard Routley, "The Durability of Impossible Objects," *Inquiry*, 19 (1976), 247–250.

63. The problem was put to me by Don Mannison.

64. This objection was raised by Tom Richards. I am indebted to him and to his colleagues at LaTrobe University for helpful discussion of an earlier version of this paper.

65. Max Cresswell voiced this objection; it is also touched on by Stalnaker in "Possible Worlds."

66. This point was raised by Phil Quinn; Stalnaker also hints at it in "Possible Worlds," but instead argues rather neatly that his Actualist world-surrogates, "ways things might have been," are just as efficacious as sets of propositions and have a slight edge in economy. I think his argument can be resisted, but I would be almost as happy with his candidates as I would be with Plantinga's.

67. I have suggested this in "Could Propositions Explain Anything?" *Canadian Journal of Philosophy*, 3 (1974), 427–435.

PART SEVEN

PRAGMATICS

INTRODUCTION

This section, on some views of the subject, takes us, in a sense, outside of semantics proper into pragmatics—the study of the manner in which context, including such diverse phenomena as speaker or audience identity, time of utterance, background information presupposed by conversational participants, and perhaps a host of other possible nonlinguistic determinants of meaning contribute to the interpretation of an utterance. Though this may be an excursion out of the city center of semantics, it certainly keeps us well within the suburbs, and it is arguably impossible to draw firm boundaries. One cannot, arguably, interpret an actual utterance (or at least a large range of actual utterances) without pragmatic information, and if semantics is the discipline concerned with the assignment of meaning to linguistic strings, it must then at least pay close heed to, if not incorporate much of, pragmatics. This is explicitly said at the beginning of "On Specificity" by Annabel Cormack and Ruth Kempson. Their subject is specific vs. nonspecific interpretations of indefinite noun-phrases, e.g., of Quine's "a sloop" in "I want a sloop." They argue that specific interpretations, interpretations that take the "a"-phrase to be about one particular thing or person, are pragmatic having to do with the way the hearer seeks to verify what is said. Verification unlike the truth that is its quarry is hence outside *pure* semantics, despite its semantic character. So too, according to some, with figurative or nonliteral usage, the subject of the papers by Harold Skulsky and Merrie Bergmann.

Indefinites are not, then, say Cormack and Kempson, semantically ambiguous between specific and nonspecific readings. It is not that "a sloop" is an existential quantifier when its scope is inferior to the desire, but a (nonquantifying) rigid designator of a particular sloop when its scope is superior. The difference, instead, lies in the way the hearer comes to grasp the truth-conditions of the proposition expressed. Issues such as these, that concern the assignment of meaning, but that require attention to more than the meanings of individual words and the form of the sentences in which they figure, requiring attention to what lies in the understandings of speakers and hearers are traditionally assigned to pragmatics. Cormack's and Kempson's extensive, detailed and amply illustrated discussion of the behavior of indefinites and other determiners in transparent, opaque, and counterfactual contexts not only serves their argument but also serves to review the literature.

The topic of metaphor unhappily attracts linguistic ideologues. Its importance in facilitating linguistic change, in the extension of workaday to technical uses of words, and in the immemorial arts of language, however, calls for cool and careful appraisal. The tortured distinction between figurative and the literal meaning, despite its genuinely pragmatic character is another of those pragmatic distinctions semantics cannot afford to ignore, defining as it does its very subject matter. The reader may also had occasional qualms about the semantic data in the essays above: Was that * indicating ill formedness really justified? One cause of variation in semantic intuition is figurativeness, figurativeness that is only sometimes strictly to be called metaphor. A sentence we may find literally false, or even ill formed may be felt to be nonetheless well formed and even true on a "metaphorical" reading.

Skulsky is learned in the antiquities of metaphor and more particularly in those elaborate renaissance taxonomies of figurative tropes that serve as a caution against metaphor mania. He and Bergmann provide excellent reviews of the salient current literature on the subject, and provide quite different proposals for understanding the nature of figurative meaning.

Skulsky says that "the figurative speaker is engaged in . . . demonstrating a new language, recruiting speakers, and establishing subtle rapport with the prospective recruits." A great advantage of Skulsky's novel language theory of figurative utterance is that it allows for figures other than the standard semantic ones, e.g., the syntactic (?) trope mentioned by Kiteley, "a solitary mister in the park." If new rules are being inculcated, there is no reason that they all have solely to do with the criteria for the application of individual words. To illustrate again from an essay above, Kiteley suggests that zeugma is a combined figure in which the yoking grammatical construction forces a verb simultaneously to have two different meanings.

Bergmann, on the other hand, argues that metaphorical utterances often are assertions; that this is, in John Austin's terminology, their illocutionary force; and that it is wrong to think that there is a separate speech of, say, figuration. It is a way, a nonliteral way of asserting a proposition, with assertion understood as in Stalnaker above. This compares interestingly with Skulsky's notion of metaphorese. One can both demonstrate a use while at the same time employing that usage, the way, e.g., one both names and gives a name in an introduction. So the two accounts are not incompatible. One could be both saying things in Metaphorese and inculcating the new language at the same time.

Bergmann's discussion of the machinery of metaphor turns on the interesting and important notion of salience, thus emphasizing the pragmatic character of this corner of semantics, and her elaboration of the conditions of success in metaphorical assertion employs ideas from Grice's theory of conversational implicature. These two essays, despite their present location in this volume could well serve as a beginning of a course in semantics mobilizing as they do many of the issues of the technical semantic theory.

John Perry's essay may seem to be more about the structure of such propositional attitudes as belief than about language, but Frege, Russell, and Quine have shown how consideration of one ineluctably leads to consideration of the other. Modern semantics can plausibly be traced to a perception of the anomalies in belief sentences, anomalies that only became visible in the light of the new logic of Cantor, Peano, and Frege. Dasein, self-awareness, is rooted in the semantics of reflexive pronouns, those peculiar vernacular devices of self-identification. Such pronouns are paradigm cases of indexicals—terms whose reference is determined by their context of utterance. In the case of "I" this phenomenon is clear, though as Perry notes, puzzling. "I" refers always to its utterer. One might expect then, that one could replace any occurrence of "I" with the name of the utterer *salva veritate*—that indexicals are always eliminable in favor of nonindexical expressions, and hence that indexicality is a linguistic convenience, but an inessential feature of a language. Perry, in this enormously influential paper—one that has spawned a large and fascinating literature—argues otherwise: In many contexts, he argues, the indexical is essential. There are statements that can only be made—knowledge that can only be expressed—using indexical expressions.

The implications of essential indexicality for the relation between semantics and pragmatics are enormous. For the fixation of the denotation of indexicals is pragmatic if anything is, and if indexicals are essential to a wide range of linguistic expressions, it follows that pragmatic considerations are essential to the enterprise of semantics. It is this unwillingness of semantics to be neatly contained that runs through this entire volume and that makes the discipline so exciting.

ANNABEL CORMACK
AND RUTH KEMPSON

ON SPECIFICITY

PROLOGUE

The following paper is an exercise in semantic analysis, showing there is no easy route from the data of speakers' intuitions to the correct semantic analysis. All expressions may in use give rise to a variety of interpretations. There are always two possible routes of analysis to explore. The variety of interpretations might be merely a case of language-specific lexical ambiguity, each interpretation in use corresponding to a discrete lexical item. But it might rather be due to an interaction between the intrinsic content of the expression used and general principles underlying language use. The question for the analyst is, which is the correct choice? In order to resolve this choice, the array of interpretations has to be analyzed into the various component contributions made by the intrinsic content of the lexical item, the linguistic environment in which it is contained, and general principles of how utterances are interpeted. Moreover, making such a choice has a significance over and above the mere descriptive task of giving the best characterization of the facts. In seeking to give a characterization of the language faculty, linguists need to characterize as part of grammar all and only those properties which are intrinsic to the language faculty. Phenomena that display interaction between grammar-internal specification and more general cognitive principles are of particular significance because they give us insight into the interface between the language faculty and such general processes.

The particular problem under consideration in this chapter is one aspect of the analysis of indefinite noun-phrases. Not only are there utterances in which the indefinite article is interpreted like the existential quantifier of predicate calculus. There are also a number of seemingly discrete "specific" interpretations in which the indefinite noun-phrase seems to be acting as a referring expression picking out a particular individual. However we shall argue, contrary to other analyses, that the phenomenon of "specificity" is exclusively pragmatic, and arises from the way in which speakers and hearers interact in communication. All that is given in the grammar is the lexical specification of the indefinite article as an existential quantifier.

At the time this article was written, in 1982, the only sufficiently developed pragmatic framework was the Gricean one in terms of speaker's intentions, and the analysis is presented in these terms. Since that time, two advances have been made. A substantial new pragmatic theory has emerged which provides an entirely new hearer directed perspective on utterance interpretation—Relevance Theory (Sperber and Wilson, 1986). And a new analysis of the quantificational force of indefinite noun phrase has been proposed as part of two closely allied semantic theories of natural language—Discourse Representation Theory and File Theory (Kamp, 1984; Heim, 1982—we shall refer to them jointly as DR/File Theory). According to this theory, indefinites are not quantifiers but introduce variables: The quantificational force in all cases arises not from intrinsic specification of the article itself but from the syntactic environment in which the expression occurs. Despite its novelty as an account of indefinite NPs, this new DR/File Theory of indefinites as variables is not incompatible with the more orthodox quantificational analysis adopted in this paper. DR/File Theory and the orthodox theory differ over whether the quantificational property intrinsic to the interpretation of indefinites is due to lexical specification of the indefinite article or to the larger clausal environment in which the article occurs. They are ad idem in assuming that the interpretation which indefinites give rise to IS invariably quantificational. So if the ambiguity claim that indefinites are intrinsically both "specific" and "nonspecific" were correct, the DR/File Theory would be shown to be inadequate in the same way as the orthodox theory. And contrarily, if the explanation of the specificity phenomena as pragmatic is correct, the DR/File Theory can be preserved without change. So the arguments that the specificity phenomenon is purely pragmatic in nature will buttress the new account of indefinites as much as the old. Moreover, the observations contained in this paper apply to a wider set of data than DR/File Theory has yet characterized, so the conclusions are still relevant to current research.

For these reasons, we present the article as it was written without change other than a few stylistic alterations. In closing we shall point out in more detail the way in which the analysis would apply within a DR/file perspective; and the way in which the problem of the "specificity" phenomenon could be addressed in the new Relevance Theory of pragmatics.

1. SPECIFICITY—THE PROBLEM POSED

It has often been observed in the literature that sentences such as (1)

(1) A student in the syntax class was accused of cheating in the final exam

appear to have distinct interpretations. On the one hand, someone uttering (1) might be intending to assert merely that there was at least one member of the syntax class who was accused of cheating in the final exam; or he might be wishing to make this assertion with respect to some particular student, whom he does not identify. The problem presented by sentences such as (1) is that indefinite noun phrases are used by speakers with a particular individual in mind in relation to that noun phrase; this we shall take to be the defining characteristic of the so-called specificity phenomenon. The question is whether this specificity phenomenon should be reconstructed by analyzing such noun phrases as having a truth-conditionally distinct referential use, in which the expression refers to that unnamed individual, in addition to the more orthodox interpretation as a quantified expression; or whether the specificity phenomenon should be explained some other way, leaving the semantic analysis of these expressions as unambiguously of a quantifier type. An analysis of indefinite noun phrases as ambiguous between specific and nonspecific interpretations was first proposed by Fillmore (1966). More recently, a number of people (of whom Fodor and Sag, 1982, have given the most detailed articulation) have taken up Kripke's work on rigid designators (Kripke, 1972) and Kaplan's on directly referential terms (Kaplan, 1977) and have proposed that indefinite noun phrases have two logically distinct sets of properties, and specific interpretation being a directly referential rigid designator akin to a proper name. Indefinite noun phrases are thus argued to have one interpretation which is subject to scope variation like any other quantified expression, and one which is effectively immune to it. In this paper, we shall seek to argue that the apparent behaviour of indefinite noun phrases as scopeless rigid designators[1] is spurious and due to a confusion between the proposition(s) a sentence can express in a context and the evidence one might bring to bear in verifying the propositions(s) that sentence expresses.

The arguments in the literature have been constructed, in the main, around opaque-context phenomena. One reason for this is that evidence in nonopaque contexts might at first glance seem nondecisive. Consider in this connection (2):

(2) John painted three cars

and Table I, where the diagram is an informal representation of a model-state:
Suppose in uttering (2) a speaker has in mind three particular cars A, B, and C, but the event that his utterance is purporting to be a partial description of is that in Table I. Is the proposition that his utterance of the sentence expresses true or false? According to the account of indefinite noun-phrases as ambiguous, it is true if the utterance is taken as a quantified proposition, but also simultaneously false if the utterance is taken as a proposition about the particular individuals A, B, and C. According to the nonambiguity account, (2) is of course simply true. The problem is that, given the notorious difficulty of assessing conditions under which propositions are false in difficult

Table I

cases (as witness the entire presupposition literature), it is arguable that speakers cannot be expected to have reliable judgments about the falsity of the proposition a sentence expresses in the face of a competing true proposition which that sentence expresses. Hence the move to opaque contexts as evidence for the case.

2. SPECIFICITY IN NONOPAQUE CONTEXTS

The move to opaque contexts is too swift. There are four different types of evidence which suggest that any analysis of indefinite noun phrases in nonopaque contexts as truth-conditionally ambiguous is incorrect.

2.1. Indefinites and Scope Variation

First, the interaction of this apparent specificity phenomenon with scope variation. Accoording to an ambiguity analysis of indefinite noun-phrases, in which specificity is analyzed in terms of there being a distinct interpretation involving a contextually fixed referential expression, the possibility of interpretations in which a speaker has unnamed but specific individuals in mind should never arise when the indefinite noun-phrase in question has narrow scope with respect to other quantifiers, since a referential terms is one which does not allow for scope variation, being fixed with respect to the context directly.[2] However, despite claims to the contrary (Rodman, 1976; Fodor and Sag, 1982), it seems to us clear that the so-called 'specific' interpretations in which speakers may have in mind an individual but fail to identify to the hearer who that individual is are available on narrow scope quantifiers. The issue here concerns the relevance of the insertability of the lexical items *certain* and *specific*. While it is possible that *certain* invariably induces a wide scope interpretation, *specific* does not.[3]

(3) I gave two students each a $\left\{ \begin{array}{l} \text{certain} \\ \phi \\ \text{specific} \end{array} \right\}$ book to read: I gave Maria Dowty, Wall, and Peters, and Susan *Word Meaning and Montague Grammar*.

(4) Every professor accused a (specific) student of cheating and I know who the accused were but I'm not going to tell you.

There is thus a lexical indication that specificity of itself does not induce wide scope. If this is so, then the existence of specific understandings do not in themselves provide evidence for an analysis involving the necessity of wide scope. Consider now (5)

(5) Each teacher has sent in two potentially damaging reports that a pupil of mine has been cheating.

If the indefinite noun-phrase has an interpretation like a proper name, this sentence should have only one interpretation corresponding to that specific interpretation, namely 'There is a specific pupil of mine that each teacher has sent in two reports about'. However there is also an intermediate interpretation which can be represented as[4]

$$\exists T_n \ \forall t \ \exists P_1 \ \forall p \ \exists R_2 \ \forall r \ Strp$$

'For each of the teachers there is some specific pupil of mine about which she/he has sent in two reports'. Again, it is certainly available with *specific* inserted. If the specific-nonspecific distinction were truth-conditional and analyzed with the nonspecific understanding as a genuine quantifier but the specific understanding in parallel with proper names, it should lead to a multiplication of truth-conditionally distinct ambiguities along the following lines: nonspecific interpretations of indefinite noun-phrases should be subject to the same range of interpretations as other quantifiers; specific interpretations of indefinite noun-phrases, however, should be subject to the same restrictions as a proper name—viz., having an interpretation fixed with respect to the context and not varying according to scope. What this example, on the contrary, suggests is that the range of specific interpretations is identical to the range of nonspecific interpretations: in other words the specific-nonspecific distinction is available in just the number of ways that scope ambiguities provide. It is thus not an explanation of scope difference as many have supposed (e.g., Fillmore, 1966).

Example (5) is interesting for another reason. It has been argued (by Rodman, 1976; Cooper, 1979) that quantifier scope is subject to island constraints, in particular that quantifiers cannot have scope beyond relative clauses or noun-complement clauses in which they are embedded. (5) is an example whereby Fodor and Sag purport to show that indefinite noun phrases are exceptions to this general constraint precisely because they display proper name like behavior. Such an argument is taken by them to be evidence that indefinite noun phrases are unlike true quantifiers in an important respect which is of truth-conditional relevance. However, if we are correct in attributing a specific interpretation to the indefinite noun phrase in (5) that has narrow scope with respect to the subject though wide scope with respect to the head noun in which it is embedded as part of the complement, this suggests that whatever the explanation of the phenomenon of specificity, it is quantifier-like behavior that is apparently exceptional in violating island constraints. However, a closer look at the Rodman suggestion reveals that it is probably mistaken.

(6) Ford recalled as many '75 models as they could which were put out by (all) their factories in Texas.

(7) Mary has dated half the men who know a producer I know.

(8) Charles bought half the dog biscuits which each shop had on display.

(9) Up to half the stems on any one rhubarb plant may be picked.

(10) Anne has interviewed secretaries who have worked with all the top BBC women.

(11) John has souvenirs that come from all corners of the world.

(12) Each of my students has dated some of the men who know a producer I know.

(6)–(12) all, we suggest, allow interpretations in which the quantifier in the relative clause has scope over the head noun of that clause ((8) and (11) would only have bizarre interpretations unless these alternatives were also available). And (12), which unlike (6)–(11) has a quantified matrix subject in addition to the problematic complex noun phrase in question, allows an interpretation in which the quantified expression in the relative clause has wide scope with respect to the head noun of that relative clause but narrow scope with respect to the matrix subject—viz. 'For each of my students there is at least one producer I know such that she has dated some of the men who know them'. But if Rodman's suggestion that quantifier scope is subject to island constraints is incorrect, then the apparent specific interpretation of noun phrases is no longer exceptional; it is merely part of the general pattern.

2.2. Indefinites in Counterfactual Conditionals

The second argument concerns counterfactual conditionals. If some expression is a rigid designator, then in counterfactuals, the individual denoted by that expression remains by definition constant and fixed. Thus in (13) the identity of the individual denoted by *John*, and indeed by *I*, is fixed independently of the range of counterfactual situations under consideration:

(13) If John had drowned, I would have been appalled.

If indefinite noun phrases had one interpretation analogous to proper names they should, in parallel fashion, be able to have an interpretation which remains fixed independently of the range of counterfactual circumstances, envisaged in exactly the same way. But they cannot. Consider (14):

(14) If a student in my group had cheated, I would have lost my job, but if Bill, who is also a student in my group had cheated, it wouldn't have affected me.

Under the analysis of specificity as having an individual in mind, there is no reason to predict (14) to be inconsistent, for the speaker could have some other person in his group in mind.[5] However, (14) is inconsistent. (14) is of course predicted to be inconsistent under a unitary analysis of indefinite noun phrases.[6]

2.3 Indefinites and Only

The third piece of evidence against invoking ambiguity of indefinite noun phrases is presented by *only*. The interpretation of *only* operates over indefinite noun phrases as though they were orthodox, unambiguous, existentially quantified expressions: The specific understanding is not available at all for *only* to range over. That is to say, (15) can be interpreted as asserting that it was a child who did that and not a member of some other class, but even though it may be said having some individual in mind, the interpretation of *only* itself cannot operate on that individual in contrast to all other individuals:

(15) It was only a child who did that.

In other words, (15) has no interpretation like that of (16):

(16) It was only John who did that.

(15) cannot be interpreted as 'It was only John who did that, not Angie, Mark, or Vanessa (all of whom are children).' Similarly, (17):

(17) It was only a boy who did that.

(17) can never be used to mean it was only Dylan who did that, and not Hugh, Bill, or Tom (all of whom are boys). Thus, even cases which are often taken to indicate a specific individual do not allow logical operations over a representation of the individual. This fact is extremely puzzling for an analysis of indefinites as ambiguous; and is in contrast entirely compatible with the view that the account of indefinites should be unitary.

Independent evidence that indefinite noun phrases are not lexically ambiguous is presented by (18)–(19):

(18) Only John washed his dog.

(19) Only a student washed his dog.

It was pointed out by Partee (1974) that (18) has three different types of interpretation, whereas (19) has only two. The three interpretations involve (i) indexical use of *his*: 'John washed that man's dog and no one else washed that man's dog; (ii) *his* coreferential with *John*: 'John washed John's dog and no one else washed John's dog'; (iii) bound-variable use of *his*—*his* is bound by *John*: 'John washed his own dog and no one else washed their own dog'. (19) only has interpretations corresponding to the first and last of these. If indefinite noun-phrases are analyzed as semantically ambiguous between a specific, referential use and a genuinely quantificational use, this nonexistence of the third interpretation of (19) is problematic in not patterning in parallel with proper names.

On the contrary however, the facts fall out automatically from a non-ambiguity analysis of indefinite noun phrases. Consider the pronoun *his* in (18) and (19). For independent reasons, we know that the so-called E-type pronouns, which to put it informally pick up semantic information from a computation over the entire clause containing the antecedent (cf. Evans, 1980; Cooper, 1979), are excluded from simple one-clause sentences. Thus, these cases, where there is an asymmetry between the referential properties of the anaphor in question and the quantificational nonreferential properties of the antecedent, do not arise in the syntactic conditions provided by either (18) or (19). The only two types of pronominal interpretation available for *his* are (i) an indexical use, indicating some person independently assumed to exist in the context, (ii) a bound-variable pronoun whose interpretation is fixed by some quantifier which c-commands the pronoun. In the case of (18) it is predictable that the instance of *his* can refer to the individual named 'John' directly, i.e., indexically, and so coincidentally be coreferential with the subject expression. This possibility is not available in the case of (19): the indefinite noun phrase is not according to the analysis a referential term, and does not therefore refer to an individual in context to whom the indexical use of the pronoun might refer directly. The range of data is thus predicted within the analysis in which quantified noun phrases are analysed as unambiguous quantified expressions.

2.4 Indefinites and Negation

The final argument concerns negation, and requires that we independently establish that negative sentences are logically ambiguous between external and internal negation. This can be straightforwardly demonstrated, since internal negation is logically independent of external negation in the case of plurals. (20) is true only on an internal negation reading in which *three cars* is taken as the logical subject if out of six cars, John painted only three of them, and it is true only on an external reading if out of four cars, John only painted two of them (cf. Table II):[7]

Table II

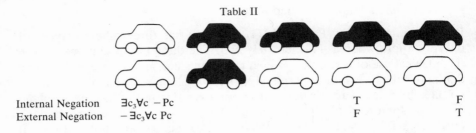

			T	F
Internal Negation	$\exists c_3 \forall c - Pc$			
External Negation	$- \exists c_3 \forall c\ Pc$		F	T

(20) John didn't paint three cars,

With this distinction in mind, consider now (21) and Table III:

(21) Justin didn't blow out three candles.

In Table III we have given truth-value assessments against informally presented model-states of the world as before, assuming the necessity of postulating ambiguity of the quantified noun phrase between a quantified interpretation and a rigid designator analysis. In this latter case, the speaker is assumed to be using the indefinite noun phrase with the intention that his expression rigidly designates the first three candles (underlined with $_{xxx}$). The notation is again that of Kempson and Cormack (1981) and we use an asterisked group variable 'X*' as the symbol of the specific interpretation. This quantification is merely a mnemonic device to give content to the label "specific." As it is subject to a referential interpretation, it will of course invariably be interpreted as equivalent to the same expression having wide scope with respect to all sentence operators (though cf. note 1). Since we are seeking to establish whether or not the apparent phenomenon of specificity is truth-conditionally independent of the internal/external negation distinction, we give independent truth-value assessments for each putative reading in the first instance.

What the table gives is all the possible different truth-value assignments against appropriately differing sets of worlds, which sentence (21) would have if specificity did not give rise to discrete propositions involving a rigid designator uniquely picking out the individuals the speaker has in mind. There are two chief views about specificity as a semantic phenomenon which have their advocates in the literature. One is that specificity is independent of scope phenomena (Fodor, 1979; Ioup, 1977): the other is that specificity correlates invariably with internal negation (for example Dowty, Wall, and Peters, 1981) and their explanation of the Montague analysis of *John seeks a unicorn*). Table III provides evidence that both these views are incorrect. Take first the position that specificity is semantically independent of scope reordering. At first glance, it might seem that Table III on the contrary confirms this, since there is one square where specific external negation has a value distinct

Table III

C_n: set of n candles,
$C_n{}^*$: some specific set of n candles
marked with 'xxx'
ceC

lit candle   blown-out candle

		(a)	(b)	(c)	(d)
Line I		xxx	xxx		
(i) $\exists C_3 \forall c - Bc$	internal negation	T	T		
(ii) $-\exists C_3 \forall cBc$	external negation	T	F		
(iii) $\exists C_3{}^* \forall c - Bc$	specific int. neg.	T	T		
(iv) $-\exists C_3{}^* \forall cBc$	specific ext.neg.	T	T		
$(=\exists C_3{}^* - \forall c \, Bc)$					
Line II		xxx	xxx	xxx	xxx
(i) $\exists C_3 \forall c - Bc$	internal negation	T	T	F	F
(ii) $-\exists C_3 \forall cBc$	external negation	T	F	T	F
(iii) $\exists C_3{}^* \forall c - Bc$	specific int. neg.	F	F	F	F
(iv) $-\exists C_3{}^* \forall cBc$	specific ext.neg.	T	T	T	T
Line III			xxx		xxx
(i) $\exists C_3 \forall c - Bc$	internal negation		T		F
(ii) $-\exists C_3 \forall cBc$	external negation		F		F
(iii) $\exists C_3{}^* \forall c - Bc$	specific int. neg.		F		F
(iv) $-\exists C_3{}^* \forall cBc$	specific ext.neg.		F		F
		(a)	(b)	(c)	(d)

from each of the three possibilites—Line II, column (d)—and also one square where specific internal negation is distinct from each of the others—Line II, column (a). Furthermore, there is independence of a stronger sort. None of the readings as stated can be defined as a boolean combination of the others, thus if the representations genuinely correspond to distinct interpretations of the sentence, then no one of them can be reduced to any of the others.[8] However it is not necessarily correct that each representation *does* correspond to an interpretation of the sentence. Bear in mind that we are considering these models in connection with (21). The question that remains is whether this sentence can mean what these distinct propositions and their values correspond to. Take, for example, Line II, column (d). Intuitions about falsity are notoriously harder to be clear about than intuitions of truth. This being so, it should be straightforward to understand (21) as a description of the picture in II(d) and yet meaning of those three candles, it is not the case that they were all blown out. But it isn't. Against the circumstances presented in the model given by Line II, column (d), (21) is false. The same is also true of Line II, column (a), but here the one distinct value is false; which predictably makes it a less clear case. But the evidence is the same—the one distinct value is impossible to separate from the other three. The conclusion to draw from this part of the table is that if the phenomenon of having individuals in mind in using a quantified expression did give rise to a genuine semantic phenomenon, then it would be truth-conditionally independent. But, as the only cases where either of the specificity interpretations have to be assigned a value distinct from the other possibilities can not in fact be isolated from the other propositions as an interpretation of the sentence, the evidence suggests that this apparent specificity phenomenon is not a truth-conditionally independent one.

According to those who believe specificity correlates with scope phenomena, such a conclusion is not surprising. But Table III provides no support for analyzing specificity as a semantic phenomenon that is coextensive with internal negation either. If the specificity phenomenon was to be the semantic explanation of internal negation (or vice versa), then the truth-value assignments of specific interpretation of internal negation (form (iii) in each line) and internal negation itself (form (i) in each line) should always coincide. They do not. In Lines I(b) and II(c) they do—the two internal negations go together; but in Lines II(b) and III(b), it is the middle two formulae that go together—specific internal negation is distinct from internal negation in this case, but not from external negation. This fluctuation of specificity formulae between sometimes agreeing with internal negation and sometimes with external negation can be seen even in the simplest of singular cases, as witness Table IV, and example (22):

(22) John didn't eat a fancy cake.

What conclusions then do Tables III and IV lead to? They suggest that specificity is not a truth-conditional phenomenon with respect to utterance interpretation at all. The correlation between specificity and the relevant quantifier having negation internal to its scope is not one that can be reconstructed by a logical analysis at all, for to do so leads on the one hand to postulating truth-value judgments that do not exist—as in Line II(d)—and on the other hand to forcing a distinction of truth-value assignment between

Table IV

		A		B	
External Negation	- c Ec	F		F	
Internal Negation	c -Ec	T		T	
Specific ExternalNegation	-c* Ec* = c* -Ec*	F		T	
Specific Internal Negation	c* -Ec*	F		T	

internal negation and specificity (Table IV), which then cannot form the basis for a semantic explanation of their undoubted correlation.

3. SPECIFICITY—A PRAGMATIC ACCOUNT

We are left with several puzzles. Why does this elusive phenomenon of specificity tend to correlate with negation internal to the quantified expression itself? More generally, why does the phenomenon tend to coincide with the expression's being interpreted as having wide scope with respect to other elements in the sentence? But why is it only a tendency? The explanation we suggest is straightforward. Consider the simple sentence (23):

(23) John painted a car.

together with a simplified logical representation: '$\exists c\ P(c)$'. Upon hearing an utterance of this sentence, assuming its logical form to be as given, what minimal addition could the hearer make to the model of the world that she already has which would make it conform to the proposition which the sentence expresses? The clue lies in the semantic rules assigned to the interpretation of the existential: Find a value assignment g such that the variable ranging over cars is assigned a value which makes the formula '$P(x)$' true. If this be so, then one needn't look to some other variable assignment differing only in the value assigned to the variable x. In other words, and less formally, if the first car you pick out has the property of having been painted by John, then no further addition to the model is needed—the proposition '$\exists c\ P(c)$' is confirmed as true. What has this to do with communication, since on-line processing is not normally thought to involve verification procedures of this sort—we take on trust what people say to us most of the time: we assume that people have evidence for what they say. The connection is this: if we assume as hearers that some speaker uttering a sentence which expresses a proposition of the form '$\exists x\ F(x)$' has evidence for what he says, then since the most straightforward evidence is to be able to pick out some such individual, we assume in many cases that he has some such individual in some sense in mind as evidence for what he says even though that individual does not constitute part of what he has literally said.

This bears on the data we have considered so far in the following way. Any proposition containing an existential quantifier can only be construed as having supporting evidence in the form of some particular individual that the speaker may have in mind if one of two conditions pertain. Either (i) it has widest scope with respect to other sentence operators such as negation, *if*, etc., or (ii) it is within the scope of some other quantifier which is also supported by the evidence of its being satisfied by some fixed set of individuals. The first of these we have already covered. *If* and negation have in common that any proposition containing such sentence-operators with widest scope cannot be confirmed as true by isolating any particular individual. It is only if it is the existential quantifier which is understood as having wide scope with respect to these operators that such a verifying process is available. The case of *only* might seem to be a counterexample to this claim. For *only* is a sentence operator which can contain an existential quantifier within its scope, as in (15), and yet such a sentence can be uttered with both speaker and hearer knowing that a particular individual is in question. However, unlike *if* and negation, any simple positive sentence containing *only* entails the truth of that sentence without *only*. Thus a sentence such as (15) is in effect a two-part assertion—an assertion of *A child did that* plus an assertion that no-one else did. The verification analysis would thus predict that though the second part of this assertion cannot be substantiated by fixing on one particular individual the first part can. Hence there can be an individual in the mind of speaker and hearer in this case without the utterance as a whole showing real specificity effects.

The second type of case concerns examples such as (3) and (4) (repeated here for convenience):

(3) I gave two students each a (specific) book to read: I gave Maria Dowty, Wall, and Peters, and Susan *Word Meaning and Montague Grammar*.

(4) Every professor in the department accused a (specific) student of cheating and I know who the accused were but I'm not going to tell you.

These are the cases where the existential quantifier associated with the indefinite singular noun-phrase can be interpreted as having as extension particular individuals, while yet having narrow scope with respect to the other quantified expression in the sentence. This is incompatible with a rigid designator analysis of specificity, but on the contrary predicted to be a possibility by an explanation in terms of evidence the hearer may construe the speaker as having in mind. If a speaker can itemize the individuals satisfying the quantified expression with wide scope, then it is possible that he may be able to itemize each of the individuals satisfying both quantified expressions. Thus the range of data are predicted entirely correctly by an analysis of quantified noun phrases as quantified expressions, if we construct an explanation of the apparent specificity phenomenon in terms of evidence the speaker may have in mind for the quantified proposition he is asserting.[9]

4. SPECIFICITY AND OPAQUE CONTEXTS

The question that now arises is whether the explanation of specificity suggested for nonopaque cases can be extended to the notoriously cloudy domain of opaque contexts. Arguments about indefinite noun phrases and specificity invariably employ the so-called opaque contexts, where many semantic arguments founder because the data seem so unclear. We shall argue that with a natural extension of the explanation already suggested in terms of evidence for the proposition expressed, much of the difficulty of characterising specificity in opaque contexts can be resolved. In an attempt to stave off whatever obscurity may arise, we shall distinguish between two types of opaque contexts, the *want*, *look for*, *try* predicates and the predicates that make explicit reference to beliefs or utterances of other people. In the first place, we shall consider the former.[10]

4.1 The Opacity of Want Predicates
Let us start from the familiar case:

(24) John wants to marry a girl his parents disapprove of.

With two approximate paraphrases: 'There is a girl John's parents disapprove of and John wants to marry her' (the transparent reading) and 'John wants to marry some or other girl that his parents disapprove of' (the opaque reading). There are three problems. (i) What existence claims might be made by such a sentence—is the existential quantifier of standard logic suitable for expressing such claims? (ii) Can such a sentence be used to express propositions about specific individuals separately and in addition to whatever existence claims are expressed by a representation of the indefinite noun phrase as an existential quantifier? (iii) To what extent is such a sentence able to express the desires and beliefs of the individual denoted by the subject of the sentence, about whom a claim of desire (or belief) is being made? The variety of claims made in the literature is tantalisingly rich. Perhaps the standard position as expressed for example in Dowty et al. (1981) is that the specific interpretation coincides with the transparent reading and the nonspecific interpretation with the opaque reading. However Fodor (1979) and Ioup (1977) argue that an existence entailment is not a necessary property of either the transparent or the opaque reading. Furthermore Ioup argues that specific interpretations are separately available on both the transparent and the opaque reading; and Fodor argues that the descriptive content of both the transparent and the opaque reading are the responsibility of the speaker.

4.1.1 Want Predicates and the Analysis So Far

Before tackling these claims, let us anticipate what one might expect on the basis of the result of considering nonopaque contexts. Firstly, the evidence of internal and external negation, with the consequent need for some procedure of NP extraction can be straightforwardly extended to opaque contexts. Just as we had logical independence between two readings of *Justin didn't blow out three candles*, so we get at least the two corresponding readings of (25) clearly separable as (25') and (25"):

(25) John didn't try to answer three questions.

(25') It's not the case that John tried to answer three questions

(25") There are three questions that John didn't try to answer

Whatever the problems involved in representing the opaque reading, there is no doubt about the existence of reading in which a claim is made about a set of at least three questions such that John didn't try to answer them. In other words we must allow for a proposition exactly parallel to internal negation in the nonopaque case, with the quantification with respect to *three questions* having wide scope with respect to the remainder of the proposition. Accordingly, we have to allow in these cases for logical forms in which the quantifier is extracted from the environment indicated by the linear sequence of the sentence. Any such process will automatically yield two nonequivalent logical forms for positive sentences involving an opaque context and three nonequivalent logical forms for the corresponding negative. As exemplification of this, consider (26) and (27):

(26) John tried not to step in three icy puddles.

(27) John didn't try to step in three icy puddles.

If for the moment we use only the paraphrases and approximate logical forms, then the interaction of an opaque context, a quantifier extraction rule and negation will produce the following possibilities for (26) and (27) respectively:

(26') try' $(j, \wedge [- \exists P_3 \forall p \ Sp])$
John tried to make true that it's not the case that he stepped in three puddles (he didn't want to make his boots dirty)

(26") try' $(j, \wedge [\exists P_3 \forall p -Sp])$
John tried to make it true that there were three puddles that he didn't step in (he thought he should leave a few for his brother)

(26″ ′) $\exists P_3 \, \forall p[try' \, (j, \wedge[\, -Sp])$
There were three puddles that John tried not to step in (they had unbroken surfaces)

(27′) $-[try' \, (j, \wedge[\exists P_3 \, \forall p \; Sp])]$
It's not the case that John tried to step in three icy puddles

(27″) $- \exists P_3 \, \forall p[try' \, (j, \wedge[Sp])]$
It's not the case that there were three puddles that John tried to step in

(27″ ′) $\exists P_3 \, \forall p \, -[try' \, (j, \wedge[Sp])]$
There were three icy puddles of which it's not the case that John tried to step in them.

(26′)–(26″ ′) seem clearly distinguishable and are in fact logically independent. (27′) and (27″) are harder to separate since they involve negation of the opacity-inducing predicate itself; but given the existence of (27″ ′) and the clarity of (26′)–(26″ ′), and too the existence of the two corresponding readings of the positive sentence, there is no reason not to assume that three logical forms should be postulated for (26) and (27) equally. Thus one would predict that while positive opaque sentences are logically two ways ambiguous, opaque sentences involving negation will be three ways ambiguous.

Secondly, if the phenomenon of specificity is not a semantic one, but arises in virtue of a verification type of strategy used by speakers and hearers, then one would predict at least that the transparent reading of an opaque-context sentence[11] such as (24) would invariably be subject to the possibility of a specific understanding in use.[12] This is uncontroversial. Indeed it is almost the sole point of agreement between the various writers on this problem. The one advantage that the current analysis has over others which incorporate specificity into the logical structure is that the specificity of the transparent reading is not postulated *ad hoc* without explanation of why it should arise in this case—it follows automatically from the account given of specificity, together with the assumption that the logical form of the transparent reading involves existential quantification for the noun phrase in the complement of the opaque predicate with the remainder of the proposition falling within its scope. Apart from the problem of whether one should give up such standard quantification (a problem we return to below), there is no disagreement over this type of case, and we shall not dwell on it further at this point.

4.1.2 Indefinites and Want Predicates

We come then to the question of the logical structure to be assigned to the opaque reading of (24). Early attempts at assigning semantic representations to sentences of this type dwelt on whether a representation such as (28′) was appropriate as a representation of the opaque reading of (28):

(28) Janet wants to find an armadillo.

(28′) want′ (*j*, ∃*x*[armadillo′ (*x*) & find′ (*j*, *x*)])

Even bypassing the problem of whether one might expect &-elimination to apply in opaque contexts, it is clear that such a representation of opacity depends on there being an embedding of some proposition inside and subordinate to the main proposition. Yet as Partee pointed out (1974) this is not always appropriate, even making the nowadays unpopular assumption that semantic representations may involve lexical decomposition. By far the most sophisticated analysis of such opaque contexts is that in Montague's *Proper Treatment of Quantification* (PTQ) (Thomason, ed. 1974), which assigns a logical structure to a simple sentence (29) as in (29′):

(29) Janet is looking for an armadillo.

(29′) look for′ [*j*, ^λ*P*[∃*x*[armadillo′(*x*) & P{*x*}]]]

If we assume that specificity is to be explained by a verification strategy then in the case of (28′) it is not clear whether or how such a strategy might be applicable. Perhaps it could be compatible with some specification on the part of the individual denoted by the subject of the sentence? However, in the case of the Montague analysis, the consequent prediction about specificity seems on the face of it unambiguous. If the phenomenon of specificity only arises as the result of a verification strategy assumed by hearers, then it should be inapplicable to cases such as (28) and (29) on an opaque reading, for the same reason as in the earlier counterfactual, negation and *only* cases—the existence of more than one operator preceding the existential quantifier should guarantee that there is no possibility of a speaker-hearer confirming such a structure by the existence of one individual taken at a single world.

This prediction is problematic. There is, as predicted by earlier arguments, a transparent understanding of (30) which can readily be assumed to concern a particular individual, represented as (30′):

(30) Janet is looking for Marxist English lord.

(30′) ∃*x*[M(*x*) & look for′ (*j*, ^λ*P*[P{*x*}])]

On this interpretation, there may—relative to the beliefs and assertion of the speaker of any such utterance of the sentence—be a particular individual he has in mind as being the individual that the individual denoted by the subject is looking for though it is not part of the propositional content of his utterance. But this is not the critical interpretation. The interpretation apparently predicted not to exist by the combination of a Montague analysis of opaque contexts and the present analysis of specificity is one in which the individual denoted by the subject of the sentence has a particular individual in mind, whose existence is not granted by the speaker of the sentence. But consider (30) as a description of the following scenario:

A: Janet is looking for someone quite specific whom she identifies as Lord Wrotham and who she believes to be a Marxist English lord, which is the reason why she's looking for him. However, contrary to Janet's beliefs and expectations, there is no such man as "Lord Wrotham" and no such thing as a Marxist English lord.

The question is whether (30) can constitute a true description of such circumstances. Despite the falsity of the transparent reading, which as standardly stated involves an existential commitment, the answer surely is "Yes." People can certainly have in mind (nonexistent) individuals in a way which can be described by a sentence such as (30).

Two questions then arise. (i) Is the phenomenon of specificity in opaque contexts the same as that in nonopaque contexts? (ii) Can predicates such as *want*, *try*, *look for* be used as descriptions of the content of other people's beliefs? In both cases we shall argue against the evidence apparent so far. We shall argue that the phenomenon of specificity is unitary, and that the opacity-inducing predicates do not provide descriptions of the precise content of other people's belief structures. There are two ways in which one might seek to incorporate into the logical representation of such sentences a representation of some specific individual which only exists relative to the belief of the individual depicted. The first is to assume that the opaque reading has to be split up into two logical representations, one involging specificity, the other not. This would yield the answer "No" to question (i) above for the following reasons. Since, let us assume, the Montague analysis does indeed capture the nonspecific understanding of (30), the specific understanding would on this analysis require some other operator specially constructed for the phenomenon of specificity in opaque contexts in order to represent the distinction between the two understandings both of which are opaque. On economy grounds alone, we assume that this is not an attractive solution. The alternative analysis of the understanding which involves a specific individual relative to the beliefs of the individual denoted by the subject of the sentence is to conflate it with the transparent reading of the sentence. That is, one might argue (as do Fodor and Ioup) of (30) that the question of whether an individual actually exists is irrelevant—what is common to the apparently distinct specific understandings of (30) and critical to their analysis is that the subject believes that there is a specific individual such that he is a Marxist English lord and she is looking for him. On this account, even on the transparent reading, the sentence is a description *only* of the beliefs of the individual denoted by the subject, and the only way in which the speaker expresses *his* beliefs in uttering such a sentence is in reporting what are the beliefs of the individual denoted. In between these two extremes, one can envisage other intermediate positions, namely that the opaque context sentences may either constitute a description of objects relative to the speaker's set of beliefs or relative to those of the individual denoted by the subject. For example, Fodor argues that the specification of the entity being looked for by the individual denoted by the subject may be relative to the beliefs of the subject-denoted individual (and for this reason she argues that the existential quantifier with its implication of existence is inappropriate). But, she argues, the description of that individual is invariably relative only to. the beliefs of the speaker of the sentence. We shall argue that all views involving specification of an individual relative to the beliefs of the individual denoted by the subject as part of the proposition expressed are incorrect. The demonstration that this is so then leads directly to a unitary account of specificity along the lines suggested for nonopaque contexts.

Suppose we attempt to represent the beliefs of the individual denoted by the subject with an additional operator B_j. One might then represent the transparent reading as '$B_j x(. . .)$'. Consider then (31):

(31) John wants to marry a member of the National Front.

with its two logical forms:

(31′) want′ $(j, \wedge \lambda p[\exists f[\text{marry}'(j, f) \ Y \ P\{f\}]])$

(31″) $\exists f[\text{want}' (j, \wedge \lambda P[\text{marry}'(j, f) \ \& \ P\{f\}])]$

Suppose we modify (31″) to reflect the analysis suggested, giving (31″ ′):

(31″ ′) $B_j \wedge \exists f[\text{want}'(j, \wedge \lambda P[\text{marry}'(j, f) \ \& \ P\{f\}])]$

Some of the problems of this notation are familiar from Fodor (1979)—in particular that such a proposition only expresses John's belief that he wants to marry some member of the National Front and is not a representation of John's desire itself at all.[13] Moreover, to represent John's belief in some member of the National Front separate from the representation of his desire to marry such a woman is not possible. (31iv) is not a well-formed formula:

(31iv) $B_j \wedge (\exists f) \ \& \ \text{want}'(j,. \wedge \lambda P[\text{marry}'(j, f) \ \& \ P\{f\}])$

The second and third of the variable f are not bound. But this is by no means the end of the problem. The evidence of negation suggests that any attempt to represent the beliefs of the subject as part of the proposition expressed is a mistake. The negation of (31″ ′) is either (31v), (31vi), or (31vii):

(31v) $- B_j \wedge \exists f[\text{want}'(j , \wedge \lambda P[\text{marry}'(j, f) \ \& \ P\{f\}])]$

(31vi) $B_j \wedge - \exists f[\text{want}'(j, \wedge \lambda P[\text{marry}'(j, f) \ \& \ P\{f\}])]$

(31vii) $B_j \wedge \exists f - [\text{want}'(j, P[\text{marry}'(j, f) \ \& \ P\{f\}])]$

None of these represent anything approximately representing the propositions expressible by *John doesn't want to marry a member of the National Front.* Just as (31) itself is not an assertion about what John believes, but about what he wants, so also its negation is not about what John does or does not believe.

It might be argued that any such criticisms are criticisms against incorporating into the logical form a syntactic belief operator, and do not hold against some model-theoretic rule of interpretation which is subject to extension assignments relative to models compatible with the subject's belief system rather than the speaker's. However, there is additional evidence against this semantic account also. In the case of (31), a mere belief on the part of the individual John denoted by the subject in the existence of some relevant individual having the property of being a member of the National Front is not sufficient: It must be a belief that the individual would satisfy his desire for the truth of the complement sentence simpliciter. Thus neither the addition of a belief operator nor an interpretation rule relative to models other than the speaker's are in themselves adequate. Consider (31) as a description of the set of circumstances (31B):

(31B) Rose is the girl John wants to marry because she's wealthy and he's obsessed with marrying into money. He happens quite mistakenly also to believe her to be a member of the National Front but this doesn't bother him given her enormous wealth.

Under such circumstances (31′) and (31″) are false. However (31″ ′) is true, and so too would (31) itself be if interpreted via extension assignments relative to models compatible with John's beliefs. Yet (31) is surely false. The only circumstances in which the specification of an individual could be relevant as part of a representation of John's desire is if the reason why he wants to marry such an individual is because he wants to marry someone who is a National Front member—if, that is, he considers her to satisfy the complex predicate *member of the National Front* which is what he requires of the person he marries. Any such circumstances would of course also satisfy the opaque reading (31′).

This restriction on the possible relevance of an individual relative only to the beliefs of the individual denoted by the subject is quite general. Consider (32) and (33) against their respective scenarios *A* and *B*:

(32) Margot is looking for a Marxist English lord

(32A) Margot is looking for Lord Carrington, believing him to be a Marxist lord which is what she wants to find

(32B) Margot is looking for Lord Carrington, who she believes to be a Marxist, because she needs to tell him that his daughter has been assaulted on Hampstead Heath in broad daylight

(32) is surely true on an opaque reading with respect to scenario *A* but false on all readings with respect to scenario *B*, (when the speaker does not believe Lord Carrington to be Marxist).

(33) Arthur is trying to get an English *chef de cuisine minceur* to judge his menu.

(33A) Arthur is trying to get Jane Grigson to judge his menu mistakenly believing her to satisfy his requirement of having an English *chef de cuisine minceur* as his judge

(33B) Arthur is trying to get Jane Grigson to judge his menu (which is an extremely rich French menu) despite his belief that she is a *chef de cuisine minceur*, because he knows her to be an informed and intelligent critic

(33), too, is false with respect to scenario *B* and true on an opaque reading with respect to scenario *A* (Jane Grigson is informed and intelligent, but she is not a *chef de cuisine minceur*). In both of these cases, the scenarios *A* satisfy the opaque reading and a possibly separate reading in which the individual denoted by the subject has some specific individual in mind. Against their respective scenarios *B*, each sentence is false. In each of these cases, the individual denoted by the subject believes that the individual in question has the property indicated by the description but this is not sufficient to guarantee the truth of the sentence.

Furthermore, one can demonstrate that at least on the transparent reading, the object in question must actually satisfy the properties ascribed to it if the sentence is to be true—it is not sufficient that the individual denoted by the subject believes the properties are ascribed to the object:

(34) John wants to sketch a Moore statue—but he's mistaken: it's a Hepworth.

(35) John wants to sketch a Hepworth statue, mistakenly thinking it to be a Moore.

(34) cannot be used to describe the circumstances described by (35). (35) is a perfectly straightforward description of a mistake on the part of the subject where, significantly, the description *Hepworth statue* must be satisfied if the sentence is to be true (on the transparent reading). (34) on the other hand does not express a coherent proposition. On the opaque reading, the pronoun *it* has no obvious referent despite the linguistic clues that the referent has been established by the first conjunct. And on the transparent reading, the sentence is contradictory. In other words, the beliefs of the individual denoted

by the subject are not in general relevant at all to the understanding of the sentence—except in the cases already discussed.[14]

4.1.3 Want Predicates and Specificity

Earlier it was suggested that the Montague analysis of the opaque reading was not compatible with a specificity prediction internal to the intensional context. But now there are indications that the strategy of fixing the referent does bear some relation to the opaque reading. What is the precise nature of this relation? Consider the semantic properties of *try to P* and *want to P* informally in the first place. If we assume for simplicity at the moment that P is an embedded clause, we can say that *try* and *want* both indicate a relation between the individual denoted by the subject and the proposition indicated by P. In the case of *try*, the relation is one of carrying out actions among whose consequences it is hoped will be that the proposition expressed by the complement clause becomes true. In the case of *want* the relation is merely one of desiring: the individual denoted by the subject desires that the proposition expressed by the complement clause becomes true. Now in the examples we are concerned with, the interpretation of this formula is dependent on an existential quantifier. As already established, a straightforward way of guaranteeing the truth of an existentially quantified formula is to establish the truth of the same predicate with respect to a fixed individual. In exactly parallel fashion, if someone is seeking to obtain the truth of such a formula, they may well consider the most sure way of so doing is to effect the satisfaction of the predicate in question with respect to a fixed individual, thus automatically fulfilling their aim. In all these cases, there is no need to incorporate any specificiation of an individual relative to the beliefs of the individual denoted by the subject. We can anticipate exactly the phenomena displayed. If a speaker asserts of some individual John that he is seeking to make true an existentially quantified formula '$\exists x F(x)$', he might well have in mind as evidence that John was in fact trying to guarantee the truth of the existentially quantified proposition by making true the stronger proposition 'F(a)'. None of this reasoning is itself part of the proposition expressed. Consider again (31), retaining still the assumption that the complement of *want* is a full clause. John's mistaken belief that Rose was a Naitonal Front member only justifies an assertion of *John wants to marry a National Front member* if it can be established that John desires the truth of the proposition 'John marry a National Front member' *And* that he envisages marrying Rose as providing a means of guaranteeing that. Since such a verifying procedure is common ground, an utterer of such a sentence can take for granted that his hearer will deduce from the utterance that John may well have in mind someone he envisages as fulfilling the proposition "John marry a National Front member", which is what the speaker is asserting John wants.

Now in fact of course it is overly simplistic to assume that in a Montague analysis *try* and *want* take as second argument a clausal formula of type $\langle t \rangle$. Indeed they do not. Moreover the analysis of *look for* and *seek* involves yet a different syntactic category. In this latter case, the complement of *seek* in the logical representation is of type '$\langle s, \langle\langle s, \langle e,t \rangle\rangle, t \rangle\rangle$', an intensional object which is a function which at each index yields a set of properties. But the precise syntactic form of the relation between the subject and the existentially quantified expression does not significantly alter the nature of the explanation: it runs just as before. If John is trying to satisfy a complex property requiring the existence of at least one individual such that F is true of x, he may try to guarantee the satisfaction of that property with respect to a fixed individual. Taking steps to guarantee the satisfaction of such a property is in just the same way as before but the mirror image of taking steps to confirm that such a property is satisfied. In other words, the very same evidence which provides the surest means of establishing the satisfaction of a complex property that is dependent on an existentially quantified formula also provides a sure way of confirming that that property is satisfied. The principle applies exactly as in the simple cases.

Two further problems are entirely resolved by this analysis. First, there is the problem that one can look for an individual who doesn't exist, as in (36):

(36) Justin's looking for a unicorn, the one who laid her head in Queen Guinevere's lap.

The nonexistence of the required entity at the time of utterance itself is no bar to the truth of (36). Thus whether this property has a nonempty extension at the time of utterance, is irrelevant, for the item under interpretation—the complement of *look for*—is a function from indices to some complex property. The analysis given is entirely compatible with a model in which the extension of the quantified variable happens to be identical across all indices at which it does have an extension. Thus a relation between the individual denoted by the subject expression *Justin* and some complex property that is dependent on some individual, constant to all indices but not the present, falls out as just one of the possible cases of the relation between Justin and the property denoted by *looking for a unicorn*. Nothing further needs to be added about the case in which Justin is looking for some specific individual who doesn't in fact exist. This may be a perfectly reasonable way of seeking to satisfy the predicate according to the evidence Justin has at the time.

The second problem that falls out without further explanation is the fact that what people have in their minds as they seek to satisfy a property dependent on an existentially quantified expression may range from something particular, to wit a fixed individual—as in (32)—over a set of individuals—as in (37)—to a set of much less well-determined properties—as in (38):

(37) PC McGarry is looking for a member of the IRA.

(38) Bill's looking for a skirt for Joan.

Let us take (37) first. This may well be true in circumstances in which P. C. McGarry is in fact looking for the group of people who lodged in Mr. O'Casey's house last week. Being a member of the IRA is not a visually identifiable property. The only way to take steps to instantiate the property of having found such a person is to have evidence in connection with either a group or an individual that leads you to look for that set. Thus P. C. McGarry may well be going round asking about those three men who were lodging in Mr. O'Casey's house last week since he believes he has evidence that at least one of them is a member of the IRA. In his view, the most effective way at that time of finding a member of the IRA is to look for that set of three people. (38) presents an even less determinate case. The criteria people have in mind in seeking to satisfy a predicate such as 'having found a skirt for Joan' may be fairly vague. She may not be particularly fussy except that she hates pleats, but she needs it to be black with no patterns. None of this is pertinent to the semantic analysis of sentences of this type. We do not need to postulate separate analyses of the opaque understanding of *Justin's looking for an x*, depending on whether he has in mind a particular individual, an individual of a certain kind, or something yet less well-determined. Such cases are simply special cases of the combined analyses of indefinite noun-phrases as quantified expressions and specificity as a nonsemantic phenomenon concerned with on the one hand the evidence people bring to bear in forming a belief whose representation involves an existentially quantified expression or on the other hand the steps people take to guarantee the satisfaction of some complex property involving an existentially quantified expression. All that the analysis of the opaque understanding of sentences such as (28)—(38) requires is (i) the opaque reading as specified in a Montague analysis, (ii) the lexical content of the opacity-inducing predicates such as *want*, and (iii) the confirmation analysis already suggested for explaining the phenomenon of specificity in nonopaque contexts. Accordingly, we conclude that the phenomenon of specificity that arises in sentences containing opaque contexts is not expressed semantically as a part of either of the scope-differentiated propositions expressed by a sentence containing an indefinite noun phrase in the complement of an opacity-inducing predicate.

4.2 The Opacity of Belief Predicates

A similar style of explanation is equally applicable to the notoriously difficult belief cases. Here we shall sidestep the problem of whether belief involves a relation between an individual and a representation, and shall simply give logical forms of a standard intensional sort. Nothing hangs on this. Moreover in order to keep the problem within manageable proportions, we shall consider only the type of case in which a belief predicate containing an existentially quantified expression is predicated of a subject that is universally quantified, such as (39):

(39) Everyone in the Registry believes a Ph.D. student of Ruth's stole the coffee money.

Standard scope maneuvers yield at least the three forms (39a)–(39c) predicated to be interpretations of (39):

(39a) $\exists R_n \forall r$ [believe' $(r, \wedge[\exists P_i \forall p[S(p)]])$]

(39b) $\exists R_n \forall r \exists P_i \forall p$ [believe' $(r, \wedge[S(p)])$]

(39c) $\exists P_i \forall p \exists R_n \forall r$ [believe' $(r, \wedge[S(p)])$]

The first question is whether this type of sentence is ambiguous between three such scope-differentiated interpretations or whether belief sentences should be taken to be fully opaque (in the first instance we are only concerned with (39a) and (39c) since the question of (39b) only arises if these two are distinct). There are two pieces of evidence that there is ambiguity here. First, it is well known that sentences of the form (40) can report a consistent belief:

(40) Everyone in the Registry believes a student of Ruth's isn't a student of Ruth's.

Second, the two interpretations represented as (39a) and (39c) are logically independent. Compare scenarios (39A) and (39B):

(39A) There is a student of Ruth's about whom everyone in the Registry has a belief that he stole the coffee money. In addition to this, the Registry mistakenly believe that student to be a student of Deirdre Wilson's (who works in the neighbouring college).

Against (39A), (39) is true under interpretation (39c), but under the interpretation (39a) it is false. Contrariwise against (39B), (39) is true under interpretation (39a) and false under interpretation (39c):

(39B) Everyone in the Registry has a belief that some Ph.D. student of Ruth's stole the coffee money, but the only person with whom they associate this belief is in fact a student of Deirdre Wilson's whom they all mistakenly believe to be a Ph.D. student of Ruth's.

(We shall come back to the matter of the discreteness of their beliefs shortly.) Moreover, it is not simply that the forms (39a) and (39c) have those truth values against the two scenarios. (39) itself is unquestionably true against both scenarios. Thus, minimally, we must allow forms such as (39a) and (39c) as representations of truth conditionally distinct interpretations of (39) and we include also the less controversial (39b).

4.2.1 Specificity and Propositional Attitudes

The analysis of specificity we have already set up leads to unambiguous predictions vis a vis each of (39a)–(39c). (39c) is the case where the speaker may have someone in mind as evidence for his assertion of a wide scope existentially quantified proposition; and in that case each of the members of the Registry is claimed to have a belief about whatever individual satisfies that proposition, that he stole the coffee money. The case of (39b) is identical to (3)–(4) discussed initially. The speaker may have particular people in mind about whom the people in the Registry have beliefs as long as he has also a means of individuating the people in the Registry. (As in the case of (3)–(4) the implication can be brought out by adding the word *specific*.) So if the speaker of (39) knows the Registry contains the Registrar, his assistant, and two typists, he may also know that the Registar has a belief that Cliff stole the coffee money, that his assistant has a belief that Judith stole the coffee money, and the two typists that Helen stole the coffee money. Though each of these is, say, indeed a Ph.D. student of Ruth's, in each case the member of the Registry in question may hold a mistaken belief that whomever they had in mind is a student of Deirdre Wilson's at the neighboring college (since the two sets of Linguistics students float freely between the two colleges, there are let us suppose genuine grounds for mistaking any one of Ruth's students to be a student of Deirdre Wilson's). Moreover, to do so is irrelevant to the truth of (39) under this interpretation (39b) as long as each member of the Registry believes some student to have stolen the coffee money; and those students that they severally have in mind are Ph.D. students of Ruth's. Furthermore, against such a scenario, (39) is true despite the fact that it is false both under interpretation (39a) and under interpretation (39c).

The remaining case is (39a) where each member of the Registry is claimed to have a belief corresponding directly to the logical form of the complement clause: to wit '$\exists p \ S(p)$'. On the same principle as outlined earlier in this paper, each might have as a reason for knowing that they hold that belief, a belief about a particular individual that they know satisfies the predicate S. By the same principle, a speaker asserting (39) on this interpretation (39a) will know that the hearer may, equally, deduce that each person in the Registry might have some individual in mind as satisfying the predicate "being a student of Ruth's who stole the coffee money." In this case, the individuals denoted by the subject expression are assumed to recognize as distinct a belief of the form '$\exists x \ F(x)$' AND a belief of the form '$F(a)$', with their belief in '$F(a)$' constituting their evidence for holding a belief of the form '$\exists x \ F(x)$'. However there is a more indirect evidence which might justify a speaker having a belief of the form (39a). Cases can arise in which each of the individuals denoted by the subject expression does not in fact articulate to themselves anything other than a belief of the form '$F(a)$'. But since it would follow from their beliefs that they also believed '$\exists x \ F(x)$', knowing that someone has a belief of the form '$F(a)$' is sufficient evidence for asserting that they have a belief of the form '$\exists x\, F(x)$'. So it appears that a speaker may use his own belief in 'J believes $F(a)$' as evidence for an assertion of the form 'J believes $\exists x\, F(x)$'. The grounds whereby a speaker deems himself to have evidence for some relatively weak proposition are thus mimicking rules of inference such as existential introduction. In support of this consider (40)–(41):

(40) John believes that Stewart tried to rape him at a late night garden party.

(41) John believes that a man tried to rape him at a late night garden party.

(40) does not itself entail (41)—John may genuinely believe what is reported of him in (40) but not believe that Stewart is a man (Stewart being a very successful transvestite). However, if the *speaker* has grounds for thinking both that John believes that Stewart tried to rape him at a late night garden party and (mistakenly as it turns out) that John believes that Stewart is a man, then these two pieces of evidence considered jointly *do* constitute sufficient evidence for asserting (41), even though John may not himself have articulated a belief in anything like that form.

This indirect form of evidence lies at the heart of the controversial cases pointed out by Geach (Geach, 1972), in which assertions involving belief contexts allow the possibility of identity across beliefs of different individuals without being shared by the speaker of the sentence, as apparently in (42):

(42) Each of the farmers in the village believes a witch has killed his chickens.

Geach's so-called "intentional identity" problem is this. How is it that (42) can succeed in conveying a belief, not necessarily shared by the speaker, that there may be just one witch doing the various killings? The answer does not, in our view, lie in postulating a fourth nonstandard form in which existence quantifiers do not entail existence as some would have us believe. It lies merely in two sorts of evidence for the truth of (42): the evidence that might lead the individuals described to hold the belief "A witch has killed my chickens" on the one hand, *AND* the evidence that might lead the speaker to hold a belief that the individuals described have a belief that "A witch has killed my chickens" on the other hand. Consider the individuals themselves first, and the grounds whereby each one of them might come to hold the belief "A witch has killed my chickens." The evidence is not likely to be direct observation—the essence of witchcraft is that its powers involve magic. Furthermore, rumor is rife in a village, bad news travels fast, and people are always ready to believe the worst on the scantiest evidence. It is unlikely in the circumstances described that the villagers have no knowledge of each other's beliefs. In addition, the extension of *witch* at any one time was commonly assumed to be a one member set. Thus if all members of a village for whatever reason separately believe "A witch killed my chickens," by far the most likely situation is that they will all believe there is just one individual satisfying the predicate "killed my chickens" in each case. Now add to this the evidence which would justify a speaker asserting that every farmer in the village believes a witch destroyed his chickens. All that is required as evidence is that taking each individual farmer *f* in turn, the speaker has evidence that *f* believes that some particular individual stole his chickens and that individual is a witch. According to this evidence, each farmer *f* believes, "There is someone who is a witch and she stole my chickens." For the same sociological reasons as before, the evidence with respect to each farmer is likely to relate to a particular individual (i.e., the local witch). But this does not need to be characterised by a different nonstandard quantification quantifying over witches without existential commitment. And it does not commit the speaker to agreeing with the farmers that anyone is a witch either. It simply falls out as a special case covered by the proposition expressed, as long as we can assume a process mimicking existential generalization inside the opaque context. So it turns out that we have two different kinds of evidence for asserting (42), both of which involve the individuals denoted by the subject expression having beliefs with respect to a single individual (in the one case they are unable to identify her, but in the other they are), and neither of which commit the speaker to believing in the existence of any such individual himself. Hence the apparent illusion of such an individual as part of the proposition expressed.

Confirmation of this general approach whereby individual entities corresponding directly to the indefinite noun phrase are considered only to be part of the evidence for holding a belief which involves existential quantification, lies in the contrast shown by the extremely similar (43):

(43) Though there are, as far as I know, no gypsies in Scotland any more, each of the farmers on the isolated mountain holdings believes that a gypsy killed his chickens.

In this case, the relevant reading is where each farmer has a belief of the form '$\exists g$ (g killed my chickens)'. In this case, the nature of the farmer's evidence for his belief is not likely to be general, triggered by rumor. There is accordingly little possibility that in believing 'A gypsy killed my chickens' each farmer shares with other farmers a conception as to who might satisfy that predicate. Since the difference falls out from the different kinds of evidence likely to be available in the two cases (42) and (43), there is no need to analyse them as expressing different kinds of proposition.

The point deserves reiterating. We have one problem and two alternative solutions. The problem is that there appear to be interpretations in which entities are common to the beliefs of a set of individuals while not necessitating existential implications with respect to the model itself. One solution is to assume this interpretation is propositionally distinct from the other interpretations and requires a nonstandard model of interpretation to characterise it (either right-left, scope-inducing operators as well as left-right, or existence, operators, which do not entail existence, or some other unorthodox device). The other solution is to assume that this apparent interpretation is, qua proposition expressible by the sentence, illusory, arising solely from the evidence that entitles a speaker to make an assertion about other people's beliefs. Since the latter requires only a standard logical analysis and quite uncontroversial assumptions about the relation between the proposition expressed and supporting evidence, we assume that it is preferable.

4.2.2 Are Natural Language Variables Restricted?

It might be argued that part of what we have raised is an artificial problem since, at least in the case of (39), the specificity phenomenon relative to the individuals denoted by the subject can be represented in a system which allows unrestricted variables, as in (39d):

(39d) $\exists x \, \forall y \, [R(y) \supset (\text{believe}' \, (y, \wedge [P(x) \, \& \, S(x)]))]$

There are however three pieces of evidence that the restricted variable notation and unitary account of specificity are correct, and the form (39d) incorrect. First, notice, apparently in favour of the independent status of (39d), that it is possible to set up circumstances to demonstrate that the forms (39c) and (39d) are logically independent. And these circumstances are none other than (39A) and (39B). Against (39A) (39c) is true and (39d) false, and against (39B), (39c) false and (39d) true. But it is no coincidence that it is these circumstances which discriminate between (39c) and (39d), for it is these circumstances which were used to demonstrate the independence of (39c) and (39d). What is impossible is to simultaneously demonstrate the independence of (39c) and (39d) *and* the independence of (39c) and (39a). Since we know in any case that we require (39a), there is no independent reason for postulating (39d).

The second argument concerns the binary quantifiers. In the case of *every* and the indefinite article, the restricted, effectively binary, quantification is not essential. With a quantifier such as *most*, binary quantification IS essential. Suppose we now replace *every* by *most* as in (44):

(44) Most people in the Registry believe a Ph.D. student of Ruth's stole the coffee money.

Here we have three forms as before, which we represent schematically as:

(44a) $\exists R_n \, \text{most} \, r \, [\text{believe}' \, (r, \hat{} [\exists P_1 \, \forall p \, [S(p)])])$

(44b) $\exists R_n$ most r $\exists P_1$ $\forall p$ [believe' $(r, \wedge[S(p)])]$

(44c) $\exists P_1$ $\forall p \exists R_n$ most r [believe' $(r, \wedge[S(p)])]$

but no form (44d). Now if (39d) were a genuinely distinct propositional form of (39), then the circumstances of which (39d) is a description should have no parallel among the possible uses of (44) since there is no way of representing such circumstances with restricted quantification. What we find to the contrary is that the range of phenomena describable by (39) carries over in exact parallel to (44). The circumstances for which (39d) seemed to be a characterization were those where the entire Registry have some particular individual in mind whom they think is a student of Ruth's and stole the coffee money. And it is this case which we analysed as merely shared evidence for their separate belief '$\exists p$ $S(p)$'. Now just as the entire Registry can share the evidence for believing '$\exists p$ $S(p)$' so the majority can. Thus (44) can be used to describe circumstances in which most people in the Registry have some particular individual in mind. But since such circumstances have to be explained in terms of evidence rather than in terms of a distinct propositional form in the case of (44), there is no reason to postulate such a form in the case of (39).

Thirdly, there is direct empirical evidence that (39d) is not a distinct propositional form. Consider (45):

(45) Everyone in the Registry believes that a student of Ruth's who isn't a student of Ruth's stole the coffee money.

If (39d) were a proposition expressible by (39), (45) should have one non-contradictory reading, the one of that form. (It is contradictory assuming forms of the type (39a)–(39c). Moreover, since this form allows for the only noncontradictory interpretation, this should be the predominant interpretation. But it is not. (45) is irremediably inconsistent, thus demonstrating that (39d) is not a proposition expressible by (39).[15] Thus the evidence from belief contexts ultimately buttresses the explanation of specificity in terms of the reconstruction of evidence confirming the truth of the existential proposition in question.

The discussion throughout this paper has ignored what many people might deem to be the crucial data—concerning anaphora. This is deliberate: It is only too easy to set up multiple ambiguity of the antecedent to match the semantic properties of the anaphor, but any such move is a brute force solution and not an explanation. In particular, if we are to respect the constraints of compositionality and identify *John hit a woman* as a part of *John hit a woman and she sat down*, then the puzzle left at the end of this paper is to explain how an anaphor can appear to be a referential expression while its antecedent is not.

In summary, the evidence of both nonopaque and opaque contexts lead to the same conclusions: (i) indefinite noun phrases of the type we have considered here are invariably existentially quantified expressions; (ii) the apparent possibility of interpretations of such indefinite noun phrases as specific is due to evidence justifying the truth of the proposition they are contained in, and not to a distinct propositional content.

EPILOGUE

The conclusion as stated might seem to flatly conflict with the Kamp/ Heim analysis that indefinite NPs are variables, sometimes construed as dependent on an existential quantifier, at other times on some other quantification. In detail, it does. Cormack and Kempson deliberately omitted any account of the anaphora facts (and also of generics and other universals). In contrast, anaphoric dependencies set up by indefinites are the prime goal of the explanation of the DR/File Theory. These theories provide a solution to the 'puzzle' we left. If we add some of these anaphora data, we can see what problem the DR/File Theory addressed, what solution it proposes, and how the incompatibility with the analysis of specificity proposed by Cormack and Kempson is more apparent than real.

In simple sentence sequences, indefinites behave quite unlike quantified expressions with respect to anaphora. First, quantifiers in general have their scope domain delimited by the sentence in which they occur. They cannot bind pronouns in some following sentence. Hence:

(46) Every one$_1$ at the party insisted on driving home. ?*He$_1$ was stopped by the police and given a drink test, which he$_1$ failed.

Indefinites *can* provide antecedents for pronouns in some following sentence. hence:

(47) A friend$_1$ of mine insisted on driving home. He$_1$ was stopped by the police and given a drink test, which he$_1$ failed.

(Example (47) is the type of case we raise as a problem in conclusion.) Secondly, in certain embedded environments, indefinites appear to be able to bind pronouns as variables within their scope outside the domain over which as quantifiers they could coherently do so. So in (48):

(48) Every man who is wearing a green tie has put it on to show his support for the Green Party.

A green tie is the antecedent for *it*. *A green tie* is not a referring expression, it does not pick out a fixed individual, yet as an existentially quantified expression, its scope domain could only be smaller than the quantifying expression *every man* . . . in whose restrictive clause it is contained. Schematically:

$\forall x \, ((\exists y \; x \text{ wearing } y, \, y \text{ green tie}) \rightarrow (x \text{ has put } it \text{ on to} \ldots))$

But that being so, it can't bind the pronoun *it* because this is outside the possible binding domain of the existential quantifier. The only apprent way for *a green tie* to coherently bind the pronoun *it* is to analyse the indefinite NP as involving wide scope universal quantification:

$\forall x \, \forall y \, ((x \text{ man}, \, x \text{ wearing } y, \, y \text{ green tie}) \, (x \text{ has put } y \text{ on to} \ldots))$

So sometimes the indefinite seems to correspond to a universal quantifier, sometimes an existential. Indefinites even apparently vacillate according as they are in the antecedent or consequent of a conditional:

(49) If a man comes up to you and asks you to dance, ignore him.

(50) If John comes in, then a man will come up to you and ask you to dance.

In (49) the assertion is universal:

'For all entities x such that x comes up to you and asks you to dance, then ignore x'.

In (50) the assertion is existential:

'For all occasions that John comes in, there will be a man x such that x comes up to you and asks you to dance'.

To these three problems, Kamp-Heim offer the same solution: the indefinite is what is in common to these various interpretations, to wit, a variable. Its interpretation as existentially or otherwise quantified is due to the semantic properties of the environment in which it is contained. These semantic properties can either be reconstructed direct from the truth conditions of the formula in which the variable is contained, or by syntactic construction of the relevant quantificational effects at the clausal level. Kamp chooses the strictly semantic route; Heim proffers both. Whatever the choice, the effect is the same. The indefinite as a variable can be used as an antecedent for a pronoun, as long as the quantificational force which induces the quantificational interpretation is taken to have scope large enough to include both antecedent and pronoun. And its interpretation as universally or existentially construed will depend on that induced quantificational interpretation. That interpretation will be universal if construed within the restrictive clause of some universal operator such as *if* or *every*, and will be existential otherwise. Now the only cases considered in the Cormack and Kempson account of indefinites are cases with the indefinite existentially construed. In the type of case analysed as universally construed by Kamp and Heim the specificity phenomenon does not arise. It is only if the indefinite is construed as outside the restrictive clause of a universal quantifier that it is construed existentially and hence subject to specificity effects, as in (51):

(51) Every man who is talking to a friend of mine over there is laughing at her.

This vacillation of the indefinite as to whether or not the indefinite is within the scope of some larger quantifier might seem to impose a commitment to a quantificational analysis of the indefinite, because surely it is quantifiers that can vary in scope with respect to each other. But on the Heim analysis, the quantifier extraction process (which the Cormack-Kempson analysis pre-supposes) is a syntactic process, called "quantifier raising" (QR) in the GB model, applying to all NPs, moving NPs into an operator position. Indefinite NPs, AS NPs, are subject to such movement. The result of such movement will be a configuration in which their quantificational force is induced from the larger environment in which they are now contained. So we can combine the Heim analysis with the Cormack-Kempson account of specificity, pre-dicting that the specificity phenomenon will arise exclusively with existentially construed indefinites. The conclusion about the specificity phenomenon itself remains untouched.

The claim that specificity phenomena never affect truth-conditional con-tent is of considerable pragmatic interest. Within the new Relevance Theory framework, a distinction is made between the intrinsic (linguistic) content of a sentence and the truth-conditional content of propositions expressible by a sentence. This is because the intrinsic properties of many expressions under-determine their truth-conditional content. By the Kamp-Heim analysis, in-definites are a paradigm case. Linguistically speaking, indefinite NPs introduce semantic variables; the truth-content ascribable to them finally is quantified. Within this new framework, pragmatic processes not only underly the impli-cature phenomena familiar from Grice, but also the characterization of explicit truth-conditional content for all cases where the linguistically specified content underdetermines its truth-conditional content. Indefinite NPs being less than fully determinate in content, one might a priori expect that they *could* be pragmatically enriched to yield "specific interpretations." On this view, no linguistic ambiguity would have to be postulated: the "specific interpretations" would merely constitute another example of pragmatically induced truth-conditional content of the utterance. But the force of the arguments in this article is that this isn't so. The specificity phenomena do not, according to the claims made in this paper, constitute pragmatic enrichments of some under-determined input. They are extraneous to the literal meaning of the utterance.

If we put together the Heim-Kemp analysis and the Relevance-theoretic account of communication we can explain why this is so—why the specificity phenomena are never part of the truth-theoretic content of the utterance attributable to the speaker and yet seem to contribute to the overall interpretation. On the Relevance account, the intrinsic content of an expression as specified in the grammar is a fully encoded property, an essential attribute of the interpretation of every occurrence of that expression. Pragmatic principles then apply to such specification enriching it to some truth-conditional content intended by the speaker and manifestly recoverable by the hearer. This process is invariably and ONLY an enrichment. On the Heim-Kamp account of indefinites, they are intrinsically encoded in the grammar as variables. They can be enriched by some manifest quantification to yield a truth-theoretic content, because such a move *is* a legitimate enrichment of their intrinsic specification. But they could NOT be given a name as a truth-theoretic content by processes of enrichment: A variable must ultimately be interpreted as if quantificationally bound. Names stand in contrast to variables, subject to quite different processes of semantic interpretation. Insofar as indefinite NPs can be construed as conveying information about a specific but unnamed individual, then given the Heim analysis, this will *only* be possible through some indirect process of reasoning. Indirect processes of reasoning are the basis of implicatures. So, according to the Heim analysis as absorbed into Relevance-theoretic assumptions about the relation between lexical content, truth-conditional content, and implicatures, specificity phenomena could only be derived as implicatures (strictly, as "contextual implications"). Sperber-Wilson and Heim-Kamp asumptions not only jointly predict this status for the specificity phenomenon, but they can provide the basis of explaining why they are derived at all. According to Relevance Theory, the interpretation of utterances is always driven by the search for chains of inference at least processing cost to the hearer. An utterance incorporating a name *would* provide a much richer chain of reasoning than the corresponding existentially quantified expression because inferences combining the predicate provided with additional information about the particular individual selected would be derivable. In order to have committed himself to an existentially quantified assertion, the speaker must have had evidence of its truth. The commonest form of evidence is to know that the predicate holds of some fixed individual. Since this fact is known to the hearer as well as the speaker, the hearer may be able to reconstruct the evidence the speaker had in mind in making the existentially quantified assertion, and so obtain a richer set of inferential effects. The speaker knows that the hearer can reason in this way, and hence he may on occasion use the indefinite to produce these inferential effects. He can achieve the effect even in the absence of any jointly known name for the individual. This reconstruction however will always take the form of an indirect conclusion.

The details of this account of course remain to be worked out. But this characterization seems to be essentially correct. So even by manipulating the barest sketches of the Kamp-Heim theory and Sperber-Wilson's Relevance Theory, we can see that the shift in theoretical assumptions since the Cormack and Kempson paper was first written, do not disturb the force of the conlcusion. The "specificity" phenomena are not linguistic phenomena; indeed they are not even part of a pragmatically derived truth-conditional content of the utterance.

NOTES

1. The situation with respect to plural indefinites is more complicated. If we assume separate quantification over the set in question and its members as in Kempson and Cormack (1981), then though the set may be indexically fixed and hence immune to scope variation, the quantification over the members of that set may interact with other propositional operators in the sentence to give varying interpretations. However even in these cases, such distinctions are hypothetical since they are never in fact variations that can be expressed using such indefinite noun phrases *tout court* (cf. our arguments to this effect in connection with Table III). The description of such rigid designation of a set entity as scopeless is therefore harmless.

2. With the minor caveat of note 1, which does not apply in the cases considered here.

3. Even the case of *certain* is dubious: *I asked each student to bring a certain book* seems clearly compatible with my having asked George to bring *Pride and Prejudice*, Deirdre to bring *The Grand Sophy*, and Bill to bring *Superman*.

4. We assume as before the Kempson and Cormack (1981) notation: T_n is an n-membered set of teachers, $t \in T$; P_1 a one-member set of pupils, $p \in P$; R_2 a two-member set of reports, $r \in R$; S 'has sent in'.

5. In 1982 when this paper was written, we took *he* to be a neutral form of pronoun. We retain *he* to refer to speakers, but use *she* to refer to hearers for clarity.

6. Unless there is an interpretation in which the existential quantifier is deemed to have wider scope than the conditional. In this case, the unitary analysis would predict the consistency of (14) under this interpretation only. This would involve extraction of the quantified expression out of the conjunction. The extent to which this is generally possible, we leave on one side.

7. C: cars, $c \in C$, P "having been painted by John."

8. This was pointed out to us by Hans Kamp.

9. It has been suggested to us by A. Garnham (personal communication) that this analysis cannot be correct in the face of examples such as *A guest of the president is staying in that room* where Tom, the speaker of the sentence, utters it to Dick and Harry, knowing that Dick will take the subject NP to refer to the head of the KGB, whereas Harry, who is not privy to such state secrets, will take it as denoting merely whoever fills the property of being a guest of the president who is staying in that room. However this is not a convincing example. In the scenario given, only Dick and Tom are supposed to have been informed that the head of the KGB is staying in that room. Thus, for Dick, Tom's utterance will certainly violate the maxim of relevance in being so underinformative. But for Dick there is a conflicting prohibition: "State secrets cannot be mentioned in general conversation." Thus, in the circumstances described, what Tom said was the most relevant thing he could say compatible with what is permitted. He is using a nonreferring expression knowing that for Dick it is in obvious violation of the maxim of relevance, and knowing that in virtue of this violation, it will lead to Dick's recalling who is in fact staying in that room. It does not follow that what he has said is a proposition containing a referring expression, even though he may intend that proposition to lead at least one of his hearers to recover a different and stronger proposition. The case is in our view parasitic on normal use.

10. Detailed attempts to define what constitutes an opaque context are given by Partee (1974) and Klein (1978). We shall not attempt such a definition here, but as will become clear during the course of the argument, we are adopting the Montague account of opaque contexts advocated in Partee (1974) as created by an unreducible intensionality in the logical structure. Incidentally this avoids the problem noticed by Klein of predicting that negation creates an opaque context.

11. Unless that NP were itself embedded in some further opaque context. We ignore this additional complexity for the time being.

12. Given that in any complex sentence the ambiguity is more than twofold, the binary terminology of *transparent/opaque* might be misleading. But initially we consider only positive nonembedded cases, and in these cases the problem does not arise.

13. (Note added in 1989.) It might be argued that the problem could be resolved by invoking a meaning postulate guaranteeing that worlds in which an individual believes they want some proposition P are worlds in which they want that proposition P. But the only way of using such a postulate to bolster up the Fodor view that even on the transparent reading of the indefinite NP the descriptive content of that NP is relative to the beliefs of the subject is to reduce the transparent reading to the opaque reading.

14. Saarinen's claim (Saarinen, 1981) that the truth of the transparent reading of *John wants to meet an author of Principia Mathematica* remaining unchanged in 1981 as in 1951 requires an operator without existential commitments, is based on the mistaken assumption that existence claims are restricted to literally the time of utterance. This is clearly not so, as witness the current truth of: *Gareth Evans may yet prove to be one of the great philosophers of the twentieth century* [d. 1980]. Cf. Klein (1978) for further arguments.

15. Notice that this alternative is in any case ruled out if quantified expressions in natural language are taken to be generalized quantifiers.

HAROLD SKULSKY

METAPHORESE

The view of figurative utterance I will be presenting here is (roughly) that the figurative speaker or writer has switched abruptly from the vernacular to a dialect that is semantically richer. A sense of a term is figurative with respect to what the listener or reader understood, before his interpretative double take, to be the medium of communication; in this ostensible medium—the vernacular—the sense doesn't belong to the term at all: in a traditional and revealing usage, the sense is *improper*. So the task of the figurative interpreter is not to *recall* the relevant senses, but to *learn* them. One relies on one's mastery of a shared language, in this case, in the very act of mastering it. I will go on, more tentatively, to suggest that the new dialect—the metaphorese—improves on the vernacular in still a second way that underlies our talk about figurative language as "imagery." In general, if I am right, the oddity of figurative meaning is not how it is attached to language but how it attaches people to each other. What is of fundamental interest here isn't cognition or semantics but a special kind of cooperative rapport.

This view will of course need to be spelled out more fully and defended against various obvious objections, including a challenge to its usefulness. But there are two important preliminaries. The first will be a review of the classical division of tropes—the manageably small set of basic ways in which a listener or reader can operate on a vernacular sense to get a possible alternative sense in the impromptu dialect of conversation. The classical account seems to me essentially right here, and important. Forgetting it is one of the reasons for the attractiveness of recent fictive, creative, and speech act theories of metaphor. These, the main rivals to my own view, are my second preliminary order of business; if they are right, figurative utterance involves no novel linguistic sense, much less a novel dialect. So in the polemical section of this paper I've tried, in some detail, to show that they are wrong. Readers who would rather dispense with this demonstration are invited to skip Section II.

I

The ballerina danced *fluently*.
The lecture *crumbled*.
He is not only a bore but a *burr*.
It is *outside* my experience.
Their friendship is *foursquare*.

Metaphors can occur in various parts of speech, as the illustrations were picked to show.[1] Typically, the figurative meaning of the metaphorical term is a part of what the term *implies*, either by itself or as conjoined with background assumptions (to be discussed later). Something done fluently is done (among other things) continuously and unhesitatingly. What crumbled disintegrated, lost cohesiveness, etc. A burr is something tenacious, something hard to get rid of, etc. To be outside of something is not to be part of it. What is foursquare is stable, reliable, etc. This is not to say that the figurative meaning of a metaphorical adverb, say, is the literal meaning of some other adverb; there may be no such term. The point is simply that, to the extent that grammar assigns distinct types of meaning to different parts of speech, the figurative meanings will conform to type.[2]

Aristotle holds that in some cases the figurative meaning of a metaphorical term is *not* implied by the literal—is not on a higher level of generality. In such cases literal meaning is to figurative as species is to species. But his sole example does not support this claim. In "having drained away the soul with a blade," "drained away" is supposed to mean figuratively just *cut off*, both draining and cutting being species of removing ([1]: 1457b13–16). But "drained" by itself is clearly generic; it is the modification by "blade" that specifies a *sort* of removal. What Aristotle classifies as analogical metaphor also tells against the species-species analysis; "the sunset of life" picks out old age, not because "sunset" figuratively means *old age*, but because "sunset" implies, and hence here means, *final stage*; modification by "life" is what generates the definite description ([1]: 1457b16–20). Perhaps there is a species-species trope all the same; I will reserve "metaphor" for the trope based on implication. One last perennial source of confusion in Aristotle's account is his emphasis on likeness as the ground of metaphor—presumably likeness between the object of a metaphorical description and the things literally denoted by the metaphorical predicate.[3] There is such a likeness only if the object really has the property figuratively expressed by the predicate. Little Ned need not in fact be messy at meals, and hence need not have the property expressed by "pig" in a defamatory remark about him, for the remark to make metaphorical sense.

I believe that, with the noted exceptions, my account of metaphor is thus far substantially the one Aristotle bequeathed to classical rhetoric. It is true that Aristotle's successor restricted the term "metaphor" to cases in which a literal alternative is available; a metaphor coined to fill a gap in the vocabulary is called a catachresis ("eye" of a needle, "leg" of a table.)[4] But the standard of alternativeness here is lax. According to Quintilian, a metaphor is either more significant or more appropriate than the corresponding literal term ([22]: 5–6; cf. [10]); it is descriptively or evaluatively richer. But if so, the terms are not synonymous and perhaps not even logically equivalent. In fact, if we are to judge by Quintilian's illustration of a "far-fetched" metaphor, some poets go wrong precisely because it is impossible to get a metaphorical term to express no more than what is literally expressible by some other term. If all Furius Bibaculus intended when he wrote of Jupiter's bespitting the Alps with snow was that Jupiter covered them with snow, the intention was doomed;[5] the preference of "bespit" to "cover" needs to be justified by its salient implications, especially that of contempt for the object being covered. For better or worse, the metaphorical term is "more significant" than any literal one; it is ill adapted for introduction as a synonym. Classical rhetoric acknowledges this interesting fact. So it is at least misleading to dismiss that tradition as defending a naive "substitution view" of metaphor.[6]

Metaphor is not the only figure of speech, and a lot of confusion can be avoided by keeping the relevant distinctions firmly in mind—though here the classical treatment needs a bit of logical tidying up.[7] Where a metaphorical predicate is true but pointlessly true on a literal reading, it is traditionally classified as a synecdoche of species for genus: "I'm human, after all" (where the conversational assumption is that being human implies being fallible). By contrast, synecdoche of genus for species *is* properly distinguished from metaphor. No implication of "vehicle" will gloss the uninformative occurrence of the term in "His vehicle won the Indianapolis 500." In such cases of gratuitous generality, the context or background assumptions impose a hierarchical structure on the class involved (vehicles); "vehicle" means *vehicle par excellence*. As with literal terms, a sense or intension—*vehicle of the only sort worth discussing*—permits a reference or extension—the set of automobiles. The form of a metonymic sense ("He drank two *cups* of coffee") is *thing standing in relation R* (e.g., contents of) *to some F* (e.g., cup), where R is supplied by context or conversational assumptions and F is the literal sense of the metonymic term ("cup"). Other standard metonymic relations: cause, effect, product, producer, instance, part, whole.

When I warned against forgetting that metaphor is not alone among figures of speech, I had a particular confusion in mind. It consists in producing a specimen of some nonmetaphorical figure as a counterexample to ordinary notions of metaphor. Thus Searle argues that unemotional John Doe is metaphorically "cold" even though "cold" taken literally does not imply being unemotional: "I think the only answer to the question, 'What is the relation between cold things and unemotional people?' that would justify the use of 'cold' as a metaphor for lack of emotion is simply that as a matter of perceptions, sensibilities, and linguistic practices, people find the notion of coldness associated in their minds with lack of emotion" ([25]: 108). If this is right, then to be precise about the figure we need to know a little more about *how* these notions are associated. If one of them automatically recalls the other, then we have one sort of metonymy of cause for effect (or vice versa). If the notions are associated by a folklore assumtpion that people with low temperature are unemotional, or the converse, then we have another sort of causal metonymy. But suppose (to take another of Searle's examples) we are told that extraordinarily impassive Richard Roe is a "block of ice"; what figure is this? None, I think, that we have considered so far, and though it is common enough there is no traditional name for it; in this case, one of the implications of a predicate does indeed apply to the subject (who is metonymically "cold"), but only figuratively. The situation would be somewhat different if Searle were mistaken and the two senses of "cold" were linked only by "linguistic practice" and not by "perception" and "sensibility." Then "block of ice" would derive its figurative meaning from a homonym of the word it logically implies (viz., from the psychological term "cold") on no other ground than the homonymy; we would have a pun by proxy, akin to what is called metalepsis in classical rhetoric.

II

The moral of my story thus far is that figurative sense derives from literal (taken together with shared lore or assumptions) by one of a number of conventional operations. But this kind of description will not be very helpful if the distinction between senses it relies on is false or misleading. What, for example, if the only sense really involved is what we call the literal? I think that the most attractive rivals to the classical view of metaphor, and to the view I will be presenting later, are attempts to weaken or do away with the distinction. In this polemical phase of my discussion, I will try to show that these attempts fail.

We can begin with the most familiar and currently least popular of the literalist theses: that metaphor is an elliptical comparison in which the metaphorical term occurs in its ordinary sense.

Searle disposes of this view as follows:

When I say metaphorically 'Sally is a block of ice,' I am not necessarily quantifying over blocks of ice at all. My utterance does not entail literally that there is a block of ice. . . . This point is even more obvious if we take expressions used as metaphors which have a null extension. If I say Sally is a dragon, that does not entail literally that there is a dragon. Or another way to see the thing is to note that the negative sentence is just as metaphorical as the affirmative. If I say Sally is not a block of ice, that, I take it, does not invite the absurd question: What block of ice is it that you are comparing Sally with, in order to say that she is not like it? ([25]: 100–101)

This argument fails to produce a difference between the entailments of metaphors and comparisons; the similes "Sally is like a dragon (not like a block of ice)" don't entail the existence of the items mentioned either. The point of the former simile, for example, is that Sally has a trait that dragons would also have if they existed. This doesn't entail the existence of dragons. But it is partly about them, and Searle seems to me to be right in thinking that "Sally is a dragon" is not. In reply to the comparison, it would not be incoherent or irrelevant to ask: "*How* is Sally like dragons?" In reply to the metaphorical ascription of dragonhood, it would; that claim is not about dragons, not even in the capacity of what Black calls a secondary subject. The appropriate question here would be: "What do you mean by 'dragon'?"

Searle assumes that the most plausible candidate for the paraphrase of a metaphor is a simile that fails to specify the point of comparison. But this seems to be wrong. It's inappropriate to ask the metaphorical speaker to specify Sally's dragon trait (T) because "dragon" already does so; what the speaker means by "is a dragon" is not *has a dragon trait*, but just *has T*. And it is the particular trait that becomes one of the dictionary meanings of a metaphorical word when the metaphor dies. "Pest" (of a person) means *intolerable nuisance*, not *thing somehow like a pest*. If (for the sake of argument) a metaphorical word abbreviated a comparison, the specificity of dead metaphors suggests a comparison of the form exemplified by *X is like a dragon in ferocity*. But this is equivalent to *X is ferocious, and dragons would be too, if they existed*. Can a quibbler show that a speaker is mistaken in describing X as (metaphorically) a dragon by showing that dragons might not be ferocious, or that being a dragon is compatible with being meek? Surely, the quibble can't get off the ground; the subject of dragon temperament hasn't come up at all.[8] It seems that metaphorical terms don't occur literally, at least as part of an elliptical comparison.

Another way of weakening the distinction between literal and figurative meaning is to maintain, with Black, that understanding a metaphor is an image-forming process based on "interaction" between the implications of two so-called literal senses, those of a subject and predicate (or "secondary subject"). A metaphorical description is not a statement, and hence is neither true nor false; it is a juxtaposition of concepts designed to encourage the hearer to devise a way of correlating parts and features of the subject—say, man—with parts and features of the secondary subject—say, wolf—that will allow the man-concept to be treated as an image of the wolf-concept. To say that man is a wolf is not to attribute wolf-traits to man but rather to invite the hearer to "view" man as a wolf: "If man is a wolf, he preys upon other animals, is fierce, hungry, engaged in constant struggle, a scavenger. . . . Any human traits that can without undue strain be talked about in 'wolf-language' will be rendered prominent, and any that cannot will be pushed into the background. The wolf-metaphor . . . *organizes* our view of man" ([15]: 288). In the algebraic terms favored by Black, one defines a one-to-one mapping between arrays of traits belonging respectively to the primary and secondary subject. By the mapping, the arrays are "isomorphic"; some relations among members of one array are paralleled by the corresponding members of the other array. For this to work, man and wolf need not have any trait in common. The defining, like a Rorschach subject's transaction with an inkblot, is more a case of creating a likeness than of finding one.

Though Black's discussion wavers on these points, they are largely what distinguish it from the classical account. The "stronger" (that is, the more suggestive) the metaphor, the weaker the case for taking it as a statement rather than as the stimulus of an interaction: "If somebody urges that 'Nixon is an image surrounding a vacuum,' it would be inept to ask soberly whether the speaker knew that to be so, or how he came to know it, or how we could check on the allegation. . . . It is a violation of philosophical grammar to assign either truth or falsity to strong metaphors" ([6]: 40–41). It is not clear why a request for the grounds of this charge (read figuratively) would be anomalous, or how the charge could be credibly maintained against evidence that the person described is forthright and principled. Of Lincoln and Jefferson, in fact, the metaphorical predicate (read figuratively) seems to be demonstrably false. Black wavers in his pseudo-statement position, I think, because it fails to capture the efforts at validation that typically accompany metaphorical discourse and are part of the process of making it intelligible: "Nixon, if we are not mistaken, is indeed what he is metaphorically said to be" ([6]: 41). What would being mistaken on this point be like, if not an unsatisfactory answer to the various questions disallowed by "philosophical grammar"? These turn out to be sensible, however ill formed.

The wolf-traits supplied by Black for use in "interaction" with the concept of man seem to exemplify *types* of behavior that could characterize human beings; why is the metaphorical sentence not to be construed as expressing just that characterization? As Black says, "wolf-language" is an idiom in which one can talk about human traits. In another of Black's examples— "Marriage is a zero-sum game"—the "implication complex" for "zero-sum game" is "a contest between two opponents in which one player can win only at the expense of the other," and the result of interaction is "a sustained struggle between two contestants in which the rewards . . . of one contestant are gained only at the other's expense" ([6]: 30). The result is apparently Black's attempt to derive from the secondary subject, by generalization, a property compatible with that of being marriage. This fits the classical account very well. But it is one thing to scan the *literal* denotation of a predicate for the features being *figuratively* attributed to the denotation of the subject (the classical account), and quite another (on Black's pseudostatement account) to define, somehow or other, a mapping between the literal denotations of *two* subjects. Stripped of an iconic theory that would implausibly turn a metaphorical sentence into a kind of Rorschach test, Black's theory collapses into Aristotle's.

In Black, the notion that a metaphorical predicate somehow retains its ordinary meaning encourages a pseudostatement theory. The same notion, oddly enough, also inspires the contrasting theory that metaphorical assertion is a superstatement that creates the truths it expresses. In Nelson Goodman's version of this approach, the first step is to dismiss from our semantics explanatory appeals to items like properties and relations that nobody needs or knows anything about; in human reality what things "exemplify" are not universals but labels attached to things by habit and utility. To introduce a metaphor is simply to liberalize one's habit of attaching a given label: "A label along with others constituting a schema is in effect detached from the home realm and applied for the sorting and organizing of an alien realm." So metaphors don't report organization; they create it: "A set of terms, of alternative labels, is transported, and the organization they effect in the alien realm is guided by their habitual use in the home realm." "The way we apply 'high' to sounds was guided by the earlier metaphorical application to numbers (via number of vibrations per second."[9]

This account of metaphor is not very clear or plausible. On Goodman's showing, "higher than" means precisely the same thing in all three domains, which are sorted out by labels and not properties or relations. But then, how is it that habits that guided the use of labels in the home realm fit the objects in the new realm, and if they don't fit them, how do the habits guide us? And if they do fit, what do they fit if not an order already in place? In particular, what is it for old habits to guide us in extending "higher than" from altitudes to numbers? Wasn't this an easier accomplishment than it would have been to learn to talk about higher and lower flavors or odors? What made it easier was that natural numbers, like altitudes in relation to a given surface, are ordered with respect to an origin. If we follow Goodman's philology, one sound is "higher than" another by metonymy, not metaphor; here the predicate means *correlated with a higher number of vibrations per second*. There is nothing in Goodman's discussion to suggest that leaving out talk of meanings and properties improves understanding, much less that metaphor is used to create, rather than to describe, the structure of pieces of the world.

In a similar vein, Black speaks of "cases where, prior to the construction of the metaphor, we would have been hard put to it to find any *literal* resemblance [viz., between what are called the literal and figurative senses of the metaphorical term, for example, between *pig* and *messy eater*]. It would be more illuminating in some of these cases to say that the metaphor *creates* the similarity than to say that it formulates some similarity antecedently existing."[10] This might be read as a misleadingly figurative account of the fallacy of equivocation (on "coldness") that "creates the similarity" between unemotional people and blocks of ice. But Black evidently wants to be taken literally: "Some metaphors enable us to see aspects of reality that the metaphors' production helps to constitute. But that is no longer surprising if one believes that the world is necessarily a world *under a certain description*—or a world from a certain perspective. Some metaphors can create such a perspective" ([6]: 39–40).

How does a description make the world satisfy it? The aspect of an object available from a given vantage point under given conditions of observation would seem to be a dispositional fact independent of whether it is reported, metaphorically or otherwise; so what has perspective to do with Black's thesis? As Davidson says, "metaphors often make us notice aspects of things we did not notice before; . . . they bring surprising analogies and similarities to our attention." ([12]: 45). This is a fairer statement of the case, I think; we may have to experiment with perspective to *find* the shared aspect metaphorically expressed by a term. The illustrative question that, on Black's testimony, "comes the closest to what I originally had in mind by the strong creativity thesis" is: "Did the slow-motion appearance of a galloping horse exist before the invention of cinematography?" ([6]: 39). The answer would seem to be yes, if by slow-motion appearance we mean the way something *would* look if it were reproduced by cinematography. The actual instances of that look, after all, were created by adding something to the world other than a use of words.

Perhaps Black's view may seem more plausible if we think of situations like compliance with instructions to see the duck-rabbit outline first as resembling the profile of one animal and then the other. But the drawing has salient characteristics on which the success of the instructions depends; these are the ground of the resemblance, and the instructions do not create them. In a metaphorical description of the outline, "rabbit-ears" or "duck-beak" would be a reference to those characteristics, and not to ears or beaks or even to resemblance. The metaphor would not create those characteristics, and it would not simply be a transferred label but a predicate used in a generic shape-describing sense not assigned to it by current English. It would be what classical rhetoric calls a catachresis.

The "strong creativity thesis" of Goodman and Black recurs in an even more ambitious version in the last such theory I shall consider. This one is ambitious and global enough to be reviewed at some length. If I am not mistaken, it illustrates very well both the allure and the fatal weakness of "creativity" theories of metaphor. According to Lakoff and Johnson (hereafter L-J), metaphor is simply the way we "understand areas of experience that are not well defined in their own terms and must be grasped in terms of other areas of experience" ([15]: 114). Ill-defined concepts, such as those of love and time, have no intrinsic structure. Fortunately, there are clear concepts, such as that of a journey, whose structure is somehow appropriate for imposing on those that are featureless: "They [the clear concepts] provide the right kind of structure to allow us to get a handle on those natural kinds of experience that are less concrete or less clearly delineated in their own terms" ([15]: 118). It is at least partly because such concepts depend on others for structure that different cultures easily misunderstand each other by failures of recognition; one culture, for example, might "structure" the concept of argument in terms of dance rather than of conflict: "We would probably not view them as arguing at all" ([15]: 5).

The notion of "structuring" an ill-defined concept needs some clarification. We need to know what in the concept, if anything, sustains the imposed structure—how one "gets a handle on" something without a handle. What part of a concept corresponds to a (graspable) handle if not some understandable feature? No doubt "get" means *put* in L-J's idiom: we *put* a handle or understandable feature *on* a concept previously without one. So a concept apparently maintains its identity under transformations of its content. But then how can a concept ever be clearly delineated? And what is the criterion of identity here? Why in particular does a "discourse form structured in terms of battle" satisfy the same concept as a "discourse form structured in terms of dance"? I will hazard one further guess about concept-"structuring" and metaphor-"handles," but not in an effort to settle the question. It seems to me that L-J's notion of what metaphors do with, or to, ill-defined concepts is itself not very well defined. But it is clear, at least, that it was quite naturally suggested by their Goodmanesque belief that metaphorical description makes human reality.

If we say that something is "in front of" the mountain, for example, "we must project a front-back orientation on the mountain—an orientation that varies from culture to culture, is given relative to human observer, and is not inherent in the mountain" ([15]: 166). "Projection" apparently is to objects what "handle-getting" is to concepts, and may be the missing gloss: to understand what we are looking at in the landscape, we apparently need to imagine that the mountain literally has a face or something very much like one.

But this, though clear, is wrong. We need not imagine that the mountain has a quasi-face to understand the metaphor; in fact, by so doing we wouldn't be understanding the metaphor, but pretending to take it literally and hence to misunderstand it. And we could hardly project the imaginary face or front onto the correct side of the mountain unless we knew that "front" in this usage means, not *face* or *façade*, but *side nearest to us*. It is true that the property of having such a side is not implicit in the concept of being a mountain. But it is compatible with satisfying that concept. We don't merely project the property onto the mountains that have it. The "orientation that varies from culture to culture" is precisely the orientation that is literally described by an expression in each culture that figuratively means *side nearest to us*; otherwise L-J are referring pointlessly to an unspecified correlation of cultures and orientations. (This point applies mutatis mutandis to dance- and battle-structured *arguments*.) And it is only because the face is thought of (in our culture at least) as the side people we have to do with ordinarily turn toward us—only, that is, because of a relevant implication—that "front" was originally available for this metaphorical use.

L-J are apparently led to their literalist view of metaphor, and the allied belief that metaphor creates human reality, by the fact that a number of pervasive features of experience are expressible in English only by dead figures of speech. Thus one moment *precedes* or *follows* another, time *passes*, thoughts are *in* the mind, sounds are *higher* or *lower*. In some such cases it is hard to paraphrase the figurative or derived sense, in nearly all it is hard to reconstruct the original figure of speech or pattern of derivation. Failure to meet these challenges can be taken as justifying a triumphant QED to the effect that metaphor is clearly not grounded on similarity, and more fundamentally that the figurative sense is nonexistent; to understand moments of time, for example, we see them as objects moving in single file, with "front-back orientation" ([15]: 113).

While this line of thought is natural, it is mistaken. Metaphor is not the only figure of speech, and resemblance or implication is not the only way of deriving a figurative meaning. On the more fundamental point, if thoughts were "in" the mind in the same sense as objects surrounded by the limits of a given volume of space are "in" the volume, then thoughts would be in the mind in no sense at all, for the mind is not a physical object—and so for moments and sounds. But sometimes thoughts are in the mind all the same— in the sense that they are sometimes objects of thinking. By which figurative process the mental sense of "in" was derived from the physical is a historical question of some difficulty, and for that very reason irrelevant; whatever figure of speech it was, it is one no longer. In the present condition of the language—or equivalently the present language—"in" is a homonym. It may be that thoughts, as objects of consciousness, are "in" the mind by metonymy, as *being represented by parts of* a mental representation of a spatial volume. In the same way, it may be that one moment "precedes" another simply because earlier moments, like physical objects preceding others moving in single file, are conventionally indexed with lower numbers, so that we have a metaphor that relies on a cultural practice it does not create. Our inability to be sure has no bearing on the nature of metaphor; for these are no longer metaphors, if they ever were.

Like Black and Goodman, L-J overestimate the power of the Word. For better or worse, the "strong creativity thesis" in its various incarnations is wrong. But this is not to say that it is worthless. On the contrary, its high value, at least in my esteem, is twofold: it is an attempt to say how imaginative modelling fits into the process of interpreting figures; it tends to reject the distinction between figurative and literal sense. These are useful challenges; to meet them, I think, is to come within hailing distance of an adequate account of metaphor. In what remains, I will take up first the question of the two senses and then that of imagination.

III

In his rather idiosyncratic essay of 1935 on language use, A. Reichling argues vigorously that figurative utterance does not work any change in the meaning of the word involved: "When a boy is called 'monkey,' the term names a particular 'monkeyish' trait of the boy. . . . What the word means in this case is really monkey; otherwise this use would not be 'metaphorese.' " "A jailer tells forced laborers: 'Gentlemen, the game is about to resume!' The force of the expression lies precisely in the fact that 'game' really means game, but that only the activity-nuance is applied" ([23]). In short, the word names (or rather ascribes) one property in 'metaphorese' while it continues to mean (or ascribe) a more complex property of which the "named" one is a part.

Reichling's difficulty here, which seems to have defeated him, is that having displaced the figurative meaning from the relevant word, which in his view remains unchanged, he doesn't know where to put it. Recently Searle has defended the same thesis of persisting literal sense, and run up against the same difficulty. According to Searle, "whenever we talk about the metaphorical meaning of a word, expression, or sentence, we are talking about what a speaker might utter it to mean, in a way that departs from what the word, expression, or sentence actually means" ([25]: 95). What a speaker "utters [an expression] to mean," in a shorter usage of Searle's, is what the speaker means by it; or in still another, the speaker's utterance meaning.

This is Searle's corrective to the view that figurative meaning is "in the sentences or expressions uttered," which is unacceptable because "sentences and words have only the meaning they have." Here Searle is apparently denying that metaphorical meaning, like the systematically varying reference of "I" or "now," is assigned to individual instances or tokens of the expression itself. This seems right; we are alerted to the presence of a figurative meaning precisely because the meaning assigned to the *token* is incongruous; the figurative meaning somehow does not belong to the expression even as uttered on a particular occasion. If it were simply what the expression means now, what would be the point of calling it figurative? As Searle says, "to the extent that there has been a genuine change in meaning, so that a word or expression no longer means what it previously did, to precisely that extent the locution is no longer metaphorical" ([25]: 100). There is apparently a sense in which the figurative meaning doesn't belong to the figurative expression. (A bit further on, I'll spell out both this sense and another in which it *does*.)

But Searle's alternative formula—"the speaker utters the expression to mean *m*"—is obscure; which noun phrase doubles as the subject of the infinitive phrase of purpose or result "to mean *m*"? If "the speaker," then we have an absurdity: "The speaker utters the expression in such a way that the speaker means (i.e., intends) *m*." Even if we take seriously the notion that some intention of the speaker results from the way he utters an expression, we still don't know what the figurative sense *m* is assigned to, and we aren't even told just what the speaker means (or intends) to do to *m*. But if the subject of "to mean" is "the expression uttered," then we are apparently back where we started: "The speaker utters the expression in such a way that the expression means *m*." This reading looks like the thesis we began by rejecting. And the reading seems plausible; metaphorical meanings, like literal, apparently match the syntax of the corresponding *expressions*. For example, the figurative sense of a metaphorical adjective ("lazy" as modifying "river") does not seem to be an exception to the plausible rule that adjective-senses are functions (from noun-senses to noun-senses) that parallel the combinatory behavior of the adjectives themselves (terms that "take" nouns to "make" nouns). In fact, this matching seems to rule out the third possible subject of "to mean": "the act of uttering the expression"; acts are not syntactic entities.

In English idiom the infinitive after an action verb expresses either purpose or result; hence the dilemma: a fair paraphrase will capture the implications of the idiomatic construction, with embarrassing results. But one can always drum up a fake paraphrase that gets round the grammatical embarrassment by ignoring it: "I mean *y* by *x*." The trouble with this maneuver is that "mean" in this context is short for "mean to *say*"; where *y* is a denotation rather than an expression, one *says y* by uttering an expression that *means y*. It seems to me that the most plausible unpacking of "I mean *y* by *x*" is "In using expression *x* I mean (intend) to use an expression that means (denotes) *y*." If this is right, lexical "meaning" isn't really dispensed with by the appeal to speaker "meaning" in "I mean *y* by *x*."

The escape from this dilemma is to remember that meaning is relative to language. There just is no answer to the question of what a given expression means *simpliciter*. It means an infinity of things—in the countless possible languages it belongs to. We need to face this language-relativity of meaning squarely if we are ever to get clear about the epistemology of figurative uptake—about what it is to believe that an expression is figurative. *In which language* does the expression mean its figurative meaning? Clearly not in the language hitherto shared by the speaker and his hearers. The metaphoric speaker has slipped into a dialect, like Mrs. Malaprop. The difference is that she thinks the language she is speaking is that of her community. The metaphoric speaker knows that his isn't, but acts as if it were. He is giving a demonstration of it, and in the process (if he succeeds) naturalizing his hearers into a second linguistic community; the hearers rely in turn on their knowledge of a manageably small set of trope functions (surveyed in Section One) to help them move from the vernacular sense of a troublesome expression to a sense it has in the dialect being introduced. Figurativeness is a kind of foreignness; it varies with the prevailing or intrenched language. A figurative expression is an element of the impromptu dialect—of the metaphorese, shall we say—that has at least one sense not shared by its counterpart in the vernacular, and its literal senses are just the shared ones. When someone overcome with nausea says "I'm *literally* sick to my stomach," he is insuring against misunderstanding by warning you that the vernacular is still in force. In a somewhat more puzzling usage, when someone says "This toothache is literally killing me" in an effort to inform his audience that the toothache is very hard to take, he is apparently thinking of metaphorese itself as the current vernacular, a successor to English in which "killing" means both *depriving of life* and *annoying intensely*. Unlike its vernacular twin, the metaphorical term has at least one relevant sense. The sense seems to be an addition and not a replacement. If *depriving of life* turns up as the relevant sense of "killing" as used later in his speech, the figurative speaker hasn't given up his right to be understood accordingly. So metaphorese seems to contain all the vernacular meanings as well as the "new" ones. With the appropriate qualification, then, Searle and Reichling are right: the figurative meaning does not belong to the *verncular* expression; that's how we come to suspect that the expression before us is not vernacular.

To accommodate the role of metaphor in the *evolution* of languages, we can think of a vernacular as a sequence of language stages—overlapping dialects successively spoken by a community in the course of its history. Then we can think of a metaphorese as a dialect proposed, or at least made available, for future membership or stageship in the vernacular. On this view, a dialect is metaphorese with respect to a current stage of the vernacular.

The figurative speaker is engaged in a complex social endeavor. He is demonstrating a new language, recruiting speakers, and establishing a subtle rapport with the prospective recruits. The standard way of showing the relevant kind of rapport with the speaker is to adopt his metaphor, or extend it into a system. One becomes a partner in developing the metaphorese. Thus, in a rudimentary example, suppose somebody talks about the conversation itself in "journey"-language about "setting out" to discuss things or "arriving at" conclusions: you reciprocate with "path"- and "surface"-language about "following" or "straying from the path of" argument, or "covering" a lot of "ground" (where "path" will mean something like *sequence of acts*, and "ground" something like *set of accomplishments*). The journey predicates from a system in the sense that they are familiarly associated with each other in literal meaning and figuratively applicable to a given subject matter. In literature, metaphorical invention is typically a conversational response of just this kind, either to a conspicuous predecessor or to a metaphoric tradition applying, for example, "coin"-language to words, "book"-language to the world, "book"-language to the mind, "theater"-language to the world, "sea voyage"-language to life, "disease"-language to vice, "sight"-language to reasoning.

If the metaphoric response develops the figure in a sense that subverts the original speaker's, then of course we have repartee; the coordination becomes a contest. And in at least one case (irony) a figure cannot be adopted without also adopting the speaker's attitude and evaluation.

Black warns against "postulating a standard response to a given metaphorical statement—a response determined by linguistic, conceptual, cultural, or other conventions. Such a view is untenable because a metaphorical statement involves a rule violation: there can be no rules for 'creatively' violating rules"([6]: 25). But "rule," like "meaning of x," is an incomplete designation; you need to specify the game in the one case, and the language in the other. Rules of what? The violation of the rules of one game can signal the beginning of another, with different rules. Black's "interaction theory," in fact, is an attempt to show how the back-up game is played. But in fact, if I am right about metaphorese, it is misleading to say that the figurative speaker is violating rules, if these are rules of vernacular semantics. You can't break the rules of a game you are no longer playing. He isn't breaking rules but switching games, like a bilingual speaker switching languages to challenge or entertain his bilingual hearers. Indeed, this seems to be more or less what is going on, except that the bilingualism is developing on the spot.

Besides, the switching itself is constrained by rules. If your sentence is absurd, anomalous, pointless, or inconsistent with your ostensible beliefs, and I have no reason to think you mad, mendacious, or misinformed, I give you the benefit of the doubt and test for one of the standard figures of speech in ways I will say a bit more about shortly. If a reading emerges that fits your line of argument, then the test has come out positive. "Every criterion for a metaphor's presence, however plausible," says Black, 'is defeasible in special circumstances" ([6]: 36). But this is a fact about criteria, not about metaphors or the plausibility of criteria for their presence.

A metaphor, after all, is a kind of riddle: "For the form of a riddle is this: in speaking of things that are, to put together impossibilities; in combining literal expressions one cannot do this, but in metaphor one can." "In general out of well-made riddles it is possible to take metaphors that are fair [*epieikeîs*]."[11] The word I am translating by "fair" here is Aristotle's term for judicial equity—a principle of flexibility in the interpretation of law that makes an interesting parallel to the way figurative interpretation dispenses with the linguistic equivalent of legal rigor to do a finer justice to individual cases. But fairness here is a virtue of metaphors in their capacity as riddles; it is a matter of fair play, of their being adapted to what their intended audience has to go on. What constitutes a fair chance at solving a metaphor is that its clues are drawn from the fund of conversational assumptions—things the parties jointly take for granted, at least for the sake of particular kinds of argument: what might be called postulates of talk. Following the lead of Aristotle's *Topics*, classical rhetoric analyzes such postulates under the rubric of the *protasis endoxos*, or generally accepted assumption, which varies with the protocol and circumstances of the conversation.[12] Black is echoing this tradition when he speaks of the commonplaces associated with a word by a given "speech community."

Still, doesn't the response to figurative language involve a picturing activity that is quite essential to it—that accounts for our inclination to talk of "figures" or "imagery" in the first place? Overlooking this response in one's account of the transaction of figurative speech is like overlooking intimidation in an account of threatening, or inducing in an account of exhorting: to choose to communicate a figurative meaning, one typically chooses to communicate images as well. Images are (to descend to the convenient jargon) a perlocutionary effect characteristic of the figurative speech act.

It has been suggested that mental images are generated by impasses in thinking ([27]). If one reads "interpreting" for "thinking" here, this seems to be partly right: not to understand that "living tombs" means *carrion eaters* (where it does) is to be left with the grotesque image that results from trying to take "tombs" literally. But one must go further. Images tend to outlast initial confusion, as if the imagination were a demon bent on getting figures picturesquely wrong by pursuing the implications of taking them literally. If truth wears a veil, "truth" must be the name of a person—the sort of person who goes veiled in the surrounding culture. If the skipper *gives* the ship *the rein*, what is called "ship" must be an unrestrained horse in full career.

On the view of imagery I am sketching, the imagination systematically misinterprets in the interests of interior cinema. Either it interchanges figurativeness and literalness, or it creates hybrids: the unbridled ship gets an equine prow. If one identifies this subversive graphics with figurative interpretation, then metaphor is fiction—either the world-creating fiction of L-J or the subjective "truth" of Hugo Meier: "Objectively considered, that seeing-of-one-thing-in-another or fusion of two concepts in which metaphor makes us believe is ultimately always false, of course. . . . Metaphorical transference is truthful only in the sense of our subjective, human awareness, not of external reality" ([17]). If my earlier argument is right, this misdescribes the justification conditions of metaphorical assertion, which are determined by figurative sense. One is warranted in believing that x is light-fingered if and only if one is warranted in believing that x is a habitual thief. On the other hand, the first of the two descriptions of metaphoric image-making offered by Meier is worth exploring. I think it can usefully supplement the demon theory. According to Carnoy (Meier's source), the parties to figurative communication "see one thing in the other, through the other, or by the other" ([8]). Is this simply an anticipation of the Wittgensteinian notion? I think not; seeing-by is not seeing-as. What is it then?

Of course one does not see or believe one sees a ship on the basis of a horse image (in the cited example). What happens, I suggest, is that one comes to think about ships by means of such images as well as by means of more obviously linguistic entities. Tokens of the ship image are concatenated with ordinary tokens of the language. (There are children's books that function on a crude version of this principle.) Image becomes term. Perhaps the curse of oddity can be taken off talk of iconic *nouns* and *verbs* by reflecting on familiar non-metal examples of iconic *sentences*: the green traffic light ordering us to drive on, the display of a white flag notifying the enemy of surrender, the look of reproach used not as a kind of substitute pain behavior but as the visual equivalent of an evaluation. The imagination may respond to figurative speech by rebellion or truancy, but it ends by making its own inner contribution to the vocabulary of metaphorese and the rapport of its teachers and learners.

NOTES

1. The point is implicit in Aristotle's discussion, [1]: 1457^{a}11–18, ^{b}9–16.
2. For general suggestions on the specification of meaning types for nouns, quantified noun phrases, verbs, verb phrases, etc., see [11], [16], [18].
3. [3]: 1412^{a}11–16. Paul Ricoeur seems to take this view [24]: 177 and passim.
4. See, for example, [26]: 192, 208, 217, 232, 246.
5. [22]: 17. The line is "Iuppiter hibernas cana nive conspuit Alpes."
6. The *OED* definition of metaphor reflects that tradition and is thus misdescribed by Max Black, [5]: 279. Ricoeur seems to take the same view [24]: 179 and passim.
7. The treatment of metaphor in [13] does not improve on Aristotle's. It relies on the questionable species-species analysis and an unmotivated theoretical notion of mediating terms.
8. Jerry L. Morgan offers as a counterexample to the simile theory the possibility of a figurative use of "John's not just *like* a tree, he *is* a tree" ([19]). But the point, on the most obvious reading, might simply be that John is not merely *like* a tree, he is *very* like a tree (identity being the limit of similarity).
9. [14]: 72, 74–75. For "exemplification" of labels, see [14]: 56.
10. [5]: 284–285. Ricoeur [24]: 213 seems to take the same view.
11. [1]: 1458^{a}25–29, [3]: 1405^{b}2–5.
12. [2], [4], [6]: 1357^{a}34. Cf. [9], [28].

REFERENCES

[1] Aristotle. *Poetics*.
[2] ———. *Prior Analytics* 2.29.

[3] ——. *Rhetoric.*

[4] ——. Topics 1.8.

[5] Max Black. "Metaphor," in *Proceedings of the Aristotelian Society* 4 (1955).

[6] ——. "More about Metaphor," in Andrew Ortony (ed.) *Metaphor and Thought* (Cambridge: Cambridge University Press, 1979).

[7] Richard Boyd. "Metaphor and Theory Change," in Ortony (see [6]).

[8] Albert Carnoy. *La Science du mot* (Louvain, 1927), p. 276.

[9] Cicero. *De inventione* 2.46–49.

[10] ——. *De oratore* 3.158.

[11] M. J. Cresswell. *Logics and Languages* (London, 1973).

[12] Donald Davidson. "What Metaphors Mean," *Critical Inquiry* 5 (1978).

[13] J. Dubois et al. *Rhétorique générale* (Paris, 1970).

[14] Nelson Goodman. *Languages of Art* (Indianapolis, 1976), pp. 72, 74–75.

[15] George Lakoff and Mark Johnson. *Metaphors We Live By* (Chicago: University of Chicago Press, 1980).

[16] David Lewis. "General Semantics," in *Semantics of a Natural Language*, ed. D. Davidson and G. Harman (Dordrecht, 1972).

[17] Hugo Meier. *Die Metapher* (Winterthur, 1963), p. 185.

[18] Richard Montague. *Formal Philosophy*, ed. R. Thomason (New Haven: Yale University Press, 1974), Chapters 6–8.

[19] Jerry L. Morgan. "Observations on the Pragmatics of Metaphor," in Ortony (see [8]), p. 140.

[20] Friedrich Nietzsche. *Über Wahrheit und Lüge im aussermoralischen Sinn*, in *Werke* (Stuttgart, 1921), 2:10–11, 17.

[21] ——. *Jenseits von Gut und Böse*, 1:20.

[22] Quintilian. *Institutiones oratoriae* 8.6.

[23] A. Reichling. *Het Woord: Een Studie omtrent de grondslag van taal en taalgebruik* (Nijmegen, 1935), pp. 232, 332; quoted in C.P.F. Stutterheim, *Het Begrip Metaphoor* (Amsterdam, 1941), p. 339.

[24] Paul Ricoeur. *The Rule of Metaphor* (trans. Robert Czerny et al.) (Toronto, 1979).

[25] John Searle. "Metaphor," in Ortony (see [6]).

[26] L. Spengel (ed.). *Rhetores Graeci* (Leipzig, 1861), 3.

[27] Gustav Stern. *Meaning and Change of Meaning* (Goteborg, 1931), pp. 46–67.

[28] Victorinus' commentary on Cicero's *De inventione*, in R. Halm *Rhetores Latini Minores* (Leipzig, 1865), p. 234–235.

MERRIE BERGMANN

METAPHORICAL ASSERTIONS[1]

I

Metaphors can be used, and used successfully, to make assertions. The claim that there is such a use of metaphor seems obvious enough, and many authors have treated it as such. Yet the claim is incompatible with, even flatly denied by, numerous other accounts of the "nature" of metaphor. Although the antagonists hail from diverse philosophical quarters, they share a concern with one aspect of metaphor: this is the "richness," or the "pregnancy" or "expansiveness," of metaphor. There are those who maintain outright that the richness of metaphor precludes its use in the making of assertions. And there are those who stop short of this conclusion but nevertheless maintain that because of their richness, what we say when we use metaphors is in some way different in kind from what can be said literally: for example, we use metaphors to say things that are "wildly" or "mythically" true.[2]

In this paper, I provide a theoretical account of the assertive use of metaphor. One of the consequences of the account is this: not only is the richness of metaphor *compatible* with its use in making assertions; but in addition our assessments of the richness of metaphors are based on the workings of *the same linguistic mechanism* which enables us to make and understand specific assertions with metaphors. Once this mechanism is understood, there is no need to maintain that the contents of metaphorical assertions, or their truth-values, are different in kind from those of literal assertions. First, though, I shall explain how concern with the richness of metaphor has led to the conclusion that assertive use is precluded, and state why the general strategy of reasoning is mistaken.

The claim that metaphors are rich means that they invite many readings, or suggest many things, and diverse ones. Consider Romeo's "Juliet is the sun." Since Shakespeare wrote that line many plausible and interesting readings have been attributed to the metaphor. There are two reasons why this richness of metaphor might be thought to preclude assertion. First, assertions presumably have fairly well-defined contents (with fuzzy edges, perhaps, due to vagueness); and when we examine a metaphor to determine all the readings it invites, we find that what the metaphor "means" is difficult to contain. Second, if metaphors are rich in the sense of conveying endlessly many things to us, it is hard to see how anyone making an assertion with a metaphor could have a good grasp on what, exactly or *even roughly*, is being asserted. While it is true that sometimes we are not fully aware of the content of our assertions, or of what we mean when we assert something, usually we are aware enough.[3]

Thus it is tempting to draw a conclusion like Donald Davidson's:

. . . the thesis that associated with a metaphor is a cognitive content that its author wishes to convey and that the interpreter must grasp if he is to get the message . . . is false, whether or not we call the purported cognitive content a meaning.

It should make us suspect the theory that it is so hard to decide, even in the case of the simplest metaphors, exactly what the cognitive content is supposed to be. . . . [I]n fact, there is no limit to what a metaphor calls to our attention. . . . When we try to say what a metaphor "means", we soon realize there is no end to what we want to mention.[4]

The fact that metaphors "generate" further and further readings does not, however, conflict with the claim that an author *can* successfully use a metaphor to convey a fairly specific cognitive content. For a person who uses a metaphor to make an assertion typically does not intend to assert *everything* that we can "read into" the metaphor. Nor does the audience typically attribute all of those readings to the author.

Let me illustrate. Suppose I say to you, after hearing the latest report on Three Mile Island, "As far as I'm concerned, nuclear reactors are time bombs." You correctly interpret my remark as an assertion to the effect that nuclear reactors are likely to fail, at any moment—of course, with disastrous consequences. A while later you say, "That was an interesting metaphor: nuclear reactors being time bombs. Although I don't think that the guys responsible for those things *want* people to get killed by them, still it seems that, like people who use time bombs, they have a frightening disregard for human lives." This, then, is something else that I could have used the metaphor to assert. But it does not follow, from the possibility of using a metaphor to make different assertions, that anyone who does use that metaphor *is* making all of those assertions. You and I may both recognize that I could have used the metaphor to make a comment about the people responsible for nuclear reactors, and at the same time recognize that I was not doing so. The richness, or suggestiveness, of metaphors does not forestall their use in making fairly specific assertions, and it is a mistake to argue otherwise.

The grain of truth in Davidson's claim about richness is this: without knowing the context in which a metaphor occurs and who its author is, it is impossible to state conclusively what the metaphor "means" without drawing out all that it *could* mean. And here the process does seem endless. Dwell on a metaphor long enough, even a relatively uninteresting one, and numerous and varied interpretations come to mind.

But bring in a well-defined context and a real author, and matters may change drastically. Although there may be *prima facie* reasons for denying the status of assertion to certain metaphors in certain contexts—as when they occur in poetry, if we do not believe that the point of poetry is assertion— there are good reasons to give the status of assertion to others. These are the metaphors that occur in everyday conversation, and in many varieties of prose.

II

My claim is that the author of a metaphor can use that metaphor to assert something, and can do so with success. In this section I provide a theoretical account of this linguistic act. First, I characterize the assertive use of metaphor; and second, I explain what is involved in the success of this use of language. For even when an author intends to assert something with metaphor, the communicative enterprise, just like any other attempt at communication, may fail. Some of the reasons for failure are peculiar to metaphor, but others are not.

It should be clear from my remarks in the last section that I do not maintain that metaphors are *always* used to make assertions. The account that follows paves the way for a theoretical description of other uses of metaphor as well. For although I develop an account of the assertive use, I characterize metaphor independently of any particular illocutionary force.

To simplify matters, I focus on assertive metaphors that occur in conversational contexts. What counts as a metaphor, and what we should regard the metaphor as doing, both involve questions of *use*. Asking of a sentence itself—say, 'Smith is a Communist'—whether it is a metaphor is like asking of the sentence itself whether it is a lie, or whether it is a warning or an insult. In each case the question is illegitimate. What we can legitimately ask is whether the sentence is, on a particular occasion, being used as a metaphor. And an answer to this question relies on recognizing, or assuming, something about the *intentions* of the person who uses the sentence.[5] The sentence 'Smith is a Communist' is not itself either literal or metaphorical; it may be used either way.

But the classification of a sentence as a metaphor does not settle the other questions of use. The uses of a sentence as a metaphor and as a lie are not mutually exclusive; and so it is with metaphor and warning, metaphor and criticizing, metaphor and asserting. Concerning lying, it suffices to note that metaphor may be used with or without intent to deceive. And when we decide that a sentence is a metaphor we are not classifying it according to illocutionary force. Here we have three dimensions of use, distinguished from one another by the sorting criterion that operates within each dimension: sincerity (truth-telling or lying), purpose (illocutionary force), and manner: the systematic relation between the words used and the content of the illocutionary act. Identification of a sentence as metaphor is classification according to manner, and manner may be literal, metaphoric, ironic, hyperbolic, and so on. In the case of the assertive metaphor, then, we must make two distinct identifications as to use: the sentence is being used *as* a metaphor, and *to* assert.

Further, when a sentence is used as a metaphor with the intention of assertion, various propositions may be intended or conveyed, depending on the author and the context. The point of 'Smith is a Communist' used as a metaphor may be to assert that Smith is unpatriotic, that Smith advocates abolition of the nuclear family, or that Smith opposes religious freedom. What is a proposition? I take a proposition to be what the best linguistic theory available says it is: something that can be represented as a function from possible worlds into truth-values, or, equivalently, a set of possible worlds (those worlds to which the function assigns the value TRUE).[6] This concept of a proposition—one that has been applied successfully to a variety of linguistic and logical problems—has a particular virtue in the analysis of metaphor: propositions are language-independent entities. So in developing a theory of what different metaphors can be used to assert, we need not assume that we must "translate" the metaphors into language used literally, as if that were the only way to get at propositions.[7]

Whereas a proposition represents the world as being a certain way, an act of asserting a proposition is an act of saying that the world *is* the way the proposition represents it as being.[8] When language is used literally to assert a proposition, there is an intimate connection between the words used and the proposition asserted: the words literally *express* the proposition. Or, to put it another way, the proposition is the *meaning* of the sentence used.[9] But a person who uses a sentence metaphorically does not use it to assert the proposition that is literally expressed by the sentence. In the case of assertive metaphor, we must distinguish between sentence meaning and speaker's meaning.[10]

If the use is to count as *metaphor*, however, rather than as some other figure like irony or even as nonsense, a particular sort of relation must hold between the sentence used and the proposition asserted. What is distinctive of all metaphorical uses of language (whether the purpose is to assert or to do something else) is that the content of what is communicated is a *direct* function of salient characteristics associated with (at least) part of the expression—rather than of the literal meaning of that part.[11] The concept of a salient characteristic associated with an expression is a technical one, which I develop in a companion to this article, and its definition will vary with the grammatical category of the expression. Here I'll just give examples for some simple sorts of expressions.[12]

Characteristics include properties and relations. *Salience* of characteristics is partially a function of commonplaces and stereotypes. The salient characteristics of a thing include those characteristics which we would typically list on the spot if asked to state what we believe is *distinctive* of that thing.[13] So the salient characteristics associated with a name include properties that are commonly attributed to the thing named (perhaps incorrectly). Salient characteristics associated with the name 'Einstein' include the properties of being a scientist, and of being brilliant. In virtue of these characteristics, I may use 'John is an Einstein' to say that John is a brilliant scientist. The proposition I have asserted is then a function of the literal meaning of 'John' and of salient characteristics associated with 'Einstein'. I may also use 'Einstein' to *refer* to John, if he is a brilliant scientist: 'Einstein is on his lunch break'.

The salient characteristics associated with a common noun or intransitive verb include properties commonly believed to be characteristic of the things— possible or actual—the noun or verb applies to, properties that are part of the stereotype of that sort of thing.[14] One salient characteristic associated with 'encyclopedia' is the property of being a source of information. Thus I can use 'Marie is an encyclopedia' to attribute that property to Marie, to assert that Marie knows lots of things. A salient characteristic associated with 'smile' is benevolence and consequently I can use 'Uncle George was smiling at us when he wrote his will' to assert that Uncle George decided to leave us something after all. The salient characteristics associated with a transitive verb include relations that are commonly thought to hold between things standing in the relation literally expressed by the verb. A salient characteristic associated with 'cook' is the relation *prepare*. Thus I can assert that Roger has become a poet by saying 'Roger is cooking poems these days'.[15]

Salience is also sensitive to context—to matters of ongoing concern, information that has just been shared. Thus the salient characteristics associated with a name also include properties that, in the context in which the name is used, have been made conspicuous by some means or other. A certain context may bring the property of being eccentric to the status of a salient characteristic associated with 'Einstein'—for example, one in which I have just been telling anecdotes (mostly false) about Einstein. In such a context, 'John is an Einstein' may be used to assert the proposition that John is eccentric, as well as (or instead of) the proposition that he is a brilliant scientist. Or perhaps you have been complaining about the exorbitant price you just paid for a cord of wood, lamenting that you will now have to watch your budget closely. I pick up on this when the conversation turns to my new refrigerator, saying 'That refrigerator is *my* cord of wood' to indicate that it, too, was expensive and that I will be on a tight budget as well.

I want to stress that properties or relations may be *ephemerally* rather than eternally salient. By telling anecdotes about Einstein I have managed to make eccentricity a salient characteristic of the man; but tomorrow this may be forgotten. And what is salient for one person may not be salient for another. A third party who did not hear your complaint will not understand why I called my refrigerator, rather than my electric space heater, a 'cord of wood'.

Salience, then, is context-dependent. And a context, when the understanding of metaphor is at issue, is a context for a person. We may think of the context that a person brings to the interpretation of a metaphor as the set of prominent beliefs that determine salience—beliefs that may vary from person to person and from situation to situation. The context includes the linguistic exchange in which the metaphor occurs—what propositions have been asserted, what the topics are.[16] The context also includes background knowledge about parties to the conversation.

While certain salience-making factors vary from context to context, however, there are still the culturally shared beliefs—the stereotypes—that stay with us. The description of contexts as person- and situation-specific is not intended to suggest that stereotypes play no role in the understanding of metaphor; they do. Rather, it is intended to draw attention to those beliefs which are not stereotypical, or which are lately acquired, that contribute to our assessments of salience along with those beliefs which are habitual.

In metaphorical assertion, then, the proposition that we take to be asserted is a direct function of salient characteristics associated with (at least) part of the expression. And as what is salient varies, so do the propositions that a sentence, taken as metaphor, may successfully be used to assert. It is a trivial consequence of my account that metaphors may be used to make true or false assertions, where an assertion is true if the proposition asserted is true and false otherwise. But it is important that truth and falsehood be tied to the assertion made, rather than to the sentence used. For a metaphor may be used to make different assertions, and typically some of these will be true and others false. Propositions themselves, at any rate, are true or false in the same sense whether metaphorically or literally asserted; so there is no need to call the contents of metaphorical assertions "wildly" true. It is not the content of what is said, but the manner of saying it, that distinguishes metaphorical assertions from literal ones.

What can be said in favor of accepting the salience relation as the basis for determining the content of metaphorical assertions? It works. Take an assertive metaphor, and take what you assume is the content of the metaphor—and you will find that content *is* determined by salient characteristics you associate with expressions in the metaphor. Moreover, the account based on salience corresponds nicely to what we do when we set out to *explicate* metaphors. A typical way to explicate 'Life is a game' as a metaphor about life is to draw attention to our beliefs about what characteristics are distinctive of games and to attribute these characteristics to life.[17]

Now we may state the conditions for success in the case of assertive metaphor. First, the audience must recognize the author's utterance as *metaphor*. There are several familiar ways in which this may happen. The speaker may explicitly indicate that he or she is using metaphor. The expression used may be either semantically or contextually anomalous if taken literally. Following Grice,[18] we may say that in this case a conversational maxim has apparently been violated: Quality (the sentence 'Men are wolves', taken literally, is false), Quantity (you may say of our mutual friend who has long lived in California, 'Hayward is a Californian, all right'), Relation (you may answer my question about your new automobile's road performance and gas mileage by replying 'It seems I have a mule with an insatiable appetite'). In each case, the literal content of the sentence is conversationally inappropriate. Or recognition of metaphor may just involve recognition of the appropriateness of a particular reading of the expression as metaphor, rather than recognition of inappropriateness of the literal reading.

Second, the audience must recognize the author's utterance as an *assertion*. And third, the audience must properly identify the proposition the author intended to assert. The audience must identify which component expressions (if any) are to be taken literally—and will use clues from the context (for example, the topic of discussion) to do so. And the audience must identify the correct salient characteristics for fixing the content of the assertion. Here the audience will typically choose characteristics the salience of which is believed to be mutual knowledge in the conversational setting.[19] Of course, not all the propositions the audience may arrive at on the basis of salient characteristics will be *plausible* in the context; and those that are not will be rejected or ignored. Grice's maxims thus help us to choose between a metaphor's possible contents, as well as to recognize metaphor.

The responsibility for the success of a metaphorical assertion is the author's; he or she must ensure that the audience can figure out *what* proposition is being asserted. Here Grice's maxim of Manner, "Be perspicuous," is relevant: the audience must have access to the salient characteristics necessary for retrieving the intended content of the assertion.[20] The author, in short, is responsible for preventing the "richness" of a metaphor from interfering with its efficacy in asserting a specific proposition. Principles of cooperative discourse are in effect here as well as in literal discourse. This is just as one would expect, if metaphors can be used to make assertions.

III

Finally, I shall use my account to address some important issues in the Literature on metaphor, and I shall substantiate the claim that I made at the beginning of this paper concerning the relation between the richness of metaphor and its assertive use.

1. *The salience relation distinguishes metaphor from other tropes*. The relations involved in figuration differ from trope to trope. For example, the relation in irony is one of inversion: what is meant is the *opposite* of what is literally expressed; the relation in hyperbole is one of exaggeration: what is literally expressed is an exaggeration of what is meant. In this paper, the examples I have given are cases of "pure" metaphor—the use of the expression involves only the figure of metaphor. Metaphor does not interfere with other tropes or figures; but it should not be *confused* with them. 'You are the cream in my coffee' may be used at once ironically and metaphorically; 'It's the Empire State Building' may involve both metaphor and hyperbole.[21]

2. *Understanding metaphor requires more than understanding word meaning*. A while back, various attempts were made to show how metaphorical "meanings" could be generated on the basis of deleted selection restrictions of semantic features (components of literal meanings.). Thus L. Jonathan Cohen and Avishai Margalit write:

> The metaphorical meanings of a word or phrase in a natural language are all contained, as it were, within its literal meaning or meanings. They are reached by removing any restrictions in relation to certain variables from the appropriate section or sections of its semantical hypothesis. For example, *baby* has as one of its metaphorical meanings the sense of *very small of its kind*: cf. *baby airplane* as against *baby daughter*. Here it is obviously the age and human/animal/artificial/etc. variables that are being treated as if they imposed no restriction, while a restriction of size is still retained. Or if this is considered an example of already dead metaphor, consider *That old man is a baby*, where on the most straightforward interpretation the age and size variables are presumably being treated as if they imposed no restriction, and other attributes of babies are being ascribed, such as mental incapacity.[22]

Such a theory requires a broad conception of literal meanings—most of us wouldn't normally think of mental incapacity as contributing to the literal meaning of 'baby'. This objection has been raised often enough.

But there is a more severe problem with the theory. For *ephemerally* salient characteristics may not be commonplace at all; yet, as I have suggested, they can play an important role in the interpretation of metaphors. Consider:

John: Look at how blue the sky is today!
Joe: Sure is. What a great color . . . and not a cloud in sight. When the sky is that blue, the air seems fresher . . . crisper . . . it really makes you feel good.

John: Yeah, it sure is a good feeling. Like everything's gonna be great, when the sky is that blue.

Joe: Mmm. . . . Hey—even the news report was blue today for a change—lotsa good stuff.

What has happened during this brief exchange is that 'blue', which under somewhat conventional usage has the associated salient characteristic *sad* or *depressing*, has picked up a very different associated characteristic: one that will likely be lost shortly in John's and Joe's conceptual schemes. In basing my account of assertive metaphor on the concept of associated salient characteristics I have developed a theory that is sensitive to those interpretations which clearly rest on context rather than on lexical knowledge, as well as to those interpretations which are dependent on community-wide beliefs.[23]

3. *A metaphor used assertively may not admit of simple paraphrase.* The claim has often been made that metaphors are not paraphrasable in literal language. Sometimes the claim is trivial, as when we are then told that even literal expressions cannot be paraphrased. When it is not trivial, the claim takes one of three forms:

(i) There is a lexical gap in our vocabulary; there are some things that can be said by metaphor for which we have no literal words.

(ii) No literal paraphrase can capture the suggestiveness of a metaphor.

(iii) No literal paraphrase can give the "insight" a metaphor gives.[24]

I shall comment on (ii) and (iii) below; it is (i) that interests me here. My theory is consistent with both (i) and its denial.

It is important to distinguish two versions of the gap mentioned in (i):

(ia) There is some proposition that, given the available resources of our language, is not literally expressed by any sentence or set of sentences.

I have not seen any convincing example supporting the existence of a gap of this sort that has been successfully plugged by a *metaphor*. Stipulation and theoretical introduction of terms, as in scientific inquiry, may fill such gaps— but this is not metaphor.

(ib) There is some meaning of a nonpropositional sort that, given the available resources of our language, is not literally expressed by any single word.

This claim seems to be true. For example, I know of no single word that means the same as what 'brilliant and eccentric scientist' literally expresses.

Yet, under appropriate circumstances, this may be a metaphorical interpretation of 'an Einstein'.

4. *There is no one answer to the question 'Why do we use metaphors?'* Although I have focused on the use of metaphor in making assertions, we must not forget that metaphors can be used nonassertively: for example, we may question or command with metaphors. But even when the use of a metaphor *is* assertive, there may be purposes beyond that of conveying a proposition. The metaphor may be used for aesthetic reasons (it conjures up a pleasing or disturbing image), or rhetorical ones (an expression in the metaphor has strong emotive connotations). Or the metaphor may be used because it is believed to be rich, to be fecund, or to have considerable organizing power.

A metaphor is *fecund* if it suggests other, related, metaphors. From 'John is a child' we may move to talk of playing to characterize John metaphorically, or we may move to characterizing other people metaphorically as adolescents, as middle-aged, or as elderly. And we may, in the process, discover a useful new vocabulary for a certain subject matter.[25]

A metaphor has *organizing power* if it influences our orientation toward a subject matter. Organizing power is what Susan Sontag notes in metaphors about artistic style:

> Take . . . Whitman's very material metaphor. By likening style to a curtain, he has of course confused style with decoration and for this would be speedily faulted by most critics. To conceive of style as a decorative encumbrance on the matter of the work suggests that the curtain could be parted and the matter revealed; or, to vary the metaphor slightly, that the curtain could be rendered transparent. But this is not the only erroneous implication of the metaphor. What the metaphor also suggests is that style is a matter of more or less (quantity), thick and thin (density). And . . . this is just as wrong as the fancy that an artist possesses the genuine option to have or not to have a style. Style is not quantitative, any more than it is superadded. . . .[26]

The organizing power of a metaphor concerns the *directedness* and *restrictedness* of what it suggests. A metaphor may highlight certain aspects of a subject while obscuring others. Here, I think, is the heuristic value in thinking of the understanding of certain metaphors as being akin to "seeing-as": metaphors sometimes give us a new orientation toward a familiar subject matter, making us revise, ignore, or even forget, the beliefs that went along with the old orientation.[27]

5. *Our assessments of the richness of metaphors are based on the workings of the same linguistic mechanism that enables us to make specific assertions with metaphor.* The mechanism is, of course, the manner of metaphor: the

salience relation between the expression used and the content of what is communicated.

A metaphor is *rich* if it is one that causes us to notice many things. Richness is not something inherent in a metaphor; rather our judgments as to richness are based on the effects the metaphor has on us. Our perceptions of the richness of a metaphor, like those of fecundity and organizing power, may vary with time and with concentration.

Take 'John is a child' as metaphor. I may use this to assert that John is naive, but it may cause you to notice (and I may have intended this) that John has other, perhaps less salient, characteristics of children: he is small, he giggles a lot. If I had just said 'John is naive' you would probably not, as a result of my utterance, notice these other things about John. In this sense, the literal paraphrase of my assertion does not have the suggestive power of the metaphor I used.

What you are noticing are salient characteristics associated with 'child'. I have already explained how salience can vary from context to context, and this is true whether the point of metaphor is assertion, heuristic guidance, or poetry. But there is another way in which salience won't stay fixed. Namely, the act of dwelling on a metaphor long enough, teasing out all that it can "mean," will affect salience of characteristics associated with component expressions. Specifically, if we repeatedly ask of a metaphor 'What *else* might it mean?', after the propositions based on some highly salient characteristics have been noted we may begin to notice, or to *focus upon*, characteristics that initially were not salient—and this very focusing raises the salience of those characteristics.

Thus, it is not surprising, to echo Davidson, that when we dwell on a metaphor we realize that there is no end to what it can "mean." And here we find one of the makings of poetry. For the poetic context invites us to dwell, to go beyond the *immediately* salient. But the poetic metaphor does not differ from the street variety in kind, for both do their work through salient characteristics. The difference lies in the practice rather than in the principle, in the ways we allow or disallow the immediate context to determine salience and hence interpretations. The underlying mechanism is the same in both cases. And it is reliance on this mechanism, rather than the purpose for which an expression is used—be it simple assertion, the sharing of profound insight, or poetry—that makes a linguistic act a metaphorical one.

NOTES

1. Research for this paper was supported by a Faculty Fellowship from Darmouth College. I am grateful to my colleagues Robert Fogelin, Bernard Gert, and James Moor for valuable criticisms and suggestions prompted by an earlier version of this paper.

2. See, for example, Stanley Cavell, "Aesthetic Problems in Modern Philosophy," in his

Must We Mean What We Say? (New York: Cambridge University Press, 1976), pp. 73–96; and Ted Cohen, "Notes on Metaphor," *Journal of Aesthetics and Art Criticism*, Vol. 34 (1976), 669–84.

3. Arne Naess discusses definiteness of intention in literal language use in *Interpretation and Preciseness* (Oslo: I Kommisjon Hos Jacob Dybwad, 1953).

4. "What Metaphors Mean," *Critical Inquiry*, 5 (1978), 46. Davidson argues that metaphors mean only what they literally mean. So the cognitive content at issue in the quotation is something different from literal meaning—a "metaphorical meaning." Israel Scheffler makes a claim similar to the one in this quotation, in *Beyond the Letter* (Boston: Routledge and Kegan Paul, 1979), pp. 128–30.

5. The nonexclusive contrast with lying is Davidson's. The inadequacies of purely semantic characterizations of metaphor are discussed in my "Metaphor and Formal Semantics," *Poetics*, 8 (1979), 213–230, in Ted Cohen, "Notes on Metaphor," and in Ina Loewenberg, "Identifying Metaphors," *Foundations of Language*, 12 (1975), 315–338.

6. Thus Robert Stalnaker writes:

The intuitive motivation for this analysis is something like the following. A proposition—the content of an assertion or belief—is a representation of the world as being a certain way. But for any given representation of the world as being a certain way, there will be a set of all the possible states of the world which accord with the representation—which *are* that way. So any proposition determines a set of possible worlds. And, for any given set of possible worlds, to locate the actual world in that set is to represent the world as being a certain way. So every set of possible worlds determines a proposition.

"Assertion," in *Pragmatics' Syntax and Semantics* Vol. 9, ed. Peter Cole (New York: Academic Press, 1978), 315–332.

7. Whether metaphors are "paraphrasable" has long been a live issue, and I'll briefly comment on it in Section III. Here my point is simply that, using intensional concepts like propositions as sets of possible worlds, we needn't beg the question as to the paraphrasability of assertive metaphors.

8. Cf. Stalnaker, "Assertion."

9. Strictly speaking, this needs qualification of a sort that need not concern us here: qualification concerning, for example, ambiguity and the use of indexicals.

10. I agree with Davidson on this point:

Once we understand a metaphor we can call what we grasp the "metaphorical truth" and (up to a point) say what the "metaphorical meaning" is. But simply to lodge this meaning in the metaphor is like explaining why a pill puts you to sleep by saying it has a dormative power. Literal meaning and literal truth conditions can be assigned to words and sentences apart from particular contexts of use. This is why advertising to them has genuine explanatory power. ("What Metaphors Mean," p. 33.)

The fact that an expression can be used as a metaphor does not point to, or create, an *ambiguity* in the expression. When metaphors die, to be sure, we may be left with new ambiguities. But that is the point of calling a metaphor 'dead'—it has become common currency.

11. The "direct" indicates that the proposition expressed may (and indeed will) depend on the literal meaning of the expression at issue; but it does so only insofar as the salient characteristics associated with an expression are partially a function of its literal meaning.

12. The companion is "The Formal Semantics of Metaphorical Assertions."

The concept of salience has appeared now in several accounts of metaphor. In particular, I am indebted to the work of Andrew Ortony for detailed discussions of this concept. See his

"Beyond Literal Similarity," *Psychological Review*, 86 (1976), 161–180, and "The Role of Similarity in Similes and Metaphors," in *Metaphor and Thought*, ed. Andrew Ortony (New York: Cambridge University Press, 1979), pp. 186–201.

13. The "distinctive" part is important. Israel Scheffler has pointed out that an account of metaphor that appeals to commonplaces with no restrictions will allow unacceptable interpretations of metaphors:

That wolves are larger than mushrooms is not only true but also commonly held to be true by laymen within our culture. These laymen also normally hold that wolves have eyes, occupy space and have weight; they are persuaded that no wolf is a tree or an umbrella or identical with Mount Everest. Does [such an account] then imply that to call men wolves is to say that men too are larger than mushrooms, have eyes, and so forth? (*Beyond the Letter*, p. 114.)

14. Max Black's description of a 'system of associated commonplaces' amplifies the notion of a stereotype:

Imagine some laymen required to say, without taking special thought, those things he held to be true about wolves; the set of statements resulting would approximate to what I am here calling the system of commonplaces associated with the word 'wolf'. I am assuming that in any given culture the responses made by different persons to the test suggested would agree rather closely, and that even the occasional expert, who might have unusual knowledge of the subject, would still know "what the man in the street thinks about the matter". From the expert's standpoint, the system of commonplaces may include self-truths or downright mistakes (as when a whale is classified as a fish); but the important thing for the metaphor's effectiveness is not that the commonplaces shall be true, but that they should be readily and freely evoked ("Metaphor," *Proceedings of the Aristotelian Society*, 55 (1954–1955), 287.)

See also Hilary Putnam's account of stereotypes in "The Meaning of 'Meaning'," in *Language, Mind, and Knowledge*, Minnesota Studies in the Philosophy of Science, Vol. 7, ed. Keith Gunderson (Minneapolis: University of Minnesota Press, 1975), 131–193).

15. Sometimes the salient characteristics we associate with a general expression such as a common noun or a verb are characteristics thought typical or distinctive of some *prominent subclass* of the extension of the word. Consider 'He had a green thought.' I can't think of any distinctive characteristics associated with the *entire* collection of green things, save that they are green. In interpeting the sentence as metaphor we may focus on a subcollection of green things— plants, perhaps, or unripe fruit. Then we have the characteristics on the one hand of growing, or thriving; and on the other of being immature or underdeveloped.

16. This includes the topics of the metaphorical sentence. Although I do not ordinarily take their lacking consciousness as a distinctive property of vegetables, in the context of the sentence 'John's grandfather is a vegetable' the property *does* become a prominent, noticeable characteristic. (The example is Andrew Ortony's.)

17. I should also add, for those who have qualms about resting an account of metaphor on the context-sensitive concept of salience, that statements of comparison and counterfactual statements are in the same boat as metaphor in this respect. See David Lewis' *Counterfactuals* (Cambridge, Mass.: Harvard University Press, 1973), pp. 91–95 and 114–117; and also his "Counterfactual Dependence and Time's Arrow," *Noûs*, 13 (1979), 466–467.

There is, of course, a long tradition of semantically analyzing metaphors *as* comparisons; and there has also been an attempt to analyze metaphors as elliptical counterfactuals. For the latter, see Teun A. van Dijk, "Formal Semantics of Metaphorical Discourse," *Poetics*, 4 (1975), 173–198. I prefer the account based on salience since the comparison and counterfactual accounts are going to have to rely on salience anyway if they are to give fairly specific content to metaphorical assertions. Once the necessity of recourse to salience is granted, there seems to be little point in taking the intermediate step of converting a metaphor into either a statement of comparison or a counterfactual.

18. "Logic and Conversation," in *The Logic of Grammar*, ed. Donald Davidson and Gilbert Harman (Encino, Calif.: Dickenson, 1975), pp. 64–75.

19. See Stephen Schiffer, *Meaning* (Oxford: Clarendon Press, 1972) and Stalnaker, "Assertion," on mutual knowledge.

20. Considerations of perspicuity enter in another way: we should use metaphorical expressions *consistently*. If I say 'Bob is a bird and Julie is a bird', intending to assert that Bob is a light eater and Julie sings beautifully, you will probably *not* get what I intended to convey.

If you do succeed in switching salience of characteristics midsentence along with me, it may be because we mutually know that Julie is no light eater and that she has been studying opera. Cf. the "rule of accommodation for comparative salience" in David Lewis, "Scorekeeping in a Language Game," *Journal of Philosophical Logic*, 8 (1979), 339–359.

21. And some *dead* metaphors may not, when live, have been pure ones. On this point see Nelson Goodman, *Languages of Art* (New York: Bobbs-Merrill, 1968), pp. 76–77.

22. "The Role of Inductive Reasoning in the Interpretation of Metaphor," in *Semantics of Natural Language*, ed. Donald Davidson and Gilbert Harman (Dordrecht: D. Reidel, 1972), p. 735.

23. Ted Cohen has argued in "Figurative Speech and Figurative Acts," *Journal of Philosophy*, 72 (1975), pp. 669–684 that because what a metaphor "means" is not a function of its literal meaning, metaphorical meaning is therefore not rule-governed and is hence unpredictable. I have been arguing that interpretation of metaphor *is* rule-governed; but the output depends on salience determined by the context as well as on literal meanings. It is this reliance on *context*, rather than the lack of a rule, that makes for unpredictability: as what is salient changes, so do the interpretations we read into metaphors.

24. The first form has been attributed to Aristotle (the *Poetics*); an example of the second is found in Charles L. Stevenson, *Ethics and Language* (New Haven: Yale University Press, 1944); and an example of the third is found in Black's "Metaphor."

25. Cf. Goodman, *Languages of Art*, pp. 74 ff.

26. *Against Interpretation* (New York: Dell, 1966), pp. 17–18.

27. There is extensive discussion of what I have called the *organizing power* of metaphor in George Lakoff and Mark Johnson, *Metaphors We Live By* (Chicago: University of Chicago Press, 1980).

Some authors have characterized or *defined* metaphor as a linguistic act of a special sort: as an invitation to "see-as" or to view the world in a new way. Loewenberg, for example, says: ". . . I believe that 'making a proposal' distinguishes metaphorical utterances more effectively than merely 'saying something' does" ("Identifying Metaphors," p. 335). The distinction is not at all effective, for two reasons. First, metaphors can be used simply to "say something"—these are the assertive metaphors; and, second, language can be used *literally* to make proposals. Any attempt to define metaphor in terms of purpose or illocutionary force is bound to fail. The points of using metaphor, like the points of using language literally, are varied; and there is no "point" that is the exclusive domain of either.

JOHN PERRY

THE PROBLEM OF THE ESSENTIAL INDEXICAL

I once followed a trail of sugar on a supermarket floor, pushing my cart down the aisle on one side of a tall counter and back the aisle on the other, seeking the shopper with the torn sack to tell him he was making a mess. With each trip around the counter, the trail became thicker. But I seemed unable to catch up. Finally it dawned on me. I was the shopper I was trying to catch.

I believed at the outset that the shopper with a torn sack was making a mess. And I was right. But I didn't believe that I was making a mess. That seems to be something I came to believe. And when I came to believe that, I stopped following the trail around the counter, and rearranged the torn sack in my cart. My change in beliefs seems to explain my change in behavior. My aim in this paper is to make a key point about the characterization of this change, and of beliefs in general.

At first characterizing the change seems easy. My beliefs changed, didn't they, in that I came to have a new one, namely, *that I am making a mess*? But things are not so simple.

The reason they are not is the importance of the word "I" in my expression of what I came to believe. When we replace it with other designations of me, we no longer have an explanation of my behavior and so, it seems, no longer an attribution of the same belief. It seems to be an *essential* indexical. But without such a replacement, all we have to identify the belief is the sentence "I am making a mess". But that sentence by itself doesn't seem to identify the crucial belief, for if someone else had said it, they would have expressed a different belief, a false one.

I argue that the essential indexical poses a problem for various otherwise plausible accounts of belief. I first argue that it is a problem for the view that belief is a relation between subjects and propositions conceived as bearers of truth and falsity. The problem is not solved merely by replacing or supplementing this with a notion of *de re* belief. Nor is it solved by moving to a notion of a proposition which, rather than true or false absolutely, is only true or false at an index or in a context (at a time, for a speaker, say). Its solution requires us to make a sharp distinction between objects of belief and belief states, and to realize that the connection between them is not so intimate as might have been supposed.[1]

LOCATING BELIEFS

I want to introduce two more examples. In the first a professor, who desires to attend the department meeting on time, and believes correctly that it begins at noon, sits motionless in his office at that time. Suddenly he begins to move. What explains his action? A change in belief. He believed all along that the department meeting starts at noon; he came to believe, as he would have put it, that it starts *now*.

The author of the book, *Hiker's Guide to the Desolation Wilderness*, stands in the wilderness besides Gilmore Lake, looking at the Mt. Tallac trail as it leaves the lake and climbs the mountain. He desires to leave the wilderness. He believes that the best way out from Gilmore Lake is to follow the Mt. Tallac trail up the mountain to Cathedral Peaks trail, on to the Floating Island trail, emerging at Spring Creek Tract Road. But he does not move. He is lost. He isn't sure whether he is standing beside Gilmore Lake, looking at Mt. Tallac, or beside Clyde Lake looking at Jack's peak, or beside Eagle Lake looking at one of the Maggie peaks. Then he begins to move along the Mt. Tallac trail. If asked, he would have explained the crucial change in his beliefs this way: "I came to believe that *this* is the Mt. Tallac trail and *that* is Gilmore Lake."

In these three cases the subjects in explaining their actions, would use indexicals to characterize certain beliefs they came to have. These indexicals are essential, in that replacement of them by other terms destroys the force of the explanation, or at least requires certain assumptions to be made to preserve it.

Suppose I had said, in the manner of de Gaulle, "I came to believe that John Perry is making a mess." I would no longer have explained why I stopped and looked in my own cart. To explain that I would have to add, "and I believe that I am John Perry," bringing in the indexical again. After all, suppose I had really given my explanation in the manner of de Gaulle, and said "I came to believe that de Gaulle is making a mess." That wouldn't have explained my stopping at all. But it really would have explained it every bit as much as "I came to believe John Perry is making a mess". For if I added "and I believe that I am de Gaulle" the explanations would be on par. The only reason "I came to believe John Perry is making a mess" seems to explain my action is our natural assumption that I did believe I was John Perry and didn't believe I was de Gaulle. So replacing the indexical 'I' with another term designating the same person really does, as claimed, destroy the explanation.

Similarly, our professor, as he sets off down the hall, might say "I believe the meeting starts at noon", rather than "I believe the meeting starts now". In accepting the former as an explanation, we would be assuming he believes it is *now* noon. If he believed it was now 5 p.m., he wouldn't have explained his departure by citing his belief that the meeting starts at noon, unless he was a member of a department with very long meetings. After all, he believed that the meeting started at noon all along, so that belief can hardly explain a change in his behavior. Basically similar remarks apply to the lost author.

I shall use the term "locating beliefs" to refer to one's beliefs about where one is, when it is, and who one is. Such beliefs seem essentially indexical. Imagine two lost campers who trust the same guidebook but disagree about where they are. If we were to try to characterize the beliefs of these campers without the use of indexicals, it would seem impossible to bring out this disagreement. If, for example, we characterized their beliefs by the set of "eternal sentences," drawn from the guidebook they would mark "true", there is no reason to suppose that the sets would differ. They could mark all of the same sentences "true", and still disagree in their locating beliefs. It seems that there has to be some indexical element in the characterization of their beliefs to bring out this disagreement. But as we shall see there is no room for this indexical element in the traditional way of looking at belief, and even when its necessity is recognized, it is not easy to see how to fit it in.

THE DOCTRINE OF PROPOSITIONS

I shall first consider how the problem appears to a traditional way of thinking of belief. The doctrines I describe were held by Frege, but I shall put them in a way that does not incorporate his terminology or the details of his view.[2] This traditional way, which I call the "doctrine of propositions", has three main tenets. The first is that belief is a relation between a subject and an object, the latter being denoted, in a canonical belief report, by a that-clause. So "Carter beliefs that Atlanta is the capital of Georgia" reports that a certain relation, *believing*, obtains between Carter and a certain object—at least in a suitably wide sense of object—*that Atlanta is the capital of Georgia*. These objects are called *propositions*.

The second and the third tenets concern such objects. The second is that they have a truth-value in an absolute sense, as opposed to merely being true for a person or at a time. The third has to do with how we individuate them. It is necessary, for *that S* and *that S'* to be the same, that they have the same truth-value. But it is not sufficient, for *that the sea is salty* and *that milk is white* are not the same proposition. It is necessary that they have the same truth condition, in the sense that they attribute to the same objects the same relation. But this also is not sufficient, for *that Atlanta is the capital of Georgia* and *that Atlanta is the capital of the largest state east of the Mississippi* are not the same proposition. Carter, it seems, might believe the first but not the second. Propositions must not only have the same truth-value, and concern the same objects and relations, but also involve the same concepts. For Frege, this meant that if *that S = that S'*, S and S' must have the same sense. Others might eschew senses in favor of properties and relations, others take concepts to be just words, so that sameness of propositions is just sameness of sentences. What these approaches have in common is the insistence that propositions must be individuated in a more "fine-grained" way than is provided by truth-value or the notion truth conditions employed above.

THE PROBLEM

It's clear that the essential indexical is a problem for the doctrine of propositions. What answer can it give to the question, "What did I come to believe when I straightened up the sugar?" The sentence "I am making a mess" doesn't identify a proposition. For this sentence is not true or false absolutely, but only as said by one person or another; had another shopper said it when I did, he would have been wrong. So the sentence by which I identify what I came to believe doesn't identify, by itself, a proposition. There is a *missing conceptual ingredient*: a sense for which I am the reference, or a complex of properties I alone have, or a singular term that refers to no one but me. To identify the proposition I came to believe, the advocate of the doctrine of propositions must identify this missing conceptual ingredient.

An advocate of the doctrine of propositions, his attention drawn to indexicals, might take this attitude towards them: they are communicative shortcuts. Just before I straightened up the sack I must have come to believe some propositions with the structure α *is making a mess*, where α is some concept which I alone "fit" (to pick a phrase neutral among the different notions of a concept). When I say "I believe I am making a mess," my hearers know that I believe some such proposition of this form; which one in particular is not important for the purposes at hand.

If this is correct, we should be able to identify the proposition I came to believe, even if doing so isn't necessary for ordinary communicative purposes. But then the doctrine of propositions is in trouble, for any candidate will fall prey to the problems mentioned above. If *that α is making a mess* is what I came to believe, then "I came to believe that A is making a mess", where A expressed α, should be an even better explanation than the original, where I used "I" as a communicative shortcut. But, as we saw, any such explanation will be defective, working only on the assumption that I believed that I was α.

To this it might be replied that though there may be no replacement for "I" that generally preserves explanatory force, all that needs to be claimed is that there is such a replacement on each occasion. The picture is this. On each occasion that I use "I", there is some concept I have in mind that fits me uniquely, and which is the missing conceptual ingredient in the proposition that remains incompletely identified when I characterize my beliefs. The concept I use to think of myself isn't necessarily the same each time I do so, and of course I must use a different one than others do, since it must fit me and not them. Because there is no general way of replacing the "I" with a term that gets at the missing ingredient, the challenge to do so in response to a particular example is temporarily embarrassing. But the doctrine of propositions doesn't require a general answer.

This strategy doesn't work for two reasons. First, even if I was thinking of myself as, say, the only bearded philosopher in a Safeway store west of the Mississippi, the fact that I came to believe that the only such philosopher was making a mess explains my action only on the assumption that I believed that I was the only such philosopher, which brings in the indexical again. Second, in order to provide me with an appropriate proposition as the object of belief, the missing conceptual ingredient will have to fit me. Suppose I was thinking of myself in the way described, but that I wasn't bearded and wasn't in a Safeway store—I had forgotten that I had shaved and gone to the A & P instead. Then the proposition supplied by this strategy would be false, while what I came to believe, *that I was making a mess*, was true.

This strategy assumes that whenever I have a belief I would characterize by using a sentence with an indexical *d*,

I believe that . . . d . . .

that there is some conceptual ingredient *c*, such that it is also true that,

I believe that *d* is *c*

and that, on this second point, I am right. But there is no reason to believe this would always be so. Each time I say "I believe it is *now* time to rake the leaves," I need not have some concept that uniquely fits the time at which I speak.

From the point of view of the doctrine of propositions, belief reports such as "I believe that I am making a mess" are deficient, for there is a missing conceptual ingredient. From the point of view of locating beliefs, there is something lacking in the propositions offered by the doctrine, a missing indexical ingredient.

The problem of the essential indexical reveals that something is badly wrong with the traditional doctrine of propositions. But the traditional doctrine has its competitors anyway, in response to philosophical pressures from other directions. Perhaps attention to these alternative or supplementary models of belief will provide a solution to our problem.

DE RE BELIEF

One development in the philosophy of belief seems quite promising in this respect. It involves qualifying the third tenet of the doctrine of propositions, to allow a sort of proposition individuated by an object or sequence of objects, and a part of a proposition of the earlier sort. The motivation for this qualification or supplementation comes from belief report which gives rise to the same problem, that of the missing conceptual ingredient, as does the problem of the essential indexical.

The third tenet of the doctrine of propositions is motivated by the failure of substitutivity of co-referential terms within the that-clause following "believes". But there seems to be a sort of belief report, or a way of understanding some belief reports, that allows such substitution, and such successful substitution becomes a problem for a theory designed to explain its failure. For suppose Patrick believes that, as he would put it, the dean is wise. Patrick doesn't know Frank, much less know that he lives next to the dean, and yet I might in certain circumstances say "Patrick believes Frank's neighbor is wise." Or I might say "There is someone whom Patrick believes to be wise," and later on identify that someone as "Frank's neighbor." The legitimacy of this cannot be understood on the unqualified doctrine of propositions; I seem to have gone from one proposition, *that the dean of the school is wise*, to another, *that Frank's neighbor is wise*; but the fact that Patrick believes the first seems to be no reason he should believe the second. And the quantification into the belief report seems to make no sense at all on the doctrine of propositions, for the report doesn't relate Patrick to an individual known variously as "the dean" and "Frank's neighbor", but only with a concept expressed by the first of these terms.

The problem here is just that of a missing conceptual ingredient. It looked in the original report as if Patrick was being said to stand in the relation of belief to a certain proposition, a part of which was a conceptual ingredient expressed by the words "the dean". But if I am permitted to exchange those words for others, "Frank's neighbor", which are not conceptually equivalent, then apparently the initial part of the proposition he was credited with belief in was not the conceptual ingredient identified by "the dean" after all. So what proposition was it Patrick was originally credited with belief in? And "There is someone such that Patrick believes that he is wise" seems to credit Patrick with belief in a proposition, without telling us which one. For after the "believes" we have only "he is wise", where the "he" doesn't give us an appropriate conceptual ingredient, but functions as a variable ranging over individuals.

We do seem in some circumstances to allow such substitutivity, and make ready sense of quantification into belief reports. So the doctrine of propositions must be qualified. We can look upon this sort of belief as involving a relation to a new sort of proposition, consisting of an object or sequence of objects and a conceptual ingredient, a part of a proposition of the original kind, or what we might call an "open proposition". This sort of belief and this kind of proposition we call "*de re*", the sort of belief and the sort of proposition that fits the original doctrine, "*de dicto*". Taken this way we analyze "Patrick believes that the dean of the school is wise", as reporting a relation between Patrick and a proposition consisting of a certain person variously describable as "the dean" and "Frank's neighbor" and something, *that x is wise*, which would yield a proposition with the addition of an appropriate conceptual ingredient. Since the dean himself, and not just a concept expressed by the words "the dean" is involved, substitution holds and quantification makes sense.

Here, as in the case of the essential indexical, we were faced with a missing conceptual ingredient. Perhaps, then, this modification of the third tenet will solve the earlier problem as well. But it won't. Even if we suppose— as I think we should—that when I said "I believe that I am making a mess" I was reporting a *de re* belief, our problem will remain.

One problem emerges when we look at accounts that have been offered of the conditions under which a person has a *de re* belief. The most influential treatments of *de re* belief have tried to explain it in terms of *de dicto* belief or something like it. Some terminological regimentation is helpful here. Let us couch reports of *de re* belief in the terms "X believes of a that he is so and so", reserving the simpler "X believes that a is so-and-so" for *de dicto* belief. The simplest account of *de re* belief in terms of de dicto belief is this:

X believes of y that he is so and so

just in case

There is a concept α such that α fits y and X believes that α is so and so.

Now it is clear that if this is our analysis of *de re* belief, the problem of the essential indexical is still with us. For we are faced with the same problem we had before. I can believe that I am making a mess, even if there is no concept α such that I alone fit α and I believe that α is making a mess. Since I don't have any *de dicto* belief of the sort, on this account I don't have a *de re* belief of the right sort either. So, even allowing *de re* belief, we still don't have an account of the belief I acquired.

Now this simple account of *de re* belief has not won many adherents, because it is commonly held that *de re* belief is a more interesting notion than it allows. This proposal trivializes it. Suppose Nixon is the next President. Since I believe that the next president will be the next president I would on this proposal, believe of Nixon that he is the next president, even though I am thoroughly convinced that Nixon will not be the next President.[3]

To get a more interesting or useful notion of *de re* belief, philosophers have suggested that there are limitations on the conceptual ingredient involved in the *de dicto* belief which yields the *de re* belief. Kaplan, for example, requires not only that there be some α such that I believe that α will be the next President and that α denotes Nixon, for me to believe of Nixon that he will be the next President, but also that α be a *vivid name of Nixon for me* ([9:225 ff.]). Hintikka requires that α denote the same individual in every possible world compatible with what I believe ([7:40 ff.]). Each of these philosophers explains these notions in such a way that in the circumstances imagined, I would not believe of Nixon that he is the next President.

However well these proposals deal with other phenomena connected with *de re* belief, they cannot help with the problem of the essential indexical. They tighten the requirements laid down by the original proposal, but those were apparently already too restrictive. If in order to believe that I am making a mess I need not have any conceptual ingredient α that fits me, *a fortiori* I am not required to have one that is a vivid name of myself for me, or one that picks out the same individual in every possible world compatible with what I believe.

Perhaps this simply shows that the approach of explaining *de re* belief in terms of *de dicto* belief is incorrect. I think it does show that. But even so, the problem remains, Suppose we do not insist on an account of *de re* belief in terms of *de dicto* belief, but merely suppose that whenever we ascribe a belief, and cannot find a suitable complete proposition to serve as the object because of a missing conceptual ingredient, we are dealing with *de re* belief. Then we will ascribe a *de re* belief to me in the supermarket, I believed *of* John Perry that he was making a mess. But it won't be my having such a *de re* belief that explains my action.

Suppose there were mirrors at either end of the counter so that as I pushed my cart down the aisle in pursuit I saw myself in the mirror. I take what I see to be the reflection of the messy shopper going up the aisle on the other side, not realizing that what I am really seeing is a reflection of a reflection of myself. I point and say, truly, "I believe that he is making a mess." In trying to find a suitable proposition for me to believe, we would be faced with the same sorts of problems we had with my earlier report, in which I used "I" instead of "he". We would not be able to eliminate an indexical element in the term referring to me. So here we have *de re* belief; I believe of John Perry that he is making of a mess. But then that I believe of John Perry that he is making a mess doesn't explain my stopping; in the imagined circumstances I would accelerate, as would the shopper I was trying to catch. But then, even granting that when I say "I believe that I am making a mess" I attribute to myself a certain *de re* belief, the belief of John Perry that he is making a mess, our problem remains.

If we look at it with the notion of a locating belief in mind, the failure of the introduction of *de re* belief to solve our problems is not surprising. *De re* propositions remain nonindexical. Propositions individuated in part by objects remain as insensitive to what is essential in locating beliefs as those individuated wholly by concepts. Saying that I believed of John Perry that he was making a mess leaves out the crucial change, that I came to think of the messy shopper not merely as the shopper with the torn sack, or the man in the mirror, but as *me*.

RELATIVIZED PROPOSITIONS

It seems that to deal with essential indexicality we must somehow incorporate the indexical element into what is believed, the object of belief. It we do so, we come up against the second tenet of the doctrine of propositions, that such objects are true or false absolutely. But the tools for abandoning this tenet have been provided in recent treatments of the semantics of modality, tense, and indexicality. So this seems a promising direction.

In possible worlds semantics for necessity and possibility we have the notion of truth at a world. In a way this doesn't involve a new notion of a proposition and in a way it does. When Frege insisted that his "thoughts" were true or false absolutely, he didn't mean that they had the same truth-value in all possible worlds. Had he used a possible worlds framework, he would have had their truth-values vary from world to world, and simply insisted on a determinate truth-value in each world and in particular in the actual world. In a way, then, taking propositions to be functions from possible worlds to truth-values is just a way of looking at the old notion of a proposition.

Still, this way of looking at it invites generalization, that takes us away from the old notion. From a technical point of view, the essential idea is that a proposition is or is represented by a function from an index to a truth-value; when we get away from modality, this same technical idea may be useful, though something other than possible worlds are taken as indices. To deal with temporal operators, we can use the notion of truth at a time. Here the indices will be times, and our propositions will be functions from times to truth-values. For example, *that Elizabeth is Queen of England* is a proposition true in 1960 but not in 1940. Hence "At sometime or other Elizabeth is Queen of England" is true, simpliciter. (See [10] and [13], especially "Pragmatics".)

Now consider "I am making a mess". Rather than thinking of this as partially identifying an absolutely true proposition, with the "I" showing the place of the missing conceptual ingredient, why not think of it as completely identifying a new-fangled proposition, that is true or false only *at a person*? More precisely, it is one that is true or false at a time and a person, since though true when I said it, it has since occasionally been false.

If we ignore possibility and necessity, it seems that regarding propositions as functions to truth-values from indices which are pairs of persons and times will do the trick, and that so doing will allow us to exploit relations between elements within the indices to formulate rules which bring out differences between indexicals. "I am tired now" is true at the pair consisting of the person a and the time t if and only if a is tired at t, while "You will be tired" is true at the same index if and only if the addressee of a at t is tired at some time later than t.

Does this way of looking at the matter solve the problem of the essential indexical? I say "I believe that I am making a mess". On our amended doctrine of propositions, this ascribes a relation between me and *that I am making a mess*, which is a function from indices to truth values. The belief report seems to completely specify the relativized proposition involved; there is no missing conceptual ingredient. So the problem must be solved.

But it isn't. I believed that a certain proposition, *that I am making a mess* was true—true for me. So belief that this proposition was true for me then doesn't differentiate me from the other shopper, and can't be what explains my stopping and searching my cart for the torn sack. Once we have adopted these new-fangled propositions, which are only true at times for persons, we have to admit also that we believe them as true for persons at times, and not absolutely. And then our problem returns.

Clearly an important distinction must be made. All believing is done by persons at times, or so we may suppose. But the time of belief and the person doing the believing cannot be generally identified with the person and time relative to which the proposition believed is held true. You now believe that *that I am making a mess* was true for me, then, but you certainly don't believe it is true for you now, unless you are reading this in a supermarket. Let us call *you* and *now* the context of belief, and *me* and *them* the context of evaluation. The context of belief may be the same as the context of evaluation, but need not be.

Now the mere fact that I believed that proposition *that I making a mess* to be true for someone at some time did not explain my stopping the cart. You believe so now, and doubtless have no more desire to mess up supermarkets than I did. But you are not bending over to straighten up a sack of sugar.

The fact that I believed this proposition true for Perry at the time he was in the supermarket does not explain my behavior either. For so did the other shopper. And you also now believe this proposition was true for Perry at the time he was in the supermarket.

The important difference seems to be that for me the context of belief was just the context of evaluation, but for the other shopper it wasn't and for you it isn't. But this doesn't do the trick either.

Consider our tardy professor. He is doing research on indexicals, and has written on the board "My meeting starts now". He believes that the proposition expressed by this sentence is true at noon for him. He has believed so for hours, and at noon the context of belief comes to.be the context of evaluation. These facts give us no reason to expect him to move.

Or suppose I think to myself that the person making the mess should say so. Turning my attention to the proposition, I certainly believe *that I am making a mess* is true for the person who ought to be saying it (or the person in the mirror, or the person at the end of the trail of sugar) at that time. The context of evaluation is just the context of belief. But there is no reason to suppose I would stop my cart.

One supposes that in these cases the problem is that the context of belief is not believed to be the context of evaluation. But formulating the required belief will simply bring up the problem of the essential indexical again. Clearly and correctly we want the tardy professor, when he finally sees he must be off to the meeting, to be ready to say "I believe that the time at which it is true *that the meeting starts now* is now." On the present proposal, we analyze the belief he thereby ascribes to himself as belief in the proposition *that the time at which it is true that the meeting starts now is now*. But he certainly can believe at noon, that this whole proposition is true at noon, without being ready to say "It's starting now" and leave. We do not yet have a solution to the problem of the essential indexical.

LIMITED ACCESSIBILITY

One may take all that has been said so far as an argument for the existence of a special class of propositions, propositions of limited accessibility. For what have we really shown? All attempts to find a formula of the form "A is making a mess", with which any of us at any time could express what I believed, have failed. But one might argue that we can hardly suppose that there wasn't anything that I believed; surely I believed just that proposition which I expressed, on that occasion, with the words "I am making a mess". That we cannot find a sentence that always expresses this proposition when said by anyone does not show that it does not exist. Rather it should lead us to the conclusion that there is a class of propositions which can only be expressed in special circumstances. In particular, only I could express the proposition I expressed when I said "I am making a mess." Others can see, perhaps by analogy with their own case, that there is a proposition that I express, but it is in a sense inaccessible to them.

Similarly, at noon on the day of the meeting, we could all express the proposition the tardy professor expressed with the words "The meeting starts now". But once that time has past, the proposition becomes inaccessible. We can still identify it, as the proposition which was expressed by those words at that time. But we cannot express it with those words any longer, for with each passing moment they express a different proposition. And we can find no other words to express it.

The advocate of such a stock of propositions of limited accessability may not need to bring in special propositions of limited accessible only at certain places. For it is plausible to suppose that other indexicals can be eliminated in favor of "I" and "now". Perhaps "That is Gilmore Lake" just comes to "What I see now in front of me is Gilmore Lake". But elimination of either "I" or "now" in favor of the other seems impossible.

Such a theory of propositions of limited accessibility seems acceptable, even attractive, to some philosophers.[4] Its acceptability or attractiveness will depend on other parts of one's metaphysics; if one finds plausible reasons elsewhere for believing in a universe that has, in addition to our common world, myriads of private perspectives, the idea of propositions of limited accessability will fit right in.[5] I have no knockdown argument against such propositions, or the metaphysical schemes that find room for them. But I believe only in a common actual world. And I do not think the phenomenon of essential indexicality forces me to abandon this view.

THE OBVIOUS SOLUTION?

Let's return to the device of the true-false exam. Suppose the lost author had been given such an exam before and after he figured out where he was. Would we expect any differences in his answers? Not so long as the statements contained no indexicals. "Mt. Tallac is higher than either of the Maggie Peaks" would have been marked the same way before and after, the same way he would have marked it at home in Berkeley. His mark on that sentence would tell us nothing about where he thought he was. But if the exam were to contain such sentences as "That is Gilmore Lake in front of me" we would expect a dramatic change, from "False" or "Unsure" to "True".

Imagine such an exam given to various lost campers in different parts of the Wilderness. We could classify the campers by their answers, and such a classification would be valuable for prediction and explanation. Of all the campers who marked "This is Gilmore Lake" with "True", we would say they believed that they were at Gilmore Lake. And we should expect them to act accordingly; if they possessed the standard guidebook, and wished to leave the Wilderness, we might expect what is, given one way of looking at it, the same behavior: taking the path up the mountain above the shallow end of the lake before them.

Now consider all the good-hearted people who have ever been in a supermarket, noticed sugar on the floor, and been ready to say "I am making a mess." They all have something important in common, something that leads us to expect their next action to be that of looking into their grocery carts in search of the torn sack. Or consider all the responsible professors who have ever uttered "The department meeting is starting now." They too have something important in common; they are in a state which will lead those just down the hall to go to the meeting, those across campus to curse and feel guilty, those on leave to smile.

What the members within these various groups have in common is not what they believe. There is no *de dicto* proposition that all the campers or shoppers or professors believe. And there is no person whom all the shoppers believe to be making a mess, no lake all the campers believe to be Gilmore Lake, and no time at which all the professors believe their meetings to be starting.

We are clearly classifying the shoppers, campers, and professors into groups corresponding to what we have been calling "relativized propositions"—abstract objects corresponding to sentences containing indexicals. But what members of each group have in common, which makes the groups significant, is not belief that a certain relativized proposition is true. Such belief, as we saw, is belief that such a proposition is true at some context of evaluation. Now all of the shoppers believe that *that I am making a mess* is true at some context of evaluation or other, but so does everyone else who has ever given it a moment's thought. And similar remarks apply to the campers and the professors.

If believing the same relativized proposition isn't what the members of each of the groups have in common with one another, why is it being used as a principle of classification? I propose we look at things in this way. The shoppers, for example, are all in a certain belief state, a state which, given normal desires and other belief states they can be expected to be in, will lead each of them to examine his cart. But, although they are all in the same belief state (not the same *total* belief state, of course), they do not all have the same belief (believe the same thing, have the relation of belief to the same object).

We use sentences with indexicals or relativized propositions to individuate belief states, for the purposes of classifying believers in ways useful for explanation and prediction. That is, belief states individuated in this way enter into our common sense theory about human behavior and more sophisticated theories emerging from it. We expect all good-hearted people in that state which leads them to say "I am making a mess" to examine their grocery carts, no matter what belief they have in virtue of being in that state. That we individuate belief states in this way doubtless has something to do with the fact that one criterion for being in the states we postulate, at least for articulate sincere adults, is being disposed to utter the indexical sentence in question. A good philosophy of mind should explain this in detail; my aim is merely to get clear about what it is that needs explaining.

The proposal, then, is that there is not an identity, or even an isomorphic correspondence, but only a systematic relationship between the belief states one is in and what one thereby believes. The opposite assumption, that belief states should be classified by propositions believed, seems to be built right into traditional philosophies of belief. Given this assumption, whenever we have believers in the same belief state, we must expect to find a proposition they all believe, and differences in belief state lead us to expect a difference in proposition believed. The bulk of this paper consisted in following such leads to nowhere (or to propositions of limited accessibility).

Consider a believer whose belief states are characterized by a structure of sentences with indexicals or relativized propositions (those marked "true" in a very comprehensive exam, if we are dealing with an articulate sincere adult). This structure, together with the context of belief—the time and identity of the speaker—will yield a structure of *de re* propositions. The sequence of objects will consist of the values which the indexicals take in the context. The open propositions will be those yielded by the relativized proposition when shorn of its indexical elements. These are what the person believes, in virtue of being in the states he is in, when and where he is in them.[6]

This latter structure is important, and classifications of believers by *what* they believe is appropriate for many purposes. For example, usually, when a believer moves from context to context, his belief states adjust to preserve beliefs held. As time passes, I go from the state corresponding to "The meeting will begin" to the one corresponding to "The meeting is beginning" and finally to "The meeting has begun". All along I believe of noon that it is when the meeting begins. But I believe it in different ways. And to these different ways of believing the same thing, different actions are appropriate: preparation, movement, apology. Of course if the change of context is not noted, the adjustment of belief states will not occur, and a wholesale change from believing truly to believing falsely may occur. This is what happened to Rip Van Winkle. He awakes in the same belief states he fell asleep in twenty years earlier, unadjusted to the dramatic change in context, and so with a whole new set of beliefs, such as that he is a young man, mostly false.

We have here a metaphysically benign form of limited accessibility. Anyone at any time can have access to any proposition. But not in any way. Anyone can believe of John Perry that he is making a mess. And anyone can be in the belief state classified by the sentence "I am making a mess". But only I can have that belief by being in that state.

There is room in this scheme for *de dicto* propositions, for the characterization of one's belief states may include sentences without any indexical element. If there are any, they could appear on the exam. For this part of the structure, the hypothesis of perfect correspondence would be correct.

A more radical proposal would do away with objects of belief entirely. We would think of belief as a system of relations of various degrees between persons and other objects. Rather than saying I believed in the *de re* proposition consisting of me and the open proposition, *x is making a mess*, we would say that I stand in the relation, believing to be making a mess, to myself. There are many ways to stand in this relation to myself, that is, a variety of belief states I might be in. And these would be classified by sentences with indexicals. On this view *de dicto* belief, already demoted from its central place in the philosophy of belief, might be seen as merely an illusion, engendered by the implicit nature of much indexicality.

To say that belief states must be distinguished from objects of belief, cannot be individuated in terms of them, and are what is crucial for the explanation of action, is not to give a full fledged account of belief, or even a sketchy one. Similarly, to say that we must distinguish the object seen from the state of the seeing subject, and that the latter is crucial for the explanation of action guided by vision, is not to offer a full fledged account of vision. But just as the arguments from illusion and perceptual relativity teach us that no philosophy of perception can be plausible that is not cognizant of this last distinction, the problem of the essential indexical should teach us that no philosophy of belief can be plausible that does not take account of the first.[7]

NOTES

1. In thinking about the problem of the essential indexical, I have been greatly helped by the writings of Hector-Neri Castañeda on indexicality and related topics. Castañeda focused attention on these problems, and made many of the points made here, in [1], [2] and [3]. More recently his views on these matters have been developed as a part of his comprehensive system of generalized phenomenalism. See particularly [4] and [5]. Having benefitted so much from Castañeda's collection of "proto-philosophical data", I regret that differences of approach and limitations of competence and space have prevented me from incorporating a discussion of his theory into this essay. I hope to make good this omission at some future time.

2. See [11] for a critique of Frege's views on indexicality.

3. For the classic discussion of these problems, see [12].

4. Frege seems to accept something like it, as necessary for dealing with "I", in [6].

5. See [5] especially section II.

6. This two-tiered structure of belief states and propositions believed will remind the reader familar with David Kaplan's [8] of his system of characters and contents. This is no accident, for my approach to the problem of the essential indexical was formed by using the distinction as found in earlier versions of Kaplan's work to try to find a solution to the problem as articulated by Castañeda. Kaplan's treatment of indexicality was by and large shaped by considerations other than the problem of the essential indexical. So, while any plausibility one finds in what I say about that problem should be transmitted to the general outlines of his system, at least, by

providing an epistemological motivation for something like the character/content distinction, any implausiblity one finds will not necessarily be so transmitted. Nor should one take any details one manages to find in this essay as a guide to the details of Kaplan's system.

7. Versions of this paper were read at philosophy department colloquia at U.C.L.A., Claremont Graduate School, and Stanford, to the Washington State University at Bellingham Philosophy Conference, and to the Meeting of Alberta Philosophy Department. I am indebted to philosophers participating in these colloquia for many helpful criticisms and comments. I owe a special debt to Michael Bratman, and Dagfinn Føllesdal, for detailed comments on the penultimate version. Most of the ideas in this paper were developed while I held a fellowship from the Guggenheim Foundation and was on sabbatical leave from Stanford University, and I thank both for their support.

REFERENCES

[1] Hector-Neri Castañeda, " 'He': A Study in the Logic of Self-consciousness," *Ratio* 8(1966): 130–157.

[2] ——, "Indicators and Quasi-indicators," *American Philosophical Quarterly* 4(1967): 85–100.

[3] ——, "On the Logic of Attributions of Self Knowledge to Others," *The Journal of Philosophy* 65(1968): 439–456.

[4] ——, "On the Philosophical Foundations of the Theory of Communication: Reference," *Midwestern Studies in Philosophy* 2(1977): 165–186.

[5] ——, "Perception, Belief, and the Structure of Physical Objects and Consciousness," *Synthese* 35(1977): 285–351.

[6] Gotlobb Frege, "The Thought: A Logical Inquiry," translated by A. M. and Marcelle Quinton, *Mind* 65(1956): 289–311; reprinted in P. F. Strawson (ed.), *Philosophical Logic* (Oxford: Oxford University Press, 1967): 17–38.

[7] Jaakko Hintikka, "Individuals, Possible Worlds, and Epistemic Logic," *Noûs* 1(1967): 33–62.

[8] David Kaplan, *Demonstratives* (Mimeographed, UCLA, 1977).

[9] ——, "Quantifying In," in Donald Davidson and Jaakko Hintikka (eds.) *Words' and Objections* (Dordrecht: Reidel 1969): 206–242.

[10] Richard Montague, "Pragmakes," Richard Montague (New Haven, 1974): 95–118..

[11] John Perry, "Frege on Demonstratives," *Philosophical Review* 86(1977): 474–497.

[12] Williard van Orman Quine, "Quantifiers and Propositional Attitudes," reprinted in *Ways of Paradox* (New York: Random House, 1966): 183–194.

[13] Dana Scott, "Advice on Modal Logic," in Karel Lambert (ed.), *Philosophical Problems in Logic* (Dordrecht: Reidel, 1970): 143–173.

REFERENCES

Adams, R. 1974. "Theories of Actuality." *Noûs* 8: 211–231.

Allwood, J. 1972. "Negation and the Strength of Presuppositions." *Logical Grammar Report* 2. Gothenberg.

Aoun, J., N. Hornstein & D. Sportiche. 1980. "On Some Aspects of Wide Scope Quantification." *Journal of Linguistic Research*. I.

Aristotle. *Topics*.

Aristotle. *Metaphysica* (*Works*, VIII). English Translation by W. D. Ross. (Oxford, 1908).

Aristotle. *Poetics*.

Aristotle. *Prior Analytics*.

Aristotle. *Rhetoric*.

Atlas, J. 1977. "Negation, Ambiguity, and Presupposition." *Linguistics and Philosophy* 1: 321–336.

Austin, J. 1961. *Philosophical Papers*. Oxford. 1961. 89–90.

Bar-Hillel, Y. 1954. "Logical Syntax and Semantics." *Language*, 30: 230–237.

Bar-Hillel, Y. (ed.) 1965. *Logic, Methodology, and Philosophy of Science: Proceedings of the 1964 International Congress*. Amsterdam.

Bar-Hillel, Y., and B. Evert. 1963. In Schlipp 1963.

Barwise, J., and R. Cooper. 1981. "Generalized Quantifiers." *Linguistics and Philosophy* 4,2: 2.

Bergmann, M. 1977. "Logic and Sortal Incorrectness." *The Review of Metaphysics* 30: 61–69.

Black, M. 1955. "Metaphor." *Proceedings of the Aristotelian Society* 4.

Black, M. 1965. *Philosophy in America*. Ithaca, NY.

Black, M. 1979. "More about Metaphor." In Ortony 1979.

Bochvar, D. A. 1938. "On a Three-Valued Logical Calculus and Its Application to the Analysis of Contradictions." *Matematicheskii Sbornik* 4: 287–308.

Boer, S., and W. Lycan. 1975. "Review of *Counterfactuals*." *Foundations of Language* 13: 145–151.

Boer, S., and W. Lycan. 1975. "Knowing Who." *Philosophical Studies* 28.

Boer, S., and W. Lycan. 1986. *Knowing Who*. Cambridge, MA: M.I.T. Press.

Bouton, L. 1970. "Antecedent-Contained Pro-forms." *Papers from the Sixth Regional Meeting of the Chicago Linguistic Society*. Chicago: University of Chicago.

Boyd, R. 1979. "Metaphore and Theory Change." In Ortony 1979.

Bresnan, J. W. 1970. "On the Form and Functioning of Transformations." *Linguistic Inquiry*, 7.

Bresnan, J. W. 1976. "Toward a Realistic Model of Transformational Grammar." Paper presented at MIT-ATT Convocation on Communications, M.I.T.

Burge, T. 1973. "Reference and Proper Names." *Journal of Philosophy* 70: 425.

The *Cambridge History of Later Medieval Philosophy*. 1989. Kretzman, Norman. Kenny, Anthony. and Pinborg, Jan, eds. Cambridge, England: Cambridge University Press.

Carnap, R. 1937. *Logical Syntax of Language*. New York: Harcourt, Brace and Company.

Carnap, R. 1942. *Introduction to Semantics*. Cambridge, MA: Harvard University Press.

Carnap, R. 1947. *Meaning and Necessity*. Chicago: University of Chicago.

Carnoy, A. 1927. *La Science du mot*. Louvain.

Castañeda, H. 1966. " 'He': A Study in the Logic of Self-consciousness." *Ratio* 8: 130–157.

Castañeda, H. 1967. "Indicators and Quasi-indicators." *American Philosophical Quarterly* 4: 85–100.

Castañeda, H. 1968. "On the Logic of Attribution and Self Knowledge to Others". *The Journal of Philosophy* 65: 439–456.

Castañeda, H. 1974. "Thinking and the Structure of the World." *Philosophia* 4: 3–4.

Castañeda, H. 1975. "Individuation and Non-Identity: A New Look." *American Philosophical Quarterly* 12: 131–140.

Castañeda, H. 1977. "On the Philosophical Foundations of the Theory of Communication: Reference." *Midwestern Studies in Philosophy* 2: 165–186.

Castañeda, H. 1977. "Perception, Belief, and the Structure of Physical Objects and Consciousness." *Synthese* 35: 285–351.

Caton, C. 1959. "Strawson on Referring." *Mind* 68: 539–544.

Caton, C. (ed.). 1963. *Philosophy and Ordinary Language*. Urbana: University of Illinois.

Chisholm, R. (ed.) 1960. *Realism and the Background of Phenomenology*. Glencoe, IL: The Free Press.

Chisholm, R. 1967. "Identity through Possible Worlds: Some Questions." *Noûs* 1.

Chomsky, N. 1955. *The Logical Structure of Linguistic Theory*. Cambridge, MA: M.I.T. microfilm. (Published in part by Plenum, New York, 1975).

Chomsky, N. 1965. *Aspects of the Theory of Syntax*. Cambridge, MA: M.I.T. Press.

Chomsky, N. 1966. "Topics in the Theory of Generative Grammar." In Seboek 1966.

Chomsky, N. 1968. *Language and Mind* (enlarged edition). New York: Harcourt Brace Jovanovich.

Chomsky, N. 1976. "Conditions on Rules of Grammar" from Chomsky, *Essays on Form and Interpretation*. Amsterdam: North Holland, 1977.

Chomsky, N. 1981. *Lectures on Government and Binding*. Dordrecht: Forris.

Church, A. 1941. *The Calculi of Lamda-Conversion*. Princeton, NJ: Princeton University Press. (Reprinted by Kraus Reprint Corp., New York, 1965).

Church, A. 1950. "On Carnap's Analysis of Statements of Assertion and Belief." *Analysis* 10: 97–99.

Church, A. 1951. "A Formulation of the Logic of Sense and Denotation." in Henle et al. 1951.

Church, A. 1954. "Intentional Isomorphism and Identity of Belief." *Philosophical Studies* 5: 65–73.

Church, A. 1956. *Introduction to Mathematical Logic* 1: 24–25. Princeton.

Cicero. *De Inventione*.

Cicero. *De oratore*.

Cole, P. (ed.). 1981. *Radical Pragmatics*. New York: Academic Press.

Cooper, R. 1979. "The Interpretation of Pronouns." In Heny and Schnelle.

Cormack, A. 1980. "Ambiguity, Negation, and Logical Form." Ms.

Cresswell, M. 1972. "The World Is Everything That Is the Case". *Australasian Journal of Philosophy* 50: 1–13.

Cresswell, M. 1973. *Logics and Languages*. London: Methuen.

Davidson, D. 1965. "Theories of Meaning and Learnable Languages." *Proceedings of the 1964 International Congress for Logic, Methodology and Philosophy of Science*, 383–394. Amsterdam: North Holland Publishing Company.

Davidson, D. 1967. "Truth and Meaning." *Synthese* 17: 304.

Davidson, D. 1969. "True to the Facts." *Journal of Philosophy* 66: 748.

Davidson, D. 1970. "Mental Events." In Foster and Swanson 1970.

Davidson, D. 1973. "In Defense of Convention T." In Le Blanc 1973.

Davidson, D. 1978. "What Metaphors Mean." *Critical Inquiry* 5.

Davidson, D. 1982. *Essays on Actions and Events*. Oxford: Oxford University Press.

Davidson, D., and G. Harman. (eds.). 1972. *Semantics of Natural Language*. Dordecht. Reidel.

Davidson, D., and G. Harman. (eds.). 1975. *The Logic of Grammar*. Encino, CA: Dickenson.

Davidson, D., and J. Hintikka. (eds.). 1969. *Words and Objections*. Dordrecht: Reidel.

Donnellan, K. 1966. "Reference and Definite Descriptions." *Philosophical Review* 75, 3: 281–303.

Donnellan, K. 1968. "Putting Humpty Dumpty Together Again." *Philosophical Review* 77: 203–215.

Donnellan, K. 1974. "Speaking of Nothing." *Philosophical Review* 83: 3–31.

Dowty, D., R. Wall, and S. Peters. 1981. *Introduction to Montague Semantics*. Dordrecht: Reidel.

Dubois, J., et al. 1970. *Rhetorique generale*. Paris.

Dummett, M. 1958–1959. "Truth." *Proceedings of the Aristotelian Society* 59: 141–162.

Evans, G. Sept., 1977. "Pronouns, Quantifiers and Relative Clauses (I)." The *Canadian Journal of Philosophy*. 7: 467–536.

Evans, G. Dec. 1977. "Pronouns, Quantifiers and Relative Clauses (II)." The *Canadian Journal of Philosophy*. 7: 777–797.

Evans, G. 1980. "Pronouns." *Linguistic Inquiry* 11: 337–362.

Evans, G., and J. McDowell. (eds.). 1976. *Truth and Meaning*. Oxford: Oxford University Press.

Feinberg, J. 1965. "Action in Responsibility." In Black 1965.

Feldman, F. 1971. "Counterparts." *Journal of Philosophy* 68: 406–409.

Fiegl, H., and Sellars, W. (eds.). 1949. *Readings in Philosophical Analysis*. New York.

Fillmore, C. J. 1966. "On the Syntax of Preverbs." Ms.

Flew, A. 1956. *Essays in Conceptual Analysis*. New York: St. Martins.

Fodor, J. D. 1979. *The Linguistic Description of Opaque Contexts*. Garland.

Fodor, J. D., and I. Sag. 1982. "Referential and Quantificational Indefinites." *Linguistics and Philosophy* 5: 355–399.

Foster, L., and J. W. Swanson. 1970. *Experience and Theory*. Amherst, MA: University of Massachusetts Press.

Frege, G. "Uber Begriff und Gegenstand." *Vierteljahrsschrift fur wissenschaftliche Philosophie* 16: 192–205.

Frege, G. 1879. *Begriffsschrift, eine der arithmetischen nachgebildete Formelsprache des reinen Denkens*. Halle.

Frege, G. 1949. "Ueber Sinn und Bedeutung." *Zeitschrift fur Philosophie und Philosophische Kritik*. Translated (by Feigl) in Feigl and Sellars 1949.

Frege, G. 1952. "On Sense and Reference." In Geach and Black 1952.

Frege, G. 1965. "The Thought: A Logical Inquiry." (A. M. and Marcelle Quinton, trans.) *Mind* 65: 289–311. (Reprinted in P. F. Strawson, ed., *Philosophical Logic*, Oxford University Press, Oxford, 1967, 17–38.)

Friedman, M. 1975. "Physicalism and the Indeterminacy of Translation." *Noûs* 9: 353.

Gallie, R. D. 1974. "A. N. Prior and Substantial Quantification." *Analysis* 34: 65–69.

Garfield, J. 1988. *Belief in Psychology: A Study in the Ontology of Mind*. Cambridge, MA: MIT Press.

Geach, P. 1957. *Mental Acts*. London.

Geach, P. 1965. *Reference and Generality* (emended ed.). Ithaca, NY: Cornell University Press.

Geach, P. 1972. *Logic Matters*. London: Blackwell.

Geach, P. and Black, M. (eds.). 1952. *Philosophical Writings*. Oxford: Blackwell.

Godel, K. 1931. "Über formal unentscheidbare Sätze der Principia Mathematica und verwandter Systeme, I." *Montashefte fur Mathematik und Physik* 38: 173–198.

Godel, K. 1936. "Uber die Lange von Beweisen." *Ergebnisse eines mathematischen Kolloquiums* 7: 23–24.

Gonseth, F. 1938. "Le Congres Descartes. Questions de Philosophie scientifique." *Revue Thomiste* 44: 183–193.

Goodman, N. 1976. *Languages of Art*. Indianapolis. Bobbs-Merrills. 72, 74–75.

Grelling, K. and L. Nelson. 1908. "Bermerkungen zu den Paradoxien von Russell und Burali-Forti." *Abhandlungen der Fries'schen Schule* 2 (new series): 301–334.

Grice, H. 1957. "Meaning." *Philosophical Review* 66: 337–388.

Grice, H. 1961. "The Casual Theory of Perception." *Proceedings of the Aristotelian Society* 35.

Grice, H. 1968. "Utterer's Meaning, Sentence-Meaning, and Word-Meaning." *Foundations of Language* 4: 225–242.

Groenendijk et al. (eds.). 1984. *Formal Methods in the Study of Language*. Dordrecht: Reidel.

Haack, S. 1977. "Lewis' Ontological Slum." *Review of Metaphysics* 33: 415–429.

Halm, R. (ed.). 1865. *Rhetores Latini Minores* (Victorinus' commentary on Cicero's *De inventione*). Leipzig. 234–235.

Hakamer, J. 1971. *Constraints on Deletion of Syntax*. Unpublished doctoral dissertation. New Haven: Yale University.

Harman, G. 1967. "Quine on Meaning and Existence, I." *Review of Metaphysics* 21: 124–151.

Harman, G. 1968. "Quine on Meaning and Existence. II." *Review of Metaphysics* 21: 124–151.

Harman, G. 1975. "Logical Form". In Davidson and Harman 1975.

Heim, I. 1982. *The Semantics of Definites and Indefinites*. Ph.D. dissertation. University of Massachusetts, Amherst.

Hency, F. (ed.). 1981. *Ambiguities in Intentional Contexts*. Dordrecht: Reidel.

Henle, Kallen, Langer (eds.). 1951. *Structure, Method, and Meaning: Essays in Honor of M. Sheffer*. New York. Liberal Arts Press.

Heny, F., and Schnelle, H. (eds.). 1979. *Syntax and Semantics*. New York. Academic Press.

Herzberger, H. 1973. "Dimensions of Truth". *Journal of Philosophical Logic* 2: 536–556.

Herzberger, H. 1975. "Supervaluations in Two Dimensions." *Proceedings of the International Symposium on Multiple-Valued Logic*. Bloomington, IN: Indiana University Linguistics Club. 429–435.

Herzberger, H. 1976. "Presuppositional Policies." In Kasher 1976.

Herzberger, H. 1978. *True, False, Etc.* Unpublished transcript. University of Toronto.

Herzberger, H. 1980. "Truth and Modality in Semantically Closed Languages." *The Paradox of the Liar*. New Haven: Yale University Press, 25–46.

Higginbotham, J. 1980. "Pronouns and Bound Variables," *Linguistic Inquiry* II.

Hilbert, D., and Bernays, P. 1934–1939. *Grundlagen der Mathematik* (2 vols.). Berlin: Springer.

Hintikka, J. 1962. *Knowledge and Belief*. Ithaca, NY: Cornell University Press.

Hintikka, J. 1967. "Individual, Possible Worlds, and Epistemic Logic." *Noûs* 1: 47.

Hintikka, J. 1969. "Semantics for Propositional Attitudes." *Models for Modalities*. Dordrecht: Reidel.

Hintikka, J. 1972. "The Semantics of Modal Notions and the Indeterminacy of Ontology." In Davidson and Harman 1972.

Hintikka, J. 1975. "Impossible Possible Worlds Vindicated." *Journal of Philosophical Logic* 4: 455–474.

Hintikka, J. 1976a, "Language Games" in E. Saarinen, ed., *Game Theoretical Semantics*, Dordrecht, D. Reidel.

Hintikka, J. 1976b. "Quantifiers in Logic and Quantifiers in Natural Languages", in Saarinen, *op. cit.*

Hiz, H. 1962. "Questions and Answers." *Journal of Philosophy* 59.

Hofstadter, A. 1938. "On Semantic Problems". *The Journal of Philosophy* 35: 225–232.

Hornstein, N. and A. Weinberg 1981. "Case Theory and Preposition Stranding." *Linguistic Inquiry*, 12.

Hughes, G., and M. Cresswell. 1968. *An Introduction to Modal Logic*. London: Methuen.

Ioup, G. 1977. "Specificity and the Interpretation of Quantifiers." *Linguistics and Philosophy* 1: 233–245.

Juhos, B. von. 1937. "The Truth of Empirical Statements." *Analysis* 4: 65–70.

Kalish, D., and R. Montague. 1964. *Logic: Techniques of Formal Reasoning*. New York: Harcourt, Brace and World.

Kamp, H. 1984. "A Theory of Truth and Semantics Representation." In Groenendijk et al. 1984.

Kaplan, D. 1968. "Quantifying In." *Synthese* 19: 178–214.

Kaplan, D. 1969. "Quantifying In." *Words and Objections*. In Davidson and Hintikka 1969.

Kaplan, D. 1977. *Demonstratives*. (Mimeographed, UCLA.)

Karttunen, L., and S. Peters. 1979. "Conventional Implicature." In Oh and Dineen 1979.

Kasher, A. (ed.). 1976. *Language and Focus*. Dordrecht: Reidel.

Katz, J. 1975. "Logic and Language: An Examination of Recent Criticisms of Intentionalism." *Minnesota Studies in the Philosophy of Science* 7: 36–130. Minneapolis.

Kayne, R. 1979. "Two Notes on the NIC" in A. Belletti *et al.*, eds. *Theory of Markedness of Generative Grammar*: Proceedings of the 1979 GLOW Conference Pisa. Scrola Normale Superiore.

Keenan, E. 1971. "Names, Quantifiers, and the Sloppy Identity Problem." *Papers in Linguistics* 4, 2.

Kempson, R. M. 1975. *Presupposition and the Delimitation of Semantics*. Cambridge: Cambridge University Press.

Kempson, R. M., and Cormack, A. 1981. "Ambiguity and Quantification." *Linguistics and Philosophy* 4, 2: 259–310.

Kiteley, M. 1968. "Of What We Think." *American Philosophical Quarterly*. 5: 31–42.

Kiteley, M. 1981. "Substitution and Reference." *Philosophical Studies*, 40: 221–240.

Kleene, S. 1952. *Mathematical Logic*. New York: John Wiley and Sons.

Kleene, S. 1952. *Introduction to Metamathematics*. Toronto: D. van Nostrand.

Klein, E. 1978. *On Sentences which Report Beliefs, Desires and Other Mental Attitudes*, Ph.D. thesis, Cambridge.

Kneale, W. and M. Kneale. 1962. *The Development of Logic*. Oxford: Clarendon Press. 1962.

Kokoszynska, M. 1936. "Syntax, Semantik und Wissenschaftslogik." *Actes du Congres International de Philosophie Scientifique* 2: 9–14. Paris.

Kokoszynska, M. 1936. "Uber den absoluten Wahrheitsbegriff und einige andere semantische Begriffe". *Erkenntnis* 6: 143–165.

Koopman, H., and D. Sportiche, 1981. "Variables and the Bijection Principle." Paper presented at the GLOW Conference, Göttingen.

Kotarbinski, T. "W sprawie pojecia prawdy" ("Concerning the Concept of Truth," in Polish). *Przeglgd filozoficzny* 37: 85–91.

Kotarbinski, T. 1929. *Elementy teorji poznania, logiki formalnej i metodologji nauk (Elements of Epistemology, Formal Logic, and the Methodology of Sciences*, in Polish). Lwow.

Kraut, R. "Attitudes and Their Objects." *Journal of Philosophical Logic*. Forthcoming.

Kretzmann, N., Kenny, A. and Pinborg, J. (ed.) 1982. *The Cambridge History of Later Medieval Philosophy*. Cambridge: Cambridge University Press.

Kripke, S. 1963. "Semantical Considerations on Modal Logic". *Acta Philosophica Fennica* 16: 83–94.

Kripke, S. 1971. "Identity and Necessity." In Munitz 1971.

Kripke, S. 1972. "Identity and Necessity." In Davidson and Harman 1972.

Kripke, S. 1972. "Naming and Necessity." In Davidson and Harman 1972.

Kripke, S. 1976. "Is There a Problem about Substitutional Quantification?" In Evans and McDowell 1976.

Kuno, S. 1974. "Lexical and Contextual Meaning." *Linguistic Inquiry* 5.

La Galy, M., et al. (eds.). 1974. *Prepare from the Tenth Regional Meeting of the Chicago Linguistics Society.* Chicago.

Lakoff, G. 1968. "Deep and Surface Grammar." (Available from Indiana University Linguistics Club.)

Lakoff, G. 1970. "A Note on Vagueness and Ambiguity." *Linguistic Inquiry* 1.

Lakoff, G., and M. Johnson. 1980. *Metaphors We Live By.* Chicago: University of Chicago Press.

Lambert, K. (ed.). 1970 *Philosophical Problems in Logic.* Dordrecht: Reidel.

Lees, R. 1960. *The Grammar of English Nominalizations.* M.I.T. doctoral dissertation. (Published by Indiana University, Bloomington, Mouton–The Hague, 1968).

Leonard, H. S., and N. Goodman. 1940. "The Calculus of Individuals and Its Uses." *Journal of Symbolic Logic* 5: 45–55.

Lewis, D. 1972. "General Semantics." In Davidson and Harman 1972.

Lewis, D. 1973. *Counterfactuals.* Cambridge, MA: Harvard University Press.

Lindenbaum, A., and Tarski, A. 1936. "Uber die Beschranktheit der Ausdrucksmittel deduktiver Theorien." *Ergebnisse eines mathematischen Kolloquiums* 7: 15–23.

Linebarger, M. 1980. *The Grammar of Negative Polarity.* Doctoral dissertation, MIT.

Linsky, L. 1963. "Reference and Referents." In Caton 1963.

Linsky, L. 1966. *Journal of Philosophy* 63: 673–683.

Linsky, L. 1968. "Reference, Essentialism, and Modality." *Journal of Philosophy* 66: 287–300.

Lycan, W. 1974. "Could Propositions Explain Anything?" *Canadian Journal of Philosophy* 3: 427–435.

Lycan, W. 1976. "Reality and Semantic Representation." *Monist* 59: 424–440.

Lycan, W. 1984. *Logical Form in Natural Language.* Cambridge, MA: M.I.T. Press.

Lycan, W., and R. Nusenoff. 1974. "Review of Munitz's *Identity and Individuation.*" *Synthese* 28. 553–559.

Lycan, W., and G. Pappas. 1976. "Quine's Materialism." *Philosophia* 6: 109–110.

Marcus, R. 1975–1976. "Dispensing with Possibilia." *Proceedings and Addresses of the American Philosophical Association* 44: 39–51.

Margalit, A. 1979. "A Puzzle about Belief." *Meaning and Use.* Dordrecht: Reidel.

Martin, J. 1979. *Some Misconceptions in the Critique of Semantic Presupposition.* Bloomington, IN: Indiana University Linguistics Club.

Martin, R. M. 1953. "A Homogeneous System for Formal Logic." *Journal of Symbolic Logic* 8: 1–23.

Mates, B. 1950. "Synonymity." *Meaning and Interpretation.* Berkeley. 201–226.

May, R. 1977. *The Grammar of Quantification* Doctoral Dissertation, MIT.

McCawley, J. 1967. "Meaning and the Description of Languages." *Kotoba no Uchu* 2.

McCawley, J. 1970. "English as a VSO Language." *Language* 46.

McKay, A. F., and D. D. Merrill. (eds.). *Issues in the Philosophy of Language.* New Haven: Yale University Press.

Meier, H. 1963. *Die ·Metaphor.* Winterthur. 185.

Meinong, A. 1960. "The Theory of Objects". In Chisholm 1960.

Montague, R. 1974. "Pragmakes." New Haven. 95–118.

Montague, R. 1974. "The Proper Treatment of Quantification in Ordinary English." In Thomason 1974.

Montague, R. 1974. *Formal Philosophy.* In Thomason 1974.

Morgan, J. L. 1979. "Observations on the Pragmatics of Metaphor." In Ortony 1979.

Munitz, M. (ed.). 1972. *Identity and Individuation.* New York: New York University Press.

Munitz, M., and P. Unger. (eds.). 1974. *Semantics and Philosophy.* New York: New York University Press.

Murray, J. A. H., et al. (eds.). 1933. *The Oxford English Dictionary.* Oxford: Oxford University Press. Vol. 11, 253.

Nagel. E. 1938. Review of Hofstadter. *The Journal of Symbolic Logic* 3: 90.

Nagel, E. 1942. Review of Carnap. *The Journal of Philosophy* 39: 468–473.

Ness, A. 1938. " 'Truth' as Conceived by Those Who Are Not Professional Philosophers." *Skrifter utgitt av Det Norske Videnskaps-Akademi i Oslo, II Hist.-Filos. Klasse* 4 Oslo.

Neurath, O. 1935. "Erster Internationaler Kongress fur Einheit der Wissenschaft in Paris 1935." *Erkenntnis* 5: 377–406.

Nietzsche, F. *Jenseits von Gut and Bose.*

Nietzsche, F. 1921. *Uber Warheit Luge im aussermoralischen Sinn* in *Werke*. Stuttgart. 2: 10–11, 17.

Nute, D. 1976. "David Lewis and the Analysis of Counterfactuals." *Noûs* 10: 353–362.

Ockham, W. *Summa Totius Logicae.*

Oh, C. K., and D. A. Dineen. (eds.). 1975. *Minnesota Studies in the Philosophy of Science* 7. Minneapolis.

Onions, C. T. 1929. *An Advanced English Syntax*. New York. 154–156.

Ortony, A. (ed.). 1979. *Metaphor and Thought*. Cambridge: Cambridge University Press.

Parsons, T. 1974. "A Prolegomenon to a Meinongian Semantics." *Journal of Philosophy* 71: 561–581.

Partee, B. 1974. "Opacity and Scope." In Munitz and Unger 1974.

Partee, B. 1975. "Montague Grammar and Transformational Grammar." *Linguistic Inquiry* 6.

Partee, B. (ed.). 1976. *Montague Grammar*. New York: Academic Press.

Perry, J. 1977. "Frege on Demonstratives." *Philosophical Review* 86: 474–497.

Plantinga, A. 1974. *The Nature of Necessity*. Oxford: Clarendon Press.

Plantinga, A. 1978. "The Boethian Compromise." *American Philosophical Quarterly* 15: 129–138.

Popper, K. 1968. *Logic of Scientific Discovery*. New York: Basic Books. 274.

Post, E. 1921. "Introduction to a General Theory of Elementary Propositions." *American Journal of Mathematics* 43: 256–283.

Prior, A. N. 1967. *Past, Present and Future*. Oxford.

Quine, W. V. 1950. *Methods of Logic*. New York: Holt.

Quine, W. V. 1953. "On What There Is." *From a Logical Point of View*. Cambridge, MA: Harvard University Press.

Quine, W. V. 1955. "Quantifiers and Propisitional Attitudes." *Journal of Philosophy* 53: 177–187. (Also in *Ways of Paradox*, New York, Random House, 1966, 183–194.

Quine, W. V. 1960. *Word and Object*. Cambridge, MA: M.I.T. Press.

Quine, W. V. 1968. "Propositional Objects." *Ontological Relativity and Other Essays*. New York: Columbia University Press.

Quine, W. V. 1965. "Theories of Meaning and Learnable Languages." In Bar-Hillel 1965.

Quine, W. V. 1967. "Truth and Meaning." *Synthese* 17: 304–323.

Quine, W. V. 1966. "Truth by Convention." *The Ways of Paradox*. New York: Random House. 82.

Quine, W. V. 1960. *Word and Object*. Cambridge, MA: M.I.T. Press.

Quintilian. *Institutiones oratoriae.* 8, 6.

Rantala, V. 1975. "Urn Models: A New Kind of Non-Standard Model for First-Order Languages." *Journal of Philosophical Logic* 4: 455–474.

Reichling, A. 1935. Het Woord: *Een Studie omtrent de grondslag van taal en taalgebruik*. Nijmegen. (Quoted in *Het Begrip Metaphoor*, C.P.F. Stutterheim, ed., Amsterdam, 339.)

Rescher, N. (ed.). 1968. *Studies in Logical Theory*. Oxford: Blackwell.

Rescher, N. 1975. *A Theory of Possibility*. Pittsburgh: University of Pittsburgh Press.

Richards, T. 1975. "The Worlds of David Lewis." *Australasian Journal of Philosophy* 53: 105–118.

Ricoeur, P. 1979. *The Rule of Metaphor* (R. Czerny, et al., trans.). Toronto.

Rodman, R. 1976. "Scope Phenomena, 'Movement Transformations,' and Relative Clause." In Partee 1976.

Ross, J. R. 1967. *Constraints on Variables in Syntax*. Unpublished M.I.T. doctoral dissertation. (Available from Indiana University Linguistics Club.)

Routley, R. 1976. "The Durability of Impossible Objects." *Inquiry* 19.

Routley, R., and Routley, V. 1973. "Rehabilitating Meinong's Theory of Objects." *Revue Internationale de Philosophie*. fasc. 2–3.

Russell, B. "Descriptions". *Logic and Knowledge* (R. C. Marsh, ed.).

Russell, B. 1903. *The Principles of Mathematics*. London: Allen and Unwin.

Russell, B. 1905. "Critical Notice of Meinong's *Untersuchungen zur Gegenstandstheorie und Psychologie*." *Mind*, 14.

Russell, B. 1920. *Introduction to Mathematical Philosophy*. London: Allen and Unwin.

Russell, B. 1940. *An Inquiry into Meaning and Truth*. New York: Norton.

Russell, B. 1975. *My Philosophical Development*. London: Unwin.

Saarinen, E. 1981. "Quantifier Phrases Are (at least) Five Ways Ambiguous in Intentional Contexts." In Hency 1981.

Sadock, J., and A. Zwicky. 1973. "Ambiguity Tests and How to Fail Them." *Ohio State Working Papers in Linguistics*, no. 16.

Sag, I. A. *Deletion and Logical Form*. Doctoral Dissertation, M.I.T.

Sag, I. A., and J. Hankamer. 1976. "Deep and Surface Anaphora." *Linguistic Inquiry*.

Scheffler, I. 1954. "An Inscriptional Approach to Indirect Quotation." *Analysis* 14: 83–90.

Schlipp, P.A. (ed.). 1963. *The Philosophy of Rudolf Carnap*. Lasalle, IL: Open Court. 61.

Scholz, H. 1937. "Review of *Studia philosophica, vol. I*." *Deutsche Literaturzeitung* 58: 1914–1917.

Scott, D. 1970. "Advice on Modal Logic." *Philosophical Problems in Logic*. Dordrecht: Reidel. 143–173.

Scott, D. 1973. "Background to Formalization." In Le Blanc 1973.

Searl, J. 1979. "Metaphor." In Ortony 1979.

Seboek, A. (ed.). 1966. *Current Trends in Linguistics* 3. The Hague.

Sellars, W. 1955. "Putnam on Synonymity and Belief." *Analysis* 15: 117–120.

Sellers, W. 1975. "Reply to Quine." *Synthese* 26.

Sicha, J. 1974. *A Metaphysics of Elementary Mathematics*. Amherst, MA: University of Massachusetts Press.

Smullyan, A. F. 1948. "Modality and Description." *Journal of Symbolic Language* 13: 31–37.

Soerber, D., and D. Wilson. 1981. "Irony and the Use-Mention Distinction." In Cole 1981.

Spengel, L. (ed.). 1861. *Rhetores Graeci*. 3.

Sperber, D., and D. Wilson. 1986. *Relevance: Communnication and Cognition*. Oxford: Blackwell.

Stalnaker, R. 1968. "A Theory of Conditionals." In Recher 1968.

Stalnaker, R. 1973. "Presuppositions." *Journal of Philosophical Logic* 2: 447–457.

Stalnaker, R. 1976. "Propositions." In McKay and Merrill 1976.

Stalnaker, R. 1977. "Complex Predicates." *The Monist* 60: 327–339.

Stern, G. 1931. *Meaning and Change of Meaning*. Goteborg. 46–67.

Stine, G. 1973. "Essentialism, Possible Worlds, and Propositional Attitudes." *Philosophical Review* 82: 471–482.

Stich, S. B. 1983. *From Folk Psychology to Cognitive Science*. Cambridge.

Strawson, P. 1954. "A Reply to Mr. Sellars." *Philosophical Review* 63: 216–121.

Strawson, P. 1956. "On Referring." In Flew 1956.

Strawson, P. 1964. "Identifying Reference and Truth Values." *Theoria* 30: 96–118.

Tarski, A. 1931. "Sur les ensembles definissables de nombres reels. I" *Funda menta mathematicae* 17: 210–239.

Tarski, A. 1935. "Der Warheitsbegriff in den formalisierten Sprachen." (German translation of an essay in Polish, 1933.) *Studia philosophica* 1: 261–405.

Tarski, A. 1936. "Grundlegung der wissenscshaftlichen Semantik." *Actes du Congres International de Philosophie Scientifique* 3: 1–8. Paris.

Tarski, A. 1937. "Uber den Begriff der logischen Folgerung." *Actes du Congres International de Philosophie Scientifique* 7: 1–11. Paris.

Tarski, A. 1939. "On Undecidable Statements in Enlarged Systems of Logic and the Concept of Truth." *The Journal of Symbolic Logic* 4: 105–112.

Tarski, A. 1941. *Introduction to Logic*. New York.

Tarski, A. 1944. "The Semantical Conception of Truth and the Foundations of Semantics." *Philosophy and Phenomenological Research* 4, 3: 351.

Tarski, A. 1956. "The Concept of Formalized Languages." *Logic, Semantics, Metamathematics*. New York: Oxford University Press: 166.

Tarski, A. 1956. "The Establishment of Scientific Semantics." *Logic, Semantics, and Metamathematics*. New York: Oxford University Press. 406.

Thomason, R. (ed.). 1974. *Formal Philosophy: Selected Papers of Richard Montague*. New Haven: Yale University Press.

Thomason, R. 1974. "Some Complement Constructions in Montague Grammar." In La Galy et al. 1974.

van Fraassen, B. C. 1966. "Singular Terms, Truth-Value Gaps, and Free Logic." *Journal of Philosophy* 63: 481–495.

van Fraasen, B. C. 1971. *Formal Semantics and Logic*. New York: Macmillan.

Weinberg, J. "Review of *Studia philosophica, vol. I*." *The Philosophical Review* 47: 70–77.

Woodger, J. H. 1939. "The Axiomatic Method in Biology" (1937). "The Technique of Theory Construction." *International Encyclopedia of Unified Science*. II(5).

Woodruff, P. W. 1970. "Logic and Truth Value Gaps." In Lambert 1970.